A Taste of Heaven on Earth

The 93,000 square-foot Oneida Community Mansion House is a National Historic Landmark and educational not-for-profit 501c3 organization. It includes museum rooms, residential apartments, guest lodging, and banquet and meeting spaces. Construction began in 1861; the corridor to the South Tower and entire South Wing was added in 1869. A four-story North Wing was completed in 1878 and a large Lounge was built in 1914 connecting the North Wing to the dining area.

A Taste of Heaven on Earth

Harnessing the Energies of Love

CAROL STONE WHITE
foreword by Anthony Wonderley

RESOURCE *Publications* · Eugene, Oregon

A TASTE OF HEAVEN ON EARTH
Harnessing the Energies of Love

Copyright © 2020 Carol Stone White. All rights reserved. Except for brief quotations in critical publications or reviews, no part of this book may be reproduced in any manner without prior written permission from the publisher. Write: Permissions, Wipf and Stock Publishers, 199 W. 8th Ave., Suite 3, Eugene, OR 97401.

Resource Publications
An Imprint of Wipf and Stock Publishers
199 W. 8th Ave., Suite 3
Eugene, OR 97401

www.wipfandstock.com

PAPERBACK ISBN: 978-1-7252-5734-4
HARDCOVER ISBN: 978-1-7252-5735-1
EBOOK ISBN: 978-1-7252-5736-8

Manufactured in the U.S.A.   04/06/20

To our Julie, who has the loving heart that John Humphrey Noyes said is the distinguishing characteristic of the spiritual person. "This is what is needed in the world," Noyes said. "With love the world might be a very comfortable Paradise, though its external institutions should remain unchanged."

"The Oneida Community was mightily shepherded by their chief Noyes, one of those chance attempts at the Superman that occur from time to time in spite of the interference of Man's blundering institutions."

—George Bernard Shaw

Contents

List of Illustrations	ix
Foreword by Anthony Wonderley	xi
Preface	xiii
Acknowledgments	xvii
1 | The Metamorphosis of John Humphrey Noyes	1
2 | High Tide of the Spirit: Putney Community	67
3 | Implementing Heaven on Earth: The Oneida Community	97
4 | Complex Marriage	119
5 | Community Children: Many Mentors	154
6 | Education: Lifelong Learning from Youth to Young at Heart	181
7 | Mutual Criticism: a Spiritual Profile	198
8 | Music, Culture, and Community Life	249
9 | Addictions	288
10 | Humanizing Work: By Their Fruit You Shall Know Them	307
11 | Stirpiculture: Planning Parenthood	353
12 | The Loves of Tirzah Crawford Miller, a Personal Journal; Excerpts, 1873–1879	388
Endnotes	423
Epilogue	427
Appendix	433
Glossary	447
Epilogue Endnotes	449
Bibliography	451

List of Illustrations

I.	Frontispiece: *The Modern Oneida Community Mansion House*	*ii*
II.	*John Humphrey Noyes, young man*	30
III.	*Charlotte Noyes Miller*	43
IV.	*Harriet A. Noyes*	68
V.	*George Cragin*	91
VI.	*Women in short dresses with matching pantalettes, designed for mobility and ease of care, at the Summer House*	110
VII.	*Original Mansion House, built of wood in 1848*	117
VIII.	*George Washington Noyes*	131
IX.	*Mansion House from the South Garden*	135
X.	*Harriet Skinner*	146
XI.	*Two Toddlers in front of Mansion House*	154
XII.	*Mary Cragin*	159
XIII.	*Nursery Kitchen*	165
XIV.	*Children dancing in the Upper Sitting Room*	171
XV.	*The Community Classroom, now the Modern Library*	181
XVI.	*Theodore Noyes*	185
XVII.	*The Community Library*	189
XVIII.	*John Humphrey Noyes, middle age*	205
XIX.	*Family with JHN outside*	229
XX.	*Musicians with JHN*	250
XXI.	*Picnic for visitors in the Quadrangle*	260
XXII.	*Family Hall from Balcony*	266
XXIII.	*John Miller*	292
XXIV.	*Work Bee, with member reading to the group*	308
XXV.	*Train on the Midland Railroad crossing long trestle*	319
XXVI.	*Sewell Newhouse*	327
XXVII.	*Working in the Publications Room*	342

List of Illustrations

XXVIII.	*Puck magazine cartoon*	375
XXIX.	*Second Generation Leaders*	380
XXX.	*Lounge*	386
XXXI.	*Tirzah Miller*	388
XXXII.	*Edward Inslee*	395
XXXIII.	*James Herrick*	414
XXXIV.	*James Herrick playing game with grandson David Noyes*	422

Foreword

The Oneida Community (1848–1880) was the most radical and radically successful utopia in American history. It comprised more than 250 people dedicated to living together as one family sharing all property, work, and love. This community built the country's first truly collective residence, a large mansion in which men and women freely mingled under one roof. Community women pioneered a new style of clothing which permitted ease of mobility to work with men in all enterprises. They invented a unique system of raising children during the day with skilled and loving caregivers, and innovated cooperative household arrangements so women were freed to participate in all activities—lifelong education, musical groups, social activity, recreation, and solitary time for prayer. They governed by "mutual criticism," developing spiritual profiles over the years for each member, by each member. They crafted a system of accomplishing tasks and making products together in "work bees," gathering volunteers; their industries fostered spirituality over money-making, emphasizing quality work, personal growth, and practical gender equality. Their system of Complex Marriage freed women from "matrimonial bondage"—in conventional marriage, women lost all legal rights even to their own children in that era. They also corrected one of the greatest sources of human misery: unwanted, unplanned pregnancies, accomplished by prohibiting males from ejaculating during sexual intercourse in order to free women from "propagative drudgery." The Oneida Community started a new experiment during the 1870's—voluntary participation in becoming new parents, in the hope of producing a spiritual humankind over time in the great enterprise of establishing the kingdom of God on earth.

So—you are being offered a remarkable story.

This story, to be sure, has been told before but almost always in secular, sociological terms (Klaw, *Without Sin*, 1993; Wonderley, *Oneida Utopia*, 2017). Alternatively, Oneida has been described as a sex cult supervised by founder John Humphrey Noyes (Wayland-Smith, *Oneida: From Free Love to the Well-Set Table*, 2016). No history of the Community treats Noyes as an important American theologian who inspired others to embark on a thrilling journey of spiritual discovery and growth. All histories, to date, preclude an understanding of Oneida as a religious experience designed to bring heaven to earth. All neglect matters of faith and spirituality.

Foreword

Carol White takes a different and original tack. Her subject is the inspirational as well as the intellectual import of Noyes, and the spirit and heart of the Oneida Bible communists. As a person who has known Carol for over a decade in the context of the Oneida Community's home (today a museum and a National Historic Landmark), I am delighted she has written this. It is good history, good scholarship, and good Christianity made relevant to our times.

Carol is well equipped to explain Oneida in this fashion. She is a fine writer who has published extensively about climbing the high peaks of the Northeast in all seasons. In reminding us what has been forgotten about Noyes and the Community, she may be, furthermore, the only one who can do that. Within the descendants of the Oneida Community, there has long been a bent toward espousing Noyes's Perfectionist theology—I mean of valuing, studying, and living it. It ran through the veins of John Noyes's nephew, George Wallingford Noyes. It was kept alive in the person of that man's daughter, Imogen Noyes Stone. It flowers in Imogen's daughter. Carol Stone White inherits and expresses this tradition. I hope she will not take offense to learn that—in my eyes—she is the last true Perfectionist.

Anthony Wonderley
Curator of Collections and Interpretation (retired), Oneida Community Mansion House
Author, *Oneida Utopia: A Community Searching for Human Happiness and Prosperity.*
Cornell University, 2017

Preface

A Taste of Heaven on Earth explores how John Humphrey Noyes's spiritual struggle and culminating revelation led to groundbreaking practices not undertaken before or since, which have much to offer humanity today. The utopian and practical Oneida Community tackled the thorniest problems humanity faces—primarily the relationship between God and man, between men and women, and the humanization of labor—and succeeded to an extraordinary degree. This community of three hundred people lived happily, productively, and creatively together for thirty-two years. If by their fruits you shall know them, the Oneida Community was indeed "the great enterprise of establishing the kingdom of heaven on earth." They realized that God's spirit abides in all and that humanity is thus united on the deepest level, the essential foundation upon which everyone is valued and nurtured. Rich human relationships flourished and people lived in social harmony; emotional intelligence and self-examination was sought, taught, and required; work and play, loving and learning in this environment revealed nearly limitless human potential. Corporate governance was based on enlightened self-interest so that all shared the fruits of labor.

How did Noyes attract and sustain this extremely competent and love-aspiring group of men and women? I see Noyes's charismatic strength as a result of his achieving mastery in many important areas: he was a well-disciplined Phi Beta Kappa scholar at Dartmouth who studied the sciences and liberal arts and then practiced law. For two more years at Andover and Yale Theological Seminaries, he became an acute observer of his mind and emotions, refusing to settle for human shortcomings that most people take for granted as inevitable. He devoted hours daily in study and silent openness to God, and practiced the moment-to-moment benevolence of Jesus in all relationships, grieving at failures. His noble aspirations culminated in a profound heart conversion, the realization that God's spirit is a living reality within all and that the purpose of human life is to learn to hear our internal teacher. Noyes's most basic conviction was that only the power of God can transform the human heart, which alone can transform individual and collective human life. I see the fruit of Noyes's spiritual labor in his gaining mastery in sexuality following the deaths of four of the five infants his beloved wife, Harriet, carried in the next six years. Refusing to put her through further suffering, he chose to live in chastity while with admirable scientific detachment he examined all phases of sexuality for two years to determine his capacities. He may have discovered tantric contemplative love; only heart-abandonment to the grace of God teaches and gives *temperance in all things*, he taught, and connects our sexual experience with that which is sacred. Noyes's highest achievement was love in all its depth, becoming a lover of God and of his closest neighbor, his wife, practicing true love making. He became a man who spoke with authority, and for fifty years he shared his knowledge through publications and in communities that developed organically as his readers gravitated to him.

Receptivity to God was Noyes's central value and the Community's North Star. By means of short regular Home-Talks that probed the deep recesses of human nature and the world of the spirit, he taught members how to receive God into consciousness. "Let everyone go home into one's heart many times a day, and seek to know God for oneself. When we have learned to do that, we can pass unhurt through the wreck of matter and the crash of worlds. Dwell deep." The spirit of the Home-Talks was "the life and breath of the Community, food and words of healing," its editors wrote, but, they added, "Mr. Noyes expects to be judged by what he has done and not by what he has said." *A Taste of Heaven on Earth* explores Noyes's spiritual development, his teachings, and the spiritual foundations of his communities: how to receive God, implement the love described in 1st Corinthians 13, practice enlightened sexual relations, humanize work, lead a balanced life, and realize contentment and peacefulness with all.

A Taste of Heaven on Earth includes much unpublished material compiled by his nephew, George Wallingford Noyes, born in the Oneida Community in 1870, one of fifty-eight children born between 1869 and 1879 who were the result of an experiment to produce a more spiritual humanity. George Noyes graduated from Cornell University at the top of his class, a junior Phi Beta Kappa scholar, and as the most devoted disciple of John Humphrey Noyes, became the Community historian and archivist following a career with Oneida Community, Limited. His two books, now out of print, *Religious Experience of John Humphrey Noyes* and *John Humphrey Noyes: The Putney Community*, contribute many insights about this complex man and his early life. Two more volumes about the Oneida Community were planned before George's death in 1941. The Community's ultimate conversion to a joint stock corporation is discussed in other works. George's granddaughter, this author, was given copies of 1,700 pages of George's unpublished papers by his daughter, Imogen Noyes Stone; the originals are preserved in the Special Collections Research Center of Bird Library at Syracuse University. The Oneida Community Mansion House is now a living museum with community descendants and others in residence; regular tours and events are offered to the public.

A Taste of Heaven on Earth discusses how Putney and Oneida Community members lived, loved, thought, worked, played, and made music; how they educated their youth sufficiently to be accepted at Yale and Cornell and provided life-long learning for all; how women participated in all decision-making and Community affairs; how they managed three hundred persons of all ages, personalities, and proclivities, including their intimate lives; and how they survived and flourished in spite of many challenges. Their extensive weekly paper, the *Oneida Circular*, described all this and is quoted throughout this book. "What makes this book so interesting to me is that the people who lived there are speaking to me," Professor John Omohundro remarked. "As an anthropologist, I like listening directly to the participants, giving them their voice."

The Oneida Community's unique practices revealed that the complex human being has innumerable capacities and that spiritual flowering and the achievement of the loving heart is the purpose of human life. *A Taste of Heaven on Earth* assesses how Community members explored the furthest reaches of human nature and realized that heaven is within all and can be known and implemented on earth. A visitor once asked a community guide as they walked the corridors of the great Mansion House, "What is this attractive scent I perceive in your halls?"

"It is the aroma," she replied, "of crushed selfishness."

Imogen Noyes Stone described the Oneida Community this way: "There were no unwanted children, no orphans, no child abuse, no juvenile delinquency, no poverty, no illiteracy, no crime, no hunger, no alcoholism, no unemployment, no loneliness, and no oppression of women."

Acknowledgments

I traveled to the Oneida Community Mansion House library to read years of the *Oneida Circular* to add interest to my chapters in *A Taste of Heaven on Earth*. I would knock on the door of the Executive Director, Kevin Coffee, hoping I wasn't interrupting a meeting or other important business. He had the key to the cabinet that held these precious bound books of weekly *Circulars*. He always graciously stopped what he was doing and walked with me to the library. He instructed me to wear gloves that he provided to insure the preservation of this treasure of memories from a unique human experiment in living, loving, and learning how to receive God.

It is not easy to very carefully turn thin fragile pages with gloves on. I'd take them off to type articles, and then don them again. One day, Kevin came in to lock the cabinet and reported that some Circulars are now available electronically. He made it possible to do research at home. This extensive weekly publication covered the natural world, the arts and sciences, practical matters of many kinds, the thoughts of Community members on numerous subjects, a significant column with the week's world and national news, and John Humphrey Noyes's Home-Talks.

I also thank Christine Hall O'Neil, Executive Director of the Oneida Community Mansion House, for accommodating my visits and immediately responding to my questions; and Abigail Lawton, Curator of Collections, for spending considerable time selecting photographs for me to peruse for *A Taste of Heaven on Earth*. Great thanks to John Omohundro for extra copyediting expertise.

I thank David Scott White for his technical assistance, his social intelligence that always offers good advice, his wit keeping me laughing even when I view the world with alarm, and his love and support for fifty-five years. He has the loving heart that John Humphrey Noyes said "is needed for a cure of the world's miseries, the spirit that is kind, envies not, vaunts not itself and is not puffed up, doth not behave itself unseemly, seeks not his own, is not easily provoked, thinks no evil, and fits a man to live in social contact harmoniously with all."

1

The Metamorphosis of John Humphrey Noyes

A NEW ENGLAND FRONTIER OASIS

John Humphrey Noyes was the oldest son of prosperous, intellectual John Noyes and spirited, devout Polly Hayes, sister of Rutherford B. Hayes, father of a future president. John Sr. was a descendant of Nicholas Noyes, fifth in line from the emigration of Nicholas and James Noyes from England in 1634. John's grandfather Joseph moved to Atkinson, Massachusetts, where John Sr. was born on April 2, 1764. One of five brothers, he became a genial story-teller, a success in the world of business and politics, and an inspirational conversationalist about philosophy, science, and literature. John Sr. began teaching at age seventeen in eighteen district schools in Vermont (the first state to end slavery, in 1777). From 1791 to 1799, he was a student and tutor at Dartmouth College; orator Daniel Webster was one of his students. Noyes had not married, because he suffered from what may be a genetic condition—bashfulness, especially toward the opposite sex. At age thirty-five, he determined to seek his fortune in Vermont and lodged at the bustling center of industry and sociability, the Hayes Big House in West Brattleboro—a trading post, tavern, and ballroom with fourteen great fireplaces where everyone met and business was done. While learning the ropes of frontier business, he made trips to Boston by horseback and stagecoach. It was a journey of three or four days each way, and each merchant carried pistols for protection from highwaymen.

Polly Hayes was born on February 8, 1780, in West Brattleboro, one of nine surviving children of Chloe Smith Hayes and Rutherford Hayes, (grandfather of President Rutherford B. Hayes Jr.), who owned and ran the Hayes Big House. Polly grew up learning frontier chores, helping the tavern's many customers, caring for the eight younger children, and enjoying sleigh rides and singing. As the eldest, she was given the great privilege of serving gentlemen a glass of wine in the parlor. Among the boarders at the Hayes Big House was a college-bred man learned in Latin, Greek, Hebrew, science, debate, and philosophy. John Noyes became enamored of Polly but was far too reticent to disclose any personal feelings; he had animated conversations with her mother, Chloe, only one year his senior, through long winter evenings by one of the cheery fireplaces. Possessed of a powerful memory, he had one of those minds in which every newly-found fact, thought, or anecdote is carefully pigeon-holed and labeled, ready for use at a moment's notice. Twenty-year-old Polly was charmed by John's vast information on nearly every subject and liked his fondness for communicating. "I was delighted to hear him talk; and he found in me just that kind of attention that would make us never tired of being together." It wasn't until he was forty that John overcame his shyness and proposed to Polly—he'd let three years pass before declaring his love and would not have done so then, if Polly, formerly engaged, had not demanded a decision.

"Father was very reserved," his son John Humphrey later reminisced. "He was sociable and entertaining in conversation, talking philosophy and science and literature, but a determined reserve ended discussions of a personal nature. Mother told him he should stop talking philosophy and go to talking love, or they would quit; and upon that he married her. He never would talk love. He was seldom heard to express emotion of any kind; he considered it childish and feminine. He had the same reserve in religion. He was quite a theologian, a vigorous moralist who understood Hebrew and Aramaic and respected Christianity, but he was not inclined to spirituality. Go near his heart or touch his personal experience, and he was as close and guarded and impenetrable as a chestnut in its burr."

They had daughter Mary in 1806, Joanna a year later, and Elizabeth in 1809. When he was forty-seven, Noyes was elected Representative of Brattleboro in the Vermont Legislature, and Honorable John was called out of the election meeting to learn that Polly required his attention when his first son, John Humphrey, was about to be born. It was a New England holiday, "Freeman's Meeting-Day," September 3, 1811. At John's birth Polly prayed that "he might be a minister of the everlasting gospel." Noyes was elected to the United States House of Representatives in 1815, which meant eleven days of travel before railroads were in service, one way—five separate stagecoach trips and five by steamboat. These journeys were more than difficult, they were dangerous; while passing through New Jersey, passengers were warned by the stage driver that their baggage might be stolen by highwaymen. In Washington, many public buildings had been burned by the British the year before and were still in ruins. Avenues were laid out on a grand scale but passed through swampy wilderness. "I live in a large, elegant chamber fronting on Pennsylvania Avenue where President Madison's and dozens of other carriages continually pass," he wrote his family. "You would be delighted—perhaps—to see the bustle, the show and parade of great folks. I wish you were here." He ended his Congressional career in 1817, and Polly regretted later that she did not accompany her husband and make a home for him. He might have been spared the painful period twenty years later when the habit of drinking, begun in Washington, little-by-little took control of him.

Polly was deeply religious from her earliest years; in adulthood, all decision-making revolved around the religious education of her nine children. The Bible was her hourly companion and she took great pains to educate them in the love of God. Like her mother Chloe, when Polly became convinced of an idea or a principle, she would try to realize it in practice. Yet she had a strong sense of the limits of human wisdom and relied on extended prayer before making important decisions such as where to live or where to send the children to boarding school and college. The four oldest children of the Noyes household were sent to school in nearby Amherst, Massachusetts. At age nine, John writes: "I have been pretty content since you left me, except last evening I was rather inclined to be homesick. I began to think of home, and I became sad. I took my book and looked over my lesson, then went to the book-store and got me ink and paper and begun me a journal, which I intend to write in every day." He never lost the habit of recording his thoughts; his writings during his years at Andover and Yale Theological Seminaries are an invaluable look at a heroic spiritual struggle and its resolution.

In 1821 the Honorable John, by taste and early vocation a student, began to carry out his long-planned retirement from business as a Brattleboro merchant at age fifty-seven to devote his life to the education of his children; John Humphrey was age ten, and the eldest was seventeen. He had acquired what he thought sufficiency for comfortable living and the children's college education, so he quit moneymaking—though in the full tide of financial success. He sought the best location for college for his growing family, looking at New Haven or Amherst as most desirable, but Polly focused on the spiritual advantages of the locale they might choose. "I could only make it a subject of prayer, which I did for three months, and my prayer was that we choose a place that would best promote the spiritual improvement of the entire family. I was divested of any desire for worldly advantages and had the comfort of believing God directed the move when we took up our residence in Putney, Vermont, instead of Amherst where our four eldest were at school." Putney had been a favored locale for extended revivals; this far overshadowed the greatest university in the land. She hoped all her sons would be ministers and all her daughters would marry ministers. Mrs. Noyes derived great enjoyment from children and young people, and especially when guiding their thought on moral and religious subjects. Generous and vivacious, fond of reading and conversation, she had a talent of drawing out others and making them think well of themselves. She also had the rare trait so pleasing to children of never being too busy to answer their eager questions and attend to their demands for amusement.

A religious revival broke out in Putney in 1819 and swept over the region. The children of the area villages were particularly affected; at age eight John Humphrey was drawn into little praying circles and received religious impressions that he never lost, reported the April 28, 1873, *Circular*. That revival occurred under the preaching of a Congregational minister, Elisha P. Andrews, who was distinguished as a scientific as well as a religious notable. "Ministers of that day were not as exclusively clerical as those afterward. This minister had the lively curiosity of a youth, with a mineralogical collection and a chemical laboratory; he visited the village school, bringing in a stalk of Indian corn in the tassel that he dissected before us, explaining the wonderful processes and uses of the pollen, the silk, etc. We never forgot what he told us—'the golden dust of flowers flying in every wind is the essence of all fructification.' His theme well illustrated what he was doing himself—fertilizing the opening mind with a love of science."

Andrews was exceedingly fond of philosophical experiment and investigation, which appealed to John at the susceptible age of eleven when his father moved the family to Putney. Andrews was the Noyes family pastor for several years, and there was intimate friendship between the families. Andrews was a reverend gentleman of the old school, tender-hearted and often weeping when touched by eternal truths, and this characteristic made him a powerful instrument of spiritual awakening. One of his sons was John's classmate at Dartmouth and became a missionary in the Sandwich Islands. A little cabinet of labeled stones and curiosities arranged on shelves in the Noyes mansion long bore witness to the fertilizing power of this minister's genuine curiosity about the natural world. But his wide interests were the cause of his having eventually to leave this church! One of the members stirred up people to think they must have a minister more exclusively devout.

One can hardly imagine a more carefree and beneficent setting for growing up than the country village of Putney in the beginning decades of our country. John was a natural leader, "marching up the hill at the head of a company of his playmates." He loved sports, hunting, fishing, and riding, yet even as a lad he would go to bed early because he wanted to think—but not about religion, which bored him. Polly's religious instruction must have made an impression, however, because when he was twelve years old he and a friend waded across the West River and were almost swept away by the strong current; John said they ought to kneel and thank God they were safe. John went to nearby Brattleboro Academy to prepare for college and entered Dartmouth at age fifteen in 1826. Having come from New Haven, Polly was convinced that Dartmouth was a safer place than Yale for the morals of young men. In his sophomore year, famed orator Daniel Webster visited Dartmouth, and John Humphrey and other outstanding students were chosen to meet him at his hotel along with noted professors. John was introduced by Professor Chamberlain as the son of Tutor Noyes. "Young man," Webster said, "I wish I could do as much good for you as your father did for me!" John Humphrey later wrote about his father: "I have never seen his equal in conversational teaching. He charmed everybody with his practical wisdom. I can truly say that friendly discussions with him did more to make me a thinker than all the discipline of the schools and colleges."

During his junior year at Dartmouth, John's journaling habit began in earnest and we enjoy first glimpses into a seventeen-year-old's humorous, analytical, even wise mind. "Riches, fame, and pleasure are the three great objects of pursuit in life. If a few simple maxims were attended to and made the guidance of men's conduct, they would be oftener attained: Look well to your pence and the pounds will take care of themselves. Study human nature and govern yourself accordingly. Whatever may be your lot, strive to be content. These principles are a solid basis for real happiness and apply equally well to people in every situation and condition." In reality his views so often changed, John writes, that he remains a stranger to himself. First he is the fisherman and hunter, not social, and studying only out of necessity. Suddenly he desires popularity and "studies human nature and learns to live with men." Then comes a period of genuine interest in learning; the idea of philosophic stoicism seems the best state to emulate. Then, horrors, the attractions of dissipation offer a more immediate path to life's pleasures. But this youngster, who made time just to think, concluded that a person must have resources of enjoyment within himself. All the diversions of social life would ultimately not satisfy; virtue and honor are the guarantors of happiness.

He graduated Phi Beta Kappa from Dartmouth College in 1829 at age eighteen and began the study of law in Chesterfield, New Hampshire. It was a year filled with study, strong friendships, one love to whom he was "strongly tempted to make an offer of marriage," but also a period of self-criticism of his debut as an advocate, and jealousy of his "competitors in gallantry." In September 1831, looking forward to a second year of law study and practice in Brattleboro with his brother-in-law Larkin Mead, Noyes resolved to "indulge the lust of the eye and the pride of life" for the present and risk the consequences. He had become wary after observing changes in those who attended popular New England revivals; emotional religion was an almost intoxicating influence—with unknown outcomes.

Protracted religious revivals had become widespread throughout New York, Connecticut and Massachusetts in the early nineteenth century, a period known as the Second Great Awakening. Evangelists demanded unconditional repentance of all sin, taking a page from Jonathan Edwards who had led the original Great Awakening one hundred years before. Charles Grandison Finney was the most brilliant of these nineteenth century itinerant preachers; he was trained as a lawyer and later became president of Oberlin College. Counties in New York State were known as "the burned-over district";—in Rome, New York, for example, nearly the entire adult population was converted by Finney in a twenty-day campaign in 1826 during which every bar in town closed! Prayer meetings were preferred to ostentatious displays of wealth following the financial crash of 1827. New England became receptive to prolonged revivals as people questioned the true meaning and purpose of life. Religion even took precedence over business; conversion and salvation were discussed in taverns and trading posts. In 1830, a great majority of the leading men and women in Rochester, New York, were converted by Finney, who preached ninety-eight sermons between

September 10, 1830, and March 6, 1831. The character of this city was permanently changed. Shops closed during the period, philanthropic causes thrived, and churches were thronged with worshippers. Religion became the main topic of conversation everywhere. One hundred thousand people were converted and joined the church that year. Finney began revivals in New York City and Boston to share his growing belief that people could, with God, perfect themselves. Many more itinerant preachers traveled the Northeast United States and enlisted the help of converted community folks to bring ever more of the irreligious into the fold. Theological seminaries became so crowded that every few years a new one had to be started, and the religious press became active and influential. Yale Theological Seminary graduates Lyman Beecher and Asahel Nettleton were other persuasive revivalists over the years.

From 1831 to 1835, religious enthusiasm was so intense and the progress of revivals so striking, that many believed the millennium was indeed near. The height of the Second Great Awakening in the Northeast was 1831, "the year of revivals." John's mother Polly told him that a four-day revival would begin on September 18, 1831, in Putney, and she was extremely hopeful that he could come. John, just twenty, considered religion not only irrelevant but a distinct emotional danger to which anyone might be susceptible—even level-headed businessmen, physicians, and lawyers had fallen! Noyes actively did not want to attend the Putney revival, but went to please Polly, assuring her that she'd be disappointed. He was confident that his aversion to religion and his love of the world's pleasures was strong enough to defeat any evangelist's assault. He admits that he also went out of curiosity and "perhaps a twinge of my own conscience." The first two days passed as hours in church pass, with indistinct impact during conventional exercises; even calling any who sought prayer on the fourth day "was not sufficient to humble my proud heart."

WHOM TO SERVE: A FORK IN THE ROAD

The next day a somber mood overtook him. Years of Polly's training must have come to his mind, because he inexplicably wondered whether to wrestle seriously with whom to serve, God or the world. He decided to meditate on the subject, as Polly always did. *Be careful*, he warned himself, *not to get caught in this snare*! The Sunday sermon was uninspiring, directed to the church, and his unsettled mind was subsiding in favor of Mammon. That afternoon he came down with a cold severe enough to put him to bed. This sudden illness made him realize how uncertain and impermanent life is; it seemed sent to keep him home longer. "The thought came suddenly and forcibly into my mind: *I will never again have a more favorable time for submitting to God.*" After some hard thinking, "I immediately set about conquering my pride." He began reading familiar Bible verses and sweated with fever, his mind trembling at the possibility that he might not escape conversion after all and would become another hapless churchgoer. "I forced myself periodically to meditate on the character of God, his goodness, his holiness, the requirements of his word and my heathenish neglect of them." He felt indifferent and inclined to quit during the exercise, but one powerful thought kept him on course—*truth is independent of one's unstable mind and mood. Feelings are not to be trusted when they contradict the plain word of God.* The things of God were momentous and drove him back to meditations, prayers, and Bible reading.

The next day, feeling a bit better, "I feared the return of my former stupidity and forced myself to continue." As he read from the New Testament with Polly, he found himself thinking how utterly inconsequential are most human pursuits—*what could be more important than understanding the great concepts of the Bible?* While reviewing his former values and new spiritual views, "I found to my surprise an entire reversal of my tastes and affections—Christians seemed kindred spirits; the matters of God and of eternity alone seemed worth attention. Light gleamed upon my soul in a different way from what I expected. I remember that I had a strong consciousness of the approving presence of God and a confidence that his grace would lead me into all truth and righteousness." The "good news" of the gospel was complete deliverance from the power of sin, he was now convinced, not simply forgiveness of sin followed by repentance, then sinning and repenting again and again, with resignation to living a less than holy life.

"This is evidence of conversion!" rejoiced Polly. Her daughter Harriet wrote later, "Her children knew from the time they knew anything that they had higher relations than our worldly ones and that they must fear the Lord. She did not merely preach to us that we were immortal beings and that it would profit us nothing if we gained the whole world and lost our own souls—she put this truth into action in every possible way. She was ready to spoil their chances for worldly advantage, rather than that they should forget God." And coming from a long line of prosperous, educated, and socially influential families on both sides, their chances for many worldly successes were virtually unlimited.

John Humphrey Noyes had indeed experienced the Biblical *metanoia*— a reversal of one's interests and goals so profound that the course of one's life is irrevocably altered. "I determined to obtain religion," he wrote boldly in his diary. "Hitherto the world—henceforth, God!" The next day he read the Bible, prayed and meditated calmly with no regret over his state of sinfulness, and this lack of feeling perplexed him. By evening he became "so tranquil that I began seriously to fear the return of my former stupidity." Forcing himself into his new convictions on the third day of his fledgling spiritual odyssey, he remained unable to feel any mourning over his own inner state, yet he soldiered on. His conversion was intellectual, not emotional, powered by a single strong conviction that truth can and must be discovered. "Ere the day was done I had concluded to devote myself to the service and ministry of God. With much joy and zeal I immediately undertook the study of the scriptures and to religious testimony in private and public. Seeing no reason why the revival spirit might not be maintained in its full vigor permanently, I determined with all my inward strength to be a young convert in zeal and simplicity forever." This was fifteen days after his twentieth birthday.

Noyes later vividly described this momentous fork in the road—he might well have opted for a worldly life or, as he did, persevere in a struggle for spiritual insight with no guarantee of success: "When you have a lethargic sleep upon you, you know how hard it is to throw it off. You try to rouse yourself but it is almost impossible; you feel an irresistible temptation to yield yourself to the drowsy spell. You're under a magnetism that darkens your mind and the imaginations of your heart, so you do not know what you are. We are in such circumstances as people who are nearly frozen to death; it is almost impossible to keep them awake. Likewise, we feel an irresistible temptation to give ourselves up to the impressions of the senses and our superficial feelings and opinions, and lose all feeling of God and eternal life. That is sleep, the sleep of death, he warned in *The Work of God in Us*. Salvation is hearing the voice of God deep down in your spirit, calling you to awake to the knowledge of God and of yourself as the child of God. Deep down in the part of us where Christ comes and where the ear is that hears him, the work of God is going on; a life is working there that wants to come to the light. Let us be willing that God should criticize and suggest and brood over us until we do his will and not our own, and act upon his wisdom and not ours. We shall have peace just in proportion as we let God work in us. There is nothing short of almighty power that can wake us and keep us awake."

Like his mother, John no sooner held a conviction than he put it into practice. *This is the last of my labors in the law,* he said to himself. *These worldly pursuits seem like the senseless eagerness of children for the toys and trifles of an hour.* He began preparatory Hebrew studies required for entrance to the prestigious Andover Theological Seminary, the oldest graduate school of theology in the United States. Andover held a reputation for orthodox Calvinism and missionary emphasis, though its founders sought professors with varying opinions and encouraged students to read diverse literature. Moses Stuart and Edward Robinson cautiously endorsed scholarship from Germany in the 1820s, known as Biblical criticism,[1] well before Noyes began study there. In conversation with his father, who was fond of theological argument, young Noyes suggested an interpretation of a passage in scripture he thought was new.

"Take care," said the elder John. "That is heresy."

"Heresy or not, it is true."

"But if you are to be a minister, you must think and preach as the rest of the ministers do," said Honorable John. "If you get out of the traces, they'll *whip you in*!"

"Never!" the son replied, indignant at this suggestion. "Never will I be whipped by ministers or anybody else into views that do not commend themselves to my understanding as guided by the Bible and enlightened by the Spirit."

Noyes assumed that everyone pursuing the ministry felt as he did, that spiritual understanding means a radical change of heart that leads to a changed life. A theological seminary where choice young men of the churches gather must be just little less heavenly than a habitation of angels! But it turned out that Andover was a very poor place for one who had vowed to live in the revival spirit and be a young convert in zeal and simplicity forever. Where there should be education of the heart, he found superficiality and pedantry about sacred matters. Instead of zeal, he found indifference; instead of sobriety he found levity; instead of love he found bickering, jealousies, and intrigues; instead of purity he found sensuality. Such defects are not surprising in an institution of men in their early twenties, but Noyes was a budding religious genius not content to pursue a tame and safe livelihood in the ministry while remaining unchanged within. The genuine pursuit of spirituality was all too rare. To explain this sad fact, Noyes reasoned that for those studying or engaged in business, the *mental* faculties are primarily engaged; religion is a matter of the *heart*. In a theological seminary religion becomes a profession, and when intellectual faculties are devoted to pursuits that are supposed to be sacred, it is natural enough to assume that there is little occasion for a separate education of the heart. But this notion is fatal to spirituality. Noyes's motto and text of argument with anyone who thought half-way religion sufficient was Paul's expression—"bringing into captivity *every* thought to the obedience of Christ." 2 Cor 10:5.

That first winter at Andover was a season of discontent, for although Noyes superficially enjoyed the general atmosphere, his spirit grieved as he observed increasing irregularity in his habits of devotion. More alarming, he felt an insidious loss of love of prayer and meditation. He was forthright in speaking about his convictions and found others who felt the same way in a group of equally zealous students at Andover called The Brethren, whose members planned on becoming foreign missionaries. His relations with the missionary students became more and more intimate, and he was admitted into this most secret society. This society began in secret at Williams College in 1808 and was practiced in the innermost sanctuary of the Congregational Church at that time. This group met "in a sphere of its own, silent, gentle, and unknown, but operating powerfully and producing important and lasting effects." From this period with the Brethren, Noyes wrote, "my standard of Christian responsibility began to rise and the thought for the first time began to develop itself, that I must live entirely for the service of God." Two of the Brethren, Lyman and Munson, had met their deaths at the hands of cannibals in the East India Islands.

On Christmas Day 1831, on his knees in prayer, he devoted himself to the missionary cause and placed himself under the American Board of Missions. To best serve as missionaries, the Brethren sought education of the heart through honest examination of each others' faults. One of their exercises was a frank criticism of one another's character. Members took turns listening silently while other members, one by one, told them their faults in the plainest way possible for the purpose of personal improvement. There was to be no defensiveness or justification of one's defects, just a silent hearing of how others perceived you. "This exercise," Noyes wrote, "sometimes cruelly crucified self-complacency, and it was contrary to the regulations of the society for anyone to be provoked or to complain." This discipline doesn't sound heartening to most, but Noyes found it immensely helpful to see himself as others did, to become more aware of his shortcomings. He found the process so helpful and even enlightening that he introduced it later as the principal source of governance in the Putney and Oneida Communities. Mutual Criticism is discussed in Chapter 7.

Going home for spring break, he had the solitude to begin again his devotional exercises, which he found very enjoyable. "I made a public profession of religion," wrote Noyes on May 13, 1832. "I made new resolutions of devotedness to God and determined no longer to live at the low-rate piety that is so common in the Christian church." Returning to Andover, he and others established a prayer group to counter the lack of seriousness at the seminary. Noyes was heavily influenced by Professor Moses Stuart, a noted Biblical scholar, who taught that the 7th chapter of Romans describes carnal man before conversion, not the mature Christian experience, and that the apostle Paul's supposed confession of sin referred to his pre-Christian experience. This strengthened young Noyes's conviction that it is possible to live in the revival spirit and become what Paul called a new creation, 2 Cor 5:17. The spark of a thought began to lift his spirit, a possibility that he actually might—and must—be satisfied with nothing less than getting the permanent presence of the living God in his heart. Revivalists had modified several Calvinist doctrines, especially one that insists that man was created wholly depraved and incapable of righteousness except as moved by God; but many earnest people asked, wasn't Christ's mission to give men more power over sin here in this world? Noyes again felt the imperative of becoming a missionary in the Foreign Service; after a "long interval of darkness, I once more held sweet communion with God."

From the beginning, Noyes was convinced that the gospel—meaning "good news"—conveys the real possibility of complete deliverance from the power of sin. Resignation to living a less than holy life cannot be good news. The power of God would purify the heart if sought with diligence:

> It is our supreme lesson, to know where the power over all happiness is, and to become reconciled to it, for then we shall turn our attention in the right direction. If we have the love of God shed abroad in our hearts, we cannot be anxious or gloomy and regardless of our circumstances, we shall be happy. Happiness and misery depend on these conditions, far more than on any other. This power over happiness must reside somewhere—where would you choose to have that power deposited?—in your own hands or in any collection of human beings, or in the laws of nature or chance? For my part, I would like to have it deposited exactly where it is, in the hands of a God whom I know to be thoroughly good and merciful and wise.

He was to learn in the coming months the meaning of the Biblical warning about spiritual indigestion—"Strong meat for men and milk for babes." Noyes was becoming aware of his limitations regarding too much mental work and how it can result in nervous difficulties—"in this state of body it is almost impossible for a sinner of my stamp to live near God." He had found his true calling, but began to decline physically because his mind became absorbed in meditation on the goodness of God. He had to force himself away from religious reflection in order to preserve mental balance and physical health. The diet and exercise regimen of the seminary improved his physical state, but he remained scattered and irregular in devotions. Though intellectually convinced of the truth of religion, "my heart and practical principles were at variance with it. I meditated much on divine things, to little profit. Nevertheless, I was enabled to watch my heart and to feel a tenderness of conscience that is always refreshing." Still, he writes that faithful self-examination must for the time elude him, though he would gladly do it, for it takes too great a toll on the body. Milk is for babes and strong meat is for the mature only.

Wrestling with Heart and Mind

Noyes reads the Bible with increasing affection and blesses God for so precious a book, yet at the same time he laments, "Oh, that I might have more of its spirit! I do not love Christ—which ought to fill my heart with overflowing. I do not have a sense of my own sinfulness and feel no abhorrence of everything opposed to holiness. I fear there is much hypocrisy in my conversation; I pass off for zeal what is really desire for applause. O God! Cleanse me from secret faults." Noyes was gifted with a rare, intuitive insight that it is what the heart, the spirit, knows that is important, not what the mind thinks and values. Brother Lawrence wrote the same in *The Practice of the Presence of God*: "Our thoughts spoil everything; all the trouble begins with them. We must be careful to reject them as soon as we see that they are neither necessary to our occupation at the moment nor conducive to our salvation, and return to our communion with God, wherein is our only good."[2] The average person has thousands of thoughts a day, studies say, mostly repetitive and the great majority negative; meditation and mindfulness provide an ability to observe one's mental life and to become freed from recurring unwanted threads of thoughts and feelings.

Noyes found self-examination a disagreeable task. For two weeks he was plunged into gloom, in the bondage of old habits. One day he remained in a "prayerful and tender frame of mind, but in the evening I engaged in unprofitable and wicked conversation and thus fell back into a state of darkness and insensibility." He searched the Bible and the library through most of the month about a question of conscience and his utter inability to resist temptation. "I was never more deeply convicted of my *meanness*, of my wickedness before God; I prayed, I wept." July 1832: "I rejoiced in the blessed influences of the Holy Spirit in my morning devotions. I felt new joy in the thought that the Lord reigneth, knows all things and will assuredly do all things right. But I cannot send my thoughts in any direction without crossing the track of some polluted image, and a thousand needless suggestions of impurity occur daily to blast my endeavors after holiness. I find my wickedness perpetually assuming some new and subtle form, and I must believe there is a labyrinth of iniquity in my heart that would baffle everything short of omniscience." His conversion faith is the one rock onto which he holds in the sea of despair: "But blessed be God, the blood of Christ cleanses from all sin and the Holy Spirit *will* search out and slay every sin."

Days later, he writes, "I have thought much of my sins today, especially the sins of my boyish days. When I look back and see what an ocean of impurity and vice I've waded through, I almost wonder I was not cut down, though the mercy of God is infinite. Mischievous thefts and lying were among the most glorious of my boyish exploits, and because there was roguery and wit in them instead of disgrace and remorse, they were actually matters of boasting. And even my riper years (age twenty while writing this journal) have been marked not merely by general impiety but by positive and shameful crime, which reason as well as conscience condemn. There is still an account blacker than these: even since God convinced me of his goodness, I have committed over and over again deliberate, flagrant wickedness. This very day, on which I resolved to keep my heart with all diligence, has sent at least three special messages of wrath to the judgment record, besides the long list of common besetting and negative sins. *Pride* has been the warp of this day's web," he laments. "The sweet influences of the spirit of God seemed to be withdrawn," he writes the next day. "I could desire and pray for their return, but my efforts to recover them were plainly impotent, as if to convince me that I have no moral power of myself. I know that God must work in me to will and to do his good pleasure, or I shall sink forever."

If this were mid-winter, one might think Noyes was subject to what we now know to be seasonal affective disorder. But July has just passed into August at the height of a warm, sunny summer and yet his thoughts become ever more melancholy. On August 5th he writes, "A day of darkness and of gloominess; my heart, even if it could be delivered from the curse of active malignity, must forever bear the coldness and insensibility of death without the spirit of God. I have passed through all the interesting exercises and privileges of this day without one warm feeling of love for Christ, gratitude to God, benevolence to man. I have been wishing today that I could devise some patent for sin, whereby the curse would be exterminated once for all." Sometimes he thinks he has had a breakthrough and that the disease is cured; but the cancer breaks out in some other spot. "Lord, help me be willing to be saved by Thee." For the remainder of the year at Andover, Noyes wrestles with his mind and heart, not satisfied with what most of us deem acceptable and inevitable. Saints and mystics set high standards for themselves; in their search for perfect acceptability in God's view, they see that they fall short, and are pained. Noyes writes, "If God did not know all things, I would be ruined." Thought experiments between his will and God's show no resignation to the will of God, only the prayer "Lord, I will lay hold on Thy hand, and be guided by Thee, though our path lie through fire and blood. I will believe in Thy goodness at all events."

Noyes lives in self-condemnation nearly constantly, enough to cause severe depression, and yet what he discerned in his conversion remains a life-saving rock on which to hold in stormy seas. He conveys this to his community ten years hence in a Home Talk called *The Anchor Rule*: "The alterations of our spiritual experience are like the changes of the weather, or the ebb and flow of the tides. We have at one time a clear perception of the truth, and are cheerful and fruitful; at another time, without any known cause of change, our minds are beclouded with doubts and condemnation, and all our being is unsatisfactory. But like those engaged in navigation, we can learn how to take advantage of the currents and counter-currents that we meet with. A person can manage even a raft so as to work his way up the North River without sail or oar. Let him start when the tide is running upstream, and he will make headway at a good rate for six hours. Then let him cast anchor and hold still the next six hours while the tide is setting back. After that he can go on with the tide another six hours. Apply this to our spiritual experiences. When we are cheerful and bright, seeing God and good in all around us, with minds clear, then the tide is setting up, and we have nothing to do but to let the raft float. But suppose that by and by we find the tide turning and all our feelings going wrong; then what we have to do is to cast anchor and lie still; which we can do by fastening ourselves to the truth we have seen, so that we cannot deny it when our *feelings* are opposed to it. There is a great deal of needless suffering for want of this anchoring rule. In many cases, a person's experience is just like running up with the tide six hours and falling back almost as much the next six hours. There is no better rule of life than to cling, in darkness, to what we saw in the light."

The next day, after sorrow in his morning devotions, he writes, "In view of the hardness of my heart and the smallness of the evidence I have of being regenerated, I could only lie at the foot of the cross and beg for repentance, for faith, for love. In the afternoon, there was a time when I thought I love God. There was a tenderness of soul that I always hail as the effect of the Holy Spirit's influences. As I read the *Missionary Herald*, I yearned for perishing souls and longed to be in the field. In the evening I had a singular season of prayer. Being alone I paced the room and as I meditated on divine things, I began to address God and found it pleasant to commune with him, I trust with reverence, yet more as conversation than formal prayer. I talked over my want of faith and feeling. I exposed freely all the deceitfulness of my heart, such as humble pride, selfish benevolence, and love of holiness because it is necessary as an evidence of being in a state of justification. I appealed to the omniscience of God for my sincerity, whether my heart was renewed or not." Brother Lawrence recommends this: "We should establish ourselves in the presence of God, talking always with Him. We ought to act very simply towards God, speaking frankly to Him and asking His help in things as they occur; God never fails to give it."[3]

Alas, this brief respite of a refreshing communication with God was not to last. Because he holds himself to the highest standard in thought and behavior, even the slightest manifestation of egocentric feeling is to be rejected. He still loves being held in favorable estimation, while at the same time he abhors this nearly universal human state of self-pride. A heated discussion with a classmate preyed on his mind. "It is my misery to be able to conceive distinctly how a warm-hearted Christian, how Christ himself would act in my situation, and yet to find myself morally impotent in regard to attaining that ideal standard. I look back with shame, and forward with gloom, because I cannot help wondering and grieving at the worldliness and pride and unholy ambition that I see every hour in my brethren. What would become of me, if God were as uncharitable and impatient as I am! If charity for the faults of Christians grows with growth in grace, I am backsliding. I must surely crucify this sin. I intend to maintain this struggle till holiness shall become the element of my rational existence." Brother Lawrence counseled in such a situation: "When at fault, simply admit it and say to God: I shall never do otherwise if you leave me to myself; it is for you to prevent my failing and to correct what is wrong. He then felt assured of God's forgiveness and did not let failure prey upon his mind."[4]

"I tried to repent and humble myself before God, but found again that without help from heaven I am impotent," Noyes wrote later. "I thought I had given up everything, and was willing to live only for God. But when I looked at my great pattern, and asked myself what he would do in my situation, I found I had not given up all. Though I might be willing to forego a thousand pleasures, to give up father and mother and brother and sister, to deny myself and crucify my lusts, to fast and pray and study even to the extent of human ability, yet I found myself shrinking back from undertaking that ceaseless activity of benevolence here on the spot, which I knew Christ would exhibit. I can vie with monks in passive piety, but to be an active Christian is another thing." He mourned this state that most take for granted as the inevitable human condition, and refused to accept it. He knew he had been converted, and yet he saw himself as a proud, angry, self-justifying spirit. "The hypocrisy and selfishness of the motives that govern me in my best actions were set before me in frightful array."

What saves him from desertion of the path he has bravely followed is the conviction he assimilated in his conversion—that God freely offers his help to all and that salvation can and must be won by individual initiative and effort. "I cannot believe that the path that God has declared plainly is beset on every hand with metaphysical traps and snares. I believe his grace is free, abundant, and accessible." Noyes always gets back on his feet (or on his knees) and renews the fight against all that falls short of pleasing God. Coupled with his core conviction that God's grace can be won by individual effort, Noyes devised a practice at Andover that helped him walk the razor's edge without becoming morose, cynical, or mad. He would select a trait of Christ or a spiritual principle and read all four gospels at once and write down every relevant passage. He would then read over his notes and reflect on them to clearly understand the trait or truth selected. He then did this with the epistles, and by the end of the Andover year he knew the New Testament chapter and verse.

George Washington Noyes wrote that after his brother John began theological studies at Andover he was home only during vacations for the next two and a half years. "On one of the first of these visits, he and other family members and many young converts from the neighborhood joined the Congregational church. This was the harvest of the revival in our town. It continued to spread—increasing in outward show, if not in power. To be religious and attend meetings became the prevailing fashion. During the next winter I attended a prayer-meeting in another town in which over thirty young girls spoke and prayed. It was the duty of every young convert to labor for the conversion of others by prayer-meetings, distributing tracts and books, and more frequently by direct personal address. A young and fashionable woman, the bride-elect of a minister in a town where I was a stranger, came up to me during the noon intermission at church and introduced conversation with, 'Well, my dear, do you think you are a Christian?' By such means converts were multiplied, but the power to keep them and lead them on to perfection was not then developed in the church. The genuine revival spirit was soon quenched in Putney by church broils and dissensions. Our minister was a blunt, outspoken man, and his open rebuke of a quarrelsome, vindictive church member set the whole town by the ears. The offended brother did not rest till he had stirred up such a commotion that the minister was obliged to get a dismissal. The church soon settled down into its old state of cold formality.

"Not so my brother. I have a vivid remembrance of the intense and growing earnestness of his spirit and conversation during his home vacations. His talk was not remembered for its smooth and elegant phrases or fine delivery in our village meetings, but sank deep into the heart and conscience. He never used notes when speaking, but his knowledge of the Bible grew to be something marvelous. The polyglot Bible, which was published about that time, was of convenient size and contained full marginal references. This was his invariable pocket companion, and was in constant use. In those days and for some years after, he was very thin and his face pale. I remember once he was in mother's chamber, talking with her about the cause dearest to his heart. More than any of us, she could sympathize with him and respond to his earnest words. As he leaned against the mantel-piece, she said, 'Why, John, how thin you look! Yet you are well, are you not?' He smiled brightly as he answered, 'Mother, it is my meat and drink to do the will of God.'"

Almost all his free time back at Andover was spent "waiting on the Lord," observing his own mental life, and praying to be cleansed from secret faults. Setting aside a day for secret fasting and prayer, Noyes gradually came to know the difference between divine nature and human nature. After his long struggles, he writes, "God has blessed my soul." He later described to his followers how he stayed the course in *First Love and Tried Love*: "Our spiritual experiences depend almost entirely on the state of our attention. We have a multitude of sensibilities that are constantly lying in wait for our attention. We are like a choir of singers in which many voices are sounding at once: voices that address our bodily senses, voices of the world of thought, voices of the world of feeling and of spirit. The series extends in regular gradation from the lowest feeling of the body up to that pre-eminent sense by which we feel God," Noyes described. "Can we in the midst of this crashing chorus hear distinctly the still, small voice of God? Yes, if we are skilled in the attentiveness of love. That is what we were made for and what we must do if we would be happy. Faith is the wide-awake state of that deepest sense by which we perceive God. It is tried by our being in circumstances where our attention is seized by other things and we are almost compelled to look away, and yet are just able to hold on to our remembered love. God thus tries our faith to strengthen it. As a man by lifting weights strengthens his arms, so our spirits grow strong in faith by turning, again and again, against all opposing forces, toward God. We are to be disciplined in controlling our attention by graduated trials, up to the utmost capability of our endurance, until we can say *I have set the Lord always before me.*"

Yale Theological Seminary

On his 21st birthday, September 3, 1832, Noyes entered Yale Theological Seminary, where the only requirement was to attend all lectures. He would have more time to devote single-mindedly to the simple treasures of the Bible. He read the epistles of Paul repeatedly, preparing the material for every sermon by reading the whole New Testament through, with reference to the theme at hand. Noyes also plunged with ardor into antislavery work with a few pioneer abolitionists, helping establish the New Haven Antislavery Society, one of the earliest antislavery societies in the country. He became much engaged in religious labor with those few freed slaves who resided in New Haven. He then became connected with about a dozen revivalists, and as their number multiplied they called themselves the Free Church. "I loved their spirit, for I was burning with the same zeal for the conversion of souls that I found in them, but nowhere else in the city. Their numbers and courage gradually increased till they began to think of employing a regular preacher. During winter vacation I visited friends in Vermont and had heard James Boyle preach several times at Brattleboro's powerful revival. When Amos Townshend spoke to me about procuring a preacher for the Free Church, I told him that Boyle was the very man they wanted." Noyes's recommendation of Boyle as permanent pastor of the Free Church was accepted in the spring of 1833, and Boyle labored in that capacity until he became a Perfectionist in the spring of 1834. The Free Church ultimately became a large and prosperous society where zealous people from all denominations gathered and built a grand meetinghouse.

Over the next year, John experienced a great increase of faith in prayer, and in August 1833, after final examinations, he received his license to preach. Students then spent several weeks performing the duties of a pastor where congregations lacked permanent pastors. "For the first time today I have performed the Sabbath duties of a minister. It is wonderful to think how God has strengthened me," he reminisces. "A year ago my nerves were so sensitive and my voice so weak that an evening meeting would spoil me for the succeeding day. I had no expectation of ever being strong enough to preach extemporaneously three times in a day. Now it actually does me good to preach. My nerves are quiet and my voice grows strong by exercise. Bless the Lord, O my soul!" On that first Sunday he read his written sermon and disliked the reading of it intensely, so from then on he began speaking without notes. The next Sunday was "a solemn and delightful meeting."

On his 22nd birthday, September 3rd, Noyes wrote, "Spent the morning in studying the mind of Christ, and was permitted to see more of his glory than I have ever seen before. I walked out over the hills and in the solitude of the forest under the canopy of heaven poured out my soul unto God, and wept for joy. My peace was as a river. I could only exclaim: Oh, what a glorious Christ is mine!" The next six weeks were spent preaching and ministering to individuals, feeling more definitely that he could be an instrument for awakening some people. "I have learned more about the Bible and about human nature during the past nine weeks than during all my theological courses. I found myself more interested in the people than I expected." But Noyes was becoming increasingly dissatisfied with the superficial spiritual life of existing churches. The revival spirit that Charles Grandison Finney and other evangelists had awakened was coalescing in major cities as free churches with "new measures"—separating from parent denominations and establishing a new sect that called for reform of "dead orthodoxy," as it termed the religion of the popular churches.

"I began to doubt whether true Christianity in its full saving operation was as extensively diffused in this country as I had imagined. As I lost confidence in the religion around me and increasingly saw the need of a re-conversion of most of those who professed Christianity, my missionary zeal declined and my heart turned toward thoughts, desires, and projects of an internal reformation of Christendom. Quality of religion, instead of quantity, became my focus. I did not entirely abandon my design of going on a foreign mission; but I became so much dissatisfied with the religion of the churches, with their benevolent societies and missionary machinery, that I determined not to go under the patronage and direction of the American Board. My purpose was to remain unmarried and to go among the heathen without scrip or purse or at the expense of my own patrimony. Work in foreign lands was increasingly redirected to converting nominal Christians here to higher views of Christian life. In conversation with one of the secretaries of the Board, I stated my objections to the spirit and measures of the churches and their societies, and to my surprise, he admitted for the most part the truth of my views.

"My spirit rapidly increased in strength during the autumn of 1833. By constant fellowship and conversation with Boyle and Chauncey Dutton and others, reading books such as John Wesley's *A Plain Account of Christian Perfection*, and by much study of the Bible and fervent prayer, my heart was kept in steady and accelerating progression toward holiness. Dr. Fitch assigned the class to write a skeleton of a sermon based on Phil 3:13–14: *Forgetting those things which are behind, and reaching forth unto those things which are before, I press toward the mark for the prize of the high calling of God in Christ Jesus.* The passage harmonized well with the state of my mind, and in studying it I received a new baptism of zeal. I ended my sermon with these words: "Paul sought a perfect objective, by perfect means, with perfect energy."

Noyes's final year at Yale was spent preaching and debating in the seminary, combined with systematic temperance, fasting, exercise, and prayer. "I had conquered my nervous system," Noyes states with youthful optimism. He was no longer tormented by the desire to eat or other temptations. "I could now study intensely twelve or even sixteen hours a day without injury. Preaching, which once would shake and disorder my nerves, had become a delight and refreshment to me. I was constantly cheerful and often very happy. My chief delight, next to that of communing with Christ through the Scriptures, was in prayer. I was in the habit of spending not less than three hours in my closet daily. I could truly say that I entered "into the secret place of the Most High, and abode under the shadow of the Almighty." The spirit of love blotted out my transgressions, wiped away my tears, and filled me with unutterable bliss."

In *Waiting and Watching*, he wrote, "The most important experience of the spiritual life is to become fishermen in the heavenly waters—to be always on the watch for a bite, to watch and wait for the responses of the Spirit to our thoughts, feelings, and imaginations, so that we act more and more from internal influences. This waiting and watching is true prayer and constitutes the interior and most important experience of the whole Christian life. We shall walk as Christ walked, not by the light of the external world but by the light of God to bring all our common actions under the control of this internal monitor. The most insignificant exterior acts may become the sweetest and most beautiful parts of one's life, just because of the connection formed between them and this internal oracle. We must let God speak to us in that inward way to be our guide in matters of knowledge and even to the extent of his becoming a practical director of our lives—this is the peace that passes understanding. Praying with the mouth is nothing. To get a bite from heaven is better than anything we call sport. There is a great deal of entertainment in this way of living. By following this principle, instead of attending to business with an idea that you are playing a strain of your own alone, you will find that you are playing a second to another melody which is vibrating in your heart; and it then becomes a matter of great interest to you to keep in time and tune with that melody, so that you lean on it and get help from it. Your life then becomes significant and melodious.

HERESY AND HOLINESS

Noyes had begun his studies fully in accord with Christian doctrine and the conventional church, but from the beginning of his spiritual journey, Noyes's quick mind and honest heart couldn't help but question aspects of church orthodoxy. His independent spirit rebelled against any notion that he must submit to doctrine that his mind and conscience questioned. A teaching by his eminent professor at Andover, Moses Stuart, was that the 24th chapter of Matthew refers to events connected with the destruction of Jerusalem.

The Second Coming

Noyes undertook a rigorous course of independent scriptural study that resulted in his unique view about the Second Coming of Christ: "I read the New Testament through ten times with the question as to the time of Christ's second coming, and noted each reference to this event; all alluded to within a generation from the time of Christ's personal ministry. The apostles exhort the churches to look and wait for the coming of Christ; they constantly speak of the event as near at hand. Paul plainly assumes that he and some of those to whom he writes will be alive on earth when Christ returns." Christ's question in John 21:22, "If I will that he (John) tarry till I come, what is that to thee?" *is intimation by Christ himself*, Noyes thought, *that John will live till his Second Coming*. The Bible's hidden treasures are fully accessible to those who make the Spirit of Truth their guide, Noyes believed. "I had long been growing in the belief that the Bible was not a book of inexplicable riddles and I determined to solve this mystery. My heart struggled in prayer for full access to the truth. When my investigation ended, my mind was clear: I no longer conjectured, I *knew* that the time appointed for the second coming of Christ was within one generation from the time of his personal ministry. I advanced into actual heresy in summer 1833."

Christ explicitly limited the time of his second coming—"immediately after" the unparalleled tribulations of the Jewish people, culminating in the destruction of Jerusalem. At that time, Jews had come to Jerusalem to attend the Passover feast. During the siege, 111,000 people were killed, most survivors were sent to Rome, all children under age seventeen were dispatched as slaves to Egypt, the temple and the city were demolished, the daily sacrifice practiced since Moses was forcibly broken up, and all national and territorial rights were stripped away. These events were the *outward manifestation* of the second coming itself, which was to be "like a thief in the night," omnipresent like lightning. Noyes took Christ fully at his word; the second coming of Christ in its visible and invisible aspects was to him a potent reality. "As the body is to the soul, so was the awful overthrow of Jerusalem to the second coming of Christ." Because the kingdom of heaven is within, the second coming was an inner event of a world unperceived but infinitely greater. The Greek word mistranslated in the King James Version in Matthew 24:3 as the end of the *world* was corrected in the Revised Standard Version to convey the end of an *age*. The second coming meant not the end of the physical world but the end of the Mosaic dispensation of prophesy and promise, during which people obeyed religious laws and the exhortations of the prophets.

Christ introduced a radical change in the understanding of holiness and sin in a new dispensation; he insisted on the necessity of right intent while affirming right action. "Your righteousness shall exceed the righteousness of the scribes and Pharisees—*Love the Lord thy God with all thy heart and with all thy soul and with all thy mind, and thy neighbor as thyself.* On these two commandments hang all the law and the prophets." The thousand precepts of the law were reduced to one—love; the law was written on tablets of stone; holiness was written in the heart—Heb 10:16–17. The Christian dispensation is the era of fulfillment where perfect holiness is entire salvation from sin, here and now. This great object of the mission and sacrifice of Christ was attained by many in the apostolic church and must again emerge as the standard of Christian experience.

One of the first persons to apprehend this conception of holiness in its relation to salvation from sin—the doctrine of Christian perfection—was John Wesley in the eighteenth century. It was taught by many revival leaders during the second Great Awakening in the early nineteenth century, such as Charles Grandison Finney especially in New York State. New York Perfectionists were Wesleyan in origin and characteristics; leaders of the New England church leaned in this direction. Holiness is perfect love of God and man and can be attained in this life, Wesley said. Lacking Noyes's view of the second coming, he did not stress that perfect holiness was actually attained by the apostolic church in the harvest period just previous to Christ's second coming.

"The question is whether Christ predicted in the 24th chapter of Matthew his own Second Coming in immediate connection with the destruction of Jerusalem," Noyes posited. "Historians and theologians both Protestant and Catholic answer, no. The force of tradition and education current in the theological world thinks the idea that the Second Coming took place eighteen hundred years ago is an absurdity. But what else can be made of this chapter? Unprejudiced common sense answers, yes. Read it with your mind divested of any preconceived interpretation. I don't know if this is at first possible, but come as near to it as you can and I believe the Spirit of Truth will help you," Noyes said in the August 24, 1868, *Circular*. What is the result? Your answer is that the language teaches that Christ would come about the time of Jerusalem's overthrow. *But . . .* you begin; no, friend—read the chapter carefully again, asking the Spirit of Truth to help you as before.

"Is this confusion because of ambiguity in Christ's words? Christ expresses himself with great clearness and simplicity. You come to the 34th and 35th verses: 'Verily I say unto you, this generation shall not pass till all these things be fulfilled. Heaven and earth shall pass away, but my words shall not pass away.' Here is a declaration amounting to an oath. Does your mind hesitate at the word generation? If so, turn back to Matt 23:36. Read the connection. Have you any doubts as to Christ's meaning in 'generation'? Your answer is unhesitatingly, no. He evidently meant the scribes, Pharisees and hypocrites living contemporary with himself. I am aware of no commentators who question this view. The word generation used here in the Greek is *genea*—precisely the same as that used in Matt 24:34. Its definition, as given in the Greek Lexicon, is: 1st—the interval of time between father and child; a single step or succession in natural descent. 2d—an age put for the average duration of human life; the period in which the population of the earth is supposed to be successively renewed. 3d—those living in any period. I reasoned thus: Christ's declarations are emphatic and unmistakable in Matthew 24 and particularly in verses 29-30 and 34-35, viz., that his second appearing would occur within the time of that generation following the destruction of the Jewish temple; it would end the Jewish dispensation. With my faith fixed in the truth that Christ did come when he said he would, the teaching of the whole Bible and especially of the New Testament, becomes a unit."

Freedom from Sin

Sin, defined, means "missing the mark." Noyes's second great heresy followed from his knowledge that perfect love of God and man can be attained in this life because he experienced that transcendent love. As God approaches persons as father instead of law-giver, myriad laws of behavior are reduced to one imperative, love, from which springs right intention and right action. External law presupposes internal depravity. How incomparably easier to receive deliverance from all sins than to conquer one! The gospel, meaning "good news," proclaimed not only the mercy of God in pardoning sin, but also power over sin altogether. Pride, envy, anger, lust, greed, Noyes always insisted, are but limbs of the tree of sin; easier to lay the ax at the root and fell the whole tree at once.

John writes in his first letter, chapter 3: "No one who abides in him sins; no one who sins has either seen him or known him." "No one born of God commits sin; for God's nature abides in him, and he cannot sin because he is born of God." Salvation from the power of sin was the mission and sacrifice of Christ, and among its fruits are love and all fruits of the spirit, described in Gal 5:22-23. "If anyone has the world's goods and sees his brother in need, yet closes his heart against him, how does God's love abide in him?"–1st John 3:17. Paul plainly asserts his freedom from sin as the consequence of his union with Christ: "I live, yet not I, but Christ in me." Paul reiterates in Col 1:23 that holiness is achieved ". . . provided that you continue in the faith, stable and steadfast . . ." As Jesus said, "If you *continue* in my word, you are my disciples indeed, and you shall know the truth and the truth shall make you free."

"One can attain the Biblical purity of heart, but not necessarily at a first conversion; it is liable to failure because it is chiefly the work of one's will. The soft heart is chiefly the work of God in one who is fully receptive to many conversions toward a transformed mind and heart. Initial conversion is preparation to experience divine love—of neighbor, of the stranger by the wayside, even of the enemy. *Not I, but Christ in me* is purity of heart, spiritual rebirth, and deliverance from sin—the reconciliation of God and man that is forever secure from backsliding," Noyes taught. "You, therefore, must be perfect, as your heavenly Father is perfect," said Jesus in the Sermon on the Mount. "*Ask* and ye shall find; *seek* and it shall be given you"—those words in the original language connote patient, confident, continuous seeking. Christ did not command what cannot be done; *perfect* in the original language connotes full realization of the human potential to love unconditionally. Theologian Moses Stuart's interpretation of Romans 7 that St. Paul's confession of sin referred to his pre-Christian experience is proved by Paul's assertion in Rom 8:2—"The law of the Spirit of life in Christ Jesus hath made me free from the law of sin and death."

"I well remember one discourse that I preached in different places four times within a few weeks, and every time with an increasing weight of self-application," Noyes wrote. "The text was Prov 28:13, *He that covers his sins shall not prosper; but whoso confesses and forsakes them shall have mercy*. Mere confession is not enough. Confession of sin without forsaking it is the most ingenious and satisfactory way of covering it. God must abhor this whole system of sinning and confessing and sinning again, which prevails in the churches," Noyes lamented. "If a man steals from you and afterward confesses it, you forgive him. Perhaps you forgive a second time; but if he steals the third day, and confesses the third time even with tears, you account his confession as bad as his theft, insult added to injury. Yet this is the way that men who profess to be religious deal with God all over the land. From Sabbath to Sabbath and year to year, they confess the same sins over and over and never forsake them, never *expect* to forsake them. Heb 10:26 is clear—"If we sin deliberately after receiving the knowledge of the truth, there no longer remains a sacrifice for sins . . ." This thought was like a barbed arrow in my heart. Every time I handled it, it entered deeper, and I knew there was no escape except by the abandonment once for all of the whole body of sin."

How can it be, he asked himself, *that I must again be converted*? "I perceived that there are three distinct states of the heart: First, a state in which a preponderance of the affections is toward the world. This is irreligion. Second, a state in which the preponderance of the affections is toward God, though more or less attachment to the world remains—this is the double-minded state, the state of ordinary sinful religion. Third, a state in which all the affections of the heart are given to God. In *this* state there is no sin, and I was satisfied that it is attainable on earth and that some in the Primitive Church did attain it. The transition from the double-minded state to perfect holiness requires as radical a conversion as does the transition from irreligion to the double-minded state—intellectual conviction evolves to the truly softened heart from which springs a God-centered life. Thus I pressed toward a second conversion.

"I lost all relish for the revival labors in which I was engaged, not because I cared less for souls, but because I felt it was folly to try to save others while I myself was not saved. I withdrew from public effort as much as possible and gave myself up to prayer, searching the Scriptures to inquire after salvation from sin. My appetite forsook me, and for a week before I found peace, I took but very little food. *Thou shalt love the Lord thy God* with all thy heart was ever before my mind as the only standard of righteousness, the very beginning of all virtue. In the blaze of that law, all my works and experiences and hopes faded into vanity. The question with me was how shall I now fulfill the righteousness of the law?" Two and a half years ago, at his first conversion, the word "righteousness" was the first mystery in his mind. *What does righteousness truly mean*? Noyes had pondered; finding the answer to this question was the only worthy pursuit of life. Over those two years of study and meditation, he realized that the human being is so constructed that at one's highest state of development, one can commune with God.

"The ideas of faith current in that day were few and meager. I had been trained in the revival doctrines of submitting to the will of God and making benevolence the governing purpose, but my attention had never been directed to *faith* as fundamentally related to salvation from sin. Chauncey Dutton was telling me about the Albany Perfectionists, and mentioned that they made great account of faith. I immediately went through the New Testament, noting all I found on the subject of faith. I was greatly astonished at the magnitude of the subject in the Bible, and my ignorance of it hitherto. I found Christ always speaking to those who sought his help in this manner—According to thy *faith* be it unto thee. Thy *faith* hath made thee whole. O woman, great is thy *faith*. In all the epistles I saw the same idea of the agency of faith, transferred from bodily to spiritual therapeutics. This was the beginning of daylight to my soul. But it was only the beginning. It is one thing to know that faith is the medium of salvation, and it is another to actually believe. My heart still anxiously pondered—*How shall I get this faith*? That evening I was under the necessity of attending an inquiry meeting and was miserable over the prospect of instructing others, almost a despairing inquirer myself! The burden of Christian perfection accumulated upon my soul until I determined to give myself no rest while the possibility of attaining it remained doubtful.

"As I sat brooding over my difficulties, I listlessly opened my Bible and my eye fell upon these words: The Holy Ghost shall come upon thee, and the power of the Highest shall overshadow thee; therefore also that holy thing which shall be born of thee shall be called the Son of God. I opened the Bible again in the spirit of Samuel when he said, Speak, Lord, for thy servant heareth. These words were before me—Notwithstanding the Lord stood with me, and strengthened me; that by me the preaching might be fully known. . . . And the Lord shall deliver me from every evil work, and will preserve me unto his heavenly kingdom. Once more I opened the book and these words met my view—Go, stand and speak in the temple to the people all the words of this life.

"Faith as a grain of mustard seed was in my heart, but its expansion into full consciousness of spiritual life and peace yet required another step: confession. The next morning I recurred to the passage that had been my guide in my first conversion, Rom. 10:7–10—'If thou shalt confess with thy mouth the Lord Jesus, and shalt believe in thy heart that God has raised him from the dead, thou shalt be saved.' It flashed across my mind that the work was done, that Christ was in me with the power of his resurrection; it only remained for me to confess it before the world to enjoy the consciousness of it. I determined at once to confess Christ in me a savior from sin, at all hazards. It fell to my lot to preach that evening at the Free Church. I prepared myself for an unflinching testimony against all sin. When I announced my text from 1st John 3:8—*He that committeth sin is of the devil*—I felt, and I doubt not that the audience felt that I was entering upon a new field of theology." First John 3 brings the point home in the next verse, 9—*No one born of God commits sin; for God's nature abides in him, and he cannot sin because he is born of God.* "I insisted on the literal meaning of the text, noting that *commits* in Aramaic connotes *keeps on* committing, as Proverbs makes clear: whoso confesses *and forsakes* sin shall receive mercy."

Noyes did his best to prove that mature Christians, many in the Primitive Church, were not sinners. Christ Jesus came into the world to save sinners, Paul said. Not from the consequences of sin but from the power of sin itself, the fallen state that separates us from knowing divine love. "I entered upon a course of departure from popular belief that would probably end in ecclesiastical outlawry and went home feeling that I had committed myself irreversibly. That night, I received the baptism that I desired and expected. Three times in quick succession a stream of eternal love gushed through my heart and rolled back again to its source. Joy unspeakable and full of glory filled my soul. All fear and doubt and condemnation passed away. I knew that my heart was clean, and that the Father and the Son had come and made it their abode."

John Humphrey Noyes experienced that power over sin he had long sought. He seemed fully awake for the first time, identified with the goodness of the universe and able to be an instrument of the Almighty. Now he possessed sure knowledge that if we seek, we shall find love of God and purity of heart. Four days later, he wrote a letter to his mother describing his experience. His sister Charlotte, then age thirteen, remembers seeing her mother standing in the kitchen, holding the letter with wet hands and exclaiming: "What *does* John mean?"

Psychologist William James cites many dramatic examples of religious conversion in *The Varieties of Religious Experience*. He drew on *The Psychology of Religion* by Edwin D. Starbuck of Stanford University, who described two dynamics in the mind of one liable to conversion: first, the feeling of sinfulness that one is eager to escape from—a pervading sense of incompleteness or wrongness; secondly, the positive ideal for which he longs.[5] "When the new center of personal energy has been subconsciously incubated so long as to be just ready to open into flower, hands off is the only word . . . it must burst forth unaided." Striving must eventually be given up—"Let one do all in one's power, and one's nervous system will do the rest." The act of self-surrender, of yielding, "is giving one's self over to the new life, making it the center of a new personality."[6] As St. John of the Cross put it in *Dark Night of the Soul*, if you want God to enter, you have to empty yourself.

The day after John Humphrey Noyes's life-changing second conversion on February 20th, a date celebrated as the High Tide of the Spirit in the Oneida Community, a theological student who had heard his discourse at the Free Church wanted to know if he really meant what he said, that a sinner cannot be a Christian.

"I assured him," Noyes said, "that I did so mean." Then, as Noyes fully anticipated, came the expected argument.

"But don't *you* commit sin?" the student asked.

"No."

Noyes answered deliberately and firmly—knowing that his answer would plunge him into the depths of contempt. The man stared as though a thunderbolt had fallen before him. At first he seemed to doubt his own senses, and asked again, "You do not commit sin?" When Noyes explained what had happened, how his experience of the Divine had changed everything, the student went to tell the news. Within hours the word passed through the college and the city—*Noyes says he is perfect!* On the heels of this went the report—*Noyes is crazy.*

"Thus my confession was made and I began to suffer the consequences. The flood of contention that poured in upon me from the College and Seminary kept my intellectual powers in a state of intense energy for several weeks. Students flocked to my room, some to see the perfect man as they would go to see any curiosity, and others to argue with me or puzzle me with objections. I never grew faster than at that time. A feeling of fearful responsibility rested upon me. It seemed as though God in giving me the treasure of the gospel had placed me in the midst of the keenest and fiercest disputers of this world, that its defensibility might be thoroughly tested. I felt that I must carefully answer every fair objection to the doctrine of holiness."

Noyes explained to his visitors that spiritual Perfectionism did not mean being perfect in external matters such as being free from personal shortcomings and errors of judgment, or being beyond discipline and improvement of character, or possessing social refinements. On the contrary! His experience assured him that an endless prospect of improvement lay before him. But he knew that he would never again willfully do wrong. "I have a vivid consciousness of the presence of God in my heart. I claim only purity of heart that gives good conscience toward God. To be pure in heart, to be receptive, to wait on the Lord—none ever wait in vain—are nearly synonymous." Noyes described how a single conversion is only a beginning and should be followed up with continuing conversions until softness of heart is established as the permanent state described by Paul—I live, yet not I, but Christ liveth in me. "Make up your mind that you will be converted as many times as necessary to have a tender heart forever," Noyes urged, "whether anybody else has or not. A tender heart is the special gift of the gospel covenant and accompanies a spiritual discovery of God. *A new heart will I give you; I will take away the stony heart out of your flesh and give you a heart of flesh*, Eze 11:19. The most radical of all diseases is hardness of heart."

John Wesley, founder of Methodism, described what he meant by being perfect: "Scriptural perfection is pure love, filling the heart, and governing all words and actions. All inward sin is taken away. One may be filled with pure love and still be liable to mistake, but where every word and action springs from love," Wesley concluded, "mistakes both in judgment and in practice are not properly *sins*—if love is the sole principle of action. 'Thou shalt love the Lord your God with all your heart, and with all your soul, and with all your mind. This is the great and first commandment. And a second is like it, You shall love your neighbour as yourself. On these two commandments depend all the law and the prophets.' We mean one who obeys the command, 'Be ye perfect,' in whom is the mind that was in Christ. 'Blessed are the pure in heart, for they shall see God.'

Noyes's strongest belief was 'No one born of God commits sin; for God's nature abides in him, and cannot sin because he is born of God'—1st John 3:9; Wesley explains 1st John 1:7–10: "'If we say we have no sin, we deceive ourselves' and 'If we say we have not sinned, we make him a liar, and his word is not in us.' The ninth verse explains the eighth and tenth—'If we confess our sins, He is faithful and just,' not only to 'forgive us our sins,' *but also* to 'cleanse us from all unrighteousness' if we walk in the light and 'sin no more.' To be sanctified is to be renewed in the image of God; it is true holiness: 'I live; yet not I, but Christ liveth in me,' in the words of Paul. In conformity both to the doctrine of St. John and the whole tenor of the New Testament," Wesley concluded, "A Christian is so far perfect as not to commit sin."[7]

Noyes corresponded with the Missionary Brethren at Andover Theological Seminary, withdrawing his pledge to go on a foreign mission and briefly stating his reasons. His friend Champion, the missionary who afterward went to Africa, asked for a fuller explanation of his course. "I wrote him that I felt bound to withdraw my pledge for three reasons: first, because I now knew that I was not a Christian when I made it; second, because I had discovered that God was my owner and had the right to direct me by *his Spirit*; third, because I saw that I was already on missionary ground among a people who (though professedly Christian) needed to be converted quite as much as the heathen. I put on paper all references to the texts I could find in the New Testament indicating that perfect holiness is the standard of Christianity. The whole theory of Christianity is based on the assumption that character can be improved, even radically changed. It is the miracle of miracles, the wonder of heaven and earth; it is a rising above nature, an ascent into the resurrection. Let that idea gain access to a person's heart and mind, and it will continue to work until he hungers and thirsts for righteousness. The person passes over to God, and begins to work out his salvation. But one must see to it that improvement is radical and central, not merely an improvement of manner and sensibilities."

John Wesley believed exactly that. Reading about purity of intention in Bishop Taylor's *Rules and Exercises of Holy Living and Dying*, "Instantly I resolved to dedicate all my life to God, all my thoughts, and words, and actions . . . ." Thomas à Kempis persuaded Wesley that "giving even all my life to God (supposing it possible to do this) and go no further, would profit me nothing unless I gave my heart, yea all my heart to Him—simplicity of intention and purity of affection, one design in all we speak or do, and one desire ruling all our tempers." William Law's *Christian Perfection* and *Serious Call* "convinced me more than ever of the absolute impossibility of being half a Christian . . . ." I saw "the indispensable necessity of having the mind which was in Christ, not only in many or in most respects, but in all things."[8]

Noyes's first convert following his spiritual experience was Abigail Merwin, a thirty-year-old talented beauty who was active in the New Haven Free Church. They met before a prayer meeting and he asked her, "Will you receive Christ as a whole Savior and confess him before the world?" Without hesitation, she affirmed, "I will." The next day Abigail Merwin publicly professed holiness, as had John.[9] Her brother-in-law Everard Benjamin, a deacon of the Free Church, his wife, and Abigail's brother followed her in the confession of holiness. She understood what John meant when he said he was beyond committing sin, that the Biblical purity of heart is the direct experience of divine love. All things are made new when the Father and the Son enter the heart and make it their abode; the "outer man" gradually conforms into that pure inner state that affirms *Thy will be done*. A friendly printer who was interested in Noyes's views printed 1,500 handbills that were delivered throughout New Haven and to others with whom he kept in touch. Abigail Merwin dispatched packages of them to missionary stations in distant parts of the world, launching the faith of salvation from sin. The two were in close collaboration for three months.

Noyes stressed the necessity of this conformity to the will of God throughout his life. When difficulties occurred, he considered them occasions of thanksgiving, regarding them as answers to his sincere prayers for a purified heart. Noyes shared this hard-learned wisdom in his Home Talk, *God in All Things*:

> "If you watch your experience, probably you will find that you are thankful for some things that happen to you, and perhaps a little cross about other things. Paul says, In everything, give thanks. The next time anything happens that tempts you to feel cross, why not think of this and ask whether it is not God that is approaching you behind the disagreeable event; and if it is, be respectful, whether you understand or not. If it is God that is approaching you, you can be sure it is for some good, and that you had better yield him your attention."

"If I did not satisfy the objectors at Yale, they were usually silenced, and at all events I got hold of the truth for myself in the struggle. After my confession of holiness, a subject of debate was brought forward by eminent theology professor Dr. Nathanial Taylor in the Society of the Theological Seminary: *Is perfect holiness attainable in this life?*" Noyes contended that purification of the human heart and spirit is so much more prominently featured in New Testament writers than is forgiveness, that it can be concluded that spiritual purification was the *only* object of Christ's atonement. Dividing salvation into two parts in the Book of Hebrews—forgiveness of past sin: *I will remember their sins and their misdeeds no more*, and purification from present sin: *I will put my laws into their hearts, and write them on their minds*—Noyes read the tenth chapter of Hebrews, dwelling on verse 14: *For by a single offering he has perfected for all time those who are sanctified.* The sacrifice of Christ makes perfect holiness attainable in this life. The breach between man and God was and is healed. Dr. Taylor and the Society came down against Noyes's views.

"I was previously engaged to preach at a meeting and I was strongly inclined by my old habits to go through the usual ceremonies, preaching to sinners and trying to get up a revival excitement. But having yielded my whole heart to God, the infusion of his Spirit inspired me to abandon the formal machinery of religion, and confess and preach salvation from sin with a simplicity that was evidently mortifying to my old revival friends. I went home with a feeling that a child may be supposed to have when it is fairly weaned from its mother. I perceived abundant evidence of God's providential care over me. Good luck, as the world would call it, met me at every turn."

Professor Taylor called at Noyes's room to notify him that he was soon to be tried by the Association that had licensed him to preach. He was displeased that a student would promulgate new views in the Seminary without consulting him; he'd heard about the controversial sermon, and thought it too *literal*.

"Do you really mean what you said, that a sinner cannot be a Christian?"

"I did mean exactly what I said, Dr. Taylor," Noyes replied.

"If this is your doctrine," Taylor persisted, "you un-church yourself as well as others—don't *you* commit sin?"

"No."

Taylor was speechless, able only to ask, "You do not commit sin?"

"I received the Holy Spirit and its purification of my heart," Noyes began, describing the infinite divine love, joy, and peace he had experienced, which blots out all transgressions. "I cannot be turned from my course by man."

"I dealt with one other Perfectionist," Taylor exclaimed. "I convinced *him* of the reality of sin! Noyes, we're going to review your qualifications to preach the Holy Gospel. You did not consult me about your radical views before spreading them at the seminary."

Noyes insisted that Taylor's own views of man's perfect ability to obey the law of God led directly to Perfectionism.

"Yes, man is perfectly able to keep the law and God has a perfect right to require him to do so," Taylor agreed, "but a gracious system in which perfect obedience is not yet required will save a greater number than would otherwise be saved, and God in his benevolence has therefore adopted such a system."

"I discovered the reality of the Gospel in prayer. As the Bible assures us, when we earnestly seek, we find. I feel the Spirit not only in my soul," Noyes continued, "but in every fiber of my body."

"No one," Taylor laughed a bit derisively, "can physically *feel* the spirit of God!"

As Noyes and Taylor discussed John's sermon theme, *He that committeth sin is of the devil*, Noyes tried to convey to Taylor that consciousness of God heals the fundamental separation between God and man, ending sin. "And in loving God, we can manifest his kingdom on earth as the Lord's Prayer asks. The Gospel message is much more than forgiveness—it describes the end of the cycle of sin, repentance, forgiveness, and inevitable sinning again."

"This is nothing but the old Wesleyan scheme, tried and failed. You might find a few followers among women and ignorant people, but not among the intelligent," Taylor retorted. "You are young and not as wise as I . . ."

"He that doeth the will of God shall know of the doctrine," Noyes felt obliged to interrupt.

"I have as much interest in that promise as you!" Taylor rejoined.

"Then," Noyes persisted, ". . . you do not commit sin?"

"Well . . . *yes*. I do."

"What do you say about 1st John, chapter 3, No one born of God commits sin; for God's nature abides in him, and he cannot sin because he is born of God. And one who commits sin is of the devil . . ."

"You say," Taylor interrupted, "that I am of the devil, do you?"

"No, I asked your opinion of 1st John 3:8–9," Noyes replied, "and quoted those words from the Bible."

"Well, you're a sinner now if you were not when I came in," Taylor blurted out, "for you have not treated me courteously!"

Remarkably self-confident for a twenty-two-year-old, Noyes responded: "The best kind of courtesy in a situation like this is plainness of speech." He had appreciated the Andover Brethren's unvarnished speech, speaking honestly from the heart. Taylor left the room. This interview was distressing to Noyes because he had great reverence and even affection for Dr. Taylor, and dreaded a collision with him, but it left no sting. "I felt more free and peaceful afterward, as a soldier might feel after having passed the deadliest spot in the breach."

Noyes received an invitation to preach from the pastor of the Congregational Church in Prospect, Connecticut; Boyle had been there before and had shaken the church to its foundations. Noyes remained for ten days, preaching every evening and three times on each Sabbath. "The very best of the inhabitants fell under the sword of God's truth and pressed into the kingdom of holiness," Noyes recounted.

Special Meeting of the Association of the Western District of New Haven County, April 16, 1834.

"I observed at the outset that I had no objection to being examined in regard to my faith, but that if the object of the examination was to ascertain whether my license ought to be taken away, it was unnecessary. I had no disposition to avail myself of their license in preaching doctrines that I knew they did not sanction, and I would therefore resign. I was requested to state my doctrines before the Association, which I did in a discourse of considerable length. Some questions were asked by Mr. Kirk of Albany, and others, and I was dismissed." The Association remained in session. Boyle sat with them by invitation. "Returning to my room I found a quantity of the tract entitled *Paul not Carnal*, which I had sent to the printer. I went back to the Session room and gave a handful to Boyle, who sat next to the door, and he distributed them among the ministers."

On the motion of Dr. Taylor, the following resolution was adopted:

"Whereas Mr. Noyes has adopted views on the doctrine of Christian perfection that are erroneous, unscriptural, and inconsistent with his usefulness as a preacher of the gospel; therefore, resolved, that without impeaching the Christian character of Mr. Noyes, the Association hereby recalls his license to preach."

A student asked Noyes whether he would continue to preach, now that the clergy had taken away his license. "I have taken away their license to sin, and they keep on sinning," he replied. "So, though they have taken away my license to preach, I shall keep on preaching."

John Humphrey Noyes experienced a heart conversion after a year at Yale Theological Seminary, an experience that revealed the divine spirit within all. The purpose of life is achievement of the loving heart by learning to hear this internal Spirit. Heaven within all can be known and implemented on earth.

"Why is it that the very name of perfection has been cast out of the mouth of Christians, as if it contained the most pernicious heresy?" John Wesley always wondered. "It is the doctrine of Jesus Christ. Those are His words, not mine:—*Ye shall therefore be perfect as your Father who is in Heaven is perfect*.... It is the giving to God all our hearts: it is one desire and design ruling all our tempers.... It is a renewal of the heart in the whole image of God, the full likeness of Him that created it. It is to love God with all our heart, and our neighbour as ourselves. We are to expect it not at death, but every moment. Christian perfection is the potential reality in all persons here and now—only to be realized." Wesley traveled 4,000 miles a year in many adverse conditions to establish and reinvigorate churches; some preachers never spoke of Christian perfection as a real human possibility, or only in general. William Law, a major influence on Wesley, contended that the commandment to love God would not be given unless the reality of the divine nature was in him. Christians fall short of holiness because *intention* is the vital ingredient—intend to please God in all actions; the heart knows it's not through inability but because you never thoroughly intended it.

William James describes David Brainerd's experience: "Though I thought that I was aiming at the glory of God, *I never once truly intended it*, but only my own happiness." Then "unspeakable glory seemed to open to the apprehension of my soul . . . a new inward view of God such as I had never had before. My soul rejoiced with joy . . . I had no thought of my own salvation and scarce reflected that there was such a creature as myself."[10] Brainerd was also expelled from Yale in his third year for criticizing a professor (then called a tutor). Theologian Jonathan Edwards and Aaron Burr interceded for him, to no avail. Unable to preach, he became a sainted missionary to Indians in remote areas who did not know Christianity.

After his license to preach was recalled, John Humphrey Noyes could no longer preach in churches or reside at Yale Theological Seminary. He had been holding meetings at five in the morning at New Haven's Free Church, and now the officers of that church told him the premises would no longer be available. He lost the companionship of Abigail Merwin, the woman who had been his first convert and an energetic, stalwart friend for three months. "My good name in the great world was gone. My friends were fast falling away. I was beginning to be indeed an outcast. Yet I rejoiced and leaped for joy," wrote this twenty-two-year-old man who had joined the ranks of those who discover that God is not found only in churches, temples, or mosques, but in the human heart.

He wrote a profound summary of his state to his parents in May 1834: "I cannot but wonder at the insignificance of all my past attainments in knowledge, when compared with developments that I know are before me. A few months have enlarged my views of God beyond all my previous anticipations even in fancy; and when imagination stretches on millions and millions of years, I ask with trembling wonder, where will all this end? Certainly the treasures of the wisdom and glory of God will not be exhausted. The ocean on which I am afloat is bottomless and shoreless. The fullness of the Godhead is my inheritance. When I think or speak of riches, I glory in the wealth of Him who made and owns the universe, and has made me his son and heir. Christ is the first-born among many brethren; we are all heirs of God, and joint heirs with him. Are these strange and boasting words? My boasting need not excite envy, for the same inheritance belongs to all who will accept it. God and the universe are mine: I hold them without a competitor. They are yours too if you are one with Christ. I am a part of your inheritance, and you are a part of mine. If all things are yours, to compare yourself with the highest archangel in heaven would be as if a man should compare himself with his own arm or a small item of his property. Boasting will do no hurt where there is no competition. If I boast of my inheritance, I boast equally of yours; nay, I boast of God. Envy, jealousy, rivalry, will forever cease when men realize they are heirs of God. All who love the Lord are one; and what benefits one benefits all. If you have not come to him who gives rest to those who labor and are heavy laden, let me tempt you, by recording his faithfulness, to prove him and see if he will not pour you out a blessing so great that there shall not be room enough to receive it. I assure you God is true; my peace is like a river, and my righteousness like the waves of the sea. God has wiped away all tears from my eyes: in Him I shall live for ever and ever. May he clothe you with immortality. Amen. –Yours, J. H. N."

He traveled to New York City with preacher Charles Weld to attend a meeting of ministers and theologians; he noticed that several speakers alluded "in a manner that indicated ill-suppressed anxiety and bitterness" to the activities of the New Haven Perfectionists. Evangelist Charles Grandison Finney believed fully in the attainment of perfect love of God and man. According to Whitney Cross, author of *The Burned-Over District*, Finney was "one of those rare individuals who of their own unaided force may on occasion significantly transform the destinies of masses of people . . . . No more impressive revival has occurred in American history" than the transformation of Rochester, New York, which Finney accomplished in six months.[11]

Noyes called on Finney in New York, but he had left three months earlier on a sea voyage to improve his health, which had been weakened by the first cholera outbreak in New York City in 1832. Mrs. Finney cordially invited Noyes in and conversed with him with interest on spiritual subjects, saying that she and her husband were thinking much on the subject of holiness, but were fearful of errors and fanaticisms connected with it. She was referring to the Pauline message of freedom from law, the mature Christian's achievement of absolute liberty; but to naïve people—or to those with baser motives—this meant worldly freedom, such as pursuing free love, known as antinomianism (glossary). Noyes had experienced groups like this and avoided them; "any attempt to revolutionize sexual morality before settlement with God is out of order," he always insisted. "The first thing to be done in any attempt to redeem man and reorganize society is to bring about reconciliation with God." Noyes was bitterly disappointed to miss an interview with Finney, for he would have relished discussion on this issue.

Charles Weld sent Noyes to an interview with James Latourette, regarded as the emperor of the scattered groups of New York Perfectionists that had grown out of revivals led by Finney and others in the Second Great Awakening. Finney and Latourette agreed with most other Perfectionists, who believed that all persons can backslide into the former state of sin. But Noyes staunchly believed in the security of the saints, i.e., that one who has attained perfect holiness cannot backslide. "Him that overcometh, I will make a pillar in the temple of my God, and he shall go no more out," Noyes reminded Latourette, who replied that he'd received that promise but thought it inexpedient to preach the doctrine lest it should beget carelessness. Nevertheless, he invited Noyes to speak at his meeting.

"If I speak," Noyes said firmly, "I shall preach security."

"Speak what the Lord gives you," Latourette replied.

"Duplicity of purpose makes the heart impure and prevents clear vision," Noyes explained to the audience. "If your life is divided, there is not strength enough in it for the intense, interior vision required to see God. Single-mindedness throughout life is possible. Purify your hearts, ye double-minded, James exhorted. The heart is the germ and center of the whole life and there is connection and reciprocal action between the heart and all parts of man. The life of the heart goes outward through all the ramifications of the body, and then the life of the body reacts upon the heart. If your life is organized so that it has but one purpose, then the whole life contributes to that one purpose. Blessed are the pure in heart, for they shall see God. We talk about unitary systems; God wants unitary men!—men of one principle. Seek first the Kingdom of God and his righteousness, and all necessary prudence, property, health, morality, and every good thing shall be added unto you." Noyes added, "He that sinneth hath not seen him, neither known him," and Latourette often interjected "Amen" or "Hallelujah." There was considerable murmuring about Noyes's testimony after the meeting.

"If that doctrine is true," one person yelled out, "I am no Christian."

"I know the doctrine is not true!" another agreed, "I have been converted and backslidden two or three times." So the word went around, and Noyes left the meeting "overborne not by argument, but by clamor." Latourette thereafter opposed the doctrine of security strenuously, but Chauncey Dutton, converted to Perfectionism by Albany Perfectionist leader John B. Foot, embraced security and asked Foot, "Why did you not teach this? This is what I've wanted from the beginning." Boyle also believed in security and it became the accepted view among New Haven Perfectionists.

DARK NIGHTS OF THE SOUL

Because Noyes no longer had his room at Yale Theological Seminary, he rented a room in a boarding house near the Battery in New York City. He endured three strange, terrifying weeks that tested everything he believed. "Often this crisis occurs among the religious at the threshold of manhood," Robert Allerton Parker noted in his biography of Noyes, *A Yankee Saint*. When Noyes sat down to write about Perfectionism, his mind would not focus. "I soon became convinced that God was calling my attention to other subjects—the thinking I had to do was for myself, instead of for others. The gospel I'd received and preached was based on faith that identified the soul with Christ, so that by his death and resurrection the believer dies and rises again spiritually. Truly, truly, I say to you, if anyone keeps my word, he will never see death, John 8:51. The true body, that which is within flesh and blood, is already risen from the dead by the power of Christ's resurrection; he will pass into the inner mansions clothed with his immortal body.

"I began to think that I'd given this idea but half its legitimate scope—a spirit of wrestling prayer for victory over death came upon me. It was not so much the act of dying that I wished to be delivered from, as the spiritual power of death that broods over all men." Noyes ruminated on 1st Corinthians 15—"What you sow does not come to life unless it dies. And what you sow is not the body that is to be, but a bare kernel.... It is sown a physical body, it is raised a spiritual body. If there is a physical body, there is also a spiritual body. Jesus said, No man taketh my life from me, but I lay it down of myself. The power he had with respect to his own life, he has with respect to the lives of those who believe on him. I passed one night in unspeakable happiness. But I soon found that the spiritual transition I'd made placed me in new relations to evil as well as good spirits; that I'd entered a region where the powers of darkness were to be encountered face to face as I had never encountered them before.

"The following day a strange, murky spiritual atmosphere began to gather around me. Strange thoughts coursed through my brain not from my own reflections, and uncontrolled by my will. The multitude of involuntary thoughts that fermented in my mind finally settled into a strong impression that I was about to part with flesh and blood either by ordinary death or by an instantaneous change. But my heart failed not. I still found refuge in God and felt that I could defy the universe of evil to injure me. Ere long I began actually to feel a suffocating pressure on my lungs. This was not the effect of physical disease, for my organs of respiration were healthy before and afterward. Nor was it the effect of excitement, for I had no fear of death and was entirely calm in heart. I put my room in decent order and lay down to die. The pressure increased till my breathing stopped, and my soul seemed to turn inward for its flight. At this crisis, when I had resigned myself wholly to the consciousness of dying, the pressure was instantly removed and I arose with the joy of victory in my heart. To my imagination, the transaction was as if I had been enclosed in a net and dragged down to the very borders of Hades, and then in the last agony had burst the net and returned to life. This transaction was repeated several times.

"Sleep was for the most part a nuisance. It seemed to be the condition in which the powers of darkness had most advantage of me, and I avoided it many times as I would avoid fire. Partly for this reason and partly because a spirit whose will I could not resist constrained me, I spent many nights in the streets. Often after a day of wearisome labor of mind and perhaps of body, I would retire to my room, hoping to enjoy a night of repose, if not of sleep. But suddenly a horror of sleep would come upon me, and a spiritual impulse would summon me with an importunity not to be denied to a night journey in the city. When weariness overcame me so that sleep became inevitable, I would lie down on a door-stone or on the steps of City Hall or on the benches of the Battery and forget myself for a few minutes. In this way most of my sleep for three weeks was taken."

Noyes's boarding house was on Leonard Street near the infamous Five Points in Lower Manhattan. "In my night excursions I was sometimes led into the vilest parts of the city. I went alone at midnight into streets I'd been told were dangerous even in daytime," Noyes wrote. He describes his visit in the Five Points slum: "I descended into cellars where abandoned men and women were gathered and talked familiarly with them about their ways of life, beseeching them to believe on Christ, that they might be saved from their sins. They listened to me without abuse. One woman seemed much affected. I gave her a Bible. To another I gave a Testament. Sometimes, when I had money, I gave that to the wretches whom I found in those dark places. These were the only dealings I had with them." One month later, Anti-abolitionist riots occurred there over four nights, beginning July 7, 1834.

Five Points originally was a paradise; Paradise Square remains. Fresh Water Pond spread over forty-eight acres along Manhattan's southern tip—a sixty-foot-deep, spring-fed pool of pristine water that provided New York City's drinking water, complete with freshwater fish to feed the populace. In the early 18th century, businesses contaminated this pond. A plan was devised to clean it up and make a park with this body of water its superb centerpiece. This plan was rejected in favor of filling it in with dirt from a nearby hill. It lacked adequate storm sewers, which caused the unpaved streets to be buried in mud, often mixed with human and animal excrement. Mosquitoes bred in myriad stagnant pools created by poor drainage. Middle and upper class inhabitants fled the area. Two years before Noyes boarded on Leonard Street, a cholera outbreak in Five Points spread rapidly throughout crowded, unsanitary dwellings and spread on to the rest of the growing city. By 1835, some 30,000 Irish had arrived annually in New York after Great Britain repealed legislation restricting emigration from Ireland in 1827. Gang riots spread. European immigrants kept pouring in to these mean streets, known for inhumane overcrowding, disease, unemployment, violent crime, prostitution, and infant mortality. Escaped slaves had been hanged here. One wonders whether Noyes's receptive mind had absorbed some of the tragic history and current reality of this place.

Erastus Hamilton, architect of the Oneida Community Mansion House, wrote about New York City in the October 12, 1868, *Circular*: "Passing along city thoroughfares I noticed the misery and degradation of poorly clothed, forlorn-looking men and women and neglected children, and have often thought, *What a storm of censure would be poured upon the Community if even a single instance of such neglect should be found among us.* People say they'd like to help the poor if they knew how. I will tell you one easy way. When a woman comes to wash, iron, or scrub, ask her how she's situated—go home with her, or let your wife go, and you will find things that would make thrilling newspaper or magazine articles. I found in a garret a poor woman with two children—one five years old, paralyzed from its hips down and crawling on her hands, dragging her paralyzed body; the other was eighteen months old. That woman had to work and could not take her children with her. You have met little girls selling penny songs and you never thought that those children lived somewhere. I met one about six years old who hobbled on a crutch, her right leg dangling from her body. She made a quarter of a cent on each song she sold—her only profit, except when a generous man gave her a five-cent stamp said 'never mind the change.' I asked her why she sold songs; 'to get money for my mother!' I went with her to a rear tenement of the worst description, passed through a cellar with several people into a rear cellar with no window and no means of receiving light or ventilation except what the door opening into the front cellar afforded. There was lying the mother of that child. Who is responsible for all these hopeless people? Is not society also coming to judgment? By our fruits we should be known." Hamilton's entire account is well worth reading.

"During my inexplicable three-week New York City experience," Noyes recounted, "I went through involuntary thoughts and feelings that I can describe by no better name than a spiritual crucifixion. All the events of Christ's death were vividly pictured in my mind and realized in my feelings. I went through them as a victim. At length came the resurrection, and for a time I was released from suffering." Noyes's mind continued to range over boundless regions of thought. "Reduced to universal doubt, my previous scholastic theories and conceptions of truth were turned topsy-turvy; when all that the schools had taught me had been reduced to chaos, I said to myself: *The Bible stands firm nevertheless.* But objections to the inspiration and credibility of the Scriptures began to force themselves upon my mind. With merciless and more than human ingenuity, the spiritual intelligence that directed my thoughts arrayed before me all the apparent inconsistencies and immoralities of the Bible, till at last I cast it from me with abhorrence. Still I clung to Jesus Christ, but ere long this refuge also failed me. On being subjected to the diabolical spirit of analysis that had taken possession of my intellect, even His character was gradually stripped of its glory. Finally I said in my heart, *still there is a God in whom I may trust.* Then the cloud of doubt began to gather about the idea of God. Nothing but my own experience was left to me, and when that was perceived as a series of deceptions, my belief in God was overclouded and the darkness of atheism fell upon me. It seemed to me that no human being ever drank so deeply of the dregs of the cup of trembling."

William James wrote: "Our normal waking consciousness, rational consciousness as we call it, is but one special type of consciousness, whilst all about it, parted from it by the filmiest of screens there are potential forms of consciousness entirely different."[12] Noyes felt that he had discovered that the universe is a battlefield between good and evil—"an eternal conflict between impersonal forces of the outer world and frailties of the human psyche within." Noyes experienced a phenomenon that he'd encountered at Andover: "One physical effect of the spiritual change that had passed upon me was loss of appetite. Until I left New York I took but little aliment and at times had a special and excessive loathing of all animal food," Noyes wrote. "Indeed I had a strong impression (not derived from physiological theories) that meat eating was a barbarism that would be abolished in the kingdom of God; the feeling did not extend to marine food. My general rule was to follow instinct; strong stimulants such as cayenne pepper suited my appetite best and I used them for a time freely. I had been long dyspeptic, but after this process my stomach became a peaceable member of the corporeal community.

"There was an instinctive consciousness of strength and an imperishable hope in my heart," Noyes realized. "When the spirit of darkness had done its worst, I said within myself: If the universe is a blind chaos without a God and the destinies of all beings are to be worked out by their own strength, I have as good a right to try what I can do for existence and happiness as anybody. I will yet wrestle for victory over evil. Then my heart began to burn with indignation against the spirit that was abusing me. Isaiah was much in my mind; its beautiful promises were applied to my spirit with healing and consoling power. My will lifted and I acted in the spirit of Isaiah's words: '. . . mine own arm brought victory unto me; and my fury, it upheld me.' When I finally emerged from my sufferings, I had a satisfying consciousness that my life was fireproof. I could say, Hell has done its worst, and yet I live!

"The net gave way and immediately. I found myself in an atmosphere of confidence and peace. The effect of the mental overturn was permanent," wrote this youth of twenty-two years. "I could hardly tell afterward what I believed on any subject till I'd investigated it anew. The rule of mental economy I adopted is this: What we positively know is all the mental capital we can count upon as safe and available. What we guess, believe, and hope to be true is paper capital, and may be genuine or not. It is well enough to have on hand a great heap of guesses, but we must not think of living on them. We should look over the whole mass of our thoughts," Noyes concluded, "and select out all that we absolutely know. If it is but a small store, never mind—a little silver and gold is worth more than a bushel of counterfeit bills."

Regarding what he absolutely knew, philosopher René Descartes finally could say only: *I think; therefore I am.* Following a profound insight, theologian Thomas Aquinas concluded, "What I have seen makes all that I have written mere chaff."[13]

"My spirit passed into a state of permanent peace," rejoiced Noyes. "Thus closed a series of trials which, though they seemed grievous and left me almost without a remnant of a reputation, nevertheless worked the peaceful fruits of righteousness, established me in the liberty of the truth, weaned me from all earthly resources, enlarged my acquaintance with the spiritual world, confirmed the strength of my intellect, and gave to my body a vigorous power of endurance that it had never possessed before and that fitted it for subsequent labors and trials. I began to feel freedom in examining the credentials of invisible powers and soon arrived at a conclusion that has since been a valuable rule to me: If any spirit attempts to hurry and drive me into belief and obedience, I may be sure that it is false; I am bound to suspend belief till I can ascertain whether an impression comes from God or otherwise.

"During my career in legal religion, I'd been a zealous temperance man and like other such zealots, regarded the use of intoxicating drinks as a sin. The temperance law had fixed itself in my conscience more firmly perhaps than any others. My New York experience taught me that my old principles of morality, however useful they had been in ordinary life, were not competent to guide me in this new world. I began to search for a new system of ethics on which I might depend for security from defilement. Whatever might be true of others, for me safety lay in transferring the keeping of my soul to the Spirit of God. God keeps me from intemperance and all other evil without the help of pledges or the influence of human combinations. To assert my liberty from all legality handed down from Puritan ancestors, I drank ardent spirits. This established me in freedom from the petty tyranny of fashionable morality, which no pressure of public opinion has since been able to subvert. To the charge of intoxication, I offer my own absolute denial. It would be unwise for anyone to attempt an external imitation of the course I pursued; it would be like someone taking another's medicine."

The new system of ethics Noyes discovered was the basis for one of his foundational convictions—"God's plan is to take *all* the passions into his service, not to suppress them. He is not going to reign over negative morality and the dry bones of intellect. He is going to reign over living beings and be glorified in a passional kingdom, giving scope to the strongest of the passions and to all of them. Men can be virtuous in spite of every opportunity to be vicious; men with their understandings and their hearts shall *choose* to be temperate in all things, though they have every opportunity to eat and drink; men will be chaste from simple choice as far as rules are concerned with the enthusiasm of artists, though they have unlimited opportunity of licentiousness. Men will be enterprising and industrious without being driven by fear of poverty or love of money." Chapter 9 on addictions shows how the Community transcended rules and legalism to achieve true inner freedom.

Noyes's brother, Horatio, was studying at Yale and had also become a convert to Perfectionism. He'd become somewhat concerned as John's period in New York lengthened and there was no word from him, and he sent friends from the Free Church to check on him. Afterward, John stayed with Horatio for two weeks; he knew that Horatio would be most likely to understand the spiritual and psychic assaults he'd endured in New York. John said he couldn't fully convey the depth of those sufferings, but shared that he emerged from the trial much edified from what he learned about himself. After his ejection from Yale Theological Seminary, followed by the New York City episode, his family and close friends were worried about his emotional well-being. Horatio wrote home that all was well: "I hope hereafter you will lay aside your prejudices and fears about him, and believe him still to possess his right mind, and hear what he has to say with a sincere desire to know the truth."

Returning to New Haven by stagecoach after a three-week vacation in Putney, with plans to publish his views, Noyes found himself seated beside clergyman Dr. Cogswell, who said he'd become aware of an unorthodox group called Perfectionists in Meridan, and he'd like to meet one of them. A lady on the opposite seat immediately announced that she was from New Haven and knew all about Perfectionists. She described them as monsters of impiety and concluded, "As for that John Noyes, I know that he is nothing less than a blasphemer, for he said in a public meeting that he was as perfect as God, and my own sister heard him!"

Noyes thought it would be well to let the lady go on without the embarrassment of knowing who he was, and answered in a mild manner, "I think you must be mistaken about Noyes. I'm somewhat acquainted with him and have never heard him say anything of the kind."

Dr. Cogswell, on learning that I was acquainted with Perfectionism, concurred that they must be outrageously self-righteous. "They explain themselves quite plausibly," Noyes replied, "by saying that holiness is entirely the gift of God, no more to be credited to self than a garment given to a beggar."

"Well," said Dr. Cogswell, "if that is their doctrine, I see nothing very frightful about it."

During their sixteen-mile stagecoach ride, the doctrines of Perfectionism and my own character were pretty thoroughly canvassed. As the lady from New Haven occasionally broke in with her speeches, Noyes noticed that a young woman who sat beside her (and Noyes later learned, knew him), was continually laughing behind her bonnet. Just as the coach drew up before the hotel, Dr. Cogswell said, "May I be so bold as to ask your name?"

"My name is Noyes."

"Ah!" said he, with a hearty laugh, "you are the very preacher we've been talking about!"

"Yes." Casting a glance at the New Haven lady, she seemed to be hiding herself in the corner of the coach.

Amos Smith was a New Haven schoolmaster much devoted to his profession and distinguished for his spirituality. He had been connected with the Free Church and showed considerable interest in Perfectionism. "He did not decidedly embrace our views nor did he directly oppose them, but he brought one charge against my colleague Chauncey Dutton and me that I found exceedingly difficult to answer. He perceived that our minds were in a state of dissipation; I *was* distinctly conscious of intellectual habits relaxed from the classical and legal discipline enforced in college life," Noyes admitted. "Judged by pedagogical standards, I acknowledged that I was in some degree liable to the charge he brought against me. Having studied the mental habits of young men extensively, and one who loved to rule boys, Smith insisted that we were only babes in spiritual truth and ought not to think of publishing at present. His spirit was strong, his will obstinate, and his knowledge of human nature on a small scale was unusually complete, and so he was one to be respected. But on a faithful inspection of my internal state, I saw nothing to be censured or regretted. We are passing from the schools of human discipline," I ventured to explain, "to the school of the Spirit of Truth. As more-or-less anarchy always attends revolutions, it is not to be wondered that our minds are not exactly in that orderly, mechanical state that suits a schoolmaster in this transition period. It is better to move into a new house, even at the cost of temporary confusion and discomfort, than to live in an old one that cannot shelter us and is ready to fall on our heads."

Noyes and Abigail Merwin had forged a deep spiritual bond in the New Haven Free Church following his spiritual experience; she was his first convert and had enthusiastically spread his views in this country and abroad. Though a chaste relationship, John had fallen in love over those fruitful months and always hoped that he and Abigail would marry. But after John lost his license to preach, followed by gossip about his weeks in New York, her parents disallowed further contact. When she married Merit Platt three years later, it devastated Noyes; however, the unbreakable spiritual bond forged between him and Abigail could never be severed through a legal procedure! "When the will of God is done on earth, as it is in heaven, there will be no marriage," he wrote to a friend. "Conventional marriage is but a flawed human ordinance, a necessary evil, not a spiritual state in the kingdom of heaven according to Matthew 22. And that kingdom is here and now, if one communes with God." The Platt marriage lasted only one year, and Merit died in 1843, but Noyes's and Abigail's relationship never revived.

LAYING THE FOUNDATION

Martin Luther was not any more eager to nail his 95 Theses to the Wittenberg Church to reform the Roman Catholic Church than was Noyes to proclaim that complete deliverance from the power of sin was the gospel's good news. His primary message was that our true relationship to God comes not from church teachings or even study of God's word in the Bible, but from what direct inspiration reveals. Noyes's friend, preacher James Boyle, had likewise contended that Perfectionists are taught by God and will not be taught even by each other, or by anti-Christian churches. Noyes, Boyle, and Chauncey Dutton were determined to begin a new publication explaining the true meaning of Perfectionism, because no paper communicated a tone that satisfied them. Selecting a name for the paper was problematic; Boyle and Dutton suggested equivocal titles. Noyes insisted on "hoisting our colors boldly," and on August 20, 1834, he and Boyle launched *The Perfectionist*, a free gospel offered in a free paper, relying on God for support and making love its medium of exchange. Whitmore and

Buckingham printers in New Haven, with whom Noyes had worked, agreed to print it. It was available in grocery stores, post offices, wherever people assembled, and found its way into the homes of many of the well educated in the church—though generally tabooed by the ministers. An edition was published on the twentieth of each month and there were 675 subscribers at the close of the fifth volume in 1836; its growing popularity furnished constant and lively interest. Noyes then wrote dozens of articles published in several periodicals with which he was connected as contributor or editor, and these articles are gathered in *The Berean*, the complete exposition of the religious doctrines of the Putney and Oneida Communities.

"My father was a theoretical believer in the paper's doctrines and much interested in its discussions," John wrote, "but he abhorred debt amid unthrifty speculations as most men do perdition." He sent John a warning when the *Perfectionist* was three months old; John's views at barely age twenty-three about "getting a living" are revealed in his letter home:

New Haven, Oct. 8, 1834.

"Dear Father:

I have received your advice that I should leave New Haven if I am not getting a living. I think it evidently is the will of God that I should remain here for the present, as it is my desire. I have employment here in various ways, which I cannot immediately have elsewhere. New Haven has become the center of business in the spiritual and intellectual world. We receive many visits from persons residing in various parts of the country who desire to understand the gospel, and desirable opportunities to circulate the knowledge of Christ far and wide continually present themselves. Correspondence is flowing in due to this paper's circulation, and will unquestionably increase rapidly. The monthly preparation of the paper is no great task; I am much interested in the work and wish to devote my immediate personal attention to the sustaining of its interest. We receive occasional invitations to preach in this vicinity, and I find it very profitable to visit the several companies of believers in Prospect and Meriden. I spent a few days at Prospect last week with exceeding pleasure and profit. That place contains the most remarkable instance I have ever seen of the continuance of a fervent but steady religious impulse for six months.

"As to getting my living, the case stands thus: Money is sometimes offered me by those who love the truth; I tell them that I have no occasion for it at present—that my father has supplied me—but Br. Boyle or Dutton could use more support. I would unquestionably be supported if it were understood that I desired it. I have received a little money and many offers of a home at Prospect and Meriden, which I would accept if constrained to leave New Haven. My expense for boarding with Mr. Boyle will be probably $2.00 per week. What has been given I have received as a gratuity, with thankfulness both to you and to my Father in heaven. I have now no claim upon you; if you are not interested in the object for which I live, I cannot ask or expect you to assist me. That object is that the will of God may be done on earth as it is in heaven. For the furtherance of this object, it seems to me desirable that I should remain here until I am directed to a more suitable place. If the object is a good one, and you consider me a person fitted to further it, you will not account money bestowed upon me as thrown away. It will not perhaps yield a profit as immediate and tangible as that of bank stock, but it will help the building of that kingdom in which you hope to dwell forever. -Your son, J. H. N."

Following its sixth issue, the *Perfectionist* newspaper "has gloriously prepared the way to hear John preach. Many testify that it is the most interesting paper they've ever read." He returned to Putney in February 1835. "Backword Glancings," in the January 6, 1873, *Circular* provided the following interesting history: "Pastors did not open their churches to him, but people came eagerly to hear him in schoolrooms, tavern halls, and private homes. Curiosity was mingled with genuine hunger for nourishing spiritual food. Silas Morgan, a Methodist who had been converted on John's first Putney visit after his New York episode, promoted and attended the meetings. He subscribed to the *Perfectionist* and had convinced everyone around him of the truth of the doctrine. The area's leading physician, Dr. Alexander Campbell, and his wife Achsah, became deeply interested in the new doctrines and opened their house for evening meetings. This example was followed by James Crawford, a lawyer; he and his wife had never professed religion, but having "tasted of the good word of God" as preached by John, now manifested all the simplicity and enthusiasm of young converts. The company who assembled at these meetings embraced a variety of classes and denominations, some members of the most orthodox and influential families in town, and others were Universalists, Methodists and Nothingarians (those of no belief, creed, or particular sect). 'I see the fruit of our labors and the wisdom of God in the publication of that paper,' John exalted. 'Truly we have been scattering the seed of the word of God with a broad cast, and even now the harvest is at hand.' The meetings were generally informal, not given to vocal praying, personal appeals, much singing, or other techniques of the professional revivalist. John stood with polyglot Bible in hand and discoursed upon a text or topic, treating it in an original, soul-searching way and interspersing familiar conversation and questions.

"The interest growing out of those evening discourses was intense and lasting. Many persons who had never cared much for the Bible began to study it, even cherish it, and felt that with the new understandings furnished by John, they were able to converse in a fruitful way with ministers and conventional church members. Those who had been seeking religion for years, but were chilled by unsatisfactory hopes held out by churches, heard the glad tidings of a full salvation with joyful surprise and became steadfast followers of John through evil and good report. Many Putney and Oneida Community members were brought into the faith directly or indirectly by *The Perfectionist*. The interest spread to the suburb of Putney on the Connecticut River—the East Part, as it was called—a neutral ground where all religions and no religion by turns held sway. The Pierces, who belonged to no church but thought John's doctrine the best they'd ever heard, invited him to preach at the East Part Methodist Church, which was not in a very flourishing or harmonious state. A revival followed this preaching. Several of the most religious and substantial families became interested and opened their houses for meetings. Converts were remarkably whole-hearted and steadfast in most cases. The rumor of these events reached neighboring areas, and invitations to preach came in almost daily."

"Harriet and I generally accompanied John to meetings in town and occasionally to those out of town, greatly to the consternation and grief of our fashionable friends," John's sister Charlotte wrote. "To forsake our regular church meetings and assemble with miscellaneous company in an out-of-the-way schoolhouse or at some remote private house was a grievous derogation from the family rank. Loss of caste was held up to us as a threat and a warning, but we pursued our course, caring little for remarks of those who would keep our attention upon considerations of that kind. Toward the end of April, Simon Lovett of New York and the Reverend Charles H. Weld of Hartford came to visit John. Lovett was a beloved and enthusiastic co-worker with John, and Weld claimed a leading position in the new dispensation. They remained at our house for three weeks, attending the meetings and occasionally making remarks. Lovett was abrupt in manner and in testimony very positive and apparently whole-hearted, but he had little power to attract or convince hearers. Weld had been a minister for many years and an associate of Finney, Boyle, Lansing, and other eminent revivalists. He had the polish and prudence of a city clergyman, but did not make any clear confession of salvation from sin himself. There was a lack of living earnestness in what he said, which made John's words so effective.

Charlotte Noyes Miller, with a heart large enough to take in the whole family, was adviser to the younger class of women in the Oneida Community.

"My father's sensitiveness on the subject of reputation was extreme and he could not endure to see his eldest son, once his pride and hope, suffer undeserved and overwhelming reproach," Charlotte recounted. "He was distressed by malicious lies told about Perfectionist doctrines and followers, and insisted that John defend himself and set the record straight. John should not be an outcast from respectable society! John said that he would not spend time and strength caring for worldly reputation—he would accept reviling and false accusations as a part of the inheritance of a son of God in this world." His father became angry and John withdrew from the Noyes residence and went to live with Mr. Cutler, a new convert to Perfectionism, who gladly offered a home to John and his two friends. They remained there for ten days and then John and Weld went to New Haven.

"This separation from John was painful to all the family," Charlotte wrote. "After John left, the excitement produced by curiosity and novelty subsided, but seed had fallen into good and honest hearts, and in them it sprung up and bore fruit—these young converts were simple and teachable." The January 20, 1873, *Circular* reprinted this history. "They met often in their own homes to read and study the Bible and the doctrines published in the *Perfectionist*. Letters were circulated and visits exchanged with believers in other towns; the Palmers, Lords, Whites, Shaws, Pierces, and Lovells of the East Part received with joy all those who confessed salvation from sin; their brotherly kindness was unbounded. Mrs. Palmer, one of the first to accept the new faith, still lived in her old Putney homestead at age eighty-four. In spite of changes and infirmities, she remained as she was forty years ago—steadfast and immovable, always rejoicing in the work of the Lord.

"While the revival was thus quietly progressing in Putney, there was a similar work commencing in the neighboring town of Westminster. The wife of the Congregational minister of West Westminster, Mrs. Field, wrote Mother a long letter denouncing the hypocrisy and lukewarmness of the clergy and churches. Mrs. Field confessed a wholehearted belief in salvation from sin. Her position as a minister's wife, as well as eloquent descriptions of her experience, bordered always upon the marvelous," Charlotte added, "and gave greater currency to her testimony. The Clark family resided nearby, influential in the church and society. Their daughter Maria was a person of superior mind and the brightest ornament of the church. She was prepared by her experience to be an interested hearer of spiritual truth, and her conversion was followed by that of a cousin of the same name. Not only was Maria Clark a great acquisition in herself, but her circle of influence was large and important."

Harriet Holton

"Maria's dearest friend and correspondent was Harriet Ann Holton, who resided in the neighboring parish of East Westminster. Miss Holton was the flower of the church, like her friend. Orphaned, she was adopted by her maternal grandparents and was now wealthy and highly connected; her grandfather, the Honorable Mark Richards, had been Lieutenant Governor of Vermont and a congressman. She was much sought after in marriage and had every inducement to a life of fashionable ease and respectability. Harriet attended a protracted revival meeting in 1831, the year Noyes left his brother-in-law Larkin G. Mead's law office in Brattleboro to attend the nearby Putney revival at his mother's request. One wonders if they attended the same life-changing revival, because it wrought enormous changes in both their lives—after it, Noyes left law to study theology, and Harriet broke off an engagement to Edmund Burke, a law student in William Czar Bradley's Brattleboro office, to devote her life to God. Her friend Maria Clark wrote her an excited letter about a strangely gifted young man, Mr. John Humphrey Noyes from nearby Putney: "He teaches the doctrine of complete salvation from sin, that we can exterminate the curse of sin, once and for all, and can implement the kingdom of heaven on earth!" She had obtained copies of two of his articles—one on the Second Coming of Christ.[14]

"I was happy in the confession of my belief of the truth contained in these articles," Harriet remembered, for an article in the October 7, 1872, *Circular*, "and searched the New Testament to see if the church to which I belonged had availed itself of all the salvation offered by Christ, who required faith in those he cured of disease or whose sins he forgave. I prayed earnestly for faith." Nine months later, Maria told Harriet that Noyes was coming to preach at the West Westminster schoolhouse. Looking back, Harriet could still vividly recall his blue coat, his sandy-red hair, and his face that shone like an angel's. "He did not take a text from the Bible, as is customary," she recounted, "but read the title page: *The New Testament of our Lord and Savior Jesus Christ*. He spoke about the difference between the old and new covenants—the word 'testament' was identical with what elsewhere was translated as 'covenant'—and under the old covenant the law was written on tablets of stone, but under the new it is written on the heart. This seemed to me like a light shining through a long vista of darkness, and it encouraged me," Harriet reminisced. "I listened eagerly to all I heard, for I instinctively felt that through his faith I would find an answer to my desires for faith. Not only did his words convey light and life, but his very personal bearing convicted those who saw him of his earnest devotion to the truth. His manner convinced me that he had a single eye to the cause he espoused.

"I was accustomed to see clergymen write their sermon, preach on Sunday, and attend a prayer meeting during the week; their general demeanor and conversation was similar to those around them. Mr. Noyes used his own words, determining to be a young convert forever. Such devotion would be tolerated in a revival, but now churches were cold, engaged in pursuing worldly business; a person who had the zeal of a young convert was considered a fanatic. Mr. Noyes was so filled with his desire to make known to all that Christ is a complete Savior, that he was called crazy by some," Harriet remembered. "John Noyes had the air of a warrior full of determination, bold and even stern against not only wickedness but against self-righteousness and pious insincerity. When I heard him preach thereafter, I realized that there was spiritual power in his words that communicated light and peace to my soul, especially when he sang the hymn beginning, 'Jesus, I my cross have taken, all to leave and follow thee . . .' and it lifted a great burden of bashfulness and egotism from me." Someone had suggested that she might marry John Noyes. "I should as soon think of marrying the morning star!" Harriet exclaimed.

He preached at East Westminster on Harriet's invitation and was the guest of her grandfather. Later she heard him preach in a schoolhouse in Putney and met him at his home, where she became acquainted with the other Putney Perfectionists. John Ransom Miller, aged twenty-one and not a church member, was boarding with Maria Clark's family while working in a store, and Maria's conversations interested him in the subject of faith. Miller joined with Miss Clark's brother in inviting John to preach in the Westminster schoolhouse. John presented a pleasant appearance, his thinness making him seem taller than his 5'11", broad-shouldered frame; his high forehead, sandy-colored hair, earnest blue-gray eyes, and powerful lower jaw were striking, but it was the way he spoke that riveted his hearers. With no notes, his originality, empathy, Biblical knowledge, mundane examples illustrating points, and sharing his own spiritual journey made him one who speaks with authority. The Westminster converts were not as numerous as in Putney, but all were persons of influence and position. Miller, whose abilities and character made him popular and respectable, became exceedingly interested and he espoused and advocated Perfectionist doctrines with great enthusiasm. He joined the Putney Community six years later in 1841, married Noyes's sister Charlotte, and later became business manager of the Oneida Community. In a few months the Honorable John Noyes resumed his kind relations to John Humphrey and continued them until his death in 1841.

John wrote a remarkable letter to his mother Polly on September 9, 1835, just after his twenty-fourth birthday: "During my spiritual infancy I have been compelled to fight for purity. Now I am strong enough to proclaim peace, and to keep the peace, whether my proclamation is heeded or not. Charity thinketh no evil. That charity is mine. I see nothing but good in the universe. All that is called evil is good, to one whose head is above the clouds—evil to him who evil thinks. When I speak well of my own estate, you will understand that I magnify only the grace of God, by which alone I am what I am. God claims me as his own property, and I admit the equity of his claim. My body, soul, and spirit with all that belong to them are his. I can never have goodness, or greatness, or glory separately from him . . . .

"Like a man climbing a mountain, as I have reached one eminence after another the prospect around me has widened, the coloring and appearance of the scenery has changed. But my eye has still rested on the summit; I have never taken a step backward, and never shall, till I sit down with Christ on his Father's throne. I thank God for the varied scenery of my course; and I thank him for the immutability of its direction . . . .

"Some of the practical conclusions to which I have been led are as follows: I have learned that the love of God, the love of mankind, and self love are all one—enlightened self-love is and ought to be the mainspring of the human machine; that in blessing and perfecting myself, I glorify God and bless mankind. I have learned that perfect self-possession stands first in the list of blessings that God gives, and that self-knowledge is the first lesson. To this lesson I have been devoting my attention, and my discoveries have been such that I have given up all thoughts of undertaking the business of teaching others until I have attained perfect self-knowledge and perfect self-control. A preacher by implication professes to know important truth, and also to know how it should be communicated. I shall therefore never again assume the place of a public teacher till I am certain that I possess such an amount of important truth and such a knowledge of the human mind, that I can honestly fulfill the promises of such a profession. When I compare myself with those who walk in the shadows of this world, I perceive that I know much; but when I cast a glance at the unexplored fields of knowledge comprised within the first lesson that God has put into my hands, I know I am but a sophomore and I lose all relish for the enterprise of instructing others.

"Having thus studied myself out of friends and business, and being without money, I began not long since to inquire the will of God concerning temporal support. I found that the love of independence was one of the strongest cravings of my nature, and that this could never be gratified till I earned my bread as other people do. I found that the love of money, which I know is the root of all evil, the reigning idolatry especially of New England, was forever extinguished in myself, and that I need not fear to seek money lest I should adore it. In view of these considerations I came to the deliberate and fixed determination to engage in business for worldly sustenance. An acquaintance in this place employed me for a time in collecting his debts, and I am about to commence with him tomorrow a survey of the town for the purpose of making a map, which will occupy us several weeks....

"The people here are very friendly, and insist upon my preaching to them on Sunday. I shall give them a talk. I can at least tell them I know nothing, and am not a preacher. I have courage enough to believe that I can gain the confidence of this community sufficiently to teach at school this fall. The man with whom I am now connected is much attached to me, and wishes to keep me here and forward my goals in every way possible. Let me say for those who prize the wisdom of this world, that in my own opinion I never was so sober and considerate as at this present time.... I have learned that logic is worth more than poetry, and matter-of-fact industry is more than building air castles. My head is now full of Yankee notions about money-making and economy, and I have become a great admirer of Dr. Franklin. Is not this a wonderful metamorphosis? I hope you will all have a hearty laugh over it, and that no suspicion of deception or fear of disappointment will shade your anticipations of my success and welfare.... I know more fully than you can know the chaotic ocean of change over which I have been tossed. Yet I have lost no confidence in myself, because

I know that God has been and is my pilot; and as I now perceive myself riding quietly at anchor in the haven of God's peace, I fear neither ocean, nor storm, nor quicksand, nor whirlpools. Innocence cannot fear . . . .

"We shall all, men, women, and children, find the necessity of studying metaphysics before we shall secure the end of our being. Horatio, Harriet, Charlotte, and George have studied almost everything save the A, B, C's of useful knowledge; they know much about the solar system and the fixed stars, but how much do they know about their own nature, the machinery in the midst of which they live? If God ever qualifies me to write a book, my subject shall be self-knowledge. I have begun to discover that I am fearfully and wonderfully made; that I am a glorious kingdom in myself, a kingdom that has long lain in ruins through misrule and darkness, but is yet capable of glorifying its maker. When I have completely ascertained the limits, character, and resources of this kingdom, quelled all the rebellions that waste it, and secured the revenue that is due to its king—I shall be prepared to assist others. Till then I shall not write a book.

"You perceive that I have grown selfish and egotistical. That love of souls that hurries and worries to save others, while self remains in ruins, is baby benevolence, foolish and fatal kindness. Charity begins at home. It is my purpose to make the most of myself. Call this selfishness if you will; it is selfishness that requires perfect benevolence. While I would exhort all not to think more highly of themselves than they ought, I would also exhort all not to think more meanly of themselves than they ought to think. Independently of God all flesh is grass, but as creatures of God you rank among the noblest of God's works . . . . I care not to pamper curiosity or mere family affection, but if we may hold such correspondence as becomes immortal beings, I shall most joyfully fulfill my share of the task. Take care of yourselves. Be quiet about me. The peace of God be with you. J. H. Noyes."

Spirit, Bible, Church

So began John's three-year odyssey in New England and New York meeting other Perfectionists, debating doctrine, gathering converts, printing religious periodicals that included topics considered forbidden ground, and conveying his basic message—all persons may be directly taught of God. Professors and ministers taught that the Bible is God's revelation to man, not crediting the Holy Spirit's vital influence in understanding the Bible. Scholars contended that understanding the ancient languages in which the Bible's books were written and the history and cultures of the ancient world are vital for unlocking vast stores of truth. This knowledge is necessary, but not sufficient, said Noyes. "It is only when the Biblical message is received *as from God* that its spiritual energy is apprehended. Believing thoughts about the gospel or being excited by reading the Bible without discerning the spirit of God cannot be said to truly assimilate the gospel." The natural man receives not the things of the Spirit of God, said Paul, because they are spiritually discerned.

Psychologist William James cites Henry Alline's experience: *You have been seeking, praying, reforming, laboring, hearing, and meditating,* a still but powerful voice asked the young man, *and are you any nearer to conversion now than when you first began?* "I opened a Bible at random at the 38th Psalm," Alline said, "and it was the first time I ever *saw* the word of God. It took hold of me with such power that it seemed to go through my whole soul as if God was praying in, with, and for me. When I gave up all to him to do with me as he pleased, redeeming love broke into my soul; my whole soul seemed to be melted down with love." He became a Christian saint and minister who never got his taste back for even the most innocent pleasures.[15]

The September 1868 *Circular* adds this note: "Sufi and Islamic scholar, Ahmad Sidi Kostas shares insights: To the Sufis, God cannot be known through the mind only. The mind is like a horse that carries you to the door of the sultan's palace, but cannot enter it with you. So the mind can lead you to knowing the existence of God, but not to communicate with God and know the essence of God—that's a different dimension."

Because the Bible reveals much that no human language can adequately convey, "we must look to the Giver of it as the ultimate guide of understanding," Noyes stressed. "Let us try to understand the true place of the Bible. Salvation reaches us by successive mediations. Its end is union with the eternal Father, but we do not reach this end by a single leap; Christ comes as mediator—we receive him first, and he brings us to the Father, but the chain of mediation has more links: the apostles help us to Christ; the Primitive Church helps us to the apostles; the Bible helps us to the Primitive Church. This is, undoubtedly, the Bible's true place. We labor to overcome infidelity that would set its value too low, but we must also keep clear of the formalism that would set it too high. It must not be placed higher in the succession. For, consider how salvation proceeded in the Primitive Church. That Church had not the Bible in our sense of the word. The Old Testament was in existence, but copies were few and costly. The New Testament was in the process of formation, but there was no printing press. Many believers were illiterate, so the use of the Bible as a general means of salvation was impossible. Christ and the apostles were the Bible for that time—acting and speaking and writing the things that make up the New Testament. Many learn primarily from the spoken word to this day; deep spiritual learning occurs between teacher and disciple. The Bible is no revelation to those who cannot read; it is a revelation of certain introductory truths to those who can only read; it is a revelation of much curious wisdom to those who read with the help of human learning; it is a revelation of the deep things of God to those who read with the help of inspiration from the Holy Spirit. Inspiration alone reveals our true relationship to God, not church teachings or even study of God's word in the Bible. The Bible assists the personal instructions of our internal teacher, and in the chain of mediation it is not above but below the apostles and the Primitive Church.

"Many churches believe that once converted, one is saved—but a single conversion is only a beginning. Often unbeknownst to themselves, those converted can became harder after their first conversion than they were before if they think conversion is a through-ticket to heaven—for they feel at liberty to go about business as before. My impression is that revivals failed in permanently breaking up hardness of heart." Noyes had observed his cold heart in theological seminary, far from loving God and man. As long as those who shape public understanding in the religious world hold up the 7th chapter of Romans as the standard of legitimate Christian experience, "it cannot be expected that vigorous and permanent advances will be made in any department of moral reform," Noyes insisted. "They announce that they are approving and desiring to keep God's commandments but are prone to break them—slaves to sin and powerless against temptation, according to the supposed apostolic model in Romans 7:7–25. This spiritual impotence, if tolerated in the church, will surely manifest itself with irresistible power of corruption in all those classes of society that surround the church and depend on it for moralizing influences."

Edson Smith, son of the Reverend Dexter P. Smith of Dorset, Vermont, wrote for the July 12, 1869, *Circular*: "I became so disgusted at times at the recital of the 7th of Romans experience by church members that I could not refrain from taunting them in a way that rendered me very unpopular. I frequently attended the monthly meetings of the Baptist Church, where it was customary for each to relate his experience for the last month. A general testimony of failures was the invariable program. Once or twice near the close of the meetings, I was invited to add my testimony. When I stated that in reviewing my life for the preceding month, I could not see but that God had given me strength to fulfill all his requirements of me; and that if I had sinned, it was my own fault. This kind of testimony caused me to be looked upon with great contempt. I'd never heard of a Perfectionist nor did I claim that I was saved from sin," Smith said, "but I delighted in reading the second chapter of Acts and longed for God's kingdom to be set up on earth, and for brotherly love to take the place of selfishness. I felt that a greater freedom from sin could be attained than was usually professed, and was forced to reason that God does not require of us more than we are able to perform. But he does require of us to forsake our sins and be holy. Therefore there must be a way to do it." He joined the Oneida Community in 1867.

"What avails the clergy to preach against various forms of external sin," Noyes asked, "while the great radical vice of the heart, moral imbecility, is openly tolerated and defended by them? Those who stigmatize the supposed self-righteousness of Perfectionists expect redemption from sin and evil at death while they daily displease the Giver. Like the Pharisees who had become like whitewashed tombs that outwardly appear beautiful, but within are full of dead men's bones and all uncleanness, Jesus said, you *appear* righteous to men but within are full of hypocrisy and iniquity. You shut the kingdom of heaven against men—you neither enter yourselves, nor allow those who would enter to go in! Myriad laws and rules neglect the weighty matters of mercy, faith, and justice while the trappings of piety are taught, such as observing the Sabbath." (A man in Brookline, Massachusetts, was arrested for nailing up a vine on Sunday, the *Circular* noted.)

"The church ladens men with burdens grievous to be born while they themselves touch not the burdens with one of their fingers; they turn on poor sinners and require them to keep the Sabbath, to abstain from profanity, lewdness, and intemperance, to forsake all their darling lusts and lead a life of prayer and benevolence. But they are bereft of guidance how to experience the Spirit within. The conventional church disseminates just enough religion to make their parishioners comfortable in the service of Mammon," Noyes lamented. His personal experience of the dynamic life-giving Spirit made him staunchly oppose religious legalism. "Law attempts to check sin by lopping off numerous branches of pride, envy, anger, greed, gluttony, lust, and sloth that only re-grow or send their juice into other limbs," Noyes contended. "It is incomparably easier to lay the ax at the root."

John spent the 1836 winter in Putney rekindling the flames of spiritual awakening. "John felt most at home in Mother's room," his sister Charlotte wrote. "She was a frequent invalid and spent most of the time there. Her interest in true religious experience was never cold. Her whole soul was hungry for salvation, for an experiential acquaintance with God.... My sister Harriet began to spend her evenings in Mother's room, listening and reading with them; if I continued to be indifferent to the discussions, she and I who had been inseparable from childhood, must here part. I felt in my heart that Harriet had left me—that she had set out in earnest to be religious. This broke up my indifference. My heart melted toward God. I must go with her. She had opened the way, and I would follow with all my heart. I joined her in spending all my leisure time in that upper chamber. George came too. This was the beginning of a new era in our family. John commenced his home-talks there with us; it was a revival on a small scale that lasted all winter. We studied the Bible in a practical, self-applying way. The truth that has before been held as a theory was laid to heart. John watched the process of conviction, and warned, exhorted, and encouraged us, and led us along step by step."

Polly struggled to understand and fully implement John's counsel. She wrote to a friend at the beginning of that winter: "Sometimes I think John may preach the everlasting gospel with a power greater than anything he has yet done. I have had interesting conversations with him, but my long discipline only proves that like the law, he can enlighten and condemn, but cannot give peace to the troubled mind nor renew and purify the heart." But two months later, she wrote to an anonymous correspondent: "I say to you frankly, that I believe John has received the glorious gospel—that a testimony has already gone forth from him that will shake the world and the church—that God is preparing him to go forward with the testimony that confession of Christ in us saves from sin and all evil, and if we have more light and higher motives set before us, we must act consistently with that light. I know that the dearest earthly relations will be dissolved and every interest and worldly attachment converged; like the children of one common family, the children of God will have no exclusive interests."

In March Noyes was leaving home for an extended trip, but first visited his eldest sister Mary in nearby Chesterfield, New Hampshire, where his older sister Joanna was visiting. Charlotte said: "From Mary he met no opposition, and nothing occurred to interrupt the friendly relations existing between them. But Joanna was too independent, too proud and self-confident to conceal or suppress her displeasure at John's course. A battle royal ensued between him and her—not a vulgar contention about external trifles, but a life and death struggle for mastery between the favor of God and the praise of this world—between faith and unbelief. The result was a glorious victory for faith. Joanna broke entirely down. Her pride and love of the world gave way. After a few days of deep repentance and heartfelt searching for God, she came forth exceedingly happy and overflowing with the love of God. Seeing with the clear light of inspiration her union with Christ, and his righteousness hers, she exclaimed to mother: "You cannot think how I love myself!" The conversion of this beloved sister was a joyful surprise to us, and brought wonder and dismay to a large circle of worldly friends and to the church in Putney of which she was a member. Soon after, Joanna returned to her home in New Haven. During the few weeks of her stay with us she gave evidence of a genuine change of spirit. She met in the circle of believers in Putney a young woman who had formerly been haughty and ambitious like herself. As leaders and rivals in society there had been something like jealousy and coldness between them. But now the power of truth had swept away their pride, and love and humility had taken its place. One of the first things Joanna did was, by confession of her fault, to seek and obtain reconciliation with this woman."

Before he left home, John helped craft this letter, in his handwriting:
"Petition of the Junior Members of the Noyes Family to their father. Putney, March 9, 1837.

Dear Father:

"We think it our duty as members of your household and family to present you a respectful expression of our united desires, and we see no way to secure the object of our petition without using great plainness of speech. We therefore frankly declare that our object is to persuade you to redeem yourself from ruin, and release us from the slavery of solicitude concerning you by wholly abandoning the use of ardent spirits. That we have good reason for this effort you will not deny, if you recall several memorable scenes of the past winter. We are all compelled, however reluctantly, to regard you as a man slowly but surely sinking in the mire of intemperance, and we are sure the melancholy truth cannot long be concealed from the world. Our only hope, that you will escape the public disgrace of drunkenness and we the mortification of a drunkard's family, rests on the success of this last effort for your reformation . . . .

"The beguiling and enslaving power of habit has long been exhibited before our eyes. You have often apparently been checked in your descent, and you have as often resumed your course with increased momentum and decreased self-control. We see you now in the harvest of your days, a time that should be honorable to yourself and honored by us, daily and almost hourly indulging a degrading appetite, and manifesting your own sense of its degradation by vainly attempting to conceal it. We see the marks of your slavery in your countenance, in your gait, in your speech. We recognize the same evil in the unreasonable temper that you manifest at times, and we sadly contrast it with the kindness and consistency of your former behavior. We see and attribute to the same cause a rapid loss of intellect and health. We reasonably fear the loss of your property and life by fire or other casualties incidental to intoxication. We can by no means feel confidence in you as a counselor and guide of the family that your former character was wont to inspire. We can have no faith in your religious character, knowing that "no drunkard shall inherit the Kingdom of God." For all these reasons we can have no pleasure in your society, neither can you in ours.

"What then can we do but exercise the right of petition? What ought we to do, as children dealing with a beloved father, but beseech you for your own sake, for our sake, for God's sake to renounce wholly and forever the use of intoxicating liquors? We will wait on the Lord with submission and patience, whatever may be the result, knowing that the God of the widow and the fatherless will befriend us if this our united and last effort fails, and giving praise and thanksgiving to him who alone can change the heart if it succeeds.—*Harriet H. Noyes, John H. Noyes, Charlotte A. Noyes, George W. Noyes, Mary Mead, Horatio S. Noyes, and Joanna Hayes.*"

This appeal of his children enabled the Honorable John Noyes at age seventy-three to break the chains of habit. Thus a life that was drawing to a close in misery and disgrace was permitted to end in harmony with its early ideals. He died October 26, 1841, at the age of seventy-seven years.

Two months after the youngsters had written this painful letter to their father, John Humphrey Noyes wrote a letter to Joanna dated May 4, 1837: "I am persuaded that your reconciliation to the gospel of salvation from sin will finally reconcile you to my conduct; I doubt not that I am as great a wonder to myself as I am to you, and the time has been when I was ready to murmur at the Lord's dealings with me because I understood them not . . . . During the past three years I have not been my own master. The God, whose I am and whom I serve, is the proper respondent to every accusation against me. To me he has fully justified himself in respect to my works, and in due time I know he will satisfy every honest mind. I cannot now attempt a vindication of myself, for a big book would not suffice for such an undertaking. I will only say that in my own consciousness I am the reverse of a false prophet—a sheep in wolf's clothing. Joanna, I love your masculine, independent temperament; only give it full scope by setting the whole world at naught for the excellence of the knowledge of Christ, and you and I will yet be happy together. But oh, beware of pride, self-will, independence in respect to God! Be a giant against the world but be a new-born babe toward God. Seek a personal and familiar acquaintance with God, not such an acquaintance as you attain with great men of history, but such as you have with your husband by daily association. To know God is eternal life. Jesus Christ has so reconciled the world unto God by assuming our nature that we may draw nigh unto him not as serfs to an emperor but as children to a father. We approach him by a voluntary movement of our hearts and find him where we leave the world . . . . You must take the lover's leap—a leap from the heights of the haughtiness of this world into the ocean of the love of God. If such a leap seems too formidable, take the testimony of one who has tried it; there is no danger and no difficulty. When the deed is done, you will wonder that you made yourself so much trouble about it."

"John is certainly a remarkable person," wrote Joanna to her mother. "I never knew anyone so self-denying, so divested of all worldly feeling." Joanna had married Samuel Hayes—a kinsman of Rutherford Hayes—who was later appointed United States Consul at Trinidad. In July 1837, Joanna sailed with her husband to the West Indies in fine health and spirits. A bad fever was raging in the Island, but she wrote to her sister Mary: "Though death reigns everywhere, I'm mercifully in peace. I think just as I did about the great doctrine of Perfectionism, and could never feel satisfied to go back to the old way." Her husband had unexpectedly been called away to Puerto Rico, and Joanna suffered a slight attack of the fever but rebounded somewhat. She was stricken again, however, and eight days later, before her husband could reach her, she breathed her last at the age of twenty-nine. The night before, she sent this message to Putney, "I am perfectly resigned to the will of God in this trying hour. I know that Christ is mine and he is precious to my soul. In the world I have had tribulation, but in him I have peace."

THE INTERNAL TEACHER

Noyes realized that to attain full growth, one must pass through four stages—infancy and young childhood, primarily concerned with self; then the period of friendship or general companionship; then the period of love. "If the growth should stop there, there would be no full fruition," he wrote in his Home Talk, *Full Growth*. "Like fruit trees or plants, where all degrees of care may be bestowed, producing all degrees of fruitfulness, so human beings may grow up in a state so wild and weedy that the fourth stage will scarcely manifest itself at all. Because they do not generally see the full growth, people may think that it is unnatural for it to come. We give up expecting full fruition and see nothing more in human nature than green fodder. In the first three stages there must be restraint, dependency, and a disagreeable state of things to a certain extent. It is only when a person reaches the fourth stage and becomes a spiritual being, that the human being is prepared for absolute freedom. Therefore I should say that human beings are not really born until they come into relationship with God; they should be considered in embryo until their spiritual character is awakened. We may say that becoming children of God is our real birth. So we may consider those who fail of becoming spiritual, as *still-born*.

"Just as we develop through successive stages from birth," Noyes elaborated, "in our second birth we likewise do so. On the first confession of Christ within, the believer enters a new realm and finds himself cut loose from old moorings, obliged to make headway through bewilderment, perplexity, and temptation. His old life—egotism, self-centeredness—blinds him for a while. One tries to save oneself through one's own strength, but after repeated failures learns dependence on the love, wisdom, and power of Christ working in and through the self." In *The Day Star*, Noyes wrote, "We perceive matter by smell, sound, taste, sight, and feeling, and our spirits have the same variety of perceptions. We may be said to feel after God before we see him. Our hearts are blind to begin with. A blind person feels around with his hands, using all the senses he has. So we may feel after God, for our hearts are fashioned with reference to seeing God. The beauty of the case is that if we use what senses we have, and do the best we can to find God by groping, the time will come when our hearts will be purified and we shall see him. To know God in this way is eternal life. The heart opens itself to God and becomes purified and the day star of his love rises in it. We may be certain that God will meet us if we seek him. *I stand at the door and knock: if any hear my voice and open the door, I will come in to him* . . . . We are not at work alone; he is feeling after us; and we may be sure that the feelers will meet. We must not aspire to anything less than getting the permanent presence of the living God in our hearts."

Three States of the Heart

Noyes perceived that there are three distinct states of the heart: first, irreligion or worldliness; second, the double-minded stage in which the affections are toward God, though more or less attachment to the world remains; and third, in which all the affections of the heart are given to God. The transition from the double-minded state to perfect holiness requires as radical a conversion as does the transition from irreligion to the double-minded state. Noyes always stressed that there could not be two standards of morality, one for the world and the other available only to monks and clerics. Noyes had sought and served God with zeal after his initial conversion, but he kept pressing toward spiritual love, love of God and man, and the peace that passes understanding. "When a human being becomes a spiritual being, one is prepared for absolute freedom," Noyes wrote. 'The fruit of the Spirit is love, joy, peace, patience, kindness, goodness, faithfulness, humility, and self-control; against such there is no law.'—Gal 5:22–23. "Only those who have become naturalized citizens of the kingdom of heaven know the glorious sensation of unshackled freedom of will," Noyes said. "The highest experience and most glowing conceptions of liberty in the world are but meager shadows of the liberty we achieve when realizing our highest human potential. God made the universe after the pattern of his own heart, and adapted it to a state of love. The whole machinery of it runs directly across selfishness, and for that reason evil men can never be free. God will reign in natures like his own, not as a lawgiver and tyrant but as a helper to free man from an unnatural, selfish disposition, thereby putting an end to the war that exists as described in the 7th of Romans—the essence of bondage. With one undisturbed principle within, coinciding with the will of God, we have perfect liberty. 'Your pleasure is mine,' says the Spirit that promises the life more abundant.

"A distinguishing characteristic of the spiritual person is a *loving heart*," Noyes continued. "First John is almost exclusively devoted to defining the character of the regenerate man, and constantly makes brotherly love the leading test-mark. The renewed heart dwells in love, has gained the crown of all attainments, charity. Carnal believers may have external gifts of the spirit, but only the spiritual have that loving heart that is kind, envies not, vaunts not itself and is not puffed up, doth not behave itself unseemly, seeks not her own, is not easily provoked, thinks no evil, rejoices not in iniquity but rejoices in the truth. This unquestionably is the grand attainment that divides the full-born son of God from the babe in Christ. It is just that quality that fits a man to live in social contact with his fellow men *without giving offense, and without taking offense* [Emphasis, Noyes's]. It implies a thorough extinction of selfishness, a perfect appreciation of the interests of others, and a quiet reliance on the faithfulness of eternal love. He cannot be drawn into an envious, grudging, murmuring, evil-eyed spirit. This unobtrusive spiritual quality is what is needed for a cure of the world's miseries. Whoever has looked into the world reflectively, knows that selfishness engendering jealousies and strife is the most universal and inveterate malady. With charity the world might be a very comfortable Paradise, though its external institutions should remain unchanged. Without it, the most perfect organization can only be a well-disciplined Bedlam.

"Another characteristic of the spiritual man is a *renewed mind.* You 'have put on the new nature that is being renewed in knowledge after the image of its creator,' Col 3:10. 'Be renewed in the spirit of your minds, and put on the new nature, created after the likeness of God in true righteousness and holiness,' Eph 4:23–24. 'Be transformed by the renewal of your mind,' Rom 12:2. This renewed mind is strong and penetrating. Like the Word of God by which it is created, and to which it is assimilated, it is quick and powerful, sharper than a two-edged sword. Hence it readily apprehends divine mysteries that mere human intellects are unable to see or hear. 'Eye hath not seen, nor ear heard, nor the heart of man conceived, what God hath prepared for those that love him. . . . For the Spirit searches everything, even the depths of God.' 1st Cor 2:9–10.

"Third, a reborn person has an unquenchable desire for spiritual improvement—perfection is not attained once and for all. Without a quiet, loving heart, a discriminating and stable mind, and an energetic ambition for improvement, no one reached the perfection described by Paul in the Primitive Church. Paul spoke about the *nepioi*—babes in spirit—and the *teleioi*, fully realized Christians. 'We speak wisdom among them that are perfect,' said Paul, a clear statement of the reality of Christian perfection. 'Conversion is not putting in a patch of holiness; with the true convert, holiness is woven into all his powers, principles, and practice,' wrote New England Puritan Joseph Alline. 'The sincere Christian is quite a new fabric, from the foundation to the top-stone. He is a new man, a new creature.'[16] Noyes explained it this way in his Home Talk, *The Internal Teacher*:

"The Holy Spirit, coming from the Father, passes through the Son, and the experience of the Son, being photographed so to speak on that Spirit in its passage, is thereby transferred to believers and becomes a sort of memory with them. The very essence of all Christ's history is taken into that spirit, so that it comes to us charged with his character and deeds. It enters the pith of our spirit, so that it is the life of our life and becomes our ever-present teacher, preaching Christ to us day and night. Christ's disciples heard his words *forgive seven times seventy-seven* while he was with them, but this was a superficial operation, only preliminary to the final and real teaching that he was to give them. Their salvation was to come by a spiritual infusion that had in it not only the same truths that he taught by word, but all his unspoken wisdom and all his hidden experience. It is very beautiful to think that besides our personal memory, we have, in that good Spirit that whispers within us, a great transferred memory, or, we may say, an opening of our memory into the great memory of Christ; we have access to all the experiences that are in the memory of Christ—in fact, to that vast reservoir of words and deeds of which it is said, that if they had been recorded, the world itself would not contain the books that should be written. An internal teacher is present within us, watching all the motions of our spirits, all our thoughts and feelings, waiting to seize the lucky moment when some sympathetic point rises within, to bring the fitting word of Christ to our remembrance, and infuse his thoughts into our thoughts, his experience into our experience, and so by ten thousand fibers of connection weave our spirits into unity with his."

The pure in heart shall see God

Noyes came to know that the pure heart and mind is the *normal* state of humanity, only to be discovered. "When the Spirit of God is realized, the innermost life becomes infused with new vigor and efficiency in every part of one's nature," Noyes wrote. "The gospel is a proclamation issuing from God, not word nor speech but *power*. It is spiritual *energy* emanating from the Almighty. The heart not only hears information but feels spiritual power applied directly to the will. The presence of Christ in the soul, instead of taking away the power of willing, greatly increases it. Our will is not superseded but quickened and actuated by Christ's will.

"If I watch in my heart and discover the will of God concerning any external thing that I am about to do—so that I feel sure I get a vibration and response and am acting under his direction—then my external actions become a part of my internal experience. The most insignificant exterior acts may become the sweetest and most beautiful parts of my life, just because of the connection formed between them and this internal oracle. It is a perfectly feasible thing, as well as a true theory of Christian life, to do all things in the name of the Lord Jesus, to bring all our common actions into the sphere of the internal reckonings. The internal teacher can guide our life to such an extent that we will live by God's inspiration. The state of unbroken communion with God is our true nature, Noyes concluded in his Talk, *Waiting and Watching*.

"The interior world is sometimes called the shadow land, but it is neither shadowy nor unreal," Theodore Pitt wrote in the September 15, 1875, *Circular*. "The outward world is but a part of the universe and ranked as an interior part—'look not at things seen but at things not seen,' says Paul, 'for things seen are temporal, but things not seen are eternal.' The inner world seems unsubstantial and vague to the materialistic conception, yet who has not gazed into a realm of truth and beauty and unspeakable harmony, where the soul, unconscious of evil, is subdued with the deepest joy at mere existence? Was it an illusion, such stuff as dreams are made of, or is the outward world an illusion and a sham? One thing is certain, cloud-capped towers and gorgeous palaces dissolve; what one would believe eternal melts at the touch of time and changes with the passing year. We believe that the realm of the real lies toward the interior; that the outward that seems so substantial is real only where it touches the interior. Man stands at the confluence of two vast worlds: the convergent lines of life and spiritual space leading to God, and the outward stretching far away from him till it fades into the inane. The center of all life and good is God—the reality of all realities, the essence of all that is substantial. In proportion as we approach the interior, we touch and drink in life and find truth and solidity. To all things there is an interior and an exterior: spirit and letter. If we deal with the exterior, the surface or form of things, we find but shadow and deception. *The letter killeth, but the spirit giveth life*. Only as we turn to the interior vitality of things do we find the central good—happiness and health for soul and body. All the struggling of the soul after rest—longing for some immortal aliment—are instincts inviting us to the better land of interior life and reality. These yearnings are the tokens of an accessible reality. Our own interior, the soul-center of our being, is all that we are—it is the substance that makes us realities. We live and move and have our being in God. The only things that do us any good are those that enter into us and touch our interior life."

"Christ said to his disciples, '*The words I speak unto you are spirit and they are life*'; they touched the core and soul of their being. Such words have a soul in them that conveys to us their real effect," Noyes taught the Community. "The simple word will do us no good: it excites expectations that will never be fulfilled, giving a show of truth that turns out to be chaff. God is the source of all good, knowledge, truth, beauty, and enjoyment, and in him only are these things to be found. If in our search after these, we stop on the outside and take up with the fleeting show of the sensuous world, we shall inevitably be disappointed and find cheats and not realities. In this great interior where God and Christ are, is all that is of worth in the universe. There are hid all the treasures of wisdom and knowledge. The kingdom of heaven is within; all the great things of the kingdom of heaven must be perceived by interior vision. Directing the attention of the head to the heart is required; the external senses of observation and perception must be directed toward the heart—toward the interior our being. We can learn to watch our heart just as persistently as the astronomer watches the heavens, the sailor watches against storms and collisions, the soldier watches against the approach of the enemy, or the street-watchman against the approach of thieves. We find here, I believe, the grand difference between a spiritual man and a common moralist. The moralist is governed by external inducements, but the spiritual person watches internal phenomena."

The Reverend W. H. H. Murray, pastor of the Park Street Church in Boston, was a good elocutionist and one of Boston's most popular preachers. He received a note from a young church member: "Dear Mr. Murray: In your Friday evening lecture you exhorted the church to prepare for fellowship with Jesus at the approaching Lord's Supper and to expect that love for him would fill their hearts. I do not know how to love a person whom I have never seen nor heard speak. To me Jesus is a myth. I hear him often spoken of but know nothing about him. How is it possible for me to think and feel otherwise?" Reverend Murray replied: "We have nothing reliable touching the person of Christ except what we can glean from the Scriptures. How is it possible for us to know and love Jesus Christ? By and through the imagination. Our imaginations of the person of Christ may vary with our different individualities, but this does not prevent our fellowship with him through such means."

"I could not but feel solicitude for that young man," Noyes wrote, "and a fear that his uncertainties had not been fully met. If he would consider that there is a realm of facts in our inner world not cognizable by the five senses but even more palpable than the facts of physical science, he might then have fellowship with such a being as Jesus Christ, feel his love in his heart without essentially drawing on his imagination at all. Man has an inward spiritual nature as well as outward; the quickening power of that spiritual nature is Jesus Christ himself. Christ is in all flesh, in us personally. This is the fundamental teaching of the New Testament. To realize this, you and I and that young man must have faith—faith is itself *substance* as much as bread, a spiritual element within us; Paul says it is the *evidence* of things not seen. It is a substantial thing, not a mere thought or abstraction. It may be compared to the fibers of a root that the plant shoots into the earth, strengthening itself and deriving nourishment from the process. In our union with God there is a reciprocal action. His word comes to us, shooting forth the fibers of his life toward us; and by the recognition of his goodness, by responsive acts of faith, our spirits shoot forth toward him, and each way fibers multiply, perfecting the union. Every little act of faith in our past experience is a fiber connecting us with God; but it is a great secret to know how to generalize, how to make a strong bond by twisting all the fibers into one.

"In spinning flax, at the point where the twist commences there are a great many little separate fibers and each alone is weak—the least pull will break them; but combine and twist all the fibers together and they make a strong cord. So we may have ten thousand fibers of faith in a loose, flax state; they will be easily pulled apart—they cannot bear any strain, till we find a way to twist them. We are in the constant exercise of little acts of faith and have been accumulating in long experience the fibrous material connecting us with God. Faith is the medium of connection between our spirit and God; let us learn the art of twisting, that we may make a cable of strength. If we can combine the strength of all our faith, it will hold anything. The exercise of the *will* rather than the imagination is necessary on our part to call it forth. God is a rewarder of those that diligently seek him, but in coming to him we must believe; and if you do not believe this, confess what you do believe and go forward. Keep stepping, and you will finally attain your heart's desire. Each one's faith is a distinct fiber connecting him with God; the strength of masses can never be known till their faith is combined and twisted into one cord. Then their union with one another and with God will be such that nothing in the universe can break or put any injurious strain upon it.

"Consider what Paul says: Fight the good fight of faith; lay hold on eternal life. Let us understand what *lay hold* on eternal life means, Noyes taught in *Realism of Christianity*. I believe it means something just as real as though Paul had said to a man who had fallen overboard, *Lay hold of that rope!* The thing for us to lay hold of is a reality, and the laying hold is a real act of taking hold of something—not indeed with the hands, but with the heart. Eternal life is one of the things unperceived, but it is a thing as real as money or blood. If you study Christ and Paul and the Primitive teachers, you will find their great distinction—they hugged realities. They did not deal in nonentities, but grasped things they could see and feel. That which was from the beginning, which we have heard, which we have seen with our eyes, which we have looked upon and our hands have handled of the Word of Life, John says, declare we unto you. This is the way they all talked, as though they would beat it into us by repetition—they were not talking about nothing. The word Spirit meant a real substance in Christ's mind, just as palpable to him as water and wind. If any man thirst let him come unto me and drink. He that believeth on me, as the Scripture hath said, out of his belly shall flow rivers of living water. On the day of Pentecost, the Spirit came like a mighty rushing wind from heaven, and filled the whole place where they were sitting, and produced not only intellectual, moral, and spiritual changes in people, but also great physical effects.

"The ideas of spirit-substantiality that pervaded primitive Christianity are gone from modern theological teachings. Our faith will be true or false, firm or futile, in proportion as it fastens on or neglects the real and substantial view of spiritual matters." Noyes used an apt analogy: "Because a thing is very refined, we must not imagine that to be a reason why it is nearer to nothing. Comparing two pieces of the same substance—one of great bulk and the other a pinhead—you may say that one of these pieces is a great deal nearer to nothing than the other. But in comparing the reality of spirit with other things we are comparing not bulks of the same substance, but things that differ from one another in the fineness of their ultimate particles; the particles of water may be finer than those of sand and the particles of electric fluid finer than those of water. Instead of finding that the smaller and finer the particles are, the less real they are and nearer to nothing, you will find the contrary—as you pass to things that are finer and finer, you are going toward the most powerful concrete realities, and receding further and further from nothing. A man's soul is further from nothing than his body, and God is further from nothing than the great worlds we see in the study of astronomy.

"Science is what we know, and there are many ways to knowledge," Noyes tells us in *The Center of Science*. "We discover some existences by the senses, by seeing, hearing, smelling, feeling; we get at others by testimony, and still others by reasoning. Last of all, there is heart-perception. I can see and feel and hear God in my heart. That is a matter of science to me just as much as anything that is discoverable with the microscope or telescope. If others say they have not seen or heard or felt God, and do not know there is such a being, I say to them, I am certain of it. I shall take what I know as a part of science. The scientific world, without the power of heart-discovery, must be very circumscribed in its domain of research—quite as limited as though it had no telescope.

> "Of all that I know, this is the surest--that I know but very little; everything persuades me to humility," Noyes emphasized in *Two Certainties*. "The second surest thing that I know is that the universe is full of somebody else's intelligence, which, compared with my intelligence, is as the ocean to a drop. Here is the true recognition of the *me* and the *not-me*. The *me* must subside into the *not-me*, and then by virtue of the partnership it knows all things: but the moment it relapses into itself it knows nothing.

"Desire earnestly to know God," Noyes urged his followers in *God's Bargain*. "Be contented with nothing less than such an acquaintance as will enable you to speak with him and hear him speak to you. Physical laws govern us in the material world—for example, the radiating power of a lamp affects us inversely as the square of the distance we are from it; at two feet its light is only one-fourth as much as at one foot. The same law of proportion governs gravitation and all radiating forces. Conceive of God as the center of a radiating influence of love and care which manages the machinery of the universe. In drawing near we find ourselves affected by his love and care according to the universal law of radiation, that is, inversely as the square of our distance from him. Nearness multiplies communication and affection in a rapidly increasing ratio. Believe that God is a personal, intelligent, sensitive being who is as much above mere arbitrary law as you are, as much a personal, affectionate agent as you are, and a great deal more so. We can know him as such, and approach him and have intelligent connection with him, not merely by words in a distant way but by receiving his Spirit. We can know him for ourselves, and come where we feel that he loves us better than we love our children or father or mother. It is a reality that will manifest itself in facts. It is a law as rational as geometry."

"God is as much of a reality, as much of a presence, as much of a power, as much of an entity and individuality as we are," wrote spiritual teacher Joel Goldsmith,[17] "and God can be just as well known by us as we can know ourselves or one another." George Fox inspired the Society of Friends known as Quakers, and taught that all people have the divine light within, an ever-available source of wisdom with no need for ministerial intervention to converse with God. This divine essence can be realized so its presence becomes a reality in daily life, wrote Meister Eckhart. "It must not remain hidden under the covering of our everyday personality. To discover this spark of the divine in our hearts is life's real and highest goal. When we realize this goal, we discover that the divinity within ourselves is one and the same in all—all individuals, all creatures, all of life."[18] Soldier Nicolas Herman joined a Carmelite order following an experience that in an instant showed him the Divine foundation of all things. "Perseverance is required at first in making a habit of converse with God, of referring all we do to Him, but after a little His love moves us to it without any difficulty," Brother Lawrence said. "In the beginning of the spiritual life it was necessary to act faithfully, and renounce one's own will, but after that there were joys indescribable . . . . [w]e ought not to get tired of doing little things for the love of God, because he looks at the love rather than the work."[19]

"The heart is thrilled with the discovery of the love of God," wrote Noyes. "This love gives birth to gratitude; the heart expands and the mind grows as communion with God is established. Spiritual perceptions gradually become acute as one begins to discover that love is the true medium through which faith works; realizing some of the fruits of this faith, persevering efforts are stimulated. Continuous growth is now understood as one's work. One now discerns the spirit of God—his plans, movements, and modes of thought and action in oneself and others, and in the universe. The Ark of the Covenant was long the place where the people of Israel consulted God. What was then locally true is now a universal principle. You will find in your own nature a sanctuary—a holy of holies, an ark of the covenant, a place where God reveals himself; and it is your privilege in all transactions to ask counsel of God and talk with him about your purposes. We must search out this central sanctuary and be in a condition to recur to it, he wrote in *Deep Soundings*.

"It should become the habit of our lives to turn to God. Let every individual go home into his heart many times a day and seek to know God for himself or herself," Noyes counseled in his Home Talk, *Go Home*. "When we have finished our work and have nothing else to do, go home and talk with God. We are sure to find nourishment and rest there, and so get ready to go out again. Let everyone have a place to retire and reflect and watch in his heart. It is a great attainment to abide serenely with God, let outside distractions be what they may. When we have learned to do this we can pass unhurt through the wreck of matter and the crash of worlds. Dwell deep. Live in your hearts, where the world cannot come; for then the Lord who is your shepherd will lead you by the side of still waters."

Most people must live active lives, as did the founder of the Jesuits, Ignatius Loyola. Though not by nature a contemplative, he regularly undertook what he called the "examin," several times daily assessing to what extent he'd been caught up in surface duties and enjoyments and the time it would take him to recover the essential contact; he retreated to prayer every quarter hour because life does "de-ordinate" one, he said. To meet the fluctuations of circumstance with inner guidance, he recommended making an honest checkup three times a day to know how far you are out on the surface.[20]

Noyes echoed this teaching in his Home Talk, *Where and How to Pray*. "Instead of going from one thing to another on the circumference, I go to the center; even though I go out again right away, if I stay out too long I lose my inspiration. The only rule I find for myself is to go home when a job is done; pray in this way twenty times a day if necessary. Much as we have to do, there is still no hurry; we need not recklessly drive on for fear our work will get ahead of us, or think we have no time for reflection. When you have got counsel from God you will go forth to action with a sure heart. You must give yourself up to this interior reflection with the understanding that as soon as your reflection shows you a thing to be done, do it swiftly and with all your might."

Inspiration is the natural, healthy condition of the race—that for which human nature was designed. "The present ordinary condition of mankind, living without God, is unnatural—at variance utterly with their original constitution," Noyes wrote in *The Berean*.[21] Uninspired men, even with all their intellectual resources, are utterly incompetent to interpret those parts of scripture that are concerned with the deep things of God. The Holy Spirit is the ultimate arbiter of biblical interpretation, but many scholars and even Christians assume that we are not to expect the direct teachings of the Spirit; that such inspiration is restricted to a favored few mostly in the past and is not accessible to all. Franciscan Richard Rohr cites Alan Watts, a former Episcopal minister who interpreted Eastern philosophy for the Western audience: ". . . [i]nstitutional Christianity has hardly contemplated the possibility that the consciousness of Jesus may be the consciousness of the Christian . . . .The truth that religion, to be of any use, must be mystical has always been denied by a seemingly large number of people, including theologians, who do not know what mysticism is . . . . Its essence is conscious of union with God."[22]

"I always know when someone has been holding central converse with God, by his coming forth with some new glowing enterprise fresh from heaven," Noyes said, in his Home Talk, *Deep Soundings*. "By meditation you get access to a fountain of pure inspiration and necessarily become original in your ideas and movements; you find in yourself continually new purposes which cannot be traced to any connection with others or to ordinary motives." Noyes believed in lifetime spiritual growth, a continuous process that could never be a final achievement. Always rekindle the desire to become the mature Christian of which Paul spoke.

"De Tocqueville came to the United States in 1831 to learn all he could about our Republic, its laws and institutions, the manners and customs of the people, our social conditions, in order to improve the French Constitution," Noyes wrote in the September 14, 1868, *Circular*. "This is the kind of study we want: Learn living facts and have fellowship with the spiritual Primitive Church, as De Tocqueville learned about our country. Enter into personal communication with the citizens of that spiritual kingdom. First get all the information we can—if going abroad, we should acquaint ourselves with a country's history, geography, and what could be learned before traveling there; and from the New Testament we obtain preliminary knowledge of the Primitive Church, which is to have its counterpart set up on earth. The prayer of Christ, *Thy will be done on earth, as it is done in heaven* will be answered. The God-centered life can power a lasting spiritual regeneration of mankind. The human intellect alone can never develop the true idea of social perfection, but with the love of God and man written in the heart and mind (Heb 10:14–16), and with the instruction of heavenly artists, we can go forward with strong hearts. The noblest destiny of mankind is rebirth into holiness, to be co-workers with God in ushering in the last period of man's education."

How reminiscent of John Winthrop's sermon to the colonists as they sailed to an unknown land in 1630. He spoke of their new covenant and commitments to God and to one another. The Bible, familiar to all literate persons, was often quoted—*Do justice, love kindness, and walk humbly with your God.* Winthrop urged all to abridge ourselves of our superfluities for the supply of others' necessities, and work together in brotherly affection with meekness, gentleness, patience, and liberality with one idea for the good of all and for posterity, because we shall be as a City on a Hill, the eyes of all people upon us. Winthrop warned that if we pursue false gods of pleasures and profits, we shall surely perish out of the Good Land. *I have set before you life and death, blessing and curse; therefore choose life, that you and your descendants may live.*

Noyes learned that Charles Grandison Finney was in New York, whom he'd missed three years previously, and wrote him a brief note. "Dear Brother Noyes," Mr. Finney replied, "I have this moment received your letter and thank you for it. I have often heard of you and of your extravagances, of course. But, precious brother, I have learned not to be frightened if it is rumored that anyone has received any light that I have not myself. It is true that I have supposed *from report* [emphasis is Finney's] that you carried some of your views too far, but whether this is true or false I would consider it a great privilege to possess myself thoroughly of your views. It would give me great pleasure to see and converse with you . . . and learn whether you have discovered any hidden rocks on the coast and dangerous quicksand upon which one inexperienced is in danger of falling. I have no fear of the doctrine of perfect, instantaneous, perpetual holiness; and know full well that like justification, sanctification is to be received by faith, and that we are as much at liberty and as much bound to reckon ourselves dead to sin as unto damnation. I would be rejoiced to see you at my study in the Tabernacle, entrance 95 Anthony Street. Your brother, C.G. Finney." Noyes immediately went to New York and had an interview of several hours with Mr. Finney. "The candor and kindness of his behavior toward me," Noyes wrote, "was surpassingly beautiful and refreshing."

William James related Finney's conversion: In an unlighted back room ". . . it appeared to me as if it were perfectly light . . . it seemed as if I met the Lord Jesus Christ face to face . . . and I fell down at his feet and poured out my soul to him." Returning to his office, "I was about to take a seat by the fire that was now nearly burned out. The Holy Spirit descended upon me in a manner that seemed to go through me, body and soul. I could feel that impression, like a wave of electricity, going through and through me. Indeed, it seemed to come in waves and waves of liquid love; for I could not describe it in any other way. It seemed like the very breath of God. I can recollect distinctly that it seemed to fan me, like immense wings. No words can express the wonderful love that was shed abroad in my heart."[23]

This fruitful meeting with Finney opened doors for Noyes; he was given the hand of friendship by William Green, one of Finney's intimate associates and husband of the editor of *The Advocate of Moral Reform*. Noyes spent several weeks with the Greens, and this may be how the Cragins learned about Noyes and became early community members. Noyes and three friends set off to visit Perfectionists in central and western New York; a kindred spirit encouraged Noyes to start a paper and gave him the means to publish the first edition.

"I present myself as a simple witness for the truth, the whole truth, and nothing but the truth in relation to the great controversy between God and the human race," Noyes wrote in *The Witness*, published on August 20, 1837, at Ithaca, New York. "*The Witness* will not be confined within the limits usually occupied by religious periodicals. I have long traversed unshackled the broad field of universal truth. I shall therefore pass and re-pass the usual boundaries of technical theology, knowing that the theology of heaven includes every other science. Regarding man as a spiritual, intellectual, moral, and physical being, I account it the proper object of his existence to glorify his Maker by the proportionate and unlimited development of each of these departments of his nature. With a single eye therefore to the glory of God by the redemption of man, I may properly—nay I must necessarily—examine and discuss not merely the spiritual and moral but also the intellectual and physical relations of mankind." In the first issues he printed many of the twenty articles he had contributed to *The Perfectionist*, and the following year he republished them all in a pamphlet called *The Way of Holiness*, which he sent to all his subscribers.

"I look to God and not my subscription list for support. The laborer is worthy of his hire but he should be paid by his employer, not by his fellow servants. I have not the least anxiety about the future either in respect to my spiritual or temporal necessities. I know God will never order me to testify without giving me the means. Whenever therefore my means fails, I receive an order to keep silence. If you wish for the paper without money and without price, send me simply your name. If you prefer to pay for it, send me your name with one dollar for twenty-six issues. If you dislike modes of subscription, another that I prefer myself is, send me your name, with a gift of any amount, more or less; your money shall be a love-token to me, and my paper shall be a present to you and not an article of merchandise. I can buy and sell with an enemy, but I can exchange gifts only with a friend. If any withhold their names because they can send no money, let me assure them that in my code of morality, poverty is not a crime. I have reason to believe that there are many worthy persons who would be glad to receive the paper, but for some cause or other can not pay for it. Most heartily I desire such to put away all squeamishness, and send me their names without delay. For one, I am not ashamed to make my wants known to God or man, and I have no fellowship with the spirit of those persons who starved to death in the city of New York last spring because they were too proud to acknowledge their poverty. *Ask and ye shall receive.* If any withhold their subscriptions because they fear the paper will stop for lack of funds, I am determined to give my subscribers twenty-six issues sooner or later, at all events.

"I shall publish communications sent to me that in my judgment hit the mark at which I aim. I insert the following extract from a letter, honorable to its author and pleasing to me—Dearly beloved: Having no money, not even enough to pay the postage of this letter, I ask you to send me the Witness in the name of the Lord. Yours, &c. I have no fear of failure of a run upon me in consequence of thus opening the doors of my bank, for I believe the time is not distant when all who receive my testimony will have but one heart, and of course but one purse."

2

High Tide of the Spirit: Putney Community

MARRIAGE, SEXUALITY, AND THE ELEVATION OF THE RACE

"Westminster, Vermont, Sept. 1, 1837. On receiving *The Witness* I felt desirous to write and send you a love token. I feel a desire to speak to you of what I have been learning of late. I am emptied of that kind of knowledge that puffeth up and desire to be filled only with that which edifies. . . . I see before me a heavenly disinterestedness where self-will is slain. . . . I shall rejoice to receive a printed letter from you once in two weeks. . . . I desire to be made what the Lord would have me to be. While thinking of receiving *The Witness* from you, I desired that your spirit might be written upon my heart. . . . Yours through the gospel, Harriet A. Holton." Enclosed was $80.00.

One month before Harriet's letter to John, a controversial letter he'd sent to close friend David Harrison had found its way into public print. In it, Noyes rejected the concept of monogamous marriage. There is no marriage in heaven (Matthew 22), and when the will of God is done on earth, there will be no marriage. "After a deliberation of more than a year in patient waiting and watching for indications of the Lord's will," John wrote to Harriet on June 11, 1838, at age 26, "I am now permitted, and indeed happily enabled by a combination of favorable circumstances to propose to you a partnership that I will not call marriage till I have defined it. As believers, we are already one with each other and with all the saints; this primary and universal union is more radical and more important than any particular and external partnerships, and with reference to this it is said there is neither marrying nor giving in marriage in heaven, neither male nor female. Therefore we can enter into no engagements with each other that shall limit the range of our affection as they are limited in matrimonial engagements by the fashion of this world. I desire and expect my yoke-fellow will love all who love God, whether man or woman, with a warmth and strength of affection that is unknown to earthly lovers, and as freely as if she stood in no particular connection with me. In fact, the object of my connection with her will be not to monopolize and enslave her heart or my own, but to enlarge and establish both in the free fellowship of God's universal family. I respect and love you for many desirable qualities, spiritual, intellectual, moral, and personal, especially your faith, kindness, simplicity, and modesty. I am confident that the partnership I propose will greatly promote our mutual happiness and improvement. It will also set us free, at least myself, from much reproach and evil surmising occasioned by celibacy. It will enlarge our sphere and increase our means of usefulness to the people of God. I know that the immortal union of hearts, the everlasting honeymoon that alone is worthy to be called marriage, can never be effected by a ceremony; and I know equally well that such a marriage can never be marred by a ceremony."

"I only expect to be placed in a situation where I can enjoy your society and instruction," Harriet replied to John's proposal, "as long as the Lord pleases and when he pleases." They spent their honeymoon searching for a reasonably priced printing press to resume publication of *The Witness*. They built a house in Putney, Vermont, and wanted a family. "In the next six years, my wife went through the agonies of five births," John wrote. "Four were premature and only one child lived." Theodore was born in July 1841 after the beginning of the Putney Community. Miscarriage, stillbirth, infant death, maternal death, or death of children before age five was commonplace before modern medical interventions. Neighbors commiserated with Harriet and recounted in harrowing detail their own ordeals in childbearing. John refused to evade his responsibility, refused to accept that he was a mere slave of nature and that Harriet must be subjected to the recurring pain and possible early death experienced by many women who underwent repeated, difficult pregnancies. *Such is the destiny of womankind; nature must take its course*, were common refrains. He brooded over Harriet's long martyrdom of childbearing and rejected the conventional silence about the fruitless suffering of women.

Harriet A. Noyes, John Humphrey Noyes's wife, was known as "Mother Noyes" to the Oneida Community. She was an important and humble role model for kind, unselfish living.

"We do not believe that motherhood is the chief purpose of woman's life—that she was made for the children she can bear," Noyes proclaimed. "We are opposed to involuntary, excessive, and therefore oppressive procreation. Why should we be enslaved by this ceaseless, automatic repetition of desire, by ruthless impersonal instinct, and suffer the destruction of freedom and the limitation of progress? Was it not just here that humanity had been brought into slavery, degraded below the level of the brute? Yet we are spiritual beings of infinite depth and potential—the long march of humanity has improved upon Nature! I pledged my word to Harriet after our last disappointment that I would never again expose her to such fruitless suffering. I made up my mind to live apart from my wife in the summer of 1844 rather than break this promise."

From ages thirty-two to thirty-four, Noyes assiduously studied all the details of this great conundrum of central importance to humanity. "I conceived the idea that the sexual organs have a social function distinct from the procreative function, and that these functions may be separated practically." His practice of entire abstinence from ejaculation revealed real appreciation of the first stages of intercourse, well short of male climax. "I found that the self control it requires is not difficult, that my enjoyment was increased and that my wife's experience was very satisfactory as it never had been before. We had escaped the fear and the horrors of repeated involuntary propagation." Sexual intercourse short of what was called the propagative crisis becomes a prolonged and richer experience, fruitful of social magnetism. Its refining effect increased the pleasure of sexual love in subtle ways. It elevated sexual intercourse to an expression of mutual love instead of an act of unrestrained sensual indulgence. Noyes discovered that amative love, as he termed it—prolonging the union of persons, making "of twain one flesh"—is a distinct and independent function that can be a portal to divine communion. The exercise of any human function in the spirit of purity is superior to sensuality, and it is also superior to the disuse of this natural function—as Shakers and others practice. "Love and parentage can be exercised without sensuality and for the good of humanity. This was a great deliverance. It made a happy household. I communicated my discovery to a friend. His experience and that of his household were the same." He wrote about his discovery of what he termed Male Continence four years later.

One chapter dealt in analytical detail about the amative and propagative functions of the sexual organs.[24] When no offspring is planned, amative intercourse is the conjunction of the organs of union and is an interchange of social magnetism, contrasted with the organs of procreation, the testicles and the uterus. These are *physiologically* distinct, Noyes noted. The communication from the seminal vessels to the uterus, which constitutes the propagative act, is distinct from, subsequent to, and not necessarily connected with, amative intercourse. These two functions are confounded in the world, both in the theories of physiologists and in universal practice. The sexual organs are termed organs of reproduction or generation—not organs of love or organs of union; the amative function is regarded as bait to the propagative, and is merged in it. Discharge of semen is the sequel and termination of sexual intercourse.

Suppose that a man in lawful intercourse with woman, choosing for good reasons not to beget a child, should stop at the primary stage and content himself with simple *presence* as long as agreeable? Would there be any harm? It cannot be injurious to refrain from voluntary excitement. Would there be no *good*? I appeal to the memory of every man who has had good sexual experience to say whether, on the whole, isn't the sweetest and noblest period of intercourse with woman that *first* moment of simple presence and spiritual effusion? But we may go further. Suppose the man chooses to enjoy not only simple presence, but also the reciprocal motion, and yet to stop short of the final crisis. Physiologists might say, and I would acknowledge, that the excitement by motion *might* be carried so far that a voluntary suppression of the commencing crisis would be injurious. But what if a man, knowing his own power and limits, should not even *approach* the crisis, and yet be able to enjoy the presence and the motion? If you say that this is impossible, I answer that I *know* it is possible—nay, that it is easy. In the normal condition, men are entirely competent to choose in sexual intercourse whether they will stop at any point in the voluntary stages of it, and so to make it simply an act of communion, or go through to the involuntary stage and make it an act of propagation." Noyes likened this to swimming in a mild current, avoiding close approach to a waterfall.

"As long as the amative and propagative are confounded, sexual intercourse carries with it physical consequences that take it out of the category of social acts. If a man under the cover of a social call on a woman should leave in her apartment a child for her to bear and provide for, he would do a mean wrong. Law, or at least public opinion, should frown on such proceedings even more than it does. We believe that good sense and benevolence will soon sanction and enforce the rule that women shall bear children only when they choose . . . . Women have the principal burdens of breeding to bear, and they rather than men should have their choice of time and circumstances." Society must charge itself with the crime of producing many more children than it can take good care of with all the surroundings of health—good air, good food, and wise nursing. And it is not to be wondered at that women, to a considerable extent, look upon ordinary sexual intercourse with more dread than pleasure, regarding it as a stab at their life rather than a joyful act of fellowship. Sexual communion should be for love, forbidding the propagative act except when conception is intended. Ordinary sexual intercourse, i.e., the performance of the propagative act without the intention of procreation, is properly to be classed with masturbation, Noyes said. "To Noyes, ordinary custom in sexual intercourse seemed to be on a par with the drinking habits of the English country gentleman of earlier times; at that period it was esteemed decent for a man to end his dinner under the table," Robert Allerton Parker noted in his superb and often humorous biography, *A Yankee Saint*. "Lust for filling the belly with food in a greedy spirit, hurrying over preliminaries, corresponded to the lust for the propagative crisis."[25]

Noyes studied both Robert Dale Owen's approach, and the Shakers, concluding that Male Continence has more real affinity with Shakerism: "It is based on self-control, as Shakerism is based on self-denial; while Owenism is the usual self-indulgence." Owen, son of the founder of New Harmony, published *Moral Physiology* in 1836, describing the withdrawal method as a reasonable answer to unplanned pregnancy and unsustainable population growth, and not much diminishing the pleasure of sexual intercourse. "But the integration of sexual love with the life of the spirit vastly increases that pleasure," Noyes reported after twenty-five years of Community experience, "and it has nearly exterminated masturbation by the reflex influence of Male Continence. The Community has had no trouble from the retention of seed," he replied to the query whether Male Continence is a difficult and injurious interruption, as some asserted. "Every instance of self-denial is an interruption of some natural act. The man who contents himself with a look at a beautiful woman is conscious of such an interruption. The lover who stops at a kiss denies himself a natural progression. Sexual experience involves self-denial throughout the spectrum of relationship from the first touch of respectful friendship. Brutes—animal or human—tolerate no interruption of this natural progression. Shall their ideas prevail? Nay, it is the glory of man to control himself, and the Kingdom of Heaven summons him to self-control in all things. Every human passion may be expressed in the spirit of purity; in my view, our method crucifies the fleshly lust of men and elevates sexual communion into a social and spiritual act."

How involuntary processes become subject to voluntary control

"It belongs to human destiny to get full possession of oneself," George Washington Noyes added to his brother's studies of sexuality, published in June 1873. "The power of a man's will over his own body is a circle of power interior to, and therefore more important than, his power over external nature. His body with its various faculties and functions is the set of tools with which he enters universal nature's vast workshop, and he must gain mastery of those tools. By attention and painstaking investigation and practice in some mechanical art, people gain a power over their muscles for certain purposes that might seem impossible, even miraculous. Great violinists and pianists are an example, expressing themselves in the motions of the body to a perfection that is in proportion to the painstaking and discipline applied. The influence of will and education to control the body is universally admitted as far as voluntary outward habits are concerned. We know that regarding half-voluntary functions such as coughing, sneezing, and breathing, the involuntary impulse can be suppressed by an effort of the will. A man was saved from the consumption by being persuaded to stop coughing—he found that the tendency, however inveterate, could be controlled, and he accordingly put it down with his will. We have had a striking accumulation of evidence in our Community over the years showing that the stomach and bowels are subject to the same control, and that such operations as vomiting and bilious disorder may be suppressed. Sea-sickness has been met and conquered as have cholera symptoms.

"But there is a step further than this," George continued. "A desire, a thought, or a motivation arises in the mind or in the emotions with an energy that is smaller than the smallest of seeds and is realized not at its origin but only after it develops somewhat. As a desire or a thought develops, it becomes more difficult to control, suppress, or eliminate; if one cannot perceive the early stages of a desire or an idea, and realizes these only when they become well-developed, one may lose voluntary control over desires and have to submit. We believe that investigation and experience are now ready to demonstrate the power of the will over what have been considered the involuntary processes of the body. The mind can take control of them certainly to a great extent, and while not yet shown to what extent, neither is it apparent that there are any limits whatever. It must stand as an open question, unless the contrary is proved, since discoveries point to the conclusion that there are strictly no involuntary departments in the human system, but that every part falls appropriately and in fact within the dominion of mind, spirit, and will."

We now know that Yogic practices demonstrate mastery over heat and cold, heart rate, oxygen consumption, and more. Tantric theory postulates that we each have a subtle body, known also as an energy body or emotional body, with operations unknown to the conscious body/mind. Each experience we have is an energy pattern that passes through our subtle body. With practice in meditation and self-observation, human beings are capable of developing awareness of the small beginnings of desires, thoughts, or motivations and up to a certain point have the freedom to allow or end their further development. Once developed, as we fall under their influence, we lose control. The unobserved self is like a human on a beach seeing a tidal wave approaching without power to turn the gigantic wave back. Tantric experience illuminates what John Noyes must have discovered in his two years of studying sexuality and practicing Male Continence, and what George Noyes learned in meditation.

"Propagation and sexual passion are matters fully within the province of the will—subject to enlightened control," John Humphrey Noyes affirmed. "These facts, a legitimate conclusion from the general truth that man is the destined master of nature, lay the foundation for great social, moral, and scientific changes. When the principle of the mind's control over the body is seen to include interior processes, as well as superficial ones, there is the basis for an entirely new system of medicine based on faith and power of will. The discovery of the scientific fact that propagation is within the limits of spiritual and moral control opens a new era in human progress—the key to a new and improved state of society. We may observe in conclusion that the whole plan of salvation by Jesus Christ is based on this view of the rightful control of the soul over the body. Our hopes in all directions turn on our understanding in regard to the power of the spirit over the flesh. Human nature does not reach its normal condition till it is the temple of the Holy Spirit, filled with all the fullness of God. A nervous system in that condition can bear a weight not only of suffering but of glory," Noyes always stressed. "The ultimate way to escape nervous injury will be found not in the direction of abstinence from excitement, but in the toning of the nervous system to the divine standard of health by fellowship with resurrection-life."

A comment in the August 15, 1872, *Circular* adds an interesting note on this theme: "Does everybody know the pleasure there is in self-denial—the happiness to be found in turning from a thing when you most enjoy it? Our life is one series of discoveries in this line. It is an excellent rule to leave the table while the appetite is still good . . . . Cultivate the habit of sagacious, reflective observation. So shall the spirit of truth go with you and perfect you in the heavenly art." As an exercise, Community members were advised to notice clinging to a habitual pleasure and to deliberately refrain from it with no regret—to await another pleasure that God surely provides.

We need not run away from the world and its activities. "You do not know God now, but if you think of him, fill your mind with the constant reminder of Him, you will come to know that He is love. . . . Out of loving devotion to God there comes a normal and natural control of all the passions—the more you advance toward God the less will be the strength of your cravings and desires for the objects of the world . . . ." In Sanskrit, *ojas* means the "energy that accumulates in the brain of one who has completely conquered the sex impulse . . . . Psychologically, sex energy can be transmuted into spiritual energy.[26] To see the Divine in oneself and in all men and women is the only solution for the world-problem of sex and the relation between the sexes," Ramakrishna said. "The Divine is in me, in all, in everything. I am not a man, I am not a woman; I am the Self. It is love if you have the idea of God in your beloved."

"We must connect our sexual experience with that which is sacred," Noyes wrote in his 1852 lectures on social freedom. "In the world there is a great gulf between sexual love and divine love, and as long as this exists, sexual love must be profane. Love is a science and a fine art, no less than a sacrament comparable to the Eucharist," Noyes knew, for it integrates sexual love with the life of the spirit. It is a power that can awaken complete realization of divine unity—an experience "through which humanity could experience the ecstasy of true communion and break through the dark isolation of egotism and selfhood."

Male Continence was natural and healthy because "God cannot have designed that men should sow seed by the wayside where they do not expect it to grow or in the same field where seed has already been sown and is growing; and yet such is the practice of men in ordinary sexual intercourse. They sow seed habitually where they do not *wish* it to grow. This is wasteful of life and cannot be natural . . . . It is seriously believed by many that nature requires a periodic and somewhat frequent discharge of the seed and that the retention of it is liable to be injurious. Even if this were true, it would be no argument against Male Continence, but rather an argument in favor of masturbation; for before marriage men have no lawful method of discharge but masturbation. But it is not true that the seed is like urine, which does require periodic and frequent discharge. Nature has provided ways of disposing of the seed. It has *immanent value* [italics Noyes's] and is in its best function while retained. Masturbation is a disreputable branch of the same seed-wasting business that is carried on in matrimonial intercourse and lacks magnetic contact and interchange of life."

Social magnetism and spiritual interchange

"The amative function—a simple union of persons, making of twain one flesh and giving a medium of magnetic and spiritual interchange—is a distinct and independent function as superior to the reproductive as amativeness is to propagation. Our theory has defined the sexual organs as conveyancers not only of seed but of social magnetism, a vital element as real as the seed and as really limited in its supply. To be magnetic is to be porous, so as to admit the infusion of the life of God. A soft heart toward God and a soft heart in relation to the attraction between the sexes are nearly alike, being in a condition to be permeated by another spirit whether human or divine," Noyes writes in a Home Talk in 1873. "Chemical attraction—admitting other particles into combination—makes us magnetic, charges us with love and life, and so makes us fruitful. This is what is meant by softness of heart. A heart characterized as hard means that it is compact—cohesion exists between its own particles so there is no room for another life to come in. Cohesion in chemistry is opposed to combination or chemical attraction. Cohesive attraction between particles of the same body is egotism. A person charged with the Spirit of God, with inspiration, is magnetic toward human beings.

"Animalism in the sexual department works in two equally lamentable extremes—sensual, fiery; or dead. The second form of animalism is a seeming continence that passes for virtue, horrorstruck whenever sexual matters are alluded to, considered a high state of grace. This condition revolts from the study of an important branch of human nature, and the Spirit of Truth cannot be at home with him. This reactive form of amativeness so much commended is really a disease, repulsive to real purity. A person who has lost the natural activity of the passion of amativeness cannot be in health. I do abhor this kind of touchy virtuosity that the world is so full of. Even we cannot talk on sexual matters without making the waters turbid. We must be able to think on this subject and speak of it in a way that is really natural. There is no more reason why sexual intercourse in a holy community should be restrained by law than why eating and drinking should be, and there is little occasion for shame in either case. We can judge what is natural by children; their minds are full of curiosity about sex. This subject is the vital center of society. It is the soul of the fine arts. It will be foolish for us to undertake to cultivate music or poetry or painting or sculpture, until we set the center and soul of them in its true place. Our capability of serving God acceptably in anything depends on our being magnetic. Our usefulness will be in proportion to our magnetism; we are dead and barren except as we are charged with electric life. We may be charged with life inwardly, yet be dead outwardly to a certain extent; the soul may be in one state and the body in another, but still there is action and reaction between the two.

"Shakers are persuaded that the celibate condition is superior and raises them above the generative stage of human evolution to a purer spirituality. Yes, God has placed a wall of partition between the male and female during the apostasy for good reasons, which will be broken down in the resurrection for equally good reasons, but woe to him who abolishes the law of the apostasy before he stands in the holiness of the resurrection," Noyes stressed. "The Shaker's insistence on abstinence fails to address an imperative instinct of human nature that demands frequent congress of the sexes, not only for procreation but for spiritual uplift," Noyes contended. "Ordinary sexual intercourse, in which the amative and propagative functions are confounded, is a short-lived affair; if it begins in the spirit, it soon ends in the sensual. In contrast, lovers who use their sexual organs as the servants of their spiritual natures, abstaining from the propagative act except when procreation is intended, may enjoy the highest bliss of sexual fellowship for any length of time without satiety or exhaustion; and thus married life may become permanently sweeter than courtship or even the honeymoon. In society trained to these principles, propagation will become a science and amative intercourse will rank above the fine arts, for it combines the charms and benefits of them all. There is as much room for cultivation of taste and skill in this department as in any. The practice that we propose will give new speed to the advance of civilization and refinement. The self-control, retention of life, and ascent out of sensualism will raise the race to new vigor and beauty, moral and physical."

"We mention the universal feeling and testimony of the Community in its favor," Noyes wrote, as evidence of the good effects of Male Continence. "It seems incredible that so large a body of sober persons as the Oneida Community in an experience of twenty-five years should be entirely mistaken in thinking, as they certainly do, that Male Continence has more than fulfilled its early promises." The New York *Medical Gazette* of October, 1870, in a review of the article on Scientific Propagation published in the *Modern Thinker* of that year, criticized the practice of Male Continence as likely to prove injurious—avoidance of the seminal crisis in sexual intercourse would so increase and prolong the excitement, it was contended, as to induce excesses that would lead to various nervous conditions. They wished to see the statistics of nervous diseases in the Community. The experience of the Community did not confirm that apprehension. A professional examination was instituted and a report was issued by Theodore Richards Noyes, M.D., in which it was shown, by careful comparison of Community statistics with those of the United States census and other public documents that the rate of nervous diseases in the Community was considerably below the average in ordinary society. This report, published by the *Medical Gazette*, was pronounced by its editor "a model of careful observation, bearing intrinsic evidence of entire honesty and impartiality."[27] The report did note one or two cases of nervous disorder in the Community that could be traced with probability to a misuse of Male Continence in the way suggested by the *Gazette*. Noyes suggested that the greatest danger attending the practice of Male Continence is the temptation to make a separate hobby of it and neglect the spiritual conditions out of which it issued and to which it belongs. "To cultivate self-control in respect to the seminal crisis, but neglect it in other sexual indulgences, is evidently Male Continence in a spurious and dangerous form. Only heart-abandonment to the grace of God that teaches and gives *temperance in all things*, can release us from the old tutelage of suffering. The spiritual view is perhaps different from the medical one," Noyes noted. "Writers on sexual pathology generally seek examples of nervous phenomena exclusively among the weaklings of debauchery. A degree of excitement that would injure a sick man may be harmless and even invigorating to the healthy.

The physiological principle of male continence as applied to the relation of the sexes is destined to work a great revolution in society as it spreads:

- Boundless, ever-improving respect and love between men and women as exponents to each other of the life and love of God. It reconciles the sexes, promoting true fellowship and union between them.
- It removes the curse from women and beautifies instead of blasting them. It is healthful for man, diminishing his cares and burdens and doubles his resources and happiness. It will tend to elevate marriage.
- To thrive, stop having children and take your wife into partnership. No more broken-down women worn out by over-breeding and excessive family care. No more neglected children growing in vice and want from the inability of parents to look after them. No more over-worked men toiling alone for the support of an undesired but ever-increasing family.
- Limitation of propagation will not exhaust society but be consistent with its highest vigor and beauty.
- It solves the population question, by placing propagation under full and natural control.
- Children are born by choice under the best conditions attainable with the care and interest of an entire Community exercised on their culture and welfare.
- With a due amount of religion, it makes community practicable.

"Woman is made for God and herself, with the right to choose when and how often she shall bear children," Noyes insisted. A young man who had lived in the community and learned the art of love, wrote: "This Yankee nation claims to be a nation of inventors, but this discovery of Male Continence puts you, in my mind, at the head of all inventors." Famed author of the dystopian *Brave New World,* philosopher Aldous Huxley, visited Noyes's descendants at the Oneida Community Mansion House to study the utopian Heaven on Earth. He thereafter wrote an Appendix to *Tomorrow and Tomorrow and Tomorrow,* praising Noyes's scientific analysis of the sexual act and Noyes's training of all the Community men in male continence. This was a singularly happy Community of three hundred people, Huxley wrote.

During his two years of study, meditation, and self-observation, Noyes learned that the human being is so constructed that, at one's highest state of development, one transcends self-centered consciousness and is able to receive God consciousness. *The pure in heart shall see God.* That is holiness, or perfection, as Perfectionists understood it: leaving behind the state of sinning, repenting, and sinning again—never expecting life to be more than that, though life's purpose is full happiness in "good conscience before God." The complex human being, usually fragmented and pulled in many directions, becomes unified through the experience of divine love. To be created in the likeness of God is comprehended.

BEGINNINGS OF COMMUNAL LIFE

> *All who believed were together and had all things in common; and they sold their possessions and goods and distributed them to all, as any had need. Acts 2: 44–45.*

When all that we think and do springs from love of God and neighbor, *Thy Kingdom come, thy will be done on earth* is reality here and now. Noyes shared his convictions with others after his religious experience in February 1834, and for four years gathered converts. In 1838 Noyes established a Bible School in Putney, Vermont, with his wife Harriet. A Quaker preacher from Westmoreland, New Hampshire, John Langdon Skinner, heard Noyes preach and joined the Putney Association in 1839. He came from a family eminent in the legal and ministerial professions since arriving in America from England in the mid-1600s. He was a Restorationist, a church reform movement that sought the unification of all Christians in a single body patterned after the Primitive Church, similar to Noyes's view. John Skinner became a writer, editor, and printer of the Putney Association periodical, *The Witness,* and later, *The Oneida Circular.* He married Noyes's sister, Harriet.

George and Mary Cragin joined Putney in 1840; George was General Publishing Agent for *The Advocate of Moral Reform* of the Female Moral Reform Society. That publication was formerly *McDowell's Journal*—a relentless chronicle of vice compiled by Reverend John McDowell including lists of two hundred and twenty brothels complete with addresses. Cragin, a revivalist under evangelist Charles Grandison Finney, co-labored with McDowell in reform work. Moral Reform Society leader Mrs.

William Green, an equally resolute crusader, astounded everyone by converting to Perfectionism. Wasn't that equally licentious? John Noyes had written a tome against conventional marriage!

Noted New York City citizens were establishing preschools and hired Mary Johnson, a teacher and Sunday school instructor with a special talent for inspiring young children. In charge of dozens of little pupils, one day she was searching for a child's mother in a squalid section of the city when George Cragin offered to help her—the rest was history. A zealous revivalist, Mary had read some of Noyes's early writings and now reread them, spending much time in prayer to know the truth of his declarations. She finally announced, very much in Noyes's words, "I confess Christ in me a savior from all sin. I shall never sin again." She subscribed to Noyes's paper *The Witness*, which George also read, though he opposed Perfectionism as a license for promiscuity. He'd always felt the dryness of church preaching and longed for real spiritual leadership. When he read Noyes's *Way of Holiness*, his life changed forever; he converted to Perfectionism and offered his resignation to the Female Moral Reform Society. They met with New York State Perfectionists, and Mary wrote an effusive letter to John Humphrey Noyes; burning their bridges behind them, they eventually met Noyes. George Cragin worked day and night for decades raising funds for Noyes's communities.

John Ransom Miller, born at Westminster, Vermont, grew up with strict religious beliefs and became interested in Noyes's doctrines at age twenty-one. A dedicated Perfectionist Christian, he joined the Putney Association in 1841, became its financial manager, married Noyes's sister Charlotte, and worked himself hard to support the press at whatever cost. He was the financial genius who later managed the fledgling Oneida Community when it operated on a shoestring; he found funds to pay the Brooklyn community's bills for operating a printing press, always Noyes's chief goal. "The Oneida Community's first business is to see that God has a press," Miller said. "If it does that, it will have God's blessing as I have had it." Miller was also business manager of their Putney general store and of several branch Communities. He and Charlotte and their children, ages one, three, and five, joined Noyes at the Oneida Community in 1849—the five-year-old being this author's great grandmother. Miller was so genial and gentlemanly that he handled with ease neighborhood dissensions at Putney and later Oneida. One time, a rowdy crowd gathered late at night outside the Mansion House yelling threats. Miller met them under the butternut tree, and his neighborly and frank dialogue satisfied them—that this community was decent, law-abiding, and hardworking! The mob dispersed.

The Putney Community met at first on Sundays; then in 1840 it expanded to Wednesday and Thursday evenings. They studied the Bible from 5:00 to 5:30 a.m., tended the two Noyes farms and their general store, and wrote and printed their paper *The Witness*. Each member had a position in the business organization. Miller, as the financial officer, was in charge of food and clothing for all. Twenty-eight adults gathered at one of the three houses owned by the Noyes siblings for three hours each afternoon to cultivate spirit and mind. By the end of March 1843, there were thirty-five persons being supported by the common purse. For the first hour they read books analyzing the Bible, commenting on them and asking questions. For the next hour they searched the Scriptures, preparing for the discussion of a question asked the previous day. During the last hour each individual offered his or her views as to Scripture, being in the affirmative or negative of the question, with the aim of arriving at a unanimous conclusion.

After the completion of the Chapel, the study session was changed to 9:00 a.m. to noon because, they reasoned, the freshest part of the day should be devoted to education. In the afternoons they worked in the store, farmed, and wrote articles for *The Witness*. They enjoyed evenings singing, debating, reading or writing, and praying while younger members studied. They ran a school for their nine children starting in 1843, offering all branches of study including Hebrew, Greek, and Latin.

In February 1841, Squire Noyes divided his estate among his surviving children, and the four Perfectionist siblings received a total of nearly $20,000, including two farms, dwellings, and investments. He died later that year at age seventy-seven.

Putney's True Purpose: A Spiritual Harvest

"We constitute ourselves a Society for the purpose of making an open and united confession of this our belief, and that we may ever more effectually assist each other in searching the Scriptures. We believe that the Bible is the word of God and that we ought to search it with diligence and respect," Noyes wrote in *The Witness*, February 22, 1841, after a year of discussion. "We also believe that the chief object of the Bible is to make known to mankind a way of present and eternal salvation from all sin; by reconciliation with God comes a complete renovation of the whole person. Recognize Christ in you, seek first his kingdom, and all other good things for soul, body, and social estate shall be added. Its modus operandi is the confession of Christ *in us*; we forsake our sins with assurance that in doing so we have God for our helper and that by him we are well able to imitate Christ. Our faith is that of the Primitive Church, which changes the heart. Through spiritual life comes social and material regeneration. It is an act of annexation to the kingdom of Heaven." In 1841 a chapel was built in which daily discussions were held after August 1st. They always "waited on the Lord for signs concerning its expediency."

Article I stated that all acts of the Society shall require for their validity the unanimous vote of the members when the acts are proposed. "This first article of our Constitution is a rule which, so far as I know, is adopted only in one case, viz., that of trial by jury. Certainly it ought to be taken for granted that a community of Christians may by the grace of God escape the disorders of selfishness. We are sure that in heaven, all acts are passed by unanimous vote. How is it possible that minds should disagree under the same divine influence, each having the one mind of Christ? As 'fellow citizens with the saints,' we should look for such unanimity and make our regulations accordingly. First, this secures the full liberty of every individual. The society cannot domineer over the will or conscience of one of its members; a majority cannot vote away the rights of the minority. It may fairly be said that there is not democracy where majority rules, for a majority may be and often is as tyrannical as an emperor. The shifting balance of parties in the pursuit of majorities is the cradle of party spirit and demagoguery. In corporations where a majority governs, unanimity is not necessary and therefore is not sought. Indeed, the favor of a majority may often be sought most successfully by stirring up strife with the minority; the drive to succeed is a stimulus of contention. Men of the world may be expected to scatter and cross each other in every direction.

"Our rule tends to peace. Making success depend on unanimity, our rule places the mover of a measure under the strongest possible inducement to seek the harmony of the whole society. As long as there is one honest heart and cool head among us, the impulses of blind enthusiasm and the machinations of demagogues will be kept in check. The principle of Article I is better adapted to an association like ours, whose chief object is the investigation and application of moral and spiritual truth, than to one of a more executive character. Whoever proposes to carry a measure will see to it that he is able to demonstrate its utility, knowing that it must pass the ordeal of every understanding in the Society. The unanimous jury verdict carries with it far greater assurance of truth than the decision of a bare majority. The ruling majority, though it has power of action, is generally embarrassed and enfeebled by the opposing minority. Under the rule requiring unanimity, our decisions will carry with them the strength of the whole Society."

"The Community consists of persons who are determined to have spiritual unity at any outward cost. We aver that the doctrine of holiness tends to unity," wrote Noyes in the September 27, 1845 *Perfectionist*, citing 1 Cor 12:12–30. This article appears in the August 17, 1868, *Circular*. "Holiness is love, a uniting principle, *the more excellent way*, 1 Cor 13. It is the love of God shed abroad in the heart; and, as God loves men, so whoever has God's love in his heart, loves men. Love makes them modest in regard to themselves, respectful toward one another, patient in discussion, ready to appreciate each other's truths, anxious for agreement. Thus the heart draws the head after it; and if the heart is in the truth, the closer the head follows it the better. Holiness, then, is an attracting, harmonizing principle making all who possess it one in heart. Persons who are in love with each other easily learn to think alike. The unity of their light, the clearness of vision it gives them and the love that goes with it, all tend to make them of one heart, one mind, and one voice. When we planned to build our new house, for example, some advocated one style and others preferred different materials and architecture, but no one wished to carry his measure against an unsatisfied minority, so the subject was dropped to be taken up again in a cooler spirit and re-discussed. The minority gradually changed and finally a decision was reached that satisfied all."

From the beginning the fledgling association wrestled with the distractions inherent in making a living. When head farmer George Cragin told Noyes about their monetary problems, Noyes simply said, "I would rather our land should run to waste than that we should fail of a spiritual harvest."[28] As the success of their businesses threatened to overshadow spiritual growth, Noyes always reminded the Community, "If we have primarily in view to make money, we shall get no enthusiasm from heaven, for we shift from our true purpose. Our business is to be co-workers with God in ushering in the last period of man's education—the victory and reign of spiritual wisdom and power," he wrote in the *Berean*. Noyes always stressed the *power* of spirit, indestructible in its essence, eternal, the dynamo of the body, animating all humanity. Human beings should not be understood as inherently conflicting and destructive; they are immortal spirits and sharers of this common life, and to know this is to implement the kingdom on earth. "The kingdom of God is within you," Noyes wrote in his Home Talk, *Where is God*? "If the kingdom is within, then I can imagine how a rich man, whose mind is engrossed and identified with his possessions and money, should not be able to enter the kingdom. He can have no conception of the inner spiritual existences; the more his attention is confined to those external things, the less is the possibility of his retiring within himself and seeking the central life."

Noyes's message resonated over the decades. Augusta E. Hamilton wrote thirty years later in the November 1872, *Oneida Circular*: "The Christian, wisely seeking first the righteousness of God's kingdom, sometimes wonders why wealth has come to be the first love of the mass of mankind, the chief ambition of nations. Why is not mankind's first love ever for the honor of God? Why is not spiritual wealth and power the first ambition of nations? The derivation of the word *wealth* explains somewhat this monstrous diversion of mankind's true ambition. Wealth is from *weal*, meaning well-being, soundness; it had originally referred exclusively to the condition of the individual. That which is now comprehended in the word wealth once had specific names—so many cattle, so many camels and asses, so many man-servants and maid-servants, so many shekels of gold and silver, and so on. Gradually, by one of those subtle laws that govern language, the word that expresses the state of the individual came to be used (under a slightly different form) to describe his external surroundings—that which well-being had produced; and at last it came to be considered the means by which that well-being is to be gained. What a perversion of meanings! The word is completely materialized," Augusta continued, "and mankind now puts its hope of happiness first in wealth, or riches, second in health, lastly in religion.... Has this perversion of so important a word wrought wisdom or foolishness to the human heart? Foolishness, it seems to us. The wisdom of the Christian leads him to seek first righteousness; second, health; thirdly and lastly, riches. Yet well-being (or wealth) in the broadest significance comprises all these three conditions of the individual, and the promise of Scripture is that all shall be had if we seek them in their true order. Surely, one whose policy is as provident and far-reaching as eternity will not seek first the riches that only gild our mortal existence, but rather the riches of God's immortal love and truth. Such wealth is indeed well-being, and both are eternal."

"We cannot carry out our social theory with merely human power," Noyes said in establishing the Putney Association. "For man alone to undertake to establish such a system as ours would be fanatical—quixotic—certain of miserable failure. We must know the power of God as Christ knew it if we expect to find our social theory safe and satisfactory. In all branches of the subject we shall find the knowledge of the power of God is the one thing necessary. Suppose you set in the midst of a company some valuable thing, and say that it belongs to all of you. In the imagination of the world they will fall to grabbing and quarreling, and the results will be very mischievous. Or if they are more civilized than to quarrel, there will be great difficulty in disposing of the matter. But suppose this company of persons all have the charity that Paul describes, that seeketh not its own, envieth not, and thinketh no evil. There cannot be jealousy or quarrelling where all are sincerely disposed to prefer each other's rights and claims. But you say, such a state of things is impossible—there are no such people! Don't you believe there are such in heaven? How do you know there cannot be such people in this world? We believe that Jesus Christ came into this world to make people of that sort and establish a society of that description. If we believe in the power of God over the human heart to abolish selfishness, to make persons who seek not their own, then community of property will not be the occasion of dispute and jealousy. The only way to remove this mountain that stands so firm in the imagination of mankind is by knowing the power of God."

The Putney Community evolved between 1842 and 1846 into an organization not unlike the Primitive Church, ending the isolation and selfishness in which the mass of men exist. "A spirit of love naturally led us into a community of goods. We trample underfoot the domestic and monetary customs of the world, ending separate households and property." The total amount of property invested by the members was an interesting number: $33,333.00. A slight gain was reported over the next year, but "a very considerable increase of love to God and one another, which is our most valuable capital" was duly noted.

"Our principles are stated in our First Annual Report, *God's ownership primary; other ownerships subordinate.* All things are ours in union with God and with each other, and the sense of that ownership is satisfaction enough. It is as if a father comes to his children with a book, and tells them that none of you own it personally and exclusively; I give it to you all together. None of you can say that book is mine. Each has the privilege of reading it and each are owners, for all the good you can get from it. That is precisely the kind of ownership, and the only ownership there is in the Kingdom of God. That is the grand constitutional law of our society. I urge everyone to study the power of God and believe that our hearts can really be conformed to that law. Be not discouraged by past failures; trust not to your own strength but believe that God gives us hearts that are harmonious with the truth, so that we shall not want to claim anything as our own."

Hard times came upon Putney in 1844. Noyes had lent $300.00 to a Perfectionist preacher, Joshua Longley, funds that were needed by the store. After the death of Noyes's friend David Harrison, his widow and four children crowded into the Campbell house. Trade at their store had decreased because of their new policy of selling only for cash. Noyes modified that policy to allow credit, urged economy on the members, and secured pledges from subscribers to *The Perfectionist*. By 1845, Noyes wrote the following: "An examination of our accounts reveals that our expenses exceed our probable income. We must therefore change our course or within a short time fail and be scattered," reported in the November 30, 1868, *Circular*. "To those who value the privileges of our Association and are willing to make sacrifices for its continuance and prosperity, I address the following suggestions:

"First, luxury and intemperance in eating and drinking are enemies of temporal prosperity; they are expensive and they enervate the faculties of mind and body concerned in the production of value, thus increasing the need of money and diminishing the power of getting it. A full stomach generally carries with it weakness, love of ease, disease of body, and depravity of soul. A person's strength is proportioned to the mind's freedom and health and this is promoted by abstinence and simplicity. There is a great deal too much eating and drinking in the world generally and we are not free from this evil. I recommend to everyone to restrain appetite habitually and not be afraid of occasional fasting. Tobacco, tea, and coffee are injurious when used habitually. I therefore recommend to all who have power over their own will to abstain from those articles, at least for a time sufficient to fairly test the value of abstinence.

"Second, we have a store of our own and most of us freely resort to it, as though what we got from it cost nothing. We soon found that our idea of common stock led to an expensive liberty by most of our young men of going behind the counter. It was finally agreed that we would abstain wholly. This habit ensnares us into luxury and wastefulness, and instead of diminishing our expenses it will increase them until we are involved in debt and sink in ruin. Let everyone determine to go to the store for goods as little as possible. Let us live as much as possible on the productions of our own farms. Let us especially eschew all vanity in dress, be content to go without the costly contrivances with which the fashionables disfigure their persons. Let simplicity be the beauty of our apparel.

"Third, we have hands enough to do all our own farm work and most work in every other department. Let us avoid hiring help as much as possible, and let everyone be ready to help in any department in an emergency. When their business presses, let them call out hands from the store, the printing-office, and the work-shops. Occasional labor in the open air will promote the health of those who work in the house. All that's necessary is courage and accommodation to make this plan entirely successful. My reliance is on the grace of God and on the hearty faithfulness of all of us. I appeal not to your fears, but to your love. The cruel machinery of motives that drives people to economy and industry is inconsistent with love, and can have no place among us. Do you wish for the continuance of our brotherhood? Are you willing to deny yourselves, that God may be glorified by our increasing unity and fruitfulness? If we avoid luxury and wastefulness, and are industrious and helpful, there is no danger of our failure. Notwithstanding the present pressure, the future is full of hope. God has brought us into difficulty that he may wake us up and improve our characters."

The Putney Community had for some time attracted public attention as an Association or Community. In *The Perfectionist*, Jan. 1, 1844, "The Spirit and Principles in which the Community Originated," Noyes explained: "Our establishment, such as it is, exists in the midst of an ordinary village, and differs not in its relation to the community from a manufacturing corporation or any other association. A few families of the same religious faith, without any formal scheme or written laws, have agreed to regard themselves as one family, and their relations to each other are regulated as far as possible by this idea. The special object of the association is not to make money or to exemplify the perfection of social life, but to support the publication of the gospel of salvation from sin by papers, books, and tracts. Formal community of property is expedient with reference to our present circumstances and objectives; we are attempting no scientific experiments in political economy or in social science. Our highest ambition is to be able to preach Christ without being burdensome to any, and to act out as far as possible the family spirit of the gospel. When we find a better way to attain our objectives than our present plan, we shall freely change our mode of living."

A month later, an article appeared in a publication called *Olive Branch* about the early days of the Putney Community: "They have 500 acres of good land, seven dwelling houses, a store, printing office, and several other buildings. Any person who is favorable to their belief can become a member if he wishes, whether he puts money into the treasury or not—provided that he sustains a good character. They have no particular rule to abide by, except the rule of the gospel, 'love thy neighbor as thyself.' There are eight families in the community who have sold their possessions after the manner of Acts 4:32–34. They are engaged in several branches of business—farming, mercantile, printing, each at his own trade. A chapel belongs to the community, in which they hold their meetings, and there is a large library for the use of all who attend their meetings. All who feel disposed can go to the chapel and spend three hours every day in study from November to May, yearly. The old as well as the young attend for the improvement of the mind and to keep the spirit in a state of health. Those who do not belong to the community can avail themselves of the benefits of their library during the time the chapel is open, free of expense. If a person is disposed to leave, he receives whatever he brought with him, and nothing more, considering the advantages he has had—clothes, board, etc., equivalent to his labor. The object is not to gain, but to improve the mind, to gain strength of the inner man. During the summer months, they do not labor more than eight or ten hours a day, either on the farm or in the shop; the remainder of the time being spent in study or otherwise."

The Community's egalitarianism was obvious from the beginning. As new disciples joined the Community, they decided that only one meal would be served each day, so every woman could take full part in spiritual studies. Harriet Noyes and other volunteers cooked and prepared food for the day and a printed card on the pantry door announced the plan:

> Health, Comfort, Economy, and Woman's Rights
>
> Believing that the practice of serving up in a formal manner three meals of heated food daily is a requirement of custom and not of nature—unnecessary and injurious to health and comfort, and subjecting females almost universally to the worst of slavery—we hereby notify our friends that we shall omit, in our ordinary domestic arrangements, two of the usual meals, viz., dinner and supper, and instead of them shall keep in this pantry a supply and variety of eatables, which we invite them to partake of at such times and in such manner as appetite or fancy may suggest.
>
> John H. Noyes, Harriet A. Noyes

Even with this arrangement, the women had to manage many domestic duties, as did the men in the farms and store, in order to devote three hours a day to spiritual pursuits. There were babies and toddlers to be cared for; volunteers helped, to allow the mothers to share in the chapel school, moderated by John Skinner. Noyes and George Cragin went on tours by invitation to preach and to introduce their publications. Growth toward communal ownership of property and money was gradual. "The spirit of love naturally led us into a sort of community of goods," Noyes wrote. "We have found it necessary to investigate many new problems in social economy, but it is difficult as yet to tell what form of social life we shall ultimately take. We shall follow the leadings of God and, I doubt not, find a way to live as becometh saints." In 1845 Putney believers were conformed to conventional marriage and had a truly Puritan standard of manners.

"For a year before my engagement to Fanny White, my mind was very much exercised on the subject of marriage," Mr. Leonard's story began, in the January 11, 1869, *Circular*. "Two elements were at work in me—love for woman, and a querying concerning God's will—by what course I should please him. I lived in Mr. Noyes's family at this time, and my wife lived there also. I began to feel an attraction toward her and thoughts of marriage came up, but I never hinted any such thing and she supposed I was totally indifferent. The attraction increased; my heart was drawn out very much, but I was bashful and reserved. It went on, my affection gathering intensity the more I suppressed it, until I began to be very much tried. In my perplexity I made up my mind to give it up to God. I had no wisdom to go forward myself. If my instincts were true, God would open the way; if he did not open the way I should have nothing to do about it, and so I dismissed the subject from my mind, and was free. The close of the year drew nigh, when I thought of leaving Putney for a season. The evening before I was to leave, Mr. Noyes in some conversation wished to know what my intentions were for the future, and among other things he asked me if I ever thought of getting married. I opened my heart to him; when he asked me if I had any particular person in view, I mentioned Fanny; and behold he was of the same mind. He suggested that I should write to her while I was gone. I did write, offering marriage. I had left it with God to determine my course, and I acknowledge the match as one that he made. I had dismissed the question so completely from my mind that I was taken entirely by surprise."

"When Mr. Leonard first came into Mr. Noyes's family, I thought he was such a still, sober young man that I would never get acquainted with him, and I did not for a good while," Fanny's story began. "You would not believe he ever looked at a woman. In the course of the summer I began to love him. A secret love burned in my heart, but I would hardly let myself know it. It was his spiritual character and his faith that made me love him. I thought to myself, he would suit me pretty well. I was afraid somebody would find it out, and I would not have it known for all the world because I thought he did not care for me. One evening while he was speaking before a Lyceum in the village, my heart kindled with love to him and I felt that it was from God, and I resigned it back to God. I said, Lord, take it into thine own care—do thine own will. I could not do anything about it. I gave it up to God, and it went out of my mind. I thought no more about it till I received a letter from him to my great astonishment, offering marriage. I said immediately, God has had a hand in all this; all this time there has been a mutual attraction, unsuspected by either of us. I acknowledged God in it, and felt that it was worthwhile to give up our dearest wishes to him. Mr. Noyes said he liked the aspect of this love-experience very much—the kind of love that is strong, deep, burning, fervent, yet modest, patient, submissive to God, is sure of success—God will favor that kind of love and bring it to a good issue."

TO HAVE ALL THINGS IN COMMON

On February 26, 1844, Noyes, his brother George, John Miller, and John Skinner formed a Contract of Partnership, whereby all property of every kind shall be held as the property of the Corporation. In August 1844, Harriet Noyes's grandfather died and left her $9,000. The financial crisis had passed. On March 9, 1945, they wrote a constitution, superseding their contract, to include members who invested time but not property, and those who invested both.[29] The Putney Community never took to written rules and regulations. "Life is developed from within outwards," stated Noyes in the Perfectionist of Sept. 27, 1845. "In the present dead state of humanity, the first business of the reformer is to proclaim the Word of Life and start a resurrection-energy at the center, which may ultimately unfold itself in the true order, from seed to fruit—from holiness of heart to external righteousness and beauty. Thus we stand, as a school, upon the quickening Word of God, assimilating faith, inward holiness, and vital union of man with God and with his brother, which are the spiritual basis and germ of true human life. Scientific external order must come after these are established and will not consist in arrangements fitted to fallen, selfish humanity, but will be the embodiment of perfect love. Meanwhile, every man can labor for the victory of the gospel of spiritual life in the fullest conviction that he is thereby hastening the advent of that external harmony that will ultimately make this world the Paradise of God."

Love for the truth and love for one another had been nurtured and strengthened at Putney until it could bear any strain. This six-year discipleship prepared them for instituting the Mutual Criticism system in 1846 (see chapter 7). Any person wishing to be criticized offered himself for this purpose at a meeting of the Association. His character then became the subject of special scrutiny by all the Association members until the next meeting, when his trial took place. Each member in turn was called on to specify as frankly as possible everything objectionable in his character and conduct. One or two prominent features would usually elicit censure from all. This person had the advantage of a many-sided mirror in viewing himself, placed in the focus of a spiritual lens. It very rarely happened that any complaint of injustice was made by the subject; generally he received his chastening with fortitude, submission, and even gratitude, declaring that he felt himself relieved and purified by the process. Any soreness from the operation was removed at the succeeding meeting by giving the patient a round of commendations. This system of open and kindly criticism became so attractive by its manifest good results that every member of the Putney Association submitted to it in the winter of 1846–47. To this may be attributed much of the accelerated improvement that marked that period of their history. Instead of offenses, abounding love and good works followed the letting loose of judgment.

"We were studying the true expression of our principles and working out salvation from selfishness," wrote a member. "The year 1846 was known among us as *the year of revival.* There was a spring-like awakening of the affections, and a baptism of the spirit of unity that was new and supernatural. Six years ago we began the experiment of living in community sharing money and property. This experiment has always been a secondary matter with us. Our primary project has been to publish the gospel of salvation from sin—the only hopeful nucleus of a divine external order. Yet we are deeply interested in the problems that our new social arrangements have presented us, and have solved many of them in a practical way with much satisfaction. We feel that we have gained wisdom by many past trials and are prepared to advance, as Providence shall call, to more systematic and extended organization. With patience, and yet with enthusiasm, we look forward to the time when we shall have but one home as we have but one heart, and shall present to many brethren an asylum of comfort and peace, and to the world a model of Christian Association."

"The new social life, heaven ordained, was to the heart what the advent of spring is to the earth; the frost and ice of selfishness and exclusiveness melted and disappeared under the warm rays of unselfish brotherhood. We believe that the kingdom now coming is the same that was established at the Second Coming of Christ; the church was then emancipated from the institutions of men and commenced existence under the sole management of God," Noyes declared in the July 15, 1847, *Spiritual Magazine*. "That kingdom, withdrawn to heaven, has been strengthening and enlarging itself ever since. God commenced a kingdom in human nature, independent of the law of the world. We look for its establishment here, for its complete extension into this world—and this extension is what we think and speak of as the kingdom of heaven now at hand. The destruction of evil will be effected by a spiritual infusion from the Primitive Church and the light and energy of God. The kingdom of heaven will be established here by a process like that which brings springtime: On the 20th or 21st day of March, spring officially begins by progress of the sun's power on the earth, though there remains a prevalence of wintry weather.

"God first begins to operate on the person while in a state of sin. The spirit works its way into his character, and predisposes his heart to faith in spite of himself. Christ shines in the darkness for a time, and the darkness comprehends him not. Suddenly the darkness is brought to the question, *Is Christ in me*? Is a person to wait for feeling, for perfection of character, for abundant good works, as evidence to compel his confession? No: confession must be the beginning of all this, the first great step toward securing these splendid results. The first responsive action is like taking a step in the dark as far as feelings are concerned, but the work of spiritual development is going on steadily and silently until we finally know that the kingdom of God is *in us*." Through his spiritual work at Yale Theological Seminary, Noyes was enabled to speak with authority, inspiring profound and permanent loyalty so intense that people followed him from well-settled lives into radically new ways of living and loving, working and relating.

"With a mighty hand, and marvelous wisdom, God has gathered us together here. It has not been effected without constant and complete crucifixion of worldly values. We have cut our way through the isolation and selfishness in which the mass of men exist; separate household interests and property exclusiveness have come to an end with us. Before heaven and earth, we trample underfoot the domestic and pecuniary fashions of the world."

COMPLEX MARRIAGE CONSIDERED, AND HOW IT BEGAN

These close economic, emotional, and spiritual bonds over six years evolved to deep love of one another. "There was much glorious testimony of the love and union that exists among us," John's sister Harriet Skinner wrote in the *Spiritual Magazine*. "The improvement that has been made among us is so palpable and universal that I cannot forbear acknowledging it," an article begins in the August 31, 1868, *Circular*, titled "A Sober Statement of Truth," reminiscing about the Putney Community. "There has been among us a marked increase of union, the ripened fruit of influences that have been operating for years—producing a healthy community of feeling and interest and the true harmony of love. To dissolve and remove the hard shell of selfishness and prejudice, which encases men in the world and keeps everyone isolated from his neighbor, requires a miracle, and nothing less. It is a disease, a sort of spiritual ossification, which mere reorganizations of society may ameliorate, but cannot cure. There has been a mutual enlargement of heart, and a throwing of sympathy and interests into a common stock. The very length of time that has been required for the development of our present union, assures us of its origin and value. We know in our souls that it is not transient in its nature, that we've grown into it through a long course of discipline, and that time will but confirm and extend the brotherly love that exists."

In May 1847, George Cragin wrote from New York: "I learned from a reliable source, that all of the social communities formed within a few years past in New Jersey, Pennsylvania, and elsewhere have experienced a total failure. In unregenerate humanity, the virus of self is death and damnation in every social pot, whether cooked by Fourier or Robert Owen, and nothing but the sail of the faith of Christ will destroy it."

Complex Marriage Considered

Nine years had passed since Noyes avowed his principles in his letter opposing conventional marriage. The Putney Community had practiced strict monogamy, because a foundation of true holiness must be solidly laid before any attempt to revolutionize the union of man and woman. Six years of daily Bible study and sharing all things including their hearts and minds made members internally honest and pure of heart. Noyes always stressed the integrity of the inner life—nothing should be done that anyone would feel was in any way wrong in the sight of God. "The soul must go down into the body and have fellowship with its pleasures just as far as God and the heavens send it and no further; and the body must go down into the businesses and pleasures of the material world just so far as the soul sends it and no further. "When God's inspiration is discerned within, life works rightly," Noyes taught.

Harriet Noyes received a letter from George Cragin on a cold January day in 1846: "I'll be home after stops at Southampton and Belchertown. Sales are going very well. My dearest Harriet, I love you as a sister in Christ, George." Harriet showed Cragin's letter to John, and she made known to him her love for George. Noyes approved of her feelings and appointed a meeting of the four on a Saturday evening. John gave the letter to George to read aloud and afterward said, "Thanks for reading your letter to Harriet out loud, George; I love Mary just as you love Harriet. We have all professed our deep love for each other in writing, speech, and actions, and I'm glad for our increasing unity of hearts. I feel that we should talk about our community and how our growing closeness may affect our relationships. What we need to do is very openly talk about all our thoughts and feelings." He added words of caution that George confessed were needed. He called upon Harriet to speak and she said that she was pleased by George's letter and that her heart was drawn out toward him by it. He confessed a similar feeling toward her, which prompted the letter. John then asked George's leave to tell Mary that he loved her and he heartily consented.

"I've loved Mr. Noyes so much that I feared he would find it out," Mary Cragin responded. "I was not certain, my awe of him was such, that he wanted me to love him so much." After these avowals the couples considered themselves engaged to each other, expecting to live in all conformity to the laws of this world. "The effect was most refreshing to our spirits," Mary wrote in her journal. "We find this evidence that our love is of God: it is destitute of exclusiveness, each one rejoicing in the happiness of the others."

Days later, Noyes said that he wanted to extend the blessing to all as fast as they were able to receive it. He talked with Harriet Skinner and found her nearer ripe for a community of hearts than he had supposed. Also at an incidental interview, Mr. Miller gave a satisfactory testimony. Noyes gave a lecture upon the proper bounds of demonstrations of love between the sexes. He disallowed kissing and everything that would be considered as leaning toward licentiousness. While rejoicing at the deepening of love, yet he cautioned everyone, himself included, to remain circumspect in all actions. On March 15th eight senior Community members met: John and Charlotte Miller, John and Harriet Skinner, John and Harriet Noyes, and George and Mary Cragin. Nothing was hidden in this loving circle.

Charlotte Miller spoke up: "Well, I do confess that I don't think John loves me as well as formerly. Mary has—no doubt unconsciously—attracted John to her." Noyes read to them the fourth chapter of First Thessalonians, dwelling with emphasis upon the sixth verse: "That no man go beyond and defraud his brother in any manner."

"I did turn to John for consolation quite a lot last year," Mary admitted. "He was like a brother toward me for which I felt very grateful." Miller had happened by when she was distraught and her husband George was away on a sales trip. "Trifling familiarities took place, which gave me uneasiness," she wrote in her diary. "I was not so much on my guard as I should have been, and you were right, Charlotte, to sense this. I will just add that I think Charlotte has not been jealous of me without a cause. I do love John more than I was aware, more than I've allowed myself to admit, but with a firm determination not to infringe on anyone's rights—I would seek your happiness before my own! Love worketh no ill to his neighbor. Alas!—that I should be an apple of discord in a family to whom I am under such untold obligation."

Mary had opened her heart to George when he returned from his trip, asking him for advice and rebuke if needed. "I also told Mrs. Noyes, from whom I had no secrets," she wrote. "Mr. Noyes called, saying he had noticed how things were going. He did not condemn anyone, but wished such intimacies put to an end before they went too far." Noyes's core principle was that no one should do anything about which they would not be in good conscience toward God.

"One evening in May, Mrs. Cragin and I went for a stroll," John recounted. "Coming to a secluded place, we sat on a rock and talked. The circumstances invited advance in freedom, and yielding to the impulse, I took some personal liberties. The temptation to go further was tremendous. But serious thoughts came at this point. I stopped and resolved in my mind as before God what to do. I said to myself, *I will not steal*. After a moment we arose and went toward home. On the way we lingered. But I said, 'No, I'm going home to report what we have done.' On reaching Mr. Cragin's house I called a meeting of the four. A searching talk ensued. He and my wife expressed approval. The last part of the interview was as amicable and happy as a wedding, and the consequence was that we gave each other full liberty." Relations were to be on the basis of Male Continence.

George Cragin joined the Putney Association in 1840 with his wife, Mary. He was an indefatigable fundraiser and advocate for Noyes. He accompanied Noyes on tours to inform the public about their convictions, and participated in publications and most other Community businesses.

George Cragin thought deeply about Perfectionism and its relation to the body, as did all Putney members. He wrote in *The Body for the Lord* that when the doctrine of perfect holiness was proclaimed as the core of the gospel, the clergy were the most violent opponents of Perfectionism. Perfect holiness is at variance with human experience, they insisted. And it is entirely incompatible with life in the body, for the body with its animal appetites is the natural if not inevitable enemy of the soul, and consequently, perfect holiness must not be regarded as an attainable state this side of death. The clergy concluded that the body with all its functions is beyond the possibility of salvation. "Without light from heaven, conventional clerics know of no better way to deal with bodily appetites than to suppress them by legal measures. Even to many religious people, the idea of living holy, blameless lives in this selfish world appeared absurd. The theological notion that man cannot keep from sinning came from the writings and traditions of the early fathers," Cragin thought, "and they received it from the hermits and monks of ancient Egypt where religion consisted chiefly in persecuting the body as the very devil incarnate. But convert bodily appetites into *allies*! If not converted by the grace of God into *servants* of the soul, passional forces within us will surely be its masters."

Perfectionists contended that any theology that leaves the body in possession of greedy selfishness can claim no right to be called Christian. Cragin and Noyes pointed to 1st Cor 6:19: *Your body is a temple of the Holy Spirit within you, which you have from God*. The Kingdom of Heaven is within you, they reminded these clerics. "Christ's spirit was poured out upon all flesh and the Holy Spirit worked mightily in the souls and bodies of the Primitive Church. This great enterprise of establishing the kingdom of God on earth was to redeem man through union with God," Noyes wrote. "Seek the gospel that is in the heart of Christ, that the power of God can make us new creatures." "Those few persons who had become totally sanctified would identify sex expressions and all others with their supreme religious devotion and through them would glorify God," wrote Whitney Cross. "Since all the saints were on a par together, in equal dedication to faith, communism among them in the sex relation as in all others was the only logical arrangement."[30]

Complex Marriage Begins

Thus Complex Marriage began in May 1846, in the Putney Community's seventh year of existence after four months of family discussion and deep soul searching, and nine years after Noyes's declaration that conventional marriage was not a holy institution. John Miller did not decisively adopt these principles, and yet said that Noyes's "whole past life has been such as to inspire me with confidence. I can point to no act that I do not think was right and directed by the spirit of God. I believe that God is able and willing to show me the whole truth on this subject in due time, and I will wait patiently." He wrote a letter to Henry Burnham in October 1846: "What will the world think of this? But I've learned that to the children of God, what my Father thinks of this is the only question. And when we have once learned his will, the world is nothing more to us than if we were inhabitants of some other planet. We should keep distinctly in mind that nothing is of any value to us that is not valuable to God." The Putney Perfectionists consolidated their separate households.

Statement of Principles, November 1, 1846:

We, the undersigned, hold the following principles as the basis of our social union:

1. All individual proprietorship either of persons or things is surrendered, and absolute community of interests takes the place of the laws and fashions that preside over property and family relations in the world.
2. God as the ultimate and absolute owner of our persons and possessions is installed as the director of our combinations and the distributor of property. His spirit is our supreme regulator.
3. John Humphrey Noyes is the father and overseer whom the Holy Spirit has set over the family thus constituted. To John H. Noyes as such, we submit ourselves in all things spiritual and temporal, appealing from his decisions only to the spirit of God, and that without disputing.

We pledge ourselves to these principles without reserve; if we fall away from them, let God and our signatures be witnesses against us.

It was signed by the Noyes's, Cragins, Skinners, and Millers.[31]

On November 4, 1846, Mr. and Mrs. Noyes moved into the Campbell house with Mr. and Mrs. Cragin and William H. Woolworth. The Skinners, Millers, and Leonards took possession of the Noyes homestead. The Skinners gave a party at which all were present the night before the move. Miller wrote about it to Mrs. Polly Noyes: "The evening until about nine o'clock was spent in reading and conversation. It was then proposed that Mr. Skinner should make a speech on the occasion of leaving the J. H. Noyes house. This proposal called out a speech from everyone present. There was much glorious testimony of the love and union that exists between us. At eleven o'clock we returned to our homes."

Another consolidation of households occurred in March 1847. The Noyes, Cragin, Skinner, and Miller families occupied the Noyes homestead; the Leonard family moved into the Campbell house with William Woolworth. Henry W. Burnham and his wife joined the Noyes homestead from Belchertown, Massachusetts. The families began having a daily evening meeting at eight o'clock.

OPPOSITION AND SUPPORT

Dr. Alexander and Mrs. Achsah Campbell had been followers of Noyes for twelve years and, because of their long association with the Community, John Miller corresponded with their daughter Helen, a student at a Massachusetts seminary in 1847. That May, Miller urged Helen and Emma, twenty and twenty-four, and their friend Lucinda Lamb to attend meetings at the Chapel and talk with Mr. Noyes. These young women were reportedly the flowers of the village, and those already somewhat antagonistic to the Community were upset about this prospect; gossip and dissention increased. When Dr. Campbell died, his position as a leading physician in Putney was taken over by his son John, Helen's step-brother. John's wife Lydia and his step-mother

Achsah urged him to talk with Noyes, but young Dr. Campbell refused and thereafter fomented a growing opposition to the Putney Community.

Noyes was arrested for adultery on October 26, 1847, and released on bail with an April 1848 trial. He was treated with great courtesy afterward, and Community members enjoyed life in the vicinity as usual. Dr. William C. Gould, associated with Central New York Perfectionists, visited Putney in early November after John's arrest to assess the state of that community and expected his stay would be short. "But I find an important and useful school in Putney," he wrote to Jonathan Burt. "I am perfectly satisfied that the Kingdom of Heaven is come in reality . . . . I have found the one in whom the spirit of the Lord resides and through whom God intends to reign over this kingdom, a most splendid and joyful discovery to me. I would say to you that Brother Noyes, instead of claiming too much confidence and dependence upon him as a leader has claimed too little."

Harriet Skinner wrote her mother: "Something inspires awe—we think it is the majesty of truth and innocence, and a lurking fear in some minds that we are the Kingdom of God. If a man's ways please God, he maketh his enemies to be at peace with him. The excitement in this place has passed away and a full tide of favor is setting in upon us from every quarter. We have miracle upon miracle in the quelling of the tempest that shook this place. Mother, there is no worst to write, but better, better, better. The town is in a spiritual magnetism and with full knowledge of our principles and practices are quieting themselves. It is as though it were said to them: Touch not mine anointed. Mouths that have breathed out threats and even slaughter are giving again the friendly greeting. Houses that have been blocked now invite us to their doors. Through the whole of this affair we have neither said nor done anything to take back. We have overcome evil with good, and carried out the principles of non-resistance in the most sublime manner. Mr. Miller has displayed the magnanimity and self-possession of a Christian hero."

On November 1st she wrote in *The Spiritual Magazine*: "We see God's power not so much in outward signs as in moral miracles, in spiritual changes, in daily providences. Stripes and imprisonment impend, and not a heart quails. Iron wills have broken, excessive self esteem has bowed, acquisitiveness has opened its hand, the affections have withdrawn from outward affection and gathered within the charmed circle. Our daily interchange is rapidly condensing life and intensifying the power of love. John's commission is to establish the kingdom of God. The Primitive Church formed the new heavens, we the new earth. They reconciled man and God; we shall reconcile man and woman."

But after committing an assault against John Miller, Dr. John Campbell shouted, "If there is no law that will break them up, the people of Putney will make law for the occasion!" Miller wrote, "Some people here are determined to do all in their power to break up the community and push us till we divide all our property and live as the world lives." There were frightful threats of violence, wrote Polly Hayes. Brattleboro lawyer Larkin G. Mead and his partner William C. Bradley heard rumors of a possible mob. On November 26th they requested Noyes and Miller to come at once to Brattleboro.

"I was content to abide the issue at Putney and settle with the law as best I could, but John Campbell could not wait on the law," John wrote. "Who then were the law abiders, and who the law breakers? I had no thought of leaving Vermont when I went to Brattleboro; I carried with me a written proposal to surrender myself to the custody of the law (without bail) on condition of peace for the rest of our Society." After a long discussion, Mead recommended that all Community members who were not residents should leave, and that Noyes should not return to Putney but leave that evening for Boston. Others left for homes throughout New England and New York, but many of the Community family remained to continue writing for *The Spiritual Magazine*, to educate their several children, and to run the store.

But by December 11th, John Miller wrote, "Our trade at the store has got about as low as possible. Yesterday we traded twenty cents and made four cents profit. Two weeks later he wrote, "Thursday night I received an anonymous letter through the post-office, saying that I would be tarred and feathered and ridden on a rail, if I did not leave town immediately. But it was evidently done only to frighten." Weathering these storms of opposition at Putney, their mother Polly was reassured by her children and their spouses, and other friends in the community. Noyes and George Cragin soon went to New York City, where they had always intended to establish a small association to publish their periodicals. They stayed with a longtime friend of Perfectionism. "If we cannot publish in Putney, God will find another place for our press," Noyes wrote to John Miller. "I am perfectly willing that you should sell our possessions in Putney. We have friends in all parts of the country who will be glad to give us refuge and help us to plant ourselves where we can grow with less molestation. I leave you to watch the signs and judge whether we can hope to keep our foothold in Putney without sacrificing our principles. As to abandoning the testimony that the kingdom of God has commenced, or acknowledging that we have done wrong, that is out of the question with me."

Noyes wrote to his wife Harriet, "Though absent in body, yet am I present in the spirit, joying and beholding your order and the steadfastness of your faith. The world imagines that our Association is dissolved, but we know that our enterprise moves steadily on. It is a satisfaction to think that even our apparent breaking up has been caused not by mismanagement and corruption, but by external violence. We have done the will of God; now we wait for his promise. Though the vision tarry, it will surely come."

George Noyes was informed by William Spencer Hatch of East Hamilton, New York, of a great movement toward community of the Ackleys, Nashes, Hatches, Waters, and Holmes, and the Hamilton family would like to join en masse. Syracuse architect and staunch Perfectionist Erastus H. Hamilton wrote a letter to Harriet Noyes at Putney. "My confidence in you is undiminished—I am not with those who step aside until the storm is over. That which thou sows is not quickened except it die," he reminded us. "This may reconcile us to the apparent dissolution of the Putney Association. It was certainly a perfect seed. Mr. Hamilton identified himself with us understandingly and been blessed exceedingly in so doing, and he is willing to abide the result."

Jonathan Burt's house contained sixteen souls. On November 26 a new house was planned. "Mrs. Burt is exceeding kind and has invited myself and Hannah to take up lodgings in 'Burt's Hotel,' Mr. Hatch wrote. "All on board are in high glee." Later it was realized that this was the very day of the dissolution of Putney, when Noyes was advised to leave the area.

When he returned to Central New York from Putney, Dr. William Gould wrote Noyes that things were progressing much faster than he'd expected. "In spring we shall have about three hundred acres adjoining Jonathan Burt's property of arable and pasture land, and an association house is commenced. I don't understand your objective to locate in New York City. I talked with John and Harriet Skinner and invited them into this part of the vineyard. When you get through in the City, if you and the Cragins wish a home, my wife and I will endeavor to make Oneida Depot as comfortable for you as we can during your expatriation, and will share with you the opprobrium and persecution with which the enemies of righteousness are now so hotly pursuing you." A note from Mrs. Gould added, "I have just read my husband's letter and fully endorse all he says. I feel one with you and the persecuted saints of Putney. I am not one of them that draw back to perdition. The more I lose, the more I find I gain. I believe I have put everything I had on the altar, but if I find anything hid I will put that on also. I rejoice that my character has gone by the board and I am not afraid of the result. Yours in like faith, C. Gould."

John Miller wrote Noyes on January 19, 1848, that "the people of Putney, all the better part, have more confidence in us now than ever. Several have inquired about you with apparent interest and I tell them frankly where you are and answer any proper questions. There are many things now that look encouraging. To my great surprise, when I got my little stock of new goods, customers began to flock in and buy. Every hour would present some new face. Even those who have been bitterly opposed and have said much to injure us began to show themselves at the store, both ladies and gentlemen. It has been amusing. Ladies would come into the store with faces as long as a yardstick and leave with their prettiest smile. One lady will come in, and that gives another courage to come. The store being open in the evening so ladies could come under cover of night, we had our store full all the evening."

3

Implementing Heaven on Earth: The Oneida Community

From his remarkable spiritual odyssey, a long-lasting utopian community was born. Noyes held that the chain of evils that holds humanity in ruins is first and primarily a breach with God; second, a disruption of the sexes involving a special curse on women; and third, oppressive labor, bearing especially on men. "I have settled it in my heart as a sober matter of fact these fifteen years that the business of life is to seek first the Kingdom of God and his righteousness," Noyes stated on November 14, 1849. "I stand on this platform at all hazards, and get others to do the same as fast as I can. All relationships must come in their true order, the order of things in the kingdom of heaven." Sincerely seeking to know and do God's will in every endeavor and thought must precede any attempt to establish right relationship between the sexes. Only when the will of God is done on earth, Noyes believed, will a new marriage covenant commence. "No one should attempt or could succeed in revolutionizing the relationship between man and woman before reconciliation with God."

Noyes believed that the true civilization of Heaven can be attained through common ownership of all goods in communal living, because God owns all things and we enjoy them as a loan or gift from him. He considered selfishness the besetting sin of mankind. The chain of redemption includes sharing of property, as Luke reported in the Acts of the Apostles: "All that believed were together and had all things in common." Paul wrote to the Corinthians: "As a matter of equality, your abundance at the present time should supply their want, so that their abundance may supply your want, that there may be equality." Each member owned all the property in the Community. "They empty their selfishness into one cauldron of common interest," a visitor wrote. Their final great goal was the humanizing of labor and transforming the nature of work and leisure. "We must see ourselves and others as they are in their innermost essence—immortal spirits, sharers of a common life and a common hope, never as conflicting and destructive egos." Noyes's primary conviction was that the kingdom could be implemented here and now, and the fruits of that conviction soon became evident in the uniquely successful Oneida Community.

INVITATION TO CENTRAL NEW YORK

Central New York Perfectionist conventions, both called by John B. Foot in September 1847, supported Noyes. At Lairdsville, Oneida County:

"*Resolved*, That we heartily approve of the general course of the press at Putney, and believe it to be an appointed and useful agency of God.

"*Resolved*, That we will cooperate with the brethren at Putney by circulating their publications, procuring subscriptions, and furnishing means and matter for the paper."

At Genoa, Cayuga County, continuing three days:

"*Resolved*, That we will devote ourselves exclusively to the establishment of the kingdom of God; and as that kingdom includes and provides for all interests, religious, political, social, and physical, that we will not join or cooperate with any other association.

"*Resolved*, That as the kingdom of God is to have an external manifestation, and as that manifestation must be in some form of Association, we will acquaint ourselves with the principles of heavenly association, and train ourselves to conformity to them as fast as possible.

"*Resolved*, That one of the leading principles of heavenly Association is the renunciation of exclusive claim to private property.

"*Resolved*, That it is expedient immediately to take measures for forming a heavenly association in Central New York."

"A new door is opening for us," Noyes wrote to Harriet on January 24, 1848, enclosing the brotherly invitation from the Perfectionist association located in the Oneida Valley of Central New York. Many families there were subscribers to *The Witness* and *The Spiritual Magazine* and had heard of the Putney disturbance, but their confidence in Noyes as an inspired expounder of Bible truths remained unshaken. "I am ready to imagine that God has been preparing to transplant us from Putney as he transplanted the gospel from New Haven at the beginning," Noyes wrote. "I will go to Oneida this week and see what can be done there. The association commencing there will need my help, and whether we join our forces with theirs or not, my visit there will be profitable. I would prefer to keep our foothold in Putney, if possible, and also to establish a post in New York City. If the reprobates in Putney continue to reign, our better way will be to make a lateral movement and join our friends in Oneida. You who are in the disputed territory will take these things into consideration, and speak your mind."

Noyes arrived at Jonathan Burt's on January 26, 1848, and after a crew stopped a leak in the dam, everyone gathered in the new house to hear his story. "Mr. Noyes explained the principle of Male Continence and related the circumstances that led to its discovery, and opened to us the fact that they had introduced a new relation between the sexes," wrote Burt in his journal. "He spoke in a spirit and manner that evinced great purity of thought and feeling, and though the subject was new to me, I had data in my spiritual experience that enabled me to accept what he presented as God's truth; and at the close of the meeting, I so expressed myself. The women were somewhat disconcerted, but on the whole there was a good deal of candor . . . . The next day Mr. Noyes went to Dr. Gould's at Oneida Depot, where it was supposed he would find a warm welcome," Burt wrote. "Mr. Nash, young Hial Waters, and I went there expecting a good meeting. The Doctor invited me to a private interview, persuading me to take sides with him against what he termed Mr. Noyes's restraint against personal liberty. I told him plainly that my confidence in Mr. Noyes was not to be shaken. My conference with Mr. Noyes lasted over an hour and there was great flow of heart between us. I told Dr. Gould that I'd made my decision that I would cleave to Mr. Noyes, who gained my thorough confidence. Mr. Noyes took from his pocket five hundred dollars in ten dollar gold pieces."

"There, Mr. Burt," Noyes said in response. "If that will help you in any way, it is at your service. I offer it as my first contribution to a New York Community."

"This was indeed aid from a source I had not expected," Burt wrote, "and I accepted it thankfully as from the Lord. The next morning I invited Mrs. Burt to look at the small bag of gold coins. She asked what I have given for security. Not anything, I said. Mr. Noyes has given it to me as a first contribution to the Community interest. I said I wanted him to come into our family and make it his home for a time; Mrs. Burt did everything she could to make it pleasant and comfortable. At about the same time, my brother Horace, whose insanity had continued without abatement," Burt wrote, "was miraculously cured under Mr. Noyes's influence. The coming of Mr. Noyes was not only for my personal deliverance but also for the success of the movement toward an association in Central New York."

In a letter to his Putney Community written when he was a guest of the Burt family, Noyes summarized his deepest values: "Our warfare is an assertion of human rights: first, the right of man to be governed by God and to live in the social state of heaven; second, the right of woman to experience her sexual nature by attraction instead of by law and routine, and to bear children only when she chooses; third, the right of all to diminish the labors and increase the advantages of life by association. These would be the three grand pillars of the kingdom of God on earth." It was here that Noyes wrote his *Bible Argument Defining the Relations of the Sexes in the Kingdom of Heaven*. In Mr. Burt, he found a right-hand man whose heart and soul were wholly enlisted in the new enterprise before them.

INTO THE WILDERNESS

The one-room log hut had only recently become available to white settlers. "The Oneida tribe descended from two persons who left the Onondaga tribe and located at the mouth of Oneida Lake. Later the Oneidas located at the outlet of Oneida Creek, where they erected fortifications as a protection against other tribes' assaults, but a compact of confederation between the Oneida, Cayuga, Mohawk, Onondaga, Seneca, and Tuscarora converted hostile tribes into friendly neighbors. Only the Oneidas adhered to the cause of the colonies during the Revolutionary War, and treated Europeans who were beginning their westward march beyond the border of civilization with kindness and civility. In their log hut the Oneida Community began." This is part of the history of this region, recounted in an issue of the October 1868 *Circular*.

March 1st seems like an unlikely time to travel from Vermont to the Central New York wilderness in 1848 to establish a new Community—winter would still be in full force! "Harriet Noyes and George and Mary Cragin, with three children and sixteen trunks, boxes, bags and bundles, arrived at 3:00 p.m. at the Oneida Depot," the October 5, 1868, *Circular* informed the later Community. "After anxious minutes standing in the wind, cold and hungry, they saw two sleighs pull up; they loaded bags and boxes on them and traveled four miles across the windswept snowy landscape into the old Oneida Indian Reserve territory. They squeezed in overnight at the Burt home; the next day the Putney pioneers took possession of the log hut, happy to do so. It consisted of one room on the ground floor about fifteen feet square with a huge fireplace, small windows and wide doors. Under the low roof was a sleeping chamber where tall folks could not stand erect except directly under the ridge-pole. A small hole under the ground floor was called a cellar, and a lean-to on the west side was a wood house.

"How delighted the older children were with their new home! The old saw-mill, the logs and lumber scattered in wild confusion, the dyke, the dam, the creek with its icy covering near our snug little cabin; forest trees nearby and stumps for hide-and-seek presented rare materials for sport without fear of hearing 'You mustn't touch.' It seemed like the beginning of a new life. Late troubles were more than counterbalanced by the influx of faith and renewed enthusiasm for the work ahead. It would be more completely consecrated to God, and made more fruitful to his honor and praise. How thankful and happy the women were with the new providential situation; kings in their palaces might have envied their peace and contentment!

"Dishes with knives, forks, and spoons were found in the boxes, placed there by the ever-thoughtful provider Harriet A. Noyes, the mother of the Oneida Community. In the mammoth fireplace, the corners of which would accommodate all the juveniles at once, hung a single borrowed iron pot; a huge fire dispelled icy cold blasts seeping under window sills; plenty of wood was available. With the addition of a table and chairs that other families of the colony could well spare, this made us feel rich. A sleeping area in a loft was reached by a narrow ladder, but we needed more beds. We determined to keep our external wants small and to make the domestic articles we needed rather than purchase them, so we set our wits to invention. Basswood boards being cheap and on hand, we produced the required furniture entirely of that article and succeeded so well that we were surprised at our own ingenuity. We might obtain a patent on our invention! The bed-posts were so constructed that they would stand alone, each on its own individual base, so if other parts gave way there would be no general tumble-down of the whole structure; the posts would maintain their integrity. Another advantage was that it was not necessary for the head and foot posts to stand at right angles, as they would admit of quite a divergence from a straight line from head to foot. It was convenient to be able to move one end of the bedstead without moving the other, in availing ourselves of limited dormitory room.

"Cooking over an open fire was a novelty we indulged in for only a few days, because more time and fuel were required to prepare meals than by using a stove; finding that we had just enough funds to procure a cooking-stove, we made an investment accordingly," reported the October 5, 1868, *Circular*. "It required but a few days to put our log-hut in good habitable order. Mary Cragin, always alive to her ruling passion, the instruction of children, proposed to Mr. and Mrs. Burt the opening of a school for their children and her own. A nearby unoccupied shoe shop measuring twelve feet by twelve was ideal for a school, thought Mary, who had received a certificate as an assistant teacher by age fifteen and developed a special talent for governing young children. She had worked in downtown Manhattan in an impoverished area when several influential women created schools for the very young. Mary said nothing of her plan till the time arrived for action. The proposition met with a unanimous response and the little cobbler's house was converted into a comfortable school-room. The fixtures required were soon finished and without much ceremony the school was inaugurated by Mrs. Cragin, with scarcely a trace of the 'school-marm' about her. A dozen bright-eyed boys and girls from three to twelve years of age listened with breathless attention to her musical voice as she read to them from that book of story and song she sometimes playfully called the Bible, illustrating the reading by allusions to everyday incidents. While Mrs. Cragin mothered and taught the children, Mrs. Harriet Noyes counseled and led the grown folks with her noteworthy example as a doer of the word of truth; so quietly and cheerfully did she discharge her duties of mother to the Oneida Community in its infancy that its success is largely indebted to her influence. Mr. Noyes was writing the *Bible Argument of our Social Theory* and Mrs. Noyes spent her afternoons copying it in her very legible hand, to be sent to Putney where quite a family of Perfectionists were still in camp.

"We had built a chapel in Putney in which we held Sunday meetings, mostly for the benefit of outside friends; our 144-square-foot shoe-shop answered the same purpose. The Sunday previous to the opening of the school, that space was informally dedicated by our assembling there for the free, mutual expression of our minds on whatever subjects were deemed most instructive and edifying. We remember that gathering well. Several friends from distant places were present and the meeting was characterized by a calm but earnest spirit conveying that we've met for business, for action, for sacrifices—whatever obedience to God and the truth requires. Several in the colony had already enlisted as students of the new faith, reading the writings of the

Putney Community with a serious spirit of inquiry. We had not been long in session that Sunday morning before Miss H., a young schoolteacher, then and there surrendered her heart to Christ and confessed him within, a Savior from all sin. This act was the termination of a mental conflict of several weeks duration. The most memorable feature of that meeting was Mr. Noyes's talk.

"The object to which I am devoted in cooperating with others in establishing an Association in Central New York is that of *education* in its deepest, broadest sense, embracing the spiritual, intellectual, physical, moral, and social interests of humanity," John told them. "So far as my influence goes, it will be exerted in making the Association a school or university in which the Spirit of truth, as manifested in Christ, in Paul, and in other apostles of the Primitive Church, will be fully recognized as our teacher in all the stages of our experiences, and on all possible subjects. This Spirit of truth alone can lead us into true freedom—freedom of the affections, freedom to control our passions and appetites, freedom of the will to obey God in all things. It is from that alone that we receive the disposition and moral strength that will enable us to live a life of fruitfulness that Paul describes in the 13th chapter of 1st Corinthians."

Those early Sunday gatherings were earnest discussions of the business of life more than psalm-singing and ministerial discourse. "Our religion was not very showy at any time, and no more so on Sunday than on other days. These meetings were later transferred to the cow-barn, belonging to the farm purchased of Mr. Francis who had offered a twenty-six acre farm that included a barn, a shoe-shop, and a log or block house contiguous to the saw-mill water-power. During the summer months, outside hearers attended our gatherings in considerable numbers and if they had no other effect on these neighbors, they served at least to correct many erroneous reports respecting our religious and social principles.

"The Depot, as Oneida was then called, offered the only convenient touching-point with the business and traveling public. About the first of April we began to make daily trips to Oneida Castle (our post-office address then) and the Depot a mile and a half farther north, four miles from the Community. Instead of possessing a stud of twenty-four horses from which to select a team for the Depot business, as we did later, we had one span of team-horses previously owned by Mr. Burt, and one additional horse, somebody's contribution, at our service when not required elsewhere. The gift horse had seen younger days and might have been 'swift o' foot,' but now with a breathing apparatus sadly out of fix, he was very 'slow o' foot,' and hardly sure of any feet at all while descending a hill. When the animal did trot (a rare circumstance), the exercise was so distressing to both parties that the luxury of traveling at a greater speed than three miles an hour was rarely indulged." Twenty years later, noted the October 5, 1868, *Circular*, "every department would like one more horse. 'A horse, a horse, my kingdom for a horse,' was the song. Folks at the packing-house are losing money for want of horses to ship fruit paid for and incurring interest. Contractors for the Midland [Railroad] complain that they're losing money for want of our keeping ahead of them in clearing our woods and lands. Then one fine horse up and dies, and another gets loose in the barn and is terribly wounded by remorseless heels. So three new horses purchased this week are but a slim addition."

"Our business at Oneida Depot and the Depot village was not much at first, but there was one quite extensive store for so small a place, the proprietor of which treated us with great civility. Indeed, we are happy to say that the same is true of every citizen of Oneida with whom we had occasion to transact business. It was fortunate that our Putney Corporation adopted the cash system in trade, previous to its emigration. In doing so from principle, without reference to its profitableness, we had no serious difficulty in adhering to it under subsequent temptations to deviate. As our new neighbors and the villagers understood, one feature of the business platform of the 'peculiar people' on Oneida Creek was that very attractive one of early pay. They looked upon our rustic appearance with a good degree of complacency, knowing full well whenever they saw the old white horse harnessed to a four-wheeled vehicle, once called a buggy, slowly advancing through their muddy streets, that it signified the distribution of *cash*.

"April is upon us in fickle moods. Including two or three single persons, the Perfectionist Colony consists of six families occupying two frame houses, a board shanty, and the Log Hut," reports the October 5, 1868, *Circular*. "The small dwelling on the last purchase is dubbed the 'white house,' and into it Messrs. Abbott and Baker move their families. The total number of adults and children to be provided for is between thirty and forty. The saw-mill, with circular saws and a shingle-machine, gives employment to most of the men and boys. The eighty-acre Francis farm is in our possession, for which we are to pay $3,550.00. Mr. Abbott, who has been in the colony since February, paid the first installment, and Mr. James Baker, who arrived from Putney, has paid the second—these two payments cancel about half the purchase. Not much is attempted in agriculture; facilities for land cultivation and men to use them to best advantage are not yet provided. The man who would give the Oneida Community an enviable reputation for cultivating and canning the choicest fruits had visited our place, not so much for joining us to share his passion for horticulture, but to converse with Mr. Noyes on the more vital question of a sinless gospel and its cultivation in the soil of his own heart.

"The location was anything but attractive to persons who were looking for an earthly paradise already prepared for them, and fortunately we had no applications from that class of society. Most who contemplated joining us understood tolerably well that much hard work and plain fare, physically, and still harder work spiritually, were in store for them. The fare to sustain their souls in doing spiritual work was liberally supplied by the ordinance of our Evening Meetings. Those family gatherings may be called hours of feasting the soul. Mr. Noyes was indefatigable in bringing things new and old out of the storehouse of spiritual truths in the form of Home Talks. We cannot conceive how we would have succeeded, even as a business, without those gatherings. The influence from them was not discussion, acute reasoning, or even religious talk; it often occurred that the most good was accomplished when the least was said. We freely admit that members of our colony were assaulted, more or less, with temptations to evil-thinking, evil-speaking, discouragement, and unbelief. Such attacks usually occurred during the hours of work, or when alone, or with those weaker than themselves and inclined to look on the dark side of events. But coming to the meeting, where all minds instinctively opened to the light of truth, the afflicted ones were quite sure to find the justification of Christ in their hearts, and their individual accounts became happily adjusted."

EXCEPT THE LORD BUILD THE HOUSE, THEY LABOR IN VAIN

"Finances were by no means easy with us. To meet obligations assumed by the purchase of lands required all our funds, so our means for meeting current expenses were at times extremely limited. We had assumed the debts with which the saw-mill property was encumbered, the amount of which was not accurately known. We well remember one close corner into which we were pressed. Being greatly in want of more team force, it was thought advisable to purchase a yoke of oxen with the first money that came into our treasury. In a few days we received a remittance of $150.00—and now, thought we, the ox team is sure! A competent judge of the useful bovines was on the eve of departure to secure the prize, when a stranger inquired where he might find Mr. J. Informed that he was away, he handed us a paper, saying, "Perhaps you can cancel this for Mr. J."—it was a promissory note amounting to one hundred and twenty-five dollars, besides the interest of several years, given by the brother in question. The stranger was informed that Mr. J. would soon call upon him and attend to the matter. He was satisfied, and left us.

"One may imagine the change of countenance that came over us. We were in trouble. Conflicting feelings raged within. Why had not Mr. J. told us of this debt? That ox team we were so sure of began to be a transitory vision gradually vanishing from our longing eyes; we could hear, deep within, a faint whisper that said, *Those bovines must be sacrificed upon the altar of unity.* This case must come before our evening assembly for adjudication. When our inestimable brother J. was informed of what had transpired, he was as much surprised as ourselves at this sudden demand upon our limited treasury, having an impression that the note in question had been paid. Unable to produce any voucher to justify that impression, it was believed that the obligation had not been canceled; it was the unanimous voice of the meeting to forego the purchase of the team. The change wrought in our own spirit was so great that the following day we took infinite satisfaction in redeeming our brother's promise. From that early sacrifice on the altar of brotherly love is a perfume as fresh as ever and more precious to us than gold, or cattle upon a thousand hills. The remarks of Mr. Noyes at our evening meeting were never forgotten:

"The greatest enemy to our success in pleasing God—the only success worthy of our ambition—is the spirit of the world. Even in our zeal for God, we would have a worldly spirit by denying that God cares for those who put their trust in him and says that he leaves them to chance, to the grab-game of selfishness in getting a living. This spirit must be watched with a vigilant eye, and resisted to the death, in whatever plausible dress it may present itself. We have taken our stand before heaven and earth on this promise of God: *Seek first the Kingdom of God and his righteousness, and all these things shall be added unto you.* We are called to stand firmly and resolutely on Bible truth, on the words of Christ that cannot fail as regards the question of getting a living. It is a question of vital importance to the entire human race, involving, as it does, the veracity of Jesus Christ and his heavenly administration."

The project of erecting a large Community mansion was fully discussed. Their new dwelling would serve a three-fold purpose: family, church, and school. "A unanimous vote favored its immediate construction, though funds for the contemplated edifice were not in hand and there was a printing office to maintain and many persons to feed and clothe. Preliminary steps toward the construction of a Community mansion were taken, and in spring they were ready for Erastus H. Hamilton to take command, reported the November 26, 1868, *Circular*. "He was selling his property in Syracuse; his friends, who had known him and his father, were discouraged over the departure of so promising a citizen. His services there as a practical mechanic—a master-builder—were highly appreciated. In the moral and religious fields, too, he was much esteemed. Mr. Hamilton's family understood their mission with us so well, and fell into their respective places so readily and quietly, that our limited accommodations remained as ample after they came, as before—a phenomenon noticed many times on the arrival of new members. Messrs. Hatch and Ruggles from Baldwinsville had been attentive readers of the Putney publications and came about this time, and these families found comfortable accommodations in the little white house in conjunction with Messrs. Abbott and Baker, who already occupied it, making five families in a dwelling that would be regarded in these days as sufficient for one.

"Mr. Cragin traveled to obtain help for building the Community mansion from persons expecting to join us later, and he was cautioned against coming under a worldly spirit and not to beg for funds. He should present facts relative to our present situation, and our future plans and purposes, let them understand clearly that the cause to which we were devoted was theirs as well as ours—the cause of God and humanity. Mr. Cragin succeeded far beyond everyone's expectations in receiving pledges of financial assistance. The sum to be raised was fifteen hundred dollars outside of our own labor and material, but more than double that amount was cheerfully pledged by friends who afterward became members. The decision to build was announced by letters to our friends in Vermont, Massachusetts, Connecticut, and elsewhere, and the responses were cheering indeed. In spring and summer 1848, people followed John Humphrey Noyes, leaving behind roots, family, and friends." Polly, Noyes's mother, left her home in Putney to join the Oneida Community in 1849; though she always had a mind of her own, she was a loyal and helpful member until her death in 1866 at age eighty-six.

"Another family to leave a prosperous life for Oneida were Albert and Maria Kinsley from northern Vermont. Albert had served as Justice of the Peace, sheriff, and church deacon in Fletcher; as sheriff, he brought his prisoners home for Maria's homemade dinner and a night's lodging in the stone house he built. He was inventive, having introduced the first cooking stove and boasting the best pump in the countryside. Noyes's message awakened an immediate response from both Maria and Albert, and without misgivings they severed their home ties, sold their valuable farms, and left for the unknown wilds of Central New York in a covered wagon with their two sons and two daughters, ranging in age from twelve to nineteen. Albert, a farmer, was often the most important community contact with neighbors at Oneida; his love and concern won over the farmers and merchants in the earliest days of the Oneida Community." The Kinsley family became pillars of the Community and directors of its silverware business in the twentieth century.

From nearby Oneida Castle appeared an unlikely candidate to join a community. Sewell Newhouse fell in love with Eveliza, they married, and became members of the Presbyterian Church. The minister was decrying the unhappy condition of the wicked in the realm of Satan: "There'll be no-o-o Sabbaths there, no-o-o churches there, and no-o-o ministers . . ." From a pew Sewell Newhouse retorted, "Yes there will-l-l!" In 1848, he became interested in the views of the nearby Perfectionists. Newhouse was a man of legendary strength and ability who had spent his youth exploring the Central New York wilderness. The Erie Canal was being built five miles north of Oneida Castle. It was said that Sewell knew every foot of its swamps, its thirty-six creeks, the bays of Oneida Lake, and all its wild creatures. As a hunter and trapper of enormous skills, he was dissatisfied with crude animal traps then available in the 1820s. "Use of German and English traps convinced him that he could hammer out a better article in his shop at home, so he experimented; his conscientious attention to details and great strength produced a far superior instrument. Trade sprang up among the surrounding Native Americans; Newhouse spent the winter months making a few hundred traps for his own and neighbors' use in spring trapping campaigns. After the season of trap-making, Sewell would disappear into the Northern Woods, an individualist to the point of eccentricity and a gentle, shy person who never discussed or wanted to hear discussed his feats in running and wrestling—though his friends never tired of relating tales about him. This was the state of his art when he joined the Community.

"Newhouse's trap-making was accommodated at one end of the blacksmith's shop, where an ordinary horse-shoeing and local jobbing-trade was carried on. Noyes drew in talent to assist Mr. Newhouse and every operation was done in the most laborious but painstaking way, fostered by a common interest. They produced an article fully equal to that of Mr. Newhouse's own manufacture. Enough traps were finished to warrant a venture among the wholesale hardware trade, and two members traveled to Chicago with a large chest of traps. After days of discouraging effort, they found a customer in the firm of Larrabee and North. The Oneida Community captured the American and Canadian markets by 1864, driving English and German traps out of the market." This enterprise became the cornerstone of Community prosperity. Newhouse never misused his prodigious strength, except for the fact that these traps caused pain to animals caught in them. But the culture and economy of the nineteenth century never questioned the morality of trapping animals. Some Community individuals may have been sensitive and mourned over this industry. The fact that a major aspect of the Community's economic viability was due to sales of excellent animal traps shows how even the spiritual life is intertwined with survival in this level of existence.

By the first of June the fledgling community consisted of fifty-one: thirteen men, thirteen women, twenty-five children and youths seventeen years or younger. Among other skilled people, a shoemaker, a lead-pipe maker, a carpenter and joiner, an architect and builder; a stone-mason, a landscape gardener, and two sawyers had already joined; there were few useless professions. Leader Noyes regarded his intellectual wealth as common property, handed down from his ancestors and from friends of spirituality and learning in ages past. "There was something within us that made us think and feel that we were called of God to unite with a people who we believed loved God with all their hearts," Joseph Ackley said, "and were not selfish but were laboring to build up a society where the love of God would be the prevailing spirit."

"The building of the new house was the colony's summer and fall work. Our entire force of men was not large, so little attention could be given to any other business. We handled a great deal of lumber, putting it in condition to season during the month of May. The colony had much valuable experience in trying to do, by ourselves, what needed to be done. Mr. Hatch said the first job given him was the repairing of an ox cart—putting in a new axletree—work entirely new to him. He thought it would be impossible for him to do it, not considering himself physically fit enough. But to try—believing he could do it—was his new watchword, and he succeeded according to his faith. The construction of the cellar wall to our large dwelling would be a very difficult task, and not one of our members had any practical knowledge of the art of mason work. We resolved that when the time came to commence the wall, we would not hire but don aprons and overalls and do our best. If in any new undertaking we required an experienced teacher, one would be sent to us in the nick of time. In Mr. Hamilton we had three professions—an architect, a carpenter and joiner, and a boss-builder. We found in Mr. Ruggles a first-class stone mason. A godsend, truly! In Mr. Ruggles we had as good as three—a worker, a teacher of the art of stone masonry, and a boss [stone sculptor]. Under the charge of Mr. Ruggles, the heavy job of stonework on the cellar walls was entered upon enthusiastically. Mr. Ruggles had Noyes and Daniel P. Nash for his assistants, who soon became experts at their new trade.

"Ambitious to render appreciative service aside from regular household duties (by no means neglected), the women soon acquired knowledge of the art. Especially was this true of Mrs. Noyes and Mrs. Cragin, who worked from two to four hours a day, handling the trowel, small stone and mortar, with dexterity almost equal to the sterner sex. The work to them wasn't drudgery, but sport—a pleasure that they looked back on with satisfaction. It was profitable in more senses than one—the pure fresh air, the exercise, the mingling of the sexes, and the consciousness of rendering public service all contributed to make the work attractive."

STYLE BEFITTING A TRUE WOMAN

The only problem was their dress. Women's heavy, bulky floor-length dresses and bound corset to achieve a smaller waist rendered women unable to participate actively in many enterprises. Mrs. Amelia Bloomer discussed the physiological harm done by women's dress; the combination of very tight waists and heavy weight on the hips on high heels tended to damage the spine and could result in damaged internal organs and other chronic conditions. Corsets were often so tightened that women could breathe only with the top part of their lungs and this caused the bottom part of their lungs to fill with mucus, causing slight but persistent coughing. Modern medicine stresses the importance of healthy breathing for robust health. In addition to these many impediments, care of these voluminous outfits wasted much precious time and resources. Equality of the sexes was valued in Noyes's communities—women participated in all the businesses and extracurricular activities, and woman's conventional dress made much of this impossible. Noyes also criticized the dress for revealing the bosom and otherwise making the distinction between the sexes greatly more prominent and obtrusive than nature makes it. "Women's dress is a lie!" he exclaimed. "It proclaims that she is not a two-legged human being but something like a churn, standing on castors."

"On a glowering April 3rd, 1848, Mr. James Baker's family arrived at Oneida Depot and no one was there to convey them to their new home," a December 7, 1868, *Circular* recounts. "Not caring to pay four dollars for a carriage, Mr. Baker walked the four miles, leaving his wife at Allen's comfortable hotel. When he presented himself at our log hut alone, we lost no time in getting under way with our not very swift team. We were overtaken by total darkness returning with Mrs. Baker and her baby, but our faithful pony could be trusted to be his own pilot in navigating roads that were a disgrace to any civilized country. Within a half-mile of home, we remarked to Mrs. Baker that she would soon have the pleasure of meeting her friends, but the words were no sooner spoken than one wheel almost lost itself in a deep rut-pit, which darkness had prevented us from avoiding. As the horse was urged to extricate it, one thill [either of two long pieces of wood between which a horse is attached to a carriage] gave way while the wheel remained stationary. To repair these damages in the dark was impossible; being near our destined port, we proposed to Mrs. Baker that we leave our team (knowing that our horse could not be excelled for the quality of standing still wherever you left him) and walk the remaining distance. She readily consented, but in helping her from the carriage, we mistook a thin sheet of water for dry land and handed her gently into a puddle of mud. We were very sorry indeed for the mistake.

"We pushed on as best we could with our charge—mother, babe, and bundles. Mrs. Baker had as much as she could do to manage her long skirts, dripping with mud. The babe soon manifested her repugnance to being carried by a stranger in the usual musical way babies have of making known their feelings. That demonstration induced the mother to carry the child herself. But to do so, she had to let go the 'halliards' as a sailor would say, and her dress and the entire batch of under-skirts that had been held up by her hands, came down to trip her feet. If we were half knee-deep in mud we knew we were in the road. Our progress was indeed slow—nearly every other step would be on her heavy muddy dress, almost throwing her to the ground. We again took the babe and her little will gave us more music than before. The walking became more tolerable; we could touch bottom. In a few moments more we were at the door of the hut, which was entered with greater pleasure and more thankfulness than ever filled the hearts of king or queen in entering the most gorgeous palace the world ever saw. Busy hands and loving hearts made a new woman of their sister in a brief space of time.

"However temporarily distressing that perilous experience was, it served a good end—those filthy skirts were powerful advocates of a dress revolution, adding fresh fuel to a fire already aflame in the hearts of the hut's inmates, Harriet Noyes and Mary Cragin. Noyes's common sense idea that there must be a more suitable way to dress had made a profound impression on the women, but who would take the initiative in adopting a new way to dress? Three enterprising Community women experimented and found the solution—cut women's long dresses to just below knee length and for modesty, use the cut-off part to make matching pantalets. George Cragin returned in June, 1848, from a lengthy financial tour and as his team halted in front of the white house, Harriet and Mary came running in short frocks and pantalets. George convulsed with laughter—his wife had metamorphosed into a schoolgirl! She appeared quite similar to the eighteen-year-old he'd met twenty years ago," he wrote for the December 7, 1868, *Circular*. "The new costume did indeed give the women a young appearance—but it was their victorious spirit and not the new uniform alone that made them seem young. It required a degree of moral courage not to conform to the implacable fashion of the day, but they would obey their inward conviction of right and adopt a style befitting a true woman. Then they wore this brand-new creation in front of the whole family, and a surprising number of women initially called the outfits ridiculous and absurd; they were truly distressed and shocked. Young men laughed out loud. Fortunately, the majority liked the new look."

Community women enjoying the Summer House in short dresses with pantalettes, designed for mobility and ease of care.

"Women from then on participated with ease in all activities and with their help, the cellar walls were soon completed, the building was framed and raised, and the work of enclosing it progressed quickly. Neighbors watched with increasing astonishment at the almost magical appearance of a large structure in this rural countryside where most people lived in cabins. It was sixty feet long, thirty-five feet wide, and four stories high from the lower ground on the south end.

"'Why didn't you people locate that big building on the creek,' a storekeeper asked, 'so it can be used as a factory when you break up?'

"'We may not break up; our religion unites us.'

"'What is your religion?—I thought you were Sabbath-breakers.'

"'Our religion makes us honest, do honest work, pay honest debts, and do so from choice. We practice it every day of the week.'

"'I guess you folks are honest in your business dealings,' admitted the storekeeper, 'but some say you hold strange notions about marriage.'

"'Your men come here to buy goods,' said importer Brown. 'All have the same enthusiasm for business that I have. One day it is Allen, another time it's Hamilton or Cragin, but it makes no difference. I understand how a man works and is active to make money for his own family, but for two or three hundred people unrelated to you is more than I can comprehend. If I had not seen it, I'd have said it was totally impossible.'

"'What's the secret of your Community?' asked General Jones. 'What makes you hold together so? I have tried to find out, but it is a perfect mystery; I don't understand it.'

"Gentleman, we reply, your wonder is to us the most wonderful thing of all. Instead of being the strange thing you deem it, living in Community is as natural and inevitable as railroads—every church with any life stands on the verge of it, ready to adopt it by the least forward movement. In the future, we fancy, it will seem strange that the world could have got on at all with the little one-horse style of family organization that now prevails; so narrow, illogical, and uneconomical."

Additional members arrived from the Putney Community, along with the printing-press with its manager, Mr. Stephen R. Leonard. "An oblong one-story affair resembling a horse-stable with stalls on both sides of a central alley was erected, the press in a double stall, and arriving men and boys in single ones, because sleeping areas were increasingly limited. Stories concerning the ideas of these foreigners circulated.

"On a warm summer evening in 1851 during the evening meeting, someone shouted, *Fire!* The printing office was burning and could not be saved. Noyes's chief goal in life was to promulgate what he learned from his spiritual experience at Yale Seminary in February 1834, so they soon moved the publishing business to Brooklyn in an area with which they were familiar." Noyes and George Cragin had spent time in New York City in 1847, exploring whether the Putney Community could be established there. After the Community constructed a new printing office in 1854 at Oneida, most Brooklyn Community members returned there and others went to a Wallingford branch. Months later, yellow fever decimated parts of Brooklyn.

Shoes

"I've never wondered that Chinese women allow their daughters' feet to be encased in iron shoes, nor that Hindu widows walk calmly to the funeral pyre," remarked Elizabeth Cady Stanton, "for great are the penalties of those who dare resist the behests of the tyrant, Custom." In *The Human Foot*, the *Circular* noted the cruelty of heels on women's shoes. "The heel of the period is pernicious and absurd to the eye of naturalists. In the natural foot the play of all the muscles and tendons is free, and the blood circulates freely in every part. The artificial shoe cramps every muscle and impedes the entire circulation. The natural foot expands beneath the pressure of the body; the shoe pinches it. The natural foot hangs and swings as gracefully and as freely as the hand, but the fashionable shoe holds it at a stiff right angle, forbidding ease, strength, or comfort. The natural foot has its heel equaling in diameter the thickness of the ankle, on a level with the ball of the foot, and separated from it by the natural bridge of beauty. The artificial heel is a narrow plug, inches long, pitching the toes forward into their narrow encasement, forbidding safety of posture or grace of action, dangerous on all staircases or rough pavements, and wholly inconsistent with anatomy. If all mankind were doomed to wear such heels, the human race would degenerate and sink to a worse than barbarian level. If the feet of the Romans had all been so cramped, distorted, and compressed, Carthage, Spain, Gaul, Thrace, Greece, Egypt, and Assyria would have been safe from their incursions. The wearers may wiggle, stagger, and toddle on their leather or brazen stilts, but they cannot march or even walk, in any just sense of the word. The style is one of fashion's base impositions, involving discomfort that not even the most frivolous of the vain can long afford to endure.

"'High heels were invented for ladies who sit in the parlor,' said Mr. Noyes, 'or ride in their carriages or, if they walk, go mincing along very daintily with a servant behind to pick up their handkerchiefs. Our women, who run and romp, find high heels dangerous—regular sprain-traps. The main difficulty is in the hearts and minds of those who follow fashions. A woman came today to tell me her troubles. I explained that in Christ, all are one; there is neither male nor female; all are strong. Paul says, *Put off the old man with his deeds.* Put off the old woman with her deeds, I say. If you are bound to follow fashion, tripping about in high-heeled boots to prove yourself distinct from man, you *will* be weak and must expect lame ankles.'"

"The morning after this talk, a regular crusade of vituperation against tight-laced and high-heeled boots swept through the Community," the June 8, 1868, *Circular* reported. "Not only women but all the children—boys and girls—were tottling about with their ankles in strait-jackets. The crusaders went into the children's house, and with looks and gestures that astonished the little ones, warned them that they would all be on crutches before they were twenty years old if they didn't get out of their laced boots and learn to go barefoot as their fathers did before them. The cripples about the house generally cut down their boots or put on slippers, and threw away their bandages, giving their ankles free air and a chance for free circulation, trusting to Peter's bath for strength and healing. A big poster was stuck on the dining-room wall with the following display of physiology and indignation:

> *Sprain Traps*! High and tight-laced boots and shoes: 1) obstruct the free circulation of blood, being analogous to tight-lacing of the waist, and to the bound feet of the Chinese; 2) give unnatural support to the ankle, thus debilitating it by depriving it of natural motion; 3) waste valuable time in lacing and unlacing; 4) waste material, are twice as costly as simple shoes or slippers and often cost more than their dresses; 5) are imposed upon us by fashion, keeping our women standing ankle deep in the stagnant pool of vanity and corruption. With high heels they may well be called Fashion's Superior Sprain Traps.

"The juveniles are out barefoot as a result of this campaign, and mothers were a little loath at first, afraid of broken glass, anticipating stone bruises and spreading toes, but after some talk we came to a unanimous vote, mothers and all, that children up to ten years old should go barefoot three months a year for the sake of toughening up. We hope the time will come when it will not offend the eye for adults to go barefoot in warm weather. It would have this good effect, at least, that loose shoes would be the fashion the rest of the year.

"Four years ago now, the low, unfashionable shoe replaced the high-heeled and high-laced boot, and I lift up my voice anew in gratitude for our low shoe," notes a contributor to the September 8, 1873, *Circular*. "This summer I've worn a high boot long enough to feel the difference. Yes, I have felt the cramp, the heat, the unyielding ligature about the ankles, hindering motion and stopping circulation. Walking, standing, or sitting I was painfully conscious of my pedal extremities. How gladly have I released them from their prison and returned them thankfully to their easy, natural, low shoe! I wonder now that I ever could have worn the fashionable high boot; I gaze with pity and astonishment on small children and young girls with their little feet and tender shapely limbs encased half way to the knee in these leather tormentors. The foot is a most sensitive member, and the old Scotch magistrates of a by-gone barbarous age well knew how to wrench a confession from a poor wretch when they invented the torture of The Boot. Yet now, tender delicate women for fashion's sake voluntarily submit to a foot-torture that differs not much in style and intensity from the Scotch horror.

"A correspondent of the *Graphic* says: 'Her new boots make her think she is walking down-hill . . . she never enjoys a sermon because her feet pain her so and a lecture is quite out of the question. I've suggested that a more sizable shoe would bring the desired relief, but arguments ensued proving that she never wore too small a shoe and was glad she was sensible enough not to pinch her feet. She's a young woman yet, Mr. Editor, and enjoys average health, but can't walk out even to shop without limping home as if she were rheumatic, and I don't know what to do.'"

Community women still had long hair, the prevailing fashion, and it was increasingly discerned that elaborately tended hair did not look right with short dresses, pantaloons, and comfortable footwear. It was incompatible with simpler living. Long hair wastes much time washing, rinsing thoroughly, drying, combing out and arranging. "Several women declared the whole process distasteful and burdensome a year after their short dress became universal, and the brave among them cut their hair; they found that it made them look younger—those middle-aged looked like young women to visitors, and the young women were taken for girls. Noyes, though a Bible literalist, did not object to women in the Community cutting their hair and they never had to wear hair coverings.[32]

"I admire gray hair," wrote Tirzah Miller. "My grandmother wore her locks in their natural color. Her face was sweet to kiss because it was genuine, and I never minded wrinkles. She was a sincere woman and never took advantage of the quackeries of the day to conceal changes that age wrought. Is it our feminine nature to appear, and not to be? Now we constantly seek to produce a false impression in our favor. I am going to denounce this terrible principality of deceit that has long held us. Even among us Community women who have cut our hair short, worn our dresses short and ignored fashion—a few of us began the abominable practice of hair-dying to conceal the touches of time. But the men protested with righteous indignation and the women became convicted that it was an ordinance of deception—by doing one untruthful thing they made themselves guilty of all worldly vanities and hypocrisies. It is pitiful, terrible to see the insincerity connected with coloring the hair. Those who make dyes and those who use them are a mutual-deception society. Quack doctors say it does not color the hair, O no! It penetrates to the roots and is a process of rejuvenation; it *restores* to it its youthful appearance. No one frankly says, *I color my hair*, for the deed is a deception and must be concealed or defended by such fallacies as renewing the growth of my hair. God is the master-artist, but many do not believe it. Do the venders of rouge and hair-dye believe it? Do manufacturers and wearers of corsets and palpitating-bosoms believe it? When gray hair appears, be sure that God is introducing an effect to correspond with your countenance, and don't spoil his work. A wrinkled face shaded by silvery locks has beauty as much as the smooth brow of youth crowned by luxuriant tresses. Until the resurrection shall change the whole body, no hair dye will bring back even the semblance of flown youth. The very object sought after is not attained. In the spiritual experience of the Community, it has been found that the seat of woman's vanity is peculiarly in her hair, and that it is a subtle distraction from seeking after inward beauty."

COUNTING THE COST

"The terms of admission to the Community were placed at the head of the Register of Members and published repeatedly in their papers and pamphlets: 'On the admission of any member, all property belonging to him or her becomes the property of the Association. A record of the estimated amount will be kept and, in case of the subsequent withdrawal of the member, the Association will refund the property or an equivalent amount. While a person remains a member, his subsistence and education are held to be just equivalents for his labor and no accounts are kept between him and the Association, and no claim of wages accrue to him in case of subsequent withdrawal.'

"The responsibilities and conditions of membership in the Oneida Community were often ill understood by casual inquirers," the October 20, 1873, *Circular* noted. "To persons discontented with their present situation in the world, or sanguine and curious to experiment in novelties, it looks like a very simple thing to join the Community. 'We are sick of the world; your people seem to be happy; we like your principles, as far as we know them, and now we are on hand to join.' Not infrequently persons apply for admission on the bare information that it is a religious Community without any further inquiry as to its terms and objects. Joining is a matter of serious moment to both parties and cannot be undertaken without much deliberation and a thorough understanding of the interests involved. To those who see only the pleasure-side of Community life, we will name some things that are sternly opposite to all worldly notions of comfort and that require a degree of self-denial rarely conceived of.

"First, the freedom to enjoy, which it is supposed must exist in a society where all things are held in common, has its counterpart in the giving up of all things, which Community demands of every individual. This feature is apt to be overlooked, while the imagination of the inquirer dwells only on the union and plenty that he sees involved in a Community organization. The fact that this result is based on a previous sacrifice of all private interests is not appreciated. In the actual working of Community we are led to realize the forsaking of all, and find that the *self*-denial—the sacrifice of private individuality—is quite as broad as the general and common well-being. In Community there is the largest liberty for love and generosity, but no liberty for selfishness and seeking one's own. If a person can shift his sensibility to happiness, so that it will forget private wants and find gratification in public service and the prosperity of the whole, then Community is exactly his place. Community holds out abundant pleasures and rewards, but only for the spirit that enjoys and sacrifices for the good of the whole. Those who enter with their eye mainly on private luxury and pleasure-seeking are courting special disappointment. True Communal life is the worst hell such persons can easily find. It has nothing for them but arrest and crucifixion till their motive is changed. It does not reserve even the common comforts of life for selfishness." All relationships were under the influence of the Community and open to criticism. Personal interviews, as it was termed, were conducted through a third party, a woman and long-time leader of the Community, so that women might decline proposals without embarrassment. This also provided those who regulated Community matters the means to monitor relationships, which were not to become exclusive; pairing off would jeopardize the cohesion of the Community spirit.

"The Community's system of truth-telling is essential to its existence. All members have their faults told to them and any bad spirit or insincere practice is held up to the free censure of all. The constant family contact of our society brings out all the concealed littleness, all the hard corners of character—bringing every hidden thing to light—seeing everyone just as he or she really is. This process is disagreeable to the sensitive nature and personal feeling of individuals; it should be carefully reckoned among the costs of Community life, at least by those deeply involved in egotism. To a person whose character is in a crude, unregulated state with two opposing forces in his nature, self-will resisting the will of spirit, true liberty is impossible. This clash of forces is bondage, the seventh-of-Romans state. True liberty is a state in which we have a unanimous vote within ourselves, for what we do; our whole life goes one way. The work of our School is to emancipate persons from self-bondage and misery, the net result of the two forces. Our system of mutual criticism and discipline diminishes the freedom of the cramped, selfish parts of one's nature and increases the freedom of the indwelling spirit. We go for the spirit, that part of a person's nature capable of faith and union with God that despises envy, jealousy, and all the brood of selfishness. That part of his nature really has the germ of liberty in it and if favored till it harmonizes his whole being, will bring about his entire freedom. We set before all who enter our school, perfect liberty as the termination of their education.

"We will not admit persons into our school until they have mastered our publications. A pleasure-seeker would not be found plodding through our *Berean*. If he should profess to be acquainted with our doctrines, he would betray himself. We could detect very easily the 'sounding brass and tinkling cymbal.' In our first stages of experience in Association we made mistakes, but we have made very few and those we have made were in consequence of not strictly adhering to this rule. The cases of X. and the Y. family are examples. They were scarcely at all acquainted with our publications. Folks who want to join to get a good home and for other private reasons will find that they know not what they ask. Establish good relations with the spirit of our publications, and then if you want to marry the Oneida Community there will be a chance for negotiations. In addition to a school, we are a church and a family; marriage with us is understood to be for life. To join us for any superficial, temporary purpose is impossible. We hope union with us is lasting, but we hold no persons in our society against their will and we deal fairly with them when they go.

"Our Communities are constantly receiving applications for admission that they have to reject. Some reasons are these: First, our Community at Oneida is full. Its buildings are adapted to a certain number and it wants no more. Second, Branch Communities, though they have not attained the normal size, have as many members as they can well accommodate, and must grow in numbers only as they grow in capital and buildings. Third, the kind of men and women who are likely to make the Communities grow, spiritually and financially, are scarce and have to be sifted out slowly and cautiously. We are more desirous than ever to make the acquaintance of honest people who are seeking salvation from sin. To such we say: Push on. Show your colors. Come out from the crowd of pleasure-seekers. We shall certainly sometime join external interests if our hearts are one. Anxiety for immediate union is not the best passport to our favor and it should be distinctly understood that these Communities are not asylums for pleasure seekers or persons who merely want a home and a living. As candidates for Communism multiply, it is obvious that they cannot all settle at Oneida and Wallingford. Other Communities must be formed; and the best way for earnest disciples generally is to work and wait, till the Spirit of Pentecost shall come on their neighbors and give them Communities right where they are.

The original wooden Mansion House is at far left. A stately Community House of red brick was built in 1861 and 1869. a four-story section was built on the north side in 1878. A spacious lounge was built in 1914 to connect the main Mansion House with the dining area.

"As to the right method of founding new Communities, we take our past experience as a guide. We have thus far felt our way into it by intuition and study of practical exigencies, and know no other way. If persons ask our help and look to our example for direction in starting Communities, we can tell them how we built and how we should build again. There are three main essentials that Community-founders may set before them if they propose to pattern after the model of the Oneida Community. The first is good leaders—those who can be trusted and followed with the certainty that they are true-hearted and competent. Mere well-meaning is not enough. The leaders of a Community should have cultivation and intelligence as well as spirituality; should have ability to speak successfully to an audience, and practical qualifications at least equal to those required to manage the affairs of a bank or a railroad. The second essential for the forming of a community like the Oneida Community is that the membership should have a thorough practical acquaintance with the institution of free criticism—studying each other's characters. This was the antecedent of our organization. I have no reason to think that we could have taken the first successful step in Communism without the discipline that came by criticizing and submitting to criticism. This is the art that amalgamates. The third pre-requisite of a successful

Community is a thorough acquaintance of its members with the theory and practice of male continence. Without this, Communism goes straight either to confusion or to Shakerism. Such are the necessary preliminaries of a Community organization according to our experience. We have no confidence that people will succeed in associative attempts without them. They constitute our standing answer to such as ask us for advice. As to our own action in the premises, we shall move on as fast as we can to provide these essential conditions of Community; and we shall form new families when we get orders from inspiration and providence. We shall not quarrel, if we can help it, with those who think that Paradise can be reached in a cheaper way.

"Applications in 1869 are greater than ever before, but the problem remains: how to distinguish real inquirers among the throng of careless ones. Horace Perry has noted that two classes of persons call on us, each feeling a deep interest in our movements but from entirely different standpoints. The first are persons of more or less depth of religious experience who long and pray for a conversion of the world to Christ and for the coming of the kingdom of God. They so firmly believe that the latter event will take place in a sudden great physical change that they overlook what is manifest to us—that the kingdom of God has already come. They feel a deep sympathy with us in our love and respect for the Bible and in our confession of dependence on Christ for salvation. But they hesitate and stumble in our abolishing of private property in all things, even including persons—our seeking the resurrection state of society and letting the spirit of Pentecost into this world. Nevertheless of such people we have great hope, for from this class the Community was originally organized, and from it have been drafted the great mass of our recruits. Those of the second class are greatly dissatisfied with the world, inveterate grumblers and tearers down of society without any heart or capacity for building up a harmonious state of things. They have a great deal of faith in themselves, very little in anybody else, and none in Christ. They see and feel that the world is in a bad way and fancy they have an ideal of what it ought to be, but no one else agrees with them and they do not agree with each other. Our surroundings completely charm them. Perhaps they request permission to remain overnight and attend our evening meeting, which is generally granted. Having discovered that we are a religious organization—a church—having faith in God and looking to Christ for salvation, they find that an effectual bar is placed between us; after stumbling over our 'religious notions' in the vain attempt to find some ground on which to form a junction with us, they patronizingly conclude that if we would only throw away our religious convictions we should be a very fine institution. In our secret thoughts we kindly hope they may yet discover that the hardness of unbelief is the real barrier between themselves and happiness."

4

Complex Marriage

EACH MARRIED TO ALL

"Copies of Noyes's *Bible Communism*, describing their system, were sent to the governors of Vermont and New York, to at least one member of Congress, to the editors of the *Tribune*, the *Home Journal*, and the *Rome Sentinel*, and to many distinguished lawyers in Vermont and New York. When the *Bible Argument* was first published in 1849, it noted that, although the principles discussed had never been carried into full practical embodiment, either at Putney or Oneida, they 'have been held by the Community as the principles of an *ultimate state* toward which society is advancing slowly and carefully, with all due deference to sentiments and relations established by the old order of things. We have left the simple form of marriage and advanced to the complex stage of it. The honor and faithfulness that constitute an ideal marriage may exist between two hundred as well as two.' It also noted that 'the leading members of the Putney Association belonged to the most respectable families in Vermont and had been educated in the best schools of New England morality and refinement—irreproachable in conduct as far as sexual matters are concerned—until they deliberately commenced in 1846 the experiment of a new state of society on principles that they had long been maturing and were prepared to defend before the world. It may also be affirmed that those who have *joined* the Community at Oneida are sober, substantial men and women of good previous character and position in society.'

"Known as Complex Marriage, all members were married to each other with a deep commitment to the physical, mental, emotional, economic, and spiritual well-being of everyone in the great family. Complex Marriage held to freedom of love only within their family, subject to Free Criticism and the principle of Male Continence. The tie that binds it together is as permanent and at least as sacred as that of marriage, for it is our religion. Every man's care and every dollar of the common property are pledged for the maintenance and protection of the women and the support and education of the children. These guarantees are much greater in the Community than they can be in nearly any private family: breadwinners come to poverty through hard times or sickness, or their own folly or incompetence, or early death. In every essential point of difference between marriage and licentiousness, this community of souls stands with marriage. These essential differences may be stated thus:

> Marriage is a permanent union; free love is a temporary flirtation;
> Marriage brings community of property; free love is a hireling system;
> Marriage makes a man responsible for his acts to a woman; free love allows him to impose his will and go his way without responsibility;
> Marriage provides for the maintenance and education of children; free love leaves them to chance.

"Free love, to the Community, does not mean freedom to love today and leave tomorrow; nor freedom to take a woman's person and keep our property to ourselves; nor freedom to freight a woman with our offspring and send her downstream without care or help; nor freedom to beget children and leave them to the street and the poorhouse. Let anyone who seeks signs of licentiousness in our life and manners look also for inevitable traces of faithlessness and irresponsibility—there are none. Abandonment and neglect are unknown among us. Therefore in the two grand essentials of sacred marriage—faithfulness and cherishing—our record is without spot or blemish. The results of the complex system are that men are rendered more courteous, women and children are healthier, and both sexes are personally free. We have no quarrel with those who believe in exclusive dual marriage and faithfully observe it, but we have concluded that for us there is a better way.

"We are making a great present to the world, the liberty to think and speak about marriage as about other subjects," Noyes wrote on October 18, 1867, in a Home Talk at Wallingford Community. "Conventional marriage has been considered beyond the reach of discussion, to think that there could be any radical wrong in it. There has been the same kind of feeling about it that there is in the old countries about kings. This idea of the unapproachable sacredness of marriage is kept up in full force among people who practically pay no attention to it. How many do we know that are fighting behind the fortifications of marriage, firing away at us with ammunition belonging to it, and yet practically are utterly disloyal to the institution. The really good objective of conventional marriage may be stated as the production of family blessings. The question is, can these blessings be best produced by families in pairs, or by larger partnerships? There has not been experiment enough in larger associations to settle the question, but people assume that it is to be done in pairs. This is as silly as it would be to say that all the business in New York City must be done in firms of two. The world must have liberty to test this question, to try all sorts of families and not be confined to what may be called the one-horse family. We have gotten beyond thinking that a one-horse wagon is all we can ride in; we have railroads now that carry six or seven hundred people at once. The world must have liberty to discover which combinations are best for producing family blessings. Exclusive love, when false, makes more mischief. All love at work in a private corner where there are no series of links connecting it with God, is false love; it is God-eclipsing, idolatrous attachment of two people that too often results in disharmony instead of making peace and happiness for both."

PASSIONAL RESTRICTIONS

"A professor has just married a fourth wife," noted the July 17, 1873, *Circular*. "His friends wonder why he couldn't get women that had stronger constitutions. Our doctor says their constitutions were good enough; the trouble is, the professor is a tough old parasite, and feeds on women." An editor visiting the Oneida Community had introduced a little sarcasm in commenting on its social principles, characterizing them as free love with certain restrictions, in a good-natured and quite flattering article about the Community.

"We accept the gentleman's definition; our liberty is modified by certain restrictions and so has all liberty that produces desirable results. Some such formula lies at the foundation of all good government; the solution of the great problems of social reform and reform in general is found in this nutshell—freedom, with certain restrictions. All the passions of mankind were organized under this law of restrictions, and the observance of the law results in harmony and blessedness as surely as the violation of it produces anarchy and untold misery. The final test of civilization in the passions is this: that they accept limitations and are governed by them, wrote William Woolworth. Hence the great desideratum of successful reform is moral power—the power of limitation, a resurrection force coming from God. The Oneida Community will exemplify the results of this force and distribute it to a world groaning under the curse of unrestricted passion. Amativeness is considered a passion too strong to come under the rules of civilized life, but we know that it can be tamed and civilized. Difficulties may be encountered, but every one can be disposed of in a satisfactory manner by sincere faith in the power of God. Crown all life beneficently when they become civilized enough to obey necessary restrictions.

"The Community transformed sexuality into an honored method of loving communion by placing it under more stringent regulation than it is in general society. Male Continence is a restraining discipline, requiring those who practice it to stop short in sexual intercourse of what is generally supposed to constitute its chief charm; this is closer to the self denial of the Shakers than free love. Sexual intercourse without the propagative act, except when pregnancy is intended, is all that we tolerate. This is a very different affair from that kind of sexual commerce against which all criminal statutes are directed, or the gross, sensual way too often practiced behind closed doors. A clear understanding on this point is essential for all who wish to know the inner truth about us. The principle of Male Continence shifted the responsibility of the maintenance of chastity from woman to man.

"This is right," Noyes declared. "Nature and justice alike cry out against the wrong done to woman and society by imposing upon her a task that man, with all the advantages of greater strength, shrinks from assuming. The world is certainly upside down on this point. Licentiousness is a gigantic foe, carrying havoc through the length and breadth of the land. Society places woman in the front of the army and requires *her* to fight the battle at her own cost and for both sexes. She has the enemy in front and all sides and ruin stares her in the face if she yields an inch. Man on the contrary, free and easy, has little responsibility and fears no social degradation. What but defeat and destitution, widespread and hopeless, can come from such an unequal fight? Exactly the state that actually exists in society! Women fall by thousands and tens of thousands into social ruin, disease breaks up the camp, and dismay at the enormity of the social evil seizes the stoutest heart.

"But let the responsibility be shifted," Noyes continued. "Let man assume that chastity is preeminently a masculine virtue, that his honor and courage are both at stake in this manner—that failure in chastity will involve him in social degradation and ruin, and what is the result? A new line of battle is presented to the enemy. The strongest battalions go to the front. The courage that spends its force in war and conquest finds a nobler field in conquering its own uncivilized passions. A new world, my masters!

"This principle has been practiced in the Oneida Community and its branches for twenty-five years, and we know that it is safe and healthy for all persons. There is no one in all our societies who is not enthusiastic in its praise. It requires that one shall put love of the truth before present and prospective pleasure in respect to the two strongest passions of human nature, amativeness and philoprogenitiveness [motherly love]. Those who joined the Community but became dissatisfied for various reasons and seceded, never talk against the principle of Male Continence. They cannot. They know it is healthful and effectual in saving women from the miseries of undesired procreation, and is purifying and ennobling to the amative passion. When thoroughly scientific men are ready to investigate this matter in the interest of science and humanity, we shall be happy to furnish them with all the facts at our command; and such investigation it must some day receive. It is our opinion that the principle of Male Continence is destined to become exceedingly popular in all classes of society and the world over. It is everywhere needed, from our sparsely settled territories to the over-populated countries of Eastern Asia. It offers the only effectual antidote for all forms of infanticide; it alone can relieve women from the necessity of bearing children contrary to their own wishes in a natural and healthful way. Male Continence would affect a complete revolution in love and marriage, transforming sexual relations into a fine art and a new science, and integrating sexual love with the life of the spirit to make a sacrament of physical love.

"The illumined human becomes capable of receiving and giving celestial love; carnal knowledge can be deepened indefinitely into a mode of mystical knowledge. The young should know that holiness of the heart is what they must have before liberty in love," Noyes taught. The early Community, having grown spiritually together, felt that embarking on the tempestuous ocean of amativeness without a pilot was absurd. Love's expression was managed for the greatest good by the fathers and mothers of the great family who understood sexuality not as merely sensual pleasure but as a sacred act. When rightly controlled and guided, the affections will produce far better results than if left to take care of themselves without restraint. Inexperienced and untutored especially in the principle and practice of Male Continence, youth of both sexes would require skilled guidance. Having protected Harriet from continual debilitating pregnancies, Noyes learned appreciation of the first stages of enjoyment in intercourse and discovered that this practice elevates bodily instinct to a qualitatively more elevating experience for both. Those entering maturity were naturally led into this knowledge by seasoned and spiritual members, often Noyes according to the principle of Ascending Fellowship, and guided in cultivating taste and skill.

"Young women were introduced to the Community's contemplative sexual relating soon after they had begun to menstruate, usually, by Noyes himself or later by one of his most trusted associates. Boys were required to become proficient in male continence and thus have relationships only with older women. Into the twenties, sexual relations had to be with older members to thoroughly instill in the young the wisdom that girl-and-boy infatuations too often end up 'getting into bondage to one another so as to make their love exclusive and idolatrous'—meaning not true love, but jealous, possessive, needy, or otherwise not relating to each other as they truly are, spiritual beings of infinite depth made in the likeness, or essence, of God." One of the lovers described in chapter 12, an adult, left the Community because he was unable to separate himself from the spirit of monopolizing the attentions of one other person, of loving that person more than others, and becoming morose when counseled to separate for a period and learn to love others equally. Such relationships, if allowed, would result in ever more pairing off, which would ultimately destroy the Community—part of their unity was based on Complex Marriage.

"The main mischief in reference to sexual matters is not in outward things but in the imaginations and the secret workings and feelings of the heart," Noyes instructed the Community. "If we cannot reach the heart and stop false thoughts and feelings, we cannot have good wholesome love. Something stronger than criticism and resolutions must enter into persons to regulate thoughts and passions and a cure of adultery." He would remind them that perceiving another with lust is committing adultery in the heart. "There is a love that doesn't darken the heart and harden it, doesn't bring us into bondage," said Noyes. "The only cure is actual, personal acquaintance with Christ, who takes possession of one's thoughts and imaginations and charms us away from all external things. That is holiness, salvation from sin—its true meaning is the possession of the passions of your heart by Christ, a power able to control your feelings and hold them against all seductions and temptations. The grace of God is essentially a spirit of self-control—full of enjoyment, and full of the power of self-denial. If you let that grace flow into your hearts, it will run into all your veins and passions and nature, and make you a new creature; it will make you like Christ, able to walk wisely and do what best judgment teaches you is good. You must learn to appreciate the wonderful power of the grace of God, an actual gift that can work miracles in you. When it possesses you, it will do what your purposes and resolutions have never done and never can do. Notwithstanding your failures, there is a way for you to get true righteousness, and that it will be by the grace of God. There will be more attraction toward internal experience—going home into our hearts—than toward any external thing whatever. God will rain righteousness on you, and you will be fruitful and full of the Holy Spirit and love unfeigned.

"Love is the gift of God," Noyes always said. "We should pray, Give us this day our daily love; for what is love but the bread of the heart? We need love as much as we need food and clothing, and God knows it." After his glimpse of the Divine, Noyes conveyed that "there is infinite depth and mystery in every person and in everything, if we only have discernment to see it. Everything that exists will be to us a shrine of the mystery of God. Divine love is within all, and accessible to all, and is the basis for human happiness and fulfillment. All things are bathed in the glory of God," he says in *Reverence and Love*; "in him we live, and move, and have our being.

"It is everyday truth with us, that to love God and to love him with intense feeling is as practicable as to love a spouse or a child," he said, reported in a *Circular* issue in October 1868. "People are very jealous of anything that interferes between a man and his wife, and a father is jealous of anything that interferes between him and his child. So let us be jealous of anything that interferes between us and the love of God. We can get along without any other love than that, and be comfortable and happy. If we have that love, it will provide us with all the other kinds of love, and make them safe, and good, and wholesome for us. Let us have that love! Let us help one another, support one another, and protect one another in carrying out this principle. In so doing we shall obtain joy and gladness; it is sure to lead right into happiness. I am going to wait on the Lord, and watch, and pray, and live in that interior life and world that Christ and Paul and the Primitive Church did, and I will have no distraction from it. I am determined to help others as much as I can, and to wait on the Lord wholly. I believe I can make the Community happier by helping all who look to me for instruction, to keep their hearts pure and clean and not get into distracting fellowships."

Noyes and a committee of elders, both women and men, undertook the practical working out of Complex Marriage. Any prospective new members underwent an extended probationary period before joining the Community. Wholehearted commitment to Noyes and the Community's religious convictions had to be beyond question, as well as thorough understanding of all aspects of the Community and their suitability to participate in it. Not everyone would want to commit to such responsibilities! The complete freedom of the women to accept or reject lovers kept men as alert as they are during courtship to prove themselves worthy of the favor of their sweethearts. Older women who represented the Community were conduits through whom members expressed interest in closer relations; this allowed women to be completely free to decline. This intermediary was vital for overseeing relationships, to protect women from compulsory connections. The sexes slept apart.

"One member quarreled with the Community because he could not make a certain woman respond to his invitations, and because the Community would not compel her to do so. This man, refusing to leave the Community voluntarily, was eventually carefully picked up and helped out-of-doors in mid-December. "Exclusive companionship does not exist in this Association," Noyes wrote on August 30, 1849. "In the world a woman secures her support and protection by marriage. A man becomes responsible for her and on that ground claims a right to her exclusive affection. No woman here is dependent on one man for support. While a man is a candidate for the favors of the other sex, he is under the strongest stimulus to cultivate amiable manners and honorable ambition, but in marriage in the world, there is an end of care about quality. He has got a woman, whom he has a right to make his companion whether she will or no, the right of a master over a slave, for husbands have legal and personal ownership of women." The Community protected their women not only from unplanned pregnancy but from slavery to unwanted sexual demands, and they protected all their members from less than agreeable social approaches. Every man is compelled to be a gentleman in the exercise of amativeness. He has no marital rights that he can enforce and is constantly on his best behavior. He must attract love; he cannot compel it nor demand any of its privileges.

"The Community abhorred rape, too often committed under the cover of marriage. Barbarisms exercised under cover of marriage have to be tolerated in ordinary society. We feel certain that the health of many women is ruined in marriage by sexual brutalities on the part of husbands—never described in newspapers and of which the perpetrators themselves may be ignorant, owing to the false modesty that enshrouds the whole subject of sexual morality. Receiving no polish from contact with his neighbors, remaining in a social sense uncultivated, a man is at liberty to be as much of a boor as he may choose, though compelled to practice some amenities of civilized life."

Living with three hundred people was an indispensable education! Learning social harmony, manners, empathy, and social graces benefits a person immensely. "Gentlemen, if I may offer a suggestion for our common improvement, I propose that we young men maintain our freedom from favoritism in which many of our married brethren are entangled, and study to be liberal and diffusive in our love and attention to the other sex," Noyes addressed the men. "Let it be our ambition to hasten the grand consummation of the courtship that is going on in this Association between all the men as one man and all the women as one woman. Let us be heroes in love and train our hearts to scale the heights above, as well as to enjoy the beauties of our level. There should be first a marriage of hearts, next a marriage of intellects, and last a marriage of bodies," Noyes counseled. "There is natural attraction between the spiritual and novices, the young and those older, an attraction both necessary and desirable."

The public opinion of the whole Community operated as a power of restraint upon individual selfishness and sensuality; freed to realize her true destiny as a person, woman could develop her many talents and interests. A conscientious member reported that he had spoken with many of the women to learn whether anyone felt limited or deprived of rights. All said they felt help in every way from the men and perceived no distinction of privileges; they enjoyed all the advantages for spiritual growth and personal expansion that men did. "Woman is made for God and for herself," Noyes insisted; "she has a spiritual nature that lifts her up to God, where there is 'neither male nor female.' It is her right to choose when and how often she shall bear children. She has children only by choice and her drudgery as a mother is to be reduced to the minimum. We are opposed to involuntary, excessive, and therefore oppressive procreation. She was not made chiefly for the children she can bear, but to be what she is in courtship rather than what she too often is in marriage, a propagative drudge. She is a companion and lover in the Community."

George Miller wrote about reducing the sum of human misery, citing momentous discoveries of Jenner, Harvey, and Pasteur, yet how even these pale in comparison to discovering a satisfactory solution of the darkest of all problems, how to subject human propagation to the control of reason. The following paragraphs are Miller's observations and thoughts:[33] "A family consisting of a stout, robust young man, a tall handsome woman with a fine intellectual face, and three children approach some park benches. A baby was in its mother's arms and the other two, aged three and four, caught at her skirts. The woman sank wearily upon an adjacent seat, no sparkle or smile there, only the hunted hopeless look of an animal caught in a trap from which there was no escape. Noble St. Paul said, *Love worketh no ill to his neighbor*. A man's wife is his nearest and dearest neighbor, but many a good man is sadly perplexed to see that he is unintentionally working grievous ill to this neighbor he loves best. He is exposing her to bearing children faster than her health will permit, thus undermining her strength and depriving her of the beauty and sprightliness that charmed him so greatly in his days of courtship. He sees with disappointment that the beautiful flower whose bloom and perfume he so strongly coveted, and which he had plucked with ardor, is withering in his grasp. He sees also that the constant breeding entailed upon his wife is depriving him, in great measure, of the society and help of a delightful companion.

"Do you love your wife? Do you want her to be a helper to you instead of a burden? Do you want to preserve her freshness like that of a sweet scented flower to brighten and perfume your pathway through life? Learn self-control. Do you wish to reduce the evils of poverty to a minimum, and avoid the anguish of seeing helpless objects of affection multiply around you to whom you can give neither adequate nourishment nor education? Learn self-control. Do you wish to have healthy and well-balanced children? Let them be only those that are desired by both parents. Do you wish to have your sons marry early enough to avoid a long and cruel suppression of a natural and innocent desire, and thus escape falling into ruinous habits that cloud their whole life? Teach them self-control. All interests of heaven and earth summon you to the supreme importance of the study of self-control in a department of life in which it has never been taught, and which is therefore filled with the wrecks wrought by an ungoverned force. Peace, order, and infinite happiness can be established there in this way, and this way only.

"My first rude awakening to the stern realities of married life came with the birth of my first child," a woman wrote. "The doctors said that my physical formation was not favorable to child-bearing, and my child was taken away from me dead. A year later I went through the same experience again, and was completely changed from a light-hearted, joyous girl to a sickly, nervous, irritable woman. Can you wonder that I shrank from my husband's embraces after this, and looked upon them as a cruel stab at my life?"

"Some women of a particular constitution and under certain favorable conditions (a congenial marriage is one) have thrived in childbearing," the January 10, 1870, *Circular* notes, "but how many women have broken down after having several children, and disappeared by premature death? Man and womankind are suffering from the unrestrained and misguided power of the propagative instinct in human society. Ask the woman who is in the agonies of bringing to birth her tenth child if there's not something wrong in the institution that gives man the power to impose upon her the herculean task of bearing children through the whole of the best period of her life, at that life's imminent risk?"

"A letter addressed to a lady in the Community in May 1872 recounts a sad story: 'Two years ago my daughter was married; nine months later she had a son and the next year she had a daughter; if nothing happens to prevent, she will be confined for the third time the following year. Her children are sickly, and she is sick and discouraged. When she first found she was in the family way this last time, she acted like a crazy person; went to her family physician and talked with him about having an operation. He encouraged her and performed it before she left the office, but without success. I was frightened at her looks and soon learned what she had done. She said she would never have this child if it cost her life. After a week she went to the doctor again; he did not accomplish his purpose, but told her to come again in three months. I told her that I would pray that Christ would discourage her; and sure enough she had not the courage to try the operation and came home, but cannot be reconciled to her condition. She does not appear like the same person she was three years ago and is looking forward with sorrow instead of joy to the birth of her child.'"

"Since my husband became acquainted with the Community's philosophy and practice of love and sex, he has endeared himself to me a hundred-fold, and although our so-called honeymoon was five years ago, it was no more real and far less lasting than the ecstatic, unspeakable happiness that is now continually mine. My prosaic and sometimes indifferent husband has changed by a heavenly magic into an ardent and entrancing lover, for whose coming I watch with all the tender raptures of a schoolgirl," wrote L.S.T. "His very step sends a thrill through me, for I know that my beloved will grasp me and clasp me and cover me with kisses such as only the most enthusiastic lover could give. And though years lapse, I cannot see or feel any change in the way he cherishes me. To each other we are continually objects of the deepest reverence and the most sacred mystery. Our affection deepens and our romance seems as sure and enduring as the stars. I date my marriage from the time that he became a student of the community, for that was the beginning of our assured happiness. But it is not alone as a cherishing lover that my husband has become my crown of happiness. He has grown perceptibly nobler in character, in purpose, in strength, in all the qualities that make a man God-like, so that besides a lover I have a strong friend and wise counselor and my happiness is complete."

"I am earnestly convinced that no other discovery in physical science has ever been made that is of such importance to the welfare of the human race," said a man married for fifteen years. "As a statistical and financial advisor to the government of a growing colony . . . I have had the problem of human poverty forced on my attention with terrible emphasis. I early realized that the Malthusian pressure of population was the one thing that dominated human destinies in this regard, but it was not until I became acquainted with [the Community's principles] that I could understand any entirely satisfactory solution of the problem . . . life has become wholesome and happy and these principles would be imperative for spiritual reasons even if there were no population problem to solve. It avoids the opposite evils of asceticism and self-indulgence, and does more than any other single thing to make marriage a perpetual courtship."

Noyes said that he would be glad to see the Oneida Community "come on to courting ground; to see every man put himself into the market for what he is worth. There would be a good deal more attention to quality. A man who has a wife has the privilege of being lazy; he has all that is necessary to satisfy his sensual appetite and social craving, and he is contented, though he may be as poor as poverty. In monotony the devil knows just where to find you—when love becomes a habit and loses its inspiration, it is hateful," Noyes went so far as to state. "The real happiness and beauty of love lies in the courting attitude of mind. This shrinking back from the energy necessary to become attractive is the natural outworking of the marriage system. Let us all come into the market with no rights or claims. Obtain love by love and by presenting attractiveness. Never think of paying that debt once and for all. God rewards every man according to his works. Conventional marriage is a refuge of lies that people cover themselves with to get a reward they do not earn."

"Dear Mr. Noyes:

I have been led to consider the relation that the men sustain towards the women of the Community, as contrasted with the position in which men are ordinarily placed by marriage. It has greatly increased my appreciation of our social principles, and quickened my heart with love and gratitude toward you. We men often rejoice that the women here are redeemed from social oppression. Have we sufficiently appreciated the social salvation that is being wrought out for *us*? I for one have not. The worst result of southern slavery is its effect upon slave holders, making them hard-hearted and despotic—destroying their finer sensibilities and nobler impulses. It seems to me that marriage-slavery produces quite as bad effects upon men as upon women; even more than southern slavery, it tends to cultivate selfishness and despotism in man. Man exercises the spirit of ownership toward goods and chattels, and is ready to resist any encroachments upon his property-rights; when his property rights in wife and children are touched he is ready to curse and kill. Christianity and all civilizing influences modify this relation of ownership, but the fact remains that ownership of persons, and especially the complete ownership that marriage gives, cultivates the most intense kind of selfishness. I thank God that our social relations do not give an opportunity for this wickedness to grow. I've observed the operation of marriage slavery, and have had to meet the principle in myself that desires to have a wife—one whom I could call mine—who should be sacred to me and me alone. The same influences that would tempt me to desire such possession should persuade me that I not treat a woman despotically after she became mine; but even if this were so, the case is no better than can be made out for southern slavery. Many slave-holders were merciful toward their slaves, treating them with great kindness and generosity; yet the institution of slavery naturally fosters despotism. For every merciful master there were hundreds who were cruel; so in marriage there are doubtless many who "do unto their wives as they would be done by," but probably the great majority act otherwise. Again I thank God, and you as the medium of his truth, that I own no woman; that I am in no circumstances to command love; that I am entitled to and can receive, as I pass along, only such social privileges as my character and course properly win.

—Truly yours, William A. Hinds, Oneida Community, August 16, 1868."

> "*To love is difficult, because loving's not enough: like God we must ourselves become that very love.*" —Angelus Silesius, *One Must Be Essence.*[34]

"I find in my heart commendation and gratitude toward the Community for its faithful observance of that part of our social theory that relates to propagation," Noyes communicated to his growing flock in November 1849. "Our principle of Male Continence makes a large demand on self-control and self-denial, especially in our incipient stage of education, and is doubtless the occasion of some trials and temptations.

It would not have been strange if instances of violation had occurred among us, but I'm thankful that no involuntary impregnation has taken place in this association." On October 1850, the *Oneida Journal* noted that a daughter, Grace, was born. "This was the first accidental birth or falseness to our principles. Both parties have had a sincere criticism for their unfaithfulness to Christ and the truth.

"Cases of special desire for children occurred occasionally and those persons have had their will; accidental or involuntary propagation also occurred occasionally, with results as fortunate as any," the October 5, 1868, *Circular* reported. "These cases were not numerous. A large proportion of the children were offspring of recently received members. The rearing of children is a great function but is not necessarily the highest of which woman is capable; the mental and physical development and improvement of the mother must enter into this question. 'Women know that they are capable of development in a thousand ways apart from maternity,' Noyes insisted, 'and if they are educated and act in other arenas, they cannot devote their life wholly to childbearing.'

"Community member Stephen R. Leonard wrote that on his business trips, he was occasionally drawn into conversation with someone on the train curious to learn more about the Community that he'd heard so much about. I informed him that it is our freedom from selfishness that enables us to live together in harmony. A gentleman exclaimed, 'Not even two families can live amicably together as one household!' I agreed that it is not human nature as we generally see it, but that we believe in being born again.

"'Your social position seems to be the great bug-bears—everything else but that, they can get along with,' said another gentleman. 'My acquaintance with society has been somewhat extensive, and according to my observation, happy marriages are extremely rare. When persons come together in courtship,' he continued, 'they see no evil in each other or if they do see some things they don't quite approve, they yield to one another's prejudices and try to make themselves mutually agreeable. But somehow after the parties become united in matrimony, all the little faults come to the surface and produce disagreements and unhappiness.'

"'That's it exactly,' I responded. 'As long as a loving couple remains unmarried, they strive to please each other. But marriage changes the relative standing of the parties. The law of marriage places the wife in the power of her husband, and she finds that if for any cause he is tempted to irritation or ungentlemanly conduct, he no longer feels under the same necessity to please her whom the law has made his own.[35] Hence the closer familiarity of marriage, instead of increasing love as was hoped, tends to the contrary. This state of things suggests the real difference between social life at the Oneida Community and that of ordinary society—it is the difference between courtship and marriage. One sex does not own the other, but both are put upon their good behavior; and all the politeness and tender regard for one another in little matters that are so common in courtship, with us continue to be the standard of everyday life.'"

"'If that is what you are doing,' said the gentleman, 'your example, if it could be followed, would be of inestimable value to the world.'"

"It is the free love of heaven and it is directed by the living God," Noyes wrote. "The use of amativeness is what is going to drive the devil out of the world. Eternity is before us."

THE NATURE OF PLEASURE

"There are two theories about pleasure. A true theory traces all good to its source and finds it organized in God; a no-theory enjoys the surface of things without inquiring further," explained George Washington Noyes. "The horse goes from oats to grass and from pasture to pasture, enjoying his present mouthful and caring for nothing more. This is the general mode of enjoyment of worldly men, passing from object to object in the search after pleasure, fancying that they can possess and consume a certain fixed quantity in each; an apple is an apple, disconnected and consumable. So of all good things. This dealing with things as individualities and not tracing them through to the universal, we call the animal theory of pleasure; selfish men seek to get possession of all the goods they can—the ground of exclusive property."

George Washington Noyes was John's younger brother and editorial assistant; his articles about human nature and Christianity rivaled John's for originality and depth. An early father of the Wallingford Community, he loved to walk and sketch and taught Latin to the younger generation. He especially promoted brotherly love.

To See God in All Things

"There is a better theory," George elaborated. "We may rightly conceive of all pleasure as a unit—not a scattered diversity of things, but one thing—a pervading spirit. We may conceive of the world of visible objects as a shell enclosing an ocean of life and love, and all the different forms by which we get access to pleasure as so many apertures opening into this one ocean. Pleasure is independent of particularities. The soul of pleasure and the life of all things is God; and the truly disciplined heart finds God through all the avenues of outward enjoyment. In this theory the whole circle of pleasures is organized—they not only lead back individually into the great center of being, but they are found united and organized in themselves, each after its kind.

"I have, for instance, a peach. According to no-theory—the swinish and carnal view—it is an individual lump of fiber and juice appealing to my sense of taste, an atom of pleasure that I'll consume, and that is the end of it. As a mere animal exercise—often to excess—love of food becomes idolatry. When one recognizes the Lord in the food one eats, eating is spiritualized. If my mind and taste are in an innocent state, un-perverted by devilish influences, I discern the deep and illimitable spirit of pleasure in the delight of eating the peach. My heart finds itself in the presence of God and draws nourishment from his love. The peach itself is the occasion of an interior pleasure that is eternal. The individual introduces me to the universal. Tracing the essence of its beauty to an interior, universal spirit, I understand a principle of unity connecting all fruit of that kind. All peaches are manifestations fed from that same fountain. They are therefore one in essence, and the pleasure I have with any particular specimen really links me to the whole. In a sense, all peachdom is contributing to my enjoyment—pouring itself into the union that I form with the one. Every form of external enjoyment is in truth a method of worship and interchange between us and the divine."

George Noyes has described what Plato was getting at: All forms, ideas, even things, exist in a universal reality of perfection that transcends sensory life; and Noyes mirrors the teaching of Vedanta, from ancient scriptures of India: Realize that finite attractions are in reality love and attraction to infinite God; true fulfillment and the love of all beings is found by directing the heart's love toward Him, and seeing God in everything.

> *"The rose which here on earth is now perceived by me,*
> *Has blossomed thus in God from all eternity."* — Angelus Silesius, *The Rose*.[36]

"This theory is applicable to every form of pleasure—to eating and drinking, to music, to the enjoyment of pleasant sights and sounds, the companionship of friends, and sexual love," George continued. "We are bound in all these things to rise from the special to the universal. Music should be a door through which we enter into the interior harmonies. The love of an individual should introduce us to God and bring us into rapport with the universal spirit of the sex, so that we taste the concentrated love and blessing of the whole. Any love of pleasure that stops in forms and individualities and fails to pursue it up to the universal, is blind, the sensuality of the brutes." His brother John agreed. He was opposed not to true pleasure but to settling for a pale imitation of what gives real happiness. To be able to enjoy everything and yet be dependent on nothing but God for happiness is the secure guarantee of happiness, instead of living mostly in the ephemeral pursuit of it. His counsel was not to turn people away from pleasure, but to learn true satisfaction and fulfillment. "One who remains satisfied with the barren outside of things finds meager pleasure and ultimately emptiness and even pain. Whether we eat or drink or sleep, work or play, we shall dwell in interior truth . . . in the soul of things, and consequently shall be perfectly happy without intermission.

"The more we get acquainted with God, the more we shall find it is our special duty to be happy," John continued. "It is the main focus and center of all duty to 'eat the fat and drink the sweet,' and enjoy God and his works," he said in *Table Talk* at the Brooklyn Community in 1852. "All other duties are merely preliminary and serve as protectives of these duties. When you eat, do it seriously, purposely, heartily, as unto the Lord. Do we gobble food, or fully savor many tastes and textures and aromas? And if you think it is an indulgence, if you cannot do it heartily, you defile your conscience; your nature revolts at the quarrel between your conscience and your appetite. If you eat on principle, it will steady your nerves and bodily functions. It will give stability to your stomach. Do it seriously from principle; count that you are serving God in eating strawberries more than in cultivating them. Cultivating strawberries is merely introductory to their main function. It is considered meritorious to plant and hoe, but indulgent to eat the fruit of our labor, as though everything pleasurable were wrong—as though God were stingy and wished to have us regard everything pleasurable as extra. This is the opposite of the truth. The truth is, God made man to enjoy not a part, but the whole of things, and this universality is necessary to his life. In order to thrive he must have free access to all the life-streams of the universe and wherever he touches he must be able to drink the infinite essence of the thing, finding sustained happiness in the source of all beauty. This, our theory teaches him to do.

"Cut him off from this, reduce him to half-fare so that he derives only a partial, outward enjoyment here and there, and he starves and dies or becomes cruel; this is the false sensual theory of the world. Men are sensual and destroyed by matter not because they love pleasure too well, but because they do not love it enough. They take up with a part—the barren outside of things—when God meant that they should have the whole. The property system of the world falls in with the animal theory of pleasure. Communal living harmonizes with the true theory. The two grow naturally out of these opposite views. The social system of the world gives a person a certain number of relations, and surrounds him with a certain amount of property it calls his. It partitions off the good things of the earth into little separate quantities and gives to every man a little exclusive pen of his own that he is allowed to enlarge according to his selfishness and skill. The doctrine being, pleasure is consumable and the object is for everyone to crowd his neighbor to get the largest place at the trough. But the best of them, on this system, get only a meager pittance—a mere fragment of the broad bounty that was intended for them. The richest man has but a stingy access to the sources of pleasure—his property is everywhere limited and partial; he nowhere touches the universal, except in the enjoyment of light, air, water, and those few blessed elements that God has reserved beyond the power of man to sequestrate. No wonder that people die under such a system. They are legitimately starved to death in the midst of abundance.

"Living in Community teaches a man to look upon *everything* as his," Noyes elaborated, "which is the firm truth when the gospel introduces him to unity with God and his neighbor. It teaches him that pleasure is an interior spirit and therefore indestructible—that the only use of things is to introduce him to that spirit; and that God has secured an everlasting supply of material for this purpose. Hence man in his true, universal character as the image of God has no occasion to appropriate and seclude anything for himself alone, but is free to worship and enjoy. The universal man who results from unity is reflected in every ember, and each may have the consciousness of an illimitable inheritance in persons and things to be enjoyed without encumbrance and with the sympathy of all. This is the doctrine of Community with the Father and Son, the angels and human brotherhood, in all happiness and immortality. Whatever of value or beauty a person may see, conceive of, or aspire unto, he will say in his heart *this comes from God*. However the value may seem to lie in the thing itself, this appearance is but a reflection of God's goodness," Noyes always taught. "The true way then to possess it is by seeking fellowship with the source." The source is our true nature, made in the image of God, and is the Holy Spirit, the divine spark within. Vedanta teaches that the true self of all humanity is identical with the highest Reality, Brahman, and religion is the search for self-knowledge, for Atman, God within.

"How shall we partake of the beauties of nature in such a way as to add to the graces of the soul," asks a Community member in the May 20, 1872, *Circular*, "and feel at season's end that we have laid up treasures that shall be everlasting? To view things with a chaste eye is to see God in all things and to drink in his spirit in everything we look upon. Arabelle is a beautiful example of such perception; it is very interesting as well as edifying to walk with her in the garden. Her enthusiasm over its beauties is contagious. 'O, how beautiful! –how sweet!' and then, as if moved by some unseen influence, she says, 'How good God is to give us all these beauties!' Every flower, with its beauty and fragrance, is to her emblematic of the Giver of all good gifts.

The Oneida Community Mansion House from the South Garden.

"There is a great difference in people in regard to the faculty of appreciation—where one garners pearls of untold value, another sees only uninteresting facts. To the appreciative eye, the world is full of rich treasures in all seasons. Even the etchings of the Frost Genie have their charms—the delicate lace-work that fringes the borders of brooks and the infinite variety of snowflakes. I accompanied two friends to a grove on the sunny side of which was a bank of drifted snow that flashed and sparkled in sunlight as though set with the costliest diamonds. One companion immediately appreciated these scintillating brilliants and with a rapturous exclamation called my humbled eyes to the sight. Selfishness blunts finer sensibilities, desiring only to know how much sleighing can be depended on for drawing of wood and stone, or how much water-power can be secured. I invited a friend to accompany me to view the noble proportions of a great tree. I expected he would show some emotion. But no; only a speculation as to the amount of saw-logs it would produce, or the number of cords into which it might be cut. The buttress-like roots which braced and supported its gigantic trunk were not even noticed. Its stately column was valued only as timber, and its wide-spreading branches, which it had taken a century or more to form, were estimated to be worth only a trifle for firewood! Another time, while listening to an enchanting concert of birds near the road-side, a farmer drove past; I congratulated him on having such lovely songsters.

"'Ye-es, but isn't my colt, here, a fine one?' was his query.

"'The colt will command money,' I answered, 'but the birds. . .'

"'Oh, I don't trouble myself about birds—I don't know one from another.'

"I've seen persons pass smiling meadows adorned with flowers, who only saw the future haycock. I have seen others who ate luscious Bartletts or Seckels with as little emotion as though they were baked potatoes. Cannot we learn to be appreciative of little things? Shall we not find our pathway continually strewed with things of beauty that may be joys to us forever?"

COMMUNITY'S PRINCIPLES AND PRACTICES KNOWN TO ALL

"In the world no man knows his neighbor," wrote Noyes. "Persons meet only in appearance. The customary respectability, used to hide universal misdeeds of thought, is before God a great sham." *To be and not to seem* was a community ideal. "We believe the time has come when people will be forced to see things just as they really are." Noyes and his Community were unashamed of its principles and practices, and Noyes's *Bible Communism* was dispatched to the Governor of New York, other prominent public officials, and to advanced thinkers. They promulgated their Community's convictions openly, yet with delicacy that respected a proper veil over private life. The Community welcomed visitors from its inception.

"We have learned to show hospitality without the assiduities of the world; to give the freedom of home without costly attention. Nothing puts us off our track of self-improvement," the September 1849 *Oneida Journal* noted. "In our evening meetings, there is quite a temptation to suit the exercises to the taste, curiosity, and edification of our strangers, but we find that the true way is to pursue steadily the lessons before us. Our heresies are so confessed that we cannot be afraid of disclosures; and if there is anything in the Association that calls for criticism, we are glad to be under all the motives to good behavior that the most open exposure to a carping world can give us." Noyes circulated the first Annual Report of the Oneida Association, and their sexual theory and practice became an open secret. The large city of Utica, twenty miles east, was prospering by 1850 with the greatest per capita income in the state. The powers-that-be in Madison and Oneida Counties dealt with complaints stemming from wild tales and gossip about the Community's immoralities—a collection of individuals of both sexes who did not hold to marriage. Their influence would corrupt the area!

"The Madison County Grand Jury asked many questions of the complainants and witnesses. The Community decided to invite the whole neighborhood to a grand strawberry festival as the best way to introduce themselves to the larger region. Community members picked and prepared seven bushels of strawberries from their garden; others prepared biscuits, cream, and sugar. Tables and chairs were arranged in shady spots and the children's playground, capacious enough to seat nearly one hundred people, was decorated with fragrant evergreen cedar. Some eighty families from neighboring villages began arriving at 3:00 p.m. and gathered in the arbor where an abundance of strawberry desserts were arrayed. Their great house was open and Community members joined visitors strolling in their gardens as the children entertained all with many songs. It was evident that these were industrious, peaceable, and law-abiding citizens. Some 300 people stayed until 7:00 p.m. and many left supplied with strawberries."

They circulated a statement to be sent to the District Attorney of the County of Oneida, which nearly all their neighbors signed. They stated that they regarded the Oneida Community "as honorable business men, good neighbors, quiet and peaceable citizens, lovers of justice and good order, and—so far as we know—persons of good moral character. The largest land-owner declared that they were the best class in the region and he considered their presence among them as a blessing. This District Attorney had put Community women and men through a probing examination before an unfriendly Grand Jury; they told the whole truth with dignity. The Grand Jury remained mixed in opinion, but eventually decided to abstain and see how things evolved over time. The Community had always believed that if their practices caused problems with their neighbors, they were prepared to marry conventionally within the Community, or move elsewhere. 'If possible, so far as it depends upon you,' Paul taught, 'live peaceably with all.'

"A few days later, the Community gave another Strawberry Festival to the Oneida Indians. George Washington Noyes wrote, 'The Indians have been our very good neighbors from the commencement of the Community here, and we are glad to pay our respects to the remnant of a once powerful race. We inhabit the home of their fathers.... We felt it to be appropriate to celebrate the idea of human fraternity with these descendants of the red men, on ground thus doubly devoted to the common interest.' Seventy of the 150 resident Oneida Nation and several from the Green Bay colony on their visit to their Oneida brethren were among our guests. About seventy sat down under our arbor, to partake of strawberries and cream. Among them were several members of the Indian Minstrel Company . . . who favored us with several hymns in their own tongue."[37]

"I do not look upon the Community as separate from the world; nor is it possible for it to be separated from the world. I never have had any idea of saving myself or the Community by keeping ourselves in a monkish kind of segregation. We are not a sect; we are nothing but a large family," Noyes said at an Evening Meeting six weeks later. "There is no sect in which parents allow their children the freedom of reading books written in the spirit and interest of other sects that we do; nor do they encourage them in freedom of thought as we do. We keep ourselves saturated all the time with worldly influences through our library. It is true that our people are comparatively free from personal communication with the world, but we keep our library crammed with the ideas of the world. We feel about as much sympathy with one sect as with another. We feel about as liberal towards Positivists as towards church members. We meet the world with freedom in music and in literature, and keep ourselves separate only as far as is necessary to retain our organization."

"The Honorable Timothy Jenkins, former member of Congress and lawyer, testified that by their thrift and industry, the Community vastly improved the region. Land became more valuable; the struggling rural populace was given well-paid employment and was assisted with many necessities. Their workers were also included in Community education and cultural life as the Community prospered. 'We've done as much for the morality of the sexes in our neighborhood as we have for its material welfare. The Synod will soon see that even ordinary marriage has been elevated here; that our influence has lessened obscenity and lewdness found elsewhere; and that there is fidelity in marriage corresponding to the material prosperity we have wrought.'"

"Pawtuckcet, Kansas, December 1871. Dear *Circular*: — I could not well do without the *Circular*. Its pages advocate a state of society where woman shall not be the slave of man and in which she shall not devote her time and energies to the study of fashions; where competition shall be unknown except to promote happiness; where mine and thine will not be heard, but all will be ours; where children will receive the best training in unison with their nature, and be surrounded with circumstances calculated to form a superior character; where means will be adopted to give to every child born the best organization physical and mental; where each individual will contribute according to his ability and each receive according to his needs. I perceive the Oneida Community to be in the right way to form a new order of society, wherein true principles of Christianity will be practiced. For eighteen hundred years the principles of Jesus have been preached, but where have they been fully put in practice? Respectfully, J. W. A."

"Those who objected to communitarian living seemed to agree on one point—it was the grave of individuality, the sepulcher of originality. Community living would tend to make people all alike, where a few ruling minds at the top determine everything. The Community's rejoinder appeared in the November 20, 1871, *Circular*: 'It is our candid conviction that individuality—the mannerisms, the originalities, the inventive powers, the thousand and one little peculiarities which, combined, make everyone a genius by himself—is increased by Community, and that materially. Why not? The unity that cements us together and that we confess we esteem above everything, makes gentlemen and ladies of us—makes us love harmony rather than discord and makes us provoke others to love rather than seek our own pleasure. That is all. It does not make us all alike. Because we have 'one Lord, one faith, one baptism, one God and father of us all, who is above all and through all, and in us all,' we do not think that the next step in the syllogism is that our minds should all run in the same groove or our souls be all cut after the same pattern, any more than that we should dress in uniform or have the same colored hair . . . . No, indeed! The more complex, the more varied its component parts will be. Besides all the diverse natural particularities of taste and disposition among us, do we not, spiritually speaking, have gifts differing according to the grace that is given us? Certainly, we find it so."

Harnessing the Energies of Love

"How do you know that it is impossible for all to be married to all?" asked Noyes's son Theodore, trained as a physician at Yale, who studied male continence and found that it was not difficult, with training, and produced emotions that were ennobling to both women and men. "There are men in the Community who have talents for social music and ought to be glorious distributors of God's love, but who are crippled by daintiness and cramped and made miserable by marriage adhesions. There are women who can and should love the whole Community but whose husbands are jealous and grumbling if their wives pay a cent to anyone but themselves. A man who has the marriage spirit is in the condition of a fraudulent debtor; he has given all his property to one preferred creditor and is cheating the rest."

"Many persons are starved; true love is essential to health. It is the fire of life," John Noyes said. As one Community elder put it, "Complex Marriage frees the spirit from restricted human love with all the difficulties, embarrassments, and torments that people experience in their sexual lives."

"God will not have those in his kingdom who cannot love all that he loves," Noyes added.

"A letter was received by Noyes from a young man in the Community who was just closing his college career at Yale: 'I want to tell you how much it stirs my spirit to hear our people magnify Male Continence. It seems to me that we are just beginning to say the good things that will be said of it; and it makes me happy to think of the honor that is sooner or later certain to be poured upon it. I love the principle of Male Continence with my whole soul, for I know that it has been and is a help to my fellowship with Christ. This Yankee nation claims to be a nation of inventors, but the discovery of Male Continence puts you, in my mind, at the head of all inventors. There has certainly been no higher conservation of force than that realized by Male Continence, and I am confident that the blessings that will flow from it cannot be measured by those that have followed the steam engine and the electric telegraph.'"

"The great characteristic of our times is in the utilization of power—water, steam, air, fire, electricity, and magnetism were known to the ancients but they left them as they found them, wild lawless giants of whom it was necessary to respect and beware," wrote George Washington Noyes in the July 14, 1873, *Circular*, echoing this idea. "But now, air—the giant of the tornado—drives mills and is the obedient vassal who prints the paper you look upon; fire, the terrible genius of conflagration, has now become the great metal-worker and by developing other forces, the chief agent of civilization; water, the demon of the flood, now grinds our bread and weaves our clothes; steam roars its gladness to serve us through every valley and on every sea; lightning and magnetism have been harnessed into the work of communication. Human association is also a power—its strength was mainly like that of the tornado and the torrent, by the devastating sweep of armies when some Alexander bore down on helpless nations, but this power of voluntary association is rapidly turning to useful ends. It builds factories, colonizes States, controls currency, establishes missions, and does the hospital service of armies. In Community where it is even more fully utilized, it is the great agent of social, moral, and material progress.

"One more element of power is that of amative passion, the magnetic bond between the sexes, whose utilization may be said to have scarcely begun. We state but a scientific fact when we say that here is a force, broad as humanity, always active, a ten-thousand-Niagara power, surging down in a current parallel with existence, waiting to be put to use. It runs as yet in the channel of mere nature, a channel bounded by fear and shame and selfishness. Society dreads its untamed outbreaks, and tries to curb it by law; but whether within bounds, or out of bounds, still it flows, irresistible, irrepressible, infinite, and mainly without use. Marriage does not utilize it but in a trivial degree. The cobble-dam by which marriage contrives to divert a little of its power to the amelioration of character during courtship is soon over, and it resumes its old, habitual channel. The question now presses, Shall this power be utilized? Shall its current be controlled by solid masonry and drawn off in peaceful manner to enrich the race with its service? Community answers: It can be done; it shall be done. The effect of this power, skillfully used, instead of devastating character as in its present unmastered condition it too often does, will be to concentrate upon society an elevating and perfecting influence hitherto unknown. Under it women will grow up blooming, healthy, free, the vestals of improvement, fragrant with unfading beauty and grace; men will be molded to more than knightly chivalry and honor, and both sexes will realize in each other the reflected goodness of God."

Complex Marriage would not have thrived without John Humphrey Noyes's elevated view of women and of human potential. "I've heard men say, *I know all about women*. Such an attitude toward women is an insult to human nature and to the God who created male and female. Only as we become refined in our perceptions and delicate in our feelings toward God, shall we be delicate and tender in our feelings toward our fellows, and treat them fairly. To one who appreciates God's creation, man and woman are an endless mystery. People devote a lifetime to understanding the violin and say they are just beginning to fathom it. I must be a poor wooden character of less worth than a violin, if the mystery of love can ever be fathomed and we know all about each other. No—we are fearfully and wonderfully made!

"This necessarily flows from the first admission that God is unfathomable in depths of wisdom. In him we live, and move, and have our being. There is no person for whom we have not infinite reason to feel respect. Our deficiency is to have too much reverence in some directions and not enough in others. The only thing that is really contemptible is contempt! To be contemptuous is considered a mark of loftiness, but it is a mark of lowness. The being capable of giving the most respect is the loftiest. Respect implies insight, perception of mystery and depth; and the being who can see the deepest, who has the most far-reaching insight, is capable of the most respect. Contempt implies ignorance. The greatest person will be the most respectful person. The only way to elevate love is to clear away false, debasing ideas about sex and substitute true and beautiful ones. Moralistic reform arising out of shame would keep us ignorant of sex while nature constantly thrusts its imperative upon us. Love and sex should be the most engrossing of all sciences, as well as an art. We are made to give and receive great pleasure in love. But enclosed in the dark isolation of egotism, sex for sex's sake, we miss that portal to the transcendent experience of love—awakening to the knowledge that all love is one and indivisible, an experience of unity with Humanity and God."

> "*I am not I nor you; yet you are I in me,*
> *And so my God I pay all homage sole to thee.*"
> —Angelus Silesius, *Man is Nothing, God Everything*[38]

John Humphrey Noyes discovered that we are in heaven now because nothing separates us from the love of God. We have only to realize that love and practice it. The old passes away and all things become new.

DEALING WITH JEALOUSY AND PLEASURE-SEEKING

"While the world is predicting that our principle of marriage of all to all will result in confusion and licentiousness, the difficulty has been elsewhere. There is very little warm, genial love between the married pairs. The parties are not to blame; God does not send his love in that channel because humanity is subject to the law of spiritual gravity," Noyes explained. Habit, routine, were felt to be tyrants—quite literally evil in their effects on people, for habits rob the human spirit of inspiration, creativity, growth, refreshment, and newness of life. Humans tend to get into ruts and may find familiar routine comfortable, but this inertia must be incessantly resisted because it tempts us to settle into habits of the minimal life. Noyes and the Community cultivated new experiences of all kinds. Even good *habits* are to be eschewed, for in the sight of God all attachments to fixed ways are deleterious to the spirit. Repetition must be minimally tolerated, but both bad and good habitual ways are to be avoided. Genius was defined as freedom from habit.

A helpful discussion entitled *The Conjugal Relation* appeared in the Family Register one year after the gathering of the Oneida Community, when married couples began joining the Community. It was chiefly a talk by Noyes on occasion of a criticism of certain married pairs whose life appears not to have been harmonious. The spirit of jealousy, of claiming, of contrariness—covered and veiled elsewhere—was brought into public gaze. This article appeared in the January 18, 1869, *Circular*: "If by any fault of your own there's a state of discord between you and your wife, you are not capable of loving any other woman better than her," Noyes said. "You are mistaken if you suppose you could live any more happily with someone else. There is but one love—the love of God—the love that suffereth long and is kind, that thinketh no evil, is not easily provoked, is forgetting and forgiving, willing to spend and to be spent for its object, though it gets only ingratitude in return. All other love is poetical; and if a man has not this love toward his wife, he can have it for no other woman. A pair can render no more real substantial love to the Community than is going between themselves.

"I begin to approve of marriage as a test of civilization. We speak of unfavorable influences generated by monogamous marriage, but I'm convinced that marriage does not create the evils we find, it only detects them. I thank God for giving us such a crucible. It's cowardly to back out of difficult circumstances and ask God to make us better by change of condition. You say it's exceedingly difficult to do right and act out love under the unfavorable influences of marriage intimacy. This is the very fact that would rouse my ambition. If there is a spot that it is difficult to behave right in, I want to be put there. There is a way to behave right, to secure respect, and lay the foundation of harmony and spiritual music in the unfavorable condition of marriage intimacy. Let us quit the cowardly shrinking from this test, and not be contented with anything short of thoroughly fulfilling the righteousness of God in the prison of marriage. God will not let us out of special relationships into more liberty until we've taken a thorough discipline and learned to behave well there.

"You attribute your conjugal difficulties to the fact that familiarity breeds contempt and that the close relationship compelled by marriage leads to chafing—in short, to circumstances rather than spiritual causes. I advise all persons who are parties to matrimonial discord to look at the matter candidly and carefully; if the fault be in themselves, they are not capable of harmony and love with anybody else. They should resolve without reference to the conduct of others that discord shall not exist by their fault. Establishing in their hearts the love that Christ and Paul had to the church is to cure evil at the center; carry love and the righteousness of love into present circumstances and then let love arrange circumstances. If we cannot learn to respect each other and treat each other courteously and beautifully, then we cannot on the great scale of Community."

In his Home Talk, *Reverence and Love*, Noyes speaks about courtship, the period where great reverence for one another exists. "Each speaks more highly of the other than of self. Paul says, 'Let each person esteem others better that themselves;' and in everything like genuine heart-love this is the fact. As they come in contact, they meet many disagreeable things; their imaginations collapse; and then they conclude they were mistaken in each other. Are their second thoughts best? I say their first thoughts were best. Each is an unfathomable mystery to the other still, if they did but know it; each is not a mere human being, but an image and medium of God; and both make the mistake of thinking that they know the whole of each other; when the fact is, they have stopped at the show and forget that the Godhead is behind . . . . Beauty is God, and can be seen only while we have reverence and worship. That is what gives us eyesight. There is infinite depth and mystery in everything, if we only have discernment to see it. And from this it follows that knowledge of the truth, and faithfulness to the truth, will make us respectful, not to certain persons and things, but toward all things. Everything that exists will be to us a shrine of the mystery of God."

"While the New York *Observer* was worrying about unbridled sex at Oneida, Noyes's brother-in-law John Skinner wrote a letter to his brother Alanson about very little sex in the Community. Many who joined the Community did not know about the sexual principle. Skinner had observed by March 30, 1852, that if complex marriage were abandoned, it would make little difference. There was only about one-tenth the amount of sexual relations that occurs in ordinary married life in the world. 'There has been a strong temptation on the part of Community members at times to feel a restriction far greater than exists in ordinary society. They all state that they have had intervals of several months of total abstinence from sexual connection. The ordinary practice in the Association is for men to sleep in quarters for the men and women in the women's area. The effect of the principles and practices of our Association on the passion of amativeness, instead of making it irritable and ungovernable, has been to produce the opposite result, to quiet, civilize, and purify it. The amount of smutty talk or indecent behavior of any kind is far less in our Community than in ordinary society called respectable in the world; indeed, so much so that these things are scarcely seen or heard of among us.'

"The current of universal love flowed sluggishly in the early years for two reasons: the persistence of pleasure seeking, and jealousy about one's spouse. Sewell Newhouse, one of the earliest joiners of the Community who brought his expertise in making effective animal traps, broke about a year into his new life. 'Sewell had suffered from jealousy and the marriage spirit in its most intense form for some time past; he gave way to his feelings and committed an assault on Daniel Nash and Mrs. Newhouse as they were walking in the garden after meeting,' the *Oneida Journal* noted on July 10, 1850. 'He followed them and violently demanded an explanation of their course, telling them that murder was in his heart. Mr. Burnham, hearing the noise, came to their rescue. He drew Mr. Newhouse away and slept in his quarters with him all night. The next day Mr. Burt and George Noyes labored with Mr. Newhouse. By some exertion he confessed his faults in the meeting and wrote a communication to Noyes at the Brooklyn Community exposing his past life. Two evenings later, at a meeting of the men, Mr. Newhouse's confessions were read. George Noyes spoke with earnestness and power, urging the necessity of carrying sincerity clear through to the bottom of our hearts. If we do not believe in marriage of all to all, the Association must fail. Possessiveness and pairing off in the Community would blight the widening and deepening of love for all, so it was considered unhealthy for two people to become exclusively attached—to idolize only each other—however popular this experience may be. The heart should not be contracted with idolatry or selfish love in any form, but be free to love all. The marriage spirit that claims private property in love is to be put off entirely. Civilized amativeness is as unselfish in love as Community spirit is regarding property. Others agreed. Mr. Newhouse said he was thankful for Mr. Noyes's criticism.'"

The Community developed a love that thinks no evil, envies not, and seeks not its own. Love is something to give, not to claim. Love for a particular person, they discovered, enhanced rather than excluded love of another. "We should commence by seeking a first love that has the sanction of God and religion and truth. All subsequent attractions shall be organized into the first one, be helpers to it, in the position of the secondary to the primary." Noyes counseled in the February 21, 1856, *Circular*. "Have no love that does not give you rest. Love that torments you is not the true kind," he advised in the March 2, 1874, *Circular*. "Love free from the tendency to own, hoard, or exclude is gentle and sweet and beautiful.

"I stand as the advocate of liberty. I am accused of being an autocrat; but being a promoter of liberty, I do not hold any woman under espionage and I shall not rest till there is no such oppression here," Noyes wrote in 'False Love' in the March 15, 1969 and November 1869 *Circulars*. "Let a person become jealous and that very jealousy will destroy love and generate hatred. A man loves his wife and wants her love, but he begins to watch her and to be an accusing conscience to her; he is perfectly sure to make her dislike him, and so on the other side. All experience shows that the way to make persons love us is to make them free. It is a splendid declaration—one that will revolutionize this Association before we have done with it—that a man has no rights but what spring from his own attractions. The quicker all persons put themselves on that basis, the better. If your attractions are small, begin with being contented, and set to work to be more attractive. To stretch out our hands for love beyond our attractions is like children reaching after the moon. If you have power of law and possession, you can use it to oppress and secure the outward homage of love beyond your attractions, but all your reaching and stretching and grasping is worse than nothing. Selfish amativeness is a suicidal spirit. Love doesn't grow under such operations. Nothing but loveliness will ever start it."

Another difficulty was a fear of falling into, or being accused of, pleasure seeking. Noyes, working on publications in Brooklyn, wrote a letter to William on this subject: "Brother Perry: Mr. Leonard has reported to me facts that show that your amativeness is in a bad state, and I am bound for the church's sake as well as for your own to deal plainly with you. Your sexual history previous to your connection with us reveals unusual corruption. Though you had been a church member and a Perfectionist, you had been promiscuous and had several times contracted venereal disease. Without any disclosure of these facts, and of course without any hearty repentance of them, you availed yourself of our free principles and exposed two of our women here at Brooklyn to the poison still lurking in your system. Self-seeking and concealment thus far marked you as an unclean man. Your secret was drawn from you, and you passed through a judgment that I hoped would give you a new sense of the sacredness of love and make you an honorable man toward the other sex.

"But it now appears that, in the face of my counsel and in the face of your own conscience, since you found it necessary to walk in darkness [secretiveness], you have dealt with Mrs. S. as you dealt with Mrs. W. and Mrs. L., exposing her to distress and distrust if not to disease. Sensual self-seeking and concealment are as manifest here as heretofore, and you have now added to them gross insubordination. You are not a safe man, and you will not be till you have had a far deeper work of repentance, and have thoroughly laid to heart God's judgment of lechery. In view of this discovery of your character I see why I have not been able to forward your negotiations with Mary. As an honorable man I cannot advise you to offer yourself to her in your present condition. You are diseased in spirit if not in body. Now is the time to overhaul your accounts and make a thorough settlement. The act in question is not the thing to be judged—it is the spirit betrayed in that act. That spirit has blunted your sense of honor in love, and you must get rid of it; God does not tolerate it, and you shall not bring it in among us if I can prevent it. If you ask what you are to do, I answer: Turn away from all women to God, judge yourself, and open your heart to the church. If you are faithful you will find business enough of this kind to occupy you for some time. Moreover I counsel you now and forthwith to apprize the whole Association of your past. We must demand such disclosures from every man who proposes to enter our circle, otherwise we are open to all the plagues of licentiousness spiritual and physical. Every woman ought to know your condition as evinced by the facts that I have referred to. Every man ought to know that women have had intercourse with you. If there is one thing above all others that ought to be prized in such a community as ours, it is perfect frankness, especially in sexual matters. Our only hope of safety lies in throwing all open to the light and allowing spiritual criticism to do its work. God will insist that sincerity shall go before liberty. Expose yourself to the flaming sword that guards the way to the tree of life, and you may yet win our confidence.–Yours faithfully, John H. Noyes."

"If ever there was an illustration of Paul's philosophy, 'a little leaventh the whole lump,' we are seeing it now.[39] A spark of hell-fire has come in through Mr. Perry that would sweep the Association if it were not quenched," Harriet Skinner said to Mary Cragin. "Last evening George called a meeting of the leading members, read John's letter, and brought out facts showing that a licentious spirit has been disclosed in other quarters. Mrs. S. confessed yesterday that she had been with Hyde without Mr. Skinner's knowledge while she was professing to confide everything to him. This brought Hyde into judgment. Julia and Jane confessed that he had been trying to seduce them, and he confessed to Julia that he was with Mary Pomeroy during the evening meeting. It appears that he has been completely drunk with sensuality for some time, and all the while in special fellowship with Mr. Perry. Hyde, Mrs. S., and Mary P. have of all others in the Association been close to Mr. Perry, and have had a thorough run of his spiritual disease.

Harriet Noyes Skinner, a younger sister of John Humphrey Noyes and contributor to Community publications, was said to have had a large intellect and "almost omniscient" intuition. She joined him in Niagara Falls two years after the Community breakup.

"It was thought best, as Mr. Perry had consented, to read John's letter before the whole meeting and invite the spirit of judgment," Harriet continued. "George said that this spirit of licentiousness was imported by Mr. Perry from New York City, and was foreign to the Community. Several confessed what struggles with that spirit they had lately been through, and George said he believed the whole Association had felt it. The evidence that it had been withstood in a good measure was encouraging. Hyde came out with an apparently broken-hearted confession of being under its influence and forsaking it. This forenoon the Association met by appointment. Circumstances have connected Mr. Perry directly with the present disorderly state of our youth; testimony is pouring in about him. He was observed this morning to be fondling Ellen L. in an unbecoming way, and Ellen and Ann Eliza have been identified as the leak among the youth that lets in the pleasure-seeking spirit. They have lately had all the appearance of girls brought up in the city, roving about, calling at the store and shops, and spending their time in the streets. Mr. Perry has been giving them sweetmeats at the store. He has been trying to seduce Sarah J. She came out in the meeting with a desire to separate herself from his spirit. He was not present at this meeting, but we were scarcely out when he was seen to give Ellen a bunch of wild flowers; then Philena said that last night, as she was washing her hands, he came along and said he wished somebody would wash his hands. She did not know that he was under special criticism and playfully told him she would. When she washed one, she felt an involuntary disgust and told him he could wash the other himself. But he wanted to pay her, and forced her to receive a kiss. This after John's letter, you see.

"Mrs. S. has come out openly to him and seems disposed to take sides with the judgment of God, though it is hard. She has been tempted from the first to excuse herself and throw the blame upon the Association in one way or another. She said that George, Mr. Skinner, and the rest of us made a serious matter of her affair with Mr. Perry, but she couldn't see what harm there was in it. This spirit of confounding false love with true love has been like a nightmare for us all—we could feel that city spirit that attaches no sacredness to the expression of love. Charlotte went through a judgment and self-clearing about her connection with Mr. Hyde, so that she was in a condition to criticize him in a way that she never has been before. Altogether this affair has let in the judgment most seriously. It has thrown Mr. Hatch and Fidelia into the fire for things that have come out about their freedom months ago. And Charlotte says it will throw Mary P. into perfect obscurity for a while; she is taken out of the kitchen. Mrs. S., who has been in the kitchen, has expressed her inclination to retire from observation, but Charlotte advised her to keep herself as much in the light as possible; if she retreated to her room in a spirit of pride, it would be bad for her. Mrs. S. takes the advice and is very meek," Harriet concluded.

"Two meetings were held after these meetings to dispose of Mr. Perry's case. Further investigation showed a lack of subordination to Mr. Noyes and the Association, also an absence of sincere repentance; it was determined by a general vote of the Association that he be expelled from our body until he make a full proof by deeds that he is cleansed from that false spirit. Two months later on the advice of Mr. Noyes, Mr. Perry returned to Oneida. Mr. Noyes stated that Mr. Perry had given proof of his subordination and faithfulness, and that he with the other members of the Brooklyn family could unanimously recommend him to the Association."

Noyes counseled one of the young men whose natural tendency was to claim a certain woman as his alone. "I thought I would say a few things to you by letter," Noyes wrote. "You say you cannot forget Helen. I do not wish you to forget her, nor to love her less. But cannot you love her without *claiming* her, and quarreling with us and with God about her, and almost shooting yourself on her account? This is not the right kind of love. It is not strong enough. When you love her thoroughly with the love of God, you will be thankful that God made her, not for you but for himself, not to be used up as Hyde is using up Julia but to grow forever more and more beautiful in His garden; you will be thankful for the acquaintance with her that God has already given you, and for the hope of future more intimate fellowship; you will be thankful for her privileges here, for her love toward others and others' love toward her. I cannot forget Mrs. Cragin. Yet I will not quarrel with God because I am separated from her. On the contrary, I will be thankful for the past, and patient and hopeful for the future. You and George Hatch both love Helen. With that old greedy, worldly love, how would you ever reconcile your respective claims? Do you not see that it is best she should be here away from both of you till you both learn to love her in the Community spirit? You have a good opportunity to learn the great lesson that I learned long ago by the same kind of experience you are now going through, that God owns all things, even our sweethearts and ourselves."

ASSESSMENT OF COMPLEX MARRIAGE

"Two hundred and fifty sober persons have lived together a quarter of a century under the rule of Male Continence in constant observation of its tendencies and effects," reported John and Harriet Noyes's son, Theodore, the Community's Yale-trained physician. "Their experiment has gone on through all the vicissitudes that reach from one generation to a second. Many applications of their sexual discovery that were in the far-off future when first published, are now matters of experience and found effectual, healthy, uplifting, and not injurious."[40]

"Experience proves that it originated in the mind of God," one said. "I have seen great beauty and celestial purity in it and I'm sure that nothing but omnipotence could create such blissful, soul-expanding, and mind-elevating realities," said another.

"My Dear Brother:—Ecclesiastical movements against the Oneida Community have made me desire to give my testimony on the question of the character and influence of the Community in respect to sexual morality and passional purity," wrote James W. Towner from Cleveland, Ohio, on November 27, 1873. "I have been a lawyer with quite a range of experience; and a school teacher, a preacher, and itinerant preacher who 'boarded round.' Nowhere else have I seen among men and women real chastity in word and act and bearing—the modesty, delicacy, and genuine refinement—that I have seen in the Oneida Community. The question is: what sort of a passional or sexual character does its teaching and its life tend to form? is it to lasciviousness or to chastity? to animal indulgence or to rational restraint? what is its influence? Does it lead a man to look on a woman to lust after her in his heart or does it cast out the demons of lust and sexual tyranny and fill their place with love that seeketh not her own and worketh no ill to its neighbor? In my judgment, the Oneida Community is not only immensely above ordinary society, even the best of it, but it has been the means of giving me an inspiration in respect to sexual morality that has enabled me to overcome passion and lust to an extent I often dreamed of and longed for formerly, but was never able to attain.

"During my earlier years, and most of my marriage life, my experience in sexual matters was that of the 7th of Romans—*When I would do good evil was present with me*. All the helps from religious influences, science, physiology, esthetics, and human experience availed not to lift me above the 7th of Romans. From the time that I was brought into contact with the Oneida Community in 1866, I got help. I was lifted up toward a higher plane of not only aspiration, but attainment. I well remember the first visit I made to the Community. I had been some years before to a limited extent a Berlin Heights free-lover. I was acquainted with the social theory of the Community, had abandoned my former "free love" views, and was in a state of mind well prepared to receive impressions of and influences from a higher and purer character than any I had yet felt in life; and I remember as but yesterday how hallowed and divine seemed to me the spirit that reigned in the life of the men and women I met there.

"I was with you only a few days, but the baptism I then received was a baptism of the spirit. From that time my life began to change; I soon adopted the practice of Male Continence and have never swerved from it since. I began to study the social theory as a part of God's truth about our souls as well as our bodies, and sexual intercourse in its relation to religion. I have become so filled with the idea that only as a means of glorifying God is such intercourse permissible, that I have come to hate and abominate even the virtues as well as the vices of my former sexual life and of passional indulgence, as of the devil himself. I have, through the power of Christ in you and in my soul, been enabled to "overcome the wicked one" in the amative nature. I have been all this time only indirectly and remotely under your influence; but it is through even this connection with you that the work has been wrought. I have visited you three times since 1866, remaining twelve, fourteen and twenty days at those several times. I have become familiarly acquainted with many of your prominent members, young and old; I have been treated almost as a member of the family.

"Regardless of the external form or the legal conformity or nonconformity of sexual relations at Oneida Community, the Synods and Conferences will have to grapple with it. What do those relations do for God's work in the soul? Are they helping to save from sin—from selfishness and all that is mean, low, sensual, vulgar, narrow, contemptible, unmanly, and tyrannical—and to cleanse amativeness from being a cage of unclean spirits and to lift it up into a life of worship, of love and purity? What kind and quality of men and women is the Oneida Community making, as to their relations to each other in all that is high, noble, generous, manly, and womanly? I wanted to bear my testimony," Towner concluded, "feeling called to do so by the inner monitor."

Letters from Community men to Mr. Noyes were mostly inspired by talks they had about their marriage relations, never designed for any eye but his, but they were read aloud to the family, for example:

> "Dear Mr. Noyes: Your talk about complex marriage has invested our Community relation with a new and sacred beauty, one that every honorable man will prize as he prizes his own soul. The results of your definition of our union must be to increase Community love and unity, but it may legitimately enhance self-respect. The thought of being joined in an eternal marriage union by God is exceedingly ennobling and dignifying. It makes our covenant with each other holy and precious beyond any legal ceremony, and our responsibility in being faithful to that covenant, a surpassingly sacred and honorable one.

"Living in equality with women without possessiveness or jealousy changed my character," said one Community member; "it roots out selfishness" another attested. "It brought me very near to God." The Community's social practice "delivered me from the bondage of an inordinate amativeness, which has been the torment of my life." Complex Marriage required a higher level of human interaction, truly valuing others' well-being, than was often found in ordinary life, and Male Continence was a discipline to be mastered. "I have had a new sense lately of the happiness that is accessible to us," Mr. W. wrote in the Christmas Day 1871, *Circular*. "There is a world of happiness that we can enter into if we can learn the art of doing so—happiness that doesn't depend on anything of an external nature. I have touched it from time to time. I can hardly explain it. It is not produced by anything external—I seem to have access to a spirit that is happy and victorious. It is an art to be happy, one that will bear study. The fruit of the spirit is love, joy, peace, and happiness."

"One specific and very significant sign of *moral* health resulted from Male Continence—the natural desire for children, which has almost died out in general society. Instead of continual dread of [unplanned] child-bearing, common in the nineteenth century, the demand for offspring in the Community and especially among women was far ahead of the supply," Theodore's summation concluded. "Complex Marriage gave the Community a higher-than-average happiness compared to monogamous marriage, forcing persons to develop their capacity to love and be loved with a sustained concentration rarely found in the outside world. Complex Marriage caused people to be more attractive, attentive, and engaged, as we are in courtship." Theodore found that 60 percent of Community members found the experience of Complex Marriage good. Forty percent would like more freedom in choosing partners—especially younger people in later years of the Community. A reason for dissatisfaction was written to be read at the evening meeting. In 1861, a woman expressed a chief goal of Complex Marriage—more general love. "I wish it were more popular than it is for the young to love the old, the handsome to love the less so, the educated to love the less educated—in short, that love might truly pervade all hearts."

Noyes emphasized just that: "Let us consider whether we may do good, get good, and feel good by drawing nearer to those who are not fully appreciated—and don't overlook the charms of older women. Let us be heroes in love! We can end loneliness by rooting out selfishness. To be a healthy, happy community, all we need is to let God's love have free course among us. God's love is not contracted and egotistical, but expansive and universal. Such love is a boundless ocean, unlocking a fountain in the soul. Our principles may look radical and licentious, but these testimonies show that much good has been achieved. Many have been saved from bondage, health has been secured, and the troubles of the flesh prevented. I am delighted to see so many distinctly express their social nature as sacred. To be acceptable to God," Noyes taught, "sex must be an expression of true love and respect; it must be elevating, not infatuation that excludes thought of spiritual growth through spiritual sexuality. One might as well think of loving a particular tune and no other, as to think of loving some particular woman to the exclusion of all others. What we love in the particular tune, is *music*; what we love in the particular woman, is *love*—and love is God."

"Our general morality and good behavior are admitted in late denunciations against us," the November 17, 1873, *Circular* noted. "The only allegation is that the intercourse of the sexes within our own circle is unrestricted—subject to no regulation whatever. It is the reverse of truth. The facts are well known to all who have the slightest acquaintance with our principles and practices. To those who have no such acquaintance, we offer the following advice: Do not believe this assertion by prejudiced and ignorant men who cannot really believe it themselves, for they know that human society cannot exist without some regulation of sexual passion. Take pains to ascertain the truth for yourselves. When you do, you will find that intercourse of the sexes in the Oneida Community is under more stringent regulation than it is in general society. We aver, (1) that the intercourse of the sexes in the Oneida Community is open to the criticism and controlled by the good sense of the entire body instead of being left to the mercy of each man's passions dealing with woman in single-handed and irresponsible privacy, as in marriage; (2) that the intercourse of the sexes in the Oneida Community is, next to religion, the great subject of scientific and conscientious study instead of being left to the sensual drift of fashion and ignorance, as it usually is; (3) that the intercourse of the sexes in the Oneida Community is restricted by the voice and heart of all to entire abstinence from the propagative act, except when propagation is agreed upon by the parties with the approbation of the Community; (4) that the practical result of these regulations, and others similar, is a state of society approaching much nearer to the self-denial of the Shakers than to the imaginary anarchy with which we are charged. At a regular meeting of the Community, the foregoing expression was accepted by unanimous vote and ordered to be published. —William A. Hinds, Chairman."

Most personal diaries and journals of Oneida Community members were burned in 1947, a tragedy and a significant loss to scholarship. The Oneida Community was a unique experiment in human living and thought; knowing the many perspectives of those who lived there would have been invaluable. The few diaries that survived the conflagration show complex varieties of relationships, and give us a glimpse of humans freed to develop many sides of themselves who lived that charity described in 1st Corinthians 13. They show how deeply the great family loved and valued each other spiritually, how they worked and played and studied together, made music and produced plays. Most astonishing was how extraordinarily transparent all Community members were to each other. A surviving journal describes five loving relationships (Chapter 12), some in the throes of suffering from the prohibition of exclusive love, others recovered from this state, and the joyful discovery of an unsuspected lover. Intense attachments were recognized and even encouraged in the Community, because special affinities do have the power of celestial love; but author Tirzah Miller heartily respected the Community's vigilance against exclusive love, which she acknowledged can occur all too easily. The difference between *special* love and *exclusive* love was evident by the discernment of any hint that one wishes to monopolize another person, by feelings of jealousy or possessiveness, or becoming emotionally dependent on one person. A member might be sent to live in the Wallingford Community branch in these cases.

"A lighter work is given to us than was given to the Primitive Church," Noyes said. "It is for us to get the victory over enjoyment; they had to get the victory over suffering. We possess our amativeness instead of being possessed by it. Persons are as free and polite to one another in sexual privileges as in any others; we have the same freedom on that subject as in eating and drinking, taking walks, or any other enjoyment. The feeling of exclusive love with me is a thing gone by, as far off as the shores of the Old World; I hear nothing of it in the Association and I have a quick eye to detect anything of that kind in myself or anybody else. There is not only no quarreling among us, but there is no temptation to quarrel. All troubles, too, about involuntary propagation are at an end."

"Mr. Noyes's remarks about exclusive love gone by in his Home Talk, *Our Victories*, are full of encouragement," wrote John Miller. "I can say sincerely with Mr. Noyes that exclusive love with me is also gone. Two years ago we acted with constant reference to exclusiveness—we had to watch constantly to prevent the fire of jealousy from burning up our social building. Now it never enters our heads that we can offend anyone by the expression of love, except in the case of new members. This is one of the greater miracles. Almost every married person in the Community is in love with somebody besides their married companion, sensible of an electricity not to be accounted for by the working of their own spirits alone."

"The Community's emphasis on the virtues of variety in relationships might be misconstrued as a rejection of commitment, a love them and leave them mentality. Nothing could be further from the truth. Temporary relationships were unknown in the Community. When one truly loves another, one remains faithful. 'We must not turn from one to another; God will forbid it,' Noyes said. 'Our coming into relations of love with others does not divorce us from our first love.' The Community celebrated the thirty-second anniversary of John and Harriet and their enduring love. 'The unity between them flows on like a river year after year,' the April 17, 1871, *Oneida Circular* noted. 'It has grown so wide and deep that it is a reservoir of life to the whole Community.' Yet theirs was not an exclusive love, which they explicitly and willingly agreed upon from the beginning. Their union radiated the higher love the Community valued; Noyes felt that even love that is content with one special person should be transcended. To settle for even a fully satisfying relationship was contrary to God's plan for human potential. 'I don't care how much special love there is in the sense of warmth, ecstasy, devotion,' he wrote at age seventy-two. 'Because one loves another does not in any way detract from or end the other relationship. Faithfulness to one person does not prevent loving many with equal ardor,' he wrote in the May 16, 1870, *Circular*. 'Love should be fervent, but not adhesive,' he said, 'never hankering for future and special attention, by recognizing Christ in all.'"

"Fidelity was valued perhaps more in the Community than in conventional marriage. Complex Marriage was the *marriage* of each man to each woman, caring for the other's well-being in every aspect of life. A letter was received in which the writer said he'd heard that the Community had made a physiological discovery called 'male constancy' or 'male continence'—he was uncertain which, but wished us to send him tracts on the subject. 'The physiological discovery relates to male continence, but our correspondent might have been assured that the Community has also discovered the secret of male constancy. Judging from the increasing frequency of divorces and other signs of social unfaithfulness outside the Community, instruction is very much needed. The institution of marriage is in some degree of peril if we trust the reiterations of the leading newspapers,' reports the March 1868 *Circular*. 'Blame is laid upon the growing evils of society—licentiousness and extravagance. When the Community is thought of or mentioned by outsiders,' the *Circular* notes, 'the prominent idea in the mind of the person speaking is that it is a society of people who are living in promiscuous sexual intercourse, *worse than the Mormons!* Others call it worse than a brothel, to give adequate expression of their horror of it.'"

"Complex Marriage is not what distinguishes the Community from the world or from professed Christians," the *Circular* editor stated. "The Community can exist without that theory and did so for years at Putney and at Oneida. It exists with us and in us nearer to Shakerism in the form of abstinence through Male Continence. Lamenting the low conceptions of salvation that many Christians have, a Methodist minister shared what one of his prominent members said: that if it were not for avoiding hell-fire hereafter, he would not trouble himself to serve God—but he wanted to be saved from that! Mr. Noyes and the Community have a very different idea of salvation—it is deliverance from sin itself, being saved not from anything without, but from something within us, from an evil spirit. Salvation is being separated from that spirit by having Christ's Spirit take possession of us and become our life. It is not in any sense an external but in every sense an internal and spiritual work. When the Holy Spirit has full possession of our hearts it will lead to all that is pure and useful, and we are willing to trust that Spirit, lead where it may. 'I am the vine, ye are the branches: he that abides in me, and I in him, the same brings forth much fruit.'"

> "If you are born of God, then in you God will green;
> His godhead is your sap, your beauty is in Him."
> —Angelus Silesius, *God Blossoms in His Branches*[41]

5

Community Children: Many Mentors

In this great family, all the children were loved and mentored by many adults whose varying personalities, skills, and interests enriched the children and gave respite to others. "If anyone doubts whether a woman without babies of her own can love other folk's children," said Harriet, "I wish they could spend a day in the East Room and see Sarah and Chloe with their little brood around them."

"So do I," Charlotte enthused. "If it's a miracle for a woman to love in such an unselfish way, then we have daily and hourly miracles among us! What mother ever gave more wise and loving care to her own darling, than Sarah and Chloe do to their nine two-year-olds."

Toddlers in front of the Mansion House. The North Tower is in the background, John Humphrey Noyes's apartment.

"Watch Chloe," Harriet replied. "What a warm motherly kiss she gives this one on her knee, while another at her side pulls out her comb and begins to comb Chloe's hair! How ready she is with a song or a story. What a way she has of getting up pretty plays and teaching the little ones to say their verses and rhymes."

"And listen to Sarah's soothing voice when a child is vexed or hurt," Charlotte added. "How she understands the art of smoothing down the ruffled temper and kissing the finger to make it well. She watches over their dispositions, their health, their diet, and their sleeping with a mother's care."

"Oh, their motherly arms and laps!" Harriet exclaimed. "When the lamps are lighted and the little ones get tired and sleepy, you'll often see them with a child on each knee while a soothing story or song prepares them for bed."

"How the children love them! It's no sham; all is genuine," Charlotte agreed. "I was sitting in the East Room the other evening at sunset when George Wallingford came in full of glee from his visit to his mama at the Villa. I took the little fellow on my lap and in a grandmotherly way was listening to his prattle and asking him about his visit, when Miss Chloe came in. You should have seen how quickly he climbed into her lap and what a hugging he gave her—then he began to kiss her, to stroke her face and lay his head on her, repeating little expressions of love till I really thought Chloe was almost embarrassed. I suppose according to worldly sentiment, I ought to have felt jealous to see the little boy leave me for her and give her so much love."

"O, yes!—philoprogenitiveness (see glossary) would have us feel almost indignant at Chloe, as if she had got the child's heart away from you."

"What nonsense this worldly sentiment of jealousy about love is! I am richer and the child is richer and happier for the love between him and Chloe and between him and everybody else, related or not," agreed Charlotte.

PRINCIPLES OF RAISING CHILDREN

"In their second summer at Oneida, the principles of raising children were briefly laid out in the August 11, 1849, *Circular*: first, to avoid as far as possible giving children occasion for transgression by putting them under a multitude of laws; and second, to correct their faults usually by addressing their reason and conscience, and winning them to obedience by kindness, patience, and gentle words. Once in a great while, when there is a signal occasion for it, give them a tremendous rebuke such as will leave its impression forever.

"On August 12, 1850, Noyes and senior members at the Brooklyn Community proposed that two of their number, Erastus Hamilton and Charlotte Miller, go to Oneida and undertake the spiritual education of the children. A clique of young men and women in the community consisting of Hyde, Julia, and others were in exclusive fellowship with one another. 'My plan has been to devise some method by which the church could get the lead of the children,' Noyes said, 'and thus let in upon them whatever good influences are coming down from heaven upon us. I do not expect that the children will understand all the movements of the Association. It is not possible for them to do so until their minds are enlarged. How can two persons be at peace with each other when one is a great deal wiser than the other? It is not possible if the inferior insists on understanding all that the superior does.'"

Noyes knew one thing in his bones: "There is one way for me to have fellowship with God, who presents me the chart of his infinite counsels, of which I can understand but very little. I understand enough to stake my all on the assertion that God is right and drop the idea of understanding all his ways. I will have a spirit of confidence and modesty and then no matter how high he is above me, love can flow. But what if I should say, I cannot have peace with God without understanding all his ways. That would not be a happy state of mind for me. God says: *As the heavens are higher than the earth, so are my ways higher than your ways, and my thoughts than your thoughts.* In the same way we find men who are inspired by God to such an extent that we can endorse them without reserve and without understanding them; these are one of the greatest gifts that God can give."

Ascending fellowship

Thus was born the principle of *ascending fellowship*. "I cannot have peace with God unless I keep the ascending fellowship predominant, so I have felt bound to introduce that principle into the church. I want the children to settle it in their hearts that I am a man of God, and there will be an end of the insistence upon understanding all that I am about. I found it necessary to demand that they seek fellowship with those above them, and I went right in among them offering to be their playmate and inviting them up into fellowship with the Association. I invite these boys to cooperate with God in the establishment of this feeling, assuring them that I have now in my heart more love for the boys and children than ever before.

"Modesty in conjunction with confidence in their parents constitutes the righteousness of children. Modesty and confidence should prevail over the fondness for pleasure and other feelings, and when the two different kinds of feelings come into collision, children should use all the power they have to make the right ones prevail. This is their faith—looking upward, and is the attitude of mind that will eventually let them into fellowship with God and his family. I felt as though I had found the whole of salvation, almost, when I had settled that principle of ascending fellowship between the superior and inferior. Without that principle, fellowship on any extensive scale would be impossible, so long as there is such a difference of intellect. Let a man wait patiently and he will find that the principle will give him a hundredfold for all that it requires of him and will eventually fill him with the richness of God."

"Mary Cragin's large-heartedness, earnestness, and motherly talent laid the foundation for all that is good in our children's house. She had fine natural qualifications for the government of children, being very loving and yet capable of severity. Her affection was strong, but her love of righteousness was stronger, so that she could be fond without weakness. She had rare opportunities to develop her faculty in early life as mistress of children's schools in New York City, and she was not long in the Putney Community before her particular function as a mother was discovered. When a separate family for the children was instituted at the Oneida Community, she threw herself into the work in the spirit of a pioneer, and carried through that great weaning—a weaning for all generations after it in the Community; for what in that first experiment seemed unnatural and cruel, now seems rational and desirable. Everybody will soon see how they thrive on Community affection. Mothers remembered how judicious Mary was in selecting persons for the care of the children's house—a mother who would be faithful in details, watchful of the toes and fingers; another should be an executive; another musical; another strong in the love of righteousness; and all should be mediums of the Community spirit.

"Her first principle was a good spirit. She did not rely on a multitude of rules, but on the children's confessing Christ in them a good spirit as soon as they could speak; also on Bible instruction, and on the personal influence of their guardians and of the older children on the younger. One young man who belonged to the generation that knew Mary, said he had a vivid recollection of her dislike of frivolousness in children—not that she would have them dull, but she disliked meaningless plays. Another remembered how when they were restless and giddy she would have them sit down and be still ten or fifteen minutes. Another, how she used to frolic with them in the meadow, abandoning herself for the time to their merriest mood and letting her heart all out in affectionate demonstrations, and then sending them about their business. Another remembered her teaching the children to say the eighth chapter of Proverbs and the 119th Psalm in unison, and other scriptures. Another, how she told stories with wonderful effect that left their impression to this day. Another, how she taught them to sing, drilling them while very young in reading notes and beating time. Another remembered the letters she wrote after she went to Brooklyn to work, letters by which she still presided over the welfare of the children."

"I well remember Mrs. Cragin's four-week stay at Wallingford, the spring before she died, and her labors with us children," Harriet Allen reminisced. "George in particular," she added. "He was called a very spunky boy—never could bear disappointment with good grace. He wanted to go to Hartford with Henry. Father said no, he could not go. Whereupon George threw himself down, kicked, bumped his head against the floor and screamed, 'Oh father, I shall die, I shall *die*!'—this being a favorite expression of his when not allowed to have his own way. Mary's effect on him was almost miraculous—he never had one of those passionate, screaming times again, which had previously almost daily. The change in George made a great impression upon me; Mary was different."

George Allen remembered the incident vividly, reported in an October 1868 *Circular*: "I was twelve years old when Mrs. Cragin came to our house. The day after her arrival, my elder brother was leaving for Hartford and I had a partial promise of accompanying him, but father concluded I had better stay home. This was a greater disappointment than I could quietly submit to, and as usual in times of great distress I threw myself upon the floor—rolled, thrashed, and kicked round generally. Mother tried to pacify me, but Henry evidently enjoyed aggravating me. He called me a whining bawl-baby, and applied other equally appropriate terms. I retaliated, said he was an old fool and told him to shut up. Mr. Cragin had been a quiet listener in the next room—unknown to us—and walked in when the uproar was at its height. I'd been lying on my back applying my boot-heels to the floor, but straightened up the instant he appeared and told me that Mrs. Cragin would like to see me in the other room.

"'George, let us find out what the Bible has to say about disobedience, and about the tongue—what an unruly member it is,' she said. For nearly half an hour she looked at passages and talked kindly but very earnestly to me. I read a few verses as she pointed them out, but the tears came so fast I could scarcely see. I cried bitterly from genuine grief because I had been a bad boy. The effect of her words was to make me feel humbled and penitent. The disappointment of the morning was entirely forgotten. I wanted to be good, and Mrs. Cragin's influence made it easy to be so. I left the room happy and thankful, and with a purpose in my heart to govern the unruly tongue and hasty temper that had made so much trouble. That purpose formed seventeen years ago, has been and is steadily growing."

"Mary Cragin kept in fellowship with a child in spite of little misbehaviors, but when its disobedience became flagrant she would give it a decisive criticism—a spanking, perhaps—that it would never forget. She set a high value on obedience; she was heard to say that she would rather her children should die than grow up in willfulness. She did not spare their flesh when its suffering would promote their spiritual good. She never left a child that she'd corrected under condemnation. After punishing the child with all needed severity, she would love it and expect good of it. She attended the morning meetings that she instituted, which have continued for decades; these gatherings were attractive to the children, though conducted in the most serious spirit. 'I've made a verse for you that you may learn to sing for me to the tune of *Begone Dull Care*:

> Bad temper go/You and I shall never agree, Bad temper go/You shall never stay with me;
> For I will always kind and mild/And gentle try to be, And do to others as I wish/That they should do to me.
> *I*-spirit go,/You shall never stay with me; *We*-spirit come,/You and I shall always agree;
> I have gentle love/That seeketh not her own; for it's not good to have/Things for myself alone.'

Mary Cragin taught children in New York City and introduced Noyes's writings to her husband George. They joined the Putney Association in 1840. She drowned in 1851 at age 40 when their sloop, transporting products, capsized in a storm on the Hudson River.

"She wanted to have everything done for the children from attraction, and would change attendants when necessary to secure this. Was there a weakly, unattractive child? She would advise the nurses to take it right into their hearts, doing so herself, nourishing it in the most tender manner, and in that way effecting great improvement where criticism failed. The Community women feel that after twenty years of experience, they have only now come up as a class to her standard of unselfishness and public spirit. All the children were hers; when she died, many children felt her loss as much as her own."

BEGINNING OF THE CHILDREN'S DEPARTMENT

"I offered to take care of little Theodore for a few weeks," wrote Emily Otis, one of many care-giving mothers, "because, my room being next door, I knew he'd not been very well for a number of nights; his mother's rest had been broken so much that I knew she must be nearly worn out. One night about one o'clock, I was awakened by her trying to sing him to sleep. I suppose her voice was subdued for fear of disturbing the occupants of the adjoining rooms, but it sounded so plaintive that I thought I could never go to sleep while I knew she was so in need of rest. I left the three little boys who sleep in my room and told her that I would be glad to take care of little Theodore. He soon became quiet and as I watched his precious face I felt such a warm love for him that I thought I would willingly do anything for him. I could hardly wait till morning to tell his mother how glad I would be to take care of him until she could recuperate. When I proposed it to her she said that she'd be glad to have me take him awhile, and presumed that he would do better with someone who felt strong and well. I told Father Noyes that I was going to take care of little Theodore.

"Why don't you take the four," he replied. "A strong woman like you ought to be able to manage as many as that." I replied that I would take all he gave me. He may have been jesting, but I'd often thought of simplifying the rearing of small children. When I found he thought seriously of the plan and others were enthusiastic in making arrangements for securing helpers and putting it into execution, I did not feel like retreating. My only hope of success was in the revival spirit, which would provide enthusiasm and loving hearts for our work, and insure good results. After two weeks' trial, I can truly say that I never enjoyed any business as I have my work in the nursery. The move has the approval of the heavens.

"The writer of the foregoing has had one child born in the Community in circumstances of comparative luxury. She is an enthusiast in all progress—has great strength of character—is strong in tenderness and strong in common sense. The writer of the following, Mrs. Jane Bailey, had five children in marriage outside the Community in somewhat straitened circumstances, which gives her very desirable qualifications. She knows how to make children take care of themselves all they should. She has displayed in our other infant department a remarkable faculty for making the little ones happy by making them good."

"When the new way was proposed by Mr. Noyes I felt very enthusiastic," Jane wrote, "not dreaming that I would have anything to do with it except to look on. It was with some fear and trembling that I began to help in this work. The first morning I went down to the drawing-room expecting only Theodore and Allan would be there, when the door opened and Alice came in bringing Corinna, and placed her in my arms saying to her, 'Here is your mama Bailey.' I do not know how she felt, but my own heart was full and I had hard work to keep back the tears. It seemed to me that the spirit and presence of Christ came in with that baby and her mother, and it has stayed with us. I said to myself, If God has given Alice grace and strength to give up her babe into our care, he will give us grace and strength to do the right thing by it. I had a new baptism of faith and love. The feeling that the mothers are in full sympathy with us gives us good heart. I've never felt so interested and given up to any work that I have in this, and it was never so easy for me to ask God for help in any work as this. Little Allan who cried for his mother and would hardly be comforted for the first two days, is now very happy and lets her come in and go out without any perturbation. The babies are all well. We spread an old quilt on the carpet and they sit on it with their playthings a good share of the time, and seem to think it is the nicest place in the house. Their fathers come in often and give them a tossing, and baby-lovers all through the Community find a new source of enjoyment. The four are getting into the habit of taking their naps at about the same time, which gives us a chance to rest."

"There are certain hearsays about the Community that are as inexpugnable as the Canada thistle—root them out year by year but they reappear as persistently as the daisies in the meadow," notes the June 23, 1873, *Circular* in an article about their youngest children. "One of these rumors is that we take the babies away from their mothers at a frightfully early age, and after that the poor little things never know their mothers from the rest of womankind. We have been able to repel this odious impeachment *in toto*. The mother nurses and cares for her baby with undivided attention for the first few months of its novitiate in this strange world, and then when it is nicely weaned, we've found that children a year and a half old can be brought up together to a great advantage. A child continually demanding mother's attentions, making itself sick with innocent restlessness, will go into our nursery and soon be well and happy. Mothers bring their babies back to their rooms at 6:00 p.m. and they sleep with their mothers, who next morning dress them, give them breakfast, and keep them till 7:30 a.m. when they are carried to the children's wing. Loving Community caregivers are waiting in a large, airy room, twenty-eight by twelve, carpeted and furnished with cribs, low beds, and four windows to the east. The two in charge are relieved by other motherly women at meal times and fixed hours, and fathers take the babies for a ride and girls amuse them—kind hands on every side. They have the best kind of care, far better care than a weak and over-burdened mother could give them—better care than a mother under any conditions could give them—at a vast reduction of cost.

"Community circumstances are always teaching us new economies and better ways of doing things. Why not begin at least as soon as the baby is weaned? The nursing period is somewhat shortened with us, not often exceeding nine months. Now we have four babies from seven to eleven months and are trying the experiment of putting them together through the day. Instead of each mother taking care of her own child in her own room, we put the four into one room under the care of two women not their mothers. They have the most gifted infant culturists we can find among us, and so the best kind of training is insured.

"Our reasons for this move connect with our Community circumstances and our Community principles. As to circumstances: if mothers are to have the chief care of their babies, the Community may not be as good a place as the isolated family, where the mother has numerous duties as wife and housekeeper that force her attention away from her children; a child therefore learns increasingly to entertain and care for itself. Then her second child soon crowds out the first and she cannot stop to dote. The young mother in the Community is under no such necessities. She has no cooking nor washing nor ironing to do—her housekeeping is all done for her. A toddler soon finds out how much attention it can have, and exacts more and more. Let a fond mother have no compelling cares and there is great danger that her child will enslave her and get spoiled for want of wholesome neglect. Many persons live and labor as though the great end of existence were to serve their children, and especially to see that all their superficial wants are satisfied. They have little thought of disciplining and educating them for God; that is left to take care of itself. If you let your heart be dependent on your children for happiness, they will instinctively find it out and soon act as though you were made for their pleasure. The reverse of that is nearer the truth. We must ever realize that their destiny, as well as ours, is in the hands of God.

"Our Community principles in regard to 'Woman's Sphere' have governed in this movement. We do not believe with Reverend Dr. Todd that motherhood is the chief end of woman's life—that she was made for the children she can bear. She was made for God and herself. She has a spiritual nature that lifts her up to God and there is her highest sphere, where there is 'neither male nor female.' In association with man she was not made first of all to be the mother of his children, but to be his companion and lover—to be what she is in courtship rather than what she is in marriage. Set aside sentimentalism and exceptional cases: woman's sphere under marriage is well characterized by Mr. Noyes in his Bible Argument, as that of a propagative drudge. She is not that in the Community. She has children only by choice, and her drudgery as a mother is to be reduced to the minimum. Queens and princesses are considered of too much value in themselves, too necessary as leaders, to be allowed to surrender their time and attention day and night for the care of their children. Women of rank and wealth are accorded the same privilege. Especially is it claimed by women of genius and women devoted to art or literature. The mother herself, her health, her faculties, her own wellbeing as a member of society, receives the first consideration and her function as nurse is subordinate. This is undoubtedly the law of nature and justice, which, as the world becomes enlightened and women rise to their true place, will be more and more observed. It has drawbacks. To gain her own personal freedom, the Princess of Wales must resign her newborn child to the bosom of a hireling. This is true of all women who do not nurse their children. This state is indeed unnatural and must give a true mother many a pang."

Four letters from four "bereaved" mothers:

"June 15, 1873. Dear Aunt H., You asked me to tell you my feelings and experience since giving up the care of my baby and I am glad to do so, as you knew so well my trials and temptations when the move was first proposed. My troubles were of short duration and I gave her up at last with the others, heartily, feeling that she would have every want supplied and that I should be a better and happier woman for doing so. Corinna has now been in the nursery two weeks, and as my room is nearby, I've observed the working of the new plan; I am convinced that she is happier, and has as good if not better care than when I had entire charge of her myself. When I go to get her at six o'clock, she is always delighted to see me, and I—feeling rested and fresh instead of tired and often impatient—take more real enjoyment in her than before. The love I've had for my baby has never given me the happiness that I expected to realize, with feelings of anxiety lest she should be sick or that some accident might come to her. Now that trouble has been taken from me and in its place I have a feeling of rest and thankfulness. I now realize, as I did not before, that the old way of each mother caring exclusively for her own child begets selfishness and idolatry, and in many ways tends to degrade woman. The new system works well in every respect, but particularly do I appreciate the opportunity it affords me of joining in public work and going home to God every day. —Yours for giving up all that stands in the way of improvement and the revival, Alice Ackley."

"To have the babies cared for together during the day by others than their respective mothers, seemed to me, after the first flutter of motherly feeling had subsided a little, a wise and beneficial one—good for both mothers and children. I was better prepared to accept it perhaps because I had not been strong enough to take the entire care of my child myself, and had become accustomed to leave him with others. But the advantages of this new method are much greater than I anticipated. The love between me and my boy is not lessened but rather enhanced by standing a little aloof from him. I do not suffer about him but truly enjoy my liberty; he never cries when I leave him. When I take him in the evening, instead of being tired and worn, I feel strong and fresh, and he is full of glee and baby joy. He is happier during the day to be with his mates than when alone with me. Before putting him in with the others he was a difficult child to manage about his naps—often tiring me out completely before going to sleep. I might rock him, walk with him, swing him, or draw him in his basket, it was all the same—always a struggle. Now I have only to lay him on the bed and in a few moments he is sound asleep, with seldom any resistance. The benefit to me is very great: it relieves me of a care that was too great for my strength; it gives me time and opportunity for other occupations; it chastens my affections and frees me from absorbing distractions. —A. S. H."

"Dear Aunt H. — When the plan was first proposed it took me somewhat by surprise; I hardly need tell you that I had conflicts with my motherly nature for a few days," wrote Charlotte Leonard. "But I resolved that my feelings should not govern me; that I would be obedient to the Community inspiration and trust God to take care of my feelings. And sure enough he has. After two weeks' trial I can assure you that I like it. I like it for my own sake and I like it for my baby's sake. It commends itself to me as a wise move, and as a blessing to both mothers and children. It is better for both of us in many ways. It relieves me from a long confinement and puts me again into the family current and public service, where I am always happy, while I know that my babe is just as well cared for and is happier even than when I had him all to myself. His necessary wants are all supplied, but he does not have that special exclusive attention that so often spoils a child. I enjoy my work during the day and enjoy taking my baby at six o'clock. He is always tickled to see me, and when I take him back the next morning he is glad to see his mothers and the other youngsters again. I am not afraid that the love between me and my child will be diminished at all, but it will be chastened by a higher love—a love for serving God and the Community—and that is just what I want. I am thankful for anything that will save me from idolatrous philoprogenitiveness [excessive mother-love], the weakness of many women. I attribute my good experience to the revival spirit in the family. I would have been weak by myself, but I am strong in the strength of the whole Community. I weaned my little one last week and he has scarcely known it—thanks to the new system. I do not believe a baby was ever weaned more easily."

"When the proposal came to us mothers to give up the care of our infants during the day, I had many conflicting feelings about it. Although my heart ached at the thought of separation, I had a secret feeling that it would prove a relief in the end. My own experience had taught me that the care and confinement from morning till night entailed on a mother is very wearing. As the child grows older it learns to claim the greatest share of attention and the mother is never free. I could not but feel that a change would be best for both mothers and babies. At the day appointed I dressed my babe, a boy of eleven months, gave him breakfast, and carried him into the drawing-room and left him to the care of his new mothers. The first day or two he seemed quite homesick, pining and worrying and watching the door whenever it was opened. I took him every evening at six o'clock, gave him supper and put him to bed. I concluded it was best to keep entirely away from him for a week, and invited his Aunt A. to sleep with him. This produced a wonderful change. Before the week was out he was as happy a child as you could wish to see, and when I again saw him I took real comfort with him. Since that time I have left him every morning at half past 7 o'clock with the assurance that he would be as well cared for as any mother could ask, and with a sense of rest, knowing that he would enjoy himself better than when staying with me all day. At night when I take him he is delighted to see me, but the old claiming, sticky spirit that made us both miserable is gone, and I have more enjoyment of him than all the time before. As my baby was several months older than any of the others, and took the change so much more to heart, I am convinced that the sooner children learn to love a great many beside their mothers, the surer they are of health and happiness. —M. J. H."

"Rochester, N. Y., June 30, 1873. Dear Friends: The article in the last Circular about the mothers giving up their babes touched my mother-love to its depths. My experience taught me long ago that yours is the only true way. No one can feel more than I the bad effects of the constant daily and nightly care of a child. It not only takes away the mother's best influence and authority, but forces the mother and child into such relations that relief is felt in separation and true happiness is diminished when together. Sincerely, K.S.P."

"Our method of bringing up children and placing them in a department under selected mentors has been commented upon unfavorably, and sometimes severely," reported the October 5, 1868, *Circular*. "Mothers and motherly folks are apt to think ill of such an arrangement. People say that we destroy families and extinguish natural affection, but see now! The babies here are born and grow up under the same roof not only with parents and brothers and sisters, but with grandparents, uncles and aunts, and many near relatives on both sides. The fathers and mothers of these children have their special friendships, companions, and lovers in the Community who love the child and often enjoy a partnership in its care. We set the heart high above the intellect and give the whole kingdom to it, and only exclude selfishness. These thoughts were suggested by hearing a mother say that the children's house folks thought her little boy's aunts and uncles took him out too often. There is perfect freedom for all the friends to go into the children's rooms at any time, and a good deal of liberty to take the children out; but the Community gives the people there the authority to say when they think a child suffers from what we think is too much family spirit, and to cut off unwise attention. Our main ambition for children is that they may grow up in the nurture and admonition of the Lord, and not be smothered by the too-anxious brooding of natural philoprogenitiveness. We mean that they shall become the nurslings of a universal fatherhood and motherhood, and grow up with the broadest opportunities for culture. After four or five o'clock these long evenings, the little ones are scattered all over the house and it is a feast of love enjoyed by many who have no children of their own as well as those who have.

"The nursery kitchen in the children's wing for mothers and caregivers has two open doors at either end, with steady travel. People gather to chat, rest on the comfortable sofa, or sit in the armchair near the stove and enjoy the budding tulip tree and apple tree blossoms through two large windows. Here Aunt Susan comes every morning to prepare mashed potato and barley-porridge for the babies' breakfast, and Mrs. Kelly makes mush for the juveniles; here is kept crackers that everyone likes for lunch, and where everybody can come and make any drink they want, for the tea-kettle is always filled with seething water. Hot flat-irons are ready to iron a collar. Novelty Cooking-Stove, No. 9 is in constant use.

Mansion House Nursery Kitchen

"No children have had a burn of any consequence; watchful attendants are always present when mother's attention is distracted. The Community panacea for burns was shellac. A ten-by-thirty-foot cistern, six and one-half feet deep, was dug under one end of the building for catching soft water for washing baby clothes; the sink includes a soft water faucet connected to the cistern. Theodore analyzed our spring water—a sulfate of magnesia explains the hardness of water, with the usual lime carbonate. We use filtered rain-water for drinking and cooking as a sanitary measure.

"When this south wing of the mansion was built, a new style of fastenings was put on closet doors with no knobs on the inside. Carrie Macknet was in her room with two-year olds Holton and George. She stepped into the closet and the little fellows shut the door. Both doors of her room were shut and the gravity of her situation flashed upon her, because steam was coming with full force into the long coil, wholly unprotected from their hands. The great mansion was so thoroughly inhabited from garret to cellar that there was little danger of remaining a prisoner for more than half a day, yet being shut up in a closet is hardly enjoyable. She knew it was seldom that ten minutes passed without someone calling to see her on business. She pounded with all her might on the door, shouted for help and listened—she heard nothing but the play of the children and distant noise. She again screamed for help and renewed her pounding, and now the toddlers burst into a frightened cry. Joseph, upstairs practicing the violin, heard the commotion and ran down; meeting Constance, they entered the room where they found the two little boys in tears, vainly trying to turn the door-knob and crying *mama, mama* in pitiful tones. At the evening meeting she told her story to the family, who with one accord voted an immediate reconstruction of these dangerous door-fastenings."

Helping with Community work

"Among our home industries, making boxes for the silk department has been started and is doing a thriving business in a quiet way," noted a *Circular* issue in December 1872. "One reason we started this business is that many of its operations are so simple that our children of five years engage in it. It is one of our pet ambitions to have them grow up industrious men and women. We know that their spiritual and physical welfare and growth, their very happiness even, depend upon their acquiring such habits. They second all our moves in this direction with enthusiasm. The first work bee on the silk boxes is an example. Someone entering the large west room would have found them merrily at work; the elder ones wielded the shears. From them the paste-boards pass to the hands of the youngest who deftly turn up their deeply scored sides in the shape of box or cover. With triumphant flourish, they exclaim:

"'O, see—I've made a box!'

"Roguish-eyed George, after working awhile with breathless enthusiasm, said to sturdy Anna at his elbow: 'This is twice better than going to school.'

"'So it is,' rejoins Anna emphatically; considering a moment, she adds, 'I would want to go to school too.'

"'Well,' says little Ransom, from across the table, 'it is ten times better than picking over beans, anyway!'

"'I should think it is,' cries smaller Eugene; 'Why, it is better than teetering!'

"Having thus touched the acme of childish praise, they fall to work with more enthusiasm than ever. When the work bee ends, there comes the delight of carrying their work out to Miss Constance at the box-room, and receiving from her their meed [reward] of praise. Older ones help in the more advanced stages of the business."

Sarah Burnham Campbell, a Community school teacher, wrote to the Wallingford Community on June 30, 1868: "I must tell you how our children are passing their vacation. They are not spending it in idleness, playing and seeking various methods of whiling away time, but in joining us grown folks in carrying out the true spirit of industry—attending bees and working there, too. It is not all work and no play—they work one, two and three hours and then have a fine relish for play. I happened upon a lively and happy party of thirty men, women and children from Achsah Campbell of eighty-four to four-year-olds busily shelling peas for dinner.

"'Let's see how long we can go without speaking,' suggested one.

"'Agreed!'

"When the signal was given, all hands fell to work in good earnest, and not a word was spoken for some time. The scene was amusing. Such intense silence and such nimble fingers! Occasionally, one would be anxious to communicate something and to get the attention of her companions would clap her hands, and give her ideas by pantomime. Clarence and Edith picked in the same basket as if persons working for a wager, neither of them speaking for nearly three-fourths of an hour. A team with attendants was ready to take them to Willow Place pond, where they had a nice time bathing and the older ones swimming. This is one of their richest treats. It was too far for the children to go to Willow Place to swim, so a place has now been selected in the creek nearer the house. Mr. Campbell made steps and John and George went down and picked out all the large stones that might hurt the children's feet. The spot is a nice one; deep enough above for the larger children to learn to swim, and below, so shallow that there is no chance for any of them to drown.

"We have a plank-walk between Oneida Community and Willow Place, a single line of plank beside the road fence for most of the way, and almost daily I'm reminded by the creeping things I pass of Cowper's lines:

> *An inadvertent step may crush the snail*
> *That crawls at evening in the public path;*
> *But he that has humanity, forewarned*
> *Will tread aside, and let the reptile live.*

"Especially after a shower, the plank will be literally alive with snails, horns extended, dragging their slow lengths along, each leaving a slimy trail behind; if one has a predominance of reverence for life, much circumspection is required not to 'crush the snail.' That many do get crushed by an inadvertent step is too evident. Caterpillars will be out in their comfortable-looking suits of red and black and may be counted by scores as they quietly pursue their way longitudinally or across the plank. Crickets, too, appear to think they have the right of way and come out on the plank in their shiny black suits for exercise and to feed on the remains of unfortunate snails and caterpillars. Humanity is pretty well taxed as one threads his way through so much animated matter.

"One pleasant feature is the nightly visit of the Willow Place family to attend evening meetings and hear Mr. Noyes's Home-Talks. Supper was belated one evening and a work bee was announced to quickly wash dishes. Enthusiasm kindles; a young machinist plunges his brawny arms into the dishpan; another rinses, and another carries the dishes to the dining-room where the tables are re-set in a twinkling. The large four-horse omnibus and another two-horse team drive up and thirty-five of us merrily stow ourselves away and start to mother Oneida Community. We note the fine accommodations for the children. When we young folks were children, we were pretty much confined to our play-yard and never could go to the big house where the grown people lived without asking leave of those who cared for us. Now the larger children have considerable scope about the house and range from one end to the other of the extensive lawns. Almost any hour of the day they are seen—even the four-year-olds—frolicking about on the grass, playing horse and 'King, king castle, who dare wrestle?' We noticed with interest a pleasant room devoted to the juveniles. A royal teeter lay aslant a long, high stool with cushions on both ends and a box in the middle for a tot to ride in who isn't big enough to hold on astride the board. A swing made of iron ropes is fastened to stationary posts. There is an attractive work bench with a machinist's vice attached and bars for climbing and balancing; wagons, blocks of wood, and other toys are strewn in charming confusion about the floor. Happy creatures! They live in such harmony together that one always feels lighter-hearted for having watched them in their innocent sports. After the evening meeting, the teams are again at the door to bring us back to Willow Place."

"We all love our little Harry very much," the Wallingford Community shared with us. "Though his father and mother and sisters are all at Oneida Community, he lives here in perfect contentment nestling in our hearts and making himself a real comfort to the whole family. He is a bright four-year-old, and his ways and sayings are a constant source of amusement. His most important and responsible occupations are picking up apples and feeding the chickens—both self-appointed. The most expressive testimonial of good-will that anyone can show him is to help him pick up apples; feeding the chickens is, in his mind, unequalled in importance by any post in the household. Belle told him the story of Joseph, how Pharaoh took him out of prison and made him Lord over his house and over all Egypt.

"'And did he feed the chickens?' asked Harry.

"When Chloe told him about David, how God was good to him and helped him beat his enemies and become a great king, the little fellow thought about it very earnestly for a minute.

"'Yes, God was real good to David, and loved him,' Harry said, 'and helped him to pick up apples when he wanted him to, didn't he?'"

After someone asked whether the youngsters like tomatoes, and the answer was "they love them dearly," Lilly wrote *Loving and Liking*— "We can forgive little ones for loving tomatoes or applesauce or sugar; sentiment with them has not risen above the delights of the palate; but when we hear a man declare that he loves roast mutton or mince pie, we wonder what he has to say to his sweetheart. We hear a lady say one day that she loved parched corn. Good heavens! Can love be so degraded? Let's make our distinctions more carefully and only like our food, our houses, our clothes; then for the higher sentiment with which our children, our friends, and our God inspire us, we shall have the warmer word—sweet love."

"All our youngest, from Richard almost four to Gertrude nineteen months, take their meals together in the family dining-room; they have only lately risen to this honor," the August 1873 *Circular* informs us. "At dinner they come in just as the second table is serving. The door is often left open and groups of curious and interested visitors frequently collect about the entrance to look at the youngsters. Some of our Community have felt a little restive under such *sans souci* inspection and are inclined to protest against it. During the dinner hour, a lady stepped inside the door and calmly seated herself with her eyes on the infant table.

"'How impolite!' several of us exclaimed, glancing at each other in displeasure.

"'O, no!' said H., smiling good-humoredly. 'I'd call this a nice way of furnishing cheap entertainment. It doesn't hurt us any, and it evidently delights her. We were made to be a city set on a hill. How are we to show the world our miracle of unity if we hide away from inspection?' We looked again at the lady with different eyes. She had a motherly countenance and appeared to be taking such solid comfort that we felt quite reconciled to her and said that she might look to her hearts content."

Providences

"Grown people tell our children stories most evenings when they have their frolic in the upper-sitting room," writes Tirzah Miller in *For the Children* in the April 1869 *Circular*. "We wish that all children who want to be noble men and women could hear these stories, for we expect that the world will be very different from what it now is; we shall need a great many good boys and girls to help make the kingdom of heaven. You may hear stories of providences that have happened to us: Every time something good happens to you and you hardly know where it comes from, you think, *That is a providence*. Miss Carrie told about a providence, and perhaps you've had things like it happen to you:

"'When I was twelve years old I went to school in an academy and began associating with a girl named Celia, who was not a good girl. My mother didn't like to have me play with her very much. There was another girl, Anna, who lived nearby with her aunt and was not a bad girl. One day Celia came for me to walk with her and Anna. Mother said I could go, and we called for Anna. Celia and I both had our silk capes on, and Anna wanted to wear hers, but her aunt had told her to wear her velvet one. I said if her aunt had told her to wear that, she ought to do it, so she did. We tried to find the bridge over the Passaic River, but did not come to it, so Celia said she was not afraid to go over on the railroad bridge. This bridge was made only for trains; it had no railing and only extended about a foot on either side of the track. The river was about an eighth of a mile wide. Celia said she was not afraid and wouldn't run either, but when she saw Anna and me run, she ran too and had just gotten across when the cars (train) came by as swift as lightning, frightening us terribly. We would have been crushed if the train had come an instant sooner. After catching our breath, we walked on until we came to the carriage bridge. There was a narrow foot-path beside the carriage road, but it was not used because it was out of repair. Celia said she was going across in this narrow path, so we followed her. We came to a place where the boards were gone; Celia said she would jump and she did, for she was a very reckless girl. Anna and I were more cautious, so we planned to both step at once on a board that was loose at the ends but fastened slightly in the middle, thinking we would get over all right. But she must have stepped first, for the board tipped and she went right down into the river. The bridge was very high above the water and the current was very swift. Celia was so frightened she could not say a word but I screamed with all my might—Anna was floating downstream. Men at work heard me and got a boat and went after Anna as quick as they could. They drew her up into their boat; they said that all that saved her was her thick velvet cape that kept her afloat. So if she had not been obedient to her aunt in that little matter, she would have drowned.'"

"The children issued invitations to the big folks all Sunday afternoon to attend their theater in the children's playroom after supper. Four white sheets concealed the stage and green-room from view except when the performers peeped out or made their exits by diving under the curtain. The sheets suddenly parting, two small boys favored us with the *Song of the Lambkin* by the Munson Quartet—the classic refrain of which was 'Still he answered, *Baa!*' Recitations, songs and dances followed. Eleven-year-old Harley personated Ole Bull, beseeching us to 'Away with Melancholy.' Harold mimicked in a life-like manner our late Turkish visitor's representation of the style of ablution common among the Turks. Humphrey gave the following account:

> O, what a naughty dog is that, / To quarrel with the pussy-cat
> About a little piece of meat / That sister gave for them to eat.
> O, fie! for shame, you dog and cat, / To quarrel for a thing like that!

He started off clearly and confidently, but disconcerted by applause he ended emphatically, 'O, what a naughty dorg!' bringing down the house. Rutherford told us in baby prattle to—

> See the naughty titten / Playing with the knittin';
> How she rolls the bails about. / How she pulls the stitches out.
> Naughty, naughty titten!

"Our little ones come to the Upper Sitting-Room after supper to present a play or to sing. This high, airy room embraces two stories with two large windows touching the floor soaring thirteen feet, catching the rising sun. Twenty-eight bedrooms open into the Upper Sitting-room, some off the balcony corridor and others directly into the sitting-room. There was more privacy in the Community than was enjoyed in nineteenth-century life with large extended families living together. Most people had their own small room; the sexes and even those of the same sex slept separately. We could convert the Upper Sitting Room into a splendid parlor, but then it would be a great, gloomy room and we wouldn't take half the comfort in it that we do. Nothing is better adapted to the children's comfort and freedom. Imagine the discord it would create if we continually kept them in check with: 'Willie, don't put your hands on those nice vases,' and 'Ormond, don't climb on that sofa,' and 'Anna, you must not touch that lace curtain.' And they wouldn't want to come where they'd often be scolded! Instead, Mr. Cragin tells them, 'Run and jump all you choose, children; turn somersaults and be just as free as you are at home.' So they have a grand frolic and then they're ready to sit still when he rings the bell. The new children's wing will soon be heated by steam.

Community children enjoyed presenting skits, songs, stories, and dances every Sunday evening in the Mansion House Upper Sitting Room.

"Watching the enthusiasm and delight that children manifest in learning new things is a constant source of entertainment," noted the January 6, 1873, *Circular*. "I watched our little boys: the three-year-olds have become such experts in top-spinning that they entertain papa and mama when they go a-visiting. What the three-year-olds do triumphantly, the two-year-olds try to imitate, and the contagion of top-spinning is having a run in this class. Felix set a small top in motion with his thumb and forefinger; he tried to manipulate a larger one in the same way and the little thumb and forefinger weren't equal to the attempt. He appealed to larger hands to give the motion and the method. The larger top was set going by a dexterous sliding of one palm on the other. The little fellow caught the idea at once and practiced it for half an hour. His attempts were more than half failures at first, but his perseverance was undaunted and success crowned his efforts. These ever-springing fountains of spontaneity and freshness ought to be perennial in human nature. Jesus, no doubt, had this in mind as one of the good and indispensable things to be recovered by conversion and a return to the child-spirit—'Except ye be converted and become as this little child, ye shall in nowise enter the Kingdom of heaven.'

"'This is the day we are all going to Joppa!' Three- to five-year-olds were ready with their attendants before train time, the first journey for them all. It is half a mile on a sandy road from the station to the ferry; we had baskets to carry and doubted whether the children could walk so far. Good luck attended us; a farmer with his team drove up and took our load and the little band snugly sat on a blanket in the bottom of the wagon. The farmer looked around and smiled many times before he reached the ferry. We walked behind to see that no one fell out and counted them again before starting in the boat. The pulling of the boat across the river by means of a rope stretched from shore to shore was witnessed with intense interest by the youngsters, and no doubt afforded the plot for future plays.

"'Let's move our Community here!'

"Miniature wells were dug, mounds built, and railroad embankments raised in the sand. Mr. Dutton, our gymnast, turned hand-springs and summersaults to the juveniles' delight. They somersaulted, chased grasshoppers, and waded with rolled up trousers. After lunch we had a row on the lake with permission to dip hands into the water and make ripples with fingers. After a nap all hands were ready for dinner, then the row on the river, and home they went without a tear. The exploits at Joppa are rehearsed daily. 'We went out in real deep water and jumped in,' say the little boys, and add in an impressive voice, 'and we didn't die, nor we didn't get drowned either!'

"There never was so nice a way to bring up children. The little toddler wants no better amusement all day than he gets from the three-year old. Aunt Susan has a fund of Bible stories to tell them, which please their infant minds wonderfully. Little children may be managed in flocks and are receptive to a good teacher. They teach each other to sing and say ABC, and rehearse the songs and tableaux of our evening concerts, and never whine to be amused."

THE CHILDREN'S MEETING: CHARACTER EDUCATION

"The Children's Meeting is a daily hour-long afternoon meeting held by the heads of the department. Its length is frequently shortened. We spread Sabbath exercises over all the week in our evening meeting, so in our Children's Meeting we spread the Sunday school over all the week. Begun more than twenty years ago, it has been kept up with little intermission, with the purpose of moral impact by conversation, confession of Christ within, reading, and criticism.

"The children are forbidden to tell on each other, but we give them a legitimate opportunity for making complaint from time to time in a way to get a benefit all around. In these criticisms they take lessons in the highest esthetics—esthetics of character. One of the children was criticized in the meeting yesterday, a boy of nine or ten. His spirit and manners had given offense for some time and he was advised to offer himself for criticism. He was old enough to know it would do him good and he had grace enough to want to improve, so he offered himself. Two of the adults were invited in. The children were very sincere. Every one of them had something to say about the boy's selfish, inharmonious ways. Even Ransom and Eugene, youngsters of six or seven, had been outraged in their sense of what is right and wrong. There was no malice in what the children said. They are too ingenuous to hold a grudge. A formal criticism finds one in a dispassionate frame of mind; the truth is told without any bitterness. The effect is not to provoke or discourage, but to soften and baptize a child with the Community spirit. Then with an attitude that virtually says, 'I have done wrong,' the child is forgiven.

"They tried the effect of a round of criticism on Pip, twenty months old. He is the pride of babydom, the best little fellow that ever was, but he would slip about one thing. Moderate correction did not cure him, so one day he was set in the midst of the Children's Meeting and all said what they thought about his careless habit. Richard and Humphrey were quite vehement in their disapprobation. They said, 'Pip is a naughty boy to do so.' He fell awfully solemn there in his chair, but did not cry or say a word. Well, the effect was wonderful beyond all expectation. It cured him entirely. He hasn't given any trouble of the kind since. True criticism given in love doesn't work on the understanding chiefly—it affects the spirit and the will, and makes it easy for the one who is criticized to change.

"Do any of the boys and girls who read the *Circular* have among their mates those who are quarrelsome? If they do, they may perhaps like to hear about a conversation that took place not long ago between a little boy and his mother. Howard is a bright, conscientious boy and generally kind to his mates; he occasionally likes to tease them and this propensity frequently causes unpleasant jarring between himself and his five-year-old brother Eddie, who is rather inclined to be quarrelsome. After witnessing a wrangle between the brothers, the mother called Howard to her and asked him why he plagued his brother Eddie? Howard found many excuses for his conduct; she listened patiently, and then showed him what would be the effect upon his little brother.

"'I wonder if my boy remembers the flower bed he took care of last summer,' she gently began. 'Can you tell me how you made your roses and other choice plants grow so thriftily?'

"'O, yes,' he replied, 'we put muck and manure on them just as we saw the gardener do.'

"'Did you not one day find a large thistle in your flower bed, and did you cultivate and train that as you did your roses?'

"'O, no, mamma, I pulled it out just as quickly as I saw it. It doesn't bear pretty flowers and would have covered up many other things.'

"'You did right,' responded his mother. 'Let me tell you, my child, that you are cultivating in your little brother's heart a much worse weed than the thistle when you hector him and tempt him to quarrel. Do you not see that you provoke him to a naughty spirit? Would it not be more manly for you to provoke him to a good spirit, and when he is quarrelsome help him to overcome his temptations? If you will do this you will enjoy him much better than you did your flowers, and you will feel a great deal happier yourself.' Howard hung his head, but his mother's earnestness had touched his heart; looking up in her face he said, 'Eddie is a good boy sometimes, and I want to help him not to be quarrelsome.'"

"The children were criticized this evening, being inclined to be somewhat immodest and disrespectful; they need to think less highly of themselves. Their tongues lead them into a bad spirit. The whole Community should be responsible to make the children obedient. To cajole children to be obedient and otherwise treat them so that they do not expect to obey promptly is real cruelty," notes the March 10, 1873, *Circular*. "It keeps alive in them the spirit of disobedience and whatever obedience they have is forced, so is good for nothing. It fosters cant and hypocrisy in them. Mercy and wisdom alike require that even small children should be taught to obey the first time spoken to, and never be coaxed into obedience. People ought to respect themselves too much to allow disobedience or disrespect from them. The truth can work through every person and make itself felt in the children.

"In mid-April 1872 the Children's Hour was revived again for a short time. Last evening the children were called upon to stand up and testify whether God and the confession of Christ within them had not sometimes helped them of late to overcome temptation. Wilfred said that he had trouble learning his arithmetic lesson, but he prayed to God to help him, confessed Christ in him, and then was able to understand the lesson and do the examples. Cosette said that she was sent to the dining-room on an errand. There was no one there and she saw the sugar-bowls; it would be very nice to have a lump of sugar! But she thought that it would not please the folks or please God for her to take it without asking, so she did her errand and came away without touching it. Harold said he resisted the same temptation about sugar. Harley said he was tempted to tell a wrong story but God made him feel so bad about it that he confessed his temptation, and the lying spirit left him. The children gave very good attention to the remarks made to them and seemed to have a receptive spirit."

Thoughts and behavior are determined by one's most profound conviction about oneself, perhaps determined in earliest childhood—one who regards himself as mean in his basic self-conception will behave meanly; self-respect manifests in acting rightly. *With immensely greater power*, Noyes conveyed, this principle works when we sincerely confess, realize, that Christ, the Holy Spirit, is within us as our deepest reality. All Community members confessed Christ in them. "Our character is formed by the action and reaction between our conceptions of our true nature as Spirit and our efforts to realize that conception in our daily life—then our behaving goes beyond our expectations toward superhuman goodness and proves to be really the working of Christ."

"I was called upon to substitute for Mrs. N. as teacher in our Primary School. Upon entering the room, nineteen pairs of eyes seemed to say, *What a funny thing to have a man for our school marm*. Women have monopolized this field, with the entire sympathy of the masculine fraternity. In studying children's temptations to prevaricate when found guilty of a misdemeanor, I discovered that they're usually seized with the spirit of fear, and under its influence untruths are told. A cure for this evil is often found in refusing to hear their story of self defense until they've taken time to get free from fear, and to awaken in them their love of truth. Fear of punishment, the displeasure of others, or of mortification should be made to work in favor of truth-telling. Being afraid to tell a lie because of its hatefulness is putting fear to its legitimate use." —*Reflections on my Two Weeks' Teaching*.

Mrs. Cragin compared life to the winding of a ball of yarn. "The daily children's meeting serves an admirable purpose in calling attention to the daily winding, and if necessary, unwinding and pulling out any dark threads on the day's life-ball," she wrote, printed in the January 20, 1873, *Circular*. "Frequent getting out balance-sheets in spiritual and moral account-keeping are popular in the Community, and nowhere more needed than with the children. Almost daily differences and grievances oppress the heart of a child. Faults of omission and commission come under review and criticism; who can doubt that such a daily elimination of dark threads will save the child from bitter sorrow and repentance in later years? The daily meeting provides an opportunity for sharing trials; by wise healing words, they are banished from memory. But scolding and dealing with problems are not the staples of the children's meetings; much in the children is good to think of and to praise, mingled with thanks to the Author of all good. The ultimate purpose is to develop character—to renew the mind and disposition rather than the repression or weeding out of specific faults."

"I have been a teacher of the children for the past few months, but many are the lessons that I've learned from them," Portia wrote on January 1, 1873. "The simple expression *I confess Christ in me a good spirit that will be a good boy today*, spoken with seriousness, has a controlling influence upon them and teaches me what a great helm is the confession of Christ. I see that these are not meaningless utterances to them—the little girl who confesses Christ a spirit that will get her lessons done well expects to do it and does do it. What interests me is their innocent belief in their confessions, and in the realization of their faith. We all look to the same means for salvation, but with them a Savior is tangible. Yesterday with its failures is forgotten; unbelief finds no home and they start anew in the path of improvement with the hope and confidence of childhood. Their simple faith has encouraged me, and made me appreciate anew the truth that Christ is in me stronger than evil. The simple words *I confess a spirit that will please my teacher*, has reacted upon my own heart; I too have confessed Christ a spirit that will please God and my teachers. Truly, of such is the kingdom of heaven."

"Pierrepont repeated after Mrs. N., in somewhat broken language: 'Suffer little children to come unto me, and forbid them not, for of such is the kingdom of Heaven.' The verse went round the circle and once in a while a well-rounded word came out. A funny by-play of roguish smiles, comical twistings in chairs, and irrelevant exclamations often interrupted, but the little ones hushed quickly when reproved and bright, earnest eyes watched their teacher. Finally came the evening prayer or confession of Christ—'I confess Christ in me a good spirit.' These words are the first taught and most used among the children, who could all say it or something meant for it. The whole had lasted only ten minutes. It was the happy close of their merry, romping day. Then came undressing, a scamper of bare feet over the nursery floor and the good night kiss. In ten minutes every head was on its pillow, far on its way to dreamland."

"All our efforts have not been in vain, as witness the oft-repeated testimony from one and another of the children with a radiant face: 'I am so happy I don't know what to do.' This happiness cannot be explained by outward change or circumstances; it is the fruit of the confession of Christ—the indwelling of the good spirit. A little girl was asked what the meaning of *happy* is," the October 6, 1873, *Circular* noted. "'It is to feel as if you wanted to give all your things to your little sister.' What would you think, Johnny, if the new kite Uncle Thomas gave you belonged to all the boys to fly just as much as to you? Mary, how would you like to put your little trinkets where all the girls could play with them? There was a charming scene among the little ones; each brought his store of toys and made a large collection to be used by all in common."

"They were very enthusiastic about it and enjoyed the draught of the Pentecostal spirit as much as anybody," Tirzah Miller noted. "No one says now, *me* and *mine*, but *we* and *ours*." One little fellow forgot and said, 'That's mine.' Little Maud spoke up, 'No, it is all the children's!' That is the way our children do. They have a large cupboard with glass doors where they put their playthings together. They are all better and happier than they were before these new measures were adopted.

"Our newspapers inform us that poor people in Europe must work very hard just to get bread to eat and clothes to wear, and now they are clubbing together so they can buy many more things more cheaply than they could when each man kept his wages to himself. Think a little and you'll see that children who own their playthings in common can have better things and greater variety, than if each kept his private store. If your parents were poor, they could only perhaps afford to get you new toys on Christmas or on your birthday; and then each child must have his own dominoes or doll—while for twenty or thirty children who live together, two or three toys of a kind will do for all; and you know, Charlie, it takes only a little while for you to get tired of your boat, even if it was so pretty at first, and you wish you had something new. If you lived as our children do, you might change many times a day. Better still, you'd keep learning the lesson that you are happier when you are generous than when you are selfish, and that really you can't own anything, not even your little hands that can do many wonderful things; and your papa and mama who look so big and strong to you, don't own themselves either, for God owns all things. You cannot imagine how nice it is for many little boys and girls to live together."

The October 17, 1872, *Circular* reported that "dear little Maud had such a brave spirit at the table that she deserves a cheer. There were not enough of the coveted sugared nutcakes at dinner to give each of the children one. Some would have to take plain cakes and do without the pretty frosting; it came that Maud had one of the sugared cakes:

"'I will give you half of mine,' she said to her neighbor who was not so lucky.

"'O, but I want one too,' said one of the children a little farther off.

"'Well,' said Maud stoutly, 'I will give you the other half.' The person waiting on the children said, 'Don't you want to keep part of the cake for yourself, Maud?'

"'Yes,' said Maud, 'but I had rather be kind.'

Hurrah for Maud!

"We have one among our children who might be called unfortunate. When whooping cough left her system in a debilitated state, rickets got hold of her. Though often commiserated by strangers, after six or seven years Rose is quite well and is among our happiest of the happy. She craves no pity, and best of all, she has learned to go to God for herself with all her joys and sorrows. She is universally beloved, and loves all warmly in return. Like the fragrance of a crushed flower, the sweetness of her disposition attracts all this affection. The twenty or thirty children by whom she is surrounded are ever on the alert to make her happy, especially those near her own age. If she needs any assistance, it is always at hand. If one of them has a present of fruit or anything unusual, she immediately says, 'I will save this for Rose.' If they are to make a little excursion, the first thought of the boys is to bring the hand-wagon for Rose. The spirit the children show is perfectly touching and draws tears from my eyes. There is a beauty about it that eclipses the deformity and would make us unwilling except for Rose's sake that things should be otherwise. Rose is among our most ambitious at school. Her experience has made her interior, and it is easy for her to concentrate her attention upon whatever she turns her mind to. Unfortunately, rickets finally caused her death at age nineteen.

"Our children's house has passed through twenty campaigns of measles, whooping-cough, scarlet fever, dysentery, influenza of several kinds, and diphtheria," the October 5, 1868, *Circular* noted, "without losing a child!"

"Several people from Oneida made a call and visited the children's department, expressing surprise at finding the twenty-three little ones younger than four years of age so healthy and robust," the August 4, 1873, *Circular* reported. "The doctor inquired if any of them had spasms while teething, and on being told that only one had been thus affected, said it was very remarkable."

"A visitor from Ohio, a reader of the *Circular*, visited with a strong belief that he would be able to discover evidence of selfishness among us, if others could not. He said his wife told him he must be very sure to notice the children. He went over to the children's house and sat down for half an hour, expecting to see some evil dispositions there. Not seeing any immediate manifestations, he even went so far as to try to stir up a quarrel between two children, none of their guardians being present, but failed entirely. Before leaving he had to confess that he had been unable to find any evidence of selfishness, and the Oneida Community is a greater mystery to him than ever. He said he was conscious that he could not be happy here, as he could not be saved from selfishness. It is a splendid thing to be free from selfishness according to his ideal, but as he could not reach that state himself, this would be no place for him. He was anxious to read the *Berean*."

"A request of the Community breaks the heart," writes Sarah Burnham in the August 4, 1873, *Circular*. "A fashionably-dressed lady from a neighboring city wished to know if we received children to educate. We replied that it is not our custom to take children into our family without their parents; after much experience we have proved it to be unsafe and inexpedient. She has a daughter thirteen years old whose father is dead and who has no male relative to control her. She is becoming very willful and headstrong. Business keeps the mother away from home all day and the daughter is sent to the public school where she mixes with other children, some good and many bad, and learns of them far more evil than she learns good from books. She is growing up extravagant in dress, saucy to her mother and brother, ignorant of and averse to all work, and worst of all, bent on being out late evenings with no one to guide her. Her mother feels powerless to curb her headstrong daughter and is looking anxiously for help. Some advised her to place the girl in a Catholic institution, but she could not endure the thought. The Orphan Asylum was suggested but the girl would undoubtedly be bound out—she knew not where. The mother might put her out to service, but that would be certain ruin—mistresses now-a-days have no care for their girls except to see that they get their work done. Her daughter would pick up her society in the streets, and if she is on time for her morning's work no one will care how or where she spends her evenings. There seems to be no place where such a girl can be taught to work and be kept under wholesome discipline.

"We sympathized with the mother: It contrasted so sharply with the feelings we have about our own girls, who are such a comfort to us; they add much beauty, harmony, and happiness to our home. Obedient, industrious, and enthusiastic for the Community, we have no fear for them and everything to hope. They learn young that life is a reality and that they have some higher aim than to seek their own pleasure and gratification. They are learning to hear God and to obey and honor their parents—not merely my own father and mother, but all the mothers and fathers; Community members are interested in and responsible for them as their own.

"The Commissioners of Public Charities and Correction announced that there are thirty thousand children in New York City growing up in ignorance and idleness, forlorn mortals ushered into a world where they are not welcomed or cared for, contracting vicious habits of life. The House of Refuge on Randall's Island is successfully helping a large proportion of these idlers to become useful members of society, provided that they are rescued early and taught the principles of obedience and veneration. Young vagrants have an opportunity to acquire regular habits and learn a useful trade. The utmost pains are taken to develop and cultivate their minds. They are watched over for good, not for evil. Obedience, good behavior, and noble deeds are rewarded to encourage and stimulate all to do likewise. Represented are nearly all nations, kindreds, and tongues on earth. Many children attract considerable attention: A colored lad who possesses a wonderful passion for oratory addresses the other boys on all subjects and is really eloquent. The principal asked him whom he adopted as his model; he grandly replied, 'I will have you to know, sir, that I am no servile imitator.' The Refuge found homes for 637 boys and 146 girls in 1867. No pains are spared to secure the best possible situation for these children, who are required to correspond with the superintendent for one or more years so that the institution may know about their progress. If any prove unmanageable, they are returned to the Refuge. Many respectable persons owe almost everything to the House of Refuge and regard it as their alma mater. A gentleman and lady were shown the premises and manifested a lively interest in the conveniences and improvements they saw. The gentleman turned to his lady and said, 'Now I will tell you a secret; I was brought up in this place.' The lady astonished all by quietly remarking, 'So was I.'"

"What to do with children on rainy days is a problem that every mother is compelled to study. 'What shall I play with now, mama?' asks the restless boy confined inside all day, tired of top, rocking-horse, and marbles, sighing for a race in the fresh outdoor air," the December 1, 1873, *Circular* asks. "There are inactive children who have to be urged to the rougher sports of the yard and meadow, but an all-day restriction to the parlor and sitting room is a fate most dismal. To go down cellar and see the kitty is the two-year-old idea of enjoyment nowadays, unequaled by anything unless it's the sport of throwing handkerchief-rabbits at spinning tops in Father Noyes's room. On his table is a rare collection of tall and short tops, thick and thin tops, level tops and curved tops—and to see them all going while the little fellows energetically pelt them is a sight worth beholding. In our labyrinthine cellars, a room has been fitted up for rainy days. It is warmed by steam and a nice floor of wood covers the cement bottom. There are swings and other arrangements but the most interesting feature is a carpenter's bench to learn the handling of tools. They have great plans of what they shall make—flying-machines are among the simplest of their projects.

"A foreman in the shop, down cellar the other day, thought he would take a cookie from a well-known basket that sat on one of the shelves. Certain rats had been holding a carnival on the shelf, and the kitchen folks had placed one of Newhouse's infallible traps in the basket. The result may be imagined. The unlucky foreman's fingers striking the trap, it closed on them as remorselessly as it would have done with any other predator. It is said the kitchen folks enjoyed the joke."

"Mr. Stephen R. Leonard, an original Putney member who lived at Wallingford for six years without one glimpse of Oneida, came back to stay," reported an October 1868 *Circular*. "This place is so constantly changing that one year makes quite a difference in its appearance, but Mr. Leonard says that what struck him most forcibly is the change among the children, many of whom were infants when last seen by him. 'To meet such a company of intelligent, well-behaved, and healthy children, full of life and enjoyment, without fault-finding or quarreling, and so respectful and affectionate toward one another and everyone as they manifestly are,' said he, 'is a treat that does not often fall to the lot of mankind.'"

6

Education: Lifelong Learning from Youth to Young at Heart

AGES FIVE TO COLLEGE

"Our interest in education will soon demand the erection of a building adapted to that purpose," reports the September 4, 1862, *Circular*. "Visitors here want to know if we have a school," Noyes wrote, "and I tell them, yes, but it has thus far been movable; we need a university—a building well situated and planned. Children through age five would be in the children's wing; from ages six through eleven they would study reading, spelling, manners, obedience, and prayer for five hours with the rudiments of art and industry gained by association with Community adults. From twelve through nineteen, youths would begin serious study for half a day in a Community Institute consisting of professorships: elocution would include reading, spelling, composition, and oratory; another would consist of geography, mathematics, and astronomy; another of languages.

The Oneida Community schoolroom. This is now a library for Mansion House residents and open to the public. The area beyond the archway is a children's library with crocheted Alice in Wonderland figures, which connects to the original Oneida Community library.

"Our students will become professors themselves in such branches as their inclinations and talents lead them, so while teaching others they continue to learn themselves. Professorships of other sciences and arts would in time evolve and form a fountain of instruction not only for the young but for the Community at large. This system of education would not resemble college but would move in combination with labor, practical enterprise, and social activities—harmonized and controlled by the science of the heart in relation to God. Education would continue throughout one's lifetime."

The April 11, 1864, *Circular* opined that in conventional schooling, much of the strength of the teacher is expended in counteracting unfortunate influences caused by unmonitored and undisciplined youthful behavior. Universal education is laudatory, but without character education, it can become a negative force as evidenced by bullying, racism, misogyny, and general selfishness. "By the age of ten or twelve, children's mutual influence becomes stronger than the teacher's." The Community called these *horizontal* attractions that prevail over *ascending* influences. Dubbed peer pressure now, "horizontal pressures can become an impenetrable barrier to superior influences. Moral supremacy is hard won, generally by hard measures," the Community believed. "We choose education within our large family, with each young scholar receiving special attention from a superior associate or a private teacher. In that circle there is a lively taste for knowledge and they will get their education by contagious enthusiasm."

A Special Correspondence by an *Elmira Advertiser* reporter appeared in the November 1872 *Circular* entitled, "The Oneida Community: An Inside View of the Workings of this Curious People—their Religious Belief and their Moral and Everyday Life":

"Although the sexes mingle together with great apparent freedom, there seems to be a power within them stronger than any law, controlling their relations with each other. I see vastly less of familiarity than exists in what the world considers refined society. All this compels me to admit that this people have a higher standard of purity and refinement than I have found elsewhere. The men appear continent and reserved—the women are modest and self-possessed. They 'neither marry nor are given in marriage' after the fashion of the world, yet I do not find the first indication of licentiousness. During my stay at the Oneida Community over many months, I cannot recall a single unchaste or immodest expression upon the countenance of either man or woman, nor have I heard that a single instance of it has ever been observed by the hundreds of employees at work for them. Instead of being what they are slanderously reported to be, they appear to me more like ascetics.

"The bright-eyed children here, more perfectly developed, happier, and better behaved than any I have ever seen elsewhere in the world, give proof that they are neither ascetics nor Shakers. These people seem to find rare enjoyment in their children, which are never regarded as a nuisance and left to the care of hirelings and strangers;

instead, the wisest and the best of the family are selected to take care of the children's department. While great care and labor are bestowed upon their spiritual and physical development (and this includes the highest morality), it is a labor of love; and I do not believe there is another place in the world where children are so well cared for, with surroundings so favorable for true development.

"From nothing are they so carefully guarded as from the influence of a bad spirit in themselves or in those with whom they come in contact. They grow up in an atmosphere of obedience, faith, and love. The result of this training has been apparent to me in the class of girls I have been teaching. Upon making the inquiry at the opening of school, 'What is the first condition of a good school as well as of good society?' I received the ready response, *A good spirit*. It was not the reply I expected, but time has proved to me that these three words cover the whole ground. The natural outgrowth of a good spirit is good order and many other desirable conditions conducive to rapid improvement of these pupils. I have had none of the neglected work of parents to do. Instead of spending weeks or months in preparatory work getting into good rapport with my pupils, I found myself at once in open communication with their minds, discovering in them great receptivity and earnestness with an unquenchable desire for improvement. I have never found these qualities in such perfection in any school that I've been connected with during many years of teaching. I gave a class of girls ranging in age from twelve to fourteen more than a page in Wilson's *Outlines of History* to commit verbatim; I was surprised at the ease and rapidity with which they accomplished the task, and with their enthusiasm as they became interested in history—usually awakened by a novel in girls of that age. After a term I required them to write an abstract or epitome of several pages, during the usual time occupied in recitation. They readily, almost intuitively comprehended the work desired of them, and the abstracts written by them I believe would compare favorably with any efforts made by pupils of the same age in the best schools of the world; and in saying this I am confident of speaking far within the bounds of truth. In no school have I ever found so clear a perception and discernment between the true and the false, the right and the wrong. The theory of self-government and self-control as advocated by Professor Steele and other progressive men is no longer to me a Utopian dream; for I have found it here a glorious possibility, and have seen its perfect realization. Not a doubt remains after the experience of the last few months."[42]

Portia M. Underhill offered her experience as a schoolmistress: "One of the pleasantest occupations of my Community life has been that of school-teacher. With a previous experience of four years in the common schools, I could not but contrast the children of the Community with those I'd formerly taught from ages five to twelve; children here of the same age are more easily governed. They are taught to watch inwardly for little seeds of discord that develop and cause unhappiness among themselves; they're taught to love study not for the sake of emulation and competition, but that they might come more into sympathy with God, who knows all things. For mental ability, I have found them to be rather above the average, particularly those born in the Community. Many possess knowledge of geography that older persons might envy: points of interest about Nineveh, Babylon, Rome, and other such places; noted mountains, rivers, and the ocean with its capes and islands, and locations of places. Community children know them not in a dry, mechanical way but as exciting realities—they'll tell you about them with a brightness of expression and earnestness that makes you almost feel they've been there themselves. Living together, they stimulate each other and create an enthusiasm that makes them studious and desirous of acquiring knowledge. This is caught by the little ones, who very early show a love for books. They learn their letters among themselves, and on coming to school, need restraining rather than urging. The wide range of thought in the Community is felt by the children. In general knowledge they are superior to those in the world. Their memories are excellent; a girl of ten recited a long chapter of *Hiawatha* without being prompted a word. They frequently get up little entertainments of music, tableaux, and plays that are original, amusing, and edifying. Teaching here has improved me more than any previous experience."

Schoolmaster Alfred Barron also shared his testimony: "I have taught in the common schools of Vermont, North Carolina, Michigan, and in the schools of the Wallingford and Oneida Communities, and take the measure of our children by the standards of a schoolmaster. There was idiocy in the school district in which I was born and there were cases of idiocy and imbecility in every single neighborhood in which it was my fortune to teach. There is no such in the Community and this is more than I can say of any neighborhood in which I have lived previous to joining this Association. I've always found that a class of scholars born in the Community was fifty percent brighter and more studious than those in any school I have taught. In my zeal and satisfaction, I have often said to myself: *These scholars are 100 percent better than any I ever knew in the common schools.* I am confident that the spirit and discipline of the Community, including as it does a hearty and intelligent confession of Christ as an indwelling Savior, has an effect to quiet the passions and clear the head, and cannot, if allowed a fair chance, fail to rear children of the happiest temperaments."

"It is to the credit of our social system that it guarantees to woman the possession of her own person, that it is her undoubted right to choose when and how often she shall bear children," Noyes wrote. "This right is inviolable in the Community and it is only upon the freest consultation that children are begotten. It is to this freedom that we attribute much of the attraction for children that exists here. Children are chosen with pleasure and loved with a mother's love and Community's love, looked upon as among the brightest joys of life and welcomed with surpassing desire. Society is beginning to acknowledge that the social fruits of the Community are good. We do not take credit to ourselves for this happy state of society. To us it is nothing less than a miracle wrought by Christ and one of the indubitable signs that his kingdom has come. We could not reproduce it in our own strength. We do not believe that anyone in society can repeat it by his will.

"We should do all we can to make the Community a university for the education of the whole person," Noyes wrote in the April 14, 1859, *Circular*. "We do not want to make ourselves mere horses and oxen, which the solitary, mechanical labor of common country life tends to do. We want to cultivate taste, the love of the beautiful; time spent educating this propensity is not wasted. The love of the beautiful could harmonize with and quicken all kinds of manual industry. The artist is no idler or dreamer. Artistic pursuit and the love of the beautiful are to glorify labor and make it attractive. We want the highest kind of industrial energy and at the same time keep work subordinate to superior ends."

College

The young were well prepared to enter excellent colleges and the Community guaranteed their support. Noyes warned against subtle motives for higher education—love of money-making and personal distinction instead of education of the character and spirit. Himself a Phi Beta Kappa graduate of Dartmouth, Noyes wanted their youths to learn many emerging sciences, mathematics, engineering, languages, the arts—a thorough collegiate course. The Community sent young men to Yale, and a small branch Community was established at New Haven for the accommodation of these students. The first two students sent to Yale entered the Medical School and after three years of study, including several months of practice in New York City hospitals, they received their degrees and took up the practice of medicine in the Community, including Noyes's son Theodore.

Theodore R. Noyes, son of John and Harriet, received a medical degree from Yale in 1867. His professional examination of Community members' physical and mental health was published in the N.Y. *Medical Gazette*, considered a model of "careful observation, entire honesty, and impartiality."

Theodore began a course in practical chemistry in their old ice-house. Several young men studied in New York City, and Charles S. Joslyn was admitted to the New York bar after having attended law school at Columbia University. K. wrote this letter to the Community on November 12, 1872: "My last year at Yale has opened very pleasantly: and although gladdened by the thought of the approaching end, there is a tinge of sadness about it and I hardly know why. It can't be the thought of losing friends, for I have ten times as many in the happy family circle at the Oneida Community who are ten times as dear to me. This sadness may result in part from disappointment at the amount of one's acquirements at school—when we learn one thing, we see a hundred more to be learned!

"My studies may interest you, as our class is the first large one that ever pursued Dynamical Engineering at Yale. M-W-F at 8:00 a.m. is Dana's Geology under Professor Verrill. The subject is not particularly exciting to many of the class, and Professor Verrill flunks with his customary remorselessness. Although the possible existence of fish in the Lower Silurian age may not bear directly upon building a steam engine, it is thought desirable that engineers should know enough about rocks to use various kinds intelligently when occasion requires. On T-T-S at 9:00 a.m. we have French under Professor Whitney. You doubtless well remember his fairly frightful exactness and particularity. We are learning very much more French under him than last year under the French gentleman, partly because we are obliged to behave better in class and learn our lessons more thoroughly, and partly because one who has learned a foreign tongue understands better what his countrymen wish to know, than the foreigner himself does. Every day except Sunday we have a recitation at noon under Professor Trowbridge in Rankine's *Machinery and Mill-work*. We have three works of Rankine's, supposed to contain all that a Dynamical Engineer needs to know, and very much more than most of us are ever likely to know, at once. Professor Trowbridge's recitations are partly lectures as well, and very interesting and instructive. Monday and Tuesday afternoons we work from 2 till 5 o'clock, draughting; with nothing given us the remaining afternoons, they are usually spent likewise. My remaining study is Vocal Music on Wednesday afternoons under Dr. Stoeckel, a kindly, thorough-going old gentleman with a grand, mellow voice. Standing up alone before a dozen men attempting an exercise is a little trying to my nerves, but I like it very much on the whole. We must furnish a composition this term; mine was on that strange oriental production, the *Bhagavad Gita*, of which Thoreau was so fond. Many interesting subjects are gone over in haste; many others that would be very desirable to study are omitted entirely for lack of time.

"I regard college as a hot-bed, an excellent place to make a start, but creating a strong tendency to abnormal growth if one is not transplanted in season. Constant attention to science alone tends to destroy faith in everything that may not be deduced according to mathematical formulae—like fire, formulae are good servants but terrible masters. Heaven help him who needs mathematical proof that it was of simple, innocent children of whom it was said, 'Of such are the Kingdom of Heaven!'"

"Science and religion are coming together," noted the August 18, 1869, *Circular* "—rapid progress of new ideas on education that amounts to a revolution. Both Catholic and Protestant religions had been afraid of direct contact with science, sensing a seeming opposition between them. The church therefore allied itself with literature and art, surrounded itself with colleges (professors denoting professors of faith), and put Greek and Roman learning as a buffer between itself and the cool eye and sure hand of science. The Community's religion criticizes the whole of Christendom by its purity and we're foremost in devotion to science; our young men demand to see things for themselves, to stand face to face with nature and fact." Noyes said that the experiment of sending the young men to college, though a bold one, was proving entirely safe, though they'd been introduced to the new concept of evolution and its possible ramifications on Biblical thought. "Blessings on educational institutions for they place persons in circumstances that favor constant study," continued Noyes. "Young America doesn't always take kindly to college drill but generally adapts to it and often appreciates study as the business at hand, and ceases thinking of professors as drill masters. Results are mostly good and often surprising. Mediocre but faithful students are greatly improved by habits of study and acquisitions of knowledge that fit them to meet life's duties."

"Our new Academy, now an established institution," the October 4, 1869, *Circular* reported, "promises to realize the much attempted but generally unsuccessful manual-labor school. The sixty-five students who attend daily recitations—a considerable class past their teens—divide their time about equally between work and books. In ordinary society many would consider their education finished and be already settled down to the routine of business and housewifery. The Community sets no bounds to education and improvement, and the lists are open to all classes. The inherent interest in the Community for education is stimulated by our Yale graduates, and under this impulse we see no stopping place short of a university education for all who aspire to that degree. Industry continues with its usual vigor, but all Community men and women are encouraged to attend at least one of these classes.

"Theodore, and Noyes's brother George Washington Noyes, editor of the *Circular*, were sent as Community representatives to Europe, where they placed samples of the Community manufactures in the Paris Exposition. They were received with great cordiality by Hepworth Dixon, to whom they gave a voluminous inquiry by Noyes into the causes of the decline of marriage, a document that Dixon put to use in his book, *Spiritual Wives*. They presented copies of Community publications to the British Museum, and established agencies for their sale both in London and in Paris. They explained to Professor Thomas Huxley the Community's method of birth control; Huxley thought it desirable to interfere with the natural course of things in this respect and was impressed by the experience of the Community. They attended a meeting held in their honor by the Fourierists of Paris. George W. Noyes and Charles Joslyn traveled through Switzerland, Belgium, and France, describing their impressions in a series of delightful oversea letters. At home the system of classes for the instruction of all ages was continued with no abatement of interest."

LIFELONG EDUCATION

"A visitor at Oneida, expressing her admiration of the enthusiasm for study that prevails here, mentioned that Mrs. N., in her forties, said she now cares nothing about her work but wants to be studying all the time—while she used to be all absorbed in her work and cared nothing for books. She studies grammar, German, and French, besides reading Cromwell and superintending in the kitchen. The October 19, 1853, *Circular* was pleased to note that "one of our elderly women got so absorbed in mathematics yesterday, that the premonitory stroke of the dinner bell at noon failed to reach her ear and on she plodded till past one o'clock." The 'plodding spirit' is much honored in the Community "as the first requisite to all improvement—it is the spirit that is willing to learn little by little; it has everlasting perseverance, is willing to dig as for hidden treasure, and does not despise 'the day of small things.' It enjoys the details of the process as well as the result. Persons who have felt that their natural talents and capabilities were small have surprised themselves and others with their improvement under the influence of this plodding spirit.

"We have an attraction going on between William H. and Harriet W. and it manifests itself in their sitting down together to study," Noyes noted. "It is a beautiful example. I wanted Mrs. Cragin to educate herself and become a good writer, and I insisted that she could learn any of the sciences. That element ran through our whole career at Putney and Brooklyn and the results were most splendid." Visitors to the modern Mansion House can view the bound volumes of periodicals the Community subscribed to, including *The Nation, Scientific American, Popular Science Monthly, Nature,* and *Atlantic Monthly,* to name a few. They subscribed to many newspapers and journals devoted to health, law, science, natural history, agriculture, music, and sports. "Louisa Tuttle and Chester Underwood overhauled our library. Our stock now numbers 3,200 books, all carefully re-arranged and completely indexed. Extra shelves were added for 600 volumes and 250 volumes have been re-bound. Our employees avail themselves of the benefits of this library.

"A first-rate appetite is the characteristic of our Community education at present—more spontaneous enthusiasm in studies of all kinds than ever before," the *Oneida Journal* noted on Christmas Day, 1856. "Men who have lived one life, perhaps of hard-handed toil, set themselves to studying French; during business they draw out of their pockets a sheet on which is printed the conjugation of the verb avoir. We noticed a stout striker at the anvil look at his lesson of French verbs pinned on the window at his right hand, while he waited for his partner to make the finishing strokes on the trap springs they were drawing. We heard a lad ask his father what the difference was between algebra and arithmetic; his father worked out for him two or three simple sums by the algebraic process. The boy's curiosity was excited and now we see him every night at the same hour with his book and slate, pursuing the study by himself. Knots of boys gather after supper, watching the solution of some difficult problem that has brought one of them to a stop in school. The old engage in them with all the zest of the young. A business class met evenings to study bookkeeping and all essentials for a thorough business education in 1860. "The Community sustains the school at considerable sacrifice from a business point of view," the November 22, 1860, Circular notes. "Our purpose is not to allow business to usurp the place that rightfully belongs to education, a vital interest to us that we cannot afford to neglect. But business in the shops and outdoors must be carried on, and housework cannot be dispensed with, so classes are set for the convenience of the greatest number wishing to study particular branches. Young men have half a day for study with the privilege of attending any class during that time, and popular hour-long classes are open to all in winter," the December 17, 1863, *Circular* reported. They started an evening school for trap factory and silk factory workers in 1873, and thirty scholars ranging from twelve to twenty-five couldn't get enough of it. "A great desire for improvement seems to possess all."

The Oneida Community Library contained 3,200 completely indexed books, plus newspapers, periodicals, and professional journals devoted to health, law, science, natural history, agriculture, music, sports and more.

"Starting with Astronomy at 6:45 a.m., the community organized all classes for those aged twelve to elder scholars," described the November 14, 1864, *Circular*. "Mathematics is an excellent tonic for minds in a condition of more or less disuse, and is sought as a natural regimen by those who wish to increase their mental activity. If study seems hard at first, a little patience and perseverance will soon overcome the difficulty and it will become a real pleasure. Fifty members wished to study arithmetic, so two classes met at different times, with good classes in geometry and algebra. One evening class in higher math consisted mostly of young men, taught by a young man; another class was composed chiefly of adults, including several grandmothers. A third class of boys between twelve and fifteen met at 9:00 a.m. and their teacher was responsible also for their further education, appointing them to such other classes as he thought best. Algebra, French, music, theology, and other classes were popular. An enthusiastic geography class of nearly fifty women and men of many ages met in the schoolroom at 4:30 p.m. The grammar class attracted thirty or forty, so there were two grammar classes, composition included, and twenty-six pupils studied writing. A very ambitious class of young ladies in natural philosophy will be inventing machinery before the winter is out. Smaller classes are in chemistry and thorough bass. There's scarcely a person in the Community who does not belong to one of these classes and most attend two. The enthusiasm is intense. After supper we spend three quarters of an hour in study of Greek, grammar, history, spelling, French, arithmetic, Natural Science, Geology, Physiology and other sciences. Frequently a dance was entered into with great zest by old and young." The May 12, 1873, *Circular* reported a determined effort to end bad spelling caused by the lack of early education before they joined the Community. "Every evening between seven and eight o'clock, many persons gathered in the South Sitting Room, the Upper Sitting Room, or the Large Hall to write words pronounced from a spelling book. A vigilance committee is informed of all egregious errors. We should not content ourselves until bad spelling is thoroughly weeded from the Community orthography."

The Debating Club

"A Conversation-Club was initially started to find and cultivate the highest standard of taste and beauty in literature and art, not for the purpose of debate. They were a success, besides affording the members who attended them a new source of amusement. After several gatherings of this quiet kind, certain subjects were introduced that involved interesting discussion, which evolved into a regular debating society. Considerable excitement attended these debates, in which many interested persons took an active part. The arguments were often exceedingly entertaining; many came only to listen. These debates first took place at the shoe-shop, but were soon transferred to the printing-office, then to the school-room, and finally were held in the old parlor where the whole family could be accommodated. George Washington Noyes organized a debating-club called the Young Men's Speaking Club, which met every

Sunday evening after supper. Officers were appointed, by-laws written, and these sessions were enthusiastically attended, frequently by the young women and others. These debating-clubs benefited those who belonged to them and furthered members' ambition for intellectual improvement.

"On Sunday, April 14, 1861, a Sociable was substituted. Each club member was present with a partner as well as other honorary members or constituents. A truly brilliant appearance met our astonished eyes as we were ushered into the school-room at 6 o'clock: Artistic fingers had decorated and arranged everything with an eye to beauty. Evergreens hung in graceful festoons around the room, and mottoes containing the different resolutions discussed by the Club had been handsomely copied and were tastefully suspended over them. The tables were daintily spread in the bright lamp-light. The president explained the purpose of the gathering, primarily for the benefit of the founders of the Club and also to make an experiment of having a party that would fulfill their idea of a Sociable. The guests discussed the supper in the merriest manner; then followed appropriate toasts, interspersed with songs and extempore remarks. An honorary member commented that when he was at college twenty years before, it was customary to have debating-societies, but there was not nearly the freedom of discussion or enthusiasm that he saw here.

"One closely contested question was finally settled: *Do the sorrows of this life exceed the joys thereof?* By the weight of argument after long, animated debate it had been decided *Yes*. But now by weight of actual facts, the decision was a unanimous *No*. During twilight, we brought chairs outside and held an extemporaneous debate with Mr. Henry Allen, Chairman. The subject: 'Resolved that Chinese emigration is a detriment to this country, and should be discouraged.' This is one of the liveliest questions of the times. Six speakers were appointed on a side and the toss of a penny determined their beginning. Many cogent things were said pro and con. Supporters contended that the Chinese are ignorant and anti-republican. 'Not so,' said others, 'this nation has been dependent on them for fifty years for materials to celebrate its independence; and now forsooth you would refuse to let them take part in the 4th of July popping, which their ingenuity has provided.'

"'Shall we let them in just because they're industrious and can make fire-crackers, which have cost us millions of dollars by fires they've caused?' said a third.

"'It is evident that they have qualities and acquisitions that we might well imitate,' was the reply, 'and that would make them at least as valuable as many of our European emigrants.'

"'But they have no interest in common with us. Their only object is to come here and get money, and then go back and spend it in their native land.'

"'Very well; this is Providence—they'll carry back the seeds of Christianity.'

"Lectures on Sunday and Wednesday evenings started a great interest in history, appreciated by all. A gentleman who has traveled much in China was our guest on August 15th, 1869; he told us that he'd never seen so much family affection as in

China—if a boy does anything to earn reward or fame, they give the father a higher rank or inscribe his name on tablets, which is far more gratifying to the son than any personal honor. 'Is it true,' William Hinds asked, 'that Chinese women are degraded—as reported by foreign visitors?' The visitor replied that a foreigner sees very little of women who are well brought up or well married; the ladies are small-footed and can hardly walk about the house. They go out but little, and then on the backs of slaves. Only the lowest classes of workers and abandoned characters are met. Our merchants go there, buy a girl of parents who are in debt, and live with her till they get ready to come away, when they take her back to her parents. This of course produces a very bad state of things. In spite of these objectionable customs, you will never find anyone who has been to China, lived in the interior and really got acquainted with these people of good manners, who does not speak favorably of them.

"Emily lectured on the Crusades, the first woman who had lectured and was a little frightened at first, but she did well and seemed to lose all her fear and embarrassment as she warmed up with her subject. Now that she has broken the ice, it will be easier for others. Augusta is to lecture tomorrow night on Venice, and George Noyes asked Chloe today to read up on The Age of Chivalry and give us a lecture on that. I think our lectures are a grand institution, making knowledge common property; it seems like a Community way of learning. Mother Noyes reads from Murray's *Geography* to a few of us after supper, which we are much interested in. We're reading about Europe, made doubly entertaining because George Noyes gives us many pleasant incidents about the places he visited. George makes subjects intelligible by means of diagrams, maps, and illustrations; we found before us a large, well-drawn map of Europe. He classified rivers first in respect to the countries through which they flowed: the Rhine might be called a German river, and the Rhone, French, and the Danube, Turkish. Then the Rhine might be considered as Teutonic in its origin, the Rhone as Gallic, and the Danube as Slavonic. Also the Rhine might be classified in respect to religion as Protestant, the Rhone as Catholic, and the Danube as Mohammedan. George described the scenery and cities along the Rhine so vividly that we almost fancied we were there. He reads to us from Arnold's *History of Rome*."

"All Community members played Bible games. One was reminiscent of Twenty Questions: ask a general and then more specific questions to guess where a verse is—in the Old or the New Testament? Did it emphasize love? Or a person would pick a verse and participants in turn would say book and chapter where it was (if they couldn't, it would move to the next person). They focused on one book and divided it into sections to make it easier to remember, such as, the first chapter in Matthew was called the Genealogy chapter; the 2nd, the Herod and Egypt chapter; 3rd, the John the Baptist chapter; 4th, the Temptation chapter and the 13th, the Parable chapter. Everyone including children would review every chapter and everyone found their own best way to learn. These games familiarized all with the Bible in new and interesting ways and encouraged old and young to study together. Noyes, from his theological seminary years, nearly always knew at once the book, chapter, and verse of a passage without reading over the appointed lesson; he used the Polyglot Bible, in which the Hebrew and Greek originals are exhibited along with historical translations. The Brattleboro, Vermont, English-only edition was published in 1834, the year of Noyes's religious experience, with many aids to the reader such as 60,000 Scripture cross-references."

EDUCATION OF THE SPIRIT

"We notice an infant's constant progress and improvement: first it shows intelligence in its eyes, then it finds the use of its arm, and next it creeps; at each advance we exult. Throughout childhood we see constant growth, enlargement of ideas, and extension of power," Noyes wrote in a *Circular* in late August, 1868. "According to the prevailing theory of life, our powers attain maximum growth at about age twenty-five, so twenty-one seems to be a fair proportion of life to devote to education and preparation. The prime of life is for making money, acquiring goods, and providing haply for an old age of competence. But cultivation of the mind and spirit does not diminish with age. When a farmer clears and manures his land he doesn't think his farm is now developed and he'll discontinue the process. No, his labor never was worth more—the harvest will more than ever reward good husbandry. It does an old tree as much good to bestow care upon it as it does a young one. Its increased fruitfulness rewards the laborer as much as anything he can do in his nurseries.

"The same principle applies to humanity. At a mature age there is more life to work upon; the benefits of culture may be greater than in youth. A contemplative spirit adopts love and the things that surround love for its chief good. Our life is but a short education into applying the heart as well as the mind to bear fruit unto God. All of us are babes in consideration of the whole scope of our existence. A taste for education and spiritual improvement has to be required and stimulated, for consider if we would leave children to themselves, how many would go to school? They'd choose sports and ramble for berries and grow up as the wild children of the forest. When they get out from under parents, they quit school and run after money, which is not a more worthy pursuit for our immortal minds than are the fancies of children. And the old have no more self-control. But the living spirit of God can kindle the most burning enthusiasm and impart exhaustless energy, putting young and old in a lifetime school to educate not a surface, but the whole depth of humanity in purification of the heart, discipline of the affections, and cultivation of one's spiritual nature. A student would get a poor education attending only one or two weekly lectures while most time is given to pleasure-seeking; a weekly sermon or occasional Bible study does not suffice while most time is devoted to often antagonistic pursuits. The true and the noble must be continually stimulated through inspection of all the relations of life—vigilant self watchfulness and spiritual knowledge to root out the lurking-places of selfishness."

"Human beings are capable of other and more important work than that of the body or of the brain," wrote Noyes in his Home Talk, *Three Kinds of Labor*. "Labor in prayer is as real and intelligible as farm-work or student-work. It is an action of the heart, a willing of the central life that does not consist or necessarily result in thinking or in any particular action of the brain. I was brought up to mental labor, and there has been a long, long conflict in me between the force concerned in brain labor and that which is concerned in spiritual labor. I see that the highest and best function of the brain is not a muscular one, not a function of labor, but one of receptivity in which it watches for and receives and acts upon suggestions that come to it from the heart and the spiritual world."

"My present ambition is not for fame nor any of the glittering goals usually set up as incentives to untiring effort," D. Edson Smith shared in the January 6, 1873, *Circular*. "It is that I may become thoroughly receptive to the Spirit of Truth. This ambition is the result of what I have learned in the Community. I did not know *receptivity* to be of any special importance in enabling me to attain to the highest aspirations of a Christian life. During youth I was a constant churchgoer, but I do not recollect having ever heard a minister urge upon his hearers the benefits growing from a receptive heart; I was taught obedience but not receptivity. No one taught me that it was possible to secure the guidance of superior wisdom in all things and at all times. Persons who visit the Community wonder what holds us so harmoniously together. One important element is the spirit of receptivity that pervades all hearts. Never before did I see a people with so little personal will or ambition, nor with such strong great ambitions to further the interests of the race under the guidance of inspiration. This Association furnishes one of the most marked proofs that all the affairs of life are controlled by a superhuman intelligence we call God; that it is possible for persons to receive guidance in all their thoughts and actions by this superior wisdom. It requires not a mere passive state, but a watching and waiting with cheerful alacrity to carry out the wishes of a wiser mind than our own. When the victory is won and a soft heart is established, a fruitful harvest succeeds such as can be obtained from no other source—even the gratification of all desires."

"Paul exhorts the Thessalonians to *pray without ceasing*," wrote Seymour Nash. "This implies that there is an attitude of heart in which it is easy to pray under all circumstances. I find myself in a true attitude of prayer when I have a soft heart, and then it seems as natural to pray as it does to breathe. By prayer I do not mean words or asking for special things, but the pouring out of the heart to God in a spontaneous way that keeps a current of life flowing through the heart from God, and governs almost unconsciously every action of our lives. When I desire to do something, the desire to ask God about it arises when I have a soft heart. If I follow the instinct, I am conscious of a feeling of happiness in doing—or not doing—that leaves me perfectly at rest afterwards. The assurance that God sees the end and will work all things for good frees me entirely from any feeling of anxiety as to the result; and the peace of heart that comes from waiting patiently on God is worth more than the gratification of any wish, however desirable it may seem in itself." This is reminiscent of the sacred scripture of the East, the Bhagavad-Gita: "Let your privilege be in actions themselves; never let it be in their fruits . . . . Without attachment do the work you have to do; for the man who does his work without attachment wins to the Supreme." [43]

"A part of my business is the work of laying the truth to heart," wrote Abram Burt in the April 20, 1868, *Circular*. "I stop in the midst of my leisure, labor, pain, or pleasure, and endeavor to put away every absorbing thought and emotion. Sometimes I can do this at once; at other times I can only succeed after the most agonizing effort. I do this in order to give God a hearing. Having done it, I have done all I can; my activity can take me no further. If anything comes of it, it is because the spirit of God becomes active and sends a word home to my heart. Sometimes the truth comes to me in the garb of ordinary language, sometimes in the language of Scripture, and sometimes in both ways combined. At one time it is a hint to action; at another, it is friendly counsel; it is always criticism, light, and relief. When suffering from a distress I couldn't express nor locate, I waited for what would come to me; and the word soon came that my intellect was too active; that it was trying to snatch the truth, that it had never asked for wisdom; that it was like some wild thing in a cage. Thereupon the stream of life began to set toward my heart, and on it was borne this saying, 'Come unto me all ye that labor and are heavy laden, and I will give you rest. Take my yoke upon you and learn of me; for I am meek and lowly in heart; and ye shall find rest unto your souls.' My load was gone, and I then knew how it was that Christ could give his rest—it was because he could wait to be taught; he could preach that which he heard. It gives me power to think, power to follow science, power to digest my meat. Best of all, it takes away fear and gives me a sense of having gained a foot-hold in the universe."

"I learn more and more to admire the versatility of the instructive power that comes from the Spirit of Truth," John Noyes agreed. "It may proceed in this way: I have a season of severe experience and suffering that does not seem to be profitable; I see no good end to it and it is discouraging. But I find at last that the Spirit has taken me through that course to prepare me to pursue some particular truth that will bring me into new affinity with itself. That spirit has delicate methods of working on the mind and heart, like the operations of a chemist. He knows what to put in and what to extract, and how to make chemical combinations for any process whatever. When he has brought me to where I am to take a new lesson, he goes about an ingenious course of reactions consisting of suffering and trials that make me receptive, so that his instruction will enter into my mind naturally and take full effect. An old passage of Scripture will come into my mind with an entirely new sense, as though fresh from God," Noyes relates in *Spiritual Lessons*. "No matter how familiar it has been, I see an entirely new meaning in it and discover that I never before got below the letter of it."

"Christ came into the world to purify the heart here in this world," wrote Noyes in *Before Community* on April 10, 1868. "From 1834 to 1846 we were known as

Perfectionists who believed in the possibility of being saved from sin. From that original root, everything else is secondary—growing branches and fruits. There's a tendency to get away from the root to the fruit, from the interior to the exterior, from cause to effect. Our young people are interested and occupied with Community ideas and have no direct memory of our original platform, so may neglect its religious foundation. Before we lived in Community, our whole heart was given to faith in Christ and salvation from sin and that doctrine must be thoroughly understood and studied by the young. All our discipline leads to going back to Christ as a Savior and purifier of the heart."

"People have no idea of our great vision," Tirzah Miller wrote a month later in the May 10, 1868, *Circular*. "Our ambition is to let inspiration control our business so that in the whirl of active operation, we shall have abundant leisure to think on deeper things. We build and extend our various businesses, we promulgate Community principles and practices, but it is interior things that command our full attention and make our hearts light—radical revolutions in character and the thousand evidences of hidden power at work on humanity. We would dissolve our form of society today if it were anything else but a means to an end infinitely higher, as described by Mr. Noyes one month ago. The *Community Journal* of April 8th notes that in the first glow of conversion, it seems an easy matter for self to die; external culture and a high moral education may lift a person up many rounds of the ladder of perfection. Yet by sad experience, reaped again and again in tears, we have learned that only a vital connection with the humblest being in the universe can eradicate from our natures those terrible weeds—envy and selfishness. The labor of our lives is in this direction, and mercy has been overflowing. Two young men running a high course of independence and recklessness turned square around by a sincere family criticism. The change they've undergone is marvelous; they often confess their belief in the power of God.

"Persons take much interest in our Community and our experiments in human association; some feel that our success rests on their shoulders," Tirzah continued. "People fire volleys of advice, remonstrance, and suggestions by the cannon-full. *Don't do this or that! Be sure that your foundation-pins are well stuck in on this point and that.* They might as well think of marking out the course of a meteor! We're always open to fair criticism and wise suggestions, and have been benefited by many observations from outside friends and even enemies. You needn't worry yourselves about us, good people. Our purpose is much larger than making the Oneida Community a financial or social success. It is our specialty to love the truth, let it cut where it will."

"The first grand agent of life and health stated by Christ at the close of his forty days' fast is *Man shall not live by bread alone, but by every word that proceeds from the mouth of God,*" wrote George Washington Noyes in *The Nutriment of Life*. "This connection between our life and the Word of God is stated over and over again by Christ with startling emphasis and is a subject of inexhaustible interest and depth. The Word of God is not merely a law appealing to the conscience, but is a power penetrating the heart—*The words I speak unto you are spirit and they are life.* Paul speaks of the Word of God as living and powerful, sharper than any two-edged sword. The effect of the word of God received in our nature is universal life. We see no reason for limiting Scripture language to mean life only to the soul, though here doubtless is its most important effect. Eating and drinking the living Word of God sweeps the whole circle of our nature including body as well as soul. *I am the bread of life* is offered as the sustainer of life, the living will of God going forth as a fresh inspiration coming to the heart in the form of a work to do or a new truth. How is the spiritual Word received into our nature? It is most often compared in the Scriptures to *eating*; our spiritual center has a receptive faculty and a demand corresponding to hunger and thirst. The only thing needed to secure a full and free supply in all circumstances is the appetite, and this God gives. Whether called faith, receiving, or eating, the Word of God, the bread of life, is always accessible to the hungry. Give us this day our daily bread, is the prayer of Christ. Blessed are they that hunger and thirst after righteousness, for they shall be filled. If any thirst, come unto me and drink; as Scripture hath said, out of his belly shall flow rivers of living water. A draught of the Word of God is better than food or medicine—it is the agent of health to body and soul."

"Some assert that there is a fixed limit to what can be known—certain strata of truth lie on the surface and we can discover secrets in the rocks, the earth, the stars, and chemical materials," Noyes wrote in *Limits of the Knowable*. "Suppose someone admires the exterior of a fine house. Without permission of the owner, he cannot go inside or learn the habits of the family. The interior can be known only by establishing personal relations with the party who owns and lives in the house. The most important region of truth is not on the surface and is accessible or not according as persons secure, or fail to secure, the key to it. That key is a true social relation with God. My conclusion about the accessibility of truth is that it is subject to no fixed limitations in the human mind."

The Honorable Ezra Cornell's words surrounded his portrait on a Cornell University catalog: "I would found an institution where any person can find instruction in any study."

"If I were to found an institution of higher learning," Noyes said, "it would offer systematic instruction:

>on the way to find God;
>in the art of walking in the Spirit;
>in the art of love, general and special;
>in the theory and practice of social life;
>in the art of conversation;
>in the art of managing infants;
>in the art of rearing boys and girls;
>in the art of making a happy home."

7

Mutual Criticism: a Spiritual Profile

The word criticism is derived from the Greek *krino*, to discriminate—to judge. At Andover Theological Seminary, Noyes joined a secret society of serious students planning to become foreign missionaries known as The Brethren. Two of the brethren, Lyman and Munson, were killed by cannibals on one of the islands of Sumatra in the East Indies, but Noyes nevertheless planned to work in Asia. Each week a Brethren member submitted to Mutual Criticism, a mutual inspection of character and unvarnished truth-telling to help each other improve. Called according to the alphabetical order of his name, the member held his peace and silently listened while the others recounted his faults of character and habits in the plainest way possible. This exercise sometimes cruelly demolished self-complacency, but the society's regulations prohibited anyone to be provoked or to complain. Few enjoy being told about shortcomings, but Noyes's spiritual practices probably helped him in the humility department—"I found much benefit in submitting to this ordeal, at Andover and afterward," he said. This practice began in an inner sanctuary of the Congregational Church in the early nineteenth century and was practiced by six young men at Williams College, beginning in 1808. One of them, Mills, took this society with him to Andover in the winter of 1809–10, where he and his associates took measures resulting in the formation of the American Board of Commissioners for Foreign Missions. The society had many branches at New England colleges and at Auburn and Princeton Theological Seminaries.

"Oneida Community member Henry W. Burnham obtained the names of twelve surviving members of The Brethren from Andover and wrote to them in 1874 asking about the society's history, and received nine responses. Two were reproduced in the 1876 book *Mutual Criticism*, published by the Community. One man who responded remembered only a single criticism of himself, but he seemed to have felt nearly the same emotions years later that he experienced at the time: 'Believe me, once was enough for a lifetime. Such an operation I never went through before or since. I have before me at this moment the remarks then made on my manner and way of doing things, in conversation, in prayer, etc. The process was severe and scathing in the extreme. Most of the remarks were kindly intended and just; some were, I have always thought, unkind, unjust, and rather *too severe* at least. At the same time, as I wrote in my journal, I was conscious of other faults more heinous and more dangerous to my soul and to the cause of Christ, as committed more directly against God . . . . After I went to my room, I could but weep before God over my numerous faults faithfully exposed.' A response from a former Brethren member was very different from the first one. 'It was in the meetings of that sacred conclave,' he wrote back, 'that I spent some of the happiest, and I might say some of the most profitable hours of my life.' Noyes agreed. 'That is the way to take criticism, and it is easy when you know how and have a soft heart. If you cannot calculate on something like that in your circle, do not undertake Mutual Criticism."

A WASHING APPLIED TO THE INNER MAN

Noyes introduced Mutual Criticism as the only method of government in the Oneida Community. Members learned how to love, respect, and live harmoniously with others not only in deeds, but even in thoughts. Mutual Criticism in the Community was summed up as the government of the Truth under which discipline was internal, not imposed from without. "Sixteen years to the day after Noyes's spiritual revelation, the Second Annual Report of the Oneida Association stated that the secret of the power that harmonizes the Community and constitutes its government lies not in any code of laws but in our system of *Free Criticism*. The power of the Golden Rule—Do unto others as you would have them do unto you—coursed through the whole Community, unifying all from the most spiritual to the most immature. Selfishness and disorder are annoying, and Community members were provided the liberty and the means of speaking the truth to an offender. Instead of running up a long account for settlement later, they said, we prefer to take it as we go along. The time inevitably comes when the secrets of hearts are made manifest and those who now shrink from the light will have to suffer all that we suffer, but it will be more intolerable to them because it has not been gradual as with us. People don't really get away with their shortcomings. Thought is full of criticism all through society—every person is more or less transparent to those around him and passes in the surrounding sphere of thought for pretty much what he is worth. Speech supplies the demand for criticism, too—known as backbiting. If you have faults, you can be sure they're covered in evil-speaking. Open, kindly criticism was a reversed substitute for tea-party backbiting. We might imagine others' criticisms of us—and our imaginings can be worse than what people actually think. We are a mirror to each other, presenting the whole of our characters both good and bad, for every fault has a corresponding virtue. The usual criticism in society is without method; it acts like electric current but is not applied to any useful purpose. It distributes itself and sometimes injuriously. The Community draws it off from the malicious channel of evil-thinking and gossip and conducts it through honest speech to a beneficial result. Far healthier to have things out in the open!"

"I don't know how much mortification others have endured under Mutual Criticism, but I've had a fair share of it, considering that I never knew what it was to allow man to rebuke me," wrote Abel Easton, a London lawyer. "I'd been brought up to esteem it a duty and a virtue to resent as an insult the slightest impeachment of my character or actions. I had never worked for wages, and therefore had never felt the restraint of a master. My youth had been spent in the society of those whose duty it was to obey me, and in subsequent life my extravagance surrounded me with parasites who stood ready to flatter so long as I had money to spend. I'd never received any contradiction or check on me until I came to the Community. It will therefore be seen that what to many people would have been a slight affair, to me was an overwhelming affront. I can now laugh heartily at criticism that formerly I'd thought would be utterly impossible for me ever to get over.

"My first taste of criticism was at the Moffat Building, New York City, where I met Mr. Noyes and Mr. Cragin and submitted to an operation. I was so indignant at what I considered consummate impudence, that I could scarcely refrain from resenting it in stronger terms than would have been considered polite or consistent with my Christian profession. With great effort I left without an improper expression. As I walked down those long flights of stairs from the top of the Moffat Building to Broadway, I swore in my heart that I would never again subject myself to such insult, or even so much as speak with a Community member again. Canal Street was crowded with carts and I couldn't readily cross; while I waited, a voice whispered in my heart, *Turn back; those men will do you good.* I returned, still indignant, to find my critics still there. From that time I was convinced that God had appointed criticism as an ordinance for my improvement and I decided that with God's help, I would go through the judgment come what may. I got a great deal more than I bargained for! If I had known all, I might never have summoned courage enough to take the first plunge. I don't remember the particulars of my criticisms at New York more than that they were frequent and intensely mortifying. Many things were said that seemed utterly untrue and after worrying and stewing over them for a few days, I concluded that it would not hurt me to accept the criticisms even if they were unjust—and they might do me some good. God was my judge and if ever I was saved, it would be by standing justified before God, not before man. Thus my attempts to explain away criticism appeared paltry, too small a business for a man who sought favor with God alone.

"For some years, the advantage of criticism was almost the only privilege of Community that I was permitted to enjoy. It was a thorny path; but the firm assurance that I had and have now, that through criticism I shall find salvation, enabled me to hold out and persevere. My greatest and latest difficulties about criticism are that positions are thrust upon me contrary to my own seeking and desires; though conscious of much diffidence as to my capabilities of filling different positions, I do my best to do my duty. Yet I've been jerked out in disgrace, criticized for seeking position, for affecting to know a great deal more than I did, and much more—all of which seemed untrue and unnecessarily unkind. Well! This has been exceedingly mortifying—I can't imagine anything more so. It seemed as if the Community was more unjust than capitalists, but I've come to see that it's not a question of justice or injustice but of spiritual growth and improvement. It would be the height of folly to suppose that the Community or anyone in it meant any injustice to me personally, or desired anything but the advancement of my highest interests. It may be legally a theft to take rags off a beggar's back, but it cannot be considered unjust if the object is to replace them with good clothes. I've received a discipline that I could have gotten in no other way; I will therefore thank God for the results. He has the right to use any means he pleases. If I believe heartily that everything works together for my good, I should not call into question the mode of discipline; the fact of my quarreling with the means should be proof that I needed that kind of discipline to teach me how to trust the Lord with more implicit faith. By such reasoning I have come to be thoroughly satisfied and thankful with all that has taken place, and it seems impossible for me ever to have a hard thought again about criticism. If there are any in the family who feel that I have at any time acted wrongly or spoken unjustly or intemperately at any criticism, I want to make all the reparation possible."

"When inquirers are informed that we rely upon mutual criticism as the principal means of internal government, it is probable that they get a very imperfect idea of what this mutual criticism really is," wrote Erastus Hamilton on February 10, 1873. "We can imagine them saying to themselves: 'Criticism! If that makes people harmonious, what a beautiful, orderly state of society we outsiders ought to have. Our atmosphere is as full of criticism as a summer evening of insects, and unhappily much of it is of the stinging, biting kind that one instinctively endeavors to flee from. I would as soon think of making my bed in a room full of wasps and mosquitoes as to live in a free-criticism society!' Such remarks are sometimes made by our visitors. We ourselves did not altogether understand it or enjoy it at first. Like children learning to be washed, we submitted with as good a grace as we could. When the ordinance was followed by a new sense of interior cleanliness, justification, and peace with God and man, *then* we began to be enthusiastic about criticism. Criticism is in fact a washing applied to the inner man. At this vision, *interior cleanliness*, what a prospect arises before us of hopes realized, a world redeemed, the Millennium a reality! How beautiful is purity! A pure heart—how priceless! It is related that God said of David, 'I have found a man after mine own heart.' David's character has a special interest—a man of strong passions, mighty in war, strong in friendship, and a great lover of women; but his deep, central passion was love of righteousness and internal purity: 'Cleanse thou me from secret faults. Behold, thou desires truth in the inward parts. Create in me a clean heart, O God, renew a right spirit within me.' Criticism of the inner life is

Jesus Christ's invention; his Spirit and the Bible furnish the discernment necessary to criticize faithfully: these agencies alone furnish the humility and desire for improvement necessary to a right reception of criticism and the unconditional love required in administering criticism. Love of interior purity is a passion as distinct as the love of food, but it has been trodden under foot for so long that its existence is made of no account. Love of interior cleanliness, purity, righteousness, is the deep, central, king-passion, and we have learned to rely upon it as the citadel that governs the whole man. People are governed by the passions and affections of the heart, not by the thoughts of the head. If, as we believe, criticism is an ordinance that develops and strengthens love of the truth, those who honestly consider the matter will see that mutual criticism is one of the most potent means of government. Its administration approaches the reign of perfect justice, under which all good people will be at peace."

"The *Present Age* publication describes our free criticism as a 'merciless overhauling of one another's individualities,' as though it were all censure and animadversion [blame]. Mutual Criticism is a spiritual profile; we are known and accepted for who we are in our entirety and are given respect and affirmation." All Community members knew that character assessment was done in kindness to help each other grow spiritually, to improve social harmony, and as a fine by-product, to make one's own life pleasanter. To make such a leap forward in insight and behavior, the Community studied human nature. They realized that each person is a complex package of highly-prized spiritual, intellectual, social, and physical qualities, and that the basic nature of a person should not be uprooted—even if it could be—but aspects of personality that become selfish or remain unexamined require pruning, for full flowering. They practiced self-observation without self-judgment in order to prune selfish aspects of an excellent quality. By understanding that virtues have corresponding faults, and vice versa, viewing one's shortcomings can be done with some interest, if not dispassion.

"Criticism is more than half praise; it corrects what is bad and commends what is good. Praise is sweet to receive, and even sweeter to give. There is very little of it in common society, but the love of praising and being praised finds gratification in free criticism. We have the pleasure of telling those around us what we see beautiful in their spirit and manners and personal qualities; of telling others what we know of their 'alms and good deeds,' and of expressing our esteem, affection, and admiration. At times we enjoy discriminations in our own favor that we haven't discovered of ourselves. Individualities may be agreeable as well as offensive, gifts as well as defects, and happy individualities are not ignored—on the contrary, they are stimulated and developed by praise. The *Present Age* assumes that our system of mutual criticism must 'suppress all spontaneity of individual expression.' Our criticism suppresses the spontaneity of 'weeds'—what is more spontaneous than the growth of weeds? Yet the gardener makes no scruple of suppressing them. Let others advocate the freedom of selfish individualities; we are contented to encourage those that make a happy home.

"A Congregational Church bulletin reviewed a book that discussed mutual criticism and suggested another use that might be made of it: How would criticism work as a means of grace in some of our churches? 'Our advice to all societies, churches, communities, and clubs that think of starting Mutual Criticism is, first, count the cost,' Noyes advised. 'Take our word for it—the cost will be nothing less than general humility enough to receive severe mortification and even unjust criticisms without reply and without offense.' After undergoing a criticism, a Community woman said, 'Well! This procedure is like undergoing a major operation without benefit of anesthetic!' This attitude was unusual, but an occasional person departed from the Community due to inability to fully embrace the spirit and benefits of Mutual Criticism in spite of pain felt on the ego level of mind. A visitor was most impressed after learning about many facets of Community life, but one Community member opined, 'I wonder if she would think it was a paradise after she'd undergone three or four criticisms.'"

"I once had a criticism in which I was strongly tempted to resent the remarks of one individual," a man said. "What was said was wholly unlooked for by me and seemed unjust and hard to bear. For several days it rankled in my mind, causing me great unhappiness. At length I thought I would try to put the matter out of my thoughts, but it kept continually recurring, bringing with it a feeling of bitterness that I'd never before known. Seeing that it was likely to destroy my peace of mind, I resolved that I would try no more to thrust it away from me, but to summon all the sincerity and humility I could and calmly and prayerfully reflect upon it. The result was, I saw clearly and acknowledged to myself that the bitter pill at which I was tempted to rebel was the *truest and best part of my criticism*. It was the only thing in my criticism that had really mortified and wounded my self-conceit, and that was its supreme value. I swallowed it, and have had no trouble with it since. If a person was tempted to resist criticism, he would need that which he most deserved; such a temptation was a sure sign, in most cases, that he'd been hit where he needed to be hit. My experience with criticism has led me to look upon it as a *great source of relief*."

"No doubt criticism was like taking bitter medicine or receiving an inoculation, resisted by children but understood by adults. Criticism is not arbitrary judgment of character. It is a work of mercy. Your dentist is severe and makes you suffer, but you know that this is doing you good. Probably dentists feel very benevolent in their vocation. So our system of criticism must be regarded as a real mercy. It is an attempt to relieve human suffering and promote human comfort by the severity of truth. I hope in the next years the science of the criticism of character will be carried as far as the science of dentistry.

"Let us bear in mind the great central fact of existence, that Jesus Christ is in us and that the Holy Spirit is in us," said G. in the January 20, 1873, *Circular*. "Let us also remember that the greatest foes to the remembrance of this precious truth and to its practical realization are the *feelings*. More than all other things combined, feelings will tend to dim the truth of Christ's presence and hide it, cover it up. Feelings are so often the result of a trivial, depressing circumstance or some contact with passing evil, that we know they can't be trusted. Hence, we must, day by day, deny superficial feelings and insist upon the stability of the word of God more willfully and doggedly than ever a soldier stood his ground upon the field of battle. We should confess this truth hour by hour, in every contingency and in every emergency of life. To keep this belief bright regardless of the feelings is to keep the faith.

"A friendly lawyer who visited us joined one of our evening conversations. 'There is a great deal said nowadays about science and political science, the science of civil government based on facts that have been discovered in human nature; adjusting human relations to these facts is called government. At Oneida is the strange spectacle of some hundreds of human beings living together in close relations, carrying on business of many kinds and undertaking all the various activities of human beings. Strong passions, such as acquisitiveness, must necessarily be called into exercise. This passion for money-making is ruling the world, but the Community has made it subservient to its uses. Then there is the master passion—amativeness. The Community lives together and raises and educates children without formal government or law. How is it done? Simply by the power of mutual criticism and brotherly love. These people are quiet and industrious and I believe they are the happiest people in the world. Criticism is certainly one of the greatest forces in civil government that has ever been discovered.'"

"If society cannot exist without government and especially without a system of courts and police, then Community cannot exist without Free Criticism," Noyes wrote. "Crimes are punished under legal systems, but the interior characters of people are not meddled with, and thus the real sources of crime remain untouched. Mutual Criticism undertakes to improve character, so there will be no occasion for judges or police. In ordinary life, persons may live with some degree of peace and comfort while the latent diseases of heart and mind are at work; but in a Community, persons in daily contact with each other in many ways can't avoid understanding each other's character and detecting interior maladies. Without a purification of character greater than any that exists in common society, it would be impossible to live here. Free and thorough criticism is not possible in the world because people can conceal their true characters and they do not know each other well enough to criticize truthfully. Community Criticism reveals the many forms of littleness, meanness, and selfishness of human nature; it may seem to cause useless distress and suffering because it discloses ordinarily concealed evils, even from oneself, but it provides an effectual remedy!

Mutual Criticism: a Spiritual Profile

John Humphrey Noyes taught that our internal teacher is the source of all happiness and health for soul and body. Conscious connection with this divine realm of truth and harmony within us is heaven on earth.

"When the system of mutual criticism shall be perfected so that God can use it as a lively medium of his Spirit, communities will be able to take care of themselves without special leaders, and revivals in the churches will propagate themselves without any other special measures. Perfected, our system will be the most effectual means of carrying salvation to the soul that the world has ever seen," Noyes exclaimed. "To any church that has no minister—if you want a revival, don't send for a preacher and start a protracted meeting, but organize yourselves into classes for mutual criticism; humble yourselves before God and before one another, by first confessing your own sins and then inviting, each from all, faithful sincerity in detecting your secret faults. Wash yourselves in the spirit of truth, and get your neighbors to help you; I will warrant you the best revival you ever heard of. Those who love criticism need not fear that day; it will be as pleasant to them as the dawn of morning. The truth-telling, sincere spirit sees us just as we are, and it must therefore detect faults so long as we have any; but as our faults gradually disappear, it will praise us more and more and end in everlasting praise."

D. Edson Smith wrote a testimony for the November 25, 1872, *Circular:* "Mutual Criticism produces wonderful effects on both body and mind. It has the power of the strongest tonics and can be so applied as to produce startling changes in the human body. But the most striking of all its effects is in its operations on our spiritual nature—here it is indeed miraculous. During the five years I've been in the Community, changes it has wrought in my own spiritual nature are as great as were effected in all my previous life, though I was brought up in the church and for years earnestly desired spiritual improvement. I'm convinced that the great hindering of spiritual growth is egotism, and for its removal or destruction, criticism is one of the best agencies ever put into practice. It brings to light even the most secret faults, leaving no hiding place for egotism to shelter itself in, and yet it does this in a way to make us love those who criticize us. Criticism given in love, for the sole purpose of helping one to improve, cannot but cause good feelings in the heart of the criticized, and promote the growth of earnestness and love, and all the fruits of the Spirit."

As the Community expanded, modifications of the system were devised. Four of the most spiritual and discerning judges of character, first criticized by Noyes, were appointed to criticize in due course all members. Committee members worked daily for three weeks developing a thorough and fair criticism—an individual spiritual profile. They interviewed the person's associates and discussed his or her character among themselves, then offered their best advice. Here is a typical criticism: "E. is remarkably outspoken and impulsive; consequently her faults are decided and well known. She is a fine specimen of the vital temperament, has great exuberance of animal spirits, would live on laughing and frolic, and is ardent in her affections and lively in her antipathies. In the circumstance of ordinary life she would not have been corrected of her faults; simple parental authority would not have been sufficient. She would have ruled all around her, and henpecked her husband to the last degree. But the Community is too much for her, especially as she is wise enough to give herself up to its criticism. Elderly people criticize her for disrespect and inattention. She will fly through a room perhaps on some impulsive errand of generosity, leave both doors open and half knock down anybody in her way. She laughs too much and too loudly. All of us agree that she should at least cease laughing at others' calamities. She has a touch of vanity, likes to look in the glass, and plumes herself on her power of charming. She indulges in unfounded antipathies and whims of taste, while she is likely to be carried out of bounds by her attractions. Her wonderful exuberance of life, gaiety, and impetuosity are her gift, the inheritance of her youth and constitution, and no one would have these qualities changed. Like many another good passion, these would be bad if allowed to act under the influence of selfishness, but of themselves they are much to be prized in society. Though E. is zealous, industrious, and useful, we should miss her more for what she *is* than for what she does. We must cure her of her coarseness, and teach her to be enthusiastic without being rude, respectful without being dull."

A similar criticism was noted from the 1873 Criticism Club in which all desired to participate: "S. was highly commended for the improvement she has made. She is naturally attractive, and was on that account petted and flattered when young. Criticism and suffering have made her an earnest God-fearing woman. She has found Christ in her heart and no longer depends on outward circumstances for happiness. She is very receptive to good influences and delights in the society of her superiors, one secret of her great improvement. She is vivacious and diffuses sunshine and joy wherever she goes. Her vivacity sometimes tempts her into frivolity. We would not have her less vivacious, but would have her vivacity express seriousness as well as mirth."

"If you listen to the strains that are ever sounding through creation," Mr. Noyes wrote, "you will find that God's everlasting melody is at once full of seriousness and full of mirth. If you would make the tones of your heart a harmonious accompaniment to that melody, you must first take lessons in seriousness (which is the soul of all God's music), and then you must learn to combine seriousness with mirth, as these are combined in all the harmonies of nature and the Bible."

HOW TO GIVE AND RECEIVE CRITICISM

"All members formed themselves into classes of a dozen persons at one time, and each group criticized all its members, furnished in writing. Later, a standing committee was selected by the Community and rotated among Community members every three months, to whom persons desiring the benefit of this ordinance might make application. With an ever-changing committee, everyone was given the opportunity to serve as critics as well as subjects; all members participated and were trained to be criticized without taking offense. Excessive sensitiveness, they thought, is a great fault. Instead of taking criticism personally, those criticized can strive to look at their personal faults as they might assess another's, and feel no more pain in dissecting one's own character than anyone else's.

"Humility is the spirit in which to receive criticism. Receiving criticism fruitfully is a combination of patience and enthusiasm for improvement, to watch oneself and to lie in wait. Self-observation succeeds where compelling change does not, and yet people cannot examine themselves with any degree of thoroughness by self-inspection alone," James Herrick said. "People suppose they know their own hearts, but their neighbors are likely to know them better. By seeing ourselves as others see us, we can grow spiritually; mutual criticism is the only thorough way. If one really wishes to know his own faults and continue from self-examination to thorough repentance, let him ask another to help him; then will he receive an answer to Burn's prayer:

> *O, wad some pow'r the Giftie gi'e us / To see oursels as others see us."*

"Members were also trained in how to give criticism, in the same spirit as we expect it to be received, with love, patience, and meekness. A combative spirit only provokes resistance, self-justification, and possibly retaliation. But, criticism done superficially by mixing in too much praise was to be guarded against as not effecting needed change. It was like walking the razor's edge! H. is a poor critic—he has good judgment of character, but he is fearful that he may displease by speaking the truth. 'In order to have real fellowship with the Spirit of Truth and see it go forth among us with power,' Noyes taught, 'there must be great sincerity. Speak the truth in love, but speak the whole truth. Let us not be afraid to say what should be said. Let us have more respect for the truth than for persons. Let the spirit of God's sincerity rejoice through us—rejoice in our simplicity and faithfulness one with another. Sincerity is the main thing in a good criticism—sincerity on one side, and love of sincerity on both sides. Those who receive criticism should count it as a blessing that is going to send them forward into good experience. I may truly say that I criticized myself into the gospel. I searched the Bible for sharp truths to convict others, and convicted myself. That is the way God took to work me into the faith. In the same manner I have overcome difficulties. Circumstances would set me to study some general subject in its application to others, and my studies would lead to deliverance from my own difficulties. I have great delight in my heart when I feel that I am discovering truth that criticizes my own position and character.

"Persons must entirely put away the natural feeling that they have no right to criticize an evil they see in others, unless they are free from it themselves; this is incorrect and shouldn't hinder a person from being honest," Noyes said in his talk *Prelude to a Criticism* at the Brooklyn Community in April 1852. "We may even help ourselves get rid of the fault. If I have a mote in my eye and you have one in yours, I can see to get yours out better than I can to get mine out, and vice versa; each can help the other. Assume that you are bound for freedom from all faults; and then if you have a fault that troubles you, criticize it, both in yourself and others; let loose upon it wherever you find it! The truth is not at all dependent on our personal position to it; submit to the influence of the Spirit of Truth. If an evil is in you, no matter how many others have the same evil, to be saved from it you should avail yourself of all the truth that can be said about it. Look simply at the evil under criticism, and let every one strike. What we want is to let the Spirit of Truth have free scope. We must assume that we are on the side of truth, and love it, and give it all the facilities we can. To have a *beam* in my eye is another thing—that blinds me altogether. I must first pull that out, before I can see to cast the mote out of my brother's eye. But it is to be assumed that we have accepted Christ and that his light is shining in our hearts, and that we are helping one another to get rid of motes. All personal feelings must be laid aside and our attention confined to the truth. Let the truth have free course, hit whom it may."

"We are constantly exercising an influence by our spirit on all around us," Mother Harriet Noyes wrote on March 3, 1873, "imprinting ourselves upon others. We preach by spirit as well as by word, and generally with more effect, so we are bound to be what we wish others to be. Instead of fretting at faults we see in our companions, make them inducements to attain the opposite virtues. If we would teach humility, for instance, we must attract those around us to a meek and lowly spirit, and in order to do it we must ourselves have a meek and lowly spirit. The same is true of all the fruits of the spirit." Interestingly, Harriet Noyes, the mother of the Community, was criticized for being deficient in severity. "It would do her good to scold sometimes."

Members Asked for Criticism

"Community members increasingly offered themselves for criticism, because the universal testimony was that criticism had been extremely beneficial, as Noyes had felt when criticized by The Brethren. On such occasions, whoever has anything to say

Mutual Criticism: A Spiritual Profile

freely says it, either in finding fault or of special commendation, or of both. If any member manifests a bad spirit, or faulty manners, or in any way proves annoying to the social circle, it is the privilege of the circle, either in public or private, to bring the matter to examination and seek in a kind spirit the reformation of the offender. It was a helpful look at how superficial deficiencies of manner—one's natural, unconscious way of interacting with others—detract from a good heart. A good example is the criticism of Mr. B. by a small committee:

"*Critic No. 1.*—'Mr. B.'s earnestness and strength of character make him a very valuable member of society; but he needs cultivation and refinement.'

"*Critic No. 2.*—'Mr. B. has all the solid qualities—firmness, uprightness, and sincerity; he intends to deal justly with everyone.'

"*Critic No. 3.*—'He is warm-hearted, and a man of tender, delicate sensibilities. I think he is governed by the Spirit of Truth more than most men; but his mind and manners do not fairly represent his heart.'

"*Critic No. 4.*—'He is an unselfish man; free from envy and jealousy. He needs outward refinement. The inward beauty of his character is working out, and will eventually overcome all external defects.'

"*Critic No. 5.*—'He is a philosopher, a man who thinks and reasons deeply; but he lacks simplicity in the expression of his thoughts.'

"*Critic No. 6.*—'The interior of his character is excellent; but the exterior is faulty. I would advise him, instead of being contented with inward beauty, to think it important to have a beautiful manifestation of it. We know, except when his spirit is unusually free, his utterance is labored, tedious, and awkward; I imagine the same embarrassment and ungainliness attaches to him as a lover in regard to expression. He is aware of all this and I hope he will not account it a small affair, not limit his ambition to being merely a good man. At present he does not do justice to himself; he is constantly liable to be undervalued by lack of science in expression. I believe he has in him the soul of music—he feels the glorious emotions of which music is an expression; but he is no singer. In regard to his business character, he has the reputation of perfect honesty; but there is a lack of science and tact in his business transactions that have brought him into many difficulties.'

"*Critic No. 1.*—'He has large hopes and often promises more than he fulfills; disappoints folks. I think his business habits are quite bad; his financial accounts are always at loose ends. He needs to carry his conscientiousness into business affairs.'

"*Critic No. 7.*—'It is true that he does not fulfill his promises. He is what I would call an outline character; he makes excellent plans, but is careless in executing details.'

"*Critic No. 8.*—'He is not as neat in his personal habits as good taste requires; he needs to pay more attention to outward appearance.'

"*Critic No. 6.* —'If we are going to be faithful critics, and improve our powers of discrimination and do one another good, we must not allow one part of the character to make us indulgent to another. To do him the good we wish to, a severe criticism ought to be aimed at his faults. There is no need of discord between two persons in very opposite states of cultivation; they may stand together in perfect peace. But for peace of the right kind, the inferior degree of cultivation must be modest, aware of its inferiority, and not despise the superior. And in all our aspirations we should address ourselves to the superior degree, take that for a standard, and calculate to please that, and not the inferior degree."

This criticism is a good example of the spiritual profile, discussing many good qualities along with those that require improvement. The Community not only studied how to assess adequately each others' character, manner, and temperament, but they knew that criticism must be combined with love to be healing. "Criticism bathed in love wounds but to heal. But if criticism is given with any taint of personal feelings, it leaves poison in the wound. The nerves of egotism are wonderfully delicate, and cringe at the slightest touch; it requires wisdom to criticize faithfully and yet avoid unnecessary irritation. A good margin was always left for praise, and the kind, impersonal way in which the criticisms were given caused but temporary soreness. There must be love, and *respect*—the recognition of the divine birthright of persons that will make us fear to lord it over anyone . . . . The object of criticism is only to destroy the husk that conceals inward goodness."

THE CRITICISM CLUB

Cleanse me from secret faults was the prayer of the Community heart. The practice grew so popular that a Criticism Club was established in 1872 and became so pressed with applications for truth telling that regular sessions were expanded from one to three per week; one person waited nearly three months for the coveted washing! It was indeed a washing, at times a spiritual probe into the depths of the mind, because Mutual Criticism's goal was to correct and improve *character*, not merely behavior.

"We devoted the week between Christmas and New Year's for a grand time of mutual criticism," the January 6, 1873, *Circular* reported. "A wonderful interest was manifested from the beginning. Three persons were appointed to receive the names of all applicants for criticism, name a suitable committee for each one, appoint a foreman, and time and place of meeting. The one criticized could always suggest additions to his or her committee. These committees, consisting each of about a dozen friends and intimates of the candidate, would be reported to the meeting one evening and do their work next day. Fourteen of them might meet during the day, each one of them occupying an hour if necessary, but no more. It sometimes happened that a critic at one session would be a subject at a second and critic again at a third one. In this way we have washed one another's feet. It has been simple truth-telling, pointing out faults of temper, of taste, of manner, of character, of attractions and of repulsions, faults of every kind, and all done in kindness with a view to unity and softness of heart, never for giving vent to pent-up grudges. The fruits are peace and humility, purity, and new life. The eagerness for heart-searching and truth-telling in those who received, as well as those who administered, steadily increased. At the close of the week, all were enthusiastic for continuing the work. The results were the beginning of religious experience in some, the brightening of religious experience in others, and a substantial conversion of the whole Community.

"Some persons, long regarded as hard cases of fixed character, were asked to offer themselves for public criticism in the Family Hall, which was considered the severest ordeal of all. 'I was surprised to see how many good things were said about them,' Noyes wrote in the February 20, 1873, *Circular*. 'With manifest love and sincerity, one after another would acknowledge the person's improvement until they would come out of the trial with an actual rise of reputation, and with new self-respect. It brings a feeling of thankfulness. We are conscious of real *deliverance*. Improvement may have been going on for years unrecognized by those around them and perhaps unknown to themselves, till an occasion of open criticism summons their acquaintances to reflect and specify observations on their character, and then, behold! They are found to be better folks than anybody thought —even themselves! Thus, in cases of chronic self-condemnation, public criticism given in perfect sincerity may be—nay, has been—the right hand of God to lift persons out of the slough of despond and put a new song in their hearts. This public purification would bring about almost instantaneous character changes, usually permanent. However painful at times, members agreed, the criticism process only increases our love for truth."

"Criticism—restoring, cleansing, comforting, and strengthening—is administered by loving brothers and sisters and his trouble rolls off him as surely and palpably as Christian's pack is represented to have tumbled from his shoulders," G. said. "It's a common thing to hear a man who has been through this searching ordeal say, 'My relief is wonderful. I feel as though a load had been lifted off me.' The whole aspect of the man is often changed by this wonderful purifier! Humbled and chastened, but justified and made clean, he has all the buoyant hope and elastic life of one just set free from prison. Free Criticism, Truth-telling, is our spiritual Turkish bath, cleansing and restoring the inner man. If it is sometimes sharper than a two-edged sword, it's again like the gentle rain from heaven, as tender and pitying as a father's love for his children. If it casts down evil, it exalts good with comely praise."

Much disharmony stems from unthinking speech; the criticism of A. dealt with harmony in conversation. Here is the rare instance of one being criticized speaking very briefly during the procedure:

"*D.*—'A. is very impetuous and positive in his manner, and is deficient in persuasiveness. He takes a position that you are not prepared for, and announces it with such flat assurance that it gives you a *jolt*. He has a kind of honesty that strips everything of romance, and this is apt to revolt you. He will bring out a statement quite contrary to what you suppose to be the fact, without any circumlocution whatever, and though you're not sure he's correct, you naturally resist being *jerked* into the admission of it. He might have had the same independence and honesty with more plausibility and tact.'

"*E.*—'The prevailing trait in A.'s character, amounting almost to idiosyncrasy, is *directness*. He is *direct* in everything he does—direct in his religious pursuits, as evinced by the straightforward simplicity of his testimony—direct in his thoughts, his speech, and his actions. This is in general a good quality in persons, giving intensity to all their operations, singleness of eye, and consequent success. But in our social intercourse, this trait needs some modification. It will not do in conversation to drive point-blank at a topic and think of nothing else. A.'s excessive directness sometimes causes him to overlook and forget everything but his subject, and leads him into unnecessary discord.'

"A. speaks here, unusual in a criticism: 'Before I came to the Community, I was fond of debate and had the habit of not caring whether what I said was pleasing or not—if it was incontrovertible, that was enough.'

"*D.*—'That rule will do for the rough-and-tumble of life outside, but it will not do here where the very object of our association is harmony. All our speech should be surrounded with the most delicate reference to harmony. Let every one of us please his neighbor and forbear one another. Endeavor to keep the unity of the spirit. If Mr. A. would make it more of an objective to think and speak harmoniously with others, his independence and impetuosity would regulate itself without any injury to his honesty. Suppose he forms an opinion that he wants to express, and at the same time he is wide awake for harmony and has reason to think that what he's going to say will not fall into C.'s mind pleasantly: true consideration requires not that he should suppress his opinion or that he should agree with C., but that he should broach his opinion moderately—make some stairs for C. to descend on, and not drop him right down with a jolt. With a quick ear for harmony and a heart that values it as God does, A. might be just as independent as he is now and yet always find a way to express himself musically. The generic fault with A. is that he is too *masculine*. He would be a better man if he were a little more of a woman, i.e., if his life, instead of running so much into strength, ran more into delicacy, affection, amiability.'

"Women are the legitimate critics of men in social life. They have discernment, finer sensibilities and tastes. The longer I live, the more I feel indebted to God for chastening the masculine by the feminine," Noyes said. Referring to marriage as it was when women relinquished all legal and personal rights once married, Noyes said, "In the slave-holding position of marriage, men refuse to look upon women as equals, and refuse to regard their feelings and impressions; but the dispensation *we* are called to is one in which women are not men's slaves . . . but set free to criticize men and express their own tastes and feelings. . . . Their criticism is the proper looking-glass for a man."

"Jottings from the Criticism Club, January 6, 1873: L. has a great deal of what is usually termed manliness. He has encouraged the stern side of his nature, and discouraged the gentle side. He seems to be ashamed to show the softness and tenderness he feels. He needs to know that these two phases of character are not irreconcilable. They are in fact necessary complements to each other. S. seems to be afraid that he will sacrifice strength by becoming subordinate to his spiritual superiors. Receptivity to God does not diminish true manliness; on the contrary, by being receptive, one gains rather than loses strength. No one can be like Christ without having both the lion and the dove in his character. Q. is subject to strong personal likes and dislikes, and he is so frank and fearless that he takes no pains to hide the one or the other. He should make his likes and dislikes conform to the truth. Neither our estimation of an individual's character nor our affection for him should be determined by our personal relations to him, but by his relations to general society and to Christ. If Q. would drop his prejudices and seek Christ's mind about persons, he might find good where he has never seen it before and have his heart flow out in new directions obedient to impulses from heaven.

The following criticism of Mrs. C. is reminiscent of the Biblical Martha and Mary: "Mrs. C. by nature makes more account of *doing* rather than *being*—to serve God more with her hands than her heart. We are all learning that nothing we have done or can do commends us to God; only the fragrance of our spirits pleases him. Good actions reflect back upon the heart and improve the quality of our *being*, and that is their chief value. Those who have the natural faculty of *usefulness* and a good deal of method and natural decorum, can be self-righteous and censorious toward those whose value consists more in their social qualities. The power of making society lively and musical, or of refreshing others by a sweet, gentle spirit, is often worth more than a great deal of industry with the hands. It is the temptation of *doing* natures to feel like the brother of the prodigal, as if they deserved the most . . . . Our spirit is that part of us that touches God and attracts his fellowship. If Mrs. C. would learn to appreciate character by this standard, and cultivate in herself the ornaments of the social nature, love, taste, sprightliness, it would improve her very much. She has an excellent mind, and strong ambition to overcome the defects in her character. God has a fair chance to work in her—the soil will bear a great deal. She has that spirit of faithfulness and persevering zeal . . . God will honor this spirit and this faith.

"X. has many valuable traits of character and is greatly beloved, but she is tempted to let outward things absorb her attention to the neglect of interior culture. She was advised to pray for grace to lay secure hold on eternal life, and become as efficient in spiritual labor as she has been in physical and intellectual. These are chiefly valuable as a foundation for the former, and are worthless when they prevent spiritual improvement. Those who pride themselves on industry, economy, faithfulness in external things, while they are not earnest in seeking interior culture, will sooner or later find that they have trusted in broken reeds. This theme is also applied to L. "He needs to consider that *being* is far more important than *doing*, and should seek to attract persons to his standard of excellence by his own life-example rather than to drive them to it by words. L. is very earnest, and yet his discourses in public and private are often unedifying. We involuntarily feel that his exhortations savor of legality rather than grace. In his zeal to improve others, he ignores many faults in his own character. In other ways his zeal defeats itself. It leads him to introduce the most profound religious subjects into conversation with little reference to the proprieties of time and place. We would not have him less earnest or wise, but more winning.

"More serious than criticisms of manner are those about character. V. has a serious fault, that her words are often better than her deeds. She has a bright intellect and seems to apprehend truth readily; her understanding assents to it and apparently rejoices in it, but it doesn't sufficiently modify her external conduct. Consequently her words are at a discount—like the notes of banks that have issued more paper than they can redeem. Our deeds form the basis of our characters, and if they fall behind our words, the latter will not long be taken at par. Such a condition is deplorable and must be the result of unbelief. If the heart sincerely believes in God, it will express itself in deeds truer and better than any words.

"Mr. S. is an honest, serious, conscientious man, but these elements of his character are not sufficiently embodied in artful love and emotion. Mr. S. is unpracticed, green, deficient in skill to make himself attractive—deficient and yet *promising*. He has improved very much since he came here. One person has confessed that she loves him very much now, though she could hardly endure him when she first saw him, he was so pedantic and awkward. His strong tendency to intellectual development is one hindrance. It's a saying that a book-worm is awkward in love—slow to be smitten, and likely to behave foolishly when he is. I think Mr. S. would have been predominantly intellectual and had but little development of his social nature in the outside world. His cast of mind is very unfavorable to poetical thought; he might make rhymes, but they would lack the sparkle of poetry and it is the poetic element that makes us lively and attractive in social intercourse. He has a warm heart and a geniality of feeling that counteracts somewhat the pedantic and sober element of his character; in the world the pedantic would probably have prevailed. The affection elicited in this Association is improving him very much. A second hindrance is alimentiveness—the tendency to high enjoyment of food—which is a hindrance to the development of life in the form of amativeness. Epicures and drunkards extinguish at last the sexual attraction. For the highest development of our social nature, it is desirable to be abstemious. As in religion, sensuality of appetite is a hindrance to spirituality, so it is equally an enemy to love and the development of the highest power of fellowship between the sexes.

"R. is a woman of very winning disposition. She is affectionate, kind, and sympathetic, and makes a great many friends. She is faithful and public-spirited in business, and there is an earnestness about her that draws out confidence in her spirituality; yet there is a lack in her: what is it? Studying her character and looking back upon her experience, we see that she has been one of those persons who come under conviction, after a time of straying from God, and make an apparently sincere confession of wrong-doing and consider that the matter is ended. It has often been a mystery to many that she should repeat again and again the same unprofitable experience after a season of what seemed to be earnest conviction and self-judgment. The work of judgment does not go deep enough; no real change of character takes place. She confesses, but does not forsake. Letters of confession are mockery if written without a serious idea on the part of the writers of changing their course and character. They breed cant, one of the wickedest things in the world—the more people deal in that kind of currency the poorer they will be. The way to help R. is to help her to make an end of cant. In doing this we may help others; for there are, no doubt, many persons who squander the grace of God and stop his work in them by talking about it and writing about it under the feeling that if they put their experience on paper or bring it out in meeting they need not give any further attention to it, but count it ended. The experience described is often only the beginning of what should continue. A woman after the first pain in child-bearing might think her suffering ended; but she must have pains, one after another, before the child is born, and if she is wise she will desire them. So the birth into the kingdom of heaven cannot be accomplished by a single pain—a great number are necessary; but they may be dissipated and stopped by foolish ostentation and by unnecessary talk about them. Superficial, shallow, religious experience that expresses itself in talking and writing, but does not result in deeds, will never save anybody. *Not every one that saith Lord, Lord, shall enter into the kingdom of heaven, but he that doeth the will of my Father.*"

"I've always been much troubled with a poor memory and this deficiency results in my forgetting errands and various details of business," wrote Seymour Nash for the January 4, 1869, *Circular*. "I've felt very bad about it, earnestly prayed for deliverance and realized a degree of improvement, yet the evil was not cured. I acquired a reputation for forgetfulness and was sadly annoyed by the personal inconvenience it caused, compelling me to take an indefinite number of unnecessary steps. It also tempted me to say many things in self-justification and defense. I said to myself: *This thing must be stopped*. I became conscious that I was doing injustice to God and to the Community spirit. I resolved to solve the problem within myself and discovered a serious leak: When anyone entrusted me with an errand or asked me to do a little work at a future time, I'd say, 'Yes, I will try to remember it.' Those words *try to remember* were a tacit confession that I was weak and unreliable; it was an inlet of weakness that increased and perpetuated the evil. It became clear that if I would overcome this weakness, I must say *I will do it* and trust God for faithfulness. I did so at once and the result was very satisfactory. Also, reminded of something to do but engaged in something else, I would say, 'Not now, later will be fine.' The thing would pass out of my mind and oftentimes cause me and perhaps others serious inconvenience. I became convinced that this invisible agent who was so faithful to remind me of my duty was really the voice of God. On making this discovery, I said, 'I will not trouble him to remind me of the same thing twice!' I have faithfully pursued that policy and have observed a steady improvement in my memory."

"I've had my heart stirred lately against shiftlessness," Tirzah Miller agreed. "I think some of the young men need to get more in earnest against the spirit of shiftlessness that does not pay attention to small but important details—that is satisfied with approximate instead of exact truth, especially in business."

"I too have been experiencing anew lately that it is very healthy to both soul and body to exercise ourselves in accurate, exact thinking," Erastus Hamilton shared at a July Evening Meeting. "It always makes me feel good and puts me in a fruitful state of mind. I've analyzed the state of mind where a person is in an aimless condition, not thinking definitely about anything, and contrasted it with the opposite state where a person applies himself to thinking accurately and truthfully; it seems to me that restlessness is the natural tendency of a listless state of mind and the habitual lack of accurate thinking. I hope we shall all appreciate the treasure we have in the ability to direct our minds into channels of thought to arrive at the exact truth about things."

"My mission would be to advocate *thoroughness*," wrote a member for the August 5, 1872, *Circular*. "If one thing fills the world with disappointment—even disaster—it is the want of thoroughness. Volumes are written showing what the world has suffered from this cause alone—shipwrecks, explosions, collisions, fires. Yet this plague goes on producing its bitter fruits as though it were useless to expect anything better. One can tell what to expect of a person from the way he does small things. A spirit of thoroughness shows itself on all occasions and no necessary act is trivial. If one discovers even a fallen broom he restores it to its place. If he has to deal with broken glass how careful is he to remove every vestige, because he has a thought for others—is this not one secret of thoroughness? It may be thought trivial to bestow any pains whatever upon small things, but we suggest that there may be real character in proper attention to them. Is there not sometimes a great deal of self-denial in acquiring a habit of thoroughness? It is beautiful to see a considerate spirit at work. Who does not make it a point of conscience to be as good as his word in all things, such as fulfilling promises or keeping appointments, no matter how small? When we leave a thing half done or not quite done without a good reason, we're not thorough-going. A spirit of thoroughness seeks not only to complete what it undertakes, but to do it in the very best way. Many epithets have been applied to it—laziness, carelessness, thoughtlessness, and shiftlessness; this spirit does not put itself out of the way one jot if it can possibly avoid it, though sometimes lack of thoroughness is due to a mere want of thought. A letter worth writing is worth writing well; anything worth saying is worth saying well, so that it will bear criticism; and anything worth doing is worth doing well. Away with shiftlessness and excuses for wrong and foolish doings of all kinds."

"Community notices that appear in different newspapers always mention the neatness of the printing-office, the order of the grounds, the fine bread and butter that accompany the strawberries and cream, etc. Well-organized in a community spirit, many persons would have things in better order than isolated families where a woman has to take care of children, wash and iron clothes, make beds, cook the meals, bake, wash dishes, sweep, and much more. In Communities where these duties are divided among many faithful, interested persons, there is opportunity to attend to them in the very best manner. Righteousness in the soul, too, will not allow business slighting; whatever is to be done must be well done, must be done right, done to the Lord and not to man.

"In the June 16, 1873, *Circular*, Maud Barron added further thought in *Precision in the Spirit of Life*: 'Effort toward precision in any department is commendable. It is opposed to laziness, which does its work at loose ends, and mixes things in a confused manner. The instincts of the age tend toward precision. The desire to improve, to invent, to discover, to explore, may be traced to a spirit of precision that is wide-awake, active, and flexible. Traced to its fountainhead, the spirit of precision will be found to spring from the heart of God. It is the forerunner of progress, of the awakening of life, the bursting of the bonds of ignorance, and the precursor of the destruction of physical, mental, and spiritual slavery. It may be said to be the voice of God crying unto all creation—Awake! Arise and be filled with light! In society, the direction of this spirit has been mainly toward material things, confining itself to the letter of life. Scientists exert every nerve at solving numerous problems of life's phenomena. Pleasure-seekers who seek merely the ends of material wealth and comfort try in vain to find a truly satisfactory security. The wealth-accumulating precisionist searches in vain for true success and victory. Only by getting into communication with God can we get at the true solution of life's great problems either in matter or spirit, and discover and establish a universal standard of science that will endure. While all efforts toward precision in the letter of life may be made relatively useful in the education and growth of the race, they will not result in peace to the heart of man nor rest to his spirit. Subordinating the letter to the spirit will avoid harshness, irritation, friction, and clashing of spirits. It will promote brotherly love. It will in due time and in its own way secure precision even in all things comprised in the letter of life. God is love; growth in and complete attainment of love will open all the mysteries of the universe and secure all desirable blessings.'"

THE CRITICISM CURE

"Other intriguing aspects of criticism warrant attention. Because Mutual Criticism penetrated into the innermost recesses of character, it often acted as a purifying agent capable of curing sickness. Known as the criticism cure, this curative power had a surprising flavor of Freud: "Life is a ball made up by the winding on of the thread of our passing experience, and whatever we have wound in the past, whether good or bad, is still in the ball. We are what our past lives have made us," Noyes wrote. "Wrongs in the past that had lain secret and perhaps half-forgotten, can be poisonous to present experience." Dorothy Leonard, a Community poet, wrote profound truisms about human nature in deceptively simple words:

> "Till I was free
> Of my own fate
> I could not hear
> The earth relate."

"Repressed past experiences not only blight our own life but cause societal disharmony, because unwittingly we project onto others our own faults as defense mechanisms to avoid the pain and perplexity of dealing with ourselves. We feel guilt but do not want to acknowledge that it is I, myself, who is guilty (whether true or not)—therefore this guilt must be out there in the world and not in my self. These rejected aspects of ourselves remain in the unconscious life and shape and color our assessments and judgments of others. Though some wrongs may have been inflicted upon us, we may have chosen unfortunate entanglements in youth out of naïveté or committed deliberate wrongs that that still fester and weigh on the conscience. Although forgiven and forgotten, some past wrongs or guilts can be reached only by a process that carries light and judgment and separation clear back to their beginning. Confession can often heal.

"Notable improvements in bodily health often occurred as a result of sincere truth-telling. A Community writer said, 'It is a common custom here for a person who may be attacked by any disorder, to apply this remedy by sending for a committee of persons, in whose faith and spiritual judgment he has confidence, to come and criticize him. This nearly always brings on a sweat, breaking up disease, and delivers what is needed to cleanse and purify the system. If you are sick, seek for someone to tell you your faults, to find out the weakest spot in your character and conduct: let him put his finger on the very sore that you would like most to keep hid. Depend upon it—there is the avenue through which disease gets access to you. If this process hurts, it is only a sign that the remedy is applied at the right place and is taking effect.... We have tried it and found it to be invaluable.'

The Community theorized that disease originates not in the body but in the spirit, and that a decisive operation there affects the whole system. They even became convinced that the free use of ice and criticism was the cure for an epidemic of diphtheria, because they'd tried all known remedies and consulted doctors, and nothing had helped; 112 persons were affected and five died soon after the outbreak. After this treatment, no new deaths occurred; most of the cases were cured in a few hours. Twenty-two people testified that the benefit was instantaneous. "My experience in respect to criticism was new, and to me interesting. I was taken at night with a sore throat that continued to worsen, and the next day I had all the symptoms of diphtheria. Being rather worse that night, I sent for a committee. Their criticism immediately threw me into a profuse sweat, till I felt as though I had been in a bath; and before the committee left the room, my headache, backache, and fever were all gone. The criticism had an edge to it, and literally separated me from the spirit of disease that was upon me. I slept well, and in the morning called myself *well*, as indeed I was, with the exception of weakness. I attribute my recovery entirely to the Spirit of Truth administered in criticism, and believe it to be the best remedy for soul and body."

"In our earlier years we resolved to have faith whether we lived or died and almost entirely abandoned the use of external remedies," the July 1872 *Circular* noted. "Until now, we were never prepared to combine faith and science, keeping faith foremost. Lately, enthusiasm is starting for the study of medicine; the necessary specifics for curing disease have been discovered, and what is wanted now is inspiration to rightly apply them. Science we believe to be the true handmaid of faith. The tree of life is in the world. Let there be light through the Community." That same year, however, *Thoughts on Disease* appeared in the *Circular*: "It is becoming more and more evident that the popular systems of medical practice do not sufficiently consider the mental and spiritual phenomena that accompany and indeed form part of every disease. The more we know about disease, the more certain we become that its spiritual causes must be looked after quite as carefully as its physical ones. If, for instance, a man's stomach, liver, or other organ gets out of order, some subtle influence sets his imagination at work to persuade him that his symptoms are very serious; that some strong disease has got hold of him to which he must succumb, and against which it is useless to struggle. Gradually these imaginations ripen into the direst forebodings, having almost the force of a prophecy. A diseased person could put himself into the most favorable circumstances possible for recovery by ridding himself of imagined forebodings, the lying spirits that could become breeders of disease within him."

"I had an experience that strengthened my faith," George Cragin related in a January 1869 issue of the *Circular*. "In performing some heavy work in the shop right after dinner, I strained myself internally, causing pain and distress in my stomach. I grew worse towards night, so I was compelled to lie down flat on my face to obtain even slight relief. I finally went to bed in hopes that perhaps I could get to sleep before morning. For some time the pain continued without abatement, and I had pretty much concluded that sleeping was out of the question, when I was suddenly reminded of Mr. Noyes's remark that 'the pain we feel is no indication of the amount of disease: every disease has its spirit, and there is a spirit of neuralgia that may take possession of us and communicate its own consciousness, and make us suffer out of all proportion to the physical cause: half the pain we feel belongs to the spirit of the disease.' I determined to confess my disbelief in the importance of my injury indicated by the pain I felt; and if kept awake I resolved to spend the time in meditation and prayer. In half an hour I went to sleep, and slept soundly until morning, and now feel as well as ever."

"I can testify to the truth of that Home-Talk," Harriet Skinner wrote in the December 1868 *Circular*, an article entitled *A Pain-Killer*. "I went to bed with a fierce headache, without much prospect of the rest I needed. But I thought of what was said in that piece, that we should seek alleviation of pain from the Spirit of God—that he delights to alleviate pain and I turned my desire that way. Soon I felt a soothing influence. I cannot express it better than that the Lord laid his hand on my head. I went to sleep and slept well; and I think something good passed into my head, that will strengthen it permanently. I know that certain conditions of the mind and heart will draw a current of life and health, just as surely as certain physical conditions will attract a flow of electricity. I am stirred up to believe in God more and more."

"Dear M:—I have wanted to tell you for more than a week how happy and well I feel," wrote E. "It seems almost a miracle to me. You know I was sick a fortnight ago. I felt so bad for two or three days that I could hardly sit up. One evening I forced myself to the meeting, thinking every minute while there that I must leave and go to bed, for I could not sit up; yet something held me there. The conversation turned upon health—how to get it? I soon wished to say something, thinking it might relieve me. But it seemed impossible. It never cost me such a struggle to confess Christ before. But just as meeting closed I found courage to say what I had so wished to. The effect was magical. I have felt like a different girl ever since, so strong and well. Nor is this all; this experience has led to spiritual victories. It has given me a new and practical faith in God. These two weeks of peace and happiness seem like a gift from him in response to faith. If the criticism and suffering I've been through this summer have been the means of bringing to me this new faith and trust in God (as I think they have), I thank him with my whole heart, and say that he has dealt kindly with me."

"Isn't it a blessed thing that we can trust God? There is hardly a day but that I have occasion to say to myself, *I will trust God any way; he will care for me*," C. exulted. "How thankful I am that I am brought up to know and feel that there is a God, and that he is constantly caring for us. Once when I was very sick for two or three days I felt discouraged and unbelieving. I looked at the dark side of things till I could see nothing bright or hopeful in my case. Finally it seemed that I could stand it no longer, I must have relief. I was alone in my room, and I said aloud with considerable emphasis, 'I will trust God, let come what will. He is dealing with me, why should I worry? He does not let anything happen to me but what is just right. I can and will trust him!' I shall never forget the rush of thankfulness and love that came upon me after that. I could see God's goodness in all my experience, and my heart was melted. It seemed to me that if the unluckiest thing should happen to me, I could still trust God that he would conduct me safely through. I felt so happy that several times that evening I said to myself, *I love to trust God better than anything else in the world.* I began to get better right away. Since then I have always found my way out of trouble and discouragement by firmly and in faith sticking to the motto, *I will trust God.*"

"One of our young men who had never been sick was lately reduced to a state of helplessness by a fever. 'I have had considerable experience for the last two or three weeks that has been very interesting to me, and rather new. I was never sick before, never really prostrated. I found the great lesson I was learning was to be thankful for suffering. When I was reduced clear down to the lowest, it seemed to me I got nearer to God than ever before; and I could say from the bottom of my heart that I thanked God for suffering, or anything that produced faith and turned my heart in that direction. This experience has made me feel very much in earnest to know God for myself and seek him every day. Until my late experience, I never realized the meaning of Paul's saying: *When I am weak then am I strong*. I realized what it is to be strong in the spirit when the flesh is weak. I hope I shall have any amount of this kind of experience necessary to keep me humble and soft."

George Washington Noyes added extra dimensions to this subject in his article "Excitement and Influx" in the *Free Church Circular*: "Good and evil are pervading non-sensory substances emanating from opposite sources and responding to our energy with reference to one or the other. Christ healed diseases on this principle. *Take up thy bed and walk* was his command, as if he had said, 'The power of life is present; now excite yourself into healthy action as is appropriate to health, and the spirit of health will flow into you.' The influx responds to the excitement," George explained. "It is likened to the electrical machine that by means of *frictional* excitement is charged at any time with the subtle element otherwise present only in a non-sensory degree. The miracles Christ wrought of this kind seem to have consisted more in the first step—putting the conception of healthy action into a diseased person's mind, enabling him to make effort toward self-excitement. After mind and spirit are strengthened and put into an attitude of action, attracting the spirit of health, the latter comes of its self. We've seen this operation so often that it stands as the first and fundamental principle of the faith practice. In sickness we look to God for a healthy excitement of the will, and good sensations immediately begin to flow through every channel of the system. Strength attracts strength, and it is downhill work to get well of disease after the spirit has been touched by Christ and purged of the lethargy of evil and put on the track of faith exercise. *Take up thy bed and walk*! This word given to the paralytic man eighteen hundred years ago is sounding forth now to all who can hear Christ's word in their hearts. Take up your bed and walk, you who are groaning at some fancied mountain of evil and lying down under it in despair. Take it up! You don't know the strength there is in you, hidden under this seeming paralysis. A spark of true effort at the center, in the name of Christ, will kindle the whole atmosphere about you in to a living flame of victorious energy, so that you will breathe in omnipotence. Wherever the believer is tempted to feel bound in spiritual impotence, whether of body or soul, there Christ's word comes to him: *Take up thy bed and walk*! The attractions of life that are everywhere watching and waiting for this exercise will flow in and work a cure."

"Persons frequently imagine that they are laboring under some chronic disease of the spine or kidneys," George Cragin contributed to the *Circular*, "when in reality the muscles of the back are tired out and need rest. The back and neck are abundantly supplied with strong muscles, six layers one above the other and interlaced in every direction, making a muscular system of great strength capable of enduring long-continued strains without becoming tired. But people who are on their feet from morning till night cause the back muscles to remain in a state of contraction, supporting the weight of the trunk and head through the whole day without a moment of rest or relaxation. What wonder is it that such people complain of backache? Short periods of rest, quite frequent if necessary and at the right time in a recumbent position in the middle of the day will enable a person to go through the rest of the day without fatigue. It will eventually cure the most obstinate backache unless it arises from organic disease. All muscles of voluntary motion must be relaxed and allowed periods of rest to keep them in a healthy condition. The heart, for example, consists almost entirely of muscular tissue and we think of it as being in constant motion, but one quarter of the time it's at rest doing nothing; recuperating. One-fourth of every minute, hour, day and year, the heart is still. If one lives one hundred years, for twenty-five years his heart has been at rest. Without this provision of nature, the heart would tire out and stop. Let one extend his arm horizontally and see how long he can hold it that way—five minutes will seem a long time. But if he extends his arm and then relaxes it at short intervals, the exercise can be continued for hours."

"A Villa resident thought he had a rather stern mission when he went to the Community to have the dentist file his teeth, and to have the Criticism Club file his character. When he got back he said that he never expected to like tooth-filing, but he thought it quite easy to fall in love with criticism."

COLLECTIVE PROBLEMS

"Social problems are caused by jealousy, envy, and striving to outdo one another, and this negative spirit was blighting the young women. Lily felt that unless she could be acclaimed as the best singer in the Community, she did not want to sing at all. Pianists Edith, Carrie, and Tirzah were all jealous of each other, seizing on every small event as a personal slight. Violinists dropped from many to just one first violinist by 1874, due to this destructive spirit of rivalry and envy that eats like a canker and cannot bear to be second in anything. Noyes dubbed this the 'prima donna fever.' All the women said that these were the meanest feelings they ever had. As youths schooled in Biblical principles, these young women were grieved and desired to strive for immunity from envy and contentiousness. They said they would rather give up music than continue in this spirit that indulges antipathies. One said, 'Whoso hates his brother is a murderer, and no murderer hath eternal life abiding in him.' Many difficulties are often lifelong and bitter, burdening the soul and wearing the life like a dragging ball and chain. They are practically incurable, just for the pitiful want of a meeting-ground for sincerity. Some felt that while behavior can be controlled, likes and dislikes are involuntary and uncontrollable; so what were they to do? After mutual criticism with Noyes, long analysis, and the sincere desire to change, they more clearly understood themselves. When the evil spirit was brought into the light, empathy bloomed. They began discerning that everyone has aspirations, hopes, confusions, fears, and feelings just like their own. Where dislikes had existed, they transformed into genuine affection, and the idea that feelings are uncontrollable proved on examination to be unsupported.

In a Community where free criticism prevails, envy and all spiritual temptations that flesh is heir to are necessarily short-lived. If a person is plagued with any of these ills, it is soon transparent to the sensitive, spiritual instincts of others; the individual himself may confess his trouble and ask for help."

"In the early days of our Community life we enjoyed a good degree of unity and fellowship of an outward kind, but our interior lives and characters had received little attention," Eleazer Hatch reminisced in a heartening article, "Love Better than Labor" in the May 12, 1873, *Circular*. "Our close Community relationships could develop character traits of which we had not been conscious. We were building that summer; E. and C., men as opposite in business habits as two persons could be, were appointed to assist with a Help-Distributing Committee that looked into and supplied the wants of each department. C. had formed very slack habits and appeared to have little appreciation of the value of time; E. had a restless, driving spirit that appreciated persons only for their doing, forgetting the more important part of being. Chafing and irritation was evident after working awhile together, though no discordant words passed between them. When there was any disagreement between members, we stopped work at once and set about reconciling them by advice or criticism. We've always considered unity far more important than work. So we talked with E. and C. and advised them to consider one another, to provoke unto love and good works. We had not yet learned to receive criticism and apply it so as to get its full benefit. Though anxious to overcome their faults, E. and C. had not learned to appreciate the good in each other and trust God to eradicate these faults; it was not long before they were again tempted into evil-thinking of each other. Everyone who has passed through such experience knows that giving way to evil temptations obliterates all good from the mind and fills it with darkness. Believing that the power of evil could be broken, we invited some of the more spiritual members to join our impromptu committee and sat down with E. and C., praying God to give us wisdom to deal with them. We criticized them for a lack of faith and trust in God and advised them to look away from each other's faults and open their hearts to the spirit of truth and the love of God, which would certainly flow in and fill them with love for each other.

"E was sitting in the parlor that afternoon thinking of the matter, when suddenly he resolved that he would accept the criticism and act in accordance with it; immediately the faults of C. disappeared from his mind and his heart was filled with love for him. While he reflected on his change of feelings, George Washington Noyes came and asked him to receive C. as a roommate. He answered heartily that he would be glad to do so. He then went to C.'s room and told him the change E. had passed through and the love he felt for him. C.'s countenance lighted up as he exclaimed, 'Why, that's just the way I feel!' Thus were two hearts brought together, and although more than twenty years have passed since that day not a shadow has come between them to mar their love and fellowship."

"There was difficulty between Mr. Newhouse, the inventor of traps and a mainstay of the Community's fortunes, and Mr. Inslee, an expert machinist who had owned a machine shop in Newark, New Jersey. Inslee had met Noyes, who was directing the printing press in Brooklyn. Community men were sent to Newark to learn the machinist trade from Inslee, who joined the Community in 1856. Noyes called him 'the financial founder of the Community,' who developed production techniques for mass-producing the Newhouse traps and the manufacturing machinery for making silk thread. Like most other members, Inslee discovered many unsuspected abilities and interests in himself—he became an expert violinist and dancer! But Mr. Newhouse had frequently expressed dissatisfaction with Mr. Inslee's lack of promptness in business. The two men offered themselves for criticism: Mr. Burt thought Inslee had not entered heartily into the work since he'd come from Newark, that he sought his own ease and comfort and was not willing to take responsibility. Mr. Kinsley thought Inslee was not reliable in any department and that the tendency of his spirit was to draw persons off from public service to pleasure-seeking. Mr. Cragin thought it important that each individual should be interested not only in some particular department, but in all the different departments. Reference was made to Inslee's spirit while at Newark, a spirit of pride that makes it difficult, for those afflicted, to engage in what they considered small things, such as the trap business."

Community members were always asked what they did about people who resisted doing their own share of the many tasks to be done. Lazy individuals, it was said, could not live under the Community's special system of spiritual education and mutual criticism; they either changed or left. The most common way of dealing with laziness or other bad behavior was to dismiss the offender from his group and request him to stop work. This cured the evil sooner than anything else. "We have to criticize members for working too much, rather than for being lazy!" Noyes wrote in *A True Reason for Loving Labor* in 1852: "I will not have any laziness in my heart. I believe that secretly, laziness is the motive of many who take advantage of their opportunities to shirk work and become *gentlemen*, and I know what a curse it is. Harriet Noyes is my model in regard to service—I envy her readiness for anything and everything. She had opportunities that would have allowed her to be quite a lady, but she has chosen a course that is not only useful to the Community but also to herself. My face is steadily set in that direction; life is growth and I cannot make sudden changes, but I am growing toward Harriet's simplicity of service. With inspiration from heaven, every kind of work is good with no important distinction between occupations. Failing as he did at Newark, I'd thought that Mr. Inslee would be ambitious to regain the confidence of the Community, but instead he is losing it," Noyes said. "He is the very man we want and there is plenty for him to do in our large trap business."

"Mr. Newhouse was criticized for personal feelings toward the Newark business and for his strong tendency to isolate himself in his own department. The trap-shop was brought up for criticism the following year. It was getting to be a man's shop with little opportunity for women in the dismal place, and the men were gradually getting worn out. A good deal of work was done, but in an unwholesome way. Social unity and edification were lost sight of in too direct an aim at material accomplishment, the true source of their prosperity. Noyes's primary goal of spiritual growth had been crowded out by *work, work, and more work*. R. is so full of business that he has set no regular hour for seeking knowledge of God. He practices music but makes no time for practice in spiritual music. We cannot become creditable performers on the violin or piano or do well in the orchestra without much practice; likewise we will not allow our spiritual fingers to become stiffened and unable to make harmony with the heavenly band. Shut the eyes, go to God, and practice sincere self-examination—or neglect this spiritual labor and choose criticism from others. As we take time to improve ourselves, we render criticism from associates unnecessary."

"Community friends have found it necessary to discuss the management of one of the business departments at the Villa," the *Circular* reported on July 30, 1872. "Dissatisfied with its spiritual condition, they made changes in the help that did not give satisfaction to all concerned," noted George Cragin. "Mr. Noyes called a meeting that resulted in just what was needed: a criticism of those connected with the department."

"Those criticized had grown hard, under the spirit of the world," William Hinds elaborated. "Our meeting softened them and we liked them better after it. And they felt better themselves," he added. "We'll know that if a bad spirit gets in, H. will be sincere and criticize it. What would we do without criticism? It is one of our great discoveries. We shall all feel good about that business now."

"The result of criticism sometimes is very sudden like the effect of a thunder-shower; sharp flashes of lightning clear up the air and make everyone feel better after it," Noyes said.

"Yes," Hinds agreed. "Edward said he felt that he'd been hard and under a cloud, but after his criticism he felt relieved and much happier than before,"

"Happy are they who know their faults and can put them to the mending," George Miller put in.

"In these muggy days when the mercury rises to the nineties and the atmosphere becomes almost intolerable, a good thunderstorm comes and usually makes everything pleasant; so when persons find themselves in an unsatisfactory state—and know not why—the trouble may be in the spiritual atmosphere," Abram contributed.

"Sometimes a person needs criticism himself," Hinds opined, "and sometimes he needs to criticize others."

"As we began Community life in Putney, Mr. Noyes had a great deal of spiritual labor to perform," George Cragin told the group. "We lived then in separate houses in different parts of the village. One time he called all the members together at midnight to have a criticism!"

"When you first introduced criticism, did all take it quietly or did some answer back?" Hinds asked.

"We all submitted quietly but did not know what serious business it was going to be. I remember L.'s first criticism," Cragin continued. "He would take notes of remarks made and that evening he prepared to take notes of his own criticism. For awhile he scribbled, but finally the shots came so thick and so near that he laid down his pencil and had all he could do to keep still."

"He stopped writing and went to sweating!" Noyes interjected.

"It must seem wonderful to you, Mr. Cragin, when you see from small beginnings how the Community has grown to its present condition," said Miller.

"It never could have attained its present status without such people, those of faith and spiritual earnestness," Hinds pointed out. "You, Mr. Cragin, had strong faith when there were only a dozen true believers."

"God gave me the utmost confidence in Mr. Noyes from the beginning—confidence that he was an inspired man," Cragin clarified. "Confidence in his inspiration has been what has held the Community together."

"I never appreciated such men as Mr. Kinsley and Mr. Burt as I have this summer—they've never failed or turned back; they're just as confident and full of faith now as ever. They're like granite!" Miller enthused.

"Quarrying for good men is like quarrying for stone—in opening a quarry, at first you must clear off the earth and loose stone, and finally come to good building stone," Hinds agreed. "After his departure from the old systems of theology, Mr. Noyes at first found himself surrounded with unreliable 'shale-y' men, but he was not discouraged! He kept on quarrying until he got good stone—granite."

The criticism of the Villa department was received in a good spirit. Mr. H. went into that department, all were pleased with this, and everything was settled harmoniously.

"'I have here a criticism of Mr. Reynolds,' Mr. Inslee said. 'We glanced at Reynolds and saw that he was even more amazed than the rest of us—he hadn't called for criticism lately and didn't know any was coming,'" reported the August 1873 *Circular*. Reynolds was known as a mighty man of strength who joined the Brooklyn Community in 1852 making traveling bags and later working in the Trap Shop.

"'I'd like to praise Mr. Reynolds,' Mr. Inslee began. 'I'm heartily pleased with the way he takes hold of his work in the machine-shop. He is musical, cheerful, much interested, and very efficient—ready for any kind of work. He looks out for me that I do not do all the heavy work. Mr. Reynolds is always ready to volunteer his help and is very kind to everyone. I feel edified by his spirit.'

"'Reynolds is merged in our business now,' Alfred Hawley agreed, 'so we have a new appreciation of him and are finding out how much he is capable of.'

"'I think it has been a fine thing for him—his former work isolated him from the other men and he often seemed cross,' Mary Bolles noted, 'but he is genial now.'

"'And I think he works from a pure love of the Community interest,' Mrs. Ackley added, 'not from a love of money.'

"'I have been much pleased with the thankful spirit Mr. Reynolds shows,' said Mr. Hawley, with feeling. 'The other day he asked me to assist him because his machinery was getting out of repair and he couldn't run it. I did so, and he thanked me over and over at the time and thanked me when we were washing our hands at night, and again when we met in the morning!'

"'He gets so much engaged in his work,' Mr. Inslee pointed out with some pride, 'that sometimes he can hardly stop to go to dinner!'

"'He is as enthusiastic as a little boy and seems interested to make the most of himself,' John Sears contributed, enthused by the conversation. 'I was very much pleased with the way he took hold of some brass-work on the spinners. He did much better than I expected he could do. He has nice ideas about mechanics and is very faithful in whatever he undertakes. Mr. Clark, the teamster, said to me the other day that he used to think Mr. Reynolds cross, but now he finds him very pleasant whenever they meet. The wholehearted way in which he performs his duties as fire warden is commendable,' he added. 'He took the post against his wishes, but is very faithful in it.'

"'Visitors here were gazing about on the portico in a curious way,' Mr. Miller related, 'and Mr. Reynolds came up to me and remarked that they don't see the solid gold that is here. I thought that remark was indicative of the way his mind runs, and that his attention is taken up with deep things a good deal of the time. He told me that when he first met Mr. Noyes, he knew he was the man for him to follow. His remark about solid gold shows his sense of the truth and his appreciation of it. There is a good deal of gold in Mr. Reynolds!'

"Mr. Inslee, in unison with others—'*There is!*'

"'It seems to me that such a great change as everyone can see has taken place in Mr. Reynolds's spirit is miraculous,' said William Kelly wonderingly. 'And it goes far to confirm the truth that a change of character is possible; such a change in a man of his age ought to encourage us all.'"

DEALING WITH PERSONALITIES, MANNERISMS, HABITS

Noyes said that mutual criticism was the modern equivalent of 'washing one another's feet.' Feet represented that part of our character concerned in outward affairs; though our essential character might have been washed clean, our superficial character might require frequent cleansing.

"The habits of individuals came up for remark, and many peculiarities of manner were set forth in a ridiculous light by some of our best mimics," reported the October 6, 1873, *Circular*. "O. had a way of winking and shrugging his shoulders, very disagreeable to all who saw him; L. made faces, often twisting his countenance into the most curious shape. When certain principles were up for discussion, he'd sometimes throw back his head and put on one of his odd expressions, as if to say, 'I can't swallow all of that.' D., R., T., A. and H. had the annoying practice of biting their fingernails; F. handled her fork like a drum-stick; when embarrassed, Z. stroked his beard in a distracted manner; M. pinched her ears until they were crimson! One young woman confessed to the habit of chewing paper, whereupon someone rejoined, "Indeed she does; she will often tear a strip off from paper lying on my desk, and before I know it, it's in her mouth!" This was mortifying to the young woman, but the exposure was beneficial. E. sat ungracefully in a chair; W. scratched his head nervously; K. when in thought twisted the corners of her apron; S. kept one foot swinging when sitting; B. had a very ludicrous manner of protruding his tongue; U. annoyed those near him by constantly drumming on the arms of his chair; Y. pulled out his watch and opened it as often as once in three minutes; P. with many others had a bad habit of tilting in his chair. Picture an attack made on P. for tilting his chair, to which he replies, "In what manner is it particularly offensive?"

"For one thing, it mars the walls and the floor," Q. began. "If you want to sit in any particular attitude, why not have your chairs fitted for it?"

"I generally tip my chair back after I have been sitting for some time and want a change."

"If the chair-legs were shorter behind, the difficulty would be obviated, I think," C. opined.

"Well, I don't defend it, but we often have a great deal of sitting to do. We could all get this change, and greater ease, if we only had rocking-chairs."

"Let's have rocking-chairs then," said Q. "I'd say that a man of your standing should have a rocking-chair!" (Laughter).

"I'd prefer doing without," he said.

"I've been invited to criticize the practice of sitting on one foot. I don't know what comfort there is in it, but the custom is unbecoming (several young ladies gave a conscious titter). In regard to men carrying their hands in their pockets, I think the only genteel way of disposing of your hands is this," putting his thumbs in the arm-holes of his vest.

"Among certain genteel people, much time is spent training their children in parlor etiquette, for if folks notice bad manners and are annoyed, they will ridicule them privately—lacking the chance to discuss these things openly, so it will do no harm to pay attention to manners," N. suggested. "It will have a good effect and we shall probably never forget lessons we're learning. I'd like to give the subject special attention for a while and then let it take care of itself. The improvement we're making is not trifling. The principle is the same as it is in music—we can delude ourselves that the minutia of music are not of great consequence, but success depends on the amount of our painstaking. So it is in anything. We must set a high standard and live up to it."

"The proposition was made that no person should be allowed to put his hands on or near his face for a week," reported B. Havior. "The result of this rule was amusing. Q. was caught rubbing his head on several occasions, and in desperation put both hands firmly down, remarking, 'I begin to feel as if I were in a strait-jacket.' L. coming in late the same evening created a great laugh by seating himself and stroking his beard most tenderly. The next evening, however, the scene was different. P. sat erect in his arm-chair, busying himself with folding and unfolding his handkerchief; E. sat very straight with head up and hands behind him; twice J. and D. began tilting their chairs, but numerous fingers pointing at them set them aright. For a week, the most punctilious behavior was required, after which the rules relaxed somewhat. Still to this day, the impression of that week's experience is not wholly effaced."

How to Quench Discord

Some of the three hundred Oneida Community members with John Humphrey Noyes, standing in front, center right.

"A beautiful queen named Love in the kingdom of One Heart lives in the palace called Harmony," writes H. in an instructive parable in the August 25, 1873, *Circular*, "and she lives to make her subjects happy and instructs me to watch the tongue. Where there's chit-chat, catch away seeds of discord and see that little matters of a personal kind are not repeated just for the sake of talking. If Eliza says something in a careless remark not very flattering to Mary's singing, I must quench that remark where it's made and not let it be repeated in the next gossiping circle—then in another, and at length come to Mary twenty times emphasized by transmission, and chill her heart inevitably toward Eliza. The tongue has a lust to repeat a matter. 'Where no tale-bearer is, strife ceaseth.' I'm to watch when there is a multitude of words. Many a chill and estrangement in social circles may be traced to the simple love of talking, which leads to casual personal remarks and then to its repetition. Too often what began without malice reaches its object with a poisonous sting. I am to make the tongue positively serve love and one way is to teach it sincerity. If Mary's manner has its imperfections, I'm not to discuss them with others but make my criticism sincerely to her in a way that she'll appreciate my intention and be able to improve. Where the tongue is taught such sincerity, it can provoke love by praise as well as criticism. 'Whatsoever things are true, are honest, just, pure, lovely, and of good report, if there be any virtue and any praise, think on these things.' If a friend has a peculiarity not quite agreeable to us, it is better to tell him rather than speak of it to some other associate, because that foible might be something minor that the other person may have never noticed. To illustrate: A. says to B., 'Do you notice that C. hardly ever seems to have original thoughts—only an echo of what others say?' B. respects C., and he'd never had such thoughts, but now, when he hears C. speak, that miserable idea put into him by A. will thrust itself upon his mind, and involuntarily he may hear only an echo. Again: Everyone thinks K. amiable and inoffensive, but he has one habit that has attracted the attention of Y. unpleasantly, and she, without meaning to disturb another's feelings toward him, says to Z., 'Doesn't that habit of K. distress you?' Z. had never noticed the habit in K., but now that her attention is called to it, it comes to be a grievous trial to her and she heartily wishes it had never been mentioned. One who has had such vexing characteristics brought to his attention learns by it. When tempted to say something negative about another, he checks himself by thinking *Perhaps I'm the only one who has thought of it; I won't burden another by pointing it out*. It will favor the growth of love and unity to decide that unless we can mention these faults in a way to do good, we won't speak of them at all."

"Our lives and characters are the results of struggling forces—between interior forces and exterior forces. Improvements of character come by what might be called civil war within us, that is, by the revolt of interior forces against the exterior. Long after our interior has surrendered to good, evil still entrenches itself in the exterior and holds its ground there. The point to be aimed at in all criticism is not to make war on the person criticized, but to enter into the civil war going on within him and help the interior party in its struggle with the exterior party. This we can do just so far as the interior forces are predominant within ourselves and free to enter into our criticisms. We are united in saying we will neither think evil of our brothers, nor listen to the evil-speaking of others. There are legitimate methods in which we may, when necessary, remind one another of faults needing correction; but needless, censorious remarks about one another shall be heard no more in our midst. No other topic has occupied so many hours in our evening gatherings; all are now ready to forswear evil-thinking and evil-speaking in every form. If we wish to be healthy and full of life, we must ally ourselves to the good of other people, contemplate it, and combine with it. It requires watchfulness to see the good side of a person's character and continually find good in our surroundings," said Tirzah Miller in the October 14, 1873, *Circular*. "If we give place to the spirit that inspects people closely and judges their faults harshly, separation and disunity will follow, and finally social destruction. We tend to look for faults in others, and to think of someone's blunder or wrong-doing even where there's no foundation for it. This apparently justifiable evil-thinking destroys the peace of God in our hearts, which passes all understanding."

"I yield to no man in lively appreciation of the large capabilities of woman," writes a member, "when she breaks out of the narrow routine of domestic duties, or repudiates the imperative demands of fashion and seeks greater culture and wider scope in fields long monopolized by man. I view with deep interest her steady advancement toward those callings for which she seems well-fitted by nature and in which she is as likely to excel. Latent forces within her are fast struggling into action. Mark her progress: In the practice of medicine she has won a recognized position; in theology and law she has gained a foothold; in business she is an indispensable auxiliary to man; in art and literature she successfully competes with him, and in the political arena her influence is great though exerted behind the scenes.

"But one pitiable weakness still clings to woman. Reared and living mostly indoors, she feared the startling and strange in nature and the same unreasoning dread of animate life is yet displayed by her. You're seated beneath a shade tree conversing on an absorbing theme and are inwardly admiring the good sense she displays and the variety of her information. Suddenly an appalling shriek accompanied with desperate passes at part of her mortal frame interrupts the tranquil scene. It was only a harmless insect that had alighted upon her fair neck, or perhaps an inchworm crawling over her shoulder. A company of women can be thrown into an ecstasy of fear at sight of a terror-stricken mouse capering about the room; animals wandering about seem to the masculine mind to be inoffensive objects, but to womankind many might be treacherous beasts likely to attack them with hoof, horn, or tooth. Darkness hides uncanny frightful things to the female mind; a crashing thunder-peal can cause our sensitive sister to shudder in abject terror. Crossing a low trestle makes her poor head swim. Surprises, sudden alarms, and unusual noises quite unnerve and sometimes prostrate her. Alas! But woman is not wholly to blame that this department of her nature, call it physical courage, is so deplorably undeveloped. And she's keenly aware of public sentiment that might condemn traits of courage, coolness, and self-possession as unwomanly or mannish. What wonder that her development exhibits this incongruous phase?"

Variety is the spice of life

"Think of the great variety of faces there are; this endless variation causes no irritation—we admire it! The eye quickly tires of the monotonous and is continually pleased with new forms, new expressions, and new combinations. If people could look upon other personal differences in the same way, how much happier the world might be! Instead of allowing differences of taste, feeling, or opinion to irritate us, and wanting to compel everybody to think and feel as we do, how much better to regard such minor divergences as a happy provision of Providence to give zest to life," Tirzah Miller shared in the October 14, 1872, *Circular*. "We would have a bland time of it if our ideas on all subjects were the same. Some persons can be exasperated at others who like an article of food cooked in a manner dissimilar to that preferred by themselves, and I honestly thought Q. would have liked to give me a shaking because I said I couldn't endure wide hems! If we can agree concerning our relations to God and to one another on the greatest scale, why not derive enjoyment from smaller disagreements, striving for charity that is not easily provoked and thinks no evil?"

> "My friend, if all together we utter but one tune,
> What music would that be, all sung in monotone?"
> —Angelus Silesius, *One Thing Alone Does Not Always Satisfy*.[44]

"Persons differ in judgment and taste, and if we allow differences to become too important in our minds they will make us see evil in others' characters. I have a strong desire to keep clear of that tendency. I have sometimes found when I'm interested in a thing and my happiness depends on having my own plan carried out, it injures my spiritual life; excessive care about anything drives the peace of God out of our hearts. I have to throw off all care about the matter, and regain my freedom. It is all too easy to fall into the habit of telling how things ought to be and would be if only persons were more enterprising."

"There should be some way to bring to the light the dissatisfactions that must exist where a number of people attempt to live together either in a commune or in the usual life, but which in a commune must be wisely managed," wrote student of communities, Charles Nordhoff. "I know of no better means than that which the Perfectionists call Mutual Criticism—telling a member to his face, in regular and formal meeting, what is the opinion of his fellows about him—which he or she receives in silence. Those who cannot bear this ordeal are unfit for Community life and ought not to attempt it. But this criticism, kindly and conscientiously used, would be an excellent means of discipline in most families, and would in almost all cases abolish scolding and grumbling."[45]

"I once thought I never could feel at home with and enjoy the society of persons who are of a different race, color, and habits from myself," wrote Charles Ellis on May 6, 1872. He was born in Kent, England, in 1814 and then moved to Canada. "Even after I had experienced religion, I considered absolutely impossible the idea of forming a spiritual relationship that would become as strong and enduring as the natural one. Twenty years' close companionship with those whom I regard as fathers, mothers, brothers, sisters, has wrought a change in my feelings. I have learned to appreciate and love all those around me and I am convinced that the relations of the flesh are weak and transitory in comparison with those of the Spirit. The variations of character seem as beautiful to me now as the variations we admire in a musical composition. I feel thankful that God has scattered his children all over the earth, in order that each may contribute something new for the benefit of all. . . . I have often met my relatives at my father's house with intense pleasure; but the joy that fills my soul at the hope of meeting that innumerable multitude of all nations, kindreds and tongues, with palms of victory, leave no doubt in my mind of the vast superiority of spiritual relations over those of the flesh."

EVIL-THINKING AND ITS CURE

"Everything that we do, even the smallest act, opens a door—turns a key that lets in upon us an influence from heaven or an evil wind from the world of bad spirits," Noyes wrote. "The act is often not half as important as what follows the act. We may judge anything we do by the sensations afterward, whether it has let in Christ or damnation; we can eat and drink Christ and we can eat and drink damnation. We talked last evening on the subject of evil-thinking and evil-speaking. The past winter will be remembered for the great victory achieved by the Community over these evils. Our system of mutual criticism, face-to-face truth-telling, has made an end of the more gross forms of evil-speaking—gossip, scandal, backbiting; but this still showed itself in less offensive forms and was the cause of more or less unprofitable conversation, especially in relation to individual peculiarities. It needed a deeper work of grace in our hearts to make an end of this form of evil speaking. Our experience as a Community has grown more and more earnest during the winter; our hearts were filled with revival fervor; we desired perfect unity with Christ and with one another; and just at the right time to make the victory most secure, our attention was turned toward this enemy of unity, evil-thinking."

"What can be more degrading and pernicious, more abusive of God and humanity, more suicidal to one's own peace and self-respect, than evil-thinking?" George Cragin asked in one of the March 1872 issues of the *Circular*. "To one who habitually thinks evil, the whole universe seems filled with misery, while to another in the same outward circumstances, the universe is a boundless storehouse of treasures of both wisdom and knowledge. To think evil gives one an evil eye, which sees evil, and nothing but evil, in individuals and in society generally. One who sees evil is looking on the changeable surface of things and at the apparent limitations of good; while the other has his attention primarily on the interior of things, and rejoices that good is unlimited. The evil-thinker can hardly be other than superficial and therefore unreliable, however profound he may regard himself or be regarded by others; for his attention is upon outward changes, which are deceptive."

"Conditions of the mind may be distinctly defined," Noyes wrote, "the lowest being insanity in which the machinery of the mind is deranged and acts incoherently or in a self-destructive manner. Another mental condition is one in which the machinery of the mind is sound, yet thoughts are not under control. The third is one in which the mental machinery is completely under the control of its owner. He has power to cause its action to cease from time to time; to direct it whithersoever he will, or to put the control of it into the hands of God and good spirits. There is more voluntary control in the spiritual mind than in the carnal mind. It's very necessary that a person have the power to stop thinking altogether—to not think of anything," Noyes conveyed in his Home Talk *Stopping Thought* at Wallingford Community, April 30, 1868. "When thought is going wrong, we can stop the machinery of mind and go into the heart and let the heart have full operation till we are ready to start the mind again under inspiration—which we do when we go home into our heart and seek to know God. Even good thoughts can wear on our nervous system. We can quit working our brain when we're awake as well as when we're asleep. If we can carry control into the sexual nature and have voluntary power there, the same power must be extended to cessation from thought. Folks ask me what I think upon such and such matters, and I have frequent occasion to respond that I don't think anything about them. The thing is to think neither right nor wrong on certain subjects until we have inspiration, or when God sets us to studying these subjects. When we form a regular habit of turning inward, this constitutes spirituality."

Introspections on Evil Thinking

"For years I have been the involuntary victim of evil-thinking concerning various things in my circumstances," wrote Henry J. Seymour. "I continually accused God of injustice, convincing myself that I was sadly abused. A thousand times I have brushed away these thoughts as I would a swarm of flies; but as often as I did so, they would return with increased power to suck my very life-blood. To give my mind to the study of mathematics was only a temporary make-shift, which availed me little. I suffered many of the torments of the insane, I doubt not, until finally it appeared to me that if drowning would afford me relief, I would gladly adopt that expedient. I was asked one day how I was getting on. I answered by describing the power and character of my mental temptations, without giving particulars. My interrogator endeavored to comfort me by showing that such trials are a necessary part of salvation. I asked him if I ought not to divulge my black thoughts. He replied that if I were convinced they were devilish thoughts I had better smother them. After further talk in which he showed the unreasonableness of my imaginations, he asked me in a loud, peremptory tone if I were 'willing to walk on the right side.' I replied, yes, though I saw no 'right side.' It occurred to me that the man with whom I was talking was clear above this weakness of evil-thinking, so I confessed myself united to him and said that if he were saved I should be. This declaration seemed to make a soft place in my heart. Although this soft spot appeared to be a pretty small one, it was large enough for me to get into, and I soon discovered that while there, I was safe from the shafts of evil-thinking. I find that I am getting more and more power over my mind and imagination. From time to time, I can make my mind a perfect blank and wait for good thoughts to arrive from my heart, and I feel I'm not at the mercy of influences that come from the outward world. This, I am convinced, is true, heavenly sanity."

"Someone who for a time was an educator of youth became very unpopular on account of his indulgence in evil-thinking," wrote George Cragin in March 1872. "The least opposition to his will or foolish whim, the slightest criticism of his character as a teacher, would so arouse the demon of evil-thinking within him that his friends gradually became alienated from him, and were filled with grief at his unmanly deportment. Professing religion only aggravated his moral disease, for his religion was purely of a legal sort and produced neither softness of heart nor humility of mind. Moreover, as moral diseases produce physical ones, he became a dyspeptic and that produced a morbid attention to dietetics. One given to evil-thinking is also an egotist of the chronic kind, and not infrequently a hypochondriac, to whom all things wear the most somber hues imaginable. Evil-thinking became in a great measure his lifework. Brooding over imaginary or real evils has become so involuntary with him that when he would think good, evil is present with him."

Albert Kinsley wrote a short note, *How to be Miserable*, in the July 19, 1869, *Circular*: "If you wish to be miserable, you must think about yourself; about what you want, what you like, what respect people ought to pay to you, what people think of you, and then to you nothing will be pure. You will spoil everything you touch; you will make sin and misery for yourself out of everything that God sends you; you will be as wretched as you choose." Noyes echoed this: "Egotism is not simple love of attention to yourself, it is attention to self to the neglect of due attention to other beings. 'You shall love God with all your heart and your neighbor as yourself.' Attention to self is here recognized, but reduced to its true proportion."

"A terrible spirit found access to my mind by my first yielding to the temptation to think evil of my own defective character, followed by my thinking evil of my friends, who kindly pointed out to me my faults," wrote George Cragin about a friend in March 1872. "While exercising a hypercritical judgment of myself, I'd be thinking evil of others before I was aware of it, accusing them of being the cause of my inharmonious relations to those around me; and, finally, even accusing my Creator for allowing so many imperfections in my inherited qualities. During these mad reveries of evil-thinking, my better nature seemed paralyzed and cold as marble. I became so perfectly isolated and so filled with a sense of utter loneliness, that I could not have suffered more had I been doomed to solitary confinement in a convict's cell. Evil-thinking created such a hell in me that I carried wherever I went a 'body of sin and death' truly. Finally I became alarmed at my helpless bondage, but what could I do? Resolutions not to think evil would, in the hour of temptation, fail me; despair of self-help seized me. In this dire extremity, something said to me—the Spirit of Truth?— *Your thoughts are not your own*. A ray of light entered my soul. 'I live, yet not I, but Christ liveth in me.' Evil thinking cannot enter where Christ dwells. The confession,

Christ in me the controller of my thoughts, is the only remedy that gives perfect victories over evil; my thoughts are not my own, but Christ's. I prayed for the crucifixion of the ego-life and putting on the new as often as the work of perfecting a vital union with Christ required. Evil-thinking put him to death, yet Christ could not return evil for evil. I heard these words, 'Father, forgive them, for they know not what they do.' I felt that the spirit of evil thinking in me had received its death-blow, consumed by the love God as exhibited in his Son. I could only exclaim, 'Infinite is the power of love!'"

Abram Burt's story; though short, contains a sermon: "Last winter I became conscious of many things in my character that needed the refiner's fire. Most of all was a propensity to evil thinking with which I struggled long and hard. All my efforts to get free from it seemed unavailing. The way was described and I knew what I needed, but how to really get deliverance was the point. I became very unworthy in my own eyes and despair began to work. One evening alone in my room, I was praying earnestly for light and help and it came to me like a flash of light, that all this struggle was with something that did not belong to me. With this insight came the discernment of a life in me deep down that was saved—and Christ's life flowed into me. I always regard it as a miracle—the work of that moment. The mountain-load I had been carrying and had struggled so vainly with was removed instantly, and great comfort and peace took its place. Egotism, pride, un-thankfulness—all had vanished to be supplanted by the faith and love of God."

"I had quite an experience reading *Salvation from Sin* that you left me," an outsider wrote to a Community member, reported in the April 15, 1872, *Circular*. "Passages like *Behold, I stand at the door and knock* seemed much clearer than anything I'd ever read on holiness. *I* am the house and He is knocking at my door! Everything is in dreadful confusion, not even one room in order. I thought of my condition, my soul panting after God, and this figure at the door will put it all in beautiful order if I will only bid him enter and take possession. Right here is the struggle—my will is in the way. It is my house; can I surrender it to someone else to keep? It will be mine no longer. I see the dire confusion and feel my utter weakness; my hands fall and my will is gone. I hear the voice at the door and I open it: 'Come in! Thou hast waited long and patiently. Come in, thou Heavenly Guest. All I have is thine. Set my house in order, and keep it forevermore.' There was a change—how, I know not; all was bright and clear and these words rang out, *happy . . . Happy!* Ministers could do great good by spreading far and wide these instructions for seeking deliverance from sin."

"I was thinking of a temptation to which I was exposed and was in tribulation about," George Noyes shared on June 28, 1869. "One way was to form a resolution to quit the action I'd drifted into from a kind of fascination—then I saw that what I wanted to be saved from most was the internal attraction or fascination itself. If I wasn't saved from that, there was no use setting up a rule in regard to my actions—I must first be saved from the charm that induced those actions. I thought about the passage in Hebrews, *I will put my laws into their mind, and write them in their hearts.*

If God can put his law into our hearts and so operate on our passions and attractions, I made up my mind to fall back upon that. The fulfillment of the New Covenant is changing our desires; making us more and more free to do as we have a mind to—we shall find that there is no conflict between duty and inclination. See how the New Covenant worked: it was no hardship for the people to put all their property together, because the Law of God was written in their hearts."

"After a long course of yielding to the temptations of unbelief and discouragement," wrote Charles Burt for the November 16, 1868, *Circular*, "I found myself out of sympathy with those around me, and out of the current of Community life. I was unhappy. By not resisting temptation, I was losing my faith in God's power to save, and doubting his love for me. This kind of experience continued until I cared but little whether I was saved or not. When at work one day, I commenced thinking of the condition of those around me, how different their feelings were from mine. They were happy, and I wondered what made them so. My faith in the Community doctrine of confession was still quite weak; all my previous confessions had failed to save me from discouragement and despair. While reflecting upon the subject, an impulse came over me to do what others around me were doing. They were cheerful and happy. Is it because they believe in Christ and confess him their savior? Let me try, for one day at least, to give up all my own thoughts, and testify roundly to the goodness of God. Even if I do not believe what I confess (I reasoned), and my testimony fails to bring relief, I surely cannot feel any worse than now; it won't hurt me to try it just for one day. The resolve was made. I went about my work next morning feeling much the same as usual, only remembering to repeat continually, 'God is good to me, and I believe he wants to help me.' At first it seemed like mockery, and a voice would occasionally say: *You don't believe that*. But I continued the testimony in spite of feelings. About noon, a still small voice began whispering within me: *Is not that true? Do you not believe in God's goodness?* At first, I put the thought away; but it returned and hovered around me, so still, so gentle, and yet so persuasive, that before I was aware I was repeating to myself, 'It must be, it is so, I know it is so!' The gates were opened, and a flood of love and joy rushed into my heart, the former stronghold of unbelief, and there reigned supreme. I was happy. I loved God, and rejoiced in a miraculous deliverance."

"There is very little confession in the world at present; yet how manly and noble to expose your faults and sinful ways by confessing them," wrote Cornelius Higgins. "No matter how contemptible your actions may have been; no matter if you are for a time despised and shunned. You must win your way resolutely back to respect, confidence, and love by downright truthfulness and honest doing. Don't wait to be exposed, to be dragged to judgment, to have your derelictions misconstrued and misjudged by the kind but unskillful efforts of the very friends who are trying to help you. Walk in the light, live in the light, never do or say that of which you will be ashamed. O!—if we will only roll off our burdens, give up our secrets of a month, a year, ten years, twenty years; let the truth search us, cleanse us of our little faults, our great faults, our most secret and carefully guarded faults; then after this purifying we shall rise light-hearted and happy, and peace, contentment, and joy shall be ours. The apostles give earnest exhortations on the subject of confession in their epistles, but do not let us wage this good warfare in our own strength. We have an ever-present, faithful, and loving Savior; the sole source of all truthfulness, who is himself the light that shines in our hearts. He will help us, guide us, protect us, and lead us onward in the path of light above, till all darkness shall vanish away, and heaven's glory shall illumine us forever."

THE SECRET OF CONTENTMENT

"From my earliest recollection I have been seeking for contentment but never found it till quite recently. All mankind are seeking this rare jewel," wrote Dexter Edson Smith. "I say rare, because it is so seldom found. Millions of persons toil for it all their lives and yet die without becoming its possessor. It is within the reach of all, but the road to it is a narrow one and few are found who tread so strait a path. I thought wealth would procure contentment in my younger days. But when I investigated the experience of rich men, I found no one who was satisfied, or contented, which is the same thing. I then became interested in religion and looked to the church for peace, and contentment. But here again I was disappointed. Instead of peace and quietness of mind, fears and doubts ruled the hearts of church members and I found them filled with condemnation, bemoaning their inability to cope with temptations. Their experience proved to be my experience, similar to Paul's, which he describes in the seventh chapter of Romans: 'When I would do good, evil was present with me.' I was taught that this was a description of Paul's Christian experience, although I greatly wondered at it, for I naturally supposed from other passages of scripture that true religion would entirely satisfy the heart. But the church said it did not, and so I had to content myself with the expectation of happiness or contentment after death. Like a sheep in a flock, I followed the one before me and if he jumped a fence into a ditch, I supposed I must follow.

"At last I strayed away from the old flock, and after much wandering found another leader who brought me into pastures that fully satisfied my every want. That leader was Mr. Noyes, and the pasture was salvation from sin. I found that I had been laboring under a delusion in thinking that the seventh of Romans described the experience of one begotten of God. The experience of such a one is described by Paul in the eighth chapter of Romans: 'There is therefore now no condemnation to them which are in Christ Jesus.' The point of no condemnation must be reached before contentment can be had, and this point can only be reached by a union with Christ; and a union with Christ can only be attained by faith that worketh true repentance, and a confession of Christ in us. If Christ's spirit controls me I cannot sin; and therefore I can not be dissatisfied or discontented. For as 'there is none good but one, that is God,' therefore there is no other way under heaven whereby we can become contented, except by allowing the contented spirit of God to take possession of us. When this is accomplished, we shall feel that God orders our circumstances; and we must necessarily be satisfied and happy whether we are in outward prosperity or adversity, knowing that all things work together for good to them that love God. We shall be like Paul when he said, 'I know how to be abased, and I know how to abound: everywhere and in all things, I am instructed, both to be full and to be hungry, both to abound and to suffer need. I have learned in whatsoever state I am, therewith to be content.'"

Paul's wisdom is reminiscent of Buddha's description of the usual human state, that of discontent; translated as a pervasive state of craving for more or for other than what we are or have, peacefulness and happiness elude us. "Desire constantly outruns enjoyment," Noyes always stressed. "There is no happiness is this. The great challenge of life is to enjoy the good things in life and then let go of them, not hankering for repetition of remembered pleasures or luxuries. Yet the human habit is remember what has been formerly enjoyed and to seek more happiness from that same enjoyment. When a person has made more than enough money to meet all needs and many desires, he finds himself wanting more, and when he has got more he wants still more. Due to this innate desire for ever more, nations are crippled in great depressions, families are bankrupted, and individuals enervated physically or mentally. I wish it might be impressed upon all of us that good, pleasant surroundings can never give us peace of mind, nor a good religious experience. On the contrary, they may divert and tempt us away from these, and instead of making us happy they will make us miserable. You may be in an outward Paradise but if your heart is not at rest, your outward circumstances will only make you miserable. Every beautiful thing you see will condemn you. You will feel a reproach coming upon you from the heavens and the earth, the birds and the flowers, and the more beautiful your surroundings are, the more miserable you will be.

"We must not think that it is right to pursue some particular pleasure till we have exhausted our susceptibility in that direction. We must learn to withdraw in the midst of pleasure, when our susceptibility is at its height, not only without pain but with positive enjoyment. This is carrying contentment to the mountain tops! If you study the matter you'll see we have a certain safeguard against being diverted and distracted from God by outward things. I never can forget that these outward things only increase my misery if my heart doesn't feel good; and I may say that in one sense, I am not at all tempted to rest in outward things. I must have God or else I cannot have any comfort. It is perfect nonsense to me to think of being satisfied with anything that money can buy. Money cannot buy good religious experience, money cannot buy love, and without these we cannot have any real comfort. We must learn the secret of enjoying more and desiring less. This is nothing more or less than the attainment of contentment."

"Jesus likened the kingdom of heaven unto a merchant who when he had found the pearl of great price, sold all that he had and bought it. I love this parable," wrote Alfred E. Hawley in *The Goodliest Pearl*. "Life is to us according to the pearl we seek;

we are always seeking goodly pearls. Now we think it's beauty—dress, admiration; now fame—the praise of fellow-beings; anon—riches; yet again—knowledge, deep and far-searching. Often esteeming such a pearl and selling all to get it, we find it no real jewel. Many pearls we seek are real pearls, but not the goodliest pearl; if we sell all we have for them, we are paying too high a price. After a few cheats we learn what are the gewgaws [showy trifles; pretty but worthless baubles]. Riches, knowledge, the love of those around us, are pleasant to desire yet even if we obtain them all, they will not make for us the kingdom of heaven in our hearts. At last we find the pearl of great price, the love of God—unity with Christ. When we have sold all that we have for this, we have made the great bargain of our lives. Sometimes we come across our pearl of great price unexpectedly and sell all that we have for it; but so sudden is the find that we may forget our ownership for a time and seek riches, knowledge, or somebody's love as the one thing needful. If we cannot get them, we imagine ourselves very unhappy. In the midst of a painful dream of this sort, there always comes a pleasant awakening—we recollect that we *already* have the goodliest pearl that can make us all glorious within. And like a magnet, it draws all other pearls to it. We bargained better than we knew. When we bought it, we also bought all the pearls that are worth having. Blessed is one who has the goodliest pearl."

"I was earnestly praying one day for a change of circumstances," T.M.S. wrote for the *Circular*, titled *Conquer Where You Are*. "If only *this* was different, or that obstacle removed, it would be easy to do right and I would not have to resist temptation. Suddenly beautiful words once given to the apostle Paul were given to me—'My grace is sufficient for thee.' At first my faith did not grasp the promise and I continued praying, but again those words seemed whispered in my heart and this time I thought, *Yes, those words are for me—I will believe them.* Christ is the same yesterday, today, and forever and can save me from temptation right where I am without any change of circumstances, if I will take him at his word. What if I am weak? His strength can be made perfect in my weakness. I will consecrate myself anew to him and not try to save myself. I will make good resolutions again; but instead of breaking them, I will trust God to make me keep them. This prayer and the assurance that God heard me were the beginning of victory. I found, to my surprise, that the temptations that had appeared so formidable were in reality very small. I realized the promise: Draw nigh to God and he will draw nigh to you. My weakness took hold of his strength and I no longer wished for a change of circumstances. Everything was just right. The path of duty that before was full of thorns to my feet was now smooth and easy to tread. My heart that seemed so hard and encrusted with worldliness seemed to break. I thankfully thought I will begin anew, thanking him for the simple faith that enables me to lay hold of the promise: *My grace is sufficient for thee*."

"When people get into bad experience, there is a strong temptation to think that their circumstances are unfavorable, but if we want to get at the root of the matter, we must go below our circumstances," said William Woolworth. "Our warfare is with principalities and powers, not with circumstances. We know that God is arranging things to educate us in the very best way. Outward circumstances are a kind of machinery that he uses to discipline us. Instead of seeking a change, seek to know what God intends—find out the spiritual meaning; then we shall not have to go through the same experience again. If we try to get out of it in an external way, we shall have to fight the battle again. If we were not in those particular circumstances we might be in some other that would bring out the same trials. Good soldiers do not want to slip out of the fight till they have gained the victory."

"Mr. Noyes's Home-Talk, *Salvation by Our Own Arm*, is to me saving truth," said T. M. S. "When I see a weakness or deficiency in my character, instead of sinking down into despondency and self-condemnation as formerly, I say, 'I will be thankful that I see the truth about myself; I will lay hold upon the promise, *You shall know the truth, and the truth shall make you free.* Christ is mighty in me; by virtue of my union with him I am a mighty principality and will not be brought into bondage, for I am one with Christ, who is free. I will assert my liberty; I will be free to serve God; the love of the truth is king of my passions, and the will of God shall be done in me.' I find that this action of my heart and mind and makes me free to wait on the Lord, and to follow the leadings of his spirit."

"One of our members, formerly much troubled in mind—the world went wrong with him from boyhood—has lately found a new experience," John Leonard recounted. "When you meet him now there is a new light in his eye and a genial smile on his face. Here is a composition he has been writing: 'The contented mind may be compared to a placid lake whose waters reflect the images of objects from its surface. Rocks and overhanging trees embellish its margin; birds flit through its submarine sky, and down deep the sun may be seen shining in his strength, or moon and stars in their nightly glory. The mountain's brow is reflected without a wrinkle. What is received is rendered back. But the discontented mind reflects a distorted image. Contentment implies reconciliation with God, love of truth; acceptance of our situation as we are related to the universe of facts; readiness to bear our responsibilities. Contented people are happy themselves and vibrations in their spiritual atmosphere make others happy. No murky fog of unbelief can hide their spirit of faith and improvement. They never grumble nor quarrel. They are pleased with small favors and little things, but their balance of mind will enable them to do great things.'"

"The following note to the family from H. was read at the evening meeting: 'I have had a great deliverance lately from depressing thoughts and temptation to self-accusation through words from Mr. Noyes. I had suffered so much that I thought I must find out the secret root of my trouble. He told me, with a power that gave me strength to obey, to turn my attention away from myself and look at the works of God in the Community, and they were seen everywhere! I could give my attention to them and rejoice in them without any reference to my own experience. I need not pray for myself, but pray that the work of God might go on. What he said dismissed all my worry about my own state not only in word but in deed. What a miracle was wrought! I cannot convey what a web of imaginations I was in, how helpless I was to extricate myself, and how the more I tried, the more I entangled myself. I thank God for my deliverance. I believe this is put into my heart by the Spirit.'"

"Isn't man rather like a candle undergoing the process of dipping? The bitter trials and terrible suffering into which we are dipped occasionally—essential to the growth of the inner man—are they not to us what the hot tallow is to the candle? Almost melted by the fervent heat of some trial, yet we come out alive, and lo!–find a valuable accretion to our spiritual life," Gail Hamilton wrote in 'Dip and Cool' for the October 26, 1868, *Circular*. "Each dipping enlarges us and brings the heat of the trial farther from the center until at length when we are dipped into the melted tallow of suffering, though it be ever so hot, yet at the center is a place where all is cool, firm, and undismayed, strengthening the exterior in the conflict. Is not the end worthy? How glorious to be able to give light to all that are in the house and to let our light so shine that all good may be visible and our Father glorified."

WHAT THE BROTHERS SAY OF BROTHERLY LOVE

"You all seem to be happy," said a young minister visiting the Community and joining their October 17, 1872, Evening Meeting. "And so we are," said James Herrick. "We have a happy home, and strangers are soon conscious of its genial radiation. They realize that there is a deep current coursing through all hearts, carrying away in its strong tide the roots and seeds of strife and irritation that could germinate and grow and produce bitter fruit. We find something growing and blooming in our hearts that we did not plant there ourselves. Love is of God and we are taught to love one another. That men can live in close Community as we do without jealousy and dissension is a wonder to the world; it is no less a wonder to ourselves. There is a mysterious power that comes upon us that we cannot explain; we call it the revival spirit; it washes the littleness out of us and fills us with brotherly love. The fact is fresh with us that Christ loved us and gave himself for us, and we feel the throbbing now of his great brotherly heart. The old life that we despise and abandon is selfish; it loves its own. The new life in Christ is pure; it counts the joy of others its own; it lifts us out of old ways, enlarges our hearts, and makes us know that the kingdom of heaven has begun on earth."

"It is surprising how unity and brotherly love can be cultivated where a company of men, women, and children really set about it," Frank Wayland-Smith agreed heartily. "We have been giving attention to that culture these twenty years, and the results gladden our hearts. Those angles of character that previously caused our elbows to gall the ribs of our associates (we speak metaphorically) have been so modified that we now wonder that our former disagreements were possible. No one knows until he has tried it, how much happiness is caused by learning to feel the hearts of his comrades and be continually assured of their sympathy and love. I know there is as solid comfort to be derived from the love of other men as from the love of woman, and I am continually learning to be sensitive to the feelings and wishes of those around me of both sexes."

"Christ is the magnetic power of this love," D. Edson Smith summed it up. "He had none of the emoluments of this life to offer his followers—rather, persecutions and sufferings—yet their love was so great that nothing could conquer it. That attractive power is still in the world. Christ dwells today in the hearts of men and inspires the same fervent brotherly love that he did two thousand years ago. I had thought it impossible to love man with the same intensity as woman; but Community experience has shown me that it is not only possible, but easy of accomplishment where life is given up entirely to God's spirit. One sees here as much kindness, deference, desire to aid and please, expressed by the men toward one another, as is seen in outside society between the sexes. I feel a warm love toward every man in the Community, and toward some I feel that thrill of pleasure from the pressure of the hand and that delight in their conversation that are commonly associated in the minds of men only with the gentler sex."

"Brotherly love in the Community extends to all our relations," wrote K. S. B. "a perfect unity with and faith in those with whom we are connected—faith so strong that we commit to others all interests public and private, with the assurance that they will be well cared for, and unity so perfect that nothing can separate us. Anything short of such unity and faith is not worthy to be called brotherly love. Each step I make in spirituality produces an increase of my love for those around me; I find that my heart is a sensitive indicator of my spiritual condition. Once when I was very happy, I sought to discover the reason of my happiness; it was that I loved everybody around me. I couldn't think of a single person against whom I had any cause of complaint."

"Judging the tree by its fruit, I had lost all confidence in the Christian churches and began to doubt the gospel of Christ," lamented Abel Easton, "until I fell in with loving men and women who for the sake of love and unity submitted to each other in the thousand-and-one trivial matters of private opinion and personal pleasures about which men ordinarily incessantly wrangle and quarrel. When I found men of stronger wills and superior intellect ready to forego their own opinions and join heartily with my own, my heart yearned for opportunities to show forth the love of Christ by making the same sacrifices of will and pride of intellect that others had made to me. I realized in my heart a more perfect understanding of the spirit of Christ's injunction, *Whosoever shall compel thee to go a mile, go with him twain*. Christ preached brotherly love because he knew that it was the very foundation of unity, as unity is the foundation of power. He desired that his disciples might have power to change the world. But from that time to the present, where can the brotherly love that Christ taught be found?"

"No sooner is the heart touched by the spirit of Christ, the fire of love is renewed within us and we begin to realize a quickening of life that is felt from the center to the surface of our being; old things pass away and all things become new," wrote Mary Loveland Blood in the July 22, 1872, *Circular*. "We live in a new atmosphere in which the spirit of peace and love and unity with God and one another rules us. A confession of Christ *in* us carries on the work. 'Beloved, let us love one another, for love is of God; and everyone that loveth is born of God, and knoweth God,' was John's exhortation in his first letter to the brethren. Love was John's all-absorbing message; his heart was aglow with love to God, which God received and returned to him and through him to the church, warming and knitting their hearts together. Love is the gift of God, free to all who are ready to accept it on the sole condition of a perfect surrender of themselves to the will of God, who waits for that surrender that he may possess and dwell in us, renewing us in the life of his own spirit and cleansing us of all our former self. Of all the gifts of God, I covet that of love as the choicest, whose fragrance is perennial and whose action is more blessed to the giver than to the receiver."

"I have a growing appreciation of true, unselfish love that first seeks the good of others, gives God the primary place in our hearts, and refuses to make an idol of any of his creatures," George Cragin wrote in *The Superior Love* in the June 3, 1872, *Circular*. "With a strong natural tendency to idolatrous love, the change in my own heart and in the hearts of my companions seems miraculous. I used to ask myself, is it possible for me to realize a condition in which I can love all my brothers and sisters and not love some *one* idolatrously? Can I have the love described in the 13th chapter of 1st Corinthians in place of the one love so popular in novels? Scorching experience taught me that idolatrous love, though sweet to think of, was bitter to take, and bad in its results to soul, mind, and body. I am now unreservedly devoted to promoting this higher kind of love—love that seeks unity one with another and the distribution of a good spirit as the most important work in which we can be engaged. That will bring the peace of God into our hearts, and the peace of God is Heaven."

"The distribution of love in the Kingdom of Heaven is governed by principles similar to those that govern the distribution of money," Erastus Hamilton wrote on January 20, 1873. "If one chooses a worldly course, one must learn right principles of securing money if he wishes to make an honorable career, but a large class of men seek to get money by cheating, theft, or other dishonorable action. Worldly law presents an obstacle to their getting money in all such ways. Just so in regard to love in the Kingdom of Heaven: If persons think they must obtain love directly for themselves, just as men would put their hands into the strong box, they will find that God in his providence is standing in the way. Those who get money by foul means are called scoundrels; those who desire love must remember that it belongs to God and seek it as his gift or they will be called by no better names. It is for God to inspire and direct us in loving one another. Hearts must be conscious that we do not belong to each other but belong to God, and we are his children. If we get that principle established in our hearts, it will help us to draw near to God and keep near him continually. Persons will have their hearts satisfied with love just as surely as there is a living God. 'Love is the circulating medium of the Kingdom of Heaven,' Mr. Noyes once said. It will be good for the young to take to heart that God is the distributer of love. We need to study love as a heavenly art, and set about spiritual, intellectual, and social improvement to attract love."

Brotherly Love—Notes of the July 21, 1873 Evening Meeting:

"The founders of this Community studied the 1st letter to the Corinthians, chapter 13, almost exclusively for a year," said Noyes. "I don't think our family knows how much they are indebted to Paul's chapter on charity. There was a continuing struggle, in a profound spirit of prayer and labor of heart, to get that gift."

"That chapter was printed on placards and pasted on our doors," William Hinds added. "Love is patient and kind; love envieth not; love is not arrogant or rude. Love does not insist on its own way; it is not irritable or resentful; it does not rejoice at wrong, but rejoices in the truth. It neither gives nor takes offense. Love bears all things, believes all things, hopes all things, and endures all things. These were also put into verse by Mrs. Cragin and Mr. Skinner. The spirit of that chapter permeated the greater part of the family."

"Yes," Abigail Burnham agreed. "Love neither gives nor takes offense. The spiritual mind places people beyond the possibility of quarreling; as long as people quarrel, they are carnal. They cannot call themselves spiritual until they attain such a degree of charity as will prevent friction."

"We've believed this can be done and I am anxious to accomplish it," William Woolworth agreed. "It was the foundation of the Community and is the cement that holds us together. The churches don't think it is practicable, but I believe that charity constitutes true Christian experience."

"Yes, the divine thing is *love*," said George Washington Noyes. "We cannot do without love, but we can do without everything else. We can live on brown bread and cold water with love. Love is the star of heaven in our souls, which only becomes the brighter. Let us be contented with love, seek it and drop everything else in the pursuit. Ask and ye shall receive, seek and ye shall find, knock and it shall be opened unto you. Love is the great gift from God. We need not think we must work it out for ourselves; it is Christ in us. The eternal fire is always there by our union with Christ. We are truly one—our everlasting and growing destiny is unity. Our separation is only outward, apparent, and temporary; the stronger reality is that we are members one of another. We will have the love that neither gives offense nor takes offense. Every man and every woman shall have it."

"The art of provoking to wrath seems to come by nature; people practice it without forethought. Some consideration is required to make us successful in provoking love," John Noyes wrote in his Home Talk, *Provoking to Love*. "We are to consider not ourselves, but one another. We miss happiness when we pursue it too directly. When we would pour it into another's cup, it overflows into our own. The most frequent cause of quarrel is evil-speaking, taunts, and impudent sallies. Persons begin to twit each other; every little meanness ever committed is dragged to light. We may reverse this performance, and twit each other of beauty and goodness. Facility of yielding and suppleness of manners will always provoke love. When there is truth or essential interest at stake, we are bound to be as inflexible as the oak; but this seldom occurs compared with the thousand little daily occurrences when unimportant things bring up a question of difference, and we have a chance to provoke love by giving way and promoting with alacrity the contrary side."

"If there has been neglect of proper cultivation in our nature, it is emphatically true of the heart," Robert Delatre wrote for the April 5, 1869, *Circular*. "Every faculty has been cherished more or less assiduously age after age, while the heart, chiefly concerned in molding the character, has been for the most part utterly abandoned to the mercy of circumstances. Love of neighbor that should have embraced the whole world has generally been confined to the mere hearth. If the heart is to be fully developed, there must be no boundary line short of God's great universe. The heart has also suffered from undue exaltation of the intellect, hence the poverty too often of the affectional sphere. By every righteous act we draw down the magnetism of heaven. *Habituate* yourself to good deeds, and it will eventually be easy for you to think and to feel and do aright. All heaven is at our elbow to help us. Try it a thousand times. Try it to all eternity. There's nothing else worth living for."

"'Try the experiment of winning over your friends by keeping a soft heart,' said S. to me on May 26, 1873. 'Then everyone will feel it a pleasure to try to please you.' I resolved to take his advice and soon had a chance to put my resolution to the test. I made an appointment with a friend who promised to meet me at a certain place promptly at the time set. The time came but my friend did not appear. The temptation to get out of patience was pretty strong, but remembering the advice I had received I sat down and waited. While waiting it occurred to me that praying was better than fretting, so closing my eyes to all outward things I soon forgot everything else in a whole-hearted communion with God. It was half an hour before my friend came, but it was a precious time to me. Had I spent that time in fretting, I would have met her perhaps with a clouded face and sharp words, but instead I accepted her apology in the spirit that that silent prayer had given me. This was the beginning of new experience. Many are the hours made up of odd minutes that I have spent in prayer since then, and the effect on my character and health has more than repaid me."

"I pray for a soft heart; for I have found by abundant experience that if I have that, everything else that is desirable will follow," wrote a young man on April 15, 1872. "I do not ask God for any particular blessing or for any change in my own spirit directly; but I simply ask him for a soft, receptive heart that he can work in and through. If I can attain a state of heart that God can use and fertilize with his life, then I am possessor of all the good that my soul can conceive of. He often gives me work I would not choose that requires all, and more than all, my natural courage to perform. But I find that he understands my case better than I do, and that he always makes my reward infinitely greater than I had hoped or expected. If I desire improvement in any part of my character, I have only to seek a soft heart that God may enter and strengthen the very point upon which I feel the most need. In his spirit are strength, health, and beauty. We are tempted to importune God for this or that favor because softness of heart is not controlling us. We don't work whole-heartedly for him without looking ahead a little for pay-day. When I am soft hearted, he gives me new desires that I never felt before, and no sooner am I the possessor of these desires than he satisfies me in regard to them. I find the greatest joy in his service when I do not stay too long with the good he gives me, but return early to his work.'"

"If a man says, I love God, and he hates his brother, he is a liar: for he that loves not his brother whom he hath seen, how can he love God whom he hath not seen? I had to learn many lessons before I could appreciate this last one—this cap-stone of the temple of holiness," another admitted. "Unless I can take my place harmoniously in the social economy of heaven as it is now here below, there can be no salvation for my soul. This impression is the deepest I have ever received. I might say on this 'hang all the law and the prophets.' Yes, love of neighbor is to be the test of our standing in the sight of God—indeed, it is the only means of true happiness. Paul makes a great account of the spirit of charity—a spirit so decidedly in harmony that it will love its very enemies rather than not love at all. We can imagine the blessedness that would ensue from everyone striving to make his neighbor happy. Were I to select one feature more than another of this charity, it would be: 'seeketh not her own.' Christ insisted that before we attempted to approach God we must first be at peace with our neighbor, and the only satisfactory course is to acknowledge God in one another—for if we cannot approach Him indirectly by honoring Him in one another, we are certainly not fit to entertain Him directly."

"It is natural for us when overtaken in faults to say that things try us, that our circumstances are perplexing, that our brothers offend us, but these are no excuses," William Hinds affirmed. "If persons make excuses for wrong-doing, it is the same as to say that they have failed in charity and in the grace of God."

"Let us all give place to the spirit that will bear fruit unto God from day to day," Mr. Hamilton expressed in the May 1872 *Circular*. "God's spirit is working in our hearts to save us from egotism, to make us new creatures and fill us with the peace of heaven. The spirit of heaven is powerful and able to help under all circumstances—help us to be joyful and happy. It is the Lord's strange work—to bless and make us happy."

"After several months of living in the Community," the Special Correspondent from the *Elmira Advertiser* wrote in 1872, "I have mingled freely with them at the table, about their work, in their sitting rooms and meetings where there is constant interchange, and in their evening meetings where the family spends an hour daily for religious improvement. As they seek to make their business and every act of their lives a part of their religion, many topics are introduced in these meetings and discussed with freedom. In each and all of these relations they appear to me like a band of brothers and sisters—children of one father with a mysterious bond of union existing between them, making them of one mind and heart. Instead of twin souls with but a single thought, I see two hundred souls united in the single thought of seeking to please God, and only so far as they are successful in this do they seem to succeed in pleasing one another. They possess a refinement and delicacy and a keen perception of what is fitting and agreeable to one another, which are evidently the result of great interior culture and entire negation of selfishness, by the growth of that true charity or love so fully described in the thirteenth chapter of 1st Corinthians. I cannot doubt that after living together thirty years and finding themselves more harmonious, more perfectly at peace in all their internal relations than at any previous period in their career, this people have really solved for the world the questions of most vital importance to mankind for all the future. Their system of criticism, or plain truth-telling in love (like a looking-glass in which all may see themselves as others see them), together with the strong spiritual atmosphere for good that preponderates over evil here, seem to be all that are needed in the way of government. I do not think there is any place in the world where a really wicked person would feel so ill at ease and so anxious to escape as here."[46]

"A visitor remarked that he could see how two or three could agree about one or two things; but how two or three hundred could agree on all essential points was a mystery to him," William Kelly reminisced. "He said he'd sooner undertake to govern a State than to govern two or three hundred people!"

"It is easier than brothers and sisters living in one family, because we're more nearly related in soul and spirit, the way Christ was to his disciples. There is the oneness of purpose, taste, and inward life that bonds. This connection is very strong, like chemical affinity."

8

Music, Culture, and Community Life

"Tell us how you learned to play the violin," John Humphrey Noyes was asked.

"Well, the year that I was studying in Esquire Mead's law office in 1830–31 when I was twenty years old and up to all sorts of fun, I heard that there was to be a singing-school started in the winter. I foresaw that in order to hold my place in the flirting ring and keep up with everything that was going on, I must go to that singing-school although I could hardly distinguish one note from another, and didn't know a discord from a concord. I discovered an old violin in the office closet and set about cultivating my ear with that and learning to read notes from a book of psalm tunes. I didn't dare begin to saw until everybody was out of hearing, but at night as soon as all was still, I would get the violin and practice till midnight. It took me quite awhile to learn to tune the instrument; but at last I got so I could do it, and after considerable hard work I was able to play some of the slow church tunes quite respectably. The result of these night labors that fall was that I got along very well in the singing-school, and had a good time carrying my part among the boys in school-time and carrying on with the girls in intermissions.

"The next year I was converted and went to Andover. The public singing of the Seminary was done by a very select organization and the custom was to choose a few of the best singers from each entering class of students to join. A delegate from this select society came to my room and set me to sing the bass alone to several rather difficult pieces. I did the best I could and the man went away without saying anything. I supposed that was the last I would hear of the matter, but I was soon officially informed that I was one among four or five of my class who were to become members of the select choir. So I had a good opportunity to improve that year. At Yale in 1833–34, I actually led the singing in the conference meetings of the Theological Seminary, and when I was preaching and attending revival meetings, I was looked up to as the musical fugleman, ready for anything from leading a choir to singing a solo. The drill I had on that old violin in Esquire Mead's office led to all my violin playing, and that led to the foundation of all our Community orchestras."

The Community orchestra had up to twenty-five members and gave weekly concerts to which the public was often invited. They had a choir of twenty-five, four soloists, three quartet clubs, and produced good plays, operas, humorous skits, and comic songs.

MUSIC AND DANCE

The exuberant happiness of the Oneida Community is delightfully described in the summer of 1855. "We've found it pleasant and profitable lately to march out to our work in the fields with music. At the sound of the clarinet on the lawn announcing a work bee for picking peas, weeding, or some other work, all hands gather with great hilarity and form a line under directions from Captain Kinsley. The band strikes up a lively tune, and the whole company marches in order to the field, turning corners and changing from platoons to single file as the width of their way requires it, in regular military style. At the close of our work the music again sounds a call, when all assemble and take up our line of march for home in a similar manner. For variety we sometimes sing one of our home-songs. On arriving at the Mansion, Captain Kinsley occasionally puts us through a few simple military evolutions. Sometimes we march to the reservoir and parade on its green slope, while some of the young men in bathing-suits perform sportive feats in the water.

"Evenings suggest serenades and all kinds of romance. There is a bath of pleasure for all the senses outdoors in all the exuberance of summer beauty. The moon shines on nature in the fragrant and balmy air. Last night, after the watch had retired and most of the family had fallen into peaceful slumbers, an enchanting mystery is added to the scene. Music in the distance, sweet voices, and a song were heard by some yet wakeful. Presently a light tripping through the garden, and then after a little silence the same music was heard on the lawn before the Mansion, now near enough to gently wake slumberers or mingle pleasantly with their dreams. This company of ten or twelve of the best singers of the Community sang two familiar songs and one that was new to us and very beautiful, *The Guardian Angel.*

"One April evening in 1872, our Sunday evening entertainment opened with a pleasing performance by the children. First a merry chorus as if from invisible birds filled the air. A band of youthful hunters then appeared on the stage armed with guns, evidently bent upon the slaughter of the feathered songsters, but a company of maidens approached and each in turn besought them in tuneful accents to spare the innocent birds. The appeal for mercy prevailed, and the affair terminated amidst a tumult of song from the birds. Next followed music by the small orchestra, a new organization in which the piano is included with fine effect. They played several pieces with applause. The last one, *Opera without Words* by DeBeriot and his son, exquisitely rendered, brought down the house.

"Two dancing classes are organized, which practice from six to seven o'clock on alternate evenings. We are learning the science of dancing and acquiring some perfection in the art. There are no objections to dancing as in common society—but there are no ball dresses, no late hours, wine, or revelry. As a means of improvement in health and grace and an expression of praise and worship, nothing can be better. Tables and chairs are carried into passage-ways and onto the stage, leaving room enough for the musicians, the violins, the double-bass viol, and horns. Dancers seat themselves on the edges of the Family Hall; mothers with babies and nurses with toddlers come to look on. Youngsters and those who wait for the last dance go up to the gallery and look down. Little boys from the children's house sit on the front of the stage—they want to be near the big drum. Mr. George Hamilton, six feet two with the voice of a stentor, announces the figures and "calls off." Fathers dance with their daughters, sons with their mothers, brothers with their sisters, and the young with everybody. We have quadrilles, contradances, waltzes, polkas, schottisches, one or two of each; waltzes and cotillions are most popular. Narrow-minded piety will look on our dances with an evil eye. But no heated men rush to the bar-room; no man and woman shows off the splendor of their dresses and the brilliancy of their dancing, and by their drunken devotion to each other. True sport and pleasure do not belong to the superficial and irreligious. After a quadrille or two, a waltz, a contra-dance or two, we're all cheered up but not intoxicated. We are ready for the evening meeting and the work of improvement and edification.

"Ten years ago when our men worked their ten hours a day in the trap-shop, carpenters' shop, or on the farm, music given to visitors was confined to the half hour after midday dinner, closing promptly at one o'clock, but we now take life more easily. The concert hour is two o'clock, and dire necessity no longer compels our musicians to lay aside the violin, flute, or cornet for hammer, forge, or flail. They are far from being idlers, though. They are even busier than they were ten years ago but now they can engage in pursuits more conducive to suppleness of wrist and finger. We did not call the noon performance ten years ago a concert. We had attained no such dignity as that. It was simply music by the band, with no other exercises; but now we have concert managers who make out a daily program, more or less full according to the number of visitors the Midland Railroad brings.

"The Family Hall, which had so long re-echoed its harmonies, became suddenly silent in the summer of 1865 for almost four years—violins mute; horns and flutes breathless, drums unstrung. The musicians were scattered, some in New York, some in New Haven, and some in Wallingford, Connecticut. Now all save three are here together again.

"'Come,' said one, 'let's have the orchestra revived.'

"'Let's have one play together, for Auld Lang Syne, no matter how it sounds. We'll have a laugh, anyway.' As though a fairy had waved her magic wand, at 7 o'clock twenty-two band members, instruments in hand, came onto the stage and took well-remembered seats.

"'O, won't it be a funny burlesque,' we said. 'They haven't practiced a bit and haven't the first idea what they are going to play. They never can keep together; they will break down a dozen times, of course,' and we laughed in anticipation. The leader lifted his baton amid silence, and every instrument, exactly together, struck the opening chords of *Oneida Quickstep*. Shades of the Nine! How electrifying! They swept on to the melody, to the more rapid passages, never breaking, but almost as of old, answering as one person to the swaying baton of the leader. Fingers do not forget their cunning so quickly. We greeted the finale with so much clapping that our hands tingled for half an hour after. 'It is wonderful,' we exclaimed; 'a miracle!' We've believed the professional notion that a musician must devote himself to incessant practice, perceiving that it is the spirit with which music is animated that gives it its charm; that each acquirement of the mind, each added grace of character, and above all each new gift of the Spirit, increases the musician's power to please."

"The Hampton Colored Students, nine men and seven women—slaves just eight years ago—came north to raise funds for Hampton Normal and Agricultural Institute, devoted to the education of colored teachers for the colored race in Hampton, Virginia. This school is close to where the first slaves were brought here. A Hampton student related her history, related in the April 28, 1873, *Circular*: 'I was born a slave in 1852 and spent my happiest days until at the age of seven I was taken from my mother, as all the rest of the children were. None of us went to the same place; my master had died and being in debt, we were first hired out to pay the debts. Before the hiring took place, I was struck to my heart with a scene I'll never forget. Everyone who wanted to hire, sell, or buy, would come get them a nigger, as they generally called us, and in the crowded street, sitting on the ground, was a colored woman and her children. Her husband was standing a little way off, crying. 'Have you any clothes? If you have, get them! Be quick about it, for I want to be off,' ordered the white man. 'You're going with me; you belong to me now.' With a loud cry the colored man said, 'I have nothing but my wife and children. Have you bought them too?'

"'No, I have bought none but you,' said the white man. 'What's going to be done with my wife and children?' The man only yelled at him to get in the wagon and wouldn't tell him where he was going.

"'I have bought your wife and baby, but the little boy I can't get,' said a nice-looking man. 'I will give her enough to eat and wear and she shall be my cook.'

"'Tell your mammy good-bye then,' a great ugly-looking man said. I didn't stir; bitter tears were flowing. This was my first dread of slavery. Then the day came for me to stand on the block. It did not go hard with me, but my sisters and brothers were scattered; I never saw them again until we were called to this place again to be sold. I was bought by the same one I was hired to and became quite a favorite with this family. They were good to me and taught me precious truths of the Bible, which I've found of much use. God grant that I may continue to learn of them and become wise in Christ. The war came and went without my feeling it. Then came the Emancipation, welcomed by every colored person; it was the first time they could say *Glory to God in the highest, peace on earth, good will to men* without being afraid."

DAYS AND SEASONS

"Six a.m. and the whistle sounds. Little bare feet are pattering along the main hall to the children's room to be dressed—the first glad sound of the morning. Laughing voices ringing through empty halls and corridors arouse sleepers from their dreams. Half an hour and a noise of footsteps, some light and some heavy, hurry up and down the long stairway from the Mansard; chairs and tables are shoved about. Another half-hour and women are sweeping halls, tidying parlors, mopping, and dusting the library. Three busy cooks are getting breakfast for those who file out to the dining room at seven o'clock. Some men go to the shop, some are packing silk, some are out on the farm, some are at the barn, and one or two are in the printing office. Some play croquet; a few are sitting on the portico and a few are reading in the library. At eight o'clock the whistle calls them all to breakfast. A server comes in bearing a new dish called German puffs made of Indian meal, flour, eggs and milk stirred into a batter without shortening and baked in the gem-irons in a quick oven. Overheard:

"L. (looking at bright, golden cakes)—'I suppose if you break one open you will find it full of holes.'

"S.—'Yes, but I am not aware that holes are an unhealthy diet.'

"D.—'But they're not particularly nutritious.'

"E.—'I suppose they are healthy because they're wholesome.'

"S—'True, but the whole sum of the holes would not amount to much.'

"By nine, people are scattered to the trap-shop, machine-shop, silk-room, business office, printing office, kitchen, dining room, laundry, company room, etc. The children with their guardians start off for the lot east of the road and the people who remain are tending our youngest or making their clothes, or taking care of the household. Company comes in on the train at ten—a slight bustle ensues. At noon a few more are added, and consequently more bustle with cooks and waiters stepping lively to get dinner ready at one o'clock. At twelve the bell rings; older children go to school and younger ones to nap. At three the whistle calls to dinner; there's a thronging toward the dining room and two hundred people discuss the viands temptingly laid out. Dinner over, many resume their labors until six o'clock.

Sounds on the lawn after supper—piano, clarinet, and cello playing in the Hall; a quartette singing in the cottage at the foot of the hill; children laughing; boys playing horse; the click of mallets and balls on the croquet-ground; the rolling of carts and wagons; cows lowing at the barn; sheep bells tinkling; lambs bleating; frogs peeping in the pond below the garden; birds singing; wind whistling through the trees; the roar and rumble of the train on the Midland Railroad; people meeting in the court or in sitting-rooms to share the latest news; young and old playing dominoes; reading, studying, writing, or practicing music—a time of rest and relaxation. The high note of the whistle calls us together for an hour in the Hall for the family meeting; interesting topics draw out enthusiasm. Meeting closes at eight and people disperse to the library, the sitting rooms, the nursery kitchen, and some to their own bedrooms. At ten o'clock the house is still. The watchman goes quietly round locking doors, putting out lights, and darkness and tranquility reign till morning.

"In 1856 there was a call for every member to keep daily accounts, for the improvement of time, about how their days were spent; volunteers might share their log at an evening meeting for entertainment and edification. Noyes wrote about a typical day: 'Just as the sun began to brighten the western hills, I arose and ate breakfast at the early serving. I guessed right at the Bible game in consequence of three previous persons having guessed wrong. I went to the kitchen with a good appetite for work, thankful for the variety and good company I found by my late change of occupation. At the usual morning gathering of the kitchen company, our chief Mrs. Van Velzer gave us the program for the day. A big baking was to be put through, and at the same time various dishes for dinner were to be prepared and put on the table. In the forenoon I assisted in bringing milk from the dairy, making brown bread, wheat bread, Indian puddings, fruit pies, and putting all into the oven; dissecting codfish and paring potatoes, cooking, and serving them. Withal I filled a small interval reading Miller's *Logic*. After our meal I enjoyed a little private fiddling with George Noyes and Erastus Hamilton. At one o'clock I returned to my post and received orders from Mrs. Van Velzer to prepare for a dinner of hulled corn; I brought a bushel of corn from the corn-house and put it soaking in hot lye.

"Went to my room to read and write awhile. "When I have finished one duty and there is nothing special before me," Noyes wrote in *How and Where to Pray*, "I go home to watching and waiting on the Lord in my heart. Instead of going from one thing to another on the circumference, I go to the center; go home and take a new start. Though I go out again right away, if I stay out too long I lose my inspiration. By reflecting and meditating on the Lord, I put myself into the best attitude for finding out what is the next thing to do. You must give yourself up to this interior reflection with the understanding that as soon as your reflection shows you a thing to be done, you are to go right off and do that thing. Pray in this way twenty times a day if necessary, and when you find out what there is to do, do it swiftly and with all your might. This is my principle of conservation of force.' This is reminiscent of Meister Eckhart's thought—'Wisdom consists in doing the next thing you have to do, doing it with your whole heart, and finding delight in doing it.'

"At half-past two, returned to the kitchen and helped wash the corn after its caustic baptism. I wondered if all our folks knew that hulled corn was prepared partly after the fashion of soap-boiling. At three o'clock I took the last batch of puddings and breads out of the oven. Finding a slide in the oven door broken, I took the job of tinkering it. This took me to the trap-shop where I occupied time until supper, and after supper played the violin awhile, criticized a young lady for not promptly returning things borrowed, talked with George about social philosophy, read a pleasant and edifying note, chatted with several folks, read the *Tribune*, attended the evening meeting and a skirmish of talk afterward, read awhile, and went to bed."

"The first salute to my senses this morning was an excellent smell of buckwheat cakes," another member wrote. "The next was a charming strain of music followed by the rattle of the big bell. Conscious of my ability to dress in one minute, I waited for the second bell and jumped into my clothes; but the smell of buckwheat cakes and the sound of music had called up so many that all tables were filled, and I had to wait. Had a good time after breakfast reading about Joshua and Jericho and attending the Bible-game, then went to the barn and milked four cows. At 8:00 o'clock went to the trap shop and took hold of the hammer and tongs; at 11:20, having pretty well moistened my shirt, I quit work and enjoyed Macaulay's *History of England* till the Johnny-cake luncheon. Then music with the band that gave unusual satisfaction, especially the Marseilles Hymn that one lady said went all through her like electricity. At 1:00 o'clock I returned to the shop, worked till 3:30 and then changed my clothes to be ready for the celebration at four. The scene in the parlor stirred my heart—three long tables lined on both sides with happy faces, cake, apples, bread and wine, music and cheering, toasts and speeches—especially the allusion to old times of 1834 and this progress toward the resurrection that we've made. After the banquet I milked again and then went to the mill to be weighed, an ordinance we have attended to punctually on the twentieth of every month for a year; my weight is 147 pounds. I spent time pleasantly in a chat with the boys and girls until meeting-time, during which I braided six times around a palm-leaf hat."

"My duties are to arise at 4:45 to rake the fire, open the dampers, light dining-room and kitchen lamps, measure out malt for coffee for those who drink it, break six eggs in it, pour it into the boiler, boil fifteen minutes, take it off, pour in hot water, carry milk, butter, bread, cold water, and applesauce to side tables, call two or three women, steam one pail of milk for coffee, often put heavy griddles on the stove, and ring the bells," the Bake-Onion Stew-dent wrote for the December 8, 1868, *Circular*. "After breakfast I empty the coffee-boiler, rake and replenish fires, take up and sift ashes, bring in wood and coal, get and prepare vegetables—all except potatoes; core apples, pick over beans, open cans of fruit, corn, and beans, run after sugar, syrup, and things too heavy for women to carry. The duty that taxes talents to the utmost is baking potatoes. You need not laugh, for it is so. If eaten during a certain three or four minutes, it carries a thrill of thankfulness to the center of one's body. Bear in mind that two hundred people require two hours and more for eating their breakfast. At noon, when the hungry ones all come in nearly at the same time, think of the awful weight of responsibility with which those potatoes baking in the oven bear down upon my soul! The mark can be hit exactly and when I do, there's a vibration of happiness through my whole being. Another point that interests me much is testing things by the sense of taste and smell to know whether they are sufficiently sweet, sour, fresh, salted, or spiced. I call all the experienced tasters to sample material for mince or pumpkin pies and the tub of cake-dough. The serious, abstracted way with which each one gives her whole being to the almost spiritual impression that a slight morsel makes upon her tongue conveys that this is a solemn business and a great weight of responsibility attends it. A subtle, interior faculty is being trained to the highest pitch of delicacy and usefulness. How far through a person's being, both physical and spiritual, do the vibrations of taste extend? I remain yours truly, Kitchen Man."

The Oneida Community had Brother Lawrence's spirit—resolving to do all tasks cheerfully, carefully, wholeheartedly, glad to do any work for the love of God. Work is holy when the heart of the worker is fixed on the Highest, echoes *The Bhagavad-Gita*.

Seasons

"Winter's early twilight and long evenings are no more. Now our curtains are trees, our chandeliers the sunset clouds, and the game is croquet. In the apple-orchard back of the summer-house lies the croquet ground. Anywhere outdoors you can hear the click of ball and mallet and the laughter or eager cries of the players. Croquet is the only outdoor game we have in summer. Croquet has this advantage: both sexes as well as old and young can join in it. How to conduct games in a spirit of harmony has been a special study with us the past winter. Now we find that we have so far advanced in civilization that croquet, which we dropped several years ago as not promoting the Community spirit, is not only a pleasant recreation with us, but a means of improving fellowship. The playful actions of life as distinguished from its more weighty pursuits will sustain a more prominent position in the future. Croquet is a favorite amusement all summer, but this week we laid away mallets and balls and left the ground to the birds and babies. We make the move voluntarily and unanimously when outward allurements are at the highest tide for the sake of promoting the growth of interior life at this time.

"Away over the bounding rail this bright and breezy morning for our cottage by the lake," the August 1873 *Circular* tells us. "The sun is hot, the sand deep, the luggage heavy, but the path soon ends at the water's edge and we row our boats around curved, wooded banks on the broad and deep tranquil river. Here we are! O what a cool, shady, picturesque spot! A tumble in the waves rolling in boisterously from the lake is the first thing we love; ah! what refreshment! Shall we go fishing? An old stager warns us that fish leave the river in the heat of day and go into the lake to cool off. Pshaw! In two hours we've basketed forty-five perch. We have sharp appetites and an excellent picnic dinner under shade trees. More fishing and those home-bound are taken over the river. Up the next morning at 5:30 for another raid on the perch. Caught eighteen. At half-past eight they adorn our plate—hot, crisp, and juicy. We meet a company coming on the train. More swimming, rowing, and fishing followed by a grand banquet. At six we're homeward bound, ten pleasure-fed, thankful souls. Pausing at State Bridge, our locomotive suddenly pours forth dense volumes of steam with angry roar. A pump connection is displaced. Out goes the fire in glowing coals along the track. A boiler with a broken pump must have no fire under it. A messenger is dispatched to the nearest telegraph station six miles away. An hour and three-quarters slip by. Three brave women of our party inspect the disabled engine, and actually climb up to the engineer's stand and view with awe the mechanism by which the huge machine is controlled."

"Croquet holds its ground in spite of snow—the charm of the game wins many out into the sharp, healthy winter air. The location is somewhat windswept, assisted by an occasional broom to keep the arches clear. If snow falls by night or day and covers the ground to the depth of a few inches, someone soon thereafter with shovel and broom clears it away. A stereoscopic picture of the croquet ground would exhibit it as an elliptical enclosure surrounded with a snow-white wall from two and a half to three feet in height. The frozen ground, say all players, makes an improved floor for rolling the balls. Notwithstanding the cold weather and frequent snows, croquet continues to be our all-winter, outdoor pastime with a goodly number of boys and girls and men and women. From one to four couples at a time (foremost Mr. Kinsley, in his 72nd year) may daily be seen manipulating mallets with zest. The game hardly demands enough activity to stay warm for the stern zero weather of mid-winter, but with mittens, overcoats, and warm clothing for the feet, the game is thoroughly enjoyed by many for an hour or more. Our shop boys traveling to and from Willow Place have a novel way of protecting themselves from the cold. They thrust their heads into paper flour-sacks with openings for the eyes. They look like a party of masqueraders, but declare themselves comfortable and ready for the roughest work old Jack Frost can do."

"W. G. Kelly narrowly escaped drowning," a December 1872 *Circular* issue noted. "He was walking on the frozen surface of our partially filled pond, carefully examining the ice as he proceeded, when a heavy wind struck him and carried him off the strong ice toward the channel of the river, where he broke through into deep water. After struggling for some time to get out on to the ice, which would break with every effort, he cried for help and was heard by John Conant and two hired men, at work far down the pond. They soon saw Mr. Kelly who was much exhausted, but had strength to tell them where to find a ladder on the bank. He was soon gotten out of the water, carried to a neighbor's house, and a physician was summoned. The day was cold and he'd been in the water for nearly a half-hour; he soon became unconscious and was apparently in a critical condition. He was restored enough to go home in a few hours but is still weak and sore, and suffers some from frost-bitten fingers. His escape seems miraculous, and fills our hearts with thankfulness. He says that in the water, not knowing whether he'd be drowned, he prayed earnestly to the Lord for help and felt that he received an immediate answer and was buoyed up with new strength."

"Oh—these feet!—what shall we do with them the coming winter?" wondered Robert Delatre. "What a chore it is to care for them those long months! Why don't socks and stockings keep them warm? Socks keep the feet too warm sometimes and then they sweat; your socks get damp and the first cold blast acting on the leather chills through to your skin. You seek the fire, but how is the vapor to escape? The only effectual way to remedy the evil would be to change your socks as soon as they get moist, but that's out of the question most times. I happened to be barefooted near a heap of fine sawdust and thought I would step on it. It flashed into my mind that this was the very stuff to come between my soul (sole) and the nether world—and sure enough, from that moment I became possessed of that bliss for my feet I'd longed for. It keeps your feet dry—half the battle—and if they do get cold at thirty degrees below zero, there will be nothing of that awful clamminess. I prefer dust from pine wood because of its sweetness and pleasant odor. A tablespoonful to each boot is enough. When on a long, cold ride with little walking to do, you can use it plentifully, as it will help to keep the feet warm as well as dry. The great thing is to keep the feet dry and give them plenty of room. The touch of leather is usually cold even to a dry skin and robs you of heat very fast because it is a conductor. A tight-fitting boot seriously impedes the circulation, the effect of which is to chill the feet, whereas in a roomy boot there is friction that makes heat. Change the sawdust every day. It is cheap and a few quarts will last you the whole winter, but see to it that it is dry before you use it. Where now is your eternal knitting and mending of stockings? Where the dirty drudgery of the wash-tub? Who can calculate the amount of work and money saved by the substitution of sawdust for yarn, an era indeed in the history of man's advancement!"

AN OPEN COMMUNITY

"By January 1853, Harriet Skinner noted that Oneida is distinguished from all other Associations in respect to hospitality. Its visitors are treated like family. Sympathy with the principles of the Community or a wish to become acquainted with them is the only passport required to hospitable treatment. No charges are made and compensation is seldom accepted. Entire strangers stay days and even weeks, and are made to feel perfectly welcome. It is rare that the family is without visitors. Those who stay for any period are invited into the work and everyday engagements. We may be asked, how does Oneida secure herself against disagreeable intrusion, if she keeps such open doors? Not by law but by sincerity. If visitors are treated to family fare in other respects, they are also in respect to criticism.

"We welcome a full and free comparison with surrounding society. Instead of moving out west into a wilderness frontier where comparison would be difficult, we stayed in New York and New England under the inspection of the sharpest eyes. The press has given us such world-wide publicity that our Community attracts persons from almost every country and clime. The effect of all this publicity was that six thousand visitors came during the summer of 1866; a large hotel was opened on the home domain about a quarter-mile from the Mansion. We receive visits from foreign tourists and celebrities almost weekly, as well as persons who have made their mark in science, the arts, literature, commerce, history, anthropology, and cultivated classes throughout the United States. Thus we gain knowledge of the world and its diverse inhabitants without the discomforts and expense incident to extensive travel; we have become a cosmopolitan institution that people study. Many come out of curiosity, but chiefly they want to know all about us. In summer our grounds and gardens are thronged with visitors. From ten to fifty eat daily at the Community table; 2,530 dinners have been furnished to visitors since June 1 (1873). They impart their artistic gifts and intellectual wares to us, and tell the world through publications what they saw and learned here.

"A Hungarian artist, a Danish student, a Swiss governess, a Polish gentleman formerly attached to the military staff of the Pacha of Egypt, and English tourists of all classes traveling on business or pleasure, made it a special point to visit the Oneida Community, the September 15, 1873, *Circular* noted. Following these came a superior pianist, a comic vocalist, and Parepa Rosa in a professional tour gave an impromptu concert in our Hall—a rich and rare entertainment. The world-renowned quartette, General Tom Thumb and wife, her sister, and Commodore Nutt made their first appearance on our stage, and charmed not only our own family but a large circle of neighbors and visitors. And our season is by no means over. Visitors come when we least expect them. I don't think we'd be surprised if the Archbishop of Canterbury himself should drop in on us.

"Noted author Hepworth Dixon, editor of the *London Athenaeum*, came to America in 1866 to study American socialisms and visited the Shakers in New Lebanon, the Mormons in Utah, and the Oneida Community. His book, *New America* in two volumes, was published in February 1867; the publishers stated that the account of the Oneida Community in fifty-five pages aroused more interest than any other subject. This book was translated into foreign languages and went all over the world. American editors took up the theme. Long appreciative articles with editorial accompaniments appeared in the New York *Tribune,* the New York *Herald,* and elsewhere. Ninety-nine meals were served during one week in the fall to persons of more serious purpose than casual visitors, and fifty applications for membership were received between January and June 1867. In April, ten persons were admitted at once, an unprecedented number since the first ingathering at Oneida in 1848–1850. A four-story brick wing to the Mansion House was built later.

The open Oneida Community served meals to visitors nearly daily, and picnics for up to 700; journalists and scholars could live there for weeks or months and participate in all activities, including mutual criticism. People came out of curiosity, interest, study, and to observe Community members; the evident happiness of Community members was remarked upon.

"Seven hundred people from Pulaski in ten railway coaches sought recreation and gustatory and musical pleasure in our dining rooms and concert hall," reports the August 6, 1873, *Circular*. "On this cool, bright and breezy day, we call in our branch families and regular workers and the work of preparation busily continued. Our large picnic days always remind us of a military engagement: the charge of the dinner brigade is particularly spirited and a small army of waiters and cooks with ample material prepare to meet it. Two hundred and fifty visitors called for dinner in our dining-rooms, while the remaining four hundred and fifty betook themselves with their baskets to shady nooks beneath the trees. A large number were here for the first time and the pleasure of novelty added zest to the occasion. We next strengthen our musical defense. No failure now! They are before us in one compact mass; we hold the stage on which to deploy. The three o'clock concert passed pleasantly; the Family Hall could scarcely have accommodated another individual. The Pulaski Ringold Fire Company with a brass band played frequently during the afternoon with appreciative groups of listeners at the windows or under the trees in the quadrangle. Although a small organization, these musicians displayed much taste in execution, and the pieces selected by their leader were of a style most pleasing. We have seldom heard a bass tuba that pleased us as well as the one played today. They left at six o'clock, the band playing as they went to the train; twelve little boys dressed in Zouave costume marched behind in single file and the great army followed.

"Seven hundred people spending a day on our grounds sets us a-thinking. What has been the silent Community teaching today? That business success, good order, and apparent happiness attend a body of men and women who hold property and persons in common, and who devote their energies to accumulating? We are mistaken if our external attractions most impress our visitors. Deeper and stronger than the influence of pleasant surroundings is the subtle contagion of a nimbus charged with brotherly love, unity, and unselfishness. What we freely receive, that we freely give. We are under sacred bonds to let whatever is good and true and commended by all men shine forth in deeds. If we can give dinners served by willing hands and happy hearts, if we can make music breathe our good will, if in any way we can convey to others the joy and peace and trust in our hearts, our reward is the blessed one of the giver.

"Clergymen of all denominations have visited the Community, the greater number belonging to Evangelical orders," the November 3, 1873, *Circular* noted. "We extended our hospitality to four Presbyterian and five Methodist ministers in one week. Episcopalians, Baptists, Universalists, and Catholics have been well represented. We were gratified to meet these gentlemen and their deportment in return was almost without exception cordial, not to say brotherly. A Doctor of Divinity, extensively known in the Churches for his labors and devotion, spent several days with us and concluded his visit with a lecture in our Hall. Since his return, he wrote to his son, a Community member—'I review with much pleasure the few days I was permitted to spend with your dear family. I admire the kind Christian spirit breathed by all.'"

"There have been sometimes a hundred visitors in a day, and people come here from higher motives than formerly; many from an intelligent curiosity and some from an attraction to the truth we represent. A gentleman was offered an opportunity to speak in the evening and he expressed unbounded admiration of everything he had seen, and above all the happiness exhibited on every countenance, the August 24, 1868, *Circular* reported. 'One object I had in coming here,' said he, 'was to see if people are happy. My business makes me a traveler—I have traveled sixty-five thousand miles during the last four years. Being a close observer of such things and desiring to be happy myself, I am always anxious to see others happy, and am astonished and gratified by the evident happiness here.'"

"We boldly challenge our young people to compare the Community with the world," the *Circular* notes in April 1873. "They are allowed to read what they please. The present generation of young men and women have had the run of the popular novels, magazines and newspapers—one hundred and thirty different newspapers are now found in our Library—from which they find out pretty thoroughly what the attractions of the world are. If the Community had not attractions to balance worldly seductions, this general freedom in reading would be as dangerous as college life; and our youth *are* sent to excellent colleges. When our young men are old enough, we put them into commercial agencies and send them hundreds and even thousands of miles from home; they are generally absent for weeks at a time, sometimes for months. They travel from village to village and from city to city all over the Northern States, see all the world has to offer and compare it with what the Community gives them. Most of our young men have been thus exposed to the attractions of common society, and the Community now has a greater number of agents than at any previous time. All this shows how great our confidence is in the superior attractions of Community life; that our confidence has not been misplaced is shown by the fact that nearly all our young men are loyal, and this means that they have intelligently decided that the Community is a better home than the world can offer them. These facts, as Mr. Higginson says, prove a good deal. Our confidence is either a delusion that has thus far been miraculously sustained, or it is a sober reliance on realities that will sooner or later come to light and convince all, that living as we do is an improvement as genuine as the use of steam or the telegraph.

"Visitors sometimes exclaim, 'How many old people you have among you!' This remark has been made so many times during the last year or two that we began to think there might indeed be a preponderance of the aged among us. Feeling curiosity and looking at the census taken January 1, 1873, we made the following notes: Between the ages of one and twenty we have sixty-three members; between twenty and forty, ninety-eight; between forty and sixty, sixty-eight; between sixty and eighty, forty-seven; between eighty and one hundred, four. There are 161 members under forty and 119 above forty, leaving a majority on the sunny side of middle life. Upward of fifty of our prominent men and women now approaching sixty were scarcely thirty when they put the vigor of their young life into this movement twenty-six years ago.

"The Oneida Community has been a subject of discussion in the public prints for the last quarter century. We've been happily surprised by the reasonable and generous treatment accorded to us by Central New York newspapers, whose editors must be best acquainted with us, notes the November 17, 1873, *Circular*.

Utica Daily Observer—

"The Oneida Community numbers two hundred and fifty men, women, and children, who constitute not only a Community but a religious sect, calling themselves Perfectionists or Bible Communists, receiving all of the Bible as inspired and basing their faith and practice on their interpretation of it, and the inspiration or spiritual insight they claim for themselves. They have been located on their present domain since 1848. Their property consists of 664 acres of choice land, with three excellent water powers and manufacturing interests valued at $200,000. Upon this property are located their model factories and the elegant buildings in which they reside. They live as one family, work as one family, and act as one family; attend to their own business, practicing the cardinal virtues of industry and integrity, and receiving therefore the rewards of prosperity, while experimenting in their ideas of a higher life.

"It is a positive blessing to the locality. No finer example of quiet industry and inflexible honesty can be found. Its products are the best of their class, are just what they are represented to be, and command the best prices. Its dealings are open, straightforward, and honorable, always and under all circumstances. It furnishes lucrative employment not only to its own members, but to large numbers of its neighbors. It manufactures articles of iron, silk, and lumber, carries on extensive farming operations, and sends to market vast quantities of fruits. Its cash business cannot fall far short of a million dollars yearly. Its members use neither tobacco nor strong drink, are models of good order, tenderly care for each other, and treat the world outside with uniform courtesy and respect. It would be well to reflect whether an organized body of two hundred and fifty persons, using neither tobacco nor whisky, cheating no one, injuring no one, quarreling with no one, religious, prosperous, happy, at peace with the world and harmonious among themselves, is a thing that should be abated by anybody, or anywhere. Are such bodies common among Presbyterians or Methodists or Universalists, or any denomination? Are they common outside of denominations? If not, ought we to abate a body of people whose success in cultivating the great practical virtues of life is undisputed? Are honesty, integrity, sobriety, and honor such common and worthless plants that we must trample them under foot?

"But it is said that the views of the Community in regard to marriage are shocking to our sense of propriety. Grant it; so were those of Abraham, Isaac, and Jacob. We neither apologize for nor defend their views in this respect. They form leading planks in the religious platform on which the Community stands. As religious views, these people are clearly entitled to maintain them, by the spirit if not the letter of our laws, especially when these views can hurt no one but themselves. Immorality and vice of every kind, as well as all free love notions as commonly received, are as strongly condemned by the Communists as by any others; in fact, it is a chief point of their faith that their marriage system forms the only relief from the tremendous evils of this character that have forever affected society. The Community invites no new members, nor has it for many years, as its number is filled to the point deemed wise. It has no room for more and desires no more. It is not, therefore, a proselytizing body. It regards itself as experimental and engaged in simply testing the correctness of its views as to a better life, for the benefit of all mankind, as well as its own."

The Fulton Times—

"The Community is, first of all, a voluntary association of practical religionists. The sermons of Christ and the epistles of Paul constitute the basis of their faith, and the example of the Savior while on earth is their rule of action. Their theories are not so strangely unlike the theories of most orthodox sects that they need excite apprehension, but they present a strong contrast to most other religious sects in that they exemplify their theories in everyday practice. They preach charity, kindness, forbearance in their daily demeanor; they illustrate by their dealings with men their faith in the saving power of the golden rule. They abstain from hypocrisy, dishonesty, lying, profanity, and all manner of what they conceive to be immorality, not simply on one day of the week but on the whole seven. They love one another as they are commanded not merely in theory belied by practice, but in fact. They are cleanly, frugal, industrious, temperate, and unobtrusive in their habits, and hence thrifty in their business. Their immense trade in traps, silks, and preserved fruits—and to some extent, we believe, in blooded cattle and sheep—is the result of a widespread popular conviction that they are rigidly and conscientiously honest and reliable. They do not seek to make proselytes. Their publications and particular sentiments are supplied only to those that apply for them. Their business managers are men and women who have demonstrated their fitness for and title to their positions by actual experiment. They believe that the world would be better if mankind were better; hence they make the improvement of mankind a subject of careful and intelligent study.

"Their government is that of free criticism, substantially the same as obtains in all associated bodies whether organized or unorganized. Any member whose conduct varies so much from that of the body that it becomes obnoxious, is compelled to conform or retire. Whatever may be their rules or methods governing the intercourse of the sexes, their women are absolutely free from the tyranny to which wives are too frequently subject, even in the most respectable companionship—the tyranny of involuntary maternity and of inopportune and offensive sexual association. It needs scarcely to be argued, even to the best of mothers and the most devoted of wives, how dear this freedom must be. They have illustrated the benefits and profits of co-operative industry, and the possibility of harmony and thrift under intelligent management. Be it understood that in saying this much we do not endorse nor condemn the customs or creeds of the Community; and it is not impossible that they would be quite as undecided about accepting or rejecting our notions and creeds. We keep in mind that the acceptance of rules of action different from our own is not a crime, and not necessarily an offense to the charitably disposed Christian person; and moreover it is by no means as unpopular as it used to be. Unquestionably in the light of the present day, the most that any one sect has a right to demand of another—or of an individual—is honesty to conviction and faithfulness to honestly conceived ideas of duty."

"One of many things for which we are thankful is that we have pleasant neighbors," noted the September 22, 1873, *Circular*. "The present mutual good feeling is pleasing, and we trust it will never be lost. Those around us many years ago were not always disposed to treat us with friendliness or even tolerance. The Community was always open, inviting others to tour our buildings and grounds, eat delicious dinners, enjoy our musical concerts, and socialize at strawberry festivals—but some were suspicious of the Community."

"We have published frankly our social principles and our paper is a constant exposé of our life," states the August 1, 1864, *Circular*. "If all the fruits are wholesome and good, why should persons imagine some secret of mischief?"

"I found out that people think our reservoir is a place where we incarcerate problem members," Harriet remembers. "Tirzah told me that someone asked her what it is and she said, 'our reservoir.' Marion said they likewise asked her and she explained the same, and Elizabeth, the *same thing*. Then I heard someone say, 'They all tell the same story.' And whose are these children around here?"

"To a boy walking by, a visitor queried, 'Where are your parents?'

"'My Papa Noyes and Mama Miller are at Wallingford,' he answered.

"'Miller! A nice name; what's your name?'

"'Temple Noyes Dunn Burt Ackley.'

"People ask, 'Are you perfectly contented here?' Without asking them if they are perfectly contented at home we say, 'We are.'

"'Do you have to work here, whether or no?' they'll ask, implying that some people are staying here upon compulsion—little better than galley slaves. 'Well, did not your father and mother work?'"

THE COMMUNITY MEETING

"The Evening Meeting began in the earliest days in the old log house and was a backbone of Oneida Community unity. Community member William Alfred Hinds wrote *American Communities* in 1878 and was a later editor of the *Circular*. 'In my tours among ten Communities, what impressed me was that the prosperity of the Communities depended upon their regular meetings. When they gave up their meetings or only some of their members attended, they began to have trouble, he noted in the *Circular* in July 1872. Where the Shakers were the most faithful in maintaining their meetings, there seemed to be the most unity and hope for the future. I would not want to adopt the Shaker fashion of compelling folks to attend meetings, but rather hope that it may be done from choice.'

"Years ago we held a religious meeting on Sundays for the benefit of outsiders, but it didn't amount to much, so we gave it up. We distribute our religious services equally through the week. Instead of laying in religion enough on Sunday to last for seven days, we prefer to receive our portion fresh every day—hence our evening gatherings in our beautiful Family Hall to wait on the Lord and edify one another. That nightly ordinance is quite as necessary as our daily food. At the whistle, the entire Community met every evening from eight to nine o'clock and later at seven when the Community reduced meals to two per day. They discussed their businesses, read letters from Wallingford, proposed Community entertainments, shared their spiritual experiences, how they dealt with problems of many kinds, and Noyes often offered a Home Talk. People who go to church put on their Sunday best to make a good showing of the outer man. We're not speculating as to the religion there is in all that.

The Family Hall, now the Big Hall, accommodated large numbers for their many events. Evening Meetings were held here for discussing businesses, branch communities, Mansion House life, religious principles and practices, problem solving, and to hear Noyes's Home Talks. Today cultural, educational, and family events take place here.

"We, too, have a passion for dressing up not our persons but our grounds, entrances, and out-of-the-way places. Every Sunday morning for an hour or more during summer we have a work bee that we enjoy; there is truth in the saying that work is worship. Our grounds are our meeting-house; we have consecrated them to the Lord and they are therefore as sacred as any place can be. The beds of flowers, the shrubbery, the groups of evergreens, the forest and fruit-trees, all constitute the upholstery of our spacious sanctuary. No artificial pictures or paintings can compare with them in artistic beauty and grandeur. While I write, amid evergreens and white and red roses, I hear the soft still voice of my Heavenly Father giving his home-talks in every leaf, in every flower, in every spear of grass. Truly there are sermons everywhere. We dwell, wherever we are, in the boundless sanctuary of our God, who himself is seen by the pure in heart. One mid-summer evening, someone broached the idea of holding our evening meetings on the grass and the idea was carried by acclamation. Notice was given in the Hall and when the bell rang, those in the mansion came out, book-in-hand, arm-in-arm, the pensive and the playful, and two hundred, young and old, all sat on the grass. We had time for the newspaper report and the correspondence before twilight deepened, and then we sang 'While shepherds watched their flocks by night,' and filled the hour with thanksgivings.

"The Community discussed their businesses and finances, read aloud letters from branch communities, appointed members to different departments, introduced newly-arrived members, and pondered questions about their young people at various periods. Dr. Theodore Noyes asked the family what amusements they desired and how often the Community should have an entertainment. The majority preferred having two or three good plays, well studied and presented repeatedly. This would be desirable for educational purposes and the selection should be made for the improvement of those immediately engaged and for the whole family. It was thought that a good play could be presented once a month without getting tired of it. Dr. Noyes inquired how it would please the family to have an alternation of dramatic, musical, and variety entertainments.

"John Humphrey Noyes creates the liveliest sensation by his take-off of a nasal-voiced singer in old Perfectionist times, Charley Lovett," reported in the winter of 1872. "He gave us a specimen of his singing at a Sunday evening entertainment and proposed a representation on stage of an old-fashioned Perfectionist meeting with its speech-making and singing done as true to that life as possible. Our members gifted in speaking and acting entered into the plan with zeal. When the enthusiasm was at its height and just in the nick of time to create the greatest surprise, who should appear but Brother Lovett with overcoat, hat, and cane, as though belated in his attendance. There was a general rush to greet him; being solicited by Brother Cragin, Brother Lovett soon stood up and sang in a style that beggars description—none but a Mozart or Handel could think of producing such originality of rhythm and intonation. We laughed till our sides ached; Mr. D., very appreciative of a joke, shook so violently we almost feared he'd go into convulsions.

"Though we were so tickled, this affair produced a strangely serious effect. Many declared themselves benefited in a remarkable manner by the religious enthusiasm enacted so genuinely. We all agreed to adopt the style of the Perfectionists the next Sunday evening. Mr. Cragin was appointed to keep things stirring; several of the readiest speakers were asked to prepare themselves beforehand, and the singers were instructed to fill every pause with a rousing song. We said to ourselves that the entertainment would certainly be very funny, but we knew not what we were doing. We found ourselves in the midst of a strong revival current. Singers helped with electrifying songs that were very popular in the 1830s. Those who had come to act found themselves unexpectedly nearer the hard-pan of reality than they ever were before. Those who'd prepared speeches were not shamming—they were preaching the gospel with marvelous power and their words pricked us to the heart with the Perfectionist understanding of Biblical truths. This was no acting; the whole scene was a glorious reality with the dawn of heaven upon it. The fire thus started spread through all our ranks, consuming prejudices, hardness, envy, un-thankfulness, and many another vestige of the old life. During this winter of 1872 there was a universal turning of the heart toward God in real revival fervor. There is scarcely one among us but has had his life quickened with the joy of a new conversion. This revival came about almost accidentally, though we know that all things are controlled by a wise Providence.

"I hope we shall let the Spirit of truth and love work from our hearts into our brains," said Theodore Pitt at an Evening Meeting in March 1868. "When that Spirit operates in us, it is destined to work as great a revolution for human nature as steam-power has affected in the world of industry. I know that in God's kingdom, love will be made to work health and miracles. I've been preaching covetousness a little to-day—when rightly directed it is a good thing. Paul exhorts earnestly to covetousness respecting our best gifts. I think it is legitimate to covet the treasures of heaven and the best gifts that God can bestow—covet them as much as the miser does his gold; not hoard what we obtain as the miser does and appropriate it to ourselves, but that we may bless others and do good. I want to be rich that I may have a great deal to give away, distribute, and do good with."

The Higher Standard, An Evening Conversation on October 17, 1872:

"H. remarked that he'd been tempted to wish the standard of the Community would be lowered so he could more easily conform to it," William Hinds began. "That's a natural temptation and doubtless many in the Community have encountered it. Some churches do unfortunately lower their standard to make it comport with the average daily life of their members. This was the case with the Methodist churches; their founder, John Wesley, believed in the possibility of salvation from sin and raised high the banner of Perfect Holiness. But his followers were not generally prepared for it, and so the doctrine of falling from grace became a special feature of Methodism. It is a special feature of Community Perfectionism that its standard of Christian experience has not been lowered. From our leader's first confession of holiness it has been an upward inclination. At the outset of his religious experience, his motto was to be a young convert forever, and it is true today. I find the greatest comfort and hope in the fact that our leader has never abated the zeal he had when the love of God first filled his heart; it is the Lord's purpose to perfect us and use us in introducing his heavenly kingdom. Some followers may have remained dead level, or retrograded, but his course has not been modified to suit them. He has ever called them to better experience, to higher attainments, to more perfect fellowship with God. Had our standard been lowered, we might as well abandon our hopes as far as expecting great results as a religious organization, for we would think the 7th chapter of Romans describes good religious experience—the step is short from there to worldliness."

"I have met that temptation," George Cragin admitted. "But when I overcome it I'm always thankful that our religious standard is high, for I see that salvation itself is dependent upon our conforming to the highest standard, even that of Christ: 'Be ye therefore perfect even as your Father in heaven is perfect.' Lowering the standard of righteousness is only one way of compromising with evil, and it is our business as Christ-seekers to war against it, rather than to compromise with it."

"It is the flesh[47]—the natural life—that shrinks from a high gospel standard," William Woolworth agreed. "The spiritual man loves the high standard and finds it easy to conform to it."

"The third chapter of Philippians," Hinds added, "shows what an exalted standard the Apostle Paul had."

"A true church has the Pauline standard in personal experience, and it also makes room for the most inexperienced believers," Mr. Woolworth pointed out. "Mr. Noyes reminds us that the platform of the Primitive Church was a way of holiness, reaching from the foot to the top of Zion, easily accessible to the world at one end and opening to the glories of eternity at the other. It was the special glory of the Primitive Church that its platform was broad enough to hold those who were just beginning to struggle with sin to those who had attained perfect and permanent holiness. It gave a home of union and love to all, whether weak or strong in faith."

William Hinds added a helpful enlargement on this idea at the November 18, 1872, Evening Meeting: "No system of education is considered complete that does not provide for *all* students—for those who study the lowest branches as well as those who study the highest—those who go to primary schools as well as those who go to colleges and universities; and so no system of religious culture is complete that does not provide for all who have set their faces heavenward."

"I've had some reflections about God's working in our hearts and wills," said H, reported in the November 17, 1872, *Circular*. "Theodore pointed out that to get one's mind rigidly set in following a desired course would destroy the peace of God in the heart. I reflected upon the difference between the disciplined, subordinated will in which God can work, and the animal will that is difficult to control and is incompatible with the peace of God. Persons of active minds and habits have a good deal to learn on this point. Most of our family are called into active business, called to plan ways things should be done; but if we adopt a plan and get so set in regard to it that it destroys internal peacefulness, we've perhaps unconsciously submitted to the animal will determined to have its own way, not compatible with the peace of God. It's a great lesson for me to learn how to plan and do things that best promote unity—it's not always important that things be done in what I think is the best way, but done to secure harmony. When I find that I'm so intent on a plan of my own that I'll feel disturbed if it is not adopted, I switch off from it soon. The world is full of this spirit and we all need to be wide-awake on this point."

"A.—'I've had good experience in giving up my own way for the sake of unity, and trusting God to have the right thing done.'

"K.—'I like the idea that it's more important that unity should be secured than that we should have our own way, even if I'm sure it's the best way.'

"E.—'I believe that's the true attitude of spirit to take; then we *will* be sure to have the best thing done.'

"A visitor found much to admire in the unity of our great family. It was 'very wonderful, but perhaps there must be some monotony in our lives—everyone seems to think in the same channel and to arrive at the same conclusions.' He related a tale of a man who boasted that he and his wife had lived together forty years without a quarrel, but his hearers thought *what a dreadful dull time* they must have had. We're willing to forego the pleasure of cat-and-dog quarrels, and will rather glory in the peace and harmony that come through love of the truth. If difference of opinion is necessary to the enjoyment of life, there will be a dreadful dull time in the kingdom of heaven. They offered this farce at the evening meeting:

"*Lively Times!*—Curtain rises. Scene: The supper-table.

"Mrs. Brown, irritated, is waiting for her husband and goes to the window several times; she hears his step and seats herself. Mr. Brown enters and sits down.

"Mrs. Brown (stiffly).—'Mr. Brown, I suppose you're aware that you are ten minutes late?'

"Mr. Brown.—'I am aware of it, Mrs. Brown.'

"Mrs B.—'Well, Mr. Brown, if you'd come when you should, you would've scolded like a house-a-fire—supper was ten minutes late. You know you would!'

"Mr. B.—'Very likely, Mrs. Brown.'

"Mrs. B.—'I know what made you late—you were whispering with Susan at the gate. Good-for-nothing hussy! I won't have her in the house another day.'

"Mr. B. (pushing away his plate) — 'Who wants to eat such stuff as this? I wish you'd spent the ten minutes you waited cooking this meat. It isn't half done!'

"Mrs. B.—'It is done, Mr. Brown.'

"Mr. B.—'I don't think it *is* done.'

"Mrs. B—'It is!'

"Mr. B.—'Stop disputing me, Mrs. Brown.'

"Mrs. B.—'I shan't!'

"Mr. B.—'You shall!'

"Mrs. B.—'I shall say anything I've a mind to!'

"Mr. B.— 'Take that, then.' (He throws his tea in her face).

"Mrs. B.—'O, you brute!' She jumps up and pushes the table with all its contents upon Mr. Brown, who goes over with it, and under it. In burst the children, disputing and pulling each others' hair. They tumble over Mr. Brown, who, extricating himself from broken crockery, catches them and cuffs them right and left. Mrs. Brown flies to the spot and seizes Mr. Brown by the arm, when an indescribable melee ensues. Curtain falls.

"*Dreadful Dull*—Curtain rises.

"Mr. Hamilton sits at the table; lively groups are laughing and chatting. He looks up from reading. 'Mr. Langford thinks it must be dreadful dull to live as we do year after year without any quarreling. Whom do you wish to quarrel with, Charlotte?'

"Charlotte. (catching hold of Ann in mock anger) —'I want to quarrel with Ann; she has stolen my knitting-work and won't let me have it!'

"Ann.—'Charlotte works in the spooling-room all day and I want to help her do her knitting.'

"Mr. U.—'That's a great quarrel! Beulah, with whom would you like to quarrel?'

"Beulah (holding up her work-box).—'I want to quarrel with someone who has been to my box. I found a new pair of scissors here all done up in a paper, and I want to know who did it.'

"Mr. H.—'What will you do to them?'

"B.—'I'll demand of them what I've done to deserve such treatment, and then . . . I'll give them a good hugging!'

"Mr. H.—'Whew! What a dreadful quarrel! I wouldn't much object to having somebody quarrel with me like that. Charles, whom will you quarrel with?'

"Charles.—'I don't know how to quarrel; I wasn't brought up to it. But if it's such a fine thing, I'll have to quarrel with the whole Community for not letting me learn how. I can pick a quarrel with Theodore. Don't you love Julia?'

"Theodore (looking up from his book).—'What if I do?'

"Charles.—'I love her, and she loves me.'

"Theodore.—'Ah! I'm glad to hear it. That's a point of sympathy. It makes me love you.'

"Mr. H.—'A pretty quarrel! There won't any blood shed from an affair like this. Well, if we can't quarrel, we can sing. Let's have *O, come, come away!*' Singing modulated into a dance, and the curtain fell."

"On Sunday evening, February 4, 1874, Mother Goose is sitting in a great armchair, with songs—comic and sober—and duets on the violin and piano; the children come in one by one, each representing a Mother Goose character and having something to say or sing or do. The characters that brought down the house were Jack Sprat and his wife—two year-olds Richard and Humphrey. Richard dressed as a little old man with a black swallow-tail coat and brass buttons with a stove-pipe hat and cane was a figure comical enough, and his little wife's merry face and big bonnet were irresistible. After this entertainment, we had another law discourse by Mr. James Towner, who has commended himself as a clear and effective speaker."

Spiritual Labor

"With our affording opportunity for reflection and prayer, I've been rather pleased to note a growing tendency among us to want separate rooms," Noyes said at the Evening Meeting at Wallingford on January 18, 1869. "There is a good spiritual ground for that desire and I hope every person who wants it, has a private room. To have a quiet space ought to be regarded as a birthright of every person who can pray. With this object, it seems to me that we can ask God to give us the means for enlarging our dwelling until our accommodations shall be perfectly adapted to good religious experience." (Applause.)

"The riches of heaven are here now, and what we want is to put ourselves in communication with its infinite reservoir," George Noyes shared. "This requires attention to be concentrated in a microscopic way in a listening attitude, suspending our own thoughts, and the Lord fills us with all sorts of fresh life, fresh thoughts, and inspired deeds. Christ always recognized the flow into him of another's life."

"Where your treasure is, there will your heart be also, and where your heart is, there will be your attention," agreed Robert Delatre. "It is an attitude of the heart that makes us receptive to Christ's words or Spirit within us, so that we can grow in conformity with the image of God. We are learning how important it is to get the control of our attention under all circumstances, that we may be able to turn that attention to Christ. Instead of looking for Christ in the clouds, as we fondly imagined, we feel after him in our own soul and begin to understand what he meant by the promise that he and his Father would come and make their abode with us."

"I've been tempted to curtail my hour for communion with God when business has pressed me," Edson Smith admitted. "It has been a loss to me when I've done so and I hope we'll pursue this plan to take one hour a day to receive God in our hearts until the habit becomes regular—I've received benefit from it in many ways."

"Accomplish many necessary things, yes—then go home to God within. These two things are compatible—in fact we're not fit to do business unless we do go home. The distinction between the two worlds is growing vivid to me," George continued. "In one world we feel external influences and attractions and may be awake to those and asleep to influences that come from a far deeper, more important source, the world we enter when we confess Christ's life in us. In seeking fellowship with the unseen life in our hearts, we're imbued with a power that makes us masters of our circumstances. What was a small seed grows by practice; we should consider that this is a commencement of true spirituality."

"Our relations to God may be compared to our situation with the dam we're building," Charles Burt observed. "We shall get two or three hundred horse-power by the dam, but if we do not adopt a method of utilizing this power, we'll be no better off. God's promise was that he would pour out his spirit upon all flesh. This great spiritual power exists and we get access to it only as we are earnest enough to *Sow to the Spirit*; open our hearts and minds to all ways that will make us like Christ, so that in any circumstances we shall feel and act as he would. I find that this state of receptivity does not come by merely desiring it, but is the result of earnest turning of my heart to God and refusing to let my attention be taken up by outward things. God responds to all sincere attempts to seek him. We consider it a privilege to go to college for intellectual culture, but the greatest of all privileges is to be in a school of inspiration. Everyone may expect to get an education in this school."

"Fruitfulness comes from the fertilizing of God's spirit in us when our hearts and minds are receptively present to God, to catch his pollen—the atmosphere is full of it all around us!—and it will fertilize us and make us fruitful," John Noyes agreed. "Faith opens our life for his ideas to flow into us: *Ask and ye shall receive; knock and it shall be opened unto you.* I want God to use me and every one of us—to make the most of us."

"We can see Christ shining out more and more in each other," George said at the April 5, 1869, Wallingford meeting. "I see the beauty in meeting Christ in everything we do—eating and drinking in his name, in our social enjoyment as well as everything else. The waters of life will flow freely and our hearts will be warmed and enlarged. I'm glad our religion is not one day of the week."

"This is the bread that if one eats of it, he shall not hunger, for it is from heaven," Theodore Pitt affirmed.

"I have had a deeper experience than ever before since beginning this practice of going home daily; the more time I give to prayer, the stronger my desires are for spiritual growth and usefulness," Charles Cragin responded. "I thank Mr. Noyes for suggesting the idea," he added.

"I've felt more than ever a spirit of prayer, and it's the result of taking the time for it," Chester Underwood contributed. "I find it easy to turn my heart toward God and easier to do my work than ever before."

"Mr. Inslee trains our youth in the machine-shop and there's a saying there that a boy never will learn much until he breaks something," John Noyes writes in a Home Talk titled *The Great Shop of the Universe* for the Evening Meeting in May 1863. 'Go to work at the lathe and see what you can do,' Mr. Inslee will say to him. 'If you break tools and make mistakes at first, by and by you'll learn better.' It would not do for him to stand over the boy and see that he did not make one mistake—the boy would never learn much under that treatment. Another principle is, if he breaks a tool he must go to the office and settle for it. The first principle is a good one for the foreman to act upon, to keep his temper toward an unlucky boy; and it's a good one for the boy to consider if he's tempted to discouragement when he breaks a tool. But he'd better not go to work expecting to break tools, because he will have to pay for them. After some experience, you become almost certain of what you undertake; by now Mr. Inslee is likely do things right the first time.

"God is dealing with us on that principle in the great shop of the universe. He is with us, ready to consult with and advise us whenever we ask him; he respects our liberty and expects to make more out of us by leaving us to find out many things by our own experience than he could by dictating to us. The Lord respects our free agency and individual liberty—if he made us servile followers, he could not train us to real righteousness. If we understand that this is the course of things, we ought to be wise enough not to take advantage of it by breaking tools, spoiling work, and making fools of ourselves—but learn to do things right as fast as we can. That's the only way for us to get out of trouble and keep out of it. Every false and foolish thing one does will certainly be brought to light in some way and must be settled for.

"The thing to be learned is how to speak, think, act, and love in the Spirit. God has poured out his Spirit on all flesh; it is waiting and watching around us and in us, for the seed-sowing of our lives—we either sow to the Holy Spirit or we sow to bad spirits. Only as we become refined in our perceptions and delicate in our feelings toward God, shall we be delicate and tender in our feelings toward our fellows, and treat them fairly. Paul says that there are two great fields in which to sow: When we act, think, and speak in sympathy with the world's enmity, we sow to the flesh. Anything that we do or say or think in accordance with the nature, desires, and feelings of that Spirit is seed sown to that Spirit and works reciprocal action between us and that Spirit. *Whatever a man sows, that he will also reap.*"

NOT WHITEWASHED OR PAINTED!

Mrs. J. C. Croly wrote a glowing report about the Oneida Community,[48] noting that the women were the picture of health—tanned, slender, active, bright-eyed, to say nothing of intelligent, well-informed, and poised with inexplicable *joie de vivre*. "A tone of piety seemed to me to be the only drawback to their sublunary enjoyment; far from verging upon coarseness, grossness, or sensuality, the moral tone the Oneida Community seems to be but one remove from asceticism. The individuality between the sexes is less marked; the men are generally more serious, kindly, and gentle in their demeanor, the women more free and self-possessed, intelligent, and independent. They stand in the Community precisely upon the same footing as men, subject to the same general rules and regulations, but are under special bonds to no one, and have no restraint and no pressure put upon their own inclinations or sense of duty. Yet to the prejudiced gaze of padded, overstuffed, and bustled ladies, they looked strange and even unhealthy—they made no attempts to whitewash or paint themselves! The women wear the most trying of dresses, a bloomer of medium length with straight trousers, a convenient and comfortable dress for work but neither tasteful nor becoming. They are outdoors a good deal, which tans their complexions—a discoloration they take no pains to conceal with powder. If dressed well, and frizzed, and puffed, and painted . . . they would hold their own with the belles of any fashionable assemblage." This full article is copied in the September 7, 1868, *Circular*.

Bloomer is a recognized word to this day, invented by Elizabeth Smith Miller, who strongly believed that the long dress symbolized women's great imposed limitations. Mrs. Miller wore a short skirt and trousers and "with a lamp in one hand and a baby in the other, walked upstairs with ease and grace, while, with flowing robes, I pulled myself up with difficulty, lamp and baby out of the question," said her cousin Elizabeth Cady Stanton, who watched her enviously.[49] Stanton donned similar attire after that. What incredible freedom I enjoyed for two years! Like a captive set free from his ball and chain, I was always ready for a brisk walk through sleet and snow and rain, to climb a mountain, jump over a fence, work in the garden, and, in fact, for any necessary locomotion," Stanton wrote, in Eighty Years and More. Elizabeth Smith Miller was the daughter of Gerrit Smith, a leading United States social reformer, abolitionist, politician, and philanthropist.

"It is whispered among us that though the world may at last admit that our women are virtuous and our children bright," Tirzah Miller writes, "they still reproach us on account of our style of dress: useful, but homely and mean; it has no regard for beauty. We are laughed at by men, hooted at by street-boys, and looked upon with contempt by women. We bear this opprobrium heroically, strong in our belief that the costume we choose is just the thing to cut us off from worldliness—neat, useful, and beautiful. We say that it is prettier than the fettered long dress, which we view as the very emblem of captivity—physical and moral. It has given us freedom to put our highest interests first. Women are following a sadly inverted order of things. It is the spirit that should be accounted beautiful first, and the body is more than raiment; to put the dress before both is the vainest of cheats. Place dress in subjection to other interests, and we may see some good of women's rights movements and, above all, see women rise to a higher plane of intellectual and moral culture. Is not the most useful dress in the highest sense the most beautiful, one that gives freedom to the limbs and to every natural movement of a well-formed body? Can any dress, however elaborate, compare with a perfect human shape?"

"Mrs. Croly gave the matter of women's dress considerable thought after her visit," reported the December 21, 1868, Circular. "She introduced resolutions at a meeting of the New York Sorosis, a woman's organization: 'Women want freedom to do and to be, freed from custom, prejudice, fashion, and from laws made to govern woman but not the human being. Freedom from the tyranny of dress involves her right to cultivate the inward sense by which she holds communication with God; it involves her right to mental culture and elevation; her right to the whole arena of trades and professions; her right to health and physical enjoyment, and her right to be loved without the arts of a courtesan.'"[50]

"Sir: I first liked the short dress for its healthfulness, convenience, and economy; afterwards for its looks; and now I like it most of all for its moral effect on the wearers," wrote a visitor named Bruin to the Circular editor. "It changes women; it signifies a social revolution; it increases home-happiness; it is a long step towards Eden. The long dress means falsehood, fashion-slavery, and wretchedness in the social relations of the sexes. What is that fashionably dressed woman—a mass of dry goods and millinery! Her life is in her flounces; self-consciousness is in every fold and pucker of her crinoline. Are they just right? Oh lovely! Are they a little wrong? Despair! What is the motive? She wants admiration, to be pretty. She hopes to fascinate men. Good heavens! Is man a maniac? It would seem so by the bait she throws out. No matter how unnatural or hideous the novelty, if only it will lure the eye and provoke pursuit. The plan succeeds; men are bedeviled by this nonsense as much as women, and directly or indirectly encourage it. Natural punishment follows. They pursue what they fancy encloses an angel and capture a figure of cotton, imported hair, whalebone, and silk. If a woman spends much of her life and attention on outside show, there will be little left for home enjoyment. That is what her husband gets and generally it serves him right. The short dress goes back to the honesty of nature. In it, women are what they seem. They fulfill more than they promise; acquaintance enhances their worth. The long dress cuts a figure on the street; the short dress is the pledge and uniform of home. The long dress sacrifices all for show, its human contents diminishing in proportion to its display; the short dress modestly proclaims the superior value of person and soul. The long dress tends to kill womanhood; the short dress leaves it as God made it."

A granddaughter of John Humphrey Noyes told the following two stories on her tours: A group went to New York City on a sales trip and arrived at Grand Central Station wearing their short dress and pants, with short hair. Crowds gathered around the community women, staring in disbelief. When two hundred people surrounded them for a good look, police were summoned. Such was the rigid conformity of dress in that era; only the excess of feminine harness and upholstery were approved, or known. Showing even an ankle was verboten, as it still is in much of the world today. The ridicule and scorn faced by women wearing anything else was so universal only a few undaunted sensible women attempted it: farmers' wives, reformers, skaters, gymnasts, and tourists. But the commotion persuaded the Community that gowns must be made in several sizes for a Community woman to wear traveling outside; she would go to a Mansion House closet and pick out a worldly costume.

President Rutherford B. Hayes (1877–1881), cousin of John Humphrey Noyes, invited Noyes's son Theodore and his friend, Marion Nolan, to visit him at the White House. Marion, a small woman, found that the small and medium costumes were unfortunately in use, so she wore the large one with the help of pins and gussets. Theodore had only one pair of shoes and a sole was loose, so every time he walked, it would flap slightly. They used carpetbags for luggage, one of the items the Community produced. The Community gave their members plenty of money when they traveled, so they were staying at one of Washington's fine hotels. They looked like rumpled immigrants fresh out of Ellis Island. They were assigned to an obscure room; bellboys ignored the seemingly impoverished pair and Theodore carried their carpetbags up flights of stairs. He sent a note to the White House by messenger, telling Cousin Rutherford that they'd arrived. President and Mrs. Hayes arrived at the hotel in their carriage, greeted Theodore and Marion warmly under the flabbergasted gaze of the hotel employees, and drove them to the White House to stay for the rest of their vacation.

"A casual observer would hardly suspect that the vanities of fashion had any allurements for us, noted a Community member in June 1873, but a dress-distraction generally comes in the springtime when we want to purchase new garments. The great worldly principality of fashion pressed hardest upon us in this respect. One who is remarkable for the simplicity of her attire spoke up in a meeting: 'I have had a new desire this spring for a right spirit about dress; this thought has come to me—that in our manner of dress, we can please the revival spirit or we can grieve the revival spirit. It seems to me that a great variety of dresses grieves the revival spirit—it takes up a person's attention and it commands the attention of all around who are distracted by the continual appearance of something new. It may seem innocent to get up a new style of collar, or a new style of trimming to your dress that will make everybody think and say, How pretty that looks! I must have a collar like that, or a dress trimmed like that. But it is not innocent if it is a distraction from the spirit of prayer. It is sure to start a wave that will vibrate through at least the younger part of the Community, contrary to the revival spirit and internal adornment. I wish we could come into our meetings without being diverted by something new and striking in this one's and that one's dress. It should certainly be a rule of spiritual etiquette not to attract attention in our evening meetings by frequent change of dress or by new styles. Let us all find out what Paul means by modest apparel. Our singularity as a people gives us perfect liberty to ignore fashion, and let us keep our freedom.' Mrs. Cragin penned on June 29, 1851, shortly before she drowned: *Beware of the seductions of dress; they bring darkness and nightmare. Fall back on seeking a handsome body*."

"Fashion, now almost omnipotent, is striving—successfully—for the position of presiding goddess over places of public worship," *Style in the Sanctuary* noted. "The church often resembles a theater for scanning one another's costume while they display their own, and to indulge in gossip or perhaps congratulate themselves that one day has been given to the Lord." Taken from the *Washington Chronicle*, the piece was reprinted in total in the *Circular*, which mused: "What would our good Puritan forefathers who worshiped God from overflowing hearts within rude walls say to this description of church worship?

"The hour for praise-givings is drawing nigh; gloved attendants seat the comers according to the cut of their robes. First Mrs. President Grant, who, of course, must look becomingly well. A Lyons silk, trimmed with lace of delicate make excites the admiration of those who can only afford the counterfeit of this original. No tiara could adorn her head to more advantage than the jaunty and becoming velvet bonnet. She carries her book of prayers and a timid, rather pretty form attends her, Miss Nellie, her daughter. An impalpable green silk with trimmings of Valencia lace show to advantage her petite form and a flurry is created among the rising female generation. Mrs. O. D. Barrett, attended by her blonde husband, is the next comer. A lavender silk falls gracefully and adds to the attractiveness of a wax-like countenance and flowing chestnut locks. Mrs. Judge Fisher, a blonde of the purest type, worships in a black rep silk, a loose black velvet sacque and bonnet of the same material. Mrs. Vice President Colfax, a maturity-looking face, sings 'Praise God from whom all blessings flow' in a black velvet suit, heavily mounted with puffings of satin and trimmed with rare and costly lace. Mrs. Postmaster-General Creswell listens to the man of God in a blue moire and white corduroy jacket, handsomely trimmed with black velvet. Mrs. Judge Humphreys feels at home in a plain black silk, with trimmings of lace. Mrs. Rev. Dr. Newman takes her spiritual nourishment in a brown silk, heavily flounced, and trimmed with point-lace and wrappings of velvet. Mrs. Thomas L. Tullock heeds the good tidings in a lavender silk trimmed with ruchings and box plaitings of lavender satin. Mrs. Secretary Delano is religiously inspired in a black velvet dress and coat to match. Mrs. John Delano 'lets the good angels come in' in a green silk, handsomely trimmed with a profusion of laces. Mrs. Col. D. C. Cox rivets her attention to the scriptural doctrine in a blue silk edged with trimmings of point lace."

"Noyes predicted that women's dress would become more nearly the same as men's; simple and attractive dress will be the uniform of vital society. He thought that frock and pantalets for children was in good taste. A lady visitor from New York City saw our boys and girls in a lively romp on the lawn and expressed approval of their freedom. She said it was such a luxury to see children dressed plainly, untrammeled by fashion and etiquette. 'Little girls are sent to dancing school not merely to learn steps—that's right and innocent—but to display their elegant costumes,' said she. 'It is appalling to see the folly of some mothers in dressing their children. A six-year-old was elegantly dressed and loaded down with bracelets and necklaces, and she affected all the airs of a seventeen-year-old. It is painful to see little children taught to love display, but most of all to see them contemptuous to a little mate that is more plainly dressed. Many poor children have been kept from Sabbath-school on account of the difference in dress; in some churches a rule is made that all children who attend shall dress plainly. It's no wonder that many thousands of young women are ruined, when you reflect how early they're taught to seek admiration. It is not uncommon to hear young girls talk about their beaux with all the seriousness of young women; little boys in turn swell with importance. It is indeed a sad state of things! Children are so housed and effeminate that they are sure to make delicate men and women.' Another lady of that party said, 'I've been thankful many times that I was a girl a long time ago, because children are not children nowadays.'

"A letter from New York City on August 15, 1872, by a Community member describes this misfortune: 'Yesterday I saw illustrations of woman's wrongs in both high life and low life—part of one of the dining-rooms where we eat is raised six steps above the main part and is more especially devoted to ladies. I saw a wealthy looking, middle-aged gentleman enter, followed by a son and a daughter in their teens. The father and son tripped lightly up the stairs, but the daughter! On her poor back was the heavy burden, sticking out as you have seen it in fashion-plates. It reminds you of pictures of peasant life in Europe where poor women toiled under bundles of fagots (sticks), or of Southern slaves toiling under a basket of cotton. The fagots or the cotton were covered with silk and ribbons. I wish you could have seen her weary, desponding look on reaching those stairs. The poor thing grasped her drapery on either side with her delicate hands, and bending forward under the huge hump, slowly ascended with a swinging motion from side to side that told of her exhaustion. After she reached the top without having been toppled over by her burden, she heaved a sigh of relief and sank languidly into a chair. You might have been amused at the grotesque attire, but you would have pitied the little slave—for she was a slave, probably for life. The picture is not overdrawn nor is the case a rare one. I thanked God that our Community mothers and sisters are not obliged to bow under the yoke of fashion.'

"If there is any environment that can degrade a human being or harden a young heart, it is the atmosphere of fashionable life," lamented 'Fashionable Life,' an article from the *San Francisco Pioneer* that appeared in the May 20, 1872, *Circular*. "You may take the tenderest, most lovely girl, the one that is kindest at home and loves her father and mother most; put her in the highest circle of fashionable life with plenty of money and full scope to do as she pleases; let her dress herself as she will—cover herself with diamonds and pearls; let the love of admiration become the ruling passion, and soon all the tenderness of that young nature passes away; her thoughts concentrate upon herself—what figure she is cutting, who her admirers are, what conquests she can make. By and by the youthful, beautiful modesty is gone and the way is open for vice, that in the beginning would not have been dreamed of; or, if thought of, put away as utterly impossible."

In the good old years

"In our first years as a Community, economy was often a virtue of necessity. There was a period of pretty sharp struggle for existence when the members lived very much like soldiers—contented with the shelter of log-houses and rough shanties, plain diet, and spare wardrobes. We enjoyed a certain romance and poetry of life that accompanies the pioneer and backwoodsman. Yet we envisioned our ideal Community home, and step by step we gradually surrounded ourselves with comforts. We'd learned pretty thoroughly how to "suffer need," and now it was before us to learn "how to abound." This latter was apparently more difficult. With thriving businesses and the smiles of fortune upon us, it was almost inevitable that we should imperceptibly fall into habits of luxury and even extravagance. Our temptation was not in respect to diet, for we held the principle firmly that our table should not lack a generous bill of fare. But great expenses in building the mansion and increased investment in the silk business reduced our available resources to a low point by 1871. Mr. Noyes, though a visionary, is a remarkably practical one, and he recommended retrenchment.

"If Mr. Noyes takes a pinch of snuff, it is said that all the Community sneezes. Here's a story about one pinch he took. He personally wouldn't have any new clothes for a year, and if the rest of the men were of his mind, the tailor should be drafted into another business. All the men and all the women of the Community *sneezed*—no new clothes, boots, and shoes for one year! The reaction spread through the whole

Community and the resolution of a few became by acclamation the resolution of the many. They went through the year with respectable everyday clothes and extra patching and darning cheerfully done by the mothers, with a best suit in reserve.

"Laughing about it afterward, Mr. Noyes said he called that sneeze worth at least $8,000! This is no expression at all of its worth—the effect of the fast on our treasury is not to be compared with its spiritual effect. It brought us nearer to God and added to our domestic happiness. Folks think that Community women always dress plainly, but in spring the dress breezes blowing everywhere affect us even here. We're accustomed to want two or three new dresses for summer, and they have to be made, and that's a great fuss, no matter how plain they are. Then words are wasted about them; and when you exchange familiar clothes for new, you make yourself a stranger and everybody has to get reacquainted with you. The difference last season was appreciated—we were better companions for the men in every way for not being taken up with our sewing. We went on heartily with our studies and labors, and increased our inward adorning. The moral effect of the self-denial was worth vastly more than the pecuniary saving; it purged the whole life and raised the Community into the consciousness of renewed continence and chastity."

CARING FOR 250 PEOPLE IN THE MANSION HOUSE

"Wasn't it too bad that Aunt Julia should travel to Utica on such a dreadful day?" When the clock struck four, in burst Julia Ackley with her skirts gathered up in both hands and her face expressing unmitigated disgust. "I almost lost my petticoat in the street and I believe I wouldn't have cared if I had, I felt so exasperated that there should be such a thing as the *long dress*. Just look!" as she lifted her petticoat that had once laid claim to the quality of whiteness, but now was a frightful sight to behold—mud-stained to the depth of a foot or more. The names of eighteen men and as many women were drawn last night as partners for today's washing. Mr. R. volunteered to start the fires and make necessary preparations. By half-past four this morning the company were gathered in the long washroom engaged in rubbing, wringing, and rinsing, by which our members' soiled clothes come out white and new. Darkness and tempest without, but cheerful light and a merry hum within. In two hours the breakfast bell rings and we washers have the post of honor.

Central New York has temperatures in winter ranging from well below zero to the thirties. In the good old days, Community laundry was not infrequently done outside. Sufficient water was fetched from a well two hundred feet away to fill a large copper kettle suspended above a fire. The weekly rubbing, pounding, and boiling of an accumulated pile of soiled clothes began. Spattering suds splashed on women's dresses, which often became literally frozen stiff with icicles forming around skirts. Active people sweat; little icicles decorated the hairline.

Steam-powered washers liberate women

"The steam-engine with large washing and wringing machinery and other excellent apparatus, is a credit to the inventor and a liberator of women from the most repulsive drudgery of the household, noted the March 1864 *Circular*. The washing for our family is now done in about a day and a half, dispensing with some twenty-four days of hand labor formerly required. This magical change is wrought within a stone's throw of the towering trestle-work of the Midland Railroad over which the good engine Oswego No. 1 puffed and whistled. All we do now is distribute our soiled clothes in large canvas bags hung in a room at the Tontine; clothes to be washed are deposited in compartments labeled with the name of almost every conceivable article of apparel—anyone who has sorted fifty baskets of 'foul linen' thought this plan a capital idea. At the end of the week we find them again in the same room, clean, and neatly folded in our boxes.

"We enter the thirty-by-forty foot washing-room. All mechanical operations are performed by water-power, while a twelve-horse-power boiler outside the door heats the water and also dries the clothes in unpropitious weather. On a platform about ten feet from the floor are four large tanks; two contain soft, and two hard water; one hot and one cold of each. Soft water is thrown up by a forcing-pump from a cistern situated under the ironing-room, thirty feet by ten, and seven feet deep, with a capacity of four hundred and seventy-five barrels. Hard water is brought from nearby springs and pumped in the same manner. Overhead is a network of pipes, and the number of faucets must be legion, for we counted forty at a glance. At each washing and rinsing-box there are four faucets, commanding soft and hard water, either hot or cold. Four kinds of soap in a state of solution are manufactured by steam on the spot. Two large washing machines, the Nonpareil and the Shaker, are kept in constant motion on Mondays, Tuesdays and Fridays. We could almost fancy the garments subjected to the vigorous and monotonous swish-swash of the Shaker crying out in the spirit of true martyrs—

> "Come life, Shaker life/Come life eternal;
> Shake, shake out of us/All that is carnal."

"Half-a-dozen small carts running on three wheels obviate the necessity of lifting and carrying the clothes. At the sunny southern entrance on a neat grass-plot is the drying yard. 'How handy!' we exclaimed to Mrs. M., who with bare arms was superintending the weekly process of bleaching with chloride of lime. 'Yes, we're discovering better ways for doing things,' she said. 'There's one improvement we've adopted that saves us a great deal of labor: When shirts are starched, instead of rubbing and rubbing them as we used to do, we just give them one dash into clear water, wring them out, and dry them. We used to spend hours rubbing the shirt: bosoms, and you know how hard that must be—blistering your fingers; but the shirts iron just as well from receiving this treatment. Think how much time and labor are saved!' she exclaimed.

"Next is the steam drying-room—ten feet by thirty—where you can dry the thickest woolen garments in two hours, fifteen minutes for towels. The last is the ironing-room—thirty by thirty. A mangle run by water-power presses sheets, towels, and other plain clothes, while seven hired women ply their irons at convenient tables, heated on one of Mott's excellent flat-heaters. It is astonishing to see the ease with which our immense washings are carried on. One of our men and two of our women take charge of the establishment; one man and seven women living in the neighborhood are employed five days a week; one of our men hangs out the clothes three days in the week, and Saturday morning all is done. Thanks to nineteenth century inventive genius, no more back-bending drudgery over nauseating suds!

"One of our men was walking toward the Old Mill at ten o'clock, when his attention was arrested by a flash of light near the laundry—a brick wing joining the mill. Hastening to the spot, he found two barrels of wood-ashes in flames, the blaze reaching nearly to the cornice," the July 1873 *Circular* reported. "With the assistance of Mr. M. who lives nearby, he succeeded in putting out the fire. Had he not discovered it, there is little doubt that the whole pile of buildings would have been burned. At the evening meeting, there was a united recognition of God's watchful care over us in regard to fire, and a desire was expressed to be more careful. The practice of putting ashes in barrels should be forbidden.

"There was a case of spontaneous combustion in the machine-shop at Willow Place. One of the boys employed in sweeping the shop had sprinkled the floor liberally and was sweeping into convenient piles masses of oily rags, iron-turnings, and filings that were scattered about the room. He had made one heap of such material near the stove, when suddenly steam or smoke appeared to arise from the material. The mass was speedily examined and found to be quite hot, caused by the rapid oxidation of the iron from the water thrown on the floor. At the rate at which the combustion was advancing, it would have taken but a short time to have set fire to the combustible material. If this affair had taken place during the night when the watchman was in other parts of the building, a serious fire would have undoubtedly occurred.

"October 25, 1869, is memorable in the annals of the Oneida Community by the introduction of steam to the mansion, estimated to save twenty-five percent of fuel. Thousands of feet of conducting pipe were fitted and placed in position, ramifying through the building from cellar to attic and making as complex a system as the arteries and veins of the human body. The amount of tubing employed as conductors, coils, and radiators is not less than 7,000 feet; this is of various sizes but will average about 1¼ inches in diameter. This will give an aggregate of 2,291 square feet of heating surface, equivalent to 11½ square feet to each individual, of a family of two hundred. This gives each individual the equivalent of a small stove. Thanks to our steam we have continuous summer in the house that renders us oblivious to out-of-doors cold. Our new system rivals midsummer's heat only too successfully; we must use the bounteous supply sparingly and look periodically at our thermometers, so we do not accustom ourselves to warmth that would make us too delicate to enjoy the bracing airs of winter.

"In this large society of people that did not pair off, who mended clothes? This job seemed to go to women, who like men did not want to spend much precious time doing this. So they accomplished knitting, darning, and sewing during evening meetings in the Family Hall under lights from green shaded glass kerosene lamps on small homemade tables with octagon tops. Men brought their laundered clothes from the cellar each week to the room of one of the women appointed as seamstress for a period, and buttons would be sewed on or rips repaired. One day a notice appeared on the bulletin board: 'Will the man who left his pants in my room please pick them up?'

"Because G. is your son, you don't necessarily take care of his clothes—some other woman is quite as likely to do it. Joseph lost his mother's help by frequent change of residence between Wallingford and the Oneida Community. The women held a caucus and it was asked, 'Who will take care of Joseph's clothes?' No answer! Finally, one said, 'I will take care of his shirts.' Another said, 'I will take care of his stockings.' Presently he had a mother for his pants and vests; another for his collars, towels, and handkerchiefs; and two volunteered to share the responsibility of mending and sponging his coats. A division of labor became necessary to achieve the immense tasks of maintaining this very large family; competent managers oversaw several departments. Mrs. Norton has general charge year around of all the Community bedding; although in her 68th year, she is indefatigable in her personal labors to provide for the family comfort in the very important item of good beds. Let Miss K. know if you need a better carpet, a new mattress, spread, or pillow. Was a new curtain, easy chair, mirror, or footstool needed? Just apply to Mrs. S., who has charge of furniture. Repairs or mending will be dispatched by Mrs. N. and Mrs. K. will carefully wash a new dress or bleach an item. Mrs. C. will furnish goods for your own clothing and Mrs. V. will provide for children.

"The desolation of house-cleaning," the *Circular* announced, "is upon us. What is drearier than the topsy-turvy, hurly-burly, helter-skelter, nowhere-to-sit-down feeling that comes with this bi-annual onslaught? It's somewhat like an epidemic in its working. Home life is flowing placidly on when suddenly morning house-cleaning breaks out in a remote part of the house. Out with the windows, down with the curtains, up with the carpets, hustle the beds out of doors, push every piece of movable property from its accustomed place, then "lay to" with brooms, mops, and pails. The disaster spreads; room after room catches the infection and no rest is known till every crack, crevice, and corner is most rigorously dealt with. It is in the nature of woman. After the energetic bustle comes order and quiet and a wholesome sense of freedom from dust and cobwebs as refreshing as sunshine after a fog.

"At a public school exhibition in Michigan, a reader of the *Circular* shared that a visitor addressed the pupils on the necessity of obeying their teachers and growing up loyal and useful citizens. To emphasize his remarks, he pointed to a large national flag spread on one side of the room, and inquired, 'Boys, what is that flag for?' An urchin promptly answered: 'To cover up the dirt, sir.'

"Commenting on an eight-hour strike of working-men, an exchange in the July 1, 1872, *Circular* inquires: 'How is it with the women? Will working-men agree to limit their wives to eight hours of labor? Or do they propose to adhere to the old-time dictum that woman's work is never done? American working-men's wives are more burdened with excessive labor than the working-men themselves. We shall feel a good deal more enthusiasm in the labor movement when convinced that women are to share its promised benefits.' The point is well made. Working-men stand in respect to the labor question in a relation to their wives similar to that of their employers toward themselves; only the men often require of their wives many more hours of work a day than their employers ask of them. 'What's sauce for the gander is sauce for the goose.' Let working-men who are compelling their employers to take ten and even eight hours for a day's work, turn round and say to their wives, 'You shall have the same privileges without strikes.' There must be a general movement for their relief; why should it not be a peaceable one? The first step will be to lessen their hours of labor, then will come cooperation with its labor-saving and labor-lightening arrangements, which is already taken advantage of to a considerable extent by working-men. Finally, we hope that both working men and working women may be prepared for Community living in which all forms of oppression cease."

"'What office do you hold in this institution?' a visitor inquired of a Community member who had graduated with honors from college and theological seminary, and officiated as church-pastor previous to joining the Community. 'I hold at present the office of Dish-Rinser,' was the simple reply. It never occurs to a member of the Community that one kind of work is degrading in itself while another is elevating. It is understood that the character of labor is determined by the spirit in which it is performed."

WHAT THEY ATE:

"We've been taken back to the halcyon days of our early Community life by readings from 1855 journals. Ah! —those were happy days, and though we had few luxuries and were sometimes obliged to retrench, we enjoyed ourselves as heartily as children. Those were the days of baked beans, brown bread, and milk porridge, the days when dainties were dispensed with. It's amusing to compare the following three meals a day (unusually sumptuous!) for August 26–28, 1855, with the 1872 two meals daily:

"For Sunday breakfast: Crust coffee, brown sugar, brown bread, butter, and baked beans. For dinner: Boiled chicken, milk-gravy toast, stewed potatoes without butter, and apples. For supper: Blackberry shortcake and plenty of it and cold water. For Monday breakfast was chicken soup with sliced potatoes, and bread and butter. Dinner was baked meat, potatoes, onions, apples, bread, and milk. Supper was bread, milk, baked apples, and cheese. Tuesday breakfast offered fried hasty pudding, syrup, bread and butter. Dinner was squash, cucumbers, bread, rice pudding, no butter, and supper was bread and butter, tomatoes, and apple-pie.

"Like most families, the Community had three meals daily until October 20, 1872. Dr. Noyes and Mr. Cragin presented scientific physiological reasons that better digestion, better assimilation, better sleep, and brighter faculties for spiritual receptivity are the rewards of those who limit themselves to two meals daily. Mr. Noyes elaborated on this: 'God's object in these dietetic changes is to get us into a bodily condition most favorable to good spiritual experience. If the ultimate end of what we are doing were simply good health, I would not have much interest or ambition about it, but the state of the body has a great deal to do with our religious experience. T. had been through a long course of fasting—had parted with forty pounds of total depravity, as she expressed it, and was in a bodily condition favorable for a good experience. So with H., who'd been pinched off from all sensory comforts and been kept on fever diet for seven or eight days, when she had a bright religious experience. God teaches us and shows us ways to reduce the flesh and keep our bodies in a state where we shall have just such experience all the time.' Doctors say that eating three meals per day is a habit, not a natural instinct. Community unity and flexibility is seen in the hearty readiness to change from three meals a day to two, which began without opposition—almost without discussion.

"The two-meal-day diet was breakfast, served from 8–10 a.m. instead of 6–8 a.m., and the final meal for the day, dinner at 3:00 p.m. On May 31, 1873, a typical breakfast featured malt coffee, granulated sugar, cream, mashed potatoes, fried shad, pie-plant sauce, apple-sauce, wheat bread and butter, cold wheat biscuit, milk, Graham bread gems, biscuits, crackers and mush, and syrup/molasses. Dinner offered dried beef cream gravy, steamed potatoes, bread pudding, pie-plant sauce, apple-sauce, wheat bread and butter, Graham bread gems, crackers and mush, and lettuce. On June 1, breakfast was malt coffee, cream, milk, prune sauce, wheat bread and butter, wheat and buckwheat pancakes, warmed up potato, Graham bread gems, crackers and mush, and syrup/molasses. Dinner was strawberry tea, cream, milk, wheat bread and butter, bananas, pear sauce, rolls, Graham bread gems, crackers and mush, sponge cake, and cheese. On June 2, breakfast was bountiful: Malt coffee, cream, meat gravy, Indian meal puffs, baked potatoes, wheat bread and butter, Graham bread gems, crackers and mush, milk, apple-sauce, pie-plant sauce, and syrup. Dinner offered malt coffee, cream, steamed potatoes, pot-pie, milk, wheat bread and butter, Graham bread gems, pie-plant pie, pie-plant sauce, cheese, lettuce, and syrup/molasses.

"Our small children, the youngest two years, now eat two meals a day, their breakfast at eight and their dinner at three. It's astonishing to see how kindly they take to the system. Some of us hardly believed it possible, remembering frequent lunches with which we were wont to be fortified in childhood. Much of the ease with which they adapt themselves is doubtless due to their diet, largely composed of coarse wheat flour and fruit. They go to the table with splendid appetites and are allowed to eat all they wish, often prolonging their sitting to three-quarters of an hour. They never plead for food between meals and even play with apples at the paring bee without apparently thinking of tasting. They're evidently happier for allowing their stomachs time for rest; they certainly are far less restless at night and rise in the morning bright-eyed and buoyant.

"After a ten day trial of two meals per day, Mr. Woolworth invited the family to say what they thought about it in the evening meeting. The expression in favor was at once hearty and unanimous. Some spoke of aches and pains that disappeared since discarding the third meal, and others testified to clearer heads, lighter spirits, a more equable spiritual life, and a new delight in food. Many find their appetites decidedly better, but without any uncomfortable feelings of hunger between meals. Of those who were weighed later, there was a gain on the previous month of 126 pounds over all losses. All rejoice in the era just begun, nearer to eating with gladness and singleness of heart than ever before. The evening meeting, the choicest hour of the day, is now held from seven till eight o'clock instead of from eight till nine. These changes have promoted sociability and broken up habit in a manner eminently pleasing to the Community spirit. Habit is a tyrant, and it is good to rebel against it from time to time. 'We never want to go back to the old plan of three meals,' most anybody will say if questioned. The cooks appreciate the change because it takes less time and labor to plan and prepare two meals a day than it did three; all like it because it economizes and proportions their time for personal improvement, study, and labor to better advantage.

"The major task of planning meals and cooking for many hard-working people was most appreciated, undertaken by two women and often rotated. One kitchen and dining-room can serve three hundred persons much more economically, efficiently, and safely, than can sixty or seventy small kitchens and dining-rooms with numerous fires, staffing considerations, and distribution. The steward reported that the stock of butter was nearly exhausted, and likewise the supply around here, therefore it is almost impossible to procure more of that commodity," the *Circular* noted in March 1868. "The price is high and advancing, so can we be contented with a little thinner spread for the next forty days? Of course! And butter appears on the table but once a day. We're well content with our short allowance, thankful to be independent of an article of diet whose use or disuse was once a consideration of vital interest and the occasion of many a debate.

"Seated at table with a plain meal before me, I'm reminded of the spirit in which the Primitive Church ate their meals, 'with gladness and singleness of heart,'" writes Mary Bolles. "The believer receives the food as the gift of God, discerns God in it, and in appropriating it may realize God's spirit. While the body is refreshed and invigorated, the spirit is warmed and enlivened. The spirit in which one acts determines the nature and effect of the act, whether for good or evil; without thankfulness in hearts nor discernment that the good flavor and vital element in all food is the product of God, they see it only as food, which they eat and drink as mere matter. We understand this if we consider that the body is the minor and the spirit the major party in the duality. We shall turn attention to God when eating, realizing and confessing God's life in the food and partaking of it in gladness and softness of heart. We may have sweetest communions with God, and to food given a relish altogether beyond that of former times, and attended with a quickening of spirit and vivification of the whole being."

"The Community gave up eating meat in 1855 following a visit to the Community by a Mr. Lawson from England, who practiced cooperative farming. He shared about how he became a vegetarian. William Woolworth asked him how he came to differ from most of his countrymen in regard to dietetics. 'I had been a respectable meat eater like everybody else. On October 4, 1801, a gentleman visited my father's house and I asked him if he would have a mutton-chop for luncheon; he replied that he never ate meat. I asked him if he thought it would be good for me never to eat meat, and he said yes. I determined to eat one mutton-chop and then give it up, which I did for one year, because I said I would. I found that the system agreed well with me and that I was better fitted for exercise. From my short study of comparative anatomy, I learned that man more resembles fruit eaters and grain eaters than flesh-eating animals. Chemistry taught that all the elements necessary to building up and invigorating the human system are contained in fruits, grains, and vegetables, and these considerations led me to a vegetarian life.'

At the Annual Meeting of the American Health Association on November 29, 1873, Doctor Hamlin of Bangor, Maine, said that the destiny of nations depends on the manner in which they are fed, the *Circular* reported. "Animal food contains elements of virulent poison and a change in its condition converts it into a source of disease and death," he said. "Great care should be exercised in the selection of meat for food."

"Another Englishman visiting us remarked that he was astonished at the rapidity with which Americans ate. Another who'd been a long time in this country replied: 'When I first came to America I was taking my dinner at a hotel; I had not finished my fish when I observed persons get up and leave the table. Supposing there must be a fire or some cause of excitement, I followed the crowd and they dispersed. I returned to the dining-room and found the tables cleared!' The Americans had bolted their dinners as usual, and he lost his by not understanding their manners."[51]

"One who left us eighteen years ago returns to visit the home of his youth and meets his friends and companions, all fresh and young and enthusiastic—time has changed them for the better. His relatives are all here and would not change places with him for a fortune. He feels the difference between himself and them. He inwardly regrets the impulse that led him to leave—but he is a man with business interests and a family. He feels that the Community has made a great advance and that it has a higher standard than the world in which he lives. He respects those who stayed in less prosperous days and knows that they are receiving their hundred-fold in this life. He knows that his brothers and sisters are better off than he is, but his visit is very enjoyable and he leaves with the best of feelings toward all."

9

Addictions

A TILT WITH TOBACCO

John Humphrey Noyes wrote in riveting detail about his battle with tobacco until age forty-two. "My father always chewed in the daytime and smoked evenings. My mother took snuff during my early years, but set a good example afterwards by breaking away from this habit. A cousin older than myself, with whom I worked and slept throughout my boyhood, was a steady chewer. My associates and roommates at an academy I attended when I was eleven years old thought it smart to take snuff and smoke, and I learned of them to enjoy a little excitement in these ways. But my grandmother Chloe, with whom I boarded—good soul!—reprimanded me faithfully for drinking too much tea and for carrying a snuff box, and I was temporarily frightened back into steady habits. (She and grandfather Rutherford Hayes ran the Brattleboro tavern, the center of business and social life; they were grandparents of Rutherford B. Hayes, Jr., President of the United States in 1876 and my cousin). My long slavery to tobacco began probably in my thirteenth year. On vacations, pleasant as home was, I would become bored and when I once complained of this to my mother, she suggested, not exactly as advice but rather as a sagacious reflection, that tobacco was what I needed. I remember well the very place out in a lane between the house and the barn where I tried my first chew. It made me very sick. Dizzy and trembling I ejected it, and almost renounced the attempt to find comfort in this terrible way. But I did not vomit and it rather elated me. I soon felt all right again and was ready for another chew. After a few trials my stomach and nerves submitted to their new master and I entered into a life of slavery that lasted, with brief intermissions, till my forty-second year when the Community set me free.

"The habit was always encroaching, and I was always resisting. The number of chews or pipes per day would steadily increase till intolerable disorders of the stomach and nerves would set in. Then would come a sharp struggle between reason and appetite, and I would get back to moderation to begin the course over again. When I was lodging in the third story of the Seminary building at Andover, my conscience got so stirred up that I determined to break off all relations with tobacco. I had a hand of Cavendish in my pocket. Raising the window, I hurled it out as far as I could. A rainstorm was drenching everything. It was Sunday and the stores were shut. I had no more tobacco and no possibility of getting any for that day at least. Can the reader guess the sequel? At dusk, when the old love began to whisper most seductively and conscience began to relent, I went out in the rain and searched the ground patiently for the hand of Cavendish, and found it. The lover's quarrel was made up and I passed a pleasant evening with the poor half-drowned plug.

"The pitch to which tobacco-slavery carried its exactions is truly astonishing. I often watch and speculate on its encroachments; it was satisfied with nothing short of a devotion that would have no pleasure in anything without it. The tobacco-user must think of his idol and provide for its accommodation when he sits down to study, when he visits friends, when he takes an excursion, even when he goes to a religious meeting. The wise say that we must eat to live, not live to eat! But tobacco, when it gets the upper hand of a person, says that he must live to chew and spit! The principal charm of a good meal lay in the quid of fine cut that was to come after it. Religion did at last conquer—for a time. When I was in the New Haven Seminary, prayer and Bible influence strengthened me till I broke away from tobacco and escaped. The struggle was long, and sometimes it seemed doubtful whether I wouldn't sell my soul for the morsel that was so sweet to roll under the tongue; but the good spirit prevailed and for one year I was free. During this period I did my best to raise public insurrection against tobacco-slavery. We instituted an anti-tobacco society in the Seminary and sent letters of inquiry and appeal to the heads of all the colleges. I was appointed to correspond with the President of Williams College. My letter came back scrawled with profanity and filth; on a blank space I was informed that 'a meeting of the students was to be held on the next Thursday to pray for my eternal damnation!'—doubtless penned by some student into whose hands it had fallen."

Legality and Grace

"After I became a Perfectionist, my theories about the ways and means of reform were entirely changed. I came to regard *legality* as a more subtle and dangerous seducer than tobacco. I became distrustful of laws and human resolutions, and jealous for the grace of God. Legality, which applies the will for the purpose of improving the spirit and character, is a stimulus of much the same kind as tobacco, opium, and ardent spirits. It is a method of stirring up and strengthening the nervous system without grace. It is one of the things that belong to the fashion of this world, and we may as well be trying to find the vent through which we are going to make our escape. I don't want violent efforts to get free from tobacco use; by standing in the sight of God and letting the Spirit of truth instruct us in this matter—not coming into legality on the one hand, nor restricting the course of the spirit of God, on the other—we shall put ourselves in the true attitude. It is the truth that makes us free.

"I'm charmed with Christ's treatment of the case as he shows me his mind—there is no harsh criticism at all in him. There is in him that which is heroic and helpful and certain to give us moral power and to ask nothing from us any faster than it strengthens our hearts, and establishes our wills in the right way. Tobacco stimulates the flesh and drowns the spirit; Christ's method is to stimulate the spirit till it overcomes and drowns the flesh. People need their hearts established in some way—when they find that tobacco and rum will do it for a few minutes, they take to these things. Christ will not take them away without substituting something better. The ideal will work itself into our life in many free ways and leaven the whole lump.

"I shall never cease to watch tobacco as a tremendous principality. You will find that your want of tobacco is not a merely natural want; it is a positive supernatural injection from a spirit with which you are in rapport. It is altogether more difficult to deal with than rum. It is far too subtle to be conquered by law, but it is not too subtle for Christ. In the struggle with this new enemy I went back to the use of tobacco and consented to live with tobacco a while longer and wait for an effectual release by powers above. Thackeray used to tell of a begging Irishwoman, who, when she saw him putting his hand in his pocket, cried out: 'May the blessing of God follow you all the days of your life.' But when he pulled out his snuff-box, she immediately added, 'and never ever overtake you!'

"We have adopted the confession of Christ as the best way out of trouble and confess Christ in our eating, drinking, and sleep," wrote Noyes in a November 1851 Home Talk. "I propose to Mr. Burt and George (his brother) that they confess Christ in chewing tobacco. I feel a sickly spirit in respect to that habit. Whatever there is bad in it we may as well put into Christ's hands to correct. We must have faith enough now to do that. We will chew tobacco heartily as unto the Lord, and insist that Christ shall have his way in everything. Then if there is anything evil in the habit, Christ will cure it. Let this be a Community matter; those who do not use tobacco can sympathize with those who do. I understand Mr. Burt and George a great deal better, using tobacco myself; I've been an old soldier in this war and can brag some. I would exhort those who do not use it to have compassion on those that do, and not to think evil of them. Let us see if there isn't a way for those who have this habit to be as clean and free from condemnation as those who do not have it. I offer myself as Community property in dealing with this principality, having gone back to tobacco after quitting for one year.

"There is no question but that the principality concerned in tobacco-chewing is the strongest one in this country, and perhaps in the world. It is much stronger than the old rum-drinking principality," Noyes wrote in an article titled *Tobacco*, as he struggled to end his addiction in Brooklyn in 1852. "And, by the way, there seems to be a kind of retribution going on. The Indians left tobacco behind them; we may call it the poison of the arrow they shot behind, as they fled before the Europeans. They formerly raised this weed in great quantities, and used it as white men now do. They made women do all the agricultural work—men considered it beneath them to plant and hoe corn and potatoes. But the tobacco crop was considered sufficiently dignified to command their attention. Europeans drove the Indians from their lands, and they died out or have become a mere ghost of a people—but their tobacco now reigns over the country!"

"By March 1853, an influx of new people in to the Community was causing the acquisition, emptying, and washing of numerous spittoons daily—men spat and women emptied the spittoons! The majority of the men not only smoked, but chewed tobacco and used snuff. The smell of tobacco increasingly permeated the buildings. The habit was not only distasteful but deleterious to health, and men as well as women wanted an end to what they called bondage to the tobacco principality. At times the men would sincerely try to stop, but the urge for tobacco is relentless, and they would start using it again. The time has come for us to discuss freely and thoroughly the subject of tobacco, and I shall from time to time broach the subject, give freedom of discussion, and—so far as I'm concerned—deliver tobacco slavery up to judgment. We're coming to a crisis that I've been looking for, when the truth, not obligations or the law, shall make us free. I think there is considerable credit due to those who do not use tobacco for keeping quiet and not judging those who do. The women have shown wonderful patience and willingness to accommodate themselves to things as they are.

"As a means of grace, what idea would it be to propose to the entire Community the experiment of a fast from tobacco for one day; i.e., as many as feel free, for I would have no law about it. Name a day and let those that have power over their own wills put aside tobacco for one day, and give that time to meditation on the subject. That might have a good effect if it were a free-will offering—more will be done by that than ever could be accomplished by legality. A new policy laying out specific things to be done would likely be ineffectual anyway. Appointing a fast to the Lord is a totally different thing from making solitary resolutions; I propose that the Community contemplate as the hope of their calling the entire breaking up of this bondage.

"The world seeks comfort from outward things that stimulate and sooth, and eating and drinking are the primary, universal method," wrote Noyes in a Home Talk titled *Tobacco Reform*. "But the world has found ways of stimulating the flesh more powerfully. The gospel method of reform is to take persons just as they are, in bondage to whatever evil, and set before them ultimate complete deliverance; then in such gentle, moderate ways as can be used without legality, begin to assume control. This is a combination of the two methods that are used in the world: liberals deal moderately with the passion to be overcome, but have little hope of attaining their objective; legal reformers set before people a rule of action and summon them to immediate attainment. There is a principle that makes it necessary that deliverance from evil should be gradual. If you cut any evil short off, you will cut away more or less good with it. Where the life of individuals is mixed up and interlaced with principalities that have possession of them, the process of disentangling them from these principalities requires nice dissection. Let a man cut himself off from chewing tobacco all at once by pure force of law, if you examine that man you will find the mischief is still in him in a latent form. I do not care how sudden and immediate a reformation is, if it thoroughly dissects and carries away the evil spirit concerned; but that cannot be done in most cases without labor and a process of discovery. Reform from any bad habit requires a great deal of unraveling of life. Law is effectual for a while, but has to be repeated and reinforced, and is finally sure to fail. If we throw out our whole strength on immediate reformation we shall not set our standard half high enough. Have our ideal clear in the first place, and then say that we are going to attain that ideal without law, if it takes forever. This method of reform precludes self-condemnation.

"I'd recommend first, that those who are free from tobacco should not contemplate using it; the use of it should be discouraged among those that have never begun. They should see that we expect to get rid of it, and it will save them trouble not to form the habit. There should be no law put upon them, because that would tempt them to it. I would suggest it as a matter of expediency that they keep their freedom. I feel that all things are lawful for me, but not all things are expedient. Is the use of tobacco expedient? I think we shall have to be redeemed from it. Is this to be done as legalists would recommend? I think not. Secondly, I would recommend that all persons who have not come under bondage to it so far, if they can drop the habit without any serious quarrel with themselves, should drop it. Third, to those who are thoroughly imprisoned in the use of tobacco, I would recommend the experiment of a fast next Sunday. Let's quit it for one day and give up our minds to reflection and attention to the Lord's mind about such matters." Harriet Noyes noted that most of the Community went without dinner to sympathize with the tobacco men.

"We were conscious yesterday that we had to contend with a great principality and, though we felt happy and strong, still we had to *fight*! Some are chewing today and some are fasting," John Miller wrote on the second day of the tobacco fast.

John R. Miller joined the Putney Association in 1841 and became Business Manager of the Oneida Community. His primary goal was to fund ongoing publications. His friendly personality helped build amicable relations with neighbors at both Putney and Oneida.

Noyes shared his experience in the March 1853 *Circular*: "I have not kept up the fast and used some yesterday and today, but I'm confident that the tobacco-devil, instead of leading us captive, is going to be itself led captive. You'll find that the imagination that makes you want tobacco is not merely a natural imagination of your own mind; it's an injection from a spirit that's always ready to fling evil imaginations into you. You may be well disposed to hold your mind clear of tobacco thoughts, but something flashes into you that makes you want tobacco—this willful injection of some spirit that you've come into rapport with, so it can at any time commit this imposition. You may be sure that your life is sucked by some evil spirit that has the benefit of your tobacco-chewing. So I'll say to it when the suggestion comes up to take tobacco: 'Do I want it? Am I not happy enough without it? Would it not spoil the enjoyment I now have?' We gain on that spirit every time we argue with it in this way. I want to see the Community rid of tobacco in the right way—that no one quit with the nervous system in such a state of want that hereafter the remembrance of tobacco would be pleasant and a temptation to return to it some time; that we make up our mind that God can take away the appetite."

"My late experience with tobacco has encouraged my faith in the power of Christ to break up the slavery of habit," reported Erastus Hamilton in the March 1853 *Circular*. "I was formerly much attached to smoking but had substituted chewing, as I found it gave me the same peculiar excitement with less offense to others. I changed on the suggestion of Mr. Noyes, who saw that I was delicate about smoking in the house; he said he considered that chewing had the advantage of smoking—being less solitary and trespassing less on the senses of others. Mr. Noyes said he was undermining the whole tobacco principality and fully expected to see an end of the use of tobacco in the Community. If we have contracted a habit that evil attaches to, let us keep open to the truth and let in free discussion, and the evil will be dissolved and waste away. Evil breeds in darkness.

"This talk inspired me with faith that I should not get in bondage to chewing," Mr. Hamilton continued, "but should be able to quit tobacco entirely when the right time came, and so it has proved. I became as fond of chewing as I had been of smoking and was somewhat tempted to feel condemned about it, and to resolve to quit in a legal way; but I determined to wait on God and get my discharge in the true way. The other night I took a chew that sickened me, upon which I began to reflect. It seemed to me that God was calling on me to quit using tobacco, and the effect was that my appetite for it was taken away. I had some hesitation about taking a stand to quit it entirely—knowing the power of habit—but concluded to trust God and begin. My experience is very encouraging and I am persuaded that the power of this principality is being broken. It is not as strong as it would have us think. I have had no difficulty at all in leaving off the practice, and it has not been by the mere action of will. I feel that Christ has taken away the appetite and destroyed the power of habit to propagate itself. Thanks be unto God who always causeth us to triumph in Christ.

To have Christ victorious over tobacco in the entire Community will be a beautiful tribute to the truth."

"There is but little tobacco used here now," John Miller reported on April 7th. "Several have left off entirely and others use it moderately. We keep the thing in the light by telling our experience in the meeting every evening. I have just taken a quid since I commenced this paragraph, which is the third I have indulged in since the day before the fast. I stand midway between the ultras and the conservatives, so you may judge the state of the Community on this subject; I commenced again because I felt that I was coming under a spirit of legality."

"By May 1, 1853, a large majority of the slaves to tobacco had already been liberated. A half dozen or so remained still in prison rather than give undue advantage to legality. By making this a spiritual battle—breaking away from servility to the tyrannical tobacco principality, from bondage to the tobacco-devil—thirty men gave it up with surprisingly little effort except for a period of dizziness; even those who didn't use tobacco were dizzy! They rejoiced in deliverance from narcotic servitude. The battle now died down for a few months, while fresh psychological reinforcements were being brought up.

"If you want to be saved, you must *put off the old man with his deeds*. You must put *him* off, not merely put off his deeds leaving him there to bring forth another set of deeds as bad as the first," said Noyes in an instructive and wide-ranging Home Talk on December 1st. "Living in Community is going to be a powerful auxiliary of Christ in enabling us to put off the old man. I was interested in that experience of old Mrs. H. She'd been thirty years attached to her pipe, but when she went to the Putney Community, she found herself in such close relations with persons who did not like smoking that to make harmony she gave it up—an illustration of the natural effect of close association. Whoever enters Community understandingly must go through a thorough washing and scrubbing that will end in being purified of everything that is disagreeable to those around," Noyes continued. "The fact that tobacco is not a Community element is weaning me from the appetite more than any motive I've ever had. This Community motive will root out the love of tobacco, liquor, and everything that isolates and separates. Paul worked upon this plan. He said on the one hand, *Let no man judge you in respect to meats and drinks*, and on the other, *If meat make my brother to offend, I will eat no meat*. I shall content myself with these two motives of reform—Community with Christ, and Community with one another. I believe they will work out every problem of morality.

"Another principle that will cooperate with Christ is this: The line between what we shall eat and what we shall not, will not be between clean and unclean, nor between meats and vegetables, but between those things that are adapted to Community living and those that are not. I would like to see that principle clearly defined and as fast as possible put into practice among us. Still another foundation principle is that the things best adapted to Community are the least expensive. We should put ourselves on a scale of living that is accessible to the great part of mankind. Luxuries will either be cut off by the Community or they will be taken into this Church and given to all." With this inspiring talk, the men of war rallied for a last desperate assault on the tobacco Bastille in all the Communities—Oneida, Putney, Brooklyn, and Newark. Soon a breach was made. Noyes and Daniel Nash at Brooklyn, we are told, left the crumbling walls without injury on the very day of the above Home Talk. On December 23, 1853, a message was flashed: 'Oneida uses no tobacco!' A shout of victory and thanksgiving went up from all the Communities."

"A strong, sensible writer says a sharp thing and a true one for boys who use tobacco in the *Oneida Dispatch* in April 1868, in 'Boys Using Tobacco.' 'It has utterly ruined thousands of boys. It tends to the softening and weakening of the bones, and it greatly injures the brain, the spinal marrow, and the whole nervous fluid. A boy who smokes early and frequently, or in any way uses large quantities of tobacco, is never known to make a man of much energy, and generally lacks muscular and physical as well as mental power. It injures the teeth. It produces an unhealthy state of the lungs, hurts the stomach, and blasts the brain and nerves. We would particularly warn boys who want to be anything in the world, to shun tobacco as a most baneful poison.'"

January 4, 1869, *Circular* News: "Someone has calculated that the people of the United States spend annually for tobacco and cigars nearly enough money to pay the interest on the national debt."

"Our Brooklyn journalist writes that an intelligent, respectable-looking man (probably a mechanic) came in and called for some issues of the *Circular*. 'Which would you like?' we asked.

"'Those that have the articles about tobacco; I'm going to send them to a friend of mine who uses tobacco and see if I can persuade him to leave it off.'

"'Have you been leaving it off?'

"'Yes, I've nearly ruined myself smoking. My nerves were all shattered. I had palpitation of the heart so badly that I did not know but I should drop down dead in the streets some day. I read your paper in the Cooper Reading-Room and noticed your articles on tobacco. I'd been thinking about leaving off smoking, and the testimony I found in the Circular encouraged me to try.'

"'How do you succeed?'

"'It has been several weeks since I began the trial and I have not yet overcome the temptation, so in walking Broadway, it is a great luxury to follow in the smoke of a smoker and get a mouthful of his smoke.'"

"Poor man! God help him! Meager encouragement and help will he find on Broadway to enable him to get his liberty. At a wedding in Providence, before it was too late, the bride proposed an amendment to the ceremony that the groom should agree to eschew smoking, the April 1868 *Circular* noted. With the good sense that had led the youth so far on toward matrimony, he allowed that he could do without a wife more comfortably than without a pipe or cigar. The bride bolted and the wedding ended. A correspondent writes us that there is an old man who insists that the Bible sustains tobacco-chewing. When asked for the passage, he refers to Revelation 22:11—'*He that is filthy let him be filthy still.*'"

"Dear Friends: The tobacco principality blunts the finer susceptibilities of the human race—weakens the bond of union between man and woman, entails disease and misery upon millions yet unborn, robs the widow and fatherless, and keeps souls besotted with the filth of the world," writes E. Y., a reader of our *Circular* from Fontana, New Mexico, in December, 1871. "This tobacco principality is one of the most powerful allies of the ruler of the kingdom of darkness, when we consider the almost universal thralldom of the human family it has occasioned. I found that it was useless quarreling with the weed or our appetites; that the battle must be between the principality of which tobacco is but the servant, and him who having conquered principalities and powers, is exalted to the right hand of God. Confessing Christ drove the vanquished foe away. The tobacco principality has rolled up its tent and departed under cover of smoke and darkness. An earnest confession was good for my soul in this battle with principalities and powers. You've opened a door to the hidden treasures of the Bible that no man can shut; we've been taught by you to understand and love that blessed book. Since we commenced reading the *Circular* in earnest, we've had better success in everyday life and in business. Debts that have pressed us on all sides have gradually dwindled away until we feel that in another year, we shall be paying subscribers. Disease, too, has had less hold upon us; when sickness has occurred, faithful resistance has driven the demon away. Thus dear friends, another link is forged that binds us together, so that although we may never see one another in the flesh, yet a time of union awaits us somewhere in the eternal future."

"A young man was told that he had received a valuable education in the Community that he never would have received at college or anywhere else—how to overcome his appetite for tobacco. 'Only in the Community would he have got rid of that bondage. In college it would have been perpetuated; he would have become a hopeless slave to the habit.' This was part of a general criticism of J: 'The education of his heart, spirit, and temper in the Community is worth more to him than any amount of school-learning. If he'd received a college education, it would not have helped his temper or helped him to overcome evil of any kind. A fiery, rebellious element in his nature makes him a rowdy—a reckless dare-devil. If the Community succeeds in making him a quiet, good-natured, well-behaved man, it will succeed in giving him the best education he can get in this world. I expect he will graduate at last with honor.'"

"I shall always hate tobacco for the simple reason that it is an enemy to all natural appetite; a healthy life, whether of the soul or the body, has a good appetite," Noyes shared in his Home Talk, *Healthy Appetite*. "That means that it has good digestion—a hearty strength to take hold of all things that are presented to it, and can analyze and digest them, and appropriate the good and cast off the evil. If we desire to nourish our life, so that it shall become assimilated to God's life and partake of God's immortality, we must know how to train ourselves to this universal healthy appetite. All our enjoyments—enjoyment of food, of intellectual pleasures, of love in all its forms—is the enjoyment of God. By giving yourself to any beautiful sensation, however small, you more than double it—every time you touch good and enjoy it, you touch God; and there are infinite depths there, however small the surface may appear. All is God-filled, and our attraction to the creation is really the call of the Divine."

A GIRDLING AXE FOR THE COFFEE TREE

"In spring of 1852, the Brooklyn, Putney, and Wallingford Communities began to experiment with pleasurably abstaining from coffee and tea for the present. Noyes said he would allow no legal restraint in the matter, but neither would he submit to the tyranny of habit. John Miller at the Oneida Community wrote to George Cragin in Brooklyn, 'We contrive to enjoy our fast from tea and coffee, though we find that we were more in bondage to it than we were aware of. It has really been a more serious matter than leaving off tobacco. Our experience has already convinced us that a fast of this kind is necessary. I have no quarrel with tea and coffee, and believe that they are among the good things that God gives us, but I will not be brought under the power of anything. There were not more than a dozen cups of tea drunk last night and the same number of cups of coffee this morning, though it was passed to all and all were free to drink it. A cup of coffee was carried the whole length of the long table without finding market this morning. It is interesting to see a whole Community cheerfully consent to such denial for the truth's sake. The spirit I've seen manifested on this issue has given me a new love for the family.'"

"The gospel method of reform may be compared to the girdling of trees; a tree is dead when it is girdled, though it may stand for some time and look like a living tree," wrote Noyes in January 1854 in a Home Talk that began the serious consideration of total abstention. "This is the way we handled the tobacco principality. We girdled it last summer, and this winter the wind blew it over. What do you think of the expediency of girdling the love of tea and coffee? They seem to have trouble with that tree at Oneida. They are daily finding out that the tobacco spirit has run into the coffee-bag. I had an apprehension, when the tobacco question came up, that it would not end there. My theory has been that narcotics and stimulants are naturally connected, and I've thought that when the Lord called us to quit tobacco he would probably be seeking a general breaking up of the use of such things. People resort to narcotics and stimulants mostly because they have nothing else to do that pleases them. As God is putting into our hearts the great purpose of establishing a daily press, it will be easy for us to quiet our sensual appetites. I covet a state in which I have no attachment to anything, but could live comfortably on parched corn; at the same time I would be free to use the luxuries of the world if they came to hand. In aspiring to be a man of God, a thorough impressibility to inspiration is most important, and this involves great freedom from habit.

"It is my ambition to have no habits that will interfere with my receiving God's spirit and obeying its orders," Noyes in his Home Talk *Without Impediment* continued this important theme in May 8, 1865. "If we have habits of self-indulgence that make certain circumstances absolutely necessary to our comfort, if we are accustomed to the kindness of friends in the same dependent way, and if we're in bondage to love and fellowship so they constitute an essential of our everyday life—all such habits come between us and God and make us hard of hearing like a partition between us and his voice. A person listening through a partition will hear indistinctly, and only part of the time. God can give us very few orders if he finds us in such limitation. I wish to be in a state where I can receive a good many orders. I do not count it any privilege to be in a condition where God cannot use me. I want to be in a condition where he can get the greatest amount of good out of me, and thus I want to be free from habits that hinder him from speaking to me freely and me from thoroughly understanding and obeying him. I want to be without impediment. In a great gathering as we have, where affection is a far more powerful element than in ordinary families, the tendency of natural affection is to bring one in bondage to particular circumstances and a routine of life—to put individuals under impediment and so obstruct inspiration. My purpose is to train myself and the whole Community to freedom from habit and routine, and the bondage of each other's affection, until all are freed to hear and obey God without being bound by affections or circumstances. Such is the liberty of the Kingdom of Heaven.

"When Christ told the young man to sell all and give to the poor, and follow him, it was a call to a loftier education—Christ could not do anything with him, encumbered with his habits of wealth. The young man of the aristocracy was in reality in a low, contracted, vulgar state of life, and Christ called him to something noble and dignified. If a military commander is under a load of habits, there is a chronic obstruction in his mind to bright ideas and plans. One must be freed of all personal considerations to be in a condition of mind to conceive great plans. Christ came right out of heaven, a pure specimen of the spirit there, no self-indulgence, no shrinking from rugged work or from suffering, or death. I think that's what is meant by perfection in the Bible. It is said of Christ, 'Though he were a son, yet learned he obedience by the things he suffered; and being made perfect, he became the author of eternal salvation unto all them that obey him.' I think he worked his nature by discipline and suffering into a state where he was able to hear with minute accuracy the dictates of inspiration, and obey them. I believe that the Lord will show us and help us to do one thing after another that will directly contribute to the success of our enterprise. I shall go into any kind of temperance that seems necessary, from *attraction* and not from legality."

In February 1854, the Community decided to end having daily coffee and tea. "The report of your remarks on the subject of prayer met a warm response in my heart and in the heart of the Community. I felt a desire to tell you my experience about leaving off tea and coffee," shared John Miller with Noyes about giving up coffee on March 9th: "I was conscious of a growing appetite for both drinks. When we learned a week ago that the Brooklyn family had abandoned the use of tea and coffee, I made up my mind at once to do the same. I confess it was something of a trial and seemed anything but attractive. During a weeklong fast from these drinks I suffered a good deal in my body and had a hankering for coffee till the last day of the fast. That morning I awoke early and was up some time before the bell rang, with an unusual appetite for coffee with breakfast. I knew I could go down to the table and willfully refuse to drink it and put myself under law, but this I could not bear to do. I went to God in earnest prayer for deliverance with a determination not to go to breakfast till I could go a free man. It was nearly eight o'clock when I went down, but my appetite for coffee was entirely removed, and I have not enjoyed my breakfast so well for a month as I did that morning. I have enjoyed my meals better ever since, and have not had the least appetite for tea or coffee. In my meditations that morning I felt clearly that there was no need of suffering in my body as I did before, and I asked God for such a victory over habit that I could make any change that was called for and not suffer by it. I have been conscious that my prayer was answered, for I am not aware of the least suffering in consequence of the change. During our fast of a week I wanted something for a substitute and sometimes took hot water with milk and sugar, and sometimes milk, but I've taken pure, cold water, and have had no appetite for anything else. When I gained a victory over coffee, I commenced drinking again one cup or less from choice and not from necessity. Since that time I have held the habit loosely, bearing in mind constantly that the tea and coffee trees were both girdled and must die soon."

For the first two or three years, the Community had coffee and tea only once in six or eight weeks, but gradually their consumption increased and became the chief table attraction. "A question from the kitchen five years later asked the family whether they'd like coffee oftener than once a week. No. There was unanimity of feeling: coffee once a week, cocoa and tea once a week, and abolish coffee at parties. Parties have been quite a fashion for a year or two—testimonial parties to individuals or groups for eminent services, congratulatory parties on the completion of some piece of work, birthday parties, etc., and coffee has been a favorite beverage at these honorary feasts. We concluded to stop the use of it in this way and make a clean matter of drinking it only once a week. A year later, the steward stated that there was an unusual consumption of coffee and tea lately by individuals and at select social gatherings. He suggested that the once-a-week resolution made six years ago be formally annulled if it was not to be observed. A discussion revealed that the backsliding was caused by giving their visitors coffee or tea—they had visitors all the time—and the tempting aromas of the coffeepot and teapot make it very natural to covet these stimulants. They discussed raising their standard to that which they offered visitors, or bringing down the visitor's standard to the family standard. One principle was clear, that they should aim to make the Community fare good enough for their visitors. Two weeks later, coffee and tea were banished from the premises by a unanimous vote. Not long after we abolished tea, Mrs. F., a great devotee of the cheering cup, had a racking headache and was tossing on the bed, soliloquizing as some folks do in such a condition: "Oh!" said she, "I do confess Christ in my head—but nothing except tea will cure it." Tea often takes the credit of curing headaches—which its habitual use has originally inflicted.

AVOIDING NEGATIVE INFLUENCES, TO BE ALL GOD CAN MAKE US

"In life a thousand different occupations, a thousand courses may be taken, from which everyone is compelled to choose," Noyes wrote in *The Light of Life*. "The secret of wisdom is in making the best choice, choosing the occupation for which s/he is best adapted; and to do that, one must have wisdom to withdraw from others. There are multitudes of persons from whom we must choose our friends and associates; whom shall we connect ourselves with and allow social influence over us? How shall we act in the midst of social influences to avoid bad influences? It is all-important that we know how to choose the myriad books and papers that will be most profitable to read, and no others. The difficulties we experience at a County Fair symbolize our life—to what will we give our attention amidst the great multiplicity of objects? Now contemplate the deeper recesses of our being—the world of thought: to let the mind be attracted by everything is to scatter our thoughts and destroy our power and fruitfulness. I feel that I have no more right to think in a scattered way than I have to abandon myself to any form of dissipation. I must have a mind that will pursue the right trains of thought in business, in the curiosities of life, in the associations of life, in literature, and in reflection.

The principle that is the pole-star to guide us through this vast labyrinth is that intelligence is desirable only so far as it is the servant of love. Our education should be strictly guided to making ourselves vehicles of the love of God. I conceive of myself in an eternity of interests and an infinity of worlds, and it will not do for me to commit myself to chance circumstances and external influences. *Keep thy heart with all diligence, for out of it are the issues of life.*"—Prov 4:23. How can we sail through this immensity of things without a pilot? I answer: By an appeal to Omniscience. To think of setting sail on such an ocean of attractions and temptations without virtual omniscience is more absurd than it would be for children to put to sea in an open boat. To get into communication with omniscience is the hope of the gospel: *You have no need that anyone should teach you; his anointing teaches you about all things*, 1 John 2:27. Omniscience is indispensable to being perfect mediums of the love of God and acting rightly in all things; that I can have in Christ. God only requires that we submit ourselves to him with the understanding that the influences of his Spirit shall be our controlling inducement in all things; that we shall always stand in a consulting spirit toward him—always in the attitude of prayer. We must allow the Spirit of God to come in and govern our attention. To do this we must be in a sober, chastened state of mind—one in which we do not feel that all we can do, think, read, and see is gain to us, but feel that it is our delight to withdraw ourselves from all external inducements day by day, and offer ourselves to the influences of God."

"If a young person chooses for his society chiefly those below him in refinement and intelligence," Carrie Macknet Woolworth wrote in the April 1, 1872, *Circular*, "he will lose the delicate sensibilities he once had and acquire the habits of thought and feeling of his coarse associates. Let's apply the same practical wisdom and discrimination in selecting the books and papers we read that we do in choosing our associates. Even Solomon with his vast experience could not have dreamed of the floods of books and newspapers that now afflict us. Printing, which has brought us the Bible, has also developed this new evil under the sun. A book or newspaper may be vulgar, profane, or cynical, introduce a sly sneer at religion or an artful apology for unbelief, and you are a receptacle to receive its contents whether good or bad; so let us choose carefully and fastidiously what books we will admit to our company."

"When I was a boy of fifteen with a taste for reading," wrote Horace Perry in the April 20, 1868, *Circular*, "I was unwisely left by my friends to seek whatever mental food might please my boyish fancy and I devoured books without any reference to the spirit that I was taking into my life. At that point, an influence for either good or ill could be readily brought to bear upon me. At that formative period, a young person most needs wise counsel and if necessary, a strong hand to guide him. My amative powers had just awakened into life, and very naturally I drifted into the maelstrom of literature that so greedily engulfs the thoughts and attention of the young of either sex. There is one book in particular that I look back to as the curse of my life. The landlord of a hotel in my native village had a literary turn of mind and loaned me a large volume of poetry, written by a celebrated English bard. My parents had died, but my friends took especial care to warn me against the seductive influences of the liquors this landlord sold at his bar. In this respect they succeeded, for in temperance matters I was a Pharisee of the Pharisees. It would have been better for me to have drunk a barrel of vile liquors than to have read that volume, one that is in the library of nearly everyone of any literary pretension. I reveled in the glowing verse, and drank with avidity from the poisoned cup. I see that when I finished that volume, my whole moral nature had suffered terribly. False love and worse lust took undisputed possession of my soul; many reflecting people will remember when the reading of a single book produced a great lasting effect on their character for good or ill. They will be able to trace to such reading the introduction of a spiritual influence into their heart and life that may have likely revolutionized their whole career. If my experience shall be the means of inducing parents and guardians to exercise vigilance in guiding the literary taste of those under their care, my suffering from reading false literature will not have been in vain."

Noyes distrusted pretentious façades of literary art—the Spirit must vitalize poetry. Blake spoke a language of the heart and spirit; eight columns of the May 9, 1864,

Circular were devoted to him. Noyes himself preferred to live in the spirit: "The best part of truth is unspeakable. I can see or feel at a flash a sum of truth that is perfectly legible to me, and yet that cannot be expressed in words. If these spirit-openings could be translated into words, a mountain of books would not contain them. To see things by intuition," Noyes said, "we shall find that there *is* another utterance—a language of the heart and spirit, that will condense volumes into one instantaneous glance."

"One other reading of a single volume wrought a very bad effect on my mind and heart at age twenty-one," Horace Perry continued. "God had brought influences upon my conscience that checked the previous evil that had come upon me. I had become a member of a church in my native village and was away from home at a boarding-school. I had little comprehension of the deep spiritual truths of the Bible but had great respect for its teachings, and had taken the first and very important step in confessing Christ publicly. I looked at the Bible from a materialistic point of view and that fact fitted me to become the easy prey of a writer who waged war against the Bible from the same standpoint. A fellow student handed me a volume written by an English infidel, questioning whether I'd dare read it. Forgetting the great damage done to me previously from reading a single volume, I said that I was not afraid to read any book; I devoured its contents and when finished, I threw the Bible overboard. I wandered for several years in the mazes and fogs of infidelity until, reading Mr. Noyes's writings and the *Circular*, I learned to appreciate the Bible as I'd never before done. I consider it to be of the greatest importance that young persons and everyone should jealously guard themselves from taking evil influences into their hearts from books or even some newspapers that are filled to a great extent with minute details of crime of all kinds. Editors and publishers ignore the fact that human nature is very liable to be changed into that which it gazes upon."

"Dear Children:—I will tell you a story," said Mary Cragin, reported in the February 4, 1848, *Circular*. "There is a boy here named George, a big boy. Another boy coaxed him to buy a book, and I read it and found that it was a long story about wicked folks, thieves, and liars and wicked men and women. We think it's best to talk and read about good folks. I told George this and advised him not to read it, and his mother said she wished it was burned up. It was a pretty looking book, and he thought he would like very much to read it. However, his love for his mother was stronger than his love for the book, and I opened the stove and in went the foolish book and it burned up with a furious blaze."

Noyes concluded early on that many newspapers circulated and represented the acrid selfish spirit of the world. "We see how the popular way of making newspapers develops; our Community journalists are always anxious for news that's sharp and racy and will produce a sensation. If I were a journalist I would try to deal only in what is true, and then my sensational items would have a sharper tang. I hope we'll have our fun criticizing newspapers and teaching ourselves to hate inaccuracy and unfaithfulness. It has been our duty to acquaint ourselves with newspapers; our profession and projects have demanded the sacrifice. But we've gained the general information and literary helps that we needed long enough to last us for some time. After having breakfasted, dined, and supped for years on newspaper poison, it is good to consider fasting from newspaper fare. Try it for a week and see if you don't all feel better—why shouldn't we turn our whole attention to our business of creating a new literature that shall be a medium of life and joy?"

"We have just risen from the dinner-table where we had a refreshing laugh in reviewing a scene that occurred this morning," Harriet Noyes wrote from Brooklyn to Charlotte Miller. "We gathered up newspapers in the sitting-room and had a game of ball with them. George expressed his disgust by kicking one of them, whereupon others joined and flung and kicked the papers about the room right merrily. Although it lasted but a minute or two, it was an expression of feeling that cleared the atmosphere."

"I sat near two friends recently," Seymour Nash wrote in the April 15, 1872, *Circular.* "one of whom was absorbed in the newspaper. He threw it down and with a look of disgust, said: "When there are so many good people in the world with characters that everyone desires to emulate, why should newspapers—which are mediums of good or evil—be filled with accounts of those who are disgracing themselves and their country by their misdeeds?"

"True," answered the other, "Why talk and write of evil when there's so much good to look at every day if we would only notice it. With their attention drawn to the beauties of truth and good, our young people would find a new desire growing in their hearts to free themselves from evil thoughts; evil deeds would be rarer. If we could get the standard of good raised in our newspapers, the necessity for speaking of evil would gradually die out. Evil would hide in the dark places of the earth, if there were no one to speak it. Evil is perpetuated by constant attention to it. Good surely has a better chance."

"Some persons will object on the ground that nothing succeeds that does not create a sensation," answered his companion. "Granted. But which makes the greater and more lasting sensation, rascalities of James Fisk Jr. or the inventions of James Watt? The characters of many in a city like New York would be changed in a short time if the standard of reading matter were elevated. I believe that good has many more charms than evil."

"So do I. Who knows the effect it would have on the rising generation? Who knows what talents lie hidden away that might be brought to light, if those who spend much time recording evil should seek out modest geniuses who only need a little encouragement to make themselves known to fame? How many germs of thought now unheard-of might add to newspapers the beauty they lack! Many people read only newspapers, and their thoughts, perverted by what they read, govern to a great extent their lives."

"How shall we remedy all this?"

"Conclude that there's much good in the world; notice it everywhere, hunt it up, talk about it, write about it, and encourage everyone to do likewise. Then our young folks will feel that good is at a premium and that their success in life depends upon their keeping up to the standard. Gradually every thought and wish of their lives will conform themselves to the highest truth. Their childhood will be controlled by those whose purpose will be to encourage good in them. The studies of their youth will be pursued not from motives of false ambition, but with the intention of cultivating their talents for God and for his family. Business and even pursuit of life will be carried on in an unselfish way that will yield more profit to those who engage in them than selfishness can hope to reap."

"Let us insist on a new standard of newspaper literature! Evil will then soon hide its head for want of something to live upon. Who can estimate the effect on the character and lives of all God's children, to shut their eyes from the seeing of evil and cultivate a quick perception of everything that is good? Love will no longer be governed by passion but by principle."

"A new periodical magazine, *The City*, is heralded by New York City papers with the criticism that it aims too high," the Community noted, "that the purest literary aliment is not appreciated. Articles in the monthly and weekly periodicals most read are those having the least merit, public taste requiring coarser literary food."

The Balanced Life

"Human health and peace depends on the right balance of our myriad faculties," Noyes stressed in his Home Talk, *Hygiene for the Head*. "The American people are especially subject to nervous disorders engendered by too much headwork. "The head, more than the rest of the being, is in communication with the external world and gets much involved; it would profit greatly by being withdrawn from the world from time to time by the influence of the heart. Our health and peace depend not on communication with the external world, but on communication with the internal world. The overworked head, worked greatly out of proportion to its actual merit in the scale of our faculties, gets into a false spiritual position; the true order of our faculties is inverted—the world prevails over the head, and the head prevails over the heart. The heart should have a firm hold on God; then God would rule the heart, the heart would rule the head, and ultimately the head would rule the external world. Physicians say that the right equilibrium must be established by more exercise of body. I have no confidence in keeping balance between our faculties by mere exercise of the limbs, except partially. The real loss of balance is not between the head and the external, muscular life but between the head and the inner life. It must be restored by an increased action of the heart toward God until the heart is able to take possession of the head and lead it in moderation. What we want is not more exercise of the muscles, but wise hearts. A wise heart will make a wise head. A wise heart and a wise head will make a wise and happy body."

"Old Dr. Abernethy would often declare that three-quarters of the cases of disease brought to him were caused by stuffing and fretting," wrote George E. Cragin in the January 20, 1873, *Circular*. "He'd gruffly order his rich patient to 'eat less, sir; eat less and play more.' Consider the daily habits of many great merchants, bankers, and railroad managers. The intense activity of brain through twelve to sixteen hours of mental effort is only kept up by immense quantities of rich stimulating food and tobacco, with no exercise, little relaxation, and still less sleep until everything gives way in the final crash of body and mind, and the miserable victim of this high-pressure system is hurried into the insane asylum or the grave. Nearly all the managing officers of one of our largest railroad companies had been compelled to resign their positions, within a few months, a newspaper reported, on account of ill health from overwork. This is only a polite way of telling half the truth. That such men are overworked there is no doubt, and there is still less doubt that one cause of their loss of health could be given in the words of Abernethy, 'Too much stuffing and fretting.' Cramming the brain just before college examinations is too often accompanied with cramming the stomach with rich, stimulating, highly seasoned food, and indigestion. Together with lack of exercise and insufficient sleep, this will soon break down the strongest constitution. We have colleges for expanding the brains of our young people; we have gymnasiums for drilling the muscles; will not someone found a school of hygiene for teaching the young as well as the old how to keep their health before they lose it? Prevention is better than cure."

"When we pray *Lead us not into temptation*, Christ teaches us to proportion our use of this world to our spiritual strength, [which] depends on our digestive power, to be kept from using any more of this world than we can thoroughly assimilate," Noyes advised in his Home Talk, *Spiritual Digestion*. "We do not give to an infant strong meat that we can digest with perfect safety. There is a digestive power that can spiritualize and sanctify everything. The healthy human being is omnivorous in the greatest sense—morally, intellectually, and physically—he has an eager desire for everything, God included and God principally. So you can judge what your state of health is by finding out what your appetites are. I hold that it is a real sinking of health in me when I have lost my attraction for even so small a thing as fishing. As we lose our appetite for one thing after another, we grow old, and really lose our health. One who loves ardent spirits has a great loss of appetite in all other directions, and the same thing occurs in one who becomes too absorbed in any special pursuit and loses appetite for other good things. A healthy appetite is not merely an attraction inherent in our natural life, but it is an inspiration—a breeze of the life that breathes through all existence. As long as our desires are natural, the great spirit of the living God himself dwells in us, and breathes through us, and makes us desire good things.

"God's will concerning us is that we should love everything that is good, and all things in their due proportion," Noyes wrote in the *Circular* in November 1871. He taught the Community that God is present in everything. "The nearer we can keep ourselves to the standard of appetite we had when we were children, the better it will be for us. There is no sight in this world more melancholy than that of a man who has worked all appetite out of himself and is sick of everything. He is weary of the sun, and has no pleasure in the singing of the birds, in the flowers of the field, nor in anything else that is naturally pleasant. Creation is an aperture onto the ocean of Divine being, through which man can reach and enjoy the love of God. Except ye be converted and become as little children, ye shall in no wise enter into the kingdom of heaven. I take that to mean, we must go back to the natural, pure, simple life before we were perverted with feverish, false appetites. True pleasure and happiness transcend the sensualist's frenetic but fruitless pursuit of happiness."

10

Humanizing Work: By Their Fruit You Shall Know Them

"The overseer system that exacts so many hours of labor, whether there is a spirit for it or not," wrote Noyes, "is totally discarded in the Community. "We depend on a free, inspired appetite for work. We have a notion that it is possible to really hoodwink the devil who knows how to find you in the tyrants of habit and routine, when he thinks he has got you started on some track where he will be sure to find you for all time, by suddenly switching off and making him lose the scent. I judge that about six hours of labor is as much as anybody ought to do on hygienic principles," Noyes said. "Labor reformers talk about eight hours, but I would reduce working hours to six between eight o'clock and three. A large association working in that way would accomplish more than under the eight or ten hour system. This provides hours for study, recreation, creativity, social interaction, eating and sleep. With this arrangement we can support ourselves well, do all the necessary business, and carry on home education. Everyone can get a liberal education and pay as he goes."

Many innovations were required to accomplish these grand goals to liberate the creativity and potential of the human spirit, which is capable of developing a vast array of talents, skills, and interests. The Community constantly rotated the occupations of their many businesses and myriad housekeeping tasks, child care, and farming. Men did so-called women's work and vice versa. "A typical day on January 22, 1855, describes two happy hours sharing the washing of all the clothes, then breakfast and half an hour of Bible study, then off to the barn, shops, woods, mill, and printing-office. Everyone including girls and boys worked hard outdoors, digging, hoeing, and weeding; all winter the men and boys worked in the barns and at the wood-pile. Yet everyone worked cheerfully at mundane tasks; dishwashers seemed as happy and were as much respected as those who managed the Community's businesses.

"We favor the mingling of the sexes in labor, in view of its great practical benefit," the October 1853 *Circular* reported, "but we find that the spirit of the world is deadly opposed to this innovation." Community men and women, and often older boys and girls, worked together in the mill, the machine and printing shops, at the carpenter's bench, in the manufacture of traveling bags and silk thread, the preserving of fruits, and many other work bees. Even the most odious or monotonous tasks became downright fun by having a bee, where a large number of men and women would volunteer for the upcoming task.

A member reads to the group; large numbers of men, women, and often youth volunteer for tasks, known as work bees. Six hours of labor a day is ideal, said Noyes, leaving much time for full human development in study, prayer, creativity, sociability, recreation, and good sleep."

"Dinner was served at noon precisely in the first decades. Mr. Reynolds and Mrs. Whitfield appeared in the parlor at 1:00 p.m. with piles of carpet-bag material for the carpet-bag bee, and few were absent. Doors and windows were opened for ventilation and a hundred needles were put in operation by old and young, men and women; young people waited with threaded needles, and some formed a braiding group for palm-leaf hats. At 2:00 p.m. they enjoyed a song and those who worked elsewhere left, the rest continuing for another hour. Supper was at 5:15 p.m. and afterword, classes met for study and recitation. Business consultations followed and plans were made for the industries of tomorrow. At 8:00 p.m. the evening meeting commenced, reading correspondence from branch communities, business and newspaper reports, then discussion and religious testimony until 9:00 p.m. A new list of both men and women for the boot-blacking business was called for and a long list was forthcoming, with more women than men. Weekly financial reports generally showed that the income of the Community exceeded its expenses in a satisfactory ratio."

MULTITASKING A JOY IN THE COMMUNITY

"Our Community members are destined to learn to do all things that man or woman ought to do, and do them well," the *Circular* informs us. "If one has formed an exclusive attachment toward one profession, trade, or calling, and possesses no attraction for others or any desire to cultivate them, the Community is no place for him/her. An over-ruling Providence seems to favor our Community policy requiring that able-bodied members learn to do good work at a dozen different trades. Regarding Community life as educational in the broadest sense, the variety of businesses necessarily carried on are well calculated to develop and discipline all the faculties of body and mind. Today, for instance, young H., an industrious expert in the use of edge tools, may be recognized as the managing foreman of a group of carpenters who are at work on the new wing of our dwelling. But tomorrow he is in the basement of the Tontine dyeing silk among numerous vats—or learning that valuable art. Geometry and drawing were his favorite mental studies as a carpenter, but on learning how to dye well, he will have a new interest in a practical knowledge of chemistry. In this way changes frequently occur; and, having freedom to make them, two important objects are gained, namely, a broader education of the members, and greater perfection in the manufacturing and mechanical arts.

"The idea may suggest itself that by frequently shifting persons from one business to another, the reverse of the highest attainments in skilled labor would result, but such has not been the fact. Indeed, one object in making these changes is to secure the right man for the right place, which, in ordinary society, could not well be done. Our business may be divided among our men. Mr. Inslee is very fond of his factory work but has always been bothered by having to give attention to outside concerns, getting orders, and making contracts; Mr. Miller on the other hand is exactly suited by this part of the business. We have discovered that fitness for a situation, and inspiration to fill it wisely, go hand in hand. The predecessor of H. in the dye-room would in all probability have been nothing more than an ordinary dyer, had he continued in the profession fifty years, not possessing the requisite genius for the art; but in some other calling, he may prove himself an adept.

"Having the opportunity to frequently change employments not only relieves the hardship of following an occupation after the taste for it has ceased, but it gives freshness to every department and opens the way for inspiration," notes the September 21, 1868, *Circular*. "Although it may seem a waste of talent for a machinist to be looking after milk, a carpenter to work in a kitchen, or a mechanic to pare potatoes, experience proves that such talent brings improvements where they may not reach if those departments were regarded as exclusively the province of men or women. A first-class joiner who worked in the kitchen invented a mop wringer that saves a world of work, and he also introduced a system of washing potatoes by means of a circular cage revolving in water; a young mechanic from the trap-shop saw that by introducing pieces of brick into the circular cage, potatoes can be rid of their jackets on the same principle by which we torn rust from iron. Bricks rub the potatoes while revolving and their skins are taken off more completely than by paring, with considerably less labor and much saving of the nutritious parts of the potato. Mr. Burt has beat the world with his omni-adjustable corn-cutter, and Mr. Thacker has produced a triumphant rake-hoe."

"Should an emergency or other pressing business occur, members readily stop working in one industry and help in another. You can turn out the trap-makers for a day's campaign against the weeds in the cornfield—result, twenty acres hoed at a stroke; the silk-spinners take a hand at strawberry picking—one hundred bushels of the fruit saved in the nick of time! Our members may be found at work printing, carpentering, hay-making, and harvesting strawberries all in the same day—one of the clear gains of Community organization."

Frank's Story

In just two years the Community expanded to 205 members who were not only idealistic but practical and industrious. They came to the Community as shoemakers, storekeepers, farmers, printers, manufacturers, architects, and bookkeepers. "My widowed mother brought me to the Community when I was ten years old," wrote Frank Wayland-Smith. "I well remember that sunny afternoon in September 1851 when we clambered out of the stagecoach and walked up the lawn past the great butternut tree to the mansion. I caught sight of a group of boys and girls playing merrily with little wheel-barrows, wagons, and hoops, and I was uneasy until I was allowed to join them. The Community family was comparatively poor in those days, and the children did not have all the advantages they now have. We were put to school several hours a day with a first-rate teacher who took us into the woods and fields and told us many interesting things about nature. We were taught intricate dances and to sing. We had small chores to do—getting a supply of kindling material and wood from the woodshed for stoves in the kitchen and other public rooms. The Community owned a saw-mill then, as almost all Communities do at first, and boys packed into bundles the shingles that the men sawed out. When we picked strawberries for the first time, our superintendent Mr. Perry waited a long time for me to hand in a full quart; he good-naturedly said that he guessed I ate rather more than I picked! I had not been accustomed to strawberries, and was not very skillful in saving them. We painted the horse-barn; that was capital fun. We daubed as much as we liked and studied other arts besides painting.

"We weren't allowed to quarrel; if we got angry or fought, we were criticized or punished. What most cured us of quarreling was that the older folks set us a good example. They rarely argued, for everything tended toward peace and good-nature.

In the outside world, men teach boys not to smoke or chew or drink, but they do it themselves. Every boy means to do as he sees the men do, just as soon as he can. If fathers throw away half-smoked cigars the boys will finish them. Community boys do not swear, because they never hear older folks swear or use bad language.

"My father was an amateur musician. He played the violin, taught singing school, and led the choir in church. I must have inherited a tendency for music, for I was seized with a desire to play on the violin. The man who was then Father at the children's house had a violin, and kindly allowed me to take it and taught me how to begin. I found an old music book and commenced scraping away on a tune called "What Fairy-like Music," picking it out note-by-note. In two weeks I'd mastered the first four bars. The strain of acquiring them had been so great that I relaxed and contented myself with playing these four bars over and over. I imagined I'd done a pretty fine thing, and made myself rather conspicuous with my achievement until I heard one of the ladies whose nerves it seems I'd overtaxed, speak about *that noise* as dreadful! Wholesome truths often have a bitter twang. Her remark opened my eyes to the fact that my music was not particularly fairy-like, and it also nerved me to learn another four bars. This made my performance somewhat more endurable, so I was encouraged and went ahead. Several other boys learned to play on the violin, flute, and other instruments about the same time.

"We went to school, did little jobs, and then I was assigned to work in the trap-shop at age fourteen. I began by learning to cut threads on the jaw posts of the traps, to drill, and to sweep the shop. They decided to make chains for the traps and I was taught to weld the wire links together at a little forge-fire on an anvil made expressly for the business. I was succeeded by another boy and went to work on the steel trap springs. There was some discipline in that. The great points to be learned were that steel is spoiled by over-heating or by hammering when too cold. Blacksmiths usually impress this latter point on beginners by repeating a rough old legend that only one blacksmith ever went to hell, and he was sent there for hammering cold iron. We did not use bellows such as blacksmiths ordinarily use, but had a blower driven by water-power, so all we had to do was to open a valve. For a long time I was liable to forget myself after putting some springs in the fire and leave them there until they were burned, the fire all in a sparkle with melted steel. I continued to work in the trap-shop more or less for eight years. During this time I spent two or three summers on the farm and one in the horticultural department, where I was chiefly engaged in tending grape vines. On the farm I learned to mow with a scythe, to operate a horse-rake, and to dig ditches. I also milked cows night and morning.

"When I was twenty-one, we had an extensive period struggling with diphtheria. Our dairyman was suddenly prostrated one Sunday morning by the disease. As I was sunning myself on the portico of the new brick house, I was hailed by a member of the appropriating-help-committee who inquired if I was willing to act as dairyman until Uncle Heman (Kinsley) recovered from diphtheria. I agreed to do so and was rigged out with a long white apron, engaged in straining milk. Then followed churning, and I became gradually intelligent on the subject of cream, sweet and sour. This pleasant occupation lasted only a month, because Uncle Heman recovered and resumed his place. A vacancy in the house-cleaning corps occurred at that precise time, and I filled it. The women of the corps were thorough Yankee housekeepers and had just begun the fall campaign. What zeal they manifested! I served an apprenticeship of four weeks at the business, and learned a lesson. The principal duties were bringing clean water, taking up and putting down carpets, mounting on a high stool and scrubbing remote portions of the woodwork, and sweeping down some real and many imaginary cobwebs. I'm afflicted with a slight constitutional apathy on this subject, but I managed to throw so much enthusiasm into these performances that I drew from the women an occasional eulogium. When the whole house had finally been gone over, as if to reward me for trials undergone, I was installed as subordinate bookkeeper, a position I very much desired.

"Then followed a year and a half of writing out bills, copying them into the sales-book, writing the accounts of the hired workmen into their passbooks, selling refreshment tickets to summer visitors, and more. In May 1865, I was sent to our New York Agency as bookkeeper and learned how banks do business. I also paid bills, made collections, and sold silk. Before we left for New York, I took a short course of lessons of Mr. Poznanski, the violinist. Having played the violin in the Community orchestra for several years before going to New York, I was prepared to appreciate this. I hope I've since entertained people enough to counterbalance the misery they endured while I was learning. I returned to Oneida with other Agency men in 1868, and gravitated into the trap shop as foreman of the finishing department, alternating with a comrade, each of us having a half day for education. Thus you see I have been successively, boy, trap-maker, farmer, horticulturist, dairyman, house-cleaner, and bookkeeper. Most of the other boys have progressed through an equal number of diverse employments and some through many more, and of higher rank. The fashion of change and rotation in business is so popular in the Community, that I have every prospect of sometime becoming house-builder, wagon-maker, dentist, weaver of silks, and so on, the acquirements depending mainly on my enterprise and faithfulness." Frank Wayland-Smith's diaries have many resolutions, such as *do what I can* and *love is the most beautiful thing in the world*.

"Much irksome work was performed by bees for planting, hoeing, cutting, and husking corn; bees for mowing, spreading, turning, and raking hay; bees for picking strawberries, raspberries, currants, and peas; bees for weeding onions, beets, and carrots; bees for building fence and tearing down fence; bees for digging, spading, and wheeling dirt; bees for washing, hanging out, and ironing clothes; bees for any and every job—well attended by men, women, and children." That's a very long sentence from the June 9, 1873, *Circular*. "Frequently at the sound of fife and beat of drum (at first a tin pan), a long procession stepped briskly to the scene of action and shortly accomplished the desired result. Every afternoon the children spent an hour braiding palm-leaf hats, which Mr. Hall sold at retail in nearby country towns; every afternoon the grown folks spent an hour making carpet-bags. Five women and girls set the type for the *Circular*; three women with a man did the dairy work; five women and a man had charge of the children. Housework was divided into departments, a suitable number of persons apportioned to each: eight women and two men did all the kitchen work, eight more did the regular laundry work, two women and a man did the tailoring, and bed-making, dining room work, dishwashing, and other chores were distributed among the rest. Many women went to the trap shop an hour or two each day, and in summer others tended the vegetable garden. We had no hired service then."

QUALITY IN ALL PURSUITS GAINS THE PRIZE

"The one rule of impartiality as civilization advances is that rewards should be proportioned to deeds," Noyes always reiterated, "and this rule will eventually purge competition of all personal ambition and strife and set every man to the task of accomplishing sincere, honest work. It is frankly acknowledged that the great point of competition in the commercial and business world should be—and to some extent is—not producing the cheapest goods at the lowest prices, but how to attain the highest excellence. Quality is more and more the criterion of judgment and the basis of successful competition. Shoddy is at a discount. Trade and commerce are compelled to adjust themselves in accordance with this standard. Putting every person on the basis of deeds excludes hypocrisy and deceit. Mere verbal representations, however voluble and plausible, will not suffice to win the reward. Let your works speak—let your deeds tell the story."

"Since the Civil War, commercial travelers are legion—up to sixty thousand traveling agents," wrote an Oneida Community agent in 1869. "On entering a store, it's common to find three or four of them ahead of you. In the quiet village of Amsterdam, New York, on October 18, 1869, the merchant told me that nine of my craft had come and gone, though my call was at 9:00 a.m. One buyer told me that he had more sales calls than customers. The situation as to morals is one of temptation and danger. A man may be very capable in driving bargains and effecting sales, thereby rendering himself popular and indispensable to his employers; but he must save his soul first and make money afterwards. The first requisite in selling goods is truthfulness. Your merchandise must be of good quality, otherwise the temptation is to misrepresent, and then the conscience becomes demoralized at once. Just here is the lee-shore of trade where moral shipwrecks are innumerable, and pecuniary disaster generally follows. I've known the agents of a certain house to sell weighted silk for un-weighted at enormous profits, simply because the buyer was ignorant, but an end comes to such games—the public learns the truth. That house is today hopelessly insolvent; its very name is suggestive of fraud. How can I mingle with and use the world in business, without abusing it or being contaminated by it? The answer is simple: by a soft heart and humility toward God and the universe, helped by our faithful friends' criticism at home. Few women were sent out because there was only a single long dress and hat then that was suitable for venturing out into the world.

"It is a rule that is recognized and enforced in proportion as we rise in the scale of civilization and refinement. The barbarian and savage win their rewards in the lower spheres of development through the arts of intrigue and cunning—by personal prowess and might makes right. That rewards shall be balanced by deeds greatly simplifies the business of life and the conditions of trade. It sets man on a course of spiritual improvement and animates him with the desire to perfect the quality of his productions. He need not concern himself about a market for his products, for they will create a market for themselves if he devotes himself with a single eye to insuring their quality. In pursuing this course he rises above all petty strife and competition with his fellows, and finds that the bounty is awarded to faithful, sincere endeavor, and that whoever has the purpose to excel by patient continuance in well-doing will gain the prize. This is not theory; it has been verified by much experience in the Community until it has become a settled and governing policy in all its affairs, whether pecuniary or otherwise. We find that this rule respecting rewards has a universal application, and must govern us in our dealings with God as well as with man—*whatsoever a man sows, that shall he also reap*. We find that it will also do away with proselytizing —*by their fruits ye shall know them*. If a man's work in religion, in social reconstruction, or anything else, has the ring of the true coin he need not blow a trumpet before him; no noisy heralding of his achievements is required, but his light will shine with a clear and steady flame, and men will take knowledge of him that he is building on a sure foundation. Believers as we are in the perfect gospel of Jesus Christ, nothing short of a perfect standard of execution in every branch of industry will satisfy our tastes or our principles."

"This note from a gentleman in Cleveland was received, and no better testimonial to the excellence of our preserved fruit could be given: 'The other day I bought a quart-can of cherries and brought it home without noting where it was put up; I took off the wrapping and discovered it had the Oneida Community label on it and wiping off the top, the revenue stamp on it had the cancelation *O. C, Oct. 2, 1866*, making it nearly six years old. I opened the can and found it contained yellow cherries, and the fruit was as sweet and perfect as it is possible for fruit to be.' An unexpected testimonial to the honest work of the Oneida Community! 'We have led the world in the preserving business; we've taught the farmers of Central New York how to raise fruit; and we have gained experience that will always enable us to supply our own table with the best of luxuries,' the September 21, 1868, *Circular* noted. 'This note made us think of the saying—*and their works do follow them*.'

"To learn a new trade, for the sake of usefulness to society, is almost equivalent to taking a new lease of life. Old habits are thrown off, and a fresh inspiration taken in. Most of our improved facilities for doing things in the various departments are the results of rotation in office and of learning new trades. Some trades offer so great a variety of things to be done that the artisan is constantly challenged to study new methods of doing them, thus bringing into exercise the full power of his inventive skill, which is both pleasurable and edifying. Workers in wood or iron—carpenters and machinists—are always learning something new. In dealing with mechanical powers, the almost endless variety of methods of their application is a continuous source of instruction to the mechanic.

"Prior to conquering the huge market for traps, the Community experienced lean years. Original Putney Community member John R. Miller had a mercantile education and trained men as salesmen, who covered a radius of fifty miles around the Oneida Community to sell their many early products—palm-leaf hats, pins and needles, lace, combs, collars, ink, and more. "Our men will go out not only as men of business but as missionaries," Noyes said.

"To send out our own men ostensibly to sell goods would be the best method of sending out our publications and spirit. The peddlers would ultimately turn pastors," George Washington Noyes agreed. "If we can establish such a system of distribution, God will give us wit to manufacture more and better things than the world ever saw. If the peddling cannot be made positively beneficial spiritually, we'd better not go into it." The responsibility was given to Mr. Miller to see that the peddling be done in a spiritual manner and at the same time be efficient and profitable. "The two things are not incompatible," Noyes believed. "I want him to study the experience of those who go out and learn to give advice and to criticize."

"Mr. H. was selected as an agent to go to Cleveland, Ohio, and he asked and received a criticism in the Evening Meeting. He was criticized for liability to take on the spirit of the world while peddling, for too much freedom of communication with outsiders in relation to Community matters; and for hardness of spirit and an itching to get out of the shop, and a spirit of discontent with his position there. As criticisms always included a person's good qualities, Mr. H. was commended for being a good manager in the shop and faithful to his responsibilities, and as a good, genial social companion. In pleasure-seeking, he was advised to seek spirituality."

BY THEIR FRUIT YOU SHALL KNOW THEM

"Folks in neighboring cities liked their preserved tomatoes in cans and jars, and the Community planned to enlarge this business. Mr. Pitt went on a tour of inquiry and inspection to gather the best information about everything related to raising and preserving fruit. He learned that a solution of strong vinegar, one part to nine of water, sprinkled on the branches of fruit-trees, will drive away or destroy insects that lay their eggs in the blossoms. Application must be made just before blossoms appear, with a garden engine, syringe, or common watering pot. Vast quantities of fruit may be saved by this simple means.

"Preparations for building a fruit house were in progress," announced the September 5, 1868, *Circular*. "Business is more active than ever at the packing-house; work bees for peeling tomatoes, paring peaches, sorting plums and husking corn occur all day long. Peaches usually come on the 5:00 p.m. train and they're sure to spoil by morning, so we have delightful evening bees paring them—one hundred and twenty-eight volunteers came one night. Those in charge are at their posts early and late. How much more deftly your knife will remove the velvety skin when a hundred other knives are doing the same in the enthusiasm of a great bee. These bees are our grand cure-all for aches and pains. Many an incipient disease has fled before the warmth kindled there. One man said that he was sick with a cold and thought of going to bed, but he plucked up and went to the bee and grew better all the time he was there, and his cold hasn't found him since. The irksomeness of monotonous work is also taken away by the reflection that we are not doing it for the benefit of one person or half a dozen but for two hundred or more. The labor of everyone is elevated from the character of individual self-seeking to that of public and official importance.

"We find no lack of outside help in picking our berries, much of which has been done in the rain," the *Circular* noted. "Most of our pickers are Indians and their reticent, quiet, industrious ways are worthy of commendation. The persistence with which our pickers stick to their rows without any requisition on the part of those who oversee the business, suggests the idea that people become rain-hardened after long experience in this climate. Many of our pickers come in family groups—as many as six members of a single family all work on rows side by side, the older members looking out for the faithfulness of the younger, and each helping the others out with their rows. Soon after our strawberry pickers had been paid last Wednesday, a smart little Indian boy who'd earned a new dollar bill and seemed delighted with it, went to play on the Midland trestle-work being built across our meadows and unluckily fell from the top of the structure. One of our men happening that way found him lying nearly unconscious, with the new dollar bill by his side. He had fallen a distance of twenty feet and was badly bruised and jarred, but at latest account was recovering.

"We have yet to can a lot of pumpkins for family use next spring and summer, and then our labor for this year will be done. We've bottled and canned 27,200 quarts of various kinds of fruits and vegetables fulfilling orders from customers; one-fifth is reserved for home consumption. Eighty persons attended a big bee for an hour and a quarter last evening to pare apples for drying—the first of many bees for that purpose; eighteen bushels of apples were pared, quartered, and sliced. They are carried over to the hop-house at Willow Place where, with the help of a little fire, they are sufficiently dried in two or three days, independent of weather. We had the first serious frost of the season on October 19th.

"*A bee to husk corn at quarter to six in the morning!*" announces the foreman of the fruit department at the close of our evening meeting. "We want to do a big work on the corn tomorrow and would like an early start." Six o'clock finds a busy group at the barn pulling off husks, an operation rendered easy by reason of the preliminary beheading each ear receives at the hands of D. Edson Smith, who is running a miniature guillotine with which he cuts off the stub close up to the corn. Soon the first load of twelve bushels is ready for the packing-room, quarter of a mile away. Work in the packing-room starts rather slowly as the boys are sleepy from last night's exertions, prolonged as they were till near midnight. Here come the scalders who put the corn into huge crates and lower it into the scalding vats. Fifteen minutes boiling and the steaming ears are piled into hoppers ready for cutting off. Two of Burt's corn-cutters manned by sturdy young fellows now commence shaving off corn at the rate of thirty or forty ears a minute. A third machine on which steam-power runs the treadle, cuts off sixty ears per minute with uniformity and ease, compared with the others, as anyone will say after stamping off corn for half a day. From the cutters it goes to the can-filler who by the aid of an ingenious machine fills twelve or fifteen cans a minute. The capacity of the cutter and the filler is from seven to ten thousand cans a day. Next the cans are weighed, a syrup of salt and sugar poured in, wiped clean and the cap soldered on. Place the cans in hot water for an instant; if one is leaky it sends out a stream of bubbles. After testing comes the calcium bath, a huge kettle containing a strong solution of chloride of calcium which carries the boiling point up to 240 degrees. After fifty minutes' bath, they are swung out, rinsed off, and thrown in heaps to cool. When cold, if the heads of the cans refuse to snap in, it indicates that there's a leak somewhere, and the can goes to the compost heap. The actual capacity of our packing-room, from husking to boiling, we find to be a little short of 4,000 cans per day. In two weeks we canned and bottled two thousand bushels of corn, five hundred of tomatoes, one hundred and fifty of peaches, one hundred and seventy-five of plums, besides small quantities of pears, blackberries, and crabapples.

"Walton Hall, England, once had its own corn mill, and when that necessity no longer existed, the millstone was laid in an orchard and forgotten, the May 1868 *Circular* reported, from an article in *Am. Exchange and Review*. The diameter of this circular stone measured five feet and a half, its depth averaged seven inches throughout and its center hole had a diameter of eleven inches. A bird or squirrel had dropped the fruit of the filbert tree through the hole, and in 1812 the seedling was seen rising up through that unwonted channel. As its trunk gradually grew through this aperture and increased, its power to raise the ponderous stone was speculated upon—would the filbert tree die in the attempt? Would it burst the millstone or lift it? In the end the little filbert tree lifted the millstone, and in 1863 wore it like a crinoline about its trunk, and the owner sat upon it under the branching shade.

"This is the merry month of hop-picking, the merriest time of all the glad New Year, to thousands of our country girls and boys. Yes, as the August sun ripens loaded vines and the evening breeze is heavy with the aromatic fragrance of the hop-fields, the whole country feels a thrill—a longing that is irrepressible," Stella writes. "The tired shop girl, the seamstress or schoolmistress, who through the long bright summer days has stood at her loom or plied her needle or leaned over her desk, now bursts her chains and rushes forth into the fields. Oh, the pleasure of breathing the fragrant air, of baring the face to the sun and the breeze, of handling the fragrant vines! You greet the new faces you see and the old friends of other hop seasons. The laughter, songs, long rides in the early morning in crowded wagons, the dance that sometimes closes the day's toil—all these are sensations that make hop-picking, to some classes, the pleasantest holiday season of all. The gregarious enthusiasm makes labor doubly attractive. Every pleasant Sunday in September for several years has seen large wagonloads of young people stop at our door from hop-fields ten miles around us. They ramble an hour or more in our grounds, walk or sit in our public rooms, and then drive away. This past Sunday, wagon after wagon rolled up till the house and grounds were thronged; it looked like the fourth of July. How to entertain our five hundred guests? Community helps out of all difficulties. When the visitors flock in, an impromptu concert can be gotten up in the Hall. Some of our old stock performers who could possibly be spared were hastily called together. We had our quartette, the violin and piano, and our choir of children. We feel thankful for another pleasant Community episode and rejoice that in every way our fortunes and sympathies are linked with honest labor and simple tastes."

"The Midland Railroad is quite a source of amusement to the family," reports the October 8, 1868, *Community Journal*. "The children especially are delighted with the appearance of the beautiful locomotive, Oswego, No. 1, as it travels so stately through our grounds. Its whistle sets every child on a keen run, and at the sound of its musical bell they jump with enthusiastic delight. It is a grand sight to stand on a knoll near the trestle-work, and witness the construction trains as they sweep down the incline at a speed that forty-five years ago would have made the hair of a looker-on stand on end. As the engine approaches, cattle on neighbor O.'s hill race over the ground, tails erect, and after describing a circle in their movements, stare at the train and again wheel off to repeat their evolutions. Familiarity with the snorting monster will soon occur and next summer these cattle will graze quietly as the train rushes by. Our vineyards and orchards must be tempting to Midland Railroad workers, and others, and it's wonderful how free they've been from depredation. We hope that Christ's principle, *All mine are thine and thine are mine*, shall be established everywhere, making theft obsolete. The 175 employees of the New York & Oswego Midland Railroad Company who are constructing the new railroad through our domain attended a strawberry supper on our lawn in response to our invitation and our brass band enlivened the scene," the July 1, 1869, *Circular* reported. "Speeches were made by the superintendents, to which we reply that our efforts were amply repaid by their gentlemanly decorum and expression of good will. We desire that our part may be understood as expressive of friendly feeling toward the New York & Oswego Midland Railroad, and of our hearty sympathy with working-men.

A train crossing the long trestle over Oneida Creek on the Midland Railroad, built during Community years. A station was located near the west side of the Mansion House. This helped Community travelers on business or pleasure, their many visitors, and transportation of products.

"In the spring and summer, spontaneous labor sorties are described, lasting but an hour in the purest and sweetest of morning air, with the sparkling dew, the flowers and birds to accompany. During spring, anyone with the responsibility of a job may mention it the evening before with an invitation to a general work bee for specific jobs nearly every morning at 5:00 a.m. One morning the kitchen group invited all to a bee in the meadows for gathering cowslips for dinner; another time the farmers called for the filling up of a ditch where drain tiles had been laid; a third morning the carpenters headed a party for clearing up the litter of a new building. The consensus was that no part of the day is more pleasantly spent than this gregarious hour before breakfast. All hands might meet after lunch to sew carpet-bags or to braid palm leaf hats, and someone would read from Dickens or Shakespeare to make rote work pleasanter. A great bell rang at 10:00 a.m. each morning to stop work and enjoy warm gingerbread and hot coffee sent over from the Mansion House kitchen. They enjoyed ten minutes of contra dancing on the spacious floor in the garret, then the fiddle stopped and everyone returned to their steel springs and forges. A fine coffee break indeed!

"There is not only mingling of the sexes but of the old and young. In the bee this morning there were men and women of seventy and people of both sexes of intermediate ages down to girls of fifteen," the October 22, 1872, *Circular* noted. "In this unity of the old and young there is something worth the attention of those who would make a model society. Fresh young life for sparkle and vivacity and years for wisdom and depth. The combination of these makes a happy society. A fence is constructed—making posts from trees, digging postholes, sawing the rails and pickets, putting them up, and painting half of it, all accompanied by spirited singing.

"Mother Noyes has discovered a model way to get up a rousing bee. Do you suppose it is by stirring about and expending half her energies in calling on others? No, indeed. She heard Mr. K. say the garden walks needed attention. She said nothing, but pretty soon, as some of us sat on the grass eating strawberries and ice-cream while others were playing ball and climbing the cherry-trees, out came Mother Noyes with a broom, and went busily to work on one of the paths. George Miller and Charles Joslyn soon joined her, and in another twinkling all the old brooms, rakes, and hoes were in great demand, and the merriest bee ensued. All worked with a will, and by reading time at 7 o'clock the walks were in very good order. Step in to our meeting room at whatever hour and you are sure to find Mother Noyes folding, pricking, stitching and covering pamphlets, or overlaying of wood cuts, or cutting labels. We have many a laugh at Mother Noyes and the very variety of her employments—now upstairs, anon, downstairs, always busy, and always cheerful, she makes the whole machinery of business go smoothly and helps us all to be just what she is, enthusiastic, hearty workers. The December 1871 *Circular* noted that the holidays brought the Wallingford Community the rich gift of a visit from Mrs. Harriet A. Noyes and two of our Yale students, Charles A. Cragin and George N. Miller. Mrs. Noyes had not been here for over a year, but her place in the heart of the Community can never grow cold. Whether at Wallingford or Oneida, her presence diffuses constant strength and peace.

"The last *bag-bee* today!" notes the April 17, 1868, *Circular*. "It was like bidding good-by to an old friend. For fourteen years bag-bees have been daily held with but few intermissions. Many are the memories connected with that busy hour. In the first days of the business, John Humphrey Noyes was the life of these bees. He was always there, thimble and needle in hand, applying his Yankee ingenuity to the seams, pockets, and locks. He even invented a scientific method of tying a knot in his thread! Often during the summer heats, we carried our work under the old butternut tree to sit on the cool grass. Mother Noyes used to read to us, and many are the books that occur to our memories associated with her soft, pleasant voice. How the business grew! At first only a little room of the Mansion House was sufficient for it. When the new house was built, a spacious apartment was appropriated for it, but not long after it had to be moved into two large rooms in the newly erected Tontine. Outgrowing those, it was next transported to the Mill, where it spread itself over the greater part of the building, and there it will make its final exit. The bees have been mostly carried on by the women, but of late the work has been carried into the Hall once a week and a large attendance called for. At the last one, ten hundred lively fingers were counted. Well, bags, good-by—sacks, satchels, railroads and all. The lessons of unity and public spirit learned in those bees are embalmed in our hearts forever.

"Sitting in front of the cows while husking brought reminiscences of milking when the Community was poor and employed no hired labor. The Community men were wont to take turns at it, five of them milking for six months at a time and then being relieved. It was a somewhat disagreeable chore starting at 5:00 a.m. but, it had its little perquisites. First, an extra leisure hour at noontime; second, a short piece of red soap scented with sassafras. The first of these emoluments was for the benefit of the individual, the second was for the benefit of society. Mr. Noyes suggested having a party for the boys who got up and drove the cows to pasture last summer and fall. A memorial was posted conspicuously, finally read and drunk for a toast: 'Honor to the Youthful Heroes, who, in loyal obedience to the Association, last fall quit their beds in the dark hours of the morning, and with lantern in hand, sometimes alone and sometimes through storm and mud, go to the distant pasture and gather the cows, encountering discomforts, not to say dangers, worthy of the courage of pretty stout men.' One ingenious youth who milked is now climbing the hill of Science at Yale and describes how he lightened this fragrant labor with curious calculations: He began by reckoning the number of days of his term and then determined the number of milkings he would have to perform; next he found out the number of cows he would have to milk, and finally by averaging the labor of milking his six cows, he made a nice estimate of the number of *manipulations* he would have to make in the time that remained to him. Don't you think such a boy ought to go to College?

"Studying and testing this people by the standard given by Christ to his disciples—'Ye shall know them by their fruits; do men gather grapes of thorns or figs of thistles?'—I believe that the tree of Bible Communism is a good tree, for I have found the fruit of the spirit that leads and governs this Community to be love, joy, peace, long-suffering, gentleness, goodness, faith, meekness, and temperance; all are fruits of the same spirit that was in Christ and the Primitive Church. In this their theory and practice agree, and I cannot doubt that they are what I believed them to be before coming here—a God fearing people, and that He dwells in them in the flesh," concluded the *Elmira Advertiser* reporter who lived at the Community for months.[52]

"A well-dressed lady in the garden was overheard to say to her party, 'I wonder what they do with the money when it comes in—do they divide it around, do you think?'

'I have lived in the Community these twenty years and do not possess a purse or anything that ever held money, I could have said. I do not see the currency of the nation from year to year and this is true of all but the few here whose business or function relates them to the world where money circulates. What do the rest of us want of money? Between ourselves it is so much rubbish. We live as children of a provident father and have all we need.'"

WOMEN WORKED IN EVERY ENTERPRISE

"What employment do women have in the Community? An impromptu census gives the following answer: The financier and two bookkeepers in the general business office are women, who take a large share of the duties and responsibilities connected with the accounts and money transactions of the Community. Five women spend several hours each day in the family machine-shop, running lathes and learning the use of machinery. This is a new industry and a most fascinating one, according to Harriet Skinner. She thinks she might have quite missed her vocation in life if she'd not had this opportunity to become a machinist. Still another home business is making trap-chains, well adapted to women and children, carried on in a well-warmed and lighted room in the basement. One woman is teacher in the elementary school and three others instruct classes in music, writing, and drawing. The weekly *Oneida Circular* is edited by a woman and another woman has charge of mailing the *Circular* throughout the U.S. and eastern Canada, keeps the subscription-book, and attends to foreign correspondence connected with publications. From three to four women are employed as compositors in the printing-office. Phonographic reporting (shorthand) is done by women. Making paper boxes for our silk manufacturers is a new home industry that gives employment to two women and several children. In a pleasant west room in the Tontine where the printing-office and box-room are, a woman superintends the spooling department in our silk works and two women ticket and label silk boxes. Two others have the entire business of putting up skein silk and a number of women find pleasant and profitable employment in skeining silk in the upper and lower sitting-rooms.

"As I entered the spooling-room this morning, I was pleased to see Mrs. T. there, well past her threescore years and ten who has had more than the usual share of infirmity and sorrow. She was seated in front of the parting-pin learning to part silk. But her graceful step, bright eye, and active intelligent mind have survived it all. There she sat for more than an hour patiently trying again and again to give the parted skein its peculiar twist, and then tie it up in its own double and twisted knot. Occasionally Harriet A., our superintendent, would lean over her chair and show her how to do it. I stopped to congratulate Mrs. T. as I passed by. 'Oh!' said she, her face glowing and her eyes sparkling, 'How slow I am—but I shall learn it! How I've prayed and longed to be able to come out here and learn to do something about the silk; this morning I know God inspired and strengthened me—and I came, determined that neither old age nor weakness, nor inaptitude to learn new things would keep me back. And now I know I shall succeed.'"

"Although according to the last financial report women average six hours and forty minutes of work, it's not monotonous toil and is all the more effective for being varied, reported the January 18, 1869, *Circular*. Let us look into the spooling-room at 7:30 a.m. Nine women and girls take places at the machines, while one throws on the belt and starts the winder. We ask the petit young lady at the winder: 'Do you work here all day, Mary? It must be tedious standing so long.'

"Mary P.—'O, no; at ten o'clock, I sit down at one of the spooling machines, where I work till twelve. In the afternoon I study, sew, or recreate until supper time, when

I wait on a table for fifteen or twenty minutes.' You see her lot is not a hard one. Two spoolers sit at each of the small tables fronting the west windows. Alice, that tall girl in black, is first in order. 'How long do you work here, Alice?'

"Alice.—'Till noon; and I help in the dining-room after dinner for an hour and a half.'

"'And Annie, what do you do?'

"Annie.—'I spool till noon and in the afternoon I go to school till four.'

"'Tirzah, how long do you work here?'

"Tirzah.—'Till half-past nine, and Mary V. takes it till noon. I help H. H. S. prepare copy for the *Circular*, read proofs, or do what I please.'

"'What are your occupations, Charlotte?'

"Charlotte.—'I spool till noon, when I wait on table for a short time. After supper I assist in the dining-room for an hour. Because I help Mrs. C. take charge of the women's clothing department, I'm liable to be called on at almost any moment to run and get something for someone.'

"'What do you do, Mary B.?'

"Mary B. —'My work is the same as Alice's.'

"'And you, Harriet?'

"Harriet.—'I am here till ten when Portia comes, and I go and make two beds. In the afternoon I work here from one till four.'

"'Do you stay here all the forenoon, Consuelo?'

"Consuelo.—'No, only till nine, when Miss N. takes the machine for an hour, giving place to Mary P. at ten. When I leave here, I have the *Circular* letters to look after and new subscribers' names to put in the book, or I print the wrappers for the papers. I usually come here again in the afternoon and work an hour or two.'

"'You must work here longer, Georgia, because you take more or less care of the business?'

"Georgia.—'Yes, I'm here till two or three o'clock, but I have no other regular work besides.'

"John Freeman has ascertained that a pound of the finest silk if in one continuous line would extend a distance of twelve miles. Such a strand is composed of nine of those delicate gossamer-like filaments of the raw silk; hence a pound of this latter would extend a distance, if continuous, of nearly one hundred and eleven miles. Mrs. J., who does the labeling, is engaged in the business four or five hours a day. The workers at the winder are constantly changing, some staying not more than half an hour; in the afternoon you will find a different set of girls at the spoolers, who have been otherwise employed during the forenoon. Mrs. H. C. N., who is the superintendent of this department of the Oneida Community silk-works, finds enough to occupy her mind and fingers from 7:30 a.m. till 4:00 p.m. She has the quarterly inventories to make out, the silk to size and sort, and a thousand things to look after.

"Mrs. E. or Mrs. P. need not weary themselves looking after the mending, darning, refitting, enlarging, and making clothing, and the thousand-and-one things connected with the care of little ones. No, two or three women superintend the clothing of the children and a grand campaign is instituted in the fall and spring to prepare for the coming season. Clothes that the larger ones have outgrown are tried on the next in size, and it is ascertained just how many new garments must be made and how many old ones will do by fixing over. Then the cloth for the new dresses, aprons, underclothes, etc, is cut into shape, and the old garments, if need be, washed and prepared for fixing over. On the bulletin appears a notice, reports the *Circular* in October 1868: 'A bee for sewing, in the Hall, at two o'clock.' All who are at leisure, or have an attraction for it (always a goodly number), make their appearance in the Hall at the appointed hour, work-box in hand. The lady who oversees the bee has a large basket-full of work, which she distributes to one and another with the necessary instructions. Energetic Mrs. T. always sits in one corner at her sewing-machine, stitching away as for dear life, on the work that scores of busy hands are preparing for her. The bees last an hour or two and are called as often as necessary. As for the inevitable buttons that come off, button-holes that tear out and the many rents here, there, and everywhere, the staff of women at the children's house attend to them as they daily occur. But the always-on-hand mending is often more than they can do; there are certain people ready to lend a helping hand, whom they feel free to call on in any emergency. One genial-hearted woman, Aunt Susan, who never had a child of her own but loves the little ones with all her heart, voluntarily darns the dozens of little stockings that come weekly through the wash; and this is but a specimen of the general interest taken in the welfare of the children."

Woman's Work and Wages, April 20, 1868:

"Hiring so much help as the O. C. necessarily does, we study in a very practical manner the causes of the difference between men's and women's wages—a never-to-be-settled question while selfishness exists, but one on which light will do no harm. In shops and factories where both sexes are employed, the difference is most apparent. For an equal number of hours work, a woman usually receives from one-half to two-thirds the amount paid to a man. In what's called piece-work, a man is as likely to earn four dollars a day as a woman is two dollars. Wages paid in our two principal businesses, trap-making and silk-making in which hired help is employed, shows an average difference of fifty cents a day. After several months' experience in silk-making, woman will earn seventy-five cents to a dollar a day; a man, with no greater experience in the trap-shop, will receive from one dollar to one dollar and a half. In cotton and woolen factories, women usually obtain from four to six dollars a week unless they are employed at piece-work; but it would be difficult to hire a man of average ability to do any kind of shop-work for less than a dollar and a quarter a day. Seventy-five percent of men in the country learn no trade but can earn two dollars per day as readily as a woman can one dollar. On the farm the difference is still greater; a man's price is one dollar and sixty cents a day, while two dollars a week and board equivalent to five dollars a week is the maid-of all-work's hire. Physical differences are a bar in employments such as mining, lumbering, ocean-commerce, and most iron manufactures; the farmer's argument is, why hire at an equal price a weak laborer when he can get a strong one?

"There are thousands of shops in which light machinery is used where women might be employed. But a Boston manufacturer states that the daily average of missing work is seven girls in fifty. Women never work so steadily as men. If mother is out of sorts, the baby sick, a new dress to be finished, or visiting to be done, it is very easy for a girl to step out of the shop a day or two. And generally, women learn no more of the construction and general working of a machine than is absolutely necessary; consequently, when a part breaks or gets out of order, they're forced to remain idle till a man comes along. Occasionally an enterprising female will attempt to repair a disabled machine, but she seldom does more than to repeat the last re-adjustment made by the foreman, with disregard to the cause of the breakage.

"Another serious trouble is the liability of losing an educated hand by marriage. Manufacturers feel that no matter how well suited a girl may be, no matter what inducement she may have in the matter of wages, no matter what has been the expense of education, if a chance to get married occurs she will jump at it. There are too few kinds of employment for women to engage in, so girls feel compelled to marry simply for a home. Were it not for this fact, there would be fewer marriages without love, fewer divorces and homes of perpetual discord.

"Marriage is coming to be looked upon as a quack-medicine," wrote K. "It kills more than it cures. Perhaps the reply of an extensive shirt maker strikes at the root of the matter. Asked why he paid women only a shilling a shirt, he admitted, 'They come to me in crowds and they'll do it for that—and so I let 'em have it! They'll work for less.' The supply of women's help greatly exceeds the demand, which keeps the price down, but as the world advances in civilization and true refinement, occupations for women will multiply. Their gentle, elevating influence is needed everywhere. But this can only be when man becomes a true friend of woman—a protector instead of a seducer. How many factories where men and women are employed are free from the stain of licentiousness? How many mothers would trust their daughters to work in a shop-full of men? How many girls would come out pure from such an ordeal? Free the world from selfishness, give Christ the control of the passions; then, and only then, will woman find her sphere.

"What I like about the industry here is the combination of the sexes in it; women carry a full half of the work," Mr. Noyes said at Wallingford Community's Evening Meeting on October 4, 1873. "I have not much confidence in anything that does not combine the sexes, whether in industry, politics, education, or religion. Education here is a healthy, wholesome thing with a mixing of the sexes in it. I don't think much of the Evangelical Alliance on account of its old-bachelor character. It has no women in its councils. I believe inspiration comes from a dual God—a Father and Mother. We cannot get the highest and best inspiration, 'the water of life that proceeds out of the throne of God and the Lamb,' except as there is appreciation of that dual life in them—except as we are in heart a combination of male and female ourselves. The enthusiasm in which every living thing is generated is the enthusiasm born of the commingling of male and female. The next generation will certainly expurgate everything that does not bring the sexes together. Wall Street would have done better if it had encouraged female brokers. My philosophy about the mingling of the sexes is that inspiration is the foundation of all good active improvement or prosperity in anything. Our respect for persons is measured by their real character and actions, not at all by their temporary circumstances. True merit is sure to manifest itself and be recognized. The best person to organize and guide inevitably gravitates to a high place of trust. Official position carries with it no rewards not within the reach of the faithful laborer in subordinate positions. There is no intriguing for official responsibility here; you might live in our midst for years and not hear a single word from a disappointed aspirant for office. The grand secret of our harmony in respect to the question of labor and of office is that we've learned to respect one another according to character regardless of position, and to consider that all labor may be made an ordinance of worship."

"When the Community's business manager John Miller died in 1854, times of real hardship began. Community branches at Brooklyn, Newark, Putney, and Cambridge, Vt., were closed. By spartan methods, they reduced the cost of lodging and board for each adult member to less than eighty-four cents per week. A typical breakfast would be boiled potatoes and gravy, tomatoes, and bread; the midday dinner might offer baked potatoes, butter, bread, pickles, and cocoa. Supper would be wheat bread, molasses cake and apples. One supper consisted only of blackberry shortcake and plenty of it (who'd complain of that?). A father and son traveled to New York City and the father said, "We're economizing a bit now, so please don't order the very most expensive thing on the menu." When the server came, the son ordered pickles and coffee!"

MANUFACTURING AND ECONOMIC STABILITY

"Our businesses were in their infancy and we did little more than to keep clear of debt. We were just starting the trap business in the little blacksmith's shop by the creek where Mr. Newhouse and Joel by dint of hard labor turned out three or four dozen traps a day. Noyes worked in most Community enterprises including get-down-and-dirty work of many kinds, and became interested in learning about making traps after returning from the Brooklyn Community in 1854. Trap-making was a major industry of the era and a possible Community business. Sewell Newhouse kept his successful method of trap-making top secret even to John Humphrey Noyes, only reluctantly teaching him some simpler parts of the business. Noyes found himself unaided when he tried to pick up more elements of this particular craft. Newhouse's assistant, Homer Barron, was a great friend of Noyes—the two were both interested in music and the Community band was just starting; after their noon practice they talked music in the trap-shop. Barron and Noyes became inseparable, Noyes got the help he needed, and the two of them led the family into that business until it was so enlarged that it had to be moved to the mill building. *This affection had something to do with the revolution in the trap department*, thought Noyes. Strapping young Community men joined Sewell in hammering out a few dozen single-size traps at the forge.

Sewell Newhouse was dissatisfied with crude animal traps available in the 1820s. A man of legendary strength, he hammered out a better article with conscientious attention to details and produced a far superior instrument, appreciated even today.

"Orders for traps began to arrive from major cities. Mr. Olds introduced our traps to St. Louis buyers and orders came for several hundred traps. Mr. Olds, who knew Mr. Noyes in Putney, is well adapted to a cooperative society that gives scope to all his talents and develops others still latent. Mr. Olds promotes the Community's prosperity, traveling extensively as a commercial agent; his name is as familiar as household words among businessmen. He furnishes a good example of those who would gain only a hand-to-mouth subsistence in the world, but are effective producers in a cooperative society where big fish do not eat up little ones, but all strive together for the common weal. He gives religion his first attention and thought; no sacrifices are too great to make for it.

"The trap business was later installed on the first floor in the mill building—the music of six new anvils rung in the ears of those who worked in the printing office above. When Community members made trap-springs by hand at the forge, there was a great liability to injure the eyes by looking at the bright hot steel under the hammer; a number of men had sore eyes. Noyes talked with Newhouse about the matter; Newhouse advised how one who hammers heated steel should not look at it constantly, nor even fix his eye steadily upon it at all, but get in the habit of *glancing* at it, and in that way, avoid having any difficulty with his eyes. Noyes tried this strategy and found good practical advice in it, which Noyes's creative mind developed into his Home Talk, *The Art of Glancing*—

"I have found many ways of applying this glancing philosophy to higher matters than hammering steel. For instance: the eyes of the *mind* are liable to get sore by looking too fixedly at subjects that are hot with interest. Even questions of ordinary business assume a fiery glow that makes continuous attention to them painful and dangerous. Insanity generally comes by too long gazing at some one subject that is absorbing enough to hold and compel thought, till the brain gets sore. The way to keep a healthy mind in the midst of complicated businesses and mighty issues is not to gaze long and fixedly at any one thing, but to do the looking indispensable to action by swift, well-directed glances. I find, too, that it makes my spiritual eyes ache to pore over the popular newspapers. The only safe way for me to go through them is by skipping glances; taking whole paragraphs by their first lines.

"Above all, the glancing philosophy is indispensable in love. There is a blinding radiance in magnetic beauty that cannot be stared at steadily without heart-disease. The sexes in their prime are like white-hot steel to each other. Whoever would keep his heart for God and for all must learn to practice withdrawing the gaze before it goes into bondage and idolatry. In short, we must practice the art of glancing in all our dealings with the external world if we would keep healthy eyes for things internal and eternal. It seems to me that in a true system of education, the ability withdraw the attention will be as important as the ability to fix the attention, and as worthy of systematic training; because the way for us to make the most of ourselves for God, man, and the universe, is certainly to keep our freedom; that is, to save our minds, imaginations, and hearts from all seizure and bondage to specialties. This has been God's way of training me, to always and thoroughly take lightly all things below himself. By his grace I am master of the art of glancing. For that, above all things, I am ever thankful."

"Thanks to Noyes's having lived at the Brooklyn Community establishing a new printing press after the Oneida shop burned, they came into contact with William Inslee, who educated several Community youths in mechanics at his machine shop in Newark. With these young machinists, Noyes and Newhouse devised machinery to supplant laborious, time-consuming handwork; they discovered that malleable cast-iron could be substituted for wrought iron in parts of the traps. Work with hammer and anvil to create the steel-spring became obsolete—not even one of the hundred and twenty former hammer-blows was required to shape the trap-spring from a long steel bar into a bent, bowed, finely-tempered and elastic instrument. The making of chains was now a branch of the trap business and did not require power. The smallest chain cost $1.00 per dozen and eight cents per chain, and the stock for one did not cost over one-and-a-half cents. The demand for traps would soon reach $50,000 a year and chains would be required for 60 percent of them. A net profit of six cents per chain would net $1,800.00 for our labor—easy, simple work and all the boys and girls could work at it. In March 1856, six hundred orders came in, and in April a single order for one thousand traps came from Milwaukee. The Hudson Bay Company order was so large that the farmers worried that all hands would be required in the trap-shop for the summer. And what about the manufacture of traveling bags?

"An 1871 *Circular* reported that the trap was protected by no patent, which did not long escape the attention of Connecticut firms who soon entered the field with an imitation. They've competed with us with all the advantages of unlimited capital and skillful workmen, but so strong was the hold of the Newhouse trap on the practical trapper, that the imitation has always commanded a much lower price to get a share of the trade. Among our recent visitors was a gentleman who mentioned that the 'Oneida Community had been the making of him.' He said that years ago, when he owned nothing, he bought two dozen Community steel-traps to try his hand at the trapping business. This first venture proved so successful that he continued buying our traps from time to time until he could afford to buy and pay for a good farm, well stocked with handsome cattle. Many improvements were made in the manufacturing processes, the benefits of which our competitors have always reaped, as no patent has ever been secured in the business.

"A community of interests has had much to do with the perfection of our articles of manufacture; our trap manufacture history has been repeated in at least two other lines—preserved fruit and silk goods, in which we have taken an acknowledged position at the head of the market in close competition with established firms. The Community is not prejudiced against patents and our members have taken out several for ingenious devices in minor branches of industry, but we're very sure that an account of profit and loss with them all would show a decided deficit. Our present capital was acquired in open competition with others, entirely without assistance from patent-rights.

"Looking toward God as the great employer, the only work that pays in the long run is that which is given to us by God," agreed George Washington Noyes. "What we want, to satisfy our self-respect and stimulate to successful exertion, is consciousness of a commission to do business for him we worship. This is possible by waiting on him to get such a commission; we can get jobs to do from heaven and get our pay in advance in the influx of life from God empowering us for its execution. Let all look to God for the privilege to work—thankful for the smallest favors in this line, appreciating the blessedness of a call to cooperate with the Most High. The end will be constant satisfaction, office, and emolument far exceeding any in the gift of earthly governments. We don't care so much to maintain our right to work against our fellow men as we do to secure permission to work from the government of heaven—*there* is the great capitalist who dispenses profitable jobs."

"If we have primarily in view to make money, we shall get no enthusiasm from heaven," Noyes always reminded his flock. "That's the snare that can beset the Community. They are great businessmen engaged in big enterprises, but there is a great danger of their forgetting that the object of business is the spiritual education and human development of ourselves and our children. Always the temptation is to shift from our true purpose and take up the worldly idea that the object of business is money. We start in business under inspiration and with pure and true objectives, but the spirit of the world broods over us and works among us continually, turning our attention to making money." Thinking about a Community youth, Noyes wrote about a deeply held conviction: "Let him remain free from the absurd notion that one kind of employment is more honorable than another, which causes so much mischief in the world. He will be taught in the Community that it is not the kind of work that dignifies a man, but that by good spirit and good manners the man dignifies every kind of work. The true spirit loves service—loves to be fruitful. The false spirit seeks ease and hates faithful industry—counts many kinds of labor as degrading. One kind of labor may be superior to another in furnishing better conditions for the development and exercise of talent, and one kind of labor may expose a person to greater temptations than another, but no necessary labor can be degrading."

Henry Seymour's *Heaven's arrangement for full human development* in the September 9, 1872, *Circular* is a masterpiece: "Our highest ideal of human existence is that of persons continually ripening toward a higher grade of excellence. Human nature was made for this end. We think of schooling as merely preparatory to the higher school of life in which we ought to be pressing toward happiness and improvement. When a student leaves the brightening and sharpening of his intellect at school and goes into the world for possible preeminence, he finds that the step he's taking is a downward one. We see evidence of a sorrow of heart. Certainly sharpening one's faculties is nobler than scraping together mere subsistence, but how has education come to be regarded as one thing and labor another? All labor should elevate the producer; we should liken human nature to the violin, the tone of which grows ever stronger and sweeter by use. The farmer, instead of being worn down and depressed by his labors, ought to be educated and elevated by it, knowing that he is performing a high service for himself, his fellow men, and his Maker. Farming includes gardening and horticulture, the raising of grains, grasses, and roots, and the rearing and caring for many domestic animals. But with one person's attention and labors so thinly spread, he has meager facilities for perfecting himself in any one branch; the results of his industry are correspondingly poor. Or a person may find work in manufacturing where labor is divided, working for years and years at a small monotonous branch like that of sharpening pins, a business he'd master in a few hours—this dwarfs his whole nature! It is a poor, mean idea of human nature to regard it as we do implements destined to be worn out in the work of production. I caricature the system with a picture of a great press called 'The Press of Business' into which the devil has put a lot of human beings. Many, representing factory laborers or counting-house workers, are held merely by their fingers, their feet, or their heads while his majesty turns the screw with a long lever called Human Wants and presses out the fluid of wealth, while death is pitching into the grave the pomace (anything crushed into a pulpy mass). The All-wise intended we should outgrow this barbarism."

OF THE MONEY-KING, BY THE MONEY-KING, FOR THE MONEY-KING?

"Let's assume that Community living has taken charge of every variety of industry and has divided and systemized every department, farming as well as manufacturing, so that each small branch can receive the attention it requires at the proper time. There are no separate interests and no pressure of necessity compelling individuals to devote themselves so continuously to any one branch or number of branches as to harm their physical, moral, or mental growth. The whole system of human industry would thus be as completely under human control as are keys of a piano under the fingers of a skillful performer. What would be the leading motive governing the assignment of persons to the branches of work that must be attended to? It is to secure the highest and best education for the workmen, who are at the same time the proprietors of the business. What would be valued most would be industry operating to elevate and refine human beings. The question would not be, how much and how rapidly can wealth be extracted from human effort? It would be, how much and how fast can we improve and elevate the laborers? Such a society would practically carry out the axioms of Christ, *Life is more than meat, and the body than raiment.*

"It may be objected that the attainment of wealth is a very necessary thing, and with this devotion to the mental and spiritual education of all, this interest might suffer. We reply that there is nothing that so enhances the productiveness of human industry as good tools and machinery—and the bright and sharp intelligence and strong and steady purpose of man are the most efficient tools and machinery. It may be objected that such facilities for change would lead to pleasure-seeking; that they would tempt persons to such frequency of change as to result in superficial education in whatever is undertaken, as well as in unproductiveness in business. We reply that having such facilities does not necessitate the unwise use of them; they would be controlled by judicious persons. It's this everlasting, enforced monotony in business that we complain of—this making of business a mere means of producing wealth and utterly disregarding it as a means of the elevation of mankind. When our Community began, our leader insisted that spiritual interests should occupy the first place in our attention whether we prospered externally or not. For several years we lost money and to the worldly-minded, it appeared as though our ship must inevitably sink, but we learned the truth of *Seek ye first the kingdom of God and his righteousness, and all these things shall be added unto you.*

> A vision without a task is but a dream,
> A task without a vision is drudgery,
> And a vision and a task is the hope of the world.
> —*from a church in Sussex, England (c. 1730)*

George Cragin wrote an important piece on July 5, 1869, *Doing as You Would Be Done By*. "A hired man who worked by the month, or as a day laborer, had no margin of time that he could call his own. When hiring out to a farmer, it was generally understood that the contract included the entire day, with some portion of the night too, if his employer's interests required it. If the farmer were covetous and grasping, the hired man must be prepared for a continuous drill in his master's service, taking his breathing spells, if he had any, between nine at night and four or five in the morning—a pretty narrow margin, the working man of today would imagine. Twelve and fourteen hours were demanded as a day's work in all cotton factories and other mills where children and adults found employment. Fourteen or fifteen hours of service were not infrequently required by exacting overseers. The effect of such incessant toil upon both the physical and moral natures of youth can be easily imagined.

"Occasionally a farmer adopted a very different policy in dealing with his hired help. Captain K., a well-to-do farmer, treated his hired man so considerately that he made him feel that he was managing his own farm, and was not a hired man at all. It was marvelous to see how a little sprinkling of good feeling and kindly treatment—which cost the farmer nothing—strengthened the muscles, fertilized the mind, and transformed the hireling into a partner who manifested as much interest in his employer's business as if it were his own. There was no complaint of fatigue or of being overworked. Indeed, the shrewd farmer had to caution his hired man against working too hard occasionally. "James," he would say, "you have done enough; quit work, and play, or go visiting, or fishing—better still, give your books a little attention." The farmer himself had literary attractions; but rarely did James heed the advice, so intent was he on making the most of his time for the benefit of his employer. James was made to feel that all of his time was his own. Why such grand effects from apparently trifling causes? That farmer had studied human nature, having discovered that kindness of heart—doing as you would be done by—is the best policy; it pays every way.

"Laws to protect workers changed our former barbarous conditions. The hired laborer, if he has a family to support and is industrious and frugal, can augment his yearly income by cultivating his half acre of garden vegetables in the long days of summer. Early morning and late afternoon hours are now free and are the pleasantest hours of the twenty-four for outdoor work. Time is available to improve mental culture, if so disposed; and all out of the margin of a legitimate day's work of ten hours. Farmers and manufacturers, however grasping, can now exact only ten hours as a day's work. This limitation of hours is only one of many blessings in the gift of a progressing civilization to the noble army of laborers, operatives, artisans, and skilled mechanics. Society is so dependent on them that a day's cessation of their busy hands would close the doors of the business world.

"But reform will not stop at ten or even eight hours as the limit of a day's work, provided the working classes make the most of the time already theirs. What is wanted is *profitable thinking* to fertilize the brains of this mighty army of industrious forces. They require enthusiasm for education in the broadest sense, a comprehensive idea including all truth, physical, moral, and spiritual. The prevailing idea that one can get a finished education in youth is a false one, or that one can be too old to go to school to improve the mind and heart. Youth is the time to educate the heart in thorough obedience to all truth; thus enlightened, the heart can guide the head safely into all the mysteries of knowledge. We believe that this method of imparting and receiving knowledge is to be greatly improved under the inspiration of God, the great educator of the human family.

"The unequal distribution of wealth is the source of a vast proportion of the most intense sufferings of humanity and of nearly all crimes," opined David E. Cronin, editor of the *Binghamton Times*, who proposed education as the great panacea. By all means educate everybody to the fullest extent possible and let every effort of every reformer and legislator be bent in that direction. But if the world's wealth were divided equally today, the Community is convinced that the division would again become unequal tomorrow, because the hearts of men must be educated no less than their minds. A merely intellectual education won't accomplish that desirable end if motives remain selfish; education will simply enable people to be more refined in seeking selfish ends. More or less clashing of interests and ultimate injustice will persist so long as such motives exist. We've seen that when the working person gains education not only of the mind but of the heart, he will find that truth, and not capital, is all-powerful; that sufficient capital will naturally follow the pursuit of truth. Learning to unite with a higher power will impel persons to act in the interests of one another instead of for self only. An employer who is less educated than his workers will soon find it to his advantage to make their superior knowledge a partner of his business, and this is occurring daily. The employer whose standard of education is higher than that of his highly educated men will make common cause with them in the love of science and truth. In either case workingmen have the game in their own hands, and can better afford to wait than to fight. The true friend of workingmen is not he who appeals to their avarice or to their sense of suffered wrongs, but one who stimulates a thirst for knowledge and cooperative ideas on every subject.

"Nothing can be more satisfactory than the marriage of Capital and Labor in the Oneida Community," noted the *Circular* in 1872. "The members commenced as workingmen and women without much Capital and went on sinking money the first years of their existence as a Community, yet by honest industry and prudence, without the aid of any patents or speculations, they have become capitalists. If God has put it into the hearts of a few hundred people to cooperate and has prepared them for the work, he can as easily prepare a few thousands or millions to do the same thing. Why not? Capital and Labor are naturally helpmeets, and one cannot get along without the other."

"Rochester (NY) shoe manufacturers are having much trouble this winter from insubordination among their workmen," wrote Agent William Kelly in a letter to the Community on January 18, 1869. "Employees have formed an organization called the Shoe-maker's League, which embraces all shoe employees throughout the country. They hold weekly meetings when they decide on what terms they will work, how much shall be paid for different kinds of work, and no one is allowed to accept any other rates. They will neither work themselves nor allow any one else to work until their rights are granted them. They not only claim the right of dictating what their wages shall be, but of choosing their foremen, and in fact of running the whole business of manufacturing, the manufacturers only having to furnish the capital. Some manufacturers have held out for weeks refusing to yield to their claims, but orders from western jobbers for spring work are coming in very fast; they cannot afford to hold off any longer, so workmen are getting their claims and are going to work again. One manufacturer is feeling very blue, as he has taken an order from one house in Cincinnati amounting to $30,000, at prices based on the former rates paid for work. It was almost ruinous for him to pay the advanced rates claimed by the workmen, but he had to yield to them or get nothing done."

"We care nothing for accounts between each other—one person owns the whole as much as another," wrote Abel Easton. "There is no place where there is less necessity for account-keeping than here, but we love keeping accurate accounts because they speak the truth. Many of us could not see the use of such careful estimations of the exchanges between as many as forty departments, some subdivided; in our hardware department an account is kept with each article of manufacture; each size of trap has its separate account and is charged with its separate inventory, checked every month. 'It is like the right hand keeping account with the left,' many said. But when Mr. Noyes said it was a method whereby the right hand made the left hand tell the truth, we all determined that every department and branch of business should tell the exact truth. Our financier can tell at a glance not only what department is losing or gaining, but the exact status and the actual results in dollars and cents of each article of manufacture. The consequence is that we now have as complete a system of accounts as any business organization in the world. We demand the truth from our businesses no less than from each other."

RECESSION AND EXPANSION

"In 1857, a major recession hit the United States, causing widespread unemployment with thousands on the verge of starvation and demanding work and food. News of panic selling in the stock market, the first of its kind, spread across the nation due to the invention of the telegraph. The hard times of 1857 notably diminished the Community's income from the sale of traps, and income from other sources was likewise small. They discussed their finances at the Evening Meeting in March 1858. 'We'll take a cheerful faith view of the matter, but trim our sails to the breeze—purchase nothing that we can well dispense with, do all we can to increase our income and wait hopefully for better times.' They were not extravagant in their food, but thought retrenchment could be found in the dress department. Notwithstanding considerable joking about whale bone, garters, etc., there was criticism of the spirit that follows fashion. Mr. Kinsley thought there might be improvement in respect to giving presents. If a present was something that was really needed, there might be no objection; but everyone had birthdays and each wanted a present as much as another. The subject of private parties was talked over. Mr. Noyes said he was afraid that in these, some were omitted while others were invited often; it was thought best to give up private parties. We take great satisfaction in remembering that the rigorous economy then practiced was the foundation for all our subsequent prosperity.

"By August 1st the financial situation was canvassed and it was unanimously agreed that, however straitened circumstances may be, there should be no grumbling, no finding fault with Providence. 'We will be contented and thankful, and with cheerful hearts do all we can to prosper.' In time, orders again crowded us for traps, so a one-hundred-foot brick wing was added into which we moved all the forges; finishing work on the traps spread over the room they'd previously occupied in the mill. Orders poured in daily and our traveling bags were also in great demand, so we were forced to hire help. We were wonderfully prospered as the year progressed. We sold $5,747 worth of traps; the next year the trap sales footed $26,000. The Community had a banquet in the trap-shop for the sixty men, women, boys and girls who had worked in it that winter. A great table was tastefully arranged with spotless linen and lustrous white dishes that contrasted well with the surroundings—a bench of drills and vices, a ponderous rolling machine and furnaces and forges, a punch machine, grindstone and drops on the other side. After a dance in the loft, the company sat down to a simple repast of cereals, butter, preserved fruits and coffee; music sent its thrilling sound from an adjoining room. Then there were a dozen impromptu toasts. The effect of the occasion was to encourage industry and provoke brotherly love, the product most thought of in the Community.

"Eight peddlers brought $2,000 worth of silk as far as St. Louis, Cincinnati, and Milwaukee. The topic of the moral influence of the silk-peddling business, its official management, and the conduct of the peddlers came up two months later. The temptations of trade and the seductions of money have been fully discussed. It seems almost impossible for persons to enter the great sphere of covetousness and handle its currency without losing some of their simplicity of heart. The Community principle forbids us to help ourselves to what we want—our wants are supplied from the public treasury and are controlled by its resources. The principle should extend to those whose business puts money in their pocket; successful traffic is a temptation to self-appropriation. The question of two prices has been discussed. Is it lawful to take what you can get instead of sticking to what you consider a fair remuneration? Peddlers who have tried both ways say they have more satisfaction in adhering to one price, no matter at what sacrifice, than in the system of prevarication that two prices almost compel. A question is: What shall be done with doubtful money? Another question is, whether it is the duty of persons riding in the train to hunt up the conductor and pay their fare if he fails for any reason to call for it. Some of our folks are conscientious enough to take a good deal of pains to find him; others feel justified in letting him take care of his own business. It was thought to be the meanest kind of sneaking to evade the payment of railroad fare. The whole peddling business is up for judgment in our court of criticism, and the result will be its thorough purification and reform or abandonment.

"Instructions for Community Silk Dealers were posted on November 1st:

1. Never sell a poor article of silk for a good one.
2. Adhere to the prices agreed upon for the wholesale, retail, and Jobbing trades *without deviation*.
3. Never allow a known mistake in quantity, price, or making change to go unrectified.
4. Never defraud a railroad company.
5. Guard against counterfeits but never *pass* them. If taken, return a suspected bill to the person from whom it was received; otherwise, keep it or destroy it.
6. Never offer to pass un-current money for more than its value.
7. Be prepared on return to make a full account of your transactions.
8. Be truthful in all cases, if it costs you a trade.

"It seems to me desirable that in entering upon the hiring system, we should discuss and settle the principle that is to govern us in regard to bringing workmen into our family," Noyes wrote in November 1862. "I think that the mixing up of the family with its hired men will not only be bad for the spiritual interests of the family, but will be unprofitable from a business point of view, because the free habits of the family in regard to labor are very different from those that will be necessary for men under wages."

"We began planning for a new shop and in 1864 we put up a large brick edifice at Willow Place; we've hired much of the work since its completion. The manufacture of plows and other agricultural implements was commenced and for the first time an office was established in New York City for the sale of all Community products. Silk-jobbing, which had been discontinued along with the peddling business, was resumed; the time had come to manufacture silk instead of buying it for resale. In 1865 the silk-business was started, which has been a source of great profit. Early in 1866, William Inslee commenced the construction of the necessary machinery; Mr. C. L. Bottum, a silk manufacturer in Willimantic, Connecticut, readily consented to admit one Community young man and two young women as apprentices."

How to Manufacture Silk

"Cocoons, which look like large peanuts, are put into a vessel of boiling water, which stands in a small furnace, the furnace itself being set in front of a small table on a level with the operator as she sat in a low chair. The action of the hot water in a few minutes loosened the gum that in their natural condition cements the fibers to the cocoon. Taking a brush in one hand, the youth stirred the cocoons about with it until the requisite number of fibers was detached at their ends, and clinging to the brush. From this they were quickly brought together to form a thread, passed through a fixed guide or staple at the opposite edge of the table, from this through a staple on a reciprocating bar, and thence to the reel, which was revolved by the hand of a small boy. A second thread was formed in like manner, and in the same way connected with the reel. As the reel revolved, the fibers were drawn or unwound from the cocoons, which danced about in the boiling water, united in the two threads, and conducted to the reel upon which they were distributed by the vibratory movement of the bar previously mentioned. The two threads, in passing to the reel, were made to cross each other at an angle of about twenty degrees. This was the distinguishing characteristic of the new invention, and the advantage claimed for it is that the two threads, in rubbing upon each other as they pass to the reel, causes the gum to stick the fibers more closely together, and consequently secure a smoother and firmer thread. After certain lengths of the two threads were wound upon the reel, its motion was stopped, the two threads were severed from it, and the two skeins of raw silk, bright yellow or lighter colored according to the original tinge of the cocoons, were slipped from its ends. The peculiar skill required from the attendant is shown in keeping the threads continuous as the fibers wind off and leave the cocoons, it being necessary to add the fiber from a new cocoon at the instant the fiber from the previous one is exhausted. The fibers are of course too fine to be seen at the distance of more than a few inches, and while the operator was attending to her work, it seemed as it her fingers were flying in the weaving of an invisible web.

"Harriet Allen, standing in the door of the silk factory, overheard two Irishmen talking with Mr. S.

"'Where do they get this silk?'

"'They buy it,' replied Mr. S.

"'But where does it come from?'

"'Oh,' said Irishman No. 2, 'it comes from down South.'

"'How does it grow?' continued the questioner.

"'Why, man,' he answered, with the air of one who has an infinite fund of wisdom, 'the bees make it.'

"'Bees!' exclaimed No. 1, 'I never heard of that before. I thought it grew like cotton!'"

"Following a depression due to the declaration of [Civil] war, a business boom commenced. 'It is tremendous to think of, but we're $715 behind our orders for traveling bags,' wrote the Oneida journalist. By spring 1863, men were hired for farm work and teaming, and that autumn the trap shop was swamped with orders far beyond the ability of the Community to supply by their own labor. It became necessary to decide whether to go back to self-help or forward to a new industrial system of hiring on a large scale. The Community hesitated, but began to contemplate hitherto undreamed-of profits. The most that had ever been earned above expenses in one year before was $15,000.00; the year 1863 rolled up a total of $55,000! By this date the financial department was further strengthened and there were eighty outside employees. Work was given out to a number of women in the neighborhood to be done in their homes. What was to be done with this huge surplus? The Community had passed over the line of bare self-support and had become capitalistic. From August 1866 to August 1867 was a year of unprecedented prosperity, internal harmony, and unity with Noyes among all members young and old. In August 1867, nearly every detail of Noyes's plan for establishing the kingdom of God on earth had been accomplished. The final step, the publication of a free, daily paper in New York City, would clinch success.

"But menacing specters of debt again arose, and the Community reexamined its foundations; expansions and events put the Community in debt to the tune of $81,000 by September 1867. Made cautious by experience, Noyes wanted to put the brakes on further expansion. The Communities never sought to grow beyond economic sustainability; in spite of being relatively small in number, they believed that they would be a model for humanity's potential. Noyes valued sufficiency but was always leery of seeking riches and piling up money as an end in itself, which it too often becomes. 'We must adopt the principle of limiting ourselves in the midst of prosperity,' he said. 'We must resolve that we shall be humble and I propose that we solemnly submit our business and organization to God for pruning, if and as much as is necessary, let the cost be what it may.'"

"After years of intermittent throat trouble, Noyes's former difficulty returned. Throughout winter 1868 he took a daily plunge through the ice into Willow Place Pond with twenty other Community men, hoping to repel the attack by inuring himself to hardship. His throat, however, grew worse and worse, until in the winter of 1869 it seemed many times as if he could not survive. He put Theodore, who'd completed his medical course at Yale and had expressed wholehearted religious sympathy with his father, in charge of managing the Community finances from 1869 to 1872.

"Theodore introduced promising economies and efficiencies, including reducing the New York Branch to a single room with a desk and bed for agents when in the city; the *Circular* was moved back to Oneida, the nearby hotel was closed, and the Bag and Fruit Preserving businesses were given up. These measures were so effective that the Community owed not a dollar by January 1869 and had invested $20,000.00 of surplus cash in United States bonds. But the Business Board was no longer holding its sessions. Theodore appointed all department heads and they came to him separately for consultation. The Community had little chance to review or even to know what was going on. Young men occupied nearly all the important positions. There was a good deal of talk about 'putting the older generation on the shelf,' and for the first time, running the businesses on a moneymaking basis, always discouraged. Thirty years earlier, when sufficient money for real necessities was a problem, head farmer George Cragin thought they should work more and study and pray less.

"I would rather our land should run to waste," Noyes told him, "than we should fail of a spiritual harvest."

"So a clash occurred between Noyes and his son. Noyes reiterated his chief guiding principle again in January 1872: *Seek first the kingdom of God and his righteousness and all other things shall be added unto you.* 'I had rather have all our departments of business stop than go along on any other principle than that. We must have more spirituality in our business. Theodore is tempted to rely too much on ability and financial machinery, and does not appreciate the tremendous importance of inspiration. I see more and more the necessity of a Business Board that meets weekly and helps us control one another. I would want counsel from the heads of departments every chance I could get. Let the Community discuss them and be free to alter them. I ask the privilege to look them all over myself, and see what I want done. Let us throw all these things open to the daylight. Let all the departments offer themselves for criticism and have no irritability about it.'"

MONEY AND FINANCIAL LITERACY

"It is essential that a unified Community, maintained by the good judgment of the whole body, thoroughly understand finance," Noyes declared on March 30, 1868. "Those who understand financial operations shall extend their knowledge through the whole Community, so that each member will be a financier for himself—understood by every soul clear down to the children. Finance can be taught in a nut-shell: To make money by manufactures, we must do the work ourselves, hire it done, or get it done by machinery before we can get returns. If you must have machinery and hired men to do it for you, you must first determine how much money you can put into it; if you haven't the necessary capital, you must either forego your enterprise, or borrow in the miserable way we have done. If you are sure of making money, there may be cases where it's safe and right to borrow—I won't deny that. But if you are going to start on the system of pre-payment, how much capital do you have to invest? People keep seeing enticing projects for manufactures and improvements, but without understanding the necessity of having the capital to implement them, there will be pressure from various quarters that will keep our financiers in distress. Money pressures and pinches will always be at work unless every individual thoroughly understands the great principle that we can't do a thousand things that might be done—if only we had capital. An individual in a particular business thinks all he has to do is see how he might make his business more profitable and then call for the necessary capital. He reasons that if he had money he could make machinery and lessen the amount of labor required, but he doesn't inquire whether we have the capital to put into it. He has wasted valuable time and thought on a impracticable project. If we all will seek a quiet, contented spirit that devotes thought and discussion to practical things that we *can* do, this will be a very valuable addition to the force of the Community.

"What we want now is a reform of our mental habits," Noyes elaborated. "I had proposed a way of making money; now I want to propose a way of saving money. I go for economy of thinking and talking, for reforming the speculations of our mind, chastening them and bringing them down to practicality. Then we'll have similar views and concerns, and things will take care of themselves instead of tormenting our financial managers by calling for money when we don't have it! A meek and quiet spirit is what we want, continence of spirit that is contented with small things. Excess of enterprise has been the bane of this Community. We are pushed and propelled into it by demand for our manufactures. We must not be governed by the demand for traps or silk, but by our ability to supply. One governed by demand will be ruined; his ability to supply is all he can go by. We must wisely calculate our abilities, be content, and turn away from illusory schemes based on borrowing. These schemes are really covetousness, the very covetousness that God forbids, hankering after money you do not have. Many former attempts to live communally show that where there was no patience, no compromising or conciliation over a great question connected with business, that Community broke up.

"The great lesson that our Community has learned is that the faculty of agreement—unity—is a more radical quality of character than it is considered by most people. It is a thing of the heart rather than of the mind. A man who is proud, conceited, self-willed, unscrupulous, and selfish cannot agree with others; cannot even be consistent with himself. We say of such a one, he is *hardhearted*. The soft heart makes a man humble, gentle, easily-entreated, truthful, and loving. Persons with these characteristics can form communities, and succeed; and none other. Where diversity of judgment has arisen, by being patient with each other, waiting, and submitting all minds to the Spirit of truth—we have always secured unanimity. When we built our new mansion, how many were the different minds about material, location, plan—there was the brick party, the stone party, and the concrete-wall party. How our feelings were wrought up! Yet by patience, forbearing, and submitting to one another, the final result satisfied everyone. Unity is the essential thing. It has become a settled conviction all through our Community, that when a project is brought forward for discussion we shall soon all be of one mind about it, and the best thing will be done. Secure that, and financial success and all other good things will follow. Let us see if there is the peace of God in the Community sufficient to overcome the tendency to excessive enterprise. It's a pernicious thing, thinking what we could do if we only had the money! The economical way is to be content with what we have, and give our attention energetically to what is sure and within our reach. Do what you see is a good thing to be done. After that, something else will come; avoid wasting yourself or drowning your minds in useless thought—as truly a narcotic as are tobacco or opium.

"The Community women held a meeting to devise ways and means to reduce their expenses to help solve the great financial problem, the *Oneida Journal* noted on March 28, 1868. 'We shall dismiss the hired women from our laundry and supply their places with help from our own number. Much of the house-cleaning has been performed by hired help, but this spring we are going to dispense with that also. We don't feel poor or cramped, and aside from all financial considerations, we find it a good ordinance from time to time to bestir ourselves energetically against the encroachments of worldly fashion; to resist indignantly the tendency that sometimes creeps in to make us effeminate. We want strong bodies and spirits that we may cooperate in every department of useful labor. There is hardly any limit to our opportunities for usefulness, and ready hands and cheerful hearts expect a fruitful harvest from our united industry. The Community has turned away from many amusements that have been popular in the past—amusements taken up to kill time are apt to end in weariness and disgust. We find too much serious business ahead to allow time or inclination for mere amusements. We want to find relief and relaxation in useful pursuits and keep ourselves sober and watchful. We do not feel less happy but more so. We want to make a deeper growth in spirituality.' A lively ambition was expressed by old and young to do whatever is in our power to help forward the good cause.

"Determining to get out of debt, we have arranged our businesses so that in times of extraordinary pressure from orders we shall have provided a larger stock of goods on hand than heretofore," reported the April 4, 1868, *Circular*. "Last fall, the shops at Willow Place were the scene of an extraordinary whirl of business—sixty extra hired hands besides all our people who could be spared from other quarters, and the shops running nights by a large force of volunteers from our own number, who worked their full time by daylight. We've since found that some of our weaker members injured themselves through excess of zeal and lack of proper forethought by those whose duty it was to look after them. This matter came up for criticism in our evening meeting. It was plainly seen that what we intended for a great good has proved in some cases a great evil, and needs to be repented of by all concerned. All testified that a valuable lesson has been learned—we must learn to provide time for rest and meditation at all times, even if we have to forego large sales.

"In the next eight years, the Community became a full-time industrial enterprise, producing tens of thousands of traps in six sizes and shipping them to the frontiers of the United States and Canada. The Hudson Bay Company sent an order so large that the entire Community mobilized to fill it, and school was temporarily suspended until production caught up. Forty skilled laborers from outside the Community were employed, their payroll exceeding $1,100 monthly. Mr. Hamilton reflected on their successful businesses: 'Money, in one sense, is like the circulation of the blood in the body. I don't think it is God's purpose to make us immensely rich. Individuals and corporations, when they amass property that doesn't play an important part in the business and as a moral influence in society, are like persons who are getting a big, overgrown belly. I like to be in good condition and see others so, and am ambitious to see the Community grow strong and acquire a great deal of power, but I don't believe God proposes to have us become pot-bellied.'

"We recognize the hand of God that led us through poverty and persecution into prosperity and peace, and we offer the future destiny of the Oneida Community to his keeping. Noyes assured the Community that 'the religion of heaven is not a drowsy affair of sitting on benches and psalm-singing, forever repeating things we have found good; everything we know of Christ shows that he never does the same thing twice, nor stays long in the same place. Let us not lay again the foundations that are already laid, but counting them eternally good, move forward under the guidance of the Spirit of Truth—it is mighty and magnetic, knows everything, and can do everything from teaching a child to pray to building an ironclad.

"Our profitable industries enable us to build a new mansion, to better educate our young people, and most important, to have funds to publish our paper, that we may send the truth freely into the world.

Working in the publications room, a good image capturing women's special mode of dress.

We have gained some proficiency in music. When the Community was becoming truly prosperous, expansions were made—a new trap factory, new farm with a revived fruit business, new dam, and greatly enlarged printing office at Wallingford with the best literary talent. The weekly *Circular* would now include science and art and become a more interesting paper, while keeping its spiritual character. We enjoy many luxuries that eighteen years ago we hardly dreamed of, but we'd give them all up if it were required. There's the same unity and earnestness among us now as there ever was, intensified by more depth of purpose and sincere love for living in Community.

"The Community was not born to a fortune and we have worked heartily through our narrow circumstances, but are fast growing into circumstances of ease and leisure," the March 23, 1874, *Circular* noted. "We are comparatively without care due to the division of responsibility that our system affords, and we average fewer hours of work than the industrious classes in the world. It seems to me that the great value of wealth is not that it gives us the privilege of living without work, but that it enables us to find work that is good and attractive and healthy," Mr. Noyes said in the evening meeting. "That is the use we are going to make of riches. They give us liberty and power to find good healthy work. Working ten or twelve hours a day under compulsion in the work-or-starve system I do not think is good or healthy. But for people who have abundance of means and could live without work, to turn to manual labor for profit of the soul as well as the body—that is something the Lord is pleased with and something we are going to do. It is just as displeasing to God that we cultivate exclusively our spiritual natures and neglect material things, as it would be to devote ourselves wholly to material things."

"Noyes opposed the unbalanced approach that values book-learning only and tends to despise manual labor, and likewise, specialization at the expense of education of the heart and spirit. The Community strived for education of the whole person. As the Community prospered and their businesses changed, more sedentary employments engaged many of their men; they found themselves occasionally sighing for the good old days when they hoed corn and dug ditches—no need to worry about physical development then! They gave more attention to insuring first-rate physical fitness and more importantly, to ponder about their children—will they learn physical work, get the vigorous, hardy constitution of the farmer, when there is no spur of necessity goading them on?"

THE CIVIL WAR

"At the height of the Civil War," the August 13, 1863, *Circular* noted: "When government stood with one foot upon the neck of the slave and trampled upon the rights of the red man with the other, we had no sympathy with it . . . . Our interest in the war was very deep and our sympathies were drawn out towards it as we saw it developing in the people and the government a recognition of the rights of man and providence of God in the affairs of the nation. We responded to repeated calls for aid to the soldier, loaned town money to aid in raising volunteers, and our direct United States war taxes have amounted to more than $10,000.00. Besides this, our state and county taxes have more than quadrupled, in consequence of heavy bounties paid by the state and counties for volunteers.

"By what some call luck but what we cannot but recognize as providence, the military draft that took place in the district this week passed the Community by without calling for a man. We had expected to be hit and have held our business arrangements in suspense for a considerable time to provide for the call of several of our members, but through a mistake of the enrolling officer, the names of Community men were not taken in the spring enrollment. This mistake resulted because our residence is situated on the border of two counties and two Congressional Districts in a sharp bend of Oneida Creek, which is crossed by bridges a short distance on either side of us. We are in Madison County between the bridges while our neighbors on both sides of us are in Oneida County. The enrolling officer supposed that we belonged to the other district.

"In August 1864 a *Circular* article discussed their profound conviction, *Overcome Evil with Good*. It will surely prevail in all advances of the kingdom of heaven into this world, and war will be no more. It is our business to see the peace of God in our hearts and blow peace upon the world. Our true course is to give political matters only that amount of attention that will keep us reasonably well posted in the progress of events. We find that it requires much more heroism to persevere in turning resolutely away from outside turmoil than to allow ourselves to be entirely absorbed by it. The Community knew that *lasting* peace will never come through fighting. Both sides will fight till they are exhausted and sick of war. And the North is fighting the war with the war spirit, criticizing the South for adherence to slavery, but the North is deserving of equal criticism for its love of money, which is the root of slavery. Outward reform in regard to slavery left the root of evil fully and firmly planted in the soil of the North's heart. It has fallen from grace—the love of money has swamped its spirituality. Thirty years ago during the Second Great Awakening, the North drew near to God and throbbed with the presence of his spirit, the basis of all that is righteous and noble in it today; this alone gives the North the spiritual authority to criticize the South.

"Laying the ax at the root of the tree of sin would emancipate the master as well as the slave from spiritual bondage, introducing both master and slave to a kingdom of unity and peace on an equal footing. Under the reign of such a spirit in the heart of men, slavery would have melted as ice beneath the sun of midsummer and elevated all to the privileges of heavenly citizenship, making them one heart and soul. I would have the North go into thorough self-examination and repentance of sin by prayer and seeking salvation of heart," Noyes wrote. "The nation can be truly redeemed only if its heart is purified from the love of money by the Spirit of Truth and is filled with the Spirit of God. A spiritual revival is worth more than millions of armed men on the field of battle or fleets of ironclads sweeping every ocean. But diverted from spiritual to carnal war, the result is devastation and killing; instead of building churches, communities, schools, universities, and converting souls, war without God's inspiration ended with bayonets and cannonballs. Granted that there was cause for war on the part of the North; the anti-slavery movement was a movement for righteousness between man and man. But war ruled by the spirit of West Point and not by the Spirit of Truth was a descent from interior spiritual ends.

"If slavery's fountain, the selfish heart, is not changed, not a jot or tittle of the inner store of human cruelty will be annihilated. Oppression in some other form, equivalent to slavery, will take its place. So long as the issues of the world's heart are murder, theft, covetousness, the strong will surely enslave the weak, in fact if not in form. There will be no radical and lasting reform until men get power to will healthily and to see clearly. That power belongs only to a sound heart; and soundness of heart comes only by that grace that saves from all sin. Popular religion has no power to mend the case, for it declares that *all* hearts, regenerate and unregenerate, are 'deceitful above all things and desperately wicked' and there it leaves us, neither presenting or allowing any hope of better hearts in this world. The 7th chapter of Romans is the only standard of experience licensed by the clergy, and that is the very standard of the drunkards and pledge-breakers.

"Temperance can never win a complete and permanent victory in the present state of human nature," Noyes believed. "If it gains three feet every day, it slips back at least two feet every night. Millions sign the pledge, but hardly thousands or even hundreds keep it. Zealous Temperance men in all our towns have been driven to the secret conviction, if not the open acknowledgment, that an Anti-Lying society is needed as the antecedent and basis of the Temperance Society. The unregenerate heart is in very deed 'deceitful above all things and desperately wicked.' How can the fidelity and truthfulness necessary to the efficacy of the Temperance pledge be expected from it?

"Reformers work for universal temperance, health, wealth, and education; they call for the establishment of peace between nations and strive after social unity and happiness," Noyes wrote. "We freely concede to these friends an elevated vision that catches outlines of the coming dispensation, but our confidence in their operations goes no further. Excellent as their objectives and intentions are, we can yet see no advantage to be gained by introducing a righteousness of constitutions, organizations, pledges, and petitions, at best a miserable imitation of God's righteousness and unattainable singly or by human industry. The one luminous fact to note is that the New Testament proposes to bring the power of God to grapple with evil at the very root of human character. The living word of God in the heart is the only effectual agency of reform. Effectual medicine for the diseased hearts of the people is salvation from all sin, now and forever, which substitutes for the moral impotence of the 7th of Romans. Meantime, underneath the tumult, the true seed is sown in many hearts. Enthusiasts who toil in different departments of reform seek good fruit, but a period for growth is necessary after seed is sown. Strife and its results for a time are too complex for human perception. Life is slow of growth, so faith and patience of the highest kind is requisite to the laborer in spiritual husbandry."

"Noyes wrote to William Lloyd Garrison a declaration of independence from the government, which he saw condoning slavery and treating Native Americans with cruelty; society had become antagonistic to peace, human brotherhood, and holiness. 'I called at the Boston antislavery office and introduced myself to Garrison, who spoke with great interest of *The Perfectionist*; he said his mind was heaving on the subjects of holiness and the kingdom of heaven and he would devote himself to them, as soon as slavery was ended.' Noyes wrote him days later: 'Allow me to suggest that you will set antislavery in the sunshine by making it a tributary to holiness. I counsel you and the people with you to set your faces toward perfect holiness. Your station is one that gives you power over the nations. Your city is on a high hill. If you plant the standard of perfect holiness where you stand, many will see and flow to it.' Garrison read extracts from it at a public meeting in Rhode Island and on October 20, 1837, he published it in *The Liberator*, omitting only Noyes's signature. Garrison wrote to H. C. Wright, 'There is nothing more offensive to the religionists of the day as *practical holiness*—they hate the doctrine of total abstinence from sin in this life . . . and stigmatize entire freedom from sin as a delusion of the devil! Nevertheless, *He that is born of God cannot commit sin.*'"

"We consider ourselves fellow-conscripts with the soldiers, pioneering in the noble task of making human society a better place for them on their return," the May 29, 1865, *Circular* concluded. "Ruled by the Spirit of Truth, the living Christ within us, all false institutions and relations would pass away; evil in individuals, societies, and nations would disappear by making men new creatures, giving them pure hearts, sound minds, and the beauty and power of all-controlling love. The spiritual regeneration of mankind is the only lasting foundation for remaking human society."

"If we find ourselves in a conflict with evil, we may settle it in our hearts that God is not only on our side in the conflict, but he is on the other side too; if he is on our side in the highest, final sense, he is managing the other side with reference to improving us, disciplining us, drawing us out, and making the most of our faculties and patience," Noyes spoke to the Wallingford Community on March 18, 1868. This Home Talk, *God on Both Sides*, "brings out very clearly the necessity of our getting clear above the fight into a place where we feel as God does, who 'maketh his sun to rise on the evil and on the good, and sendeth rain on the just and on the unjust'; where we can pray for our enemies and bless them that curse us; where we can take opposition as serenely as we take assistance. The work of righteousness is so complicated, so composite, that we have to know how to fight and struggle tremendously, and still recognize this principle, as Christ did. *Father, forgive them, for they know not what they do*. His faith rose above it all."

Quack Beds—A Community Parable:

"Quack is a species of grass with which many are acquainted, to their sorrow. It is very hardy and prolific and when it has once gained a foothold, its extermination is exceedingly difficult. Its deep roots spread all through the ground, forming a firm sod. Cutting it off with a hoe above the surface of the ground does no good, but rather harm, because checking the growth above ground gives new strength to the roots and causes them to send forth a multiplied number of shoots. The only way to exterminate the pest is to dig out every root and rootlet. It will not do to break off the main root and leave the branches in the ground, for they will surely spring forth again. In preparing the land for strawberry-plants, which we set out in the spring, the quack was not eradicated from one corner of the field and it soon threatened to overrun and entirely choke the strawberry-plants, in spite of thorough hoeing. So I was directed to take a spading-fork, and dig out every root and branch, and carry them off the field.

"While busily engaged in this work, it was suggested to my mind that mankind, including the majority of professing Christians, are quack beds. Each human being is a field in which the devil sows quack, that being the crop in which he deals. A great many persons do not see much harm in a little quack, or they think that some future time will do to set about killing it. Others think that all that grows in the field is good, and that at the harvest, the husbandman will gather everything into the garner. Still others see the vileness of the plant and that if not killed, it will destroy the whole field; but not knowing its nature they keep hacking away at the top of it, vainly hoping thus to destroy it. But this treatment does no good and rather strengthens the root, and up it comes again until those who are seeking to rid themselves of it, almost in despair cry out, 'Who shall deliver us from this vile weed'?

"I got hold of a work called the *Berean* that treated this subject in a masterly way and gave full instructions for the entire eradication of the plant—dig out the roots, thus leaving the ground entirely free to be occupied by good seed. Nothing short of this will save the field. The tools to work with are repentance, confession, and faith. Repentance is genuine only when it results in the forsaking of sin. Periodic repentance, implying continuance in sins repented of, is merely cutting off the tops of the plant, and is most horrible hypocrisy. 'Godly sorrow worketh repentance that needs not be repented of.' There are things which, though necessary that they should be done once, ought not to be done the second time. In order to raise a field of strawberries, it is necessary to dig out the quack so thoroughly that the work need not be done a second time, lest you destroy the plants too. Likewise, thorough repentance is essential, to entirely eradicate sin from the heart, else, in oft-repeated attempts, the seeds of grace will be unable to take root, and you will be obliged to say at last, 'The harvest is passed, the summer is ended, and we are not saved.' Perfect holiness is as consistent with growth in grace, as perfect freedom from quack in a strawberry bed is consistent with the growth in size and good flavor of the fruit."

THE GRAB-GAME, OR E PLURIBUS UNUM?

"I've had occasion to go among the poor in cities since growing up and have seen such scenes of wretchedness, the result of poverty, that I've been almost tempted to think it was a sin to be rich," said a Community member. "It does not comfort me to have people tell me that these poor people are to be blamed for their poverty—that they swear, drink, chew, and smoke; for it seems to me that all these bad habits are as likely to be the results of poverty as to be its cause. It is equally as true that ignorant and bad habits arise out of poverty, as it is that poverty grows out of ignorance and bad habits. The truth is that the whole concern is a blot on the face of God's beautiful universe.

"So, you don't like the grab-game even though you have made a successful grab?" my friend P.L.W. said. "Neither do I and I don't think the Lord does. I wish there were more of that feeling in the world. We would be a great deal happier if there were. This feeling has warmed the heart of mankind, but has never flamed up with sufficient brightness to show the true road to its attainment or what true liberty is. It consists in having universal promotion of full development of each human being. Consider what a glorious state of things it would be if the cold, separating influences that have settled over the warm hearts of God's children were banished! Each could serve his neighbors with his best talents and energies, and then each will be served by all in the best manner.

"Young William Bower has the finest talents for landscape gardening and has cultivated those talents as far as diligent study can do it. Put him on an extensive estate and give him plenty of help and he would soon make a perfect paradise of it, but he's cramped on his little half-acre lot while the estate's head gardener is throwing away thousands in cutting up the estate. I never shall have perfect liberty until I can see a brother in every face into which I look. The little morsel of liberty I can grasp by my own unaided efforts is hardly worth contending for. I want the assistance of God and the whole universe to help me to it. *E Pluribus Unum*: fix your eye on that mark. Labor and pray for it: *If any man lack wisdom, let him ask of God who giveth to all men liberally and upbraidth not*. When the time comes that God's will is done on earth, there will be no rich or poor. As long as the good things of this world are distributed by grab-game rules—each man exerting his strength and talents to magnify his own pile compared to that of his neighbor—there is no perfect liberty. Farmers never treat their land as mankind is now treated; he'd be a fool to leave his manure in a small part of his field and plow and plant and sow without spreading it. So it is with mankind. Many starve while a minority is smothered with good things.

"A farmer's superior corn won awards at the state fair year after year. A newspaper reporter interviewed him and was surprised to discover that the farmer shared his seed corn with all his neighbors! 'Why do you share your best seed corn with farmers who are going to be competing with you every year?' the reporter asked. The farmer smiled. 'The wind picks up pollen from the corn as it ripens and sweeps it from one field to the next,' he explained. 'If my neighbors grow inferior corn, I'll end up growing inferior corn. If they grow good corn, I'll be growing good corn. It's the same elsewhere: Keeping the good all to yourself can hurt you in the end, but sharing what you've got tends to come back to reward you.'"

Natural Liberty, Civil Liberty, and Laws of God

"This discussion continued in the *Circular*: The absolute rights of man, a free agent endowed with discernment to know good from evil, are usually summed up as the *natural liberty* of mankind: the inherent right of acting as one thinks fit without restraint or control, being one of the gifts of God to man when he endowed him with the faculty of free will. But when entering into society and receiving the advantages of mutual commerce, one gives up a part of natural liberty as the price of so valuable a purchase. Society establishes laws and requires obedience, infinitely more desirable than the wild and savage liberty sacrificed to obtain it. No one should wish to retain absolute and uncontrolled power of doing whatever he pleases, for everyone else would also have the same power. Therefore, *civil liberty* is no other than natural liberty restrained by laws (and no further) as is necessary and expedient for the public good. Society sacrifices an inferior kind of liberty to gain a superior kind. The Oneida Community sacrifices the liberty of selfishness and gains a liberty as much nobler than that of common society, as that liberty is nobler than the liberty of savages. William Seward enunciated a *Higher Law* in March 1850 when discussing the compact of the Constitution that bound Free States to deliver fugitive slaves to their masters: 'The Law of Nations, written on the hearts and consciences of freemen, repudiates such compacts. There are constitutions and statutes, laws mercantile and codes civil; but when we are legislating for states, those laws must be brought to the standard of the *laws of God* and must be tried by that standard, and stand or fall by it.'"

"St. Paul traces the root of all evil to the love of money, and the apostle made a center shot, laments the October 11, 1869, *Circular*. "Wall Street speculators Jay Gould and his partner James Fisk attempted to corner the gold market on the New York Gold Exchange, causing the price of gold to plummet on September 24, 1869, financially ruining many. That day was ever after referred to as Black Friday. One man is reported to have accosted another on Wall Street during this frenzy, asking, 'Where is all this to end?' The laconic answer: 'End in hell.' Why is so palpable an evil as the love of money left intact while moralists and reformers spend all their ammunition on mere branches of the great tree of evil? The whole brood of worldly diseases that curse humanity are but off-shoots of this central lust for money; reformers may hew off diseased branches, but the tree will remain corrupt while the love-of-money root remains. How shall we lay the ax at the root of this blighting evil? It is in the spirit that says, 'All mine are thine, and thine are mine.'

"We hold that all the systems of property-getting in vogue in the world are forms of what is vulgarly called the 'grab-game'—the game in which prizes are not distributed by any rules of wisdom and justice, but are seized by the strongest and craftiest. The *laws* of the world simply give rules, more or less civilized, for the conduct of this game. God the Creator has the first and firmest title to all property and no way of escape from the miseries of the grab-game will ever be found until *His* title and right of distribution are acknowledged. In the kingdom of God, every citizen is subordinate joint-owner with God of all things, and the reign of covetousness, competition, and violence is ended. In trying to establish that kingdom on earth, the Oneida Community's doctrine was that of community, not merely with each other but with God; they looked not to constitutions or compacts with each other but to the wisdom and goodness of the Spirit of Truth."

"George Cragin wrote in the *Circular* on September 29, 1873: 'The celebrated houses of Jay Cooke & Company, Fisk & Hatch, Hoyt, and New England's greatest manufacturing firm, the A. & W. Sprague Manufacturing Company, have been compelled to suspend payment, causing wide-spread business cessation and the closing of the Stock Exchange, throwing thousands of working people out of employment. The failure was caused by doing business on insufficient capital, which dragged them into a financial slough of bonds and mortgages, loans at enormous rates of interest, compromises with creditors, and an immeasurable amount of anxiety. A. & W. Sprague spread its capital and dozens of factories, manufacturing companies, mills, water-privileges, woodland by the hundred thousand acres, horse railroads, savings banks, and steamboat lines from Maine to South Carolina—and now a temporary stringency of the money market cripples them at once, and down they go. We're not opposed to moneyed institutions established to meet the needs of commerce; but beyond that, financial institutions will eventually assume the character of gambling and unjustifiable speculations that become parasitical and a prey on the vitals of healthy business. Whatever we sow, that also shall we reap—a law that applies to all classes of people and to all pursuits in life, be they moral, spiritual, or physical; the reaping-time often comes when least looked for.'"

"Such financial storms affect us unavoidably," Noyes wrote on November 10, 1873. "Our busiest time of year is September and for the first ten days of the month we received only a quarter of the money due us, ordinarily confidently counted on. It briefly seemed as if we could scarcely meet our obligations promptly. The payment of many of our small debts was delayed beyond thirty days, but we are now making collections fast enough to catch up with them. For some years we've required the use of borrowed capital during the summer and autumn, obtained from our banks, and taking four or six months' credit on our principal articles of raw material, contrary to our usual custom. The temptation is strong to make permanent use of our credit in this way, and so extend our operations beyond the limits set them, but a Community like ours cannot afford to run risks. We determined to 'pay as we go' for everything we buy. If the whole country becomes bankrupt, the worst that can happen will be temporary cessation of manufacturing. Having no debts to pay, we can live on mush and applesauce and wear our old clothes until better times. Our cause is too precious to risk in the arena with the bulls and bears, and we shall gladly bid goodbye soon to the credit system with all its allurements.

"The great evil to be avoided by the Community and by the financial board is *anxiety*, which affects the Community and all mankind. I want a system that will save us from the heart-torments of the money world," Noyes wrote. "Isn't this the objective that should prevail over our ambition to enlarge and expand our businesses, over our love of rich food and fine clothes, over our desire for more buildings and all projects that keep our expenses so large? Anxiety presses right on the pit of the stomach and is very unhealthy. It affects us in the same place as indigestion and takes the place of a feeling of happiness and buoyancy that ought always to be at the pit of the stomach. In the 6th chapter of Matthew, Jesus repeatedly says, *take no thought* for the necessaries of life; the Greek word translated *thought* is '*merimnesete*,' which means *anxious*. Not that we should go poor—*your heavenly Father knows that ye have need of these things*, but he sets himself against everlasting anxiety. If we want the love of God or of man or of woman, we must have the pit of the stomach free from anxiety. Our financiers must manage our affairs so the farmers, our elderly, and women and children of the Community, are freed from this anxiety. For the sake of the love, joy, and peace that are principal elements of good religious experience and good home life, let us take care in all things, especially in money-matters, to run no unnecessary risks. Give the heart freedom from anxiety—the freedom to love and be happy. Our present system of finance is like the young men who went out on Oneida Lake in the boat during a storm recently. They didn't capsize or have loss of lives, but they put themselves and their friends on shore in a terrible state of anxiety. If we must lie down in the boat and bail strenuously through the storm, I do not consider it a success even though we do get ashore. Our enterprising financiers are tempted to expand business, so when a storm comes it's necessary for some of us to lie in the bottom of the boat and bail. That certainly is not the best way."

On being out on the water in a storm: "Two young men sailing recently on Delaware Bay were overtaken by a squall," the September 1872 *Circular* reported. "They'd been in a Methodist Church and were familiar with how religious services are conducted. As they were about to capsize, one said, 'Bill, this is serious business, can you pray?' 'I've heard Joe do it, but I can't do it myself.' 'You can sing a hymn, can't you? Do something!' 'No—how can I sing when this boat may at any moment drown us?' 'Well, we must do something religious; if you can't pray or sing, let's take up a collection.'"

"The Community always attended to the greater happiness of their employed workers: the December 8, 1873, *Circular* noted that an evening school has been started near the Trap Factory for our employees in the Trap Shop and Silk Factory. Mr. Nelson, station-master at the Community Midland depot, has consented to act as teacher, and although it's his first attempt as a school-master, he seems well qualified both by education and character to fill the position. Two rooms were fitted up in the old Willow Place house, now partly used as a machine-shop. Conveniences are somewhat primitive, with the exception of a handsome map presented by a friend in New York. Thirty scholars ranging from twelve to twenty-five years are divided into two classes according to their attainments, and each class meets three evenings in the week from six till eight. A great desire for improvement seems to possess all.

"A young man engaged in the hardware department wrote a note addressed to the family: 'I had lost the light heart I felt at the beginning of the season. I saw it was because I had allowed business to absorb the whole of my attention, and I'd dropped my hour for prayer. I'm now resolved to be faithful to this—let business be ever so pressing. Several expressed their interest in his experience: 'It requires a good deal of earnestness to be faithful to our hour of prayer, as I have found,' William Hinds assured him. 'It is all important that we be faithful to that ordinance, no matter what the pressure of business may be. It seemed to us like an inspired suggestion and we found great benefit from it.'"

"It is very true that it takes earnestness and self-control to turn away from external things. We must find a way to have our thoughts and attention under control or it will be comparatively profitless for us to have an hour for retirement," William Woolworth pointed out. 'Christ can do this for us—he can bring our thoughts into subjection to himself.'

"It is a good idea now to read the latter part of the 6th chapter of Matthew; if people will read that every day until they get it by memory, and reflect on it, it will help control this rush of business," John Humphrey Noyes summed it up. "That is the very foundation of my business character, and it is the foundation of the business character of the Community; we shall never prosper on any other foundation. We ought always to take plenty of time and especially in busy times to thoroughly understand that constitution. We shall have to be spiritual students to harmonize meditation on God with all necessary business. Once when there was monetary pressure on us, I proposed that we go without any new clothing for a year. It relieved the pressure at once, and it would relieve the pressure of all Wall Street if those moneyed men pursued that policy. If we should have hard pressures of business this fall, it would be easy for the Community not to call for another piece of clothing for a year. That is the financial advantage and safety we have by studying Christ's principles and living them."

11

Stirpiculture: Planning Parenthood

TO A MORE SPIRITUAL HUMANITY

"Following the publication of Charles Darwin's *On the Origin of Species* in November 1859, Noyes began studying the emerging discipline of scientific breeding. Darwin discusses 'the hereditary varieties or races of our domestic animals and plants.' His publisher insisted on adding the subtitle *by Means of Natural Selection, or the Preservation of Favoured Races in the Struggle for Life*. Palaeontologist Heinrich Georg Bronn translated *On the Origin of Species* into German, and having a religious outlook, translated 'favoured races' as 'perfected races.' The word race in this context means only varieties—there is no discussion of the human race. Alfred Russel Wallace asked Darwin if *Origin of Species* would examine human origins; Darwin told him that he would avoid that controversial subject. American botanist Asa Gray showed similar interests and Darwin sent Gray a detailed outline of his ideas in 1857. Darwin's theory stated that there is a struggle for existence because many more individuals of each species are born than can survive under varying conditions of life. Therefore if any individual varies even slightly in a way profitable to itself, it will have a better chance of surviving and thus be *naturally selected*. Any selected variety will tend to propagate its new and modified form. Animals and plants with desirable traits are artfully and systematically bred and cultivated.

"There is grandeur in this view of life . . . . From so simple a beginning, endless forms most beautiful and most wonderful have been, and are being, evolved," he concluded. In 1871, Darwin examined human evolution and sexual selection in *The Descent of Man, and Selection in Relation to Sex*. Noyes studied Gregor Johann Mendel's *Experiments on Plant Hybridization*, published in 1866, a work with little impact, it was said, because it dealt with hybridization rather than inheritance—even Charles Darwin was unaware of Mendel's paper! Mendel began his studies on heredity using mice, but the bishop at St. Thomas's Abbey did not like one of his friars studying animal sex, so Mendel switched to plants. William Bateson publicized the value of Mendel's work and used the word genetics; Francis Galton, Darwin's cousin, referred to human racial improvement in the mid-1860s and published *Hereditary Genius, Its Laws and Consequences* in 1869. His work, *Human Faculty*, spoke of well-born in a spiritual sense; he lamented that the dark ages may have been caused by the celibacy of religious orders, restricting offspring of gentle natures.

"Noyes read about how much more care, thought, and money are devoted to the production of improved horses than to men and women. 'Is it possible to produce healthy, spirited human beings?' one article's author mused. "The breeding of animals under the guidance of science certainly cannot be implemented for the improvement of humans; God does not manage us in any such way," Noyes commented in a Home-Talk at the family meeting on March 15, 1869. "The final government under which human propagation will be conducted must be free self-control. Rational demonstrations and good spiritual influences instead of personal dictation are to govern. We as a Community are already well advanced in arrangements favorable to scientific propagation—our living in large numbers, our displacement of marriage, our training in male continence, our victory over special love, and the growth of public spirit among us, make it easy for us to do what is utterly impossible in ordinary society. Let us consider it our business to pioneer in this intricate possibility. I intend to study this question with all the help I can get from above, and I hope the whole Community will do so. The greatest want of the world is spiritual men and women in every department of action. The emphatic lesson that horse-breeders teach is that improvement is to proceed on two lines—take the best possible care those already born, and attend faithfully to the second imperative—to make the next generation as much better than ourselves as we can."

Noyes agreed with Galton that intellectual, artistic, moral, and spiritual proclivities are transmissible, as well as physical qualities: "The Shakers virtually castrate themselves, though they claim to be the world's noblest and purest people. If home could be enlarged to the scale, for instance, of the Shaker families, and if men and women could be taught to enjoy love that stops short of propagation, and if all could learn to love other children than their own, there would be nothing to hinder scientific propagation in the midst of homes far better than any that now exist. The Shakers claim that by making the Church the unit of society, they have the best of homes even now. Shakers live in peace and plenty and breed the best of horses and cattle. They are just the people to take hold of scientific propagation in earnest to advance the world. Institutions of the future must not injure *home*. The best part of human happiness consists in sexual and parental love, and the best part of education consists in the training of these passions in the school of home. The practical difficulties of our problem must not turn us away from the study and discussion of it."

The Community limited offspring by practicing Male Continence, demonstrating the great effectiveness and intriguing acceptance of male responsibility for birth control. They tested the implementation of continence by the entire male membership and produced less than two babies a year in the great family. Like all prudent families, they limited births until they were out of debt and economically viable, and were always able to provide well for every child. Equally important, Community women conceived children only when they chose, a truly remarkable accomplishment for those times and in that large family. The men from the original Putney Community had no children in the Children's House with the exception of George Washington Noyes, the father of a boy of seven. Applications for membership averaging about two per week in 1867 were from persons seeking refuge from the world's hardships, not from those eager to enlist in the great enterprise of establishing the kingdom of God on earth, so Noyes said he would not be afraid to try his dream of scientific propagation. "For the growth of the Community, we must look in the direction of spiritual regeneration of our own young people; have a far-reaching purpose to save the world by combining regeneration with generation."

Master Community horticulturist Henry J. Seymour wrote in *Ripe Fruit* an enlightening metaphor about the growth of this Community in the spring of 1869: "There are three distinct stages in the perfecting of good fruit: First is the short stage of blossoming, through which seed is fertilized with pollen. Then a longer period of growth of the fleshy part of the fruit occurs. Finally comes the somewhat protracted period during which the seed is ripened and this is the stage most trying to patience. Grapes very quickly get their full size, but un-ripened clusters hang on the vines for weeks and one wonders what they are waiting for. Boys many times can't abide this slow process in the case of apples and club off green fruit. The Community's flowering period was when its founder came into a close relation with God, and lived by spiritual inspiration. Its second stage was perfected when a peaceful and harmonious relation was thoroughly established among its members. Its final period, when it shall have ripened its seed, will have been completed when the system of scientific propagation is thoroughly and experimentally established. The Community had to establish first its relations to God; second, the relations of its members to each other; and third, its relations to the succeeding generation. The Community now stands in a position where the first two in this series of periods are completed. The social relations of its members seem to be in a peaceful condition and bread-and-butter questions were settled long ago. Its establishment through coming generations is not yet so clearly manifest. The question whether God has launched the Community with the purpose that it shall stand forever can only be solved by the propagation and nurturance of successors of those who first shouldered and bore its burdens. Outside friends couldn't understand why the Community did not establish other Communities, not perceiving this broad view of Communal progress. Like grapes and apples, the Community is engaged in the comparatively slow process of ripening its seed. Until that is done it cannot reproduce itself. Therefore we say to the impatient as we'd say to the boys, don't club off the green apples."

"In August 1868, a propitious visit to the Community by the editor of the *New York World*, D. G. Croly, was the tipping point for turning dreams into reality. Mr. Croly said that the Community was 'an enormous benefit' and he was particularly interested in scientific propagation. That October, Noyes published in the *Circular*: 'Prosperity inward and outward is rolling in upon us; we are studying Darwin and the Bible on stirpiculture.' He wrote *Scientific Propagation*, a long essay published in August 1870 in *The Modern Thinker: An organ for the most advanced speculations on philosophy, science, sociology, and religion*. 'We intend to build the final wing of our Mansion house next summer and give it to the children with the best equipments that science can furnish for their training; the Community has so far perfected the discipline of its affections that it is ready, as with one heart, for a faithful trial of the experiment of rational breeding. Without immodesty we may ask all who love God and mankind to pray that we may succeed, for our success will surely be the dawn of a better day to the world.'"

One hundred women and men wanted to have children and participate in the stirpiculture venture. From 1869 through 1879, sixty-two children were born, four not surviving infancy. An informal committee consisting of about a dozen central members presided over the proceedings, and later an organized Stirpicultural Committee composed of experienced and judicious persons of both sexes was placed in charge, including Dr. Theodore Noyes and a second physician, both Yale medical school graduates. Out of fifty-one applications from men and women desiring to become parents, forty-two were approved. The Committee usually interested itself in finding a combination that it could approve, and occasionally it took the initiative in bringing about combinations that it deemed ideal. John Humphrey Noyes had nine of these children.

"His niece and trusted assistant Tirzah Miller wrote in her journal on January 9, 1875: 'An aristocracy of the Noyes blood has grown up in the Community. There is no question of the spirituality of the original four—Noyes and his sisters Harriet, Charlotte, and his brother George. Where is there one among the second Noyes generation who has inherited anything like the original faith? Theodore, Joseph Skinner (first cousins of Tirzah), Constance Noyes, and I have not. George Miller (Tirzah's brother) has perhaps a greater measure of the spirit that possessed the founders, but he has few qualities of a leader. An aristocracy of blood in this Community is more unjust and senseless than the aristocracy of the nobility. It is antagonistic to many of our doctrines. One of our dominant ideas is that the natural should be subjected to the spiritual—that the Community has a right at any time to step in and set aside the natural when it interferes with the spiritual. We are taught to consider the children as belonging to all the Community with equal claims on our love. Isn't Mr. Noyes as likely and even more likely to transmit his spirit to those who have adopted his faith, than to those who are of his seed? The only kind of aristocracy possible among us is a spiritual aristocracy, the aristocracy of Jesus when he said, *They who do the will of my Father in heaven, the same are my brother, and mother, and sister.* When the members of one generation become renowned, their children may be eclipsed and paralyzed by the brilliant reputation of their fathers; they may be persons of excellent parts themselves, who, were it not for the glory of their predecessors, would rise into positions of eminence.'"

Stirpiculture did result in healthier offspring. According to actuarial computation based on the Elliott tables for 1870, of fifty-eight Community offspring growing into adulthood, forty-five deaths would have been normal by 1921, whereas only six deaths had occurred in the Stirps. Of the ninety-eight children born to these Strips, there were no still-births and only three died in their first year. The results by actuarial experts are said to be unprecedented in the records of contemporary vital statistics. Was this nature or nurture? Children cared for during infancy by their mothers were admitted to enjoy the amenities and structure of the Children's House when able to walk. The mother continued night care; both child and mother benefited from this arrangement. Until adolescence, the Children's House had complete charge, though all adults visited them and took them outside. Much attention was given to diet, sanitation, profitable activity, character education, and spiritual discussion. Because common epidemic diseases were vigilantly excluded, sickness among the children was rare. At adolescence a young person took his place in the general organization of the Community.

The Second Generation

"The first term of my last year is ended and for a brief fortnight, we three—the Chemist, the Lawyer, and the Engineer—are enjoying the blessings of our Oneida home. One of the worst things about college life is its effect on the home relations of the student," wrote one of our Yale students on January 1, 1873. "The images of father and mother and home in time grow dim. Along with the growth of independence and self reliance natural to coming manhood, his intellectual acquirements give the student a conceit that almost overbalances their value. Home looks dull and tame, and father and mother, though good folks, are old fogeyish—the simple faith of childhood is a forgotten dream. Many students in every part of Yale University, especially the brighter ones, end at last in skepticism after vainly struggling to harmonize their earlier religion with later knowledge. An old Yale graduate said that young men after graduating should spend four years more in educating their spiritual natures, not mere theological 'gerund grinding,' but discipline of the heart and soul. For such a college as this, Yale has few competent professors."

A few of the young men of the second generation sent to Yale returned to the Community as agnostics. One of the brilliant young members, Daniel Bailey, was a chair-bound paraplegic from an injury by a machine extracting roots in his youthful years. He became a leader among the rising young intellectuals, espousing German Rationalism. Bailey's influence became obvious when Harriet Skinner's son Joseph, a nephew of Noyes, became a follower of Bailey's; Theodore was influenced to a lesser extent because he wished to remain in harmony with his father. When Joseph returned from Yale in 1869, he was put in charge of the newly organized Community Academy; Rationalist or Positivist literature were not to be introduced. Joseph Skinner finally left the Community on April 10, 1873, a religious skeptic.

"Do you have any difficulty in your mind about the Bible?" Noyes asked Theodore.

"No sir, I don't know as I do, any that influence me in regard to present faith," Theodore replied. "I find that I allow myself to put a rather freer construction on the first part of the Old Testament than some folks do."

"I put on pretty free construction on that, myself," Noyes agreed. "The account of creation may be a poetic way to convey substantial truth . . . placing God supreme over matter, which is the beginning of all truth. The time has come for us to pitch into the freest discussions about the Bible among ourselves, and we shall come out with a tighter grasp on the Bible than we ever had." Noyes felt that the Community could meet attacks on the letter of the Bible by going way beyond and being more liberal and confident than scientific people themselves.

"It was the study of the Bible that gave me the best heart-experiences of my life and started me on the career that has led to results you seem to approve," Noyes shared with his son, reported in the December 1, 1873, *Circular*. "A man should not easily quarrel with the bridge that has carried him over safely. I know all that has been said against the Bible, and yet I cannot doubt that it has done me a great deal of good; it has in it stores of the deepest and noblest truth. Founded on experimental knowledge of its riches, my respect for it will not allow me to discard it because the churches use it in a narrow-minded way. The Bible has had a large place in history and is likely to hold that place in the ages to come. It was my study of the Bible that made me a Communist based on Acts 2:44–45: 'All who believed were together and had all things in common; and they sold their possessions and goods and distributed them to all, as any had need,' and Acts 4:32—'The company of those who believed were of one heart and soul, and no one said that any of the things he possessed was his own, but instead they had everything in common.'"

"Theodore was a sympathetic but detached observer of the great community experiment. Positivist thought had abated, but Theodore believed that the Community would inevitably go to pieces before many years, and that when that catastrophe occurred, he meant to be on hand to see that justice was done. He did not look upon the prospect as one of unmitigated evil and seemed to have little regret about it, but he still appreciated the communitarian spirit. He decided with deep regret in July that year that he would have to leave the Community for the same reason that Joseph Skinner had left. Noyes told him that he might be free to go or stay, and told him to take the full amount that a departing member received, $100.00—but if he considered this only an excursion with the expectation that he might return, it would be proper to take $50.00, which he did. The door would be open to him."

"I hope you will come back," Noyes told him.

"No one could wish that I could be changed more than I," Theodore responded with real sadness, "but unless I can be changed, it will probably mean a permanent separation."

"I have not determined any destination or occupation yet," he soon wrote to his mother Harriet, "because I find that my sense of the grief my course has caused you and Father and many others is too intense to allow me to enjoy anything. I don't see as I shall be able to escape this feeling, which comes between me and all plans for self-advancement. Home and the love of friends are the best things we can have. I shall not take up any permanent scientific pursuit, except as a last resort. I wish some way might be devised by which we could get along together and enjoy a reasonable degree of freedom in thinking and doing. Before I left, it did not seem to me that any compromise was possible and I do not now see any way to compromise my beliefs."

"The hearts of Mr. and Mrs. Noyes were very much touched by this letter. John Humphrey Noyes wept like a child after reading it. In the Evening Meeting he told the Community about their parting words, that Theodore could engage in any of the industries, could go to their Oneida Lake cottage, Joppa, as often as he pleased, and could live at Wallingford or at the New York Agency. 'His good sense will show him that I cannot essentially change the habits of the Community to accommodate his case, nor allow his belief to change the belief of those over whom I am placed. What further liberty I can give him, consistently with my duty to the Community, I do not see.'"

"Theodore shortly suggested several options, his favorite being the formation of a nonsectarian part of the Community. 'Why not assume that, while I may be a confirmed nonbeliever, we've entered into relations that involve too much suffering to break up, if a possible way can be found to avoid it, and let me live with the Community, partaking to some extent in its social life and occupying myself about whatever you would think best, both parties to avoid controversy. If a Community could extend its benefits to unbelievers, leaving the religious to cultivate religion and the unbelievers to their consciences, it seems to me it might do the world more good. I think some such compromise ought to be worked out to save the coming generation to the Community, for *they will think independently.*'"

"I wish most earnestly to save my son; but I must also save the Community," Noyes replied. "I can have no hope of the unity that is essential to the Community without agreement in religion. If we cannot save the coming generation without this, we must let them go." He invited Theodore to return, but the invitation was "based unalterably on my hope that you will be converted. If it were not for that hope, I should a thousand times prefer that you stay away. You said yourself that, if you did not change, your separation from us would probably be final. I have submitted my heart to that alternative, let the grief be what it may, and I think all your friends here have done this same. It is best that we and you face the emergency and not try to make a hollow peace that will end in worse miseries than those we are passing through. You leave us but the smallest encouragement to hope that you will be converted at some future time. It seems to me that now is the time for you to seek the Lord. You are evidently softened by your sorrows. If you are not converted now, what reason have we or you to expect that you ever will be? The fifth course open to you, which I advise you by all means to take, is to come back not to confess what you do not believe, but with an honest wish and purpose *now* to go through the change that you admit is possible in the future, and which is an inexorable necessity if you are ever really to rejoin the Community."

WHO SHALL LEAD THE PEOPLE?

"The Community bought a water privilege at Wallingford, Connecticut in 1870 for that branch community, and was engaged in clearing the ground preparatory to building a dam. Noyes's brother George pitched into the work with all his might, splitting rocks and felling trees. Malaria had become general in a wide belt around Wallingford. Seventeen Wallingford Community members were stricken at once, and George was assailed by pains in the back, a burning throat, disordered heart, pressure on the brain, and terrible nights. The situation was so bad that on the 18th of September, Noyes put the seven worst sufferers aboard the train for Oneida, assuming charge of the party himself. On reaching Oneida just at nightfall, they learned to their dismay that their telegram had miscarried—no one was there to meet them. They were four miles from home and the only thing Noyes could find was an omnibus drawn by mules that had just returned from the Community silk mill with a load of girls. The driver was too tired and hungry even to consider making a second trip, so Noyes climbed up on the box himself. 'Imagine,' exclaimed one of the shiverers, later narrating the story, 'mules, tired with their day's work, going the opposite way from their stables, and with *no whip!*' The journey consumed more than two hours and when the end was reached, the occupants of the bus were so weak and numb that they could scarcely get out. George rallied for several months, but was again fighting for life more desperately than ever. 'George was not depressed by his last sickness; the Lord seemed to have taken away the sting of death,' William Woolworth noted. 'He was cheerful and buoyant through the whole of it.' He died at age forty-seven on July 23, 1870, a shock to the Community comparable to the drowning death of Mary Cragin in 1851.

"Charlotte Miller, Noyes's sister, died of malaria also, at age fifty-five in 1874. For more than twenty years she had held the extremely important post of adviser to the younger class of women. She was a person with 'a heart large enough to take in the whole family. Everyone from the youngest to the oldest felt free to go to her for sympathy and counsel, sure of an appreciative ear,' William Hinds reminisced. 'All her waking hours are spent speaking of God's goodness.' George and Charlotte both died after being stricken with malaria at Wallingford. They lived for periods in both Oneida and Wallingford communities, which may explain their fatal susceptibility to malaria. Malaria never triggers lifetime immunity; those who survive repeated bouts get less sick each time, but such immunity disappears if they move out of the malarial region. If they return, the first mosquito bite may kill them.[53]

"Noyes said that the great thing we need to realize about death is that the same Lord, the same Jesus that we trust and who cares for us here is also Lord of the dead.... Let us accept Christ *now*, as the Lord of the dead and living, and believe in him as the resurrection power, both on this and the other side of the veil.... Death always makes us realize how truly we are one large family, whose members are all united to one another by ties quite as strong as those in smaller families. The memories of all who have left us are still held in tenderest regard, and their names ever recalled with sincerest affection. If we preserve our cheerfulness on the death of a brother or a sister, it is because we do not think of our friends as lost to us, but still reckon them one with us in faith and purpose—only separated by a thin partition that may soon be removed."

"In a proclamation to his great family, John Humphrey Noyes described how his quest for a successor was to choose a *fit* man—if he proved to be his son, so much the better—but that person would have to be a Bible believer as well as a person with full mental, moral, and practical competence. It was hoped that not only Theodore Noyes but the whole Community would earnestly seek humility. The question of reinstating Theodore in his community membership was put to a vote and was unanimously approved, after which the hearts of all beat more freely. On his return, Theodore undertook a virtual Cartesian self examination: Descartes questioned everything that could be considered true and was left with only, '*I think, therefore I am*.' Given his scientific mind, Theodore said it was necessary to 'strip himself down to bare rationalism in order to make a beginning of perfect sincerity.' He hoped to 'carry it through all the heights of belief between this world and heaven.' Noyes realized that what we positively know is all the mental capital we can count upon as safe and available. What we guess, believe, and hope to be true is paper capital, and may be genuine or not. If what we absolutely know is only a small store, never mind: A little silver and gold is worth more than a bushel of counterfeit bills. Theodore sincerely desired Community criticism—a probing depth analysis of his heart and mind. He was willing to accept any occupation. He would avoid argumentative debate."

Ann Hobart (known also as Ann Bailey) of the younger generation took over Charlotte's post, and William Woolworth took over Noyes's position as father of the Community, but he was not inclined to rule with a strong hand. When Ann came to William for help, he would beg to be excused. Finally, Ann became truly overburdened and talked with Harriet Skinner and Frank Wayland-Smith; strangely, the latter suggested appointing Theodore to the position. Noyes felt that discussions would be absolutely necessary before he could take the place in the heart of the Community.

Theodore's name could be nominated, and the Community would decide. Many members noted the principle that has governed the Community in the selection of leaders.

"They shall be selected from among those who represent the faith of the Community, who stand in communication with Christ," Theodore Pitt said. "Is Theodore a spiritual man? Does he in his daily life and in his testimony strengthen our faith in the living God? Does he strengthen our faith in Jesus Christ as an indwelling Savior, and lead us to the Primitive Church? I feel kind and brotherly toward him, but I am not prepared to vote for him."

"In all my contact with Theodore during the past year, I've never even once heard him mention the name of God or Christ or faith," Charles Joslyn agreed. "In considering whether persons are suitable for certain places, Theodore wholly ignores their spiritual character. I say in sorrow but in the deepest sincerity of my heart, that if we select such a man for our leader, I shall be anxious about the perpetuity of the Community. I also think it would be unfortunate to have the leadership of the Community fall entirely into the hands of the young. If the female part of the administration is from the younger generation, as at present, it seems very necessary that the man should be a person of mature years and ripe experience."

Sarah Campbell felt likewise: "I have had great confidence in and respect for Theodore and no one not intimately connected with him has rejoiced more than I at every step he has taken showing return to the truth, and the love of it. After deliberate thought and prayer, I cannot find it in my heart to vote for him as our leader, so long as there is any doubt as to his religious position. I would not be willing to put my child in a school where she would be exposed to erroneous teachings; much less would I vote for anyone to be her spiritual teacher unless I was sure he would lead her to God."

James Herrick made a surprising comment: "It seems providential that we should have a man like Theodore with a strong intellectual and scientific bias who would faithfully represent these attributes of his father in the Community; it will be broader, healthier, and have a better chance of perpetuity, than if built simply on a spiritual basis."

Erastus Hamilton added to Herrick's assessment: "The Community is founded on faith in Christ, and the main thought of the future is that our loyalty to Christ may be maintained. It is possible that Theodore is being trained to make him receptive to interior control, God's influence, which the elder Noyes called inspiration. That is all I would ask. I acknowledge Theodore as my superior in intellect and in moral nature, a large man able to fill a large place in society. He has worked honestly and faithfully for our financial prosperity. In his criticisms he seems judicious and wise. I've respected all these things in him and then again I have stood ready to criticize him. The word in my heart is, 'Blessed in he that cometh in the name of the Lord.'"

"There is no use in trying to make out that Theodore is a religious man, for he is not, and a large part of the Community knows it," Henry Burnham adamantly stated. "What is meant by saying that the Community must have greater breadth? I do not ask for greater scope of thought than I can find under the inspiration of Jesus Christ and the Primitive Church. The object of this Community *is to make us good men and women.* Is thinking God out of the universe going to make us better men and women? We all know better. I have charity for Theodore and a certain respect for his present attitude, but until he is restored to the faith that built this Community, let him wait and let the Community wait before placing him at the head."

"No considerable portion of the Community would have thought of putting Theodore into the office of leader if he were not Mr. Noyes's son," said William Hinds. "Natural relationship must be entirely subordinate to spiritual relationship. It is my conviction that the Community can perpetuate itself only by keeping alive and active the old spirit of faith in a living God and in a living personal Savior."

"There is a feeling among the older class that some of the younger people are ready to abandon the faith of the Community, almost to abandon the Community itself," said Ann Bailey (Hobart), leader of the young women. "I believe that the young folks are striving to perpetuate community life and are holding to the faith. I would rather see the Community go to pieces than have it stand on any other basis than it now does."

"We may take Theodore on his simple merits as he is now, or we may take him for what he shall be. If his fitness is to be tried on the ground of what he now is, I could not so accept him at present," stated James Towner, a relatively new member who was converted to Christianity and was a prominent lawyer from Ohio who had been a member of a free love society there. "My own experience in infidelity makes me look cheerfully and hopefully upon Theodore's case and the case of all those who want to think for themselves. I say, Let them think; help them to think—they will think anyhow, only say to them, be modest and don't ask us to put your loose thinking at the head of the Community. I sincerely believe that the Oneida Community, as it is in John H. Noyes, furnishes the broadest platform there is in the world—physical, moral, intellectual, and spiritual—because it is nearest the kingdom of heaven in whose king, Christ, are hid all the treasures of wisdom and knowledge. Until Theodore can with the abandon of Paul say, I am determined to know nothing among you save Jesus Christ, and him crucified, I must answer to the pending question, No."

Theodore responded: "My candidature as leader of the Community was uninvited by me. I have no desire to put myself forward unless it can come about without strife. I sincerely think a fanatical tendency in some of the members needs the antidote of my tendencies of mind, and I am quite confident that I could sympathize with the mental struggles that many of our children must go through, in a way that would improve the handling of them. But of course I could not help as leader without kindness and charity on the part of those who have more definite views. I am well content to wait until I am wanted by all hands. There is one thing greater than my love of unity; that is my love of truth. The Community need fear nothing from my ambition; I grasp at nothing but a place in the hearts of the whole Community." William Woolworth would remain the Community's father *pro tem* and help Ann Bailey when Noyes was at Wallingford.

"In June, 1875, three months after the Great Discussion, Theodore wrote to his father who was still at Wallingford dealing with fever and ague, another malaria outbreak. 'The one desire of my heart is spirituality, that is, a life from the interior. The Community most needs spirituality, as you say; I see it every day. Many fall back from their good experience because they have no realizing sense that they are spirits and must be about spiritual business to grow. This is what I am most ambitious to do; to tend the growth of my spirit, so that whatever may be my future circumstances I shall go higher.' Theodore joined him there until December 1875."

"Father and son came to greater appreciation of each other and agreed on all essentials, especially the father's unwavering principle that Community businesses were not for money-making but for spiritual education. When the Oneida Community asked for Noyes's advice about a proposed change of organization in the business, Noyes sent Theodore to manage it. "I have no hesitation in giving Theodore *carte blanche* to act for me," Noyes wrote in a message sent with Theodore. "At the same time, I do not send him to dictate arrangements. The best way is to have a meeting for consultation and free expression. Then if there is divergence of view, let him report to me. I hope his visit will be an occasion of new harmony.""

"The Evening Meeting in December 1875 was a frank discussion about Theodore, who said he would not attend so the family could freely to discuss whether they would have confidence in him as his father's representative. Theodore was a highly intelligent, competent administrator and physician, and the Community reported confidence in him—even the three men who had opposed him previously. James Towner summed it up: 'I heartily sympathize with Mr. Noyes's objective in business—that it is not for money-making. I sincerely believe that Mr. Noyes is the best businessman in the Community. As to Theodore's cooperation with him, I will say frankly that I would feel a good deal of distrust and anxiety, but I am highly pleased with what Mr. Noyes says about Theodore. I have so much confidence in his inspiration as to believe that he knows whether it is best to use Theodore in the reorganization and control of the business, and how far it is best. I believe that Mr. Noyes sees a great deal further than I can, and I'd be perfectly willing that he should use Theodore or anyone else he may choose.' The question was put to a vote: 'Are we ready as a family to put our entire business into Mr. Noyes's hands and accept heartily any agent he may select?' The ayes were unanimous. 'We have had a good time with Theodore,' wrote William Woolworth to Noyes, 'and I think the whole Community hails the dawn of a better day. There are many signs that the spirit of unity is developing.'"

"An important question arose under the new regime. A clash with some young men occurred when the elder Noyes thought that some of them made business trips to the detriment of their spiritual character. So Theodore obtained data regarding the amount of travel needed and met with a rebuff from one of the superintendents.

'When those of the young men who have bright faculties drift away from spirituality and take refuge in the excitements of business, shirking the struggle we must undergo to purify our souls, we're lucky to have some left of the sterner sort who make a serious study of ethical and spiritual problems,' Theodore responded. 'If I have any voice, they shall have a large place. The Community is ruined when it tucks its philosophers and spiritually minded off in a corner, and gives its heart to money-making.' Noyes came out with a powerful talk defending his right to govern the Community by deputy (Theodore); this superintendent resigned and moved to Wallingford to separate himself from worldly temptations and to seek renewed spiritual experience."

"But a rift was opening between the Oneida and Wallingford Communities. George Miller had come from Wallingford in November 1876 and delivered a course of lectures before the Oneida family on the Bible. This was followed by the formation of Bible classes led by the older revivalists Mr. Burnham and Mrs. Bushnell, and the Oneida family enjoyed a revival more powerful than any it had experienced in years. Theodore and Ann Hobart had been leaders at Wallingford with a more light-hearted secular course, so the Wallingford family held aloof from this new revival. Some in Oneida criticized the Wallingford family for infidelity and worldliness, and a good deal of feeling was aroused, especially against Theodore. George Miller, having returned to Wallingford, wrote to Oneida criticizing the revival leaders for narrowness and legality. By March, Noyes discerned the disorganizing spirit of this past revival; Miller said he had no wish to check a true revival spirit—the life-blood of the Community—and wouldn't it be best to discontinue Bible classes in the controversial form they'd assumed? The history of the Community had been a succession of such changes to attain true unity and there was no opposition to Miller's proposal; many spoke in favor of it.

"This clash between Wallingford and Oneida led Theodore to propose gathering the whole Community at Oneida. They would get rid of hired help as much as possible, devote a few years to developing home industry, and perfect the organization. 'The Community here is perpetuating the same narrowness that has given us all our trouble, and if we do not take hold now to conquer them, we shall never do it,' he wrote to Ann. 'In a few years we can live together again in such a happy family as the Wallingford Community has been. I'm convinced that unless we do this, we shall have no peace.' To the evening meeting, the elder Noyes said, 'If we can get all hearts interested in gathering together here, it will be a conversion to the whole Community. As it is now, the Community is divided up into cliques that have little to do with each other. However heretical Theodore may be thought by some, his idea of seeking unity and sacrificing financial considerations is orthodox to the core. This move of Theodore's is a continuation of the revival, only carrying it a little higher up and on a larger scale—he has really proposed not a four-day but a four-year protracted meeting. The old revivalists ought to favor that.' This view was greeted by clapping of hands and stamping of feet. In May and June the plan of concentration at Oneida was carried out.

"The son had won the confidence of his father. Theodore and the elder Noyes as its active head had jointly led the Community for a year and a half, and now John Humphrey Noyes addressed the great family: 'I find myself now engaged in the last stage of my work in this world. Through our new publication *American Socialist*, I am laying before the world a full report of what I have done and what I have learned in the evolution of a Christian Community. Whatever is valuable in my work on the Oneida Community will be turned over to the benefit of humanity, and become the seed of future communities. A father has the right to give his property to his son irrespective of that son's character; I do not claim that right. I have renounced it, and have pledged myself solemnly to the Community that I will not commit its government to an unbeliever or one who is in any way unfit to be its leader. In this I renounce the principle of transmission by natural inheritance that governs in the kingdoms of the world. I claim only the right to choose the *fit* man to be my successor. I announce this principle not only for myself but for my successor and for all his successors, and I charge them to renounce honestly before God the temptation and the rights of hereditary succession, and to be governed only by fitness in transmitting the government.

"Theodore has been our most promising young man, not only for business ability and intellectuality but for spirituality. Those who know him best, and they are the most spiritual part of the Community, think of him most highly. The Community wants a leader who is grounded in all the wisdom and in all the wiles of science. Who is there as well qualified in this respect as Theodore? He is thirty-six years old, in the fullness of strength, the same age I was when I came to Oneida. As to Theodore's probable policy of administration, we all know that it hasn't been formed by *imitation* of mine but by consulting his own genius and inspiration, which is right. I have studied it a good deal, and am now free to say that I approve of it most heartily and from rational conviction. It seems to me to be summed up in the formula, return to first principles. His purpose is to lead the Community back into home industry, hygienic habits, and above all into the subordination of money-making to spiritual interests, which is in a new form our old first principle, *Seek first the kingdom of God and his righteousness, and all other things shall be added unto you.*"

"The Editor-in-Chief of this paper has the pleasure of announcing that he has resigned the Presidency of the Oneida Community and will be free henceforth to devote himself wholly to editorial labor," Noyes announced in the *American Socialist* on May 24, 1877. "John H. Noyes parts with the Community to which he has given thirty years of his life in entire harmony, leaving his son, Dr. Theodore Richards Noyes, to be henceforth its responsible head." This short announcement electrified the press. The *Springfield Press* likened this retirement to the abdication of a monarch and was confident that Noyes would always be the Community's guiding inspiration. The *Utica Herald* opined that the Community's success was due to the founder's unique genius, and that it would likely end without him. The New York *Daily Graphic* believed its demise would be due to the younger generation's differing religious and philosophical convictions. Other observers felt that this was a healthy and natural progression—bring on the next generation to manage the Community and free Noyes to promulgate the gospel, always his primary objective. He had left the Community in internal harmony and free from external opposition, small as that had been, as a model for others to emulate in establishing the Kingdom on earth."

But who could embody all the traits of John Humphrey Noyes? Having received profound spiritual experiences through long meditation, he was a man who possessed the charisma and the authority necessary to manage several communities of up to three hundred persons, yet he was a gentle, flexible, diplomatic presence trusted by young and old. He had worked in all the enterprises, established life-long learning, and had written daily about the great problems of our relation to God and to each other and how to reconcile these. The Oneida Community was the product of John Humphrey Noyes's heart, mind, and spirit. Under his spiritual leadership it prospered harmoniously with virtually no laws or penalties.

"All the success the Oneida Community has gained is to be attributed to the love of spiritual growth," wrote William Woolworth. "Its founder has been a devotee to spiritual improvement and it has shaped his whole career and destiny. It so ruled his life that his soul revolted against a religion that did not lift its converts out of the slough of sin and selfishness. He caught the light of the primitive gospel, and in its clear beams, sin and condemnation fled away and his heart found innocence and peace. An improved social life became possible, lifted out of the time-worn grooves of tradition and habit. Shall science, invention, and discovery have free scope in the minor departments of human weal and yet be excluded from the spiritual and social domain where sin and ignorance have wrought their deepest degradation? The true light shineth with too clear a light for ignorance and intolerance to bear rule in this nineteenth century. The only claim the Community urges for itself is that it has subverted old institutions and customs under the dictates of that spirit. If our works and our innovations will not stand the test inevitably applied to all progressive measures, we ask no favors for them."

Theodore could rule only as most people do—institute laws and rules and insist upon obedience. The outward affairs of the Community went on with little apparent change. During the last week in June, more than forty members of the Wallingford Community arrived in Oneida as planned, and the confluence of the two Communities took place with scarcely a ripple. Twenty persons were left at Wallingford, and it was a very good plan not to end that Community and sell the property, because Theodore proposed that the Wallingford Community enter upon the manufacture of spoons on May 29, 1877. Very soon, Oneida Community, Limited would emerge and become Oneida Ltd., an international corporation managed by community descendants for over one hundred years.

GRADUAL DISUNITY

Signs of Community breakdown were gradual but often disheartening after Noyes left. Theodore talked to the Community on July 26, 1877 about difficulty in getting people to do their jobs. It was a new rebellious spirit by the youthful members. "Many of us are public-spirited, but others have formed the habit of refusing to do what they are asked. It seems to be one of those faults of individualism that the Community has fallen into. I object to the spirit that says, *I will* or *I won't*. That spirit is not brotherly love and it is subversive of good organization. I thought we would speak about it in public, but if necessary we shall have to bring criticism to bear on individual cases. I have been so exercised on this question that I've devised a method of statistics to find out how much we do. There are some among us who suffer from what is no more nor less than laziness. We must have a different spirit about work. I do not feel like mincing the matter at all. If we can get a revival of old-fashioned love of faithfulness in the use of our time, the financial problem will be easy; but if we go on in our luxurious habits, it is going to be a serious thing in a year or two." In 1878 the Community found it necessary to economize and saved $8,000. On February 19, 1879, the Committee on Personal Appropriations reported to the evening meeting that the elder Noyes hoped there would be a free will to keep appropriations as low or lower in the coming year: "Everyone whose heart is right about this matter will not feel that he must spend all of his appropriation," the report noted, "only what he needs and let the rest remain in the treasury where it belongs."

John Humphrey Noyes felt that the younger portion of the Community had never known what it is to suffer real need. They had known how to abound; their whole life had been one of luxury, and it seemed to him that for them to suffer need voluntarily was the better way. Members were reminded that all money earned goes in to the Community treasury, as it always had. "We do not want the Community to be divided into rich and poor," said Noyes, reiterating that the Community was founded on Acts 4:32—*Those who believed were of one heart and soul, and no one said that any of the things that he possessed was his own, but they had everything in common*. "I think that we've departed from this blessed state," Noyes continued. "If this principle is clear, the system of personal appropriations can be continued; otherwise it will become detrimental to the Community. All income, whether of cash or other property, should be turned in to the Community treasury before it can be passed to the individual.

"We have been falling away ever since we made distinct institutions of our different departments, with separate appropriations," John Noyes informed the meeting. "The departments came to have separate interests and the heads of them in many cases probably became more ambitious for their own business showing than for the Community interests. Persons who do not find place at the head of some regular department naturally are ambitious to create a department for themselves in which they may individualize. This arrangement could have been carried out by men of thorough spiritual wisdom, but to the selfish and careless, it was a temptation to fall into the feelings and ways of the world in business. Here will be found the secret of the decay of the great business committees and of the management that used to reside in the Sunday meetings, where all who chose would attend and discuss matters. This process of individualization propagated itself gradually into social matters and participation in criticism. Community interference with individual affairs of all kinds is now resented as intrusive." His right-hand man Myron Kinsley was confident that all the scattered departments would place themselves under Community control as they were originally.

"Problems small and large demonstrated the weakening of Community spirit. By October, a growing laxity of standards became the topic of an extended discussion. The boys were spending time with those outside the Community who were hired to work with the horses, and several members agreed that the horse barn is not a good school when hired help is there. Likewise, several boys became quite well acquainted with hired girls in the new dining area, which was built adjacent to the quadrangle and brought the Community into closer relations with those from the outside. The girls were allowed for a while to be off by themselves at the Fruit House, which required a change. C. was in an unsatisfactory state, keeping to her room in a frightful state of demoralization. Theodore urged Ann Hobart, counselor of the young women, to discuss matters with C."

"When I returned from Wallingford," he said, "I found that she had not done so." Ann asked Harriet Noyes to talk with her, and then C. wrote this long note to the family:

"Ever since I can remember, I have loved to get attention from hired people and outsiders. When the stone wall to the new building was commenced, I as usual looked at the hired workmen. Finally I began to notice that one man looked at me, and I began to return the look. It then went from bad to worse until I became so fascinated that I looked for him every day, and if he were not at work I took measures to find out where he was. While he was blacking brick north of the Tontine, I would sit at the window and look at him and occasionally when anything happened to laugh at, would smile at him, but no words ever passed between us. It got so overpowering that I thought nothing would be too bad. I even had thoughts of leaving the Community. I came just as near destruction as I could and escape, and realize that it was the providence of God that saved me. I think it has been a good lesson to me and hope I shall never in the future look at any hired man or outsider, and will feel contaminated if they talk about me in any way. I entirely forsook Miss Ann's and Dr. Noyes's advice, and instead of going to them as my spiritual advisors, I shunned them and never told them anything unless it was dragged out of me. I realize that I have forfeited all right to the confidence not only of my special friends but of the whole Community, and I most sincerely ask their forgiveness. I did not have the fear of God or man before my eyes, and I don't know what I was thinking. If I'd kept my heart open to my superiors,

I would probably have been saved all this trouble. I now feel thankful for *anything* that will crucify my old life and make me a God-fearing woman. I ask the prayers of the Community, that I may have the *godly sorrow that worketh repentance unto life that needeth not be repented of.*"

"James Vail and other young men are quite heavily responsible for this," said Theodore, "by throwing ridicule on the strict state in which the young women were kept at Wallingford. "They said to the girls that they were treated like children, and that they were too old for it. Two years ago I found out that C. had always known the name of every hired man we had, also of folks in the village. She has a passion for outside acquaintance, which those who dealt with her brother know was a strong passion in him. I hope this affair will demonstrate to everybody the necessity of setting up barriers that may not seem reasonable to young people. C. needs a conversion to religion. I hope this experience will show her the importance of the daily exercise of her heart in prayer. It is one of our cardinal ideas that those most in contact with the world should offer themselves for frequent criticism. It is rather awkward for Ann and me to ask folks to offer themselves for criticism," Theodore said, "but in several cases where it has seemed imperative, we have done it. I've sometimes thought that unless there is more earnestness on the part of people in offering themselves, we'd have to start a system by which everyone would come under criticism by routine. And when I've had to go away during Evening Meetings," Theodore continued, "I've always found quite a number of young people out. 'X.' made an excuse to sit near the door in meeting, so she could slip out. What's the use of having such an ordinance, if folks who need it don't go?"

Frank added that the meetings were very thin on Oneida Fair nights. Ann noted that having so many go to the Fair and watch a set of gamblers would inevitably affect the atmosphere at home. "I don't believe we can touch such things without being contaminated."

"I never knew of so much irresponsible visiting of a Fair as there was this year with so little consultation with Community leaders, who are quite distressed about it," Frank agreed. "The young folks do not have the keen ambition for education and an earnest spirit for self-improvement. They have more spare time than previous generations and yet are not so careful in the disposal of it."

"I've been distressed by what seems to me a terrible spirit of irreverence on the part of some of the young folks," Erastus Hamilton added, "especially the class of larger boys." Henry Allen agreed: "I hope the time will come when the Community will have nothing whatever to do with the Oneida Fair."

"The state of the Community is indicated by the state of this class; if any part of the Community is pleasure-seeking, this class will be," Theodore said ruefully. "I don't think they always have the best example set them by persons old enough to do better," he added. "We ought to be in earnest to labor for their improvement—one way is to improve ourselves! Those of us who are older find recreation and amusement in things that would be quite unprofitable for those who are younger. We need to be the best possible example."

"We'd be happier if we didn't care about the ways of the world but could realize that we're different," agreed Ann, "and wish to be so."

"Then there are persons older still who are not exactly spiritually-minded," Theodore continued. "They set a questionable example of seeking their own pleasure in a way that is quite pernicious. It's a serious problem—how to view an event like the Oneida Fair without causing the older and better class to feel unnecessarily restrained." No one said anything, puzzling over these problems. The deaths of John Humphrey Noyes's younger sister Charlotte and his younger brother George had been a calamity. They had always commanded loyalty from the younger generation comparable to Noyes's.

"In better times, when the Towner committee decided to make the juvenile department an entire Community responsibility, the Community would implement the plan heartily and thoroughly. Mothers who had individually cared for their own children's clothes gladly consented. The Willow Place family would join a bee to baste and stitch two large baskets of cut and rolled up and labeled aprons, drawers, and little dresses. The sewing-machine on the stage sang lively accompaniment to the chatter and bustle below. But by July 1877, mothers did not want to give up making their own child's clothes, and the committee plan was resisted. Not all clothing was put into the children's department by some people."

"It's trying to the soul to hear remarks showing that persons do this in a grumbling spirit—only because they have to—and even take back everything they can," Theodore lamented. "I'm willing to be flexible, but I want it distinctly understood that I back this committee. We likewise had to pass through a great shower of resistance when it was thought best to have school commence. I don't pretend to be such a lover of children as some are," Theodore admitted, "but I think my course would be as likely to turn out good and healthy men and women as that of the tenderest mother. But I'm subjected to the accusation of not understanding a mother's feelings; it makes my labors a great deal heavier. I think even the most sensible women need the strength of men in governing children. If the Community in passing from the old to the new form of society fails to furnish the masculine element, the true order of things will be reversed. I don't think mothers realize the danger there is if we let things go on as they have. Those of us who wish to be happy living communally will have to get rid of the idea that it can be carried on without interfering with individual liberty. This is a fact, not because I or anybody else says so, but because the logic of events proves it so. We might as well make up our minds to it."

Theodore expressed his belief that there is no modified form of the Community that will work; if his father's system is departed from, he said, we are on a sliding scale. He hoped to help make the descent safe, avoid destructiveness, and preserve cooperation when possible with four different religions he saw in the Community.

Leadership of the Community by the second generation during Theodore's reign was most problematic. He had appointed close friend Ann Hobart, a leader in the Wallingford Community, to be his chief assistant after the move to Oneida from Wallingford. She had helped lead Theodore into a deeper acceptance of the spiritual realm of life, especially desired by the elder Noyes, but Ann was a complicated personality not suited for leadership in the greater Oneida Community.

"Her friend Charlotte Maria said to John Humphrey Noyes, 'I have been with Ann considerably and have become much attached to her and ready to do anything she desired. I've always supported and obeyed her under the decided conviction that I was acknowledging a faithful agent of Mr. Noyes. When Theodore and Ann first came to Wallingford, I resolved not to allow myself to fall into evil thinking of them, and I so fortified myself that when I heard their differences, I said to myself, *It is none of my business to judge them.* I've been pained many times by their disagreements and wondered that such discord existed between persons in their position, when all the time they were the most intimate and dependent of friends. There have been times, especially when Ann was sick last fall, that she talked in a way as to almost make me lose confidence in Theodore when I was with her. She made a good deal of fun of his doctoring and really talked disrespectfully of him, as though he knew little or nothing about the proper treatment of sick folks. She was quite willful at first in refusing to do as he wanted until she had relapses in consequence of doing as *she* pleased. I can scarcely remember an instance of his besting her in their discussions—he had to defer to her judgment, for she is very strong in argument and always convinces you that she is right. Soon after we all came to Oneida from Wallingford, Ann told me emphatically with tears in her eyes that she did not feel that God called her to lead this larger Community. She'd felt it her mission to do what she did at Wallingford, but could not feel that same inspiration as leader here. She said she knew that if God did not call her to the place, she could not do right. This made a strong impression on my mind.'"

"Ann came to the elder Noyes's room on October 23rd of her own accord, quite unusual, and complained about Theodore, that he had become infatuated by a certain young woman and had tried to appropriate the young woman to himself. Frank Wayland-Smith was present. She said that there were many other things in which Theodore was acting directly contrary to the elder Noyes's wishes, and her assertions did indeed undermine Noyes's confidence in him."

"I cannot doubt that her intention was to produce that impression, and I determined not to judge him on Ann's testimony but to wait for a representation from his side; I advised Frank to say nothing about what he'd heard," Noyes said. "Two months passed. I expected further communications from Ann and hoped for something from Theodore, but nothing came. Passing Ann one day, I asked her whether they had better times and she said yes without elaboration. I learned that the day after her disclosure to me, she went to Frank and repeated her charges against Theodore with enlargements and additions; also that days *before* her talk with me, she opened her mind on the same matter to Mrs. Leonard, who urged her to open it to me. She had also spoken to Mrs. Waters about discords between her and Theodore. These facts seriously changed the aspect of Ann's leadership. Her entire right to that office rested on Theodore's choice of her, and she was destroying my confidence in him—as one in a cabinet officer position attacking the character of her chief and attempting to raise a party against him. That was the manifest intent of her going to so many of the leading Community members. I waited long and struggled hard to evade the logic of the facts, which declared inexorably that I must either give up my confidence in Theodore or my confidence in Ann. Until that day, I had not the first thought of questioning her substantial loyalty to me and to Theodore or her fitness for the place she had assumed. The Community accepted Theodore's choice and I did not feel called upon to interfere. I accepted her leadership and went along with her administration in peace, and helped it all I could until October 23rd."

"I can see that all my life I've had this heartless, cruel way of being very affectionate and demonstrative toward people at one time, and at another time being indifferent with apparently no cause for change," Ann began, describing her cavalier treatment of some men and women in the Community to the elder Noyes. "I have made men themselves suffer and sometimes their friends. There has been that in me that was willing to absorb the attention of men and careless as to whether it took them away from other friends or not. Though I've *said* I wanted them to love others, in my spirit I have been self-centered. In my relations with all these men I have had what I'd criticize in others as special love; I've been free to have frequent visits without being asked by a third party, thinking that if Theodore knew, that was sufficient; I've had this cruel spirit toward Theodore," Ann continued. "I have by my ugliness made him suffer terribly, and then I would feel impatient and as if I was the one who was abused. I have abused Theodore in a great many ways, domineering over him about his own personal affairs. I knew if we had any disagreement, that he would come to me and make up, and I've often held out until he did it; and then, instead of being softened by his better spirit and example, it only hardened me and made me tyrannize over him the more. Many things I've complained of in him I see were my own faults. I have engrossed his attention and time, taking him away from the society of those he used to love and associate with, who deserved his love much more than I. If he had not been my exact opposite, kind, forbearing, patient, tender-hearted, and forgiving, he would've shaken me off long ago; any other man would. When he came here from New York and in his suffering turned to you [his father], I believe he would have worked out an entire reconciliation if I had taken the right course. Everything seemed to indicate that the best way then was for me to go to Oneida and for him to stay here with you; the office I had filled naturally terminated. But my mean, jealous heart was afraid of losing his love and I drew on his sympathies so much that you let him have me come back here. And I have held on to him when I believe he would have been glad to get free."

"Two weeks later John Humphrey Noyes resumed the leadership of his Community, which, in order to endure, must remain a spiritual association. Theodore attempted in every way he could, without sacrificing his own principles, to come into unity with his father. The elder Noyes, worried about the Community's financial situation, decided to sell a resort cottage near the Wallingford Community, and to close the New York City office temporarily. With his characteristic creativity, he sought ways to raise money to meet all debts without undue belt-tightening. They'd entertain visitors, have daily concerts—the outdoor brass band would play twice a day and the military band would accompany marches; in the Great Hall there would be dances and the children would produce shows on the stage. All suggestions were welcomed! Noyes started Bible classes again and hoped for a genuine revival to inspire all.

"Theodore did not attend meetings and kept to his room, arguing his thoughts with his father by writing, sent through a third person. Theodore's studies of emerging sciences and new biblical interpretations, combined with his skeptical temperament, no doubt made religious conversion of his particular mindset next to impossible. Frank Wayland-Smith's journal, dated January 14, 1878, reported that Theodore believed that 'Christ was an inspired man—but not the son of God. He believes in the doctrine of evolution implicitly and will not undertake to define the Creator or First Cause. He has read the German materialists and become considerably impregnated with their ideas and modes of thought.' When his special friend Ann Hobart left the Wallingford Community to marry Joseph Skinner—Noyes's nephew who'd left the Oneida Community—Theodore left the Oneida Community for a second time. His leadership had lasted half a year."

British Anthropologist Robin M. Dunbar in 1993 revealed that when a group of people exceeds 150–200 people, it will tend to break into two to facilitate greater cooperation and reciprocity among its members. Dunbar's Number is a suggested limit to the number of people with whom one can maintain stable social relationships in which an individual knows who each person is and how each person relates to every other person. When forty of Wallingford Community's sixty members joined Oneida in June 1877, plus fifty-eight new children added during the Stirpiculture period of the 1870s, the Oneida Community may have exceeded the optimum number of people that can maintain essential unity, especially with fluctuating leadership.[54] Some members supported its breakup, and after many months of discussion and planning, it transformed into the joint stock company, Oneida Community, Limited, in 1881.

Ultimately no one except John Humphrey Noyes could inspire and manage this unique human experiment in its original spiritual form. The basis of Noyes's charismatic genius was his rich spiritual experience, his explorations into the human heart, his creativity to think anew about perennial problems, his friendly, flexible temperament, and the energy to offer indefatigable leadership to a small heaven on earth. As the great man aged, it was only a matter of time until it changed or ended, as many had predicted. The Community weakened due to several factors: the deaths of four original Putney members of the deepest spirituality and charismatic influence over the young; a second generation, many of whom attended Yale, became more interested in business and science than in religion, with an increasing desire to pair off—Complex Marriage would not endure; a splintering leadership led by James Towner; outside attacks by orthodox moralists in spite of wide knowledge of the Community's worth, purity, and splendid addition to the region; plus John Humphrey Noyes's strong desire to resume his meditations, studies, and his original love, publishing. Inability to find a comparable successor was probably the chief cause of Community breakup. George Washington Noyes, his younger brother by ten years who died at age 47 of malaria could have masterfully taken over.

In December 1873, a Presbyterian Church elder, discussing attacks of his Synod accusing Noyes of adultery, remarked, "There is nothing under heaven in the deportment of the Oneida Community toward the society where it is situated or toward the State, or the nation, that the strictest Christian moralist can complain of .

Puck **magazine was the first successful humor publication in the United States with cartoons, caricatures, and political satire. It was published from 1871 until 1918.**

Although I am a Presbyterian and have no fellowship with your [Oneida's] social theory, I have just as little fellowship with any denomination that would try to put you down by other than moral suasion and a superior example. What is the use of trying to legislate a people down when you can discern no immoral habits, actions, or censurable deeds of any kind? Heaven knows there are tangible vices and crimes enough both in church and state to be put down by Synods and Conferences that have the requisite power to do it. As long as the Oneida Community continues to conduct itself as it has done for a quarter of a century past, you may rest assured that there is no authority in this or any other Christian nation, that will molest it for the simple reason that there is nothing to complain of. Puzzling, that's a fact," he concluded.

Nellie Bly visited the Mansion House in 1889 at the height of her fame as an investigative journalist.[55] "Why did people interfere with the Oneida Community?" Nellie asked her landlord. "Why they did no one knows," he replied. "It was not the people about this part of the country that made any fuss, but ministers in other parts of the States that only knew the Community by hearsay. They were of great benefit to this country. They employed a large number and annoyed no one. They are the most honest people on earth and would rather give a man a dollar than take a cent from him, and there was nothing coarse or mean about them. For my part I can't see why they should be interfered with."

Nellie asked an old man who had lived for years beside them. "I think that John Noyes was a religious fanatic," he said, "and I didn't believe in their not marrying, but I must say they were the most honest people that I ever dealt with."

"Everywhere I inquired it was the same story," Nellie wrote. "Not one person could bring any complaint about the Community, and on all sides they praised them. None of the neighbors believed in the abolition of marriage and that is the only thing they criticized. 'We fear our own neighbors,' one woman remarked, 'but we trust the Community in all things.'"

In their early days before their neighbors knew them well, the Community was prepared to end Complex Marriage to promote harmony in the region. They valued Romans 12:18—"If possible, so far as it depends upon you, live peaceably with all." Noyes moved to Niagara Falls, Canada, to live in the Stone Cottage with a terrace overlooking the Falls; their incipient silverware business was begun at Niagara Falls to utilize water power. In late August of 1879, to promote harmony in the Community, he advised them give up complex marriage and live as celibates but with freedom to marry for the same reasons given by Paul in the 7th of 1st Corinthians. He lived with devoted members, freed to "dwell deep" and pursue his primary work, writing about how to recognize God in our own nature—the proper work of mankind and single great hope for establishing the kingdom of God on Earth.

Pierrepont Noyes, later the president of Oneida Community, Limited, lived with him there at age fifteen for a year with eight others, including his cousin George Wallingford Noyes, later the treasurer of the company who became the Community historian and archivist. "My father's religion, with all its austerities and severities, encouraged happiness—pleasure, if you please," writes Pierrepont.[56] "What he criticized as pleasure seeking was pleasure sought beyond the freedoms licensed by one's degree of spiritual development. He had a sympathetic nature which, quite outside theological sanctions, loved to see people enjoying themselves . . . .The atmosphere of holiness at his new residence, Stone Cottage, was pervasive. It grew denser as we approached [Father's] upstairs front bedroom, but thinned in the out-of-doors until it was hardly more oppressive than the blue sky and those cirrus clouds which add beauty to a scene but in no way interfere with a boy's activities."[57] His cousin Humphrey's diary recounts this: "When Mr. Noyes got up from the supper table, he came round where Pip [Pierrepont] was sitting and put his hand on his shoulder and said something like this: Conversion is not a painful thing—it is a happy thing. You will be converted when you begin to notice God's providences. That is the way I was converted and began to be religious. If you see a providence, believe in it, and confess it, and that will be conversion. From that you will go on till you see God in all the Universe."[58]

"Old members of the Community have said to me that those who got within the effective area of Father Noyes's personality were reluctant to lose him; that life seemed brighter and more worthwhile when he was about."[59] "The most vivid reminiscence I have of Father Noyes is the atmosphere of good feeling that surrounded him," James Herrick remembered. "It was a pleasure to sit near him whether he was talking or silent. A river of living water seemed to issue from him. His life was so harmonious that the effect of contact was musical. One forgot one's trouble in his presence. He had the quality of attracting all to him and making them harmonious among themselves." A long-time associate accounted for Noyes's unquestioned power to attract and hold the loyalty of both men and women: "Most people subconsciously fear life just a little or become disillusioned by its futility. Mr. Noyes had no doubts regarding life or himself. He plowed through difficulties, disappointments, and dangers with an inextinguishable faith in an Edenic world plan and the ultimate triumph of righteousness. He was a source of light and power for all about him."

"How can wisdom attained only through long suffering and laceration of the spirit be transmitted to the next generation, so mutinous in receiving the stored-up wisdom of the race?" asks Noyes's biographer, Robert Allerton Parker in *A Yankee Saint*. "To the flesh of our flesh, the bone of our bone, we bequeath not one atom of the wisdom that we buy—at what a price."[60]

"All this repeating of troubles is going to end," Noyes concluded, "when wisdom and righteousness are fixed in the blood, so the lessons that the parents have learned by experience, the children will have in them when they are born. Lord hasten the day, is my prayer."

SPIRITUAL COMMUNITY TO PARTNERSHIP CORPORATION

"By temperament, Pierrepont Burt Noyes was an optimistic, energetic extrovert who in his teens became intrigued by becoming competitive in all aspects of life, even achieving wealth. He traveled to the Big Apple on April Fools Day in 1892 on a Hudson River ferry with his half brother Holton with high hopes for success in business. Noyes Brothers was established on Warren Street, selling Community silverware, and Pierrepont had inherited John Humphrey Noyes's practicality, persistence, and charisma. He sold everything he could buy, traveling through New York State and Pennsylvania. The panic of 1893 caused Oneida Community, Limited's New York office to downsize its sales force, and Pierrepont was asked to take over territory in New England, Philadelphia, Baltimore, and Washington, while selling his own line. With an infusion of capital to Noyes Brothers from community member James Herrick who came to New York, Noyes increased his sales; more importantly, he became acquainted with Oneida's important larger silverware buyers. He found the business world to his liking and compatible with his abilities. His persistence in the face of difficulties in his early twenties served him well. On New Year's Day 1894, he was on the high road to worldly success in New York City, in full pursuit of riches *that moth and rust doth corrupt* . . . .

"I am still somewhat puzzled that a youth of twenty-three years should have developed a distaste for getting rich, but that is certainly what happened to me. Apparently the emergence of success raised a question as to what I could do with wealth, and the answer left me cold . . . . I was walking along Central Park West (then the Park Avenue of New York), beneath the towering façades of fashionable apartment houses and hotels, when a revulsion of feeling seized me." He said to himself, "This represents the normal goal of a successful career: an apartment here, living among other men who have devoted their lives to money-making and have cached the things worthwhile, to be enjoyed—sometime. My imagination, as often happens, insisted on something pictorial. When at last they open the bag, what do they find . . . . Not a damn thing in it!"[61]

"Pierrepont B. Noyes came to the realization that money-making alone does not lead to happiness. He decided that he didn't want to be rich and he didn't want to be poor; he wanted enough money to give him comfort and the real pleasures of life, but he didn't care about merely piling up wealth. His musings were reminiscent of John Humphrey Noyes's first serious question to himself at age twenty: 'What is truly of importance in this life? Worldly pursuits seemed like the senseless eagerness of children for the toys and trifles of an hour.' The elder Noyes, thinking of a community youth, hoped that 'he will ever be kept from the mercenary idea of making riches for himself.'"

Perhaps Pierrepont B. Noyes did indeed inherit the hard-earned wisdom acquired by the parents, and perhaps as Pierrepont's father so hoped and prayed, Community descendants will continue to inherit this wisdom. "Father laid emphasis chiefly on not letting a worldly spirit get into our hearts," Pierrepont remembered. The elder Noyes's values are well summarized in his Home Talk, *Economy and Taste*: "A true taste would demand that we have just what we need and no more. In reference to spending money, our view should be that all things are God's, and that we are dealing with him and his property. I want to form such a character that millions of dollars would not increase my wants. Generally the appetites and wants of men increase as they grow rich. Under the influence of the Spirit, all fondness for display and for acquisition of things will die out."

Personal success was an alien idea to young Pierrepont Noyes, a product of the Oneida Community where three hundred people held all property in common, worked without wages for the support of all, and evolved spiritually and socially. He grew up with many children who studied, played, and worked together, and he admired the competent, nurturing adults who ran multiple businesses, cared for the 475-room Mansion House, and loved each other. When he was ten years of age the Community broke up, though he continued to live nearby. He was taught—rather, caught—the communitarian spirit of working for the common good.

"A director of Oneida Community, Limited asked him to serve as a director in his place. He wanted to live with his Community peers, and for them, to help preserve this unique experiment in spiritual living—infinitely more enriching than amassing personal wealth. In the back of his mind, too, was his concern that these Oneida idealists who believed in selflessness and peacefulness might be unable to compete for the long haul in the new era of mass production with grab-all values. The long-term viability of the Community business increasingly worried him, for its profits supported the elderly Community members. If successful Community industries failed, what would happen to them and youths not yet educated and unprepared to be self-sufficient? In addition, the great vision of creating a new way of living and working could disappear! Though he had prospered, assured of personal wealth, Pierrepont decided to move from New York City and apply his business sagacity to Oneida Community, Limited.

"After much strategizing he was elected a director, changing the course of his life. Only age twenty-three, he brought his considerable experience with Oneida's customers to meetings; though disregarded by some older directors, his advice was increasingly appreciated. He rooted out inefficiencies and identified any customer who took advantage of the good-hearted Community businessmen, as superintendent of the company's three departments in Niagara Falls. In 1899 he was officially made General Manager at a salary of $2,500 with $250 for expenses. P.B. had unilaterally established the nine-hour day—then unheard of—with *ten* hours' pay in 1898 (apologizing to the Board that he'd announced this at Niagara without consulting his elders), and in 1903, the directors' minutes noted that "our wages advanced thirty or forty per cent."[62] That year, H.G. Wells visited Oneida, and in his book, *The Future of America*, he wrote about Pierrepont: 'I never met a man before so firmly gripped by the romantic, constructive, and adventurous element of business, so little concerned about personal riches or the accumulation of wealth . . . . Someday, I like to imagine, the World State, and not just Oneida corporations . . . will command such services as his.'"[63]

Second generation leaders Pierrepont Noyes, President of Oneida Community, Limited, standing second from right; and George Wallingford Noyes, Treasurer of OCL, sitting at far right."

"George Wallingford Noyes went with him to Niagara Falls as his right-hand man. From the beginning the contribution George Noyes made to the building of their new form of industrialism amounted to a great deal more then merely being a good assistant. Almost every man with creative ability is likely at some point in his life to meet another mind with a capacity for feeding and stimulating his own and serving as an anvil on which he can hammer out his ideas. George Noyes served Pierrepont Noyes in this capacity; so close was their relationship and so nearly did their objectives and personal ideals coincide that it would be hard to say in which mind the creative process began. George had led his class in Cornell, but he returned to a small job in Oneida Community, Limited, confirmed in his belief that the underlying principles of the old Community life were right and good."[64] Pierrepont said, "George is the most conscientious and consistent Christian I ever knew. An ardent disciple of John Humphrey Noyes, he believed that my father pointed the way to a more Christ-like social system."

Staying at Stone Cottage, ten years after he'd stayed with John Humphrey Noyes for a year there, Pierrepont, George, and Noyes's son Theodore had many discussions. Theodore said, "People fool themselves; they think that sharing with others will deprive them of part of their own means for happiness. They don't know, as we learned in the Community, that working for something which will benefit others as well as one's own self can multiply the pleasure of work and the enjoyment of success by the number of friends benefited."

Four young men who had been raised in the Community's Children's House—Pierrepont, George, Stephen Leonard, and Grosvenor Allen—envisioned a company committed to give their workers better conditions and a better life. But the world around them was ever-changing; mass-production was decimating small, independent businesses. This nucleus with bright minds and good souls bravely planned a new course. To survive, they had to produce a quality product capable of selling competitively on a nationwide scale: it would be centered in the silverware department. In 1910 Pierrepont was made president on the death of William Hinds, acting as his own general manager. Their chain business was sold in 1912 and the silk business in 1916. A new factory building was built near the Mansion House in Sherrill, New York, and the first silverware department moved there from Niagara Falls in 1912. In July 1914 a train with all the plant machinery, the workers and their families, and all their possessions left Niagara Falls. A week later, the factory in Sherrill was in full operation.

Pierrepont noted a cheerful man at work and assumed that this conscientious employee went home to a comfortable setting. He visited this worker after he'd been badly injured and was shocked that his extended family of seven lived in notable deprivation—four children and their mother shared one room in the small four-room house. Pierrepont determined that no man who worked for Oneida Community, Limited, would live in poverty. He and other Community leaders forged a profit-sharing partnership: Corporate leaders would sacrifice a part of their share in the business's success with the rank and file. A basic principle was based on the Community's conviction that all labor is equally honorable: All who contribute to success, from laborers to management, have the basic right to a life of sufficiency and even comfortable and enjoyable living. So began the building of many homes near the factories, rented to employees at low rates and later sold to them inexpensively. Streets were built and building lots were sold to employees for little more than farmland prices; bonuses were given to make home ownership possible. Loans were given by the company; workers were assisted in obtaining credit, normally available only to those with money. A model company town was born in the exact center of rural New York State.

The very month the business located at Sherrill, the Austrian archduke Franz Ferdinand and his wife were assassinated, precipitating World War I. Business sharply declined and other major silverware companies suffered strikes due to cutbacks. In October 1914, Oneida Community, Limited was forced to drop salaries 10 percent and cut the workweek to four days, but plans for company and club rooms for workers continued. New York State's organizer for the silver workers' union was instructed to organize Oneida Community, Limited. After a thorough survey, his report sums up why the company was so successful: "They work their men short hours, give them good pay, and treat them like human beings . . . .[t]his company is different from any company in their treatment of their employees. It is not done for advertising purposes . . . but is simply a business policy carried out by men who put the man and the woman ahead of the dollar."[65] No strike occurred; other silverware companies did have strikes, and their lost business benefited Oneida Community, Limited.

P.B. left in 1917 to serve war efforts in Washington and later as the American Delegate of the Interallied Rhineland Commission to determine the post-war Occupation of the Rhine Provinces of Germany. P.B. urged President Woodrow Wilson to advocate against a fifteen-year occupying army, which even with good intentions could provoke problems and resentments; he received a letter from President Wilson on May 27, 1919, agreeing with him. Pierrepont's letter and outline of a plan changed the occupation to a civilian one.

Albert 'Ab' Kinsley served as General Manager during Pierrepont's absence; he was the grandson of the esteemed Albert Kinsley family who packed up everything and left Fletcher, Vermont, to join the fledgling community in 1848. Ab was the son of Myron Kinsley who was John Humphrey Noyes's right-hand man in his later years. Ab's primary interest was the welfare of the factory force. He helped all the new families from Niagara Falls settle in Sherrill, and helped form the Community Associated Clubs for workers' social, recreational, health care, and insurance needs. It was run by its members after its formation. He persuaded the Company to contribute generously to an Oneida water project to assure good water for the village. Holton V. Noyes, son of John Humphrey Noyes, asked Oneida Community, Limited to provide for a professional baseball field and tennis courts adjacent to the clubhouse and they readily approved even more; later the company authorized the building of a grandstand and a bandstand and for years they gave a public concert every Monday night.

P.B. returned in the summer of 1920 after serving in the war effort; he envisioned a bright future for Central New York and beyond, carrying on Oneida Community's philosophy: "By cooperating honestly with our employees, a village can be built that will be the model for the whole country, and in which the thrifty can have the comforts of the rich—I do not mean luxuries, but they can have all the comforts as a result of their partnership with us. The spirit of partnership grew throughout the twentieth century with Oneida's policy of paying less at the top so there will be more at the bottom. We are paying a higher average of wages than others in the same line of business. We can do more if we move along only so fast as we establish this new, self-respecting relation between the men and ourselves. When this principle is established, higher wages will be recognized as part of the employees' share in our earnings." Their employees thoroughly trusted those at the top; they knew that they were respected, that management cared about their well-being, and that they would participate in the Company's success. Workers' loyalty is the reward, which is why this vision of partnership is not utopian or even philanthropic, but practical.

Theodore Skinner, grandson of original Putney Community member John Skinner, was born in the Oneida Community in 1872, received a degree in civil engineering, and returned to the Community from 1904 to 1923 to build many homes for company workers and much of the new city of Sherrill. It exploded in population from 100 to

2,500 people, employed in the immediate area, and 1,100 more in other domestic and foreign plants. The Community had given Theodore Skinner material well-being, an education, and the opportunity to acquire a vision of a larger world, and he wanted to give back to it. He gave a banquet speech at the Oneida Community, Limited's annual meeting in January 1912. He reflected the Community vision that complex human requirements and amenities can be realized in architecture. He transformed an old barn into a recreation complex with a basketball court, bowling alleys, pool, dance floor, and café, and across the road the Kenwood Park baseball field. For this new Sherrill, he created two schools for which the Oneida Community, Limited, paid half the cost and supported recruitment of excellent teachers. He designed the Sherrill-Kenwood Library, churches, gardens, and a commercial block with a dry goods establishment, grocery, barber shop, and pharmacy, so the populace could shop near their homes in the day when cars were just being invented. Nearby were a trap and chain factory, a treatment plant, and an outdoor ice-skating rink still in use. The Oneida Community family of three hundred had become a diverse small city, a prototype for business and the good society, which should be emulated nationwide.

"Mr. Toastmaster and friends," Theodore Skinner said to corporation directors and salesmen in 1912—"The germ of the Oneida Community was an ideal.... They lived in a period tense with religious fervor and in a mental state quite impossible of apprehension by many of us in this more materialistic age. They held together through thick and thin so long as the ideal of the founder was the main-spring of their thoughts and actions.... Material prosperity pushed something of the ideal back.... It looked for a time as if our family tree were done for. But after the destruction of an old blighted tree, sprouts spring up from the butt that makes a marvelous growth soon surpassing the original tree in size, beauty, and vigor, being nourished by the spreading root system of the old tree. The company inherited businesses built upon strict integrity of product and fair dealing in trade.

"We are the orchardists and the tree; we see about us new and busy factories with throngs of busy workers, new homes on every hand, each containing increasingly new comforts and luxuries, electric lights, vacuum cleaners, central heating, etc. Automobiles are replacing our horses.... We have the advantage over our imaginary tree in that we can select our own scions for grafting, can do our own pruning and shape our own top.... The Oneida Community lives in us—its spouts—and in those scions we have bound to us and grafted into our body by marriages and intimate association. To live and long endure, however, we must only graft with scions of like characteristics, capable of absorbing and assimilating our sap, and we must not grow too many branches—we must also keep high ideals ever before us and not let the desire for accretion and the pursuit of things material overshadow the obligation to grow spiritually. Let us aspire to let God's sunshine into our hearts, that our growth may be real, and our fruits, at maturity, perfection."[66]

The Dean of the Sales Force spoke feelingly about Oneida Community, Limited, at the 1912 meeting of shareholders and executives: "From almost the lone salesman of the Company, I have seen it grow to its present proportions: it has gone on step by step until now it is not only respected and admired for its commercial activity and growth, but always mentioned as the very soul of honor and integrity. How vivid are the memories that often come back to me of the kindnesses shown me when sickness and death were the portion assigned to me. When a loved one was stricken and for eight long months suffered torments until relieved by death, I was made to feel by your president that life was worth living, that corporations were not soulless."[67]

John S. Freeman, Treasurer of Oneida Community, Limited, compared Oneida's partnership model with capitalistic United States laws and customs with passionate intensity. "Quite a number of stockholders . . . do not do a thing for Oneida Community, Limited. One of them has not taken any part in the business, hasn't given a thought to the interests of the corporation. I do not say that he is to blame. He receives $4,000 automatically by reason of our country's laws and customs. Another actor in the drama is a woman working in one of our mills who comes early, before it is light. She stops work only long enough to take a cold lunch, and stays until after dark. Does she get $4,000? No, she gets about one-twelfth or one-thirteenth of what the drawer of dividends gets. Perhaps she has a mother or children to support. Is there any provision in her pay envelope for them? Not a cent. Our laws and customs do not count that mother or the children. One would think that society would protect her against overcharges; but it does not . . . . [s]he has to yield up about one-tenth of her earnings to pay her way home and back. When she gets home she yields up another slice to the landlord . . . . [t]he merchant takes a further slice of her earnings. One would think merchants might charge her less than they do others, but they charge her more. We get coal for $5.00; she has to pay $6.50, and gets two hundred and forty pounds less than we do . . . . Is this not a question in which we all have some responsibility? If we are not interested in changing these laws and customs, then we are perpetuating them."[68] John Humphrey Noyes would have said that this system is created by those with debased views of life, that a human being, blessed with infinite depth and potential, could be used as chattel, slaves, cannon fodder, poorly-paid and over-worked cogs in the wheel of industry useful only to provide wealth for a few.

"We have built up a semi-socialistic organization at the top of our business structure," Pierrepont B. Noyes said at the 1912 meeting. "Other large companies are composed of the rank and file of the workers, then the Superintendents and Officers who keep the organization going, and finally the owners or the few leaders in control who manage in most cases to get the greater share of the benefits coming from the organization. The first thing we did and the first ideal we nailed to our mast was this, that there should never be an individual or group of individuals who got the principal fruits of the general development. We were going to be socialistic to whatever extent seemed necessary to make practical the old community idea of brotherhood . . . . We have been fifteen years in building a semi-socialistic structure at the top.... Now we want to begin extending the benefits as far as practical, to the rank and file. Abundant material fruits of our work are in sight. There are two ways of taking success. One is to sit down in a fat, comfortable, selfish way and enjoy it, following which we would certainly get in the end what comes to all fat, lazy people. Money is necessary to make any institution go, but as an *end*, I despise it. The other way is to recognize that enlarged opportunities as well as new responsibilities come with success; that we have only built the preliminary and more self-interested part of our structure; that we cannot stop for the sake of our own development as well as the moral right of others in our success....

"We must take the rank and file of our working people into an honorable, if limited, partnership. That means that we must voluntarily sacrifice a part of our share in the success. On the other hand, it means a limited partnership where the sharing of benefits must be proportioned to responsibilities. I believe that our history during the past fifteen years holds the key to a practical method of accomplishing this partnership. There is no other large company that I have ever heard of where the spirit of partnership extends so far down into the organization as in the Oneida Community, Limited. In most companies, as soon as you get below the two or three principal owners, you find even in a responsible organization a barren waste of salaried officials with no sense of partnership, and little satisfaction aside from their salaries. Such a company has little ambition in the matter of salaries except as these can be shown to produce more work—and the officers have little ambition for work except as it produces more salaries. We certainly have changed all this, and we have done it in the form of partnership. As we have accomplished this in our part of the organization by making both salaries and benefits go right along with prosperity, we must accomplish the partnership with our working people by making their wages accompany such prosperity. When we are prosperous we must sit right down and raise our men's wages *without reference to whether we are forced to or not. That* is to me the proper kind of profit-sharing. While I believe that Socialism is going to leaven Society, and its principles eventually dominate it, successful Socialism will start at the top and work downward. The trouble with Socialism has been that it attempted to work from the bottom upward.

"The laboring man is to be emancipated—not from labor, not from wage labor, but from wage slavery," Pierrepont Noyes said. "He is going to earn something besides a living. A good workman is going to receive wages that will enable him if thrifty to accumulate property, to buy a house, and be as responsible and self-respecting a member of society as the manufacturer and merchant have been."[69]

In an interview in 1928, P.B. said, "A family man can expect to have leisure to enjoy his family and to develop himself. Most own their homes and we help them to do this. They have clubs, a community house, and golf links. Someone counted five hundred cars parked outside the factory, and they weren't all flivvers, either! A new definition for Oneida Ltd. would be *A Society for attaining true happiness*. Our

Society has from the beginning aimed at finding happiness, which consists in doing something for someone other than ourselves. No one is really on the road to happiness until he learns this practically. We have always paid our workers more than the union scale of wages and I am just as interested in their being happy as in being happy myself. But how *can* I be happy, if the people around me are dull and *un*happy? From a selfish point of view, then, I want to be surrounded by folks who are having a good time, getting pleasure and satisfaction out of life. Maybe it is a survival of the old Community spirit that I absorbed in my childhood. I don't believe tremendous contrasts in material wealth are good for anybody. But I don't believe in a dead-level, either. I think some people earn, and therefore deserve, more than others. But I don't believe in grabbing all you can get, just because you can get it. Give the other fellow a chance to have a share. It will be more fun to work with him, play with him, and live with him if he is an interested and happy companion."

"Better than a tonic, that man is!" Mr. Sumner, the interviewer, exclaimed. "The Kenwood community too—how they do work and play, talk and write. How they do live! Just to be with them from 9:00 a.m. until 5:00 p.m. has been like taking some newfangled electric treatment." Sumner was referring to the four hundred or so people who still lived in and around The Mansion House, how they ran the biggest business in their specialty, worldwide, yet "nobody is disgustingly rich, nobody is poor, and everybody is doing a lot of interesting things absolutely apart from the business." He describes Pierrepont Noyes as a man "who talks about everything from jigsaw puzzles to international diplomacy, a man who could have been a millionaire many times over but who is not one, because he doesn't choose to be one." In the old community everyone worked, and no kind of work was held to be less honorable than another; that philosophy permeated Oneida's modern corporation and, "to an almost incredible extent, the old feeling that no one person or no small group of persons should grab most of the rewards of work."[70]

The Mansion House Lounge was built in 1914 to connect the four-story north wing with the dining rooms. An oil painting of Pierrepont B. Noyes hangs above the fireplace on the south side of the Lounge.

A reader of the old Community's *Circular* felt as John Humphrey Noyes and his son, Pierrepont, and his nephew, George did: "I believe that Jesus taught, as he prayed, that the Kingdom of God was to be a human society on earth from which the devil of selfishness and self-seeking would be wholly shut out. *Thy Kingdom come, thy will be done.* I look upon your thoroughly cooperative society, dear friends, as 'a city set on a hill.' The tree is known by its fruits. If you have annihilated among yourselves this stupendous contradiction between our Sabbath worship and our weekday business, from which the real spirit of Jesus is so effectually excluded, you are verily doing the noblest work of this or any age. Let your light so shine that men may see that your works are good, and so glorify the Father in Heaven in the only genuine way—by building on the broad and deep foundations of Christian Socialism."

Throughout the twentieth century, Oneida Ltd. became the finest example of enlightened self-interest, a win-win business model capable of transforming the industrial order of the United States for the good of all. If it had become the dominant corporate model, it could have transformed the world, but many corporate debacles caused by the grab-all mentality brought idealism to its knees. The spiritual inspiration that created a long-lasting, flourishing community in the nineteenth century and a prosperous world corporation throughout the twentieth century sheds light on how to solve perplexing, persistent problems that plague us today. The Oneida Community's great goal of establishing the Kingdom of Heaven on earth produced much good fruit, literally and figuratively. John Humphrey Noyes taught that all things are bathed in the glory of God. In him we live, and move, and have our being. Within each person is the holy of holies, that vital connection to the divine, accessible to all; there is infinite depth and mystery in every person and in everything. All our relationships and activities, whether at work or play, love, or learning, become ordinances of worship when done with reverence and loving care. *By their fruit you shall know them.* The high-minded, great-hearted, and spirited people in John Humphrey Noyes's communities and who led its twentieth century corporate enterprise were indeed good fruit.

12

The Loves of Tirzah Crawford Miller, a Personal Journal; Excerpts, 1873–1879

Tirzah Miller was born September 13, 1843 of Charlotte A. Noyes and John Ransom Miller. Siblings were George Noyes Miller and Helen Miller Barron. Tirzah bore three Community children: George Wallingford Noyes, with George Washington Noyes; Paul Inslee Herrick, with Edward P. Inslee; and Hilda Hayes Herrick, with James B. Herrick.

The Oneida Community disallowed any relationship that Community elders discerned was tainted by feelings of jealousy, possessiveness, or becoming emotionally dependent on the other. Intense attachments were recognized, even encouraged, because special affinities do have the power of celestial love. Tirzah's journal describes these varying states of love.

Tirzah Miller was a trusted assistant to John Humphrey Noyes, who consulted her about Community affairs. An accomplished pianist, she was involved with the publishing department and wrote articles for the *Oneida Circular*. She left the Community in 1880 with her husband James Herrick to live with Noyes at Niagara Falls.

The Loves of Tirzah Crawford Miller, a Personal Journal; Excerpts, 1873–1879

LOVE THAT REQUIRED SEPARATION—HENRY HUNTER

I was dreadfully weak all day with a headache and Henry Hunter came to my room after the evening meeting to see if he could magnetize the headache away. He did so. Quite an affectionate time; kissed. We've been reading the Bible together every day. The following night Henry came to read after the meeting and stayed and talked till after midnight—I wish I could give a verbatim report of our conversation—it would do for a scene in a novel. I saw that he was repressing very strong emotion but could not guess what. He said he had for years—ever since he began to feel anything—pursued the policy of suppressing all emotion, chaining down his feelings with an iron hand, and he meant to do so. He has grown more reserved in his treatment of me lately, so I'd concluded that those who said he cared something for me were greatly mistaken. We talked on; he said finally that he *did* like someone and had for a very long time, that it was I, but that I seemed so far away that he thought it no use. Then he threw aside his almost supernatural self-control, and kissed and embraced me ardently. We had a delightful time. He said, "I don't feel any more toward you this minute than I have for a long time." I have not felt so much affected by anyone since Edward left.

Henry was very ardent last evening. He is fast making a powerfully magnetic man; but this romance is nipped in the bud, perhaps wisely, for I feel that I *could* love him intensely. Mr. Hamilton told me that he found himself feeling anxious about it and thought I'd better drop it. He had no criticism, but thought Henry ought to get into the revival spirit and he feared love would stand in the way. Mr. Hamilton's views regarding this matter had changed so suddenly that I felt sure someone had suggested these ideas to him, though I couldn't guess who. I told Homer about it this evening, and he told me that *he* went to Mr. Hamilton and told him his temptations to feel jealous of Henry. I was very much surprised, and told him it seemed unreasonable to me—my attraction toward Henry would have helped my relation to Homer. I told Henry about the probability that we should not read together. It affected him a good deal and he thought he could not stand it. Henry neither eats nor sleeps; neither do I. I hardly understand why the affair should affect my nerves so. Henry came to me today and said he could endure it no longer—he must go to Mr. Hamilton. He looked and acted very fierce, and said he felt ready to fight the whole Community. I showed him the folly of that way of feeling, and begged him to go to Mr. Hamilton in a docile, obedient spirit, ready to take any course he recommended. He reported the talk to me and he had a more subdued spirit than I ever saw in him before. He said that Mr. Hamilton criticized him a good deal, and he wept in spite of himself; but he felt nearer to Mr. Hamilton than before, and said that he left him with the liberty to read with me. We both agreed that the feeling between us is safer.

Feb. 25—It is wonderful to me the amount of emotion that Henry has aroused in me. I would never have believed it possible. I began to feel last evening as though we were expressing more to each other than was right. I spoke with Mr. Hamilton about whether Henry and I could read the Bible again; he said that Henry was doing so well that he was afraid our being together would be a distraction to him; I must not forget that I am a very powerful social magnet and that I didn't appreciate how terribly the idea of giving me up wrenched Henry. I felt mortified some at my position.

Feb. 28—I talked with Henry until eleven o'clock. Aunt Harriet came in and said she felt distressed while he was there. We had quite a talk, and I couldn't feel quite as she did. The next day I wrote to Mr. Noyes about Henry, but he would not give any definite answer as to whether we might go on. Two days later, Aunt Harriet and I had a long talk. I shared some temptations I've had about her manner of criticizing me—I tried to have a good spirit in what I said and she said she felt good about it and thought I did.

March 4—What a strange attraction this is! I never would've believed I could be affected in this way. I saw Henry in the evening, and he grows more and more urgent. When he knows his power, he will be very much such a man as Edward. The next day a communication with Aunt Harriet led to a meeting with Mr. Noyes. He thought my associating with Henry would be a snare to me and he wished me to drop it, because Henry's feeling toward me was likely to be very similar to Edward's. I told Aunt Harriet about it and that I would tell Henry myself. I spoke to him after the meeting and we went into the tower room and talked till 2:00 a.m. I told him how Mr. Noyes felt and Henry wished to know if there was no hope in the future. No, I told him. Then he talked in quite a desperate way about it, and about going away. I told him a good many times tonight that he should go to his room, but I was very weak in spirit so I let him hold me there when I knew he ought to go. Every time I rose to go, he would stand against the door. He was so thoroughly respectful to me, that of course if I'd insisted I must go, he would have relented.

March 8—Mr. Hamilton asked me to promise him that I would say nothing more to Henry. He said that Henry reported his talk with me to Clarence, who came to Mr. Hamilton about it, recounting that Henry told him that he didn't want to live any longer. Of course I gave him the promise, but told him I thought Henry should hear what I have to say. Last evening I was in the children's South Room, and Henry came to say that he felt better than when he left me, and thought he could get along very comfortably if we could be ordinary friends. Mr. Towner brought Paul to bid me goodnight; the little fellow put his arms around my neck and hugged me and then, though his lip quivered, he went with Mr. Towner without crying.

"He did well," said Henry admiringly. "If only I could do it as easily as that!" I thought this one of the prettiest compliments I ever had. Aunt Harriet saw us together and went to Mr. Noyes, sharing the full pressure of her alarm and anxiety. He sent for Henry during the meeting and gave him a very sharp talking to, even that he would send him out of the Community if he didn't stop his intimacy with me. After the meeting, Mr. Noyes sent for me and gave me a thorough criticism. The next day I told Aunt Harriet about Henry's and my long talk, how he stood against the door when I proposed to go. I assured her this not to blame him or excuse myself, but merely to show that he was a man of strong feelings, not a boy to be dealt with easily. I said that for one instant I had such a sense of his great strength that a terror went through me of what he was able to do with me—but that I immediately reproached myself for that thought because he'd treated me with such genuine respect. I knew I had no fear of him! Aunt Harriet wrote only the bare facts to Mr. Noyes without including my modifying comments. Mr. Noyes went down to the office and gave Henry a fearful denunciation. It seemed to me all day as though I would die of self-condemnation because of having gotten a young man into such a dreadful scrape. I couldn't feel good at all to have him blamed, when I am much older. It seemed to me that I ought to take the blame alone.

March 10—I wrote to Mr. Noyes and asked him to put me in the lowest place in the Community as long as I am so liable to come under influences alien to him. I called for a committee to criticize me, too. I never felt so thoroughly crushed and humbled in my life, and expected to be annihilated; but to my surprise all except Henry Burnham were very kind and charitable. Still it seems as though I ought hardly to stay in the Community, and certainly deserve no place of confidence. Though there are many things in this judgment that are very hard to bear, I can see that God is dealing with me and planned it all to humiliate my old life. Henry also had a committee criticism the next afternoon, and Mr. Hamilton told them about his blocking the door. Oh! dear! I know he will think it very unjust told in that bare way, and yet if he'd heard what I said, I don't think he would have found any fault with it, and I had no idea that Aunt H. and Mr. Noyes would feel that way.

March 16—A letter from Ann Hobart, who writes as though offended or ashamed of me. Good! I feel as though I'd got my release; I've had too much reference to Ann's good opinion of me and I am glad I've lost it. I told Mr. Hamilton that it seemed unjust to have it in any way represented that I was afraid of Henry that night or that he forced me, but both he and Aunt Harriet both thought I was inclined to justify him, and they refused to do anything about modifying the statements.

March 18—I wrote to Mr. Noyes about the part of the affair with Henry that troubled—my being afraid of his violence—and he had quite a talk with me, saying that it was a small matter for me to worry about, and he wished I would put it out of my mind: he said he would see that Henry was not abused. I went into Mr. Noyes's room after the dance, and he said he'd been thinking about me a good deal. He said I must get my affections into such obedience to God that, as dancers obey the manager's call, if I let my heart out to someone I must take it back instantly at the word of command. I told him I'd been tempted to think I must crush out of me all love, but he said if I could get this obedience to God, I could love more intensely than now.

March 24—Constance told me of a talk she'd with Henry. She said he was very soft, but it was extremely hard for him to give me up. He said he'd found out that he *could love*. I have taken considerable criticism from Constance lately. She has been a true friend to me. I've learned to love Mrs. Bushnell very much. She is a thoroughly good woman.

March 31—Harriet Worden showed me a letter from Homer in which he made quite a coarse remark about Henry and me. I told Mr. Noyes how Homer had talked and written. He was indignant and said Homer had no business to say one word about Henry and me after he knew we'd both been criticized—that was to be the end of it. Mr. Noyes wrote to Homer, reproving him. He said, "I will tell you what I think of that matter of Henry Hunter. I'm glad it all happened as it did, and considering everything, you did well about it. It is plain enough that Homer needed it." I wrote a note to Mr. Noyes; he said he could see plainly enough that God was using me to bring *men* to judgment. "It is pretty hard on you; but in one sense you ought to be glad if you are bringing the false love of men to judgment, for that is what you are doing and I can see great benefit coming out of it all.

Tossed about till half-past 12, then went up to Frank's room and we had a good talk that strengthened us in our resolve to make the most of ourselves during the next thirty years. Got to sleep about 3 o'clock. Lorenzo asked to talk with me after the evening meeting. He wished very much to have a certain embarrassment between us removed so he could feel at ease in my society; he'd felt strange ever since I declined an invitation from him two years ago. I told him that I did not suppose that he'd care because I told him how jealous Edward was—how Edward confessed to me the next day that he went into the entry outside the office-bedroom and heard and saw all he could. I was much surprised that he would feel so about Lorenzo with so little cause. He seemed ashamed of having given way to this temptation, and confessed in quite a broken way; but therefore I didn't feel that I could ever go with Lorenzo again while there was danger of Edward's feeling so.

I took Paul to walk in the meadow where the ducks are and we heard distant voices calling; Florence, Mabel, and Ida, with Henry Hunter, were engaged in a butternut-crack. I joined them, though of course I said not a word to Henry. I'd asked Theodore if he and Ann would consider allowing us liberty to speak to each other again. I told him that Henry had been extremely obedient, and the present restriction was and had been dreadfully humiliating to me.

April 13—I deliberately made up my mind to speak to Henry today, and did so. It is five weeks yesterday since we said a word to each other. I asked whether anyone told him not to speak to me. He looked astonished at first, but glad; he said from what Mr. Noyes said to him—to let me entirely alone—he took it that he must not speak to me. I said that it is foolishness to do it this way; it only makes it a great deal worse. He said he'd tried to obey Mr. Noyes as well as he knew how, and that I couldn't be any more tired of it than he was; yet he had some hope that things would be different before a great while.

April 16—I told Mr. Noyes that I wished I might be free to treat Henry as I did other young men. At first he said I might and then added that this time of year was so enchanting and romantic that it might be dangerous; he guessed that we'd better go on as we were until Theodore returns and looks after me. I told Henry this in the evening and he looked much pleased. I asked him if he had a good supply of patience, and he said "Yes." The next day, Henry came to the window at the piano house where I was practicing, his gun on his shoulder and his girdle about his waist. I talked to him a few moments and then told him we'd better not speak.

April 20—We had a picnic for people who stopped this afternoon and had a lively time waiting on them. I met Henry in the Court; he had two fragrant bunches of trailing arbutus in his hand, one of which he asked me to take, and said the other would go into the sitting-room. I'd missed him all day; he said he'd walked to Joppa and back and that he would have put the flowers in my room if he'd not met me. Paul is three years old today; will Edward remember his birthday? I can scarcely keep him from my thoughts today.

April 27—I told Mr. Noyes that I'm working in the Printing Office. He replied, "I noticed it and wondered if it was a very good plan to be there with Henry." This disturbed me a good deal and we had quite a discussion, renewed later, finally ending in his having me send word by Mr. Hamilton to Henry to give up forever any idea of loving me or my loving him, entirely and completely, and never think of it again.

May 27—I wrote to Mr. Noyes three weeks ago requesting that the law he put on me a year ago not to speak to Henry Hunter might be removed; he had long ago transferred his affections and it seemed to me to keep up a restriction of that kind was a humiliating farce. Mr. Noyes complied. I had no special wish to speak to him and so said not a word, not even informing him of the change. The law was extremely galling to me, and I resolved I would never expose myself to the possibility of being treated so again. Today he spoke to me and said he felt the same as he did a year ago. I told him that we must be very careful indeed in our treatment of each other, and that he had better go on as he was, without minding anything about me. He said he had learned a good deal by all he'd gone though.

EXCLUSIVE LOVE, AVOIDED—FRANK WAYLAND-SMITH

1874—It seems to be God's will to keep me in a humble state. Let me sympathize with his ways. Frank came into my room and we talked for an hour. It is some satisfaction to know that he had the same feelings toward me that I did toward him during that long time that we loved each other so hopelessly. He said it was a constant stimulus to him. With very new attainment, he thought *She will like this* and so urged himself forward to acquirements he would not otherwise have made. He believed his mind was far better now [with their separation] than it would have been otherwise. Nice times now practicing music with Frank.

Journaling about Frank begins on June 16, 1877—There has been considerable steady magnetism between Frank and me for a long time, though we can't stay together. He said he thought we should have a honeymoon when we are sixty. "It has been seventeen years already," said he, "and we haven't lost an atom of attraction yet, and I don't believe we ever shall." My health is superb nowadays; Frank complimented me today and said, "You look just as fresh as a rose," which is pretty well for a woman of thirty-three who has been dragged through the misery that I have with Edward. Portia told me I looked the best this summer that I ever had since she first saw me nine years ago, and Constance said, "I was thinking only yesterday that if I were a man I would be sure to fall in love with you, you are so bewitching." Am I attractive? I asked, astonished. "Yes, *very*, and I don't blame Henry for loving you. I don't see how he can help it. You seem just as you were five years ago!" My ideas of my attractiveness are so very different. I'd be insincere if I did not admit that I know I've been one of the most attractive women in the Oneida Community; yet I've thrown away with indifference so much love that has been offered me, and lavished so much on my one attraction to Edward, that I now feel quite poor in lovers, though my first love—Frank—told me yesterday that he felt more of this magnetic, electrical attraction toward me than toward anyone. Although I do not feel that consciousness of power I once possessed, yet I feel still that there are many persons whom I might attract if I cared to do so. But things of that kind do not possess the zest they once did, and it would indeed be a bore to me to be popular again.

Aug. 19—I stayed with Frank and we had a very cozy, affectionate time and a plain talk about having a child together. He said he had never found a woman before who so completely satisfied him as I do, and that if he could only stay with me a little while every day, that would be all he should want. We had a very satisfactory talk on the relation that exists between us. He says he can work and harmonize with me more easily and fully than with anyone. This is mutual, and we both agreed that it would be better to preserve our musical, literary, and magnetic relation than to have a child, if so doing would be likely to destroy this superior relation. He says he loves me more now than he did years ago, and we think we are adapted to form a lifelong intimacy that will be a mutual help.

Eliza told me this evening that Homer told her this morning that he could not get to sleep last night. He is so proud that he won't believe I love him or let me love him at all, since I do not feel just as I used to. I said to him last evening that I had not changed as much as he had. "No," he said, "it would not be at all the same to change one from degree above zero to one degree below, as it would be to change from a hundred degrees above to one below." He also said, "Your combination with Edward was not half as painful to me as having to give up last winter [trying to have a baby]." It is curious what an amount of attention, or attraction, I can feel is directed toward me. Men tell me they love me whom I had not been conscious of attracting. I suppose my having been out of circulation for so long with Edward is one cause of it.

Aug. 21—Frank and I got into the intensities a good deal last night. He says he has come to the conclusion that I understand him better than any other woman.

The Loves of Tirzah Crawford Miller, a Personal Journal; Excerpts, 1873-1879

TWO LOVES DURING THE STIRPICULTURE YEARS—ONE REQUIRED SEPARATION; ONE IN THE COMMUNITY SPIRIT

Noyes's son Theodore was a Yale-trained physician, and with his father and other Community elders planned the next generation, a program they called Stirpiculture, a coined word meaning cultivation of the human race to achieve a more spiritual humanity. The Community had largely restricted parenthood from 1849 to 1869 until it was economically strong and a mature, spiritual culture could nurture their offspring. Those twenty years thoroughly tested the equally important principle of Male Continence.

May 4-6, 1873—A stunning proposition! JHN told me this evening that he sent Mrs. Ackley to Edward Inslee to propose having a baby by me, that he liked the combination very much. Edward was pleased and overwhelmed, and said he didn't deserve it. Edward came to see me and we had a very pleasant talk. He was very affectionate and said he would love me and be faithful to me forever. Edward proposed to sleep with me tonight so we could get better acquainted.

June 18—Best time Edward and I ever had.

Nov. 6—The dear baby begins to assert itself. For an hour before rising it kicked me quite vigorously. Edward left for New York. My love and respect for him grow continually.

Edward Inslee and his father, William, expert machinists in Newark, NJ, joined the Oneida Community in 1855 and 1856, respectively. Noyes had sent Community youth to Newark learn that skill. Edward was an accomplished musician and had a complicated relationship with Tirzah Miller, described in chapter 12.

Jan. 25, 1874—Trouble began after Edward's visit to Newark. [Details are not discussed]. Edward wrote a letter to JHN and I suggested modifying parts of it; he would best express my heart by being soft and docile in his attitude. JHN told me he'd received this letter and that he thought it was written in a hard, unyielding spirit. I told Edward what JHN had said. He was feeling badly about it himself, and wished he had not given it to him. I told him I thought he had been more affected by his Newark visit than he supposed. He admitted it and said he wished he'd followed an instinct he had to go to JHN and tell him all about it. He promised he would in the morning. After talking with him, Edward came to my room and threw himself on the bed in a passion of weeping. He talked for an hour and was about to leave, feeling some better; we were standing face-to-face and the baby had just kicked him twice, when the door opened and JHN came in with my mother. JHN was very much in earnest, and after making remarks showing how serious would have been the consequences of that Newark visit, he told Edward that he must not come to my room or see me any more until that was thoroughly repented of. "All right," said Edward, looking as white as a sheet. Edward wrote a good sharp letter to Julia Inslee. JHN told me that I had better write to her, too, without letting Edward see it. He told me to send a regular bombshell among those relatives who were trying to get Edward away. I began that night and finished in the morning. JHN liked what I wrote and I sent it.

I was practicing the piano when Frank came in and seated himself on the stage. I asked him what was going on and he said that George Easton appointed a meeting of the quintet, and hadn't I been notified? I knew nothing of it and asked if all were coming; if Edward was coming, he must have consulted JHN. "Yes," Frank said. Theodore came; we heard a noise in the balcony and Frank and Theodore shouted to Edward to come down. Silence. Finally he came into the ante-room where we could not see him nor he us, and called to George; soon George returned, saying, "Edward says he is not at liberty to associate with the pianist."

"I've been in that situation toward this very pianist for the greater part of my natural life," Frank interjected. "How natural that sounds!" We all laughed.

"George said he was going to see JHN and soon returned, saying he thought it would be rather embarrassing to us to meet just now and that we might as well postpone for the present. We dispersed. My heart began to ache terribly and I felt sure that Edward must be suffering, so I asked mother to go and see him in the evening. She found him in great distress of mind. I met JHN in the hall and we went to his room. He said he'd just had a hard battle with Edward, who'd come in bringing a letter written in a demanding spirit. Edward thought he had done what JHN required of him about his relatives, and now he didn't see why he couldn't return to communication with me. JHN told him he never would have me in that spirit; it was the potentially exclusive spirit of our love that he was contending against more than anything else.

Edward sent a good, loyal, docile letter in the evening. This pleased JHN very much and he seemed ready to give us some liberty right away, but I suspect I upset it by asking whether I can sleep with Edward. "Not unless you guard against an exclusive relationship," he said. "I think it would be best to relate only to Frank for a time, who fully accepts the Community rule against exclusivity." I was quite taken aback by this and told him I hoped he wouldn't urge Frank, for he and I had gotten over our old feelings and he might not like the proposal. "I will make a better woman of you and bring you nearer to God," JHN said. "I do not quarrel with your power but I want you to have a conversion in that part of your life so you will use it for God. Have children and be a mother of the Community." My heart felt soft and broken and I wept, I hardly know why. On Sunday, Edward sent a beautiful letter to JHN.

Jan. 26—I told Ellen Nash today of the arrangement about Frank and asked her to tell Edward. She did so and he wrote a very brotherly note to Frank. When I went into JHN's room this noon, he showed me a note he'd had this morning from Harriet Worden, telling of good experience she had last night sleeping with Edward. It went through my heart like a knife! It was two hours before I could breathe naturally, there was such pain at the center of my life. Yet I told no one, and she and all concerned supposed that I felt perfectly well about it. *I did*, really. It did not seem as though I was jealous, because I had no bad feelings toward her and had a pleasant talk with her about it. It was like death. Terrible! What does it mean? I think after all, that I'm the one who is being restricted. Edward seems to have no particular trouble now. I am glad he doesn't.

Jan. 27—"I went to bed in great distress of mind last night, with a suffocating ache at my heart. The baby was uncomfortable, and my trouble seemed greater than I could bear. I tossed till after midnight. I longed for some superior strength to comfort, but dared go to no one. I slept little, awaking every half-hour to a consciousness of the pain at my heart. I felt so sorrowful in the morning that after crying an hour in my room, I talked with Harriet Skinner. I told her how I felt about Frank and also that Mr. Herrick had been very kind to me. She seemed to appreciate the situation and said she would talk with JHN about it. I finally concluded to write to him and state my case with frankness, and then take criticism from him, if that's what I needed. I carried the note to him.

As soon as he'd read it, he said, "I will go this minute and speak to Frank and Mr. Herrick." The pain at my heart disappeared immediately. Not a trace of it remained. In the library that evening I had a very pleasant, affectionate chat with Frank. There was quite a gush of good feeling. He looked upon the freedom Mr. Noyes had given us as providential, because it would be safer for him to begin socially with someone like me. I went up and told JHN all about it, and he was very much pleased. I went to my room with Georgy, and soon Mr. Herrick came in. We met affectionately and chatted very pleasantly for an hour. After meeting mother, I had a long talk with Edward, showed him my note to JHN and found that he was feeling rather badly, though he felt better before he went away.

Jan. 28—Homer told mother this morning that he and Edward had a long talk about me, and Homer is feeling so well now about me that he was able to comfort Edward a good deal. Homer told him that he'd been in a sweat for a year over his experience with me, but it had done him a great deal of good to be separated and he believed it would Edward. He had had a great deal of peace for the last two months. Edward came over from the shop in the forenoon to talk with mother and consulted her about a note he'd written to JHN asking for liberty to speak to me. She advised him not to send it.

Feb. 1—An eventful day. At noon JHN brought me a note he'd just received from Edward, asking to see me. He showed me his answer, which was that Edward might take the responsibility of seeing me if he felt himself free from temptation to idolatry (See glossary.). He would advise that the call be short and that we did not talk of late experience. JHN asked me what I thought; I hardly knew what to say. Of course I *wanted* to see Edward, but I didn't believe that JHN really thought it best. He finally left it with Harriet Skinner and me. I told her I'd rather wait till JHN invited us; I would rather not speak to him at all till after the baby is born, than fail to do what JHN wishes us to do. She wrote this to him. Edward wrote again to JHN asking to be released from the promise not to speak with me. JHN answered that he would release him from that, and he might speak to me as he would to any other woman. The more JHN thought about it, the more he felt as though Edward had a hard spirit, that he was trying to make JHN acknowledge himself mistaken in his treatment of the case; so he wrote Edward another earnest letter, and told me I must defend myself now. I had an instinct to put myself in communication with Ellen Nash, because I knew Edward would quite likely be confidential with her. I showed her as clearly as I could how the matter stood—how Edward seemed to be resisting JHN in an independent spirit, and was relying on his own strength to keep him right, and that I was sure that unless there was a change in him, we would not be associated at all even after the child is born. I told JHN what I had done, and he said I might communicate with Edward through Ellen; so she went back and forth between us until nearly 11 o'clock, and left him finally in a softer state, desiring to have God do with him as he would.

Feb. 2—JHN showed me a good letter he had from Edward this morning, which pleased him very much. Edward spoke in meeting and said he had had a new ambition to be filled with the grace of God.

Feb. 3—I communicated some with Edward through Ellen and he had a real conversion while at the shop in the forenoon and was enabled to see what all this discipline is for. He acknowledged that he has been dependent upon my society for happiness. He made a splendid confession in the evening. After the meeting, as I was sitting by Constance in the Hall, he stopped by me a moment and said: "I see it all now." This is the first word and look that has passed between us for more than two weeks. Now is the time for patience. I thank God for this change in Edward. He is very soft-hearted now. I pray for patience about seeing him.

Feb. 9—Once the bars were let down between Edward and me, we were tempted into several talks. I felt distressed about it and told him last evening that I did not think we were doing right and it made me unhappy; that I rather he wouldn't say anything more to me until JHN gave us leave. This forenoon I went into JHN's rooms and the first thing he said was: "Does Edward let you alone?" So it all had to come to light.

Feb. 12—I think I love Edward better than he does me, after all. I had written to JHN asking him to deal as mercifully as possible with Edward, acknowledging that I believed him better than myself, when JHN told me that Edward that morning threw the blame on me, at Mrs. Ackley's suggestion. JHN did not accept that, after hearing Edward's own testimony. I could not help feeling somewhat bad about this; but it shows that there is a great deal of false love mixed in with our feelings toward each other, and this fact ought to help cure me.

Feb. 22—Edward has had strange ups and downs of experience. JHN gave him a number of criticisms and about a week ago he seemed to submit himself to JHN; but for days he has looked very dark and I knew last night by my own sensations, and the baby's, that he must be suffering. This forenoon JHN brought me a letter Edward had written him, asking for renewal of a certain amount of intimacy with me. JHN asked me what I wanted to do about it. I told him I did not wish for any change in my personal relations to him at present, but wished he would associate with others and not make such a hermit of himself. JHN put what I said into his answer and advised him to offer himself for criticism. Edward said he would do so, but wrote a reply that tried JHN very much, and he had a committee get together immediately and criticize him. This seemed to produce a wonderful effect.

Feb. 26—This second generation has thus far had its attention more on its social relations than on learning to experience God. The Community will die if this continues.

March 1—I believe Edward is established in the right way. He has remained of the same mind for a week.

March 5—I was distressed to find a note in my room from Edward. I did not read it but asked Mary Pringle to give it to him and tell him I had not read it, and did not think he ought to write me without asking JHN.

March 13—Edward again in a quarrel with JHN. A committee criticized him behind his back.

March 16—Thank God! Thank God!—a letter of humble submission to the family. JHN said to me after meeting that the struggle had finally come to a good termination. He said he had been in travail of spirit about Edward for the last three days and it ought to effect something, and he believed it had. I have been tempted to feel sorry for Edward; but during this last struggle I saw clearly that JHN was the one who needed sympathy and I did pity him most. Edward has been possessed by a principality that has transformed him. For the first time in several weeks the baby let me go to sleep in tranquility very soon after retiring. There has been a mysterious connection between Edward's state and the way the baby has acted. When he has been quarreling with JHN, it has hurt me sometimes; it has not been any less lively today, but the movement has been pleasant.

March 22—Moved into the lying-in room.

March 25—O Edward, if you think I don't love you, how little you know me. You cannot have had a pang that has not struck an answering chord in my heart, and yet I know this discipline is right and that we need to be separated.

March 27—I have felt depressed for a week or more and troubled with misgivings about the baby. I know that I need to trust God more and prayed all day that I might, and felt that my prayer was answered. I called for a criticism.

March 29—I feel no jealousy about M.W., but an unaccountable disgust came over me at the idea of Edward's lying in her embrace, kissing her, and so on. I never had this feeling about anyone before. I am grieved, too, that he does not look higher. It is none of my business, I know, and perhaps my feelings are altogether wrong; but though I have nothing in the world against her, her life seems coarse to me; the idea of very close contact is repugnant. I never thought I could kiss her. Men probably think differently, though I remember that this was JHN's opinion about her. Auscultation with Dr. Noyes [endnote: listening with ear or stethoscope to sounds within the body, esp. chest and abdomen, relating to pregnancy]; 140 pulsations a minute; picture taken.

April 7—I am now passing through the greatest trial of my faith that I have ever called to endure. I wrote to JHN telling him of my wish to communicate with Edward before the child is born. I had gotten over the heartache about it and felt resigned to God. JHN answered that he would not hesitate an instant on my account, but Edward had behaved so that he would have to consider the matter. He seemed quite reluctant to give his decision. He said he dreaded another encounter with Edward and hoped he would not be called to endure one. He thought if I were wise, I would hesitate very much before putting myself in his power again. I told him it seemed to me that Edward was very much changed, and that his will was broken. He replied that Edward did not come near him at all. He told me not to worry about the matter and not to let Edward know I was asking for him. My God! It seemed as though my heart would break for a while. It is even worse than I feared. I had not supposed that JHN intended to keep us separated all the way through. I can't but acknowledge that Edward's course is not calculated to make JHN think well of him. O Edward, if you loved me half as well as I do you (to say nothing of your duty to God and the Community), you would make some effort to win JHN's confidence and love. How can you at this serious moment dissipate your time with such a woman as M., who is totally incapable of elevating you? I told JHN that I would abide by his decision and feel good about it, and *I will*, though the trials of this winter have caused me the acutest suffering I have ever known. Though Edward tortures me so, I love him perhaps far too much. I pray to God to make my heart right about him.

April 8—I had an earnest talk with mother last evening about Edward, and entreated her to talk with him. She did so for an hour and a half after the evening meeting and succeeded in arousing him to quite a sense of the situation. He said he would make an effort to get near Mr. Noyes and would testify every day, whether he was under temptation or not. He did speak well in meeting tonight. A good cry, after meeting. I never wept so much in my life as I have during the last three months. Every day or two the tears will flow. The next day I begin to feel at rest again about not seeing Edward. I desire to have my will in subjection to God's will.

April 11—JHN asked me if I still wished to see Edward. I told him I did, though I no longer felt any anxiety about it. We talked for more than an hour about the matter, which ended in his writing me the following letter: "Dear Tirzah—The hold I have upon your heart has been pretty well tested in the struggles of the past winter. On the whole you have been faithful to me, and I have confidence that you will be faithful. I feel free to say to you, in view of your impending trial, that you may follow the instincts of your heart in regard to Edward, and invite him to as much intercourse, always with the restraint of male continence, as you think you can afford. Yours faithfully, J.H.N." I felt very glad and thankful, but in no hurry to move. I long to have Edward secure JHN against anxiety, and wrote to him after meeting to that effect.

April 12—I received a good letter from Edward at 11 o'clock last night and another one this morning, took them to JHN, and he seemed quite well satisfied. I wrote to Edward in JHN's room. JHN liked the letter, and told me to say at the end that he might write his answer or come and tell me personally. It was not long before Edward came to my door, and in an instant we were in each other's arms. But I cannot describe it. It was very sweet to meet him again. Edward is carrying out his original program splendidly. We had as magnetic a time last night as ever.

April 20—I awoke at 3 o'clock with an unmistakable pain that continued without cessation, growing harder and harder. JHN sat with me and as the pains rapidly grew harder, at 12:30 it was thought best for me to undress. Eliza kindly helped me. Swift work soon followed. At 1:30 Frank came in. In a few moments I called to Mrs. Sears that the water had broken and she sent for the doctor. Edward came in and clasping me in his arms for moment kissed me passionately, and then I sent him away. At 2:10, Haydn was born, weighing eight pounds.

Tirzah's journal skips to September 20th—

My mother is perhaps dying; Dr. Carpenter says she cannot live, but we do not give up hope.

Sept. 29, 1874—My dear, good mother died at 6 o'clock this evening, at age 55. She has suffered greatly, but has never made a complaint. She has shown wonderful faith, patience, and care for others. The last thing she said to me was day before yesterday when I had rubbed her all over: "You did it nicely, nicely." The last time she saw Georgy—George Wallingford Noyes—Tirzah's first child by George Washington Noyes, she told him to ask God to cure her. Half an hour before she died, Edward came to my room in considerable agitation with white face and burning eyes, feeling very hard against Mr. Noyes. JHN has been concerned about the growing family spirit and thought Edward and I had better dissolve. We had quite a struggle and he went away somewhat mollified. He said if I released him from responsibility about the child he would leave the community, but I said I never would.

Oct. 23—Edward left for Wallingford Community this evening. He came to see baby and me. (Sweetest). God is good—better than I asked or thought.

Oct. 26—If Edward and I meet in the Great Hereafter, he will know that I loved him, and that I only left him because my conscience would not let me choose the world and have any peace.

Dec. 22—What a fearful experience has been mine for the last three months! I feel now considerable peace of heart, and trust in God's purpose to make suffering work patience, hope, and all the excellent qualities of the spirit. After Edward went to Wallingford on October 23rd he wrote me three letters that were very affectionate. I did not consider that we had any liberty to correspond, so did not answer. But when I decided to put Haydn into the Drawing-Room [Children's Department in daytime hours], I thought it would be proper for me to write to him about it; also to tell him that it was not in accordance with Mr. Noyes's idea for him to write me such love letters. So on November 2nd I asked Mr. Noyes if I might write to Edward about Haydn. "Wouldn't it be as well," he mildly asked, "for someone else to write?" I answered, "I don't see why I can't write." He expostulated with me a few moments, and I said I thought he dealt with me more severely than with others. We had quite an argument about it. "It seems to me," he said, "that you take the liberty to counter my judgment on this matter." I responded that I can't help it, though it makes me feel bad not to think as you do. We argued still further, and left it so. After dinner, Ann said that Mr. Noyes wanted to see me in his room. He said he would like to have Ann tell me something that she had divulged to him when he reported our talk to her. The night before Edward went to Wallingford, he consulted Frank about his legal rights and duties concerning me and the baby; he felt quite stiff and resolute about the matter. I've been unable to see Edward's character as Mr. Noyes did, or to believe him dishonest, but knowing that he had this talk with Frank at the same time that Edward professed to me great affection for and loyalty to Mr. Noyes, I couldn't deny that the course he'd taken was a disloyal one.

A strange, sweet dream about Edward this morning—I wished the other day when I was lying with my eyes closed during a bout with fever and ague, that I could see his face. I dreamed that he had returned to the Community and that there was a deep, bubbling joy in my heart about him. Mr. Noyes was kind and sympathetic, and left me free. I ran up to Edward's room in the garret and found him reading in the Testament, and a quiet, peaceful expression radiated from his beautiful eyes. I put my hand on my heart and said, I know in here that the child will be yours, and put up my arm to clasp his neck. He at the same instant turned, and bent on me his dark, tender eyes, full of soul-love, and I awoke. The impression left on me was one of *goodness*.

July 1877—Ann told a committee some appalling things that Edward told her just before he left the Community, about the deception Ella practiced, which he allowed. She made Mr. Noyes and the Community believe that she loved and suffered about Edward when it was really Edwin Burnham; afterward she acknowledged to Edward that she put it on him because he was already under criticism about me, and she laughed and joked with him about it. It shocked me to have to believe him capable of associating with one whom he knew to be deceiving in so flagrant a way. He would be in the Community now if he had not associated with her. Although I have no reason to think that he loved her, intimacy with her engendered willfulness, evil-thinking and independence in him. I offered myself for criticism today, July 23rd. I enjoyed Theodore's remarks very much. He was very sincere, and also very kind. He criticized me for general indiscretion. I only wish what he said had been told to me ten or fifteen years ago; but I shall do my best now to learn the lesson.

Nov. 27—Edward asked again if he might visit. Mr. Noyes wrote a kind letter to Edward and had me copy it and send it in my hand-writing, saying that he does not wish him to visit until he can rejoin the Community. He told him that he and others earnestly hoped he would return. He advised him to stay where he is at present and correspond with him.

Dec. 14—A long letter from Edward came to Mr. Noyes, and cold, cruel, and heartless it is. He seems to have no real sense of the position in which he places me and his child. His own self-will is of more consequence to him than our bleeding hearts. He tries to make out that he is really all right and shows plainly that he has no desire to return unless the government can be changed. Yet he says his heart is here, and he wishes to be free to visit. My heart sank and I felt badly for a while, but I went to bed very quietly with a feeling of hope and trust in God. *The Lord gave, he took, he will restore. Blessed be the name of the Lord*.

Feb. 28, 1878—I dreamed about Edward last night. The scene was the Hall, and we seemed to be about to hear a lecture. I took a seat by Carrie; looking up, I saw that I had sat down directly behind Edward. He soon became aware that Carrie was there but did not see me. By and by I leaned forward, and whispered: *Edward*! He turned instantly, his eyes meeting mine and melting into that humid expression of unutterable tenderness I remember so well. Then he caught me passionately in his arms, murmuring: *Oh, my precious, precious darling*! and carried me out of the room. The rest of the night, my dream was spent going with him from one place to another trying to find a room where we could talk without interruption. I thought Edward's knees and elbows were patched, and that he said he was not doing as well as he had been.

March 4—I suffer a good deal in my mind nowadays. I wish I could show Mr. Noyes all that is in my heart about Edward. I don't see how I'm ever to feel differently.

March 18—Ann left the Community and married Joseph Skinner. I can't help remembering how Theodore and Ann drove Edward out of the Community, and then showed no sympathy for me. Theodore seemed to think I ought to have no more feeling than a machine and give up Edward without a pang, and consider it good riddance.

March 20—Mr. Noyes found out that I was feeling bad. The present affair brought up all my agony about Edward afresh, and he talked with me today about him in the most encouraging way. He assured me that if any opportunity appeared, he would do everything in his power to save him. I felt that if I could be assured that Mr. Noyes had hope of him and would do his best to reclaim him, I'd not care if I never saw him again in this life.

March 29—I feel extremely unhappy, and yet my feeling about Mr. Noyes makes it impossible for me to leave him. I have sacrificed my happiness in this life to that feeling. In thinking over all the experience with Edward, it seems terrible, and I wish that I might have done differently; but I could see no other way and if I had a chance to do it all over again, it might end the same because there are two things I cannot do: *I cannot desert Mr. Noyes, and I cannot take George Wallingford away from the Community.* No matter what my temptations or how much I long to be with Edward, I always have to come back to these two fixed facts in my life. So why can't I accept the inevitable, and be happy? Why waste my life in vain wishes that things might be different? Edward and I can only come together again in one way; he must come back.

March 31—Mr. Noyes called a meeting this morning and gave a talk about a new policy regarding those who leave the Community. He does not consider them reprobates but on the contrary, better material for conversion than people we know nothing about. He spoke of sending missionaries to them, and mentioned Edward. Is there really hope that Mr. Noyes will change in his feelings toward him?

April 18—I am in continual torture of mind concerning Edward, and it seems to me I can never have any peace unless I can communicate with him. I suppose Mr. Noyes would think I am quarreling with him if he knew all that is in my mind; but I do not think it is really so. I have never felt as though I could leave Mr. Noyes, and yet I must have some things different about Edward or I shall go crazy. If he'd been treated altogether right, I believe that I would have felt at rest about him.

April 20—Paul is four years old; put pants and jacket on him for the first time and Eliza and I took him to ride. He looked very bright, and healthy, and handsome, and I would have given a great deal if his father could have seen him. Paul said to me this morning, "Mama, I wish you *would* ask Papa Noyes if he won't go and see my own papa, and talk to him, and bring him back. I want to see him." So do I, I answered. I had a long talk with John Norton and he told me all he knew about Edward's call at Wallingford four months ago—Edward met our agent, Bristol, and told him that he used to live in the Community and was obliged to leave under peculiar circumstances. Poor boy!

April 23—Mr. Noyes expressed an interest in Edward and a hope that he would come back, and said his feelings about him had very much changed. I thought I'd write to Mr. Noyes about Ann's treatment of Edward that have long troubled me; I wrote about her misrepresentations of him for three years and her final sending him away from the Community. Mr. Noyes said he had no doubt that it was all true. I believe that we shall some day have Edward back.

April 26—Frank reported that when he saw Edward in New York City last November, he felt in him a very soft, tender spirit toward the Community and that he said not a harsh word about it; he had evidently suffered a good deal and instead of being hardened, he had been softened by it. My prayer is that he may come back to Mr. Noyes. Mary Prindle, now at Wallingford, saw Theodore in New York and wrote me about what she learned about Edward. He is really out of fellowship with Julia on account of her opposition to the Community. I showed the note to Mr. Noyes and we had a pleasant chat over it; he said it would be splendid to have him back to help us in our musical campaign, if he would take hold under him. Mr. Towner also saw Theodore, who told him that Edward said his heart was in the Community, and that he never could marry Miss Ricker of whom we've heard so much. He also asked Theodore if he supposed the Community would let him see Paul. I have talked quite freely to Paul about his father lately and he speaks of him frequently, saying that he wishes his own papa would come back. Mr. Towner said Paul asked him suddenly, "When my papa Inslee comes back, will you be my papa then?" It is wonderful the way things are working and I have every reason to thank God for his goodness.

June 4—Paul stood looking out my window today at the tulip tree that's in blossom, and said, "Mama, when my own papa comes, won't you ask him to climb that tree, and get me one of those pretty flowers?" The other day he said, "I do want to see my own papa." You must pray to God to send him back, I said to him. "I do," he answered. "I did last night." I talked with Rosamond this morning and was greatly astonished at a revelation she made concerning me. She said that Ann talked to her about me *last summer*, showing without a doubt that it was her purpose and hope to have me go away from the Community. When Rosamond perceived her design she exclaimed: "You mean to drive Tirzah from the Community!" "I don't deny it," said Ann. She said she was *determined* to have me go and that she never failed in anything she undertook. Rosamond told her she would fail in this. This accounts for many things I have felt from Ann during the last four years, and if it is really true, it was a plot of a number of years. That was the cause of her persecution of Edward—the hope that I would go with him.

June 12—I received a note from Mr. Pitt reporting to me his conversation with Edward, and suggesting that he be allowed to make a visit here. I was horrified to have him write to me as I knew Mr. Noyes would not like it; but I sent the letter in to Mr. Noyes, and then followed a correspondence between us that lasted several days. It was rather stormy at first, but finally ended in a very satisfactory covenant between us. In the midst of this correspondence, Mr. Noyes received a letter from Edward, asking liberty to visit, and enclosing a letter to me that Mr. Noyes did not let me have, but wrote me the purport of its contents. He also told me that Edward wrote a letter to me a year ago that he kept from me, and when he told me that, I was at first glad that he did not let me have it then, because I was under such fearful temptation that I would have doubtless have gone to Edward. After thinking about it a while, I was tempted to feel provoked that Mr. Noyes had dared to interfere with my rights so; I went through quite a struggle, but finally saw that my first feeling was the right one, and I wrote to Mr. Noyes thanking him for not letting me know about the letter at the time.

July 10—Two years ago this evening I saw my dearly beloved Edward for the last time. Although I felt goaded on by an inexplicable impulse to do something desperate, I had no idea then that so long a time could possibly elapse ere I saw him, or that any serious obstacle could ever come between us. God grant that the days of separation may be shortened, for the sake of my darling boy!

July 20—I have had a new feeling come into my heart about Edward lately, which has been quite a comfort to me. I have been able to see that in spite of everything that has seemed so cruel and unjust in the treatment of Edward, the whole experience has been very necessary to me; and a number of times, instead of complaining *O Lord! How much longer must I endure*? I've found myself praying that God would continue the discipline until he made of me what he wished. I realize that it is one thing to recognize the fact that God arranges our circumstances, but quite another to feel good about it, and contented to have him do as he pleases. Theodore is here and we have had several chats together. He seems quite friendly and we've talked somewhat freely of the problem of life, and of the conditions we would have chosen to have existed. I told him about my temptations to leave the Community; that although I was under great temptation to do it for several years, and often came to a point where it seemed as though I could not endure the life here a day longer, I always found that an inexpugnable feeling that I have toward his father stood in the way. I could not escape from it, however I might try. That was what held me when Edward went. I felt that in giving him up that I sacrificed all hopes of happiness in this life; but I knew that if I went with him the remorse I would feel for having set aside this sense of duty toward Mr. Noyes would embitter my whole existence, so that I considered it better to sacrifice love than conscience and honor. He said that this same feeling toward his father was just what ailed him and he could not get away from it.

Aug. 2—My soul is sometimes very sorrowful because of the hope deferred so long about Edward; yet I know that God is doing the best thing. But I ask myself: How can Edward live away from the dear boy whom he certainly loved very dearly? How can he let him grow through all the prettiness of early childhood without seeing him? I wrote to Mr. Noyes about some of the trials I have had with Mr. Towner as Paul's father, on account of his legality, and what seemed to me to be a lack of love for him. Mr. Noyes had been for some time very much tried with Mr. Towner, and advised me to withdraw Paul from him, and proposed that Mr. Herrick be his father. I proceeded to change the child's sleeping, etc., and talked with Mr. Towner. He was so much offended at my high-handed outrage that he made quite a disturbance, and finally went to Mr. Noyes, who advised him to offer himself for criticism. He did so, and after a day or two had a deep conversion. This produced a great change in him that was very satisfactory to Mr. Noyes. He also came to me, and wrung my hand with tears in his eyes.

[Tirzah and Edward were separated because they had become emotionally dependent on each other, Edward was required to live at the Wallingford Community while Tirzah lived at the Oneida Community with the baby, causing both distress. Two years later on September 1, 1876, Edward finally left the Community entirely.]

LATE STIRPICULTURE PERIOD

Nov. 25—Mr. Noyes asked if I desired to have more children and I told him that my past experience was not such as to make me very enthusiastic about having more, but that I was glad to participate in the Stirpiculture program. Theodore studied multiple traits of Community men to select the best scientific combination for me. He gave Ann a list of eight men that she handed to me, written in order of preference: George D. Allen, James B. Herrick, J. Homer Barron, Frank Wayland-Smith, Henry Grosvenor Allen, William A. Hinds, Alfred Barron, and Frederick A. Marks. Ann wished it might be Homer; Theodore said he considered him about as scientific a combination as the first two names, but he thought we were not quite so sharply contrasted temperamentally. Theodore thinks I'm one of the strongest women in the Community and I can therefore afford to combine with someone who is not so strong. Of course I showed the list to Mr. Noyes, who talked with Theodore, and he told me afterward that he didn't want to have sentiment control the matter; we concluded to let the subject drop for a few days.

Dec. 2—I told Mr. Noyes that I did not feel that my heart was set on having a child by anyone in particular at all and had made up my mind to be thoroughly scientific about it. My feelings about Edward are held in suspense. I was ready to do as Theodore said. "Yes, leave it to Theodore," Mr. Noyes said, "and it will all go right."

[Tirzah tried to conceive with Homer Barron for a significant period, without results.] Mr. Noyes said he'd have no objection to my trying with Frank, but said he preferred Mr. Herrick, so I said I would. I spoke to Mr. Herrick, telling him he might feel perfectly free to decline. He said he would be glad and pleased, and wanted to have a visit with me this month, but I dread the idea very much. Weeks later, she wrote that she 'came round' on her due date, so will not have to try with Mr. Herrick any more. There is certainly an incompatibility between us, which has seemed to me more and more apparent. I wrote to Mr. Noyes saying that if he sympathized, I would prefer to give up trying with Mr. Herrick, and he said, "All right." I told Mr. Herrick what I wrote to Mr. Noyes, and was surprised to find how badly he felt about it. He asked if there would not be a chance for him again, that it would be a tremendous giving up for him and that he would rather have a child by me than by any other woman in the Community. He also said he didn't think he had quite a fair chance last month, as he was feeling badly about his criticism and I was not well. He said he knew it was asking a great favor of me, but he did wish he might try once more, and I felt so sorry for him that I said I would. But when I was away from him I found that it put a great weight in my heart, which had felt very light just before.

I feel convicted of un-thankfulness. I am continually reaching out for, and grieving because I cannot have certain unattainable things, instead of being thankful for the blessings I actually possess if I would only recognize the fact. God must look upon me as ungrateful. I have felt perfectly indifferent to the matter of having a child by Mr. Herrick and have been quite prone to see his defects; but there is certainly a great deal of good in him, and I don't know as I deserve a child by him. I certainly don't by anyone, unless I am thankful and reconciled to God for his dealings with me.

Mr. Noyes criticized me some for my feelings toward Mr. Herrick; he said he prayed that Mr. Herrick might be successful in impregnating me. "It will be the finest child you have had and the one that will give you the most comfort." (She bore Hilda Herrick; see Appendix). I asked the Doctor and Ann if I might begin practicing the piano. They left me free to do as I thought best.

Sept. 13, 1878—I'm about to begin the month with Mr. Herrick again. It does not seem right for two persons to try when one feels as I do. I dread it fearfully, and more and more every day. Mr. Herrick came without notifying me last night, and after the trial was over he said, "Poor little martyr! I know the best part of this to you is for me to go away." I decided that I'd tell him wherein it seemed to me that he had not treated me fairly and justly. I ended with that affair when he wrote to Theodore and got me into such a muss between him and his father. Mr. Herrick's motives were good—he had no intention of making trouble for me—but I thought he acted on impulse without getting a clear idea of what he was about; it made me dread to get into any relation to him where he'd feel he had a responsibility about me; I would never be able to calculate what he'd be likely to do. Mr. Herrick said he was glad to find there was a foundation for the aversion I had toward him; he's been afraid that I disliked him and could not tell why. He'd felt that I couldn't endure the idea of trying again. I told him I had not an aversion toward him in the beginning, though I never felt any spontaneous attraction for him. We left it that we would try no more until there was a better state of feeling between us. He said that when he asked me to let him try one more month, he never felt more attracted to any woman in his life than to me. Because I felt so glad to be free from the engagement with him, I treated him quite genially and naturally, but that all changed as soon as I gave him the promise to go on again.

Tossed about till half-past 12, then went to Frank's room and we had a good talk that quite strengthened us in our resolve to make the most of ourselves during the next thirty years. Got to sleep at about 3 o'clock. Lorenzo asked to talk with me last evening after meeting. He said he wished very much to have a certain embarrassment between us removed, so he could feel at ease in my society; he had felt strange ever since two years ago, when I declined an invitation he sent me. I told him that I did not suppose at the time that he would care because I refused him and I told him how jealous Edward was—how Edward confessed to me the next day that he went into the entry outside the office-bedroom and heard and saw all he could. I was very much surprised that he would feel so about Lorenzo with little cause. Edward seemed ashamed of having given way to this temptation, and confessed in quite a broken way; but therefore I did not feel as though I could ever go with Lorenzo again while there was any danger of his feeling so.

Oct. 19—Nearly two weeks over my time—can it be possible I am to have another child? Henry Hunter had a hard criticism yesterday and the fact was evolved that he is in a quarrel with Mr. Noyes about me.

Nov. 8—I was so afflicted with nausea that I wanted to get away from the Community for a while, and came to Joppa. Oh, Edward, *Edward*! Is this the end? Do you ever think of the mother of your boy? I thank God that I believe in Providence and that he orders our circumstances, and I believe good shall come of the present unpleasant arrangements. Were it not so, I would find it very difficult to be reconciled—with child by a man I do not love and the one of all others whom Edward disliked.

Nov. 10—Mr. Herrick asks me if I want anything and I generally say, No, but I did want some nuts. After a few days he brought a most munificent supply of English walnuts, filberts, pecans, almonds, and Brazil nuts. I was very much surprised, as I had not thought he was that kind of man. Is it possible that I love Mr. Herrick? A strange, sweet magnetism has come between us. What is it? Whence is it? I never could have believed it would be so, and yet I do love him, *love him*, and find in him a great deal that is pure and noble and high-toned. I hardly know whether he really loves me, though he is very affectionate and kind. He said to me last evening: "Never in all your life have you looked as pretty to me as you have today." There have been some exquisite love passages between Mr. Herrick and me. We ponder how to love each other and yet keep clear from all appearance of special love.

"It will be quite a satisfaction to me to go back to Joppa knowing that you are feeling good," Mr. Noyes said. "I was afraid that you were mad at me; I think a great deal of your good opinion. I always feel bad when you feel bad." We both wiped tears from our eyes, had a very affectionate talk, and I felt more as though I could sacrifice my life to this good old man than ever before.

Today Mr. Kinsley came to me, burdened with a message that he said came from St. Paul. Mr. Kinsley is an old man, broken with age and infirmity, and yet his soul is so devoted, his manner so earnest, that it seemed almost as though one of the prophets of old had come to me with a message from the Almighty. He said that for three weeks I had been almost continually in his mind. He had a time of prayer and heart-searching, and asking God what he should do to rise into more usefulness, and the answer came that he must go and talk with me. He resisted the impression and put it off again and again, saying that it was not his place to do anything of this kind, and that I might be offended; but he could not get rid of the idea that Paul commanded him to go and talk with me; it was the only answer he could get to all his prayers. This morning the call came again so strongly that he promised Paul he would obey. "Paul wants you to abandon all worldliness and come entirely over on Mr. Noyes's side, that you might help others to do it. There is need of a great change in order to bring the young into unity with Mr. Noyes's faith, and I have a feeling that if you don't start out and answer this call from Paul, it will not be done. There is not another woman in this Community who can do so as much as you can. Mr. Noyes needs you." I told him I had never had any ambition to lead. "I know it," he said, "but those who do not desire it are just the ones for leaders."

March 4, 1879—The Community has been quite distressing of late. There was the raid of the ministers upon us, but that was nothing compared to internal dissensions; general independence has become more widespread and outspoken. The agony of the situation comes over me occasionally in waves, though I generally manage to keep a faith-view of things. My sister Helen asked me today whether I expected to have Mr. Herrick help me to take care of the baby; he said he told her he didn't mean to get his heart set on it, as he thought I did not like him, and would probably prefer to have someone else help me. I told her to say to him that no idea of the kind had ever entered my mind, and if he would like to take care of the child, I'd certainly prefer to have him rather than anyone else. Besides, I expected that when we had a mutual interest like that, it would improve our general relationship.

March 21—Today the clouds of discouragement came down pretty heavily, and yet there was a gleam of sunshine in Mr. Herrick's love. For he *does* love me; he has told me so again and again, and many times his looks and actions have said so more plainly than words. He was in a peculiarly soft state today, his beautiful eyes often filling with tears as some emotion crossed him. I love him very dearly, and am only fearful lest I love him too much, and become too clairvoyant about him. We have had a very sweet almost uninterrupted period for several months. That evening he invited Helen, but she was engaged. At first I had a slight temptation [jealousy], but I immediately said to myself that I'd had a pleasant time with him lately and now I would stand back and let her enjoy him, and feel good about it. Consequently I began to treat him according to the agreement I'd made with myself—to be kind and respectful but to withdraw my magnetism entirely from him so that I would not affect him, nor he me. He, of course, noticed the change and asked what the matter was, and I answered good-naturedly that I was not as selfish as he thought me, and that I was only adopting a new policy [not becoming too "special," as the Community prescribed].

"You know I didn't *feel* any differently toward you?" I asked.

"Yes, I did know it; but I want you to be as you have been, darling." He went out for a walk, from which he returned in quite a different mood. We've been reading together lately between 4 and 5. At 3:15 I heard him go through the hall outside my door, and within two or three minutes afterward, I had one of my clairvoyant flashes that are so troublesome. I felt that he was having the proposed visit with Helen. Yet I felt determined to have a good spirit and behave well with God's help. I went as usual to read. He came a few moments late with a flushed face, and proceeded very smilingly to read. He tried several times to caress me, but that I could not bear and did not respond. He kept stopping to look at me with an expression on his countenance of great affection and said some things that would have been very sweet under other circumstances. As it was, it only made my heart ache to have him do so, though I tried with all my might to feel generous. We went to the kitchen to strain porridge for Hilda [their baby]. After we returned he sat looking at me a while, and then wrote something on a slip of paper he handed to me saying: "I couldn't speak it," and then left the room. I opened the paper and read: "You cannot begin to tell how beautiful you are to me." Oh, dear! Oh, dear! If he'd only done this some other day. Now it seemed to me that his apparent feelings toward me must be all inspired by his real feelings toward Helen. It was terribly humiliating, and yet I hardly could resent it without saying things that would give him the wrong impression of my real purpose of heart about him and her. Still, it was hard, it was hard.

March 22—He has been most charmingly affectionate all day today, and I have been able to put away my pride, and accept and return his love with simple hearted trust. He spoke of spending the afternoon with me, and we were together several hours.

March 24—He said this afternoon that he had never in all his experience with Helen and me been on such good terms with us both as during the past week, and he thought we both were free from all trouble about the relation. I was a little surprised that he thought so, because I knew that this week I had had my first real trouble about him, and I said enough to set him eagerly at work investigating. I was very sorry I said anything about it, for it would have been so much better to have left it as it was; and now I am afraid he will think I am hopelessly jealous of him. I had noticed that Helen felt unusually well during the last week, and I was glad it was so, and glad that I'd been able to conceal my own troubles as well as I had. I ought to have let it go. Why couldn't I?

April 1—A week of uninterrupted bliss. It is really wonderful how much romance Mr. Herrick and I have. Now that I understand him, nothing he does troubles me. I find I did not really believe him before, when he said that no woman drew his heart from me, that Christ had the first place there. I believe him now, and would not have it otherwise. He tried to find me several times yesterday but could not, and in the evening expressed a great deal of yearning of heart toward me. "I have felt more love-sick today than any day since I have known you," said he, "and I wanted to cry when I couldn't find you." He said today that I was the greatest luxury he had had since he came to the Community.

Meanwhile, although my heart is comforted about Edward in Mr. Herrick's love, I still have hopes of Edward, and cannot believe that he is a wicked man. Mr. Towner is now in a great quarrel with Mr. Noyes, acting in more open disobedience to him than anyone, for example, sitting by his wife in meeting. Mr. Towner continues to eat with Paul and to have him sleep in his room, and to pay him a great deal of fatherly affection, and I think Paul might as well have his own father as to be under the present influence. I told Mr. Noyes this morning that I'm distressed to have Paul associated with Mr. Towner and wish to make a final separation between them; he entirely justified me in doing it, but advised me to act without any reference to him.

April 12—Mr. Noyes said, "I want you to make up your mind that you are to be the mother of this Community. I say to you secretly that this is what is before you." I replied that I would never choose this position. "I shall keep after you until you do," he said. "You can direct all our young people."

April 22—Mr. Herrick and I cleaned my room today and had a charming time. In the afternoon we had an exquisite experience that seemed like a baptism of heavenly purity and continence. It put a new quality into our love.

April 26—Mr. Herrick has at last divulged to me the true state of things between him and Helen, and all that seemed so strange and contradictory and inconsistent in his behavior at times is explained. He said several times two or three months ago that he loves us equally, and could not tell which he loved best. I could see how a man might find it difficult to tell between two sisters whom he loved best, especially when he had known and loved one a long time before knowing the other. But I could not understand how it was possible that there should be the same kind of glow, magnetism, and ardent attraction between him and her that there has been between him and me. My instincts told me it was not so, and yet his words often persuaded me that it must be so. Thus the suffering I have had has been caused by the inability to prove the truth or falseness of my instincts, which, in such matters, I had supposed almost infallible. I was sometimes perfectly bewildered, dazed; I was at sea with no compass. All ordinary calculations failed. My reason is now satisfied. I respect his faithfulness to Helen, and his determination that I should get no advantage over her while I might not make a good use of it. He does not now say that he loves me better, nor do I wish it; but he shows me very frankly that he feels that inspiration has led him in loving me, and that I understand him and am nearer his heart than any other woman. I would be afraid of this did I not know that he loves Mr. Noyes far more than me, and that he would instantly leave me at a word from him.

May 6—I could write volumes about our romance; but I shall only tell occasional incidents. I gave him the first tea-violets that bloomed, and he wrote me a pretty verse in reply. Today I gave him this:

> You are so near—so near and dear—
> My life in yours so deeply dwells,
> That love has banished every fear,
> And peace I feel that no tongue tells.

He answered:

> My life in Him I deeply hide
> Who taught us both to safely love.
> In Him in peace we now abide,
> And rapture thrills us from above.

May 12—Great and ever-expanding plans about what we are going to do to entertain visitors this summer. A free concert! Some of the musicians want me to get back to playing as soon as possible after confinement. Frank said he was almost sorry I was going to have a baby soon.

May 22—Moved into the 'lying-in' room today and slept little overnight. The room is so haunted with memories of Edward that I could not get my mind off him. It seems to me that I *must* say a few things to him before my confinement.

June 2—We were advised not to cause remark by the appearance of the marriage spirit. We do love each other wonderfully.

June 8—At 3 o'clock in the morning I awoke with a pain. I went about my work as usual after breakfast, saying nothing, though the pains grew more frequent. At 10 o'clock I attended a committee and took notes for an hour. At 1 o'clock I told my nurses Belle Woolworth and Mary Van Velzer of my probable condition, and also Mrs. Conant who had promised to be with me. Near 3 o'clock Dr. Cragin was called in and at 7 minutes past 3, a little girl with dark hair made her appearance; Hilda weighed seven pounds, nine ounces. I immediately sent word to Mr. Herrick, who did not know.

June 10—"What a year of romance this has been. I never had such a romance in my life and never have had such uninterrupted happiness in loving anyone," said Jamie this evening. My answer was heartfelt: Neither have I—the story of our romance ought to be written, and it would fill a volume.

June 11—I practice from 11 o'clock till 1:00 at the Cottage. Jamie comes down frequently and plays with me, or listens to me and criticizes my playing. Today I asked him to criticize The Two Angels, but when I turned around he was weeping and said that I did it beautifully. It is a continual wonder to me that we two, who thought ourselves so incompatible, should find ourselves really better adapted to each other than we ever were before to anyone. It is true. We are constantly remarking upon the marvelous way in which we fit each other. "Nobody *ever* drew me out as much as you have," he said. He took Helen and me for a boat ride with the babies this evening, and we had a pleasant time. I have times of sitting and loving him all by myself, and love him so that my heart burns within. Sometimes I run down to the office just to see him and touch him a moment, and we glow to each other in the perfect radiance of love. This afternoon his love seemed so beautiful to me that I felt it was selfish for me to have so much of it, and I wanted others to know what a lover he is.

James Herrick received a theology degree from the University of Virginia in 1860 and was an Episcopal minister in New York City. He was a father figure for Community boys, introducing them to lacrosse and fishing. He married Tirzah Miller in 1879 and the couple joined John Humphrey Noyes in Niagara Falls after the breakup. He was Noyes's personal secretary and later, Secretary-Treasurer of Oneida Community, Limited.

June 13—Jamie and I were together last night, and were both most unexpectedly overcome. He was somewhat anxious as to consequences, and ran for a syringe. We would both consider it a terrible calamity to have an accident of that kind happen, and cannot believe that God will let it. We talked about it some today, and agreed that we will each speak at such times, so that the other can know just what is liable to take place. I am afraid I have more of his society than I deserve. He is so sweet and dear to me that I long to have him appreciated by others. My love for him has grown constantly during the past two months. "What a continual crescendo our love has been all this year!" he said.

June 16—Jamie went to New York suddenly last evening on business about his youngest sister, Louise. An unpleasant occurrence took place between us while packing his satchel that made us both miserable all the remainder of his stay. He went away with a sad face, and I lay awake a great deal with heartache. It was all a misunderstanding and there was no real cause for either of us to be offended at the other. I have felt dreadfully all day until late in the afternoon, when I got a view of my own pride; this helped to remove all bitterness from my heart toward him, and then the sun began to shine. O my darling! How terrible if anything should happen to you when we parted thus! Four days later, home again. So glad to see him! There is perfect harmony between Jamie and me.

The Loves of Tirzah Crawford Miller, A Personal Journal; Excerpts, 1873–1879

Noyes Leaves the Community

June 23, 1879—Myron Kinsley has lately come from Wallingford for a visit and told me that the situation here makes him feel very anxious. Outside parties want to arrest JHN and the bitter feeling of some in the Community toward him made him consider it best to go away. Mr. Noyes left here with Myron in the evening for parts unknown, later revealed as Niagara Falls. It has been a rather quiet day as far as outward manifestations go, but you could feel great surges of feeling rushing in the undercurrents. The majority of us who are loyal have consulted together a great deal. There is perfect harmony between Jamie and me. Mr. Noyes wrote yesterday the codicil to his will.

June 28—Jamie's and my life has been during the last four days a poem of exquisite beauty. He has said so many sweet things to me that I cannot remember them all. "How wonderful, how strange it is!" he has often said, "this magnetism between us. No matter what happens, still it flows on, and is renewed every morning." We strolled about in the garden in the evening, and he looked down at me so tenderly, and said, "Dear, dearest!—how strange it is. I shall certainly fall in love with you (playfully). You quicken my circulation and send thrills right through me." This afternoon I went to the office a moment, and got caught there in the rain. I had my white dress on, which Jamie likes very much (he calls me his little bride in it), so I waited for the rain to stop. Jamie and Helen were working at their desks, and he kept glancing at me when he could do so without observation. After a while he went to the house and brought me my black dress, and had me change in the inner office. He took Helen to the house with an umbrella and came back for me. There was a wonderful glow and ache between us. We seemed all aflame. We hurried to the house and then he wanted me to come to his room. Ecstasy, but alas! We went just too far. He says he has wanted just such a friend as I am ever since he came to the Community, and that I understand him better than any woman—even his wife.

June 29—Myron returned this morning with good news of Mr. Noyes's health and spirits, though he does not tell us where he is. Mr. Hamilton called a meeting of a number of us and we continued in session for two hours. Afterward a very pleasant visit with Myron. Jamie and I keep in constant rapport, and it does seem as though nothing in the world could come between us.

July 4—A wonderful day of magnetism with my beloved. In the morning, the afternoon, and at night. We seem to be absolutely one. "I don't believe there is another couple in the house who enjoy such rapture as we," he said. Yesterday he read a charming story to Helen and me, *Signor Monaldini's Choice*, and he told me that in the most powerful chapter, Camilla, the heroine, reminded him continually of me.

July 16—Jamie and I took Hilda in the little carriage to the Island. All the way along we recalled the many charming episodes we have had together since her birth. She has been a blessing to us every day. If it had not been for her we would never have known each other, and we would have both missed a great happiness. We referred to a charming walk we took last winter, early in January. We tramped a long distance across the meadows through knee-deep snow; but were so absorbed in each other that we never thought of fatigue. "That walk," he said, "was just as full of magnetism as it could be."

We are in exquisite rapport, even reaching new heights this afternoon. I must mention a delightful stroll we took together to the mill this morning, I with my hands clasped round his arm and both of us in a glow of magnetism. "Is this special love?" he asked. I answered that it is special, yes, but not exclusive; there's a difference. And that is the fact about it. It is a romance that we both recognize as a gift from God, and being such, is full of a divine beauty the aroma of which I would fain imprison here, that in years to come we may again inhale its sweet fragrances. I know that Jamie is a universal lover. He first loves God, then Mr. Noyes, then all women who would make themselves brides of heaven; and I have no thought of appropriating to myself either his affection or the beautiful words that express it. Returning from the mill we stopped in the flower garden, where I picked a lovely Jessamine, and as we parted, I gave it to him; "That is to remind you that you are in love or that I am," I said. "Yes," he answered, "I am in love."

July 18—We had a long, strange talk in the cooling-room of the Turkish Bath this morning. He seemed to wish to reassure me of his love, again and again promising never to do anything knowingly that would give me pain. But you must not refrain from doing what you would like to do, I assured him, just to save me from suffering. "There is nothing I could have in the world that would be good enough to compensate me for hurting you," he answered earnestly. "I cannot put a knife into your heart." There were many other things he said — very, very sweet.

July 19—E.H.H. invited me last evening. When Olive first asked me [invitations were sent by a third person], I thought I could not possibly do it, and excused myself. When I told Jamie afterward, he did not like it and thought it would have been better if I had. I went into the library and while writing there, tried to feel good about recalling the answer I'd sent to E.H.H. After a while he stopped at the door and bade me goodnight with a very pleasant smile. This was so different from the way he used to take such refusals that I immediately felt as though I could go. I slipped my hand through his arm, and told him that I would see him shortly. He was much surprised and pleased, and I never knew him to be more enthusiastic or affectionate than during this visit. I ran upstairs afterward to tell Jamie that I repented, and he was happy.

July 19—I have been preparing to go to Joppa this afternoon. Mr. Kinsley came in and said he had not been to see me for some time because he was afraid I might think he claimed too much attention. I said I had not thought so. He asked if he might kiss me. Of course he might, I answered, and put my arms around him and returned his embrace. "Now I'm going to feel free to love you all I've a mind to. Mayn't I?" Yes, I answered, I hope you will—I appreciate your love very much. "I'm an old man," he said, "and didn't know but I might obtrude; but, *once a man and twice a child*, so I can be a child again, and love." He asked me to kiss him again and said, "There! I can let you go now." I told Jamie and he was greatly pleased.

Aug. 1—A marvelous time of magnetism these last three days. This evening after reading until 10:30 we lay a while in each other's arms, when he said: "Isn't this delicious? How nice it would be for you to sleep here!" So I went down and got my nightdress. Then again we lay clasped in each other's arms while waves of heavenly ecstasy rolled over us. Wonderful! *Wonderful!* But when we tried to intensify our happiness by drawing nearer together, the exaltation passed away. We fell asleep afterward, however, and once when I rose on my elbow an instant he sprang up and caught me in his arms, calling me by the most endearing names, and repeating again and again that he loved me, *loved* me.

Aug. 10—Aunt Harriet and Mr. Hamilton both talked to Jamie some about having the marriage spirit toward me. He acknowledged that he loved me very much, but explained to them some of Mr. Noyes's directions to me, which seemed to justify more or less specialty between us. They were both very good-natured, and only wanted to talk with us as friends without offering any criticism.

Aug. 20—A pleasant ride to the Cascades with Alfred, Helen, Mr. Bradley, and Paul; I ought to mention here the constant and growing friendship there has been between Alfred and me for more than a year. He is very confidential with me—more so than any man ever was who was not a lover—and I have enjoyed very much my companionship with him.

Aug. 24—Found a sealed envelope in my P.O. Box; within was a square piece of white birch bark freshly cut from the tree on which were cut initials almost obliterated by time. Seven years ago Homer and I walked to a beautiful wood near Sconondoah and he cut our monogram on a tree under which we romanced. I guessed this was that cutting. The next day I met Homer and he gave me a conscious smile. I asked him if he went riding yesterday, and laughing, he said "Yes . . . I thought perhaps you'd like to see it." We agreed to walk there next month on the anniversary of that day, September 23rd.

Aug. 24: There is continual romance between Jamie and me, and I grow larger-hearted about him all the while. I feel as though I perfectly understand him now, and trust him implicitly.

Aug. 26—A proposition that was like a bombshell was read in meeting from Mr. Noyes. It was that we give up complex marriage and live as celibates but with freedom to marry for the same reasons given by Paul in the 7th of 1st Corinthians. It was decided that this proposal should take effect Thursday morning at ten o'clock. I slept with Jamie the next night; a pleasant visit with E.H.H. at 2 o'clock. He had such a beautiful spirit that I told Jamie afterward that I would rather have had this meeting with him (E.H.H.) than to have had a romantic reunion with Homer, pleasant as that would be. I of course could not help thinking about Homer a little, now that complex marriage is ended perhaps forever, and I thought more of it just now because, as things have progressed lately between us, it was not unlikely that we might sometime—sometime—come together again. Well, we met in a friendly way several times in the afternoon and evening, chatting confidentially about his plans with others. Just before meeting I ran downstairs to get a lemon for Jamie, and started in search of the steward. Passing by the outside bathroom I caught a glimpse of Homer and so asked him. He'd not finished dressing but said he would go in a minute. I can hardly tell how it happened, but there seemed to be a subtle fire between us and before we knew it he hurried me into the inside bathroom where we——.

Sept. 1—There has been considerable agitation about the subject of marriage during the past week. Jamie said to me this afternoon with tears in his eyes and voice: "O darling! Don't go and leave me, and marry Edward Inslee. If you want to break my heart right in two, you will do that. It will tear a great piece of me away; as much as a hundred pounds of me will go with you. I would be willing to share you with him, if he should come back, and I would let you make the division between us; but I *can't* have you go." I begged him not to talk so.

Sept. 20—The excitement about marriage has somewhat subsided. There seemed to be an anxiety and impatience on the part of many to get their relations of that kind settled. Although there has been great magnetism and attraction between Jamie and me, we would not think of marrying without Mr. Noyes's approval and desire to have us; yet it was pleasant to have him say the other day: "If I only thought of what I would *like* to do, I would marry you tomorrow. I would deliciously like to marry you." He said also that he did not think there was another couple better, and few as well adapted to derive happiness from the relation as we are. Frank and I have been practicing our music with all youthful ardor for two months and are making good progress. We play something every Sunday evening after meeting. Last Sunday was the fifth week since we began. I was made melancholy by hearing that Edward is likely to marry. They say he is courting a young lady. I would feel comparatively well now about his marrying (considering the situation) if I could have one talk with him.

Sept. 30—I think sometimes that we are not first-class celibates [practicing male continence]. We don't transgress, but we get much wrought up and go very near the edge of the abyss.

Oct. 13—Jamie left for Wallingford Community and New York.

Oct. 16—Letters from Wallingford tell that Edward had been there on a visit of several hours this week, by George Miller's invitation. The first man he met was Mr. Herrick; the family was starting off on a nutting expedition and invited him to go. On the crowded wagon, Edward held Mr. Herrick on his lap. What a situation for a novelist to work up! Everybody said he was soft-hearted and wanted to come back to the Community.

Oct. 18—Jamie returned and I ran upstairs and hid behind the door; when he came in, we met in the most affectionate manner. He embraced me rapturously, calling me his precious darling, and said I was a hundred times the nicest thing he had seen all the while he was gone. We had a charming evening with the baby, and he said

The Loves of Tirzah Crawford Miller, a Personal Journal; Excerpts, 1873–1879

he wanted very much to marry me. "Would you like to be Mrs. Herrick?" he asked. I told him I would consider it a great honor to be his wife. Homer also went to New York and Wallingford and returned last evening and came upstairs; we talked for an hour very affectionately.

Oct. 24—We had quite a solemn talk and decided that we would withdraw a little from each other, that we might see more clearly what God wishes us to do about marrying. We have been so swept forward by the power of the attraction between us that we've hardly known what to do. We felt pretty sober this morning, and I did not go to the office. I was writing in my room 10 o'clock when in came Jamie holding out a letter that he received JHN. My heart almost stood still when I read these words: "No shade of doubt as to your faith and faithfulness to Christ and to me has place in my thoughts of you. As to your intimacy with Tirzah, I am not afraid of its running into the marriage spirit. You and she both are called to a higher marriage, and he that called you will take care of you. I would not care if you were ceremonially yoked." We were very joyful—such a quick and unexpected answer to our quandary! Jamie wrote to Mr. Noyes about two weeks ago (without telling me) that he was very intimate with Tirzah—perhaps more than he would like, and asked him to advise him, expecting he would perhaps tell him to go to Wallingford; instead, he made him free to marry! Although we had such an enthusiastic talk over the matter, I didn't suppose we should do anything about it for a long time.

Oct. 25—Jamie and I were standing by the stairs at 4:30 this afternoon near the Council door. "Let's put in our [marriage] application!" We talked and acted in a whirlwind of excitement. He was for putting the matter right through; I said at first it seemed as though I could not do anything until I had either seen Edward or written to him. We both signed the paper. He said, "I'll run down and put in this application, and then we can talk." I assented, scarcely thinking of the consequences. He came back and said he marched in before them all and handed it to the Secretary. He says he sympathizes with my writing to Edward, and seeing him, too, after we are married. Our application made a great sensation in the Council, and a greater one still in the family evening meeting where it was read. Nobody dreamed of such a thing! Those like Frank, who knew the most about it, had no idea we would act so precipitously. The announcement was like a bombshell in their midst—some said they were thunder-struck. People generally have supposed that Jamie would be one of the last to marry. I cannot help having a good deal of feeling and thought about this move, but as long as it is hopeless that Mr. Noyes will ever sympathize with my marrying Edward, I believe that I shall be a happier woman to have the heart-bleeding I've had in that direction forever stopped. Jamie and I are wonderfully mated. He says he believes I am the best mate for him in the whole world. I cannot tell what wrenchings my heart would be subjected to if I saw Edward; but as things are now, I feel that I would do more cruel wrong to leave Jamie for Edward than to marry him and cut myself off from Edward. It would be perhaps hard to choose between these two men if they both had Mr. Noyes's approval, and both wished to marry me. I would probably take the one who, I thought, wanted me the most. But there are many reasons why, as things are, I should choose to be Jamie's wife. My conscience toward Mr. Noyes and my faithfulness to community are in that direction; and really, I have had so much freedom with Jamie that he has gotten deeper into my life than Edward did—and yet, and yet—I had hoped, hoped, that sometime I might once more be folded in those strong, tender arms I remember so well. If Edward loves me any, he must wish that he had stayed by the Community.

Oct. 27—The opposition has begun. Frank advised Mr. Herrick to fortify himself by getting a copy of his divorce decree, because Mr. Towner, Mr. Burnham, William Woolworth, and others are bound to obstruct, casting doubt on the validity of his divorce. Jamie wrote to Baltimore this morning for a copy of the decree *at once*, enclosing $5.00.

Oct. 28—Helen returned from Wallingford this evening and feels good about this proposition. She is comforted in Homer's love for her, which is immense. It seems a little strange to me sometimes, to have him speak to me about her the way I knew of his speaking about me to others. We three had a very pretty meeting in her room this evening, he putting his arms around both of us. In the Council yesterday, William Hinds proposed putting a committee of lawyers over Mr. Herrick to see that his divorce was legitimate. Frank stood up for Jamie, and said he did not think such a course would be delicate or brotherly toward Mr. Herrick. I never saw Jamie more roused than he was today. Once he stepped over to my desk and said very earnestly: "You won't go and marry Edward till you know whether I can marry or not, will you? Promise me, promise me." He said if they snatched me away from him he would growl as he never growled before—he felt like a lion.

Oct. 29—Mr. Inslee went to Frank to entreat that Edward's feelings be considered tenderly in regard to my marriage, and Frank brought up the matter in the Council today. They appointed Frank and Helen to confer with Mr. Herrick, Mr. Inslee, and me about it, with power to do what we agreed on. I assured Mr. Inslee that I had not thought of being married without first writing to Edward.

Oct. 30—My thoughts were on Edward a great deal today and I felt very heavy-hearted. Mr. Herrick tried to find out what the matter was, and about 6 o'clock in the evening I tried to tell him the trouble, attributing it to my feelings about Edward. There, I said—I've told you like a dutiful wife!

"And like a dutiful husband," he replied, "I will tell you that Edward Inslee has been over at the Willow Place factory all afternoon." I immediately understood my day's emotions. Mr. Herrick told me that Edward came to the shop at about 2:00 and sent word over to know if he could come here. Mr. Hamilton advised Mr. Inslee to go back to New York without coming here. Edward was docile, and allowed Charles Marks to take him to Oneida at 6 o'clock. I felt quite hurt and somewhat indignant at his being sent away without a word being said to me, and I told Mr. Herrick and Frank. I said that I thought I ought to have seen him, and I still thought I ought to do so before I married. They sympathized, and Aunt Harriet said she thought I ought to see him by all means.

Oct. 31—Between 9 and 10, word came from Theodore at Willow Place that Edward remained at Oneida overnight, feeling pretty sore about being sent away. He still asked permission to come, but promised to go if there were serious objections. Theodore thought that Mr. Herrick and I ought to take the responsibility of dealing with him. I said I wished him to come. Everybody else consulted said that was the only humane course. Mr. Hamilton agreed, and Frank went for him. He arrived a little after noon and I met him alone in my room with Paul. I found him the same tender and true love he always was, and as faithful to me in thought and act as ever man was to woman. He said he came by one of those sudden impressions that he used to have that I wanted to see him. We talked over the past and the present in a free and loving manner. Although the thought of my marrying another is distressing to him, he behaves in a noble and manly spirit about it. He says it has been his one object in life to be re-united to me, and that now that object is gone, he cannot tell what he shall do. I played music with him awhile at the cottage in the afternoon, he having brought his beautiful cornet. He and Paul seemed to take to each other as though they had always been together.

Nov. 1—I talked with Edward a great deal yesterday and today. He asked me if I married only from duty, and I told him, No, that I loved Mr. Herrick, that he had won my heart by his kindness and goodness. "Then you are choosing between us two men, and if you love him more than you do me, I have no right to say anything." I told him that I still loved him as I always had, but that I loved Mr. Herrick too, and if they both wished to marry me and had equally Mr. Noyes's approval, it would be very hard for me to choose between them, and that I would probably take the one whom I thought wanted me the most. He knew me well enough to believe that I could never be happy to marry with Mr. Noyes's disapproval, and I had little hope that he would ever feel that same sympathy with my marrying Edward that he would with my marrying Mr. Herrick. I asked him if it would not be possible to marry someone else in the Community, and so live here with me, and take care of the boy. He answered that his love for others here was so weak compared with his love for me, that he hardly believed it possible for him to do so. Then I said if he married outside, I hoped he would stipulate for freedom to come and see his son. He said he thought he would never marry. It seemed to him now that he could never love anyone as he had me. "Tirzah, you have been my guiding star, and the thought of you has kept me from falling in places of temptation. I have done nothing during these three years that I would not have been willing that you should see." I could fill a volume with what he said, but perhaps it would not be profitable. He left at half past 12, Paul going to Oneida with him. In the last words we had together he said, "I give you up. It is a bitter trial, but if this is the way it must be, I am resigned." I tried to be faithful to Mr. Noyes and Mr. Herrick in my dealings with him, and above all to my inner sense of what God wants me to do. I believe God has helped me; for I was wonderfully sustained while he was here, having no heartache or temptation, but when he was gone, the tears would come. The copy of Mr. Herrick's decree of divorce came and the Council met in the afternoon. Frank reported to us a stormy time, compromising the disagreement by allowing Mr. Towner to go to Syracuse and investigate the matter. Mr. Herrick never expressed so much love for me as he did this evening. He said he would remember this day as long as he lived. It was marvelous that I could remain faithful to him when under the magnetic influence of that handsome, attractive Edward, and yet he trusted me perfectly.

Nov. 2—Jamie said that if things had turned the other way it would have ruined all his prospects for future happiness. "It would have been by far the greatest sorrow of my life if Edward had taken your heart away from me." Oh, no, not as bad as that! I said.

Nov. 3—Mr. Towner went to Syracuse and returned with a written opinion that there was no legal obstruction to Mr. Herrick's marrying, none whatever.

Nov. 5—Jamie and I started this morning at 7:30 for Wallingford; we were heartily welcomed. My brother George and his wife Annie and many good friends are here and make us thoroughly at home. Mr. Herrick went to town and bought a license, and engaged Mr. Ira Martin, Justice of the Peace, to join us in wedlock at four o'clock. He arrived promptly and performed the ceremony, George and Annie standing up with us. The ceremony was quite a solemn one to me, and it will take me a long time to realize that I am Mrs. Herrick. They treated us to an elegant wedding supper.

Dec. 14—We've been having an almost uninterrupted honeymoon for about a month. He told me he was so glad, so *glad* he married me, and that he would rather have me than anyone in the whole world. No lover ever expressed more affection for me than my beloved husband does.

After Noyes's death, the couple returned to Kenwood where he helped form the Loomis School for the second generation's continuing education. Their daughter, Hilda, became a medical doctor and married John Humphrey Noyes II; they had six children. Here, Grandpa Herrick plays with his grandson David Noyes.

Endnotes

1. Biblical criticism, defined: "Scientific investigation of the origin, text, composition, character, and history of literary documents, especially the Bible."
2. Brother Lawrence, *Practice of the Presence of God*, 38.
3. Lawrence, 36.
4. Lawrence, 36.
5. James, *Varieties of Religious Experience,* 205.
6. James, *Varieties*, 206.
7. Wesley, Christian Perfection, 19, 29, 42–43..
8. Wesley, *Christian Perfection*, 5–6; 108–109.
9. Noyes, *Religious Experience of J.H. Noyes*. 114.
10. James, *Varieties*, 209-10.
11. Cross, *Burned-Over District*, 158.
12. James, *Varieties*, 378.
13. Isherwood, Christopher, Vendanta for Modern Man, 384.
14. Noyes, *Religious Experience*, 142–143.
15. James, *Varieties*, 214.
16. James, *Varieties*, 224.
17. Goldsmith, *Art of Meditation*, 6–7.
18. Rohr, quoting Meister Eckhart, August 15, 2019 "Daily Meditation."
19. Lawrence, *Presence of God*, 35, 40, 46, 49.
20. Vedanta for Modern Man, "Three Key Answers to Three Key Questions," 297-298..
21. Noyes, Berean, 51.
22. Rohr, Center for Action & Contemplation, *Things Hidden*, 81; *Behold the Spirit*, xix; 5–6.
23. James, *Varieties*, 250.
24. Bible Argument, *Report of the Oneida Association 1849*, 18–42.
25. Parker, *Yankee Saint*, 181.
26. Isherwood, *Vedanta for Modern Man*, 301–302.
27. New York *Medical Gazette*, October 1870: review of "Scientific Propagation," published in *Modern Thinker*, 1870 .
28. Noyes, *Putney Community*, 55.
29. Noyes, *Putney Community*, 69–72.
30. Cross, *Burned-Over District*, 248.
31. Noyes, *Putney Community*, 205–206.
32. Paul's injunction regarding veiling of women while men appear bareheaded was opposed to Jewish custom where men wore the head covered by the tallith (prayer shawl), while women were covered by long hair (1 Cor 11:5,15). Paul recommended conformity to Greek standards.

ENDNOTES

33. Miller, *After the Strike of a Sex*, 13–14, 34–35, 11, 55, 26–27.
34. Shrady, Schmidt, Angelus Silesius, 42.
35. May 5, 1873: Marriage is formed by contract and the parties henceforward are governed by the law of husband and wife. Obligations of law are imposed upon the parties. Only one thing does the law allow the parties to regulate by contract: rights of property between themselves. A woman may be free from the control of her husband and may act after marriage as an unmarried woman, but in the absence of any ante-nuptial agreement in regard to property, the law determines the rights of the parties. This legal status works changes that consist almost wholly in deprivations of legal capacity that woman suffers when she enters into this status. Marriage confers nothing upon woman except to be provided the necessaries of life—food, clothing, shelter, and the burden of lawful (legitimate) child-bearing—while it takes from her many things that she before possessed in common with all other human beings. The only real difference between the past and present legal status of married women is the difference in the kind and amount of deprivation that woman undergoes at the hands of the law when she enters this status.—T.
36. Shrady, Silesius, 44.
37. Worden, Harriet M., *Old Mansion House Memories*, 35.
38. Shrady, Silesius, 65.
39. 1st Corinthians 5:6–8.
40. From the New York Medical Gazette, reported in the October 1870 Oneida Circular. Its editor called Theodore Noyes's professional examination of the Oneida Community's physical and mental health a model of "careful observation, entire honesty, and impartiality."
41. Shrady, Silesius, 43.
42. Special Correspondent, *Elmira Advertiser*, "Oneida Community: An Inside View of the Workings of this Curious People—their Religious Belief and their Moral and Everyday Life." From the November 1872 *Circular*.
43. Bhagavad-Gita, Chapters 2:47 and 3:19.
44. Shrady, Silesius, 52.
45. Nordhoff, Charles, *Communistic Communities of the United States*, p. 413.
46. Special Correspondent, *Elmira Advertiser*, 11/1872 *Circular*.
47. The Greek word "sarx," translated as "flesh" in Paul's epistles, most often denotes the nature of man apart from divine influence, referring not to the body only, but to the psyche and mind.
48. Croly, *A Lady's Impression of the Oneida Community* from the New York *World*.
49. Stanton, Elizabeth Cady, *Eighty Years and More*, 201.
50. Croly, *Woman's True Freedom*, New York Sorosis, a woman's association.
51. To feel satiated requires twenty minutes. If eating hurriedly, more food is ingested and over-fullness, possible indigestion, and overweight result. Conscious eating reveals enhanced enjoyment of food and maintenance of healthy weight.
52. Special Correspondent, *Elmira Advertiser*, 11/1872 *Circular*.
53. Malaria never triggers lifetime immunity. People who survive repeated bouts get less sick each time, but that immunity disappears if they move out of the malarial region and back again, which Community members did from Wallingford to Oneida, repeatedly. From *New York Times*, Sept. 11, 2018, D3: "Money Needed to Develop Vaccines."

54. The average size of modern hunter-gatherer societies is 148.4 people (Dunbar, 1993). Malcolm Gladwell, *The Tipping Point*, cites Gore-Tex brand leadership's discovery that if more than 150 employees worked in one building, social problems may occur; buildings were limited to 150 employees, and then another was built. Anthropologists H. Russell Bernard and Peter Killworth estimated that a social network can maintain itself up to 290 people, based on repeated field studies using different methods in various populations. Neolithic villages in Mesopotamia had 150–200 people (Oates, 1977). The Oneida Community had 250 members living at Oneida and 60 living at the Wallingford Community in Connecticut; forty of them moved to Oneida in May and June 1877. Fifty-eight children were born in the Stirpiculture period from 1870–1879. The community broke up in 1880, due chiefly to Noyes's relinquishment of its presidency without a comparable successor, the death of key leaders, and the growing intransigence of the second generation. External and internal pressures, however, had previously been overcome. Another factor in the breakup may have been its growing size.
55. *Outline of Bible Theology*, Leaflet 30A, from letter by Nellie Bly to the New York *World*, June 2, 1889.
56. Noyes, P. B., *My Father's House*, 274.
57. Noyes, *My Father's House*, 279.
58. Noyes, *My Father's House*, 271.
59. Noyes, *My Father's House*, 297.
60. Parker, *Yankee Saint*, 264.
61. Noyes, *A Goodly Heritage*, 70–71.
62. Noyes, *Goodly Heritage*, 163.
63. Noyes, *Goodly Heritage*, 257.
64. Edmonds, Walter D., *First Hundred Years*, 35.
65. Edmonds, *First Hundred Years*, 52.
66. Noyes, G. W. *Oneida Community: Its Relation to Orthodoxy*, Appendix II, Banquet Speeches of the Oneida Community, Limited, in January, 1912, 17–19.
67. Noyes, *Oneida Community: Relation to Orthodoxy*, 16–17.
68. Noyes, *Relation to Orthodoxy*, 25–26.
69. Noyes, *Relation to Orthodoxy*, 20–24.
70. Crowell-Collier, *American Magazine*. Publication ceased in 1956.

Epilogue

A unique human experiment from which we have much to learn

Founder John Humphrey Noyes's spiritual quest at Andover and Yale Theological Seminaries culminated in a *metanoia* of the heart, an experience of the divine that revealed the purpose of human life—to love God and man as oneself and to hear the spirit within. He taught that within each person is a vital connection to the divine. In knowing our true nature, the loving heart manifests the fruit of the spirit enumerated in Galatians 5:22–23. Noyes founded free publications to convey his experience and what he learned; people who read his writings gravitated to Putney, Vermont, to study the Bible with him. They built a chapel, ran a store and farm, raised children, and loved each other. After the first four years, sharing all money and worldly goods, they lived as one big family; three years after that, the evolution to complex marriage seemed completely natural, though they discussed this for months. When a small faction in Putney opposed this community, they were invited to join a developing New York State Perfectionist community whose members supported Noyes. This group was unaware of Complex Marriage at Putney, but they so thoroughly believed in Noyes's convictions that when they met him, they listened and discerned his true spirit, and accepted his community. They built a great mansion that ultimately accommodated three hundred people who sought God, transcended selfishness, shared all things, and were married to each other with full commitment to each others' well-being and spiritual growth.

"I live, yet not I," Paul said, "but Christ *in* me." The Community's fundamental teaching was to identify with this living reality within all; by receiving wisdom directly from this source, selfishness is purged from the soul. Looking deeply into Noyes's communities, we indeed see human beings at a high state of spiritual development. They placed 1st Corinthians 13 verses throughout their spaces, striving to live these attributes in their thoughts, speech, and actions. They lived productively, creatively, and peacefully together for thirty-two years through transparency and honesty in all aspects of life. "To be and not to seem" was a Community motto. We begin to comprehend what Noyes taught, that in every person is infinite depth and mystery.

A Community parable conveys Noyes's fundamental conviction that lopping off the "branches of sin" was futile; its roots in the heart must be excavated. Community farmers struggled with quack grass, which has a system of underground rhizomes that grow quickly and spread out widely from the mother plant; if the entire root system of this plant is not completely removed, it grows back. External law presupposes internal depravity; the roots of depravity can and must be rooted out. Having experienced the love of God, which uproots the power of sin in the human heart, Noyes knew that the pure heart and mind is the *normal* state of humanity and he taught that the world's intractable problems can only be vanquished by learning to receive God. The Community's mission was the spiritual transformation of the human race. "With the loving heart, the world might be a very comfortable Paradise, though its external institutions should remain unchanged," Noyes said. "Without it, the most perfect organization can only be a well-disciplined Bedlam." Purity of heart is our true nature as we learn to discern the divine within, he always taught; character can be radically changed. How to achieve unconditional love was his life work. Jesus clarified human capacity in Matthew 5:44–48 in his clear statement that we are capable of loving our enemies. "You, therefore, must be perfect, as your heavenly Father is perfect." Noyes therefore held that "Perfect holiness is the standard of Christianity."

Radical wrong is to be condemned by mature Christians, the *téleioi* as Paul called some in the Primitive Church. Why did he not roundly condemn slavery, the owning of another person, as evil, however common that practice was? So in the unregenerate heart slavery persists;[1] racism thrives covertly or openly. "Slavery is like holding a person under water and saying, why don't you swim?" said Father Theodore Hesburgh. "Education was forbidden to a slave so that he will devote himself to his master." Paul consigned women in church to a subservient role, though many were important thinkers and great helpers in his work. This was surely another cultural assumption of Paul rather than a spiritually discerned universal principle. If women had been able to play a prominent role in the church through the centuries, how would that institution have developed differently? Paul said that some things he expressed were his personal thoughts, "not the Lord's."

Noyes was a disciple of Paul and accepted 1st Cor. 11:3 as truth, thus he held that men were more the recipient of inspiration than women. But after living for thirty-three years with spiritual women in community, Noyes said in 1873: "I believe inspiration comes from a dual God—a Father and Mother." *Let us make man in our image . . . male and female he created them.* "The duality of the Godhead is here stated, an actual specification of the first great feature in the human constitution that makes it an image of God—that feature is its bi-personality," Noyes stated. "We cannot get the highest and best inspiration except as there is appreciation of that dual life in them— except as we are in heart a combination of male and female ourselves. My philosophy about the mingling of the sexes is that inspiration is the foundation of all good active improvement or prosperity in anything and thus woman as an interdependent part of God thrives best in relationship with man. Yet Noyes said repeatedly that woman is made for God and for herself, not for the children she can bear. "A woman should not be dependent on any man because God alone must the focus of our love" if we are to continue spiritual growth, which is blighted if worldly attachments capture us, known as idolatry. Thus he believed that focus on the "woman question" was "misguided zeal for the abolishment of oppression," because there will be no deep and lasting change without heart conversion powered by God.

In practice, the sexes in the Oneida Community were as nearly equal as has ever been achieved. The *Oneida Circular* stated, "Woman has been kept in an inferior sphere by lack of education, in order to devote themselves to obeying and waiting on men." We must not judge of woman's intellectual capacities by her present state; "an enlightened society has enlightened women who contribute in many endeavors," said Noyes. "Our respect for persons is measured by their real character and actions, not at all by their temporary circumstances."[2] He instituted lifelong education for all and promoted woman's full development; he encouraged them to speak up in meetings more, and study the sciences. He even opined in 1873, "Wall Street would have done better if it had encouraged female brokers." Women headed up Community enterprises.

The Community greatly valued the tender heart that accompanies a spiritual discovery of God. "The most radical disease blighting mankind is hardness of heart," Noyes said. "Egotism is not simple love of attention to oneself, it is attention to self to the neglect of due attention to others. Selfishness is the besetting sin of mankind." *Deny your self to follow me*—allow divine pruning for spiritual growth. The meaning of sin is "missing the mark," foreclosing the *life more abundant*. The Community practiced the pruning of selfishness by creating in-depth spiritual profiles of each other carefully developed by all of them, for all of them, described in chapter 7. Mutual criticism became exceedingly popular; a Criticism Club was established!

After having all things in common as in Acts 2:44–45 and Acts 4:32–35, and working, playing, praying, and studying together for seven years, the Putney Community was essentially married—ready to leave the simple form of marriage for the complex form of it, each married to all. Complex Marriage flourished under a disciplined regime and Community life held abundant pleasures, but only for the spirit that enjoyed and sacrificed for the good of all. Like all other Community activities, sexuality was not a private matter, which may seem shocking, but sexual reality behind closed doors is no doubt more so. The Community's bedrock practice of male continence to avoid unplanned pregnancies was discovered by Noyes's studies of chastity and sexuality for two years out of loving consideration for his wife, Harriet, after they lost four children in childbirth. This was a common experience of women then and in many parts of the world today. Noyes discovered enjoyment and spiritual pleasures in all phases of sexual experience for both sexes, while avoiding the male orgasm.

More like the discipline of the Shakers than "free love," Noyes's discovery of contemplative sexuality was more akin to Tantric practice, finding the sacred in making love. The consensus was that Male Continence and Complex Marriage originated in the mind of God, having great beauty and celestial purity. Continence was adhered to faithfully by all Community men for over thirty years, according to public and private records; in the great family of three hundred, only one accidental pregnancy occurred a year. Less than two children were added per year for twenty-one years in this great family of three hundred, until the Stirpiculture period began in 1869, when fifty-eight children were born and survived in the next ten years. Complex Marriage required persons to develop their capacity to love and be loved with a sustained concentration rarely found elsewhere; people remained attentive, engaged, and attractive, as in courtship. "Love must be attracted," Noyes always insisted, "not compelled."

Mature Community women trained young men in Male Continence and the Community's young people were introduced to sexuality by wise and gentle elders at physical maturity, the common age to enter adulthood in that era and in many cultures today; Noyes entered college at age fifteen. Those unreliable in Male Continence were not included in Complex Marriage or were limited to liaisons with post-menopausal women. Until the Community family could economically support more children, pregnancies were limited as practiced by any prudent family. Physician Hilda Herrick Noyes, daughter of Community members James Herrick and Tirzah Miller, received her medical degree at age twenty-three from Syracuse University Medical College after attending Women's Medical College in New York City. She studied Community sexual experience. Not only were women freed from repeated pregnancies, often resulting in injury or early death, but Male Continence was well-liked by women, an act of sociability, and love, with extended coition. "The men prided themselves on giving women an orgasm," Hilda Herrick wrote. Noyes's son Theodore took his medical degree at Yale and studied the effects on men, published in the New York *Medical Gazette*; its editor considered the study a model of "careful observation, entire honesty, and impartiality." A lifelong practitioner of Male Continence, he wrote that it was "not injurious to either sex, while it gives rise to all those emotions that are refining and ennobling to both men and women." A gynecologist who visited Oneida learned from women he interviewed that most men had little difficulty in restraining the "propagative crisis."

Adults regarded the community as one family and all children were loved and nurtured by every adult. Child care during daytime hours after weaning was undertaken by members who had the best talent and the most interest in it. One mother was convinced that "her daughter is happier and has as good, if not better, care than when I had complete charge of her." The weekly *Circular* report noted, "A child that is bored and making himself sick with his innocent restlessness will go into our department and soon become well and happy." Noyes likened the relationship of children to adults as his was to God: we must be humble and obedient. Children met daily as a group with adult caregivers to talk over problems, as adults did in the evening meeting. Children openly described difficulties with each other, without rancor, and were surprisingly humbled when their faults were revealed. The capacities of well-treated and well-taught children and youth are revealed in this book. Youth were instructed to carefully guard themselves from taking into their hearts negative influences, for these may taint feelings and thoughts for years.

A Community teacher encouraged children to learn through plays. She would have liked what Iowa teacher Jane Elliott did the morning after Martin Luther King Jr. was assassinated. Elliot divided her third grade into blue-eyed and brown-eyed groups to provide an unforgettable lesson of empathy, which the PBS program *Frontline* aired on Station WGBH. Everyone pretended that one group was superior; after a single day, students began to internalize the sense of being superior or inferior! The experiment soon ended. Teachers everywhere could devise a similar experiment with age-appropriate classes, perhaps conceived by students themselves, to mitigate racism or any sense of feeling superior to others. Young people are idealistic; once awakened to problems, they make positive contributions to a better future.

True health, as opposed to absence of disease, is enhanced by being part of any sort of community. Social psychologist Jonathan Haidt determined that people reach the highest level of human flourishing when the isolated self becomes part of a larger group. Modern community-like living arrangements are listed in the Directory of Intentional Communities, including ecovillages, cohousing and shared housing communities, spiritual or religious communities, communes, student coops, and communities that provide employment and other supports. In Okinawa, Japan, people form a social network called a *moai*. Parents put children into a moai when they are born with a group of five friends who offer lifetime support for each other. National Geographic fellow Dan Buettner, a researcher of peoples who thrive, works with health officials in the U.S. to create moai groups in cities. In the Peruvian mountains, the community comes together from miles around to work for all, called a *minga*. A village chief announces a *minga* and hundreds of men in the midst of harvest, women with babies, and children gather by morning; they can achieve in hours what takes aid workers days or weeks to accomplish. The Oneida Community's version of this was called a work bee, gathering many hands to get work done.

Finland was named the world's happiest country by the United Nations Sustainable Development Solutions Network in 2018, based on polling in 156 nations. Inexpensive evening classes are offered in centers across Finland, anything that people are interested in, subsidized by both the state and the city. Lifelong education was valued in the Putney and Oneida Communities, with classes in the sciences, languages, mathematics, history, business, literature, art, music, drama, prayer and more. In the twenty-first century, traditional jobs may disappear; many public spaces could

EPILOGUE

be utilized more, and lifelong education could be subsidized. We can learn ways to contribute to others.

Lynne McTaggart gathers trained scientists to measure small brain and bodily changes in individuals when a group focuses together in prayer or on a healing intention for another. Brain regions that strengthen the sense of an isolated self become measurably quieter, allowing a sense of unity with others. One participant describes her intention group as more a unified energy field than individuals. Intending good for another is about giving, said another, and added that he felt better all day when working on others. This defines a "win-win" strategy for healing the world. McTaggart concludes that group intention is the basis for *Do unto others. Love your neighbor as yourself. Help the stranger in need. Love your enemies.*[3]

The Community liberated human creativity and potential because everyone worked in many enterprises and therefore discovered new skills, interests, and capacities. They worked six hours a day, leaving plenty of time for play, study, the arts, meditation, and socializing. They valued all labor as equally honorable, replacing love of money and worldly ambition with sharing the fruits of labor; they passionately believed that all who contribute to success have the right to comfortable, enjoyable living. They abolished deadening monotony at work by rotating all tasks, and enjoyed accomplishing quality work. Noyes pointed the way to a more Christ-like social system, noted his nephew and ardent disciple, George Wallingford Noyes.

The breakup of the Oneida Community began when Noyes announced that he was resigning the presidency in May 1877 to devote himself to editorial labor, although he wasn't able to leave his leadership for two more years. No successor had emerged with all of Noyes's spiritual qualities, which were developed by faithful spiritual meditation from the age of twenty. Over decades he evolved into a great-hearted, charismatic, and practical genius. The breakup into a joint stock corporation had several causes: an increasing desire to marry; a second generation that increasingly resisted community practices; some became more interested in business and science after college, than in religion; a faction desired to take over leadership as Noyes receded and became increasingly deaf. Outside attacks increased and precipitated Noyes's final departure from the Community, though these rare outbursts soon blew over in previous decades, and the latest assault did so also. The early deaths of four original members who especially nurtured the young could have been another factor that slowly weakened the Community.

With his devoted wife Harriet, one surviving sister, Harriet Skinner, and several community members and devoted teens, Noyes lived in Niagara Falls from 1879 to 1886; he died at age seventy-four. "My most vivid reminiscence of Father Noyes is the atmosphere of good feeling that surrounded him," wrote James B. Herrick. "It was a pleasure to sit near him whether he was talking or silent. A river of living water seemed to issue from him. His life was so harmonious that the effect of contact was musical. One forgot one's trouble in his presence. He had the quality of attracting all to him and making them harmonious among themselves."

Appendix

Some Community members cited in *A Taste of Heaven on Earth*

Jane Abbott was born in 1834 in Champion, New York, and entered the Oneida Community with her parents and three brothers when almost age 14. She did not have children but was a beloved assistant in the Children's House, later replacing Chloe Seymour as "mother of the children."

Alice Ackley was born in East Hamilton, New York, in 1847. She worked in the Children's House at Oneida and taught at Wallingford. At age twenty, she studied voice in New York City with Abram and Charles Burt. She had a voice that her daughter, Corinna Noyes, wife of Pierrepont B. Noyes, remembered as "of operatic quality."

George Allen joined the Wallingford Community with his parents, Henry and Emily, and became a machinist at age seventeen. He was instrumental in starting the silk business and was also a teacher, trap-maker, and salesman. Allen's parents gave their Wallingford home to the Community, which became a branch community where members lived periodically and where, on occasion, a person from Oneida Community might be sent to live if a relationship became too possessive or dependent.

Henry Grosvenor Allen was born in Wallingford, Connecticut, in 1833, the eldest child of the founders of the Wallingford Community. He founded the Community's silk manufacturing business, travel bag business, and studied fruit bottling and preservation. He was a business agent, secretary to the Business Board, and then served on the Board of Directors of Oneida Community, Limited.

Daniel Bailey, born in Hardwick, Vermont, in 1840, entered the Community with five siblings and his widowed mother who moved east from Illinois in 1856. He was a paraplegic resulting from an injury by a machine, extracting roots. He was a stenographer and became interested in German Rationalism, which denied divine inspiration of the Bible. A brilliant, strong-minded leader, he influenced several young Community men.

Alfred Barron, born in Westford, Vermont, in 1829, became a teacher in Ohio and later followed his family to the Oneida Community in 1853. He was a teacher and horticulturist, laying out the North and East lawns and refurbishing the Quadrangle. He wrote a book on walking, *Footnotes*, and was known as Community poet naturalist; he edited and wrote for the *Oneida Circular* and *American Socialist*, and edited Noyes's *Home-Talks*. He had a Community child, Maud Barron, with Elizabeth Kellogg in 1865.

Helen Miller (Barron) was the daughter of Charlotte Noyes and John Miller, born in 1847 in Putney, the younger sister of Tirzah. An editor of Community publications and a bookkeeper, she had one Community child with John Humphrey Noyes, Miriam (Earl). She married J. Homer Barron; after they moved to Niagara Falls where she served as office manager for Oneida Community, Limited, they had a daughter, Norma. Pierrepont Noyes was told "she always saw your nobility." He replied, "That's what makes nobility."

John Homer Barron was born in Westford, Vermont, in 1835. He entered the Oneida Community with his parents in 1852. He taught Noyes the art of trap-making and encouraged many others to learn it. He also worked in the silk industry and was a Community storekeeper. He married Tirzah's sister Helen after the breakup.

Maud Barron was the 38th Community child, empathetic from earliest years. She worked as a teacher and later became the head of the Cost Department at Oneida Community, Limited. As head of the Lawn Committee, she was responsible for many of the later Mansion House gardens. She helped found the Oneida Community Historical Committee and was curator of the collection. She traveled widely and loved children.

Edwin Burnham was born in Putney, Vermont, and joined the Community with his family as a child. He worked in Community farming, accounting, printing, and making traveling bags. After the breakup he married Ida Kate Kelly and worked in the printing business in New York City with Theodore Noyes and two other Community men.

Sarah Burnham was born in Jerico, Vermont, in 1822. The Burnham family joined the Community in June, 1849, and Sarah married George Campbell the day she joined the Community at age seventeen. A Community teacher, they had two Community children, Clarence in 1859 and Theodora ("Dora") in 1861. Dora became a missionary and died in China at age forty-three.

Abram Burt, eldest of Jonathan and Lorinda Burt's five children, joined the Community with his family on February 1, 1848, at age fifteen, the first recorded members of the Community. Abram helped construct the early buildings, and after Noyes's death he served as "father" to young Pierrepont Burt Noyes.

Charles Burt was the youngest of Jonathan and Lorinda Burt's five children. Charles studied chemistry at Yale and worked as a carpenter, horticulturist, and salesman. He and Ann Hobart designed the miniature chests used in the Community. He and his brother Abram studied voice in New York City and directed the Community chorus.

Jonathan Burt, born in 1806 in Long Meadow, Massachusetts, moved to Chittenango, New York, where he married Lorinda Lee. In the mid-1840s, he purchased land at Oneida Reserve, the home of the Oneida Tribe of the Iroquois Nation; most had moved to Wisconsin the year before. He operated a sawmill built by the Indians; the couple had five children. He was converted to Perfectionism by Chauncey Dutton and the writings of John Humphrey Noyes, and as a leading New York Perfectionist, invited Noyes to establish the Oneida Community on his land. He died two months after Noyes in 1886.

Candace Bushnell was born in 1817 in Catskill, New York. She became acquainted with Perfectionism during a six-week stay with the Oberlin Perfectionists led by Charles Grandison Finney. She lived in Bath with her brother, a Presbyterian minister, and converted four college girls. She and Emily Otis joined the Community in 1866; once she was criticized "for fanatical proselytizing" by Noyes himself.

Achsah Campbell was born in Templeton, Massachusetts in 1784, daughter of Captain John and Rebecca Richardson. She married Dr. Alexander Campbell, a Vermont physician, and they had three daughters. They were Unitarians, but in 1834 she heard Noyes preach and joined the Putney Community, moving to Oneida in 1849 with daughter Emma and son-in-law, William Woolworth. She was known as a charmer of children. Before her death at age ninety, she wrote a short story of her spiritual life, ending with "If my life be spared a while / Before my last remove / Thy praise shall be my business still / And I'll declare my love."

Charles Cragin graduated from Yale with an Engineering degree, worked in the Community's trap shop, and learned the silk manufacturing business in Connecticut. He persuaded Theodore Noyes to enter the silverware business at Wallingford, which moved to Niagara Falls to take advantage of water power. Oneida Community, Limited, moved that branch of the business near the Mansion House and created an ideal company town, Sherrill, New York.

George Cragin, Sr. was born in 1808 in East Douglas, Maine. He was General Publishing Agent for *The Advocate of Moral Reform* of the Female Moral Reform Society in New York City. In 1830, he worked with evangelist Charles Grandison Finney. Initially a strong opponent of Perfectionism, he was converted by his wife, Mary. The couple joined him at the Putney Community in 1840 and began Complex Marriage with other Community leaders later in the decade. He became an indefatigable fundraiser and advocate for Noyes. They traveled to Oneida in March, 1848, with Harriet Noyes. He worked in most Community businesses and wrote extensively for the *Oneida Circular*.

George E. Cragin received his medical degree at Yale in 1867. He was first a farmer, then a key inventor in the Community trap shop, serving on the Business Board. He played the clarinet, piccolo, violin, and cello, wrote in Community publications, and started the Community's genealogical cards.

Mary Johnson Cragin was born in 1810 in Portland, Maine; the family moved to New York City and she became a talented school teacher. She was the first convert of Charles G. Finney in 1831, becoming an ardent Perfectionist and converting her husband, George, whom she married in 1833. She developed the concept of the children's house at Oneida. She and Eliza Allen died in a freak storm at Rondout-on-Hudson on July 26, 1851, causing the sinking of the *Rebecca Ford*, which transported Community goods.

Robert Sparrow Delatre was born in Ceylon (now Sri Lanka) in 1808 and was an English convert to perfectionism in Canada. There, he cared for the property of Community member Charles Ellis, the latter joining in 1850. Delatre traveled to Europe in 1851 with John Humphrey Noyes and joined the Community in 1856, working as a trap-maker and gardener; he was a musician and artist, and contributed much to the *Oneida Circular*.

Abel Easton was born in England in 1830, practiced law, married, and immigrated to New York City with the family's three children; they joined the Community in 1866. He was the lawyer very upset by his criticism, cited in chapter 7, Mutual Criticism.

Augusta Hamilton was the only child of Erastus and Susan Hamilton, born in Syracuse, New York, in 1845. She had two Community children, one with George Washington Noyes, and the second with Daniel Abbott. She taught at Wallingford and was later a compositor at Oneida. She married Arthur Towner, seceding a day after her marriage; the couple rejoined the Community at the termination of Complex Marriage. They moved to Santa Ana, California, to be near Judge James Towner, a key figure in the Community breakup.

Erastus Hapgood Hamilton was an architect and Presbyterian prior before he received the doctrine of holiness through the writings of Noyes in 1843 after college in Syracuse, New York. He married Susan Williams in 1845, also convinced of the doctrine of holiness. They joined the Oneida Community with their two children in April 1848. Hamilton superintended the building of the first Mansion House, became chief of the industrial department, and managed many

Some Community Members cited in *A Taste of Heaven on Earth*

community activities and committees. He moved to Niagara Falls with Noyes, and later served briefly as President of Oneida Community, Limited.

Eleazer L. Hatch was born in Zolland, Connecticut, in 1810. He married Hannah Burnham in 1837 and was led to self-examination and much trial as an Presbyterian Church elder at Baldwinsville, New York. He joined the Community in 1848 with his wife and four children. His specialty was cabinet-making; he made the Community's first basswood violins and organized Community instrumental music.

Hilda Herrick was the daughter of James Herrick and Tirzah Miller and was the 98th and last child born in the Community on June 8, 1878. She attended Women's Medical College in New York City and Syracuse University Medical College, receiving an M.D. degree at age twenty-three. She married John Humphrey Noyes II and had six children. She became one of the first women doctors in Central New York, specializing in the care of infants and children at the Oneida Hospital. She collected and analyzed statistics on the health and growth of Community children. Along with George Wallingford Noyes's manuscripts, her records are a valuable source for Community genealogy.

James Herrick was born in New York City in 1837, one of ten children. He graduated from Columbia University and received a theology degree from the University of Virginia. An Episcopal minister, he led a prosperous New York City congregation and had a mission church. He married Sophia Bledsoe and had five children, separating from them after joining the Oneida Community in May 1868. He was especially fond of children, introducing them to many activities, and was known as "the mender of broken toys." He married Tirzah Miller after the breakup and they lived with Noyes in Niagara Falls where he was Noyes's personal secretary. They returned to Kenwood after Noyes's death, and he founded the Loomis School in 1887, a strong influence for higher education for the Community's second generation. He was Secretary-Treasurer of Oneida Community, Ltd. Eulogized in 1912, it was said that "selfishness was not of his makeup and all mankind was his family."

Paul Herrick was Edward Inslee's and Tirzah's son, adopted by James Herrick when he married Tirzah. Musical like his parents, Paul was superintendent of the Silk Department and worked in other businesses after the Community breakup. He married Eleanor Nash Kellogg, the 53rd child born in the Community, and they had three children.

William Alfred Hinds was born in 1833 and clerked at John Miller's Vermont store; with John and Charlotte Miller and their three children, he joined the Putney and Oneida Communities. Hinds had unusual mathematical ability, playing multiple chess; he memorized Noyes's *Salvation from Sin*. He was sent to Yale at age 34 and received his degree in three years. He went to Niagara Falls at the breakup and wrote *American Communities*. He was president of Oneida Community, Limited, and later was president of the Kenwood Benevolent Society; he contributed to the revitalization of neighborhoods surrounding the Mansion House.

Henry Hunter joined the Community at age fifteen with his father, William, and other members of the Berlin Heights commune who joined in 1874 as a group, including Universalist minister and lawyer James Towner, who tried to wrest control of the Community from Noyes in the late 1870s, precipitating its break-up. Henry was musical, playing the violin in a Community string quartet. One of Tirzah Miller's lovers, he was 16 years younger.

Edward Inslee married after leaving the Community because of possessive feelings toward Tirzah Miller. After working in Newark, he moved to California where he played lead clarinet, cornet, viola, and alto horn in the Los Angeles Philharmonic. "Edward Inslee is one of those gifted mortals," George Cragin said of him, "in whom the fire of music ever grows." Noyes felt that Edward's influence kept Tirzah from reaching her full potential in directions other than music. Edward and Noyes may have clashed, because Noyes was "candid to an unusual degree," as was Edward.

Eleanor Nash Kellogg graduated from Wellesley in 1894 and married Paul Herrick in 1896. The couple lived in Kenwood near the Mansion House and had three children. She had a strong interest in Madison County children and became the first woman County Supervisor in New York State in 1930.

Annie Kelly was born in Freemont, New York in 1852. She worked in the Community as a silk-spooler. She had two Community children, one with George Noyes Miller, whom she married in 1879. Their son, Kenneth H. Miller, became a noted twentieth-century painter and taught at the Art Students League of New York for forty years. In 1929 he was included in the Museum of Modern Art's first exhibition of works by American artists, "Paintings by Nineteen Living Americans."

Ida Kate Kelly came to the Community with her parents and siblings at age almost ten and had a daughter, Rhoda, in the Community with Noyes's son Theodore. At the break-up she married Edwin Burnham and they had a son, Chester.

William Kelly was born in South Dansville, New York, in 1833. In youth he was considered "a hopeless consumptive," but after joining the Oneida Community in 1854, his health improved and remained very good. "Papa" Kelly, as he was known, was Superintendent of the Children's House for years, a good disciplinarian. He also worked as a commercial salesman, gardener, and farmer. He married Emily Otis after the break-up and moved to Niagara Falls near John Humphrey Noyes.

Albert Kinsley was born in Fletcher, Vermont, in 1801 and became a Perfectionist in 1837 through the study of the Bible and Noyes's writings. He was highly regarded as a sheriff, a deacon in the Congregational Church, a member of the Vermont State Legislature, and a Justice of the Peace. He always had sympathy for the weak and was always ready to help by word and deed. He was primarily a farmer, but with his sons, Myron and Martin, he built the top two floors of the dining room, called the Tontine, in 1874. He died from Bright's Disease, caused by malaria, in 1882.

Myron Kinsley joined the Community with his family from Fletcher, Vermont. After participating in many Community industries, he became superintendent of the silverware business at Wallingford Community. Just before the breakup, this factory was moved to Niagara Falls, and later to Sherrill, near Oneida. Myron was instrumental in persuading Noyes to leave Oneida for Niagara Falls in 1879, and he served as his emissary to Oneida.

Charlotte Leonard was born in the Putney Community in 1846 to Stephen Leonard and Fanny White. She had two Community children, John Humphrey Noyes II in 1869, and Stephen Rose Leonard in 1872. Charlotte worked in the silk department and in bookkeeping and general services. She had a good voice, was very musical, and loved little children. She had an unusual memory and was self-taught in mathematics and French. She worked in the business office for several years after the breakup.

Carrie Macknet was born in Newark, New Jersey in 1837 and joined the Community in 1863 after visiting with her mother; her parents were not members. She was a bookkeeper and had a Community child with William Woolworth, whom she married after the breakup. Their son Felix Woolworth was a banker in Niagara Falls who attempted to gain control of Oneida Community, Limited, in its early years.

Frederick A. Marks was born in England in 1841 and joined the Community with his mother and brother. He worked as a Community carpenter, was a good singer, and one of thirteen Community men sent to study at Yale. He became an architect.

Charlotte Noyes Miller, a younger sister of John Humphrey Noyes, was John Miller's wife and mother of Tirzah, whose journal is presented in parts in chapter 12. She was the advisor of the Oneida Community's second generation. William Hinds described her as a person "with a heart large enough to take in the whole family. Everyone, from the youngest to the oldest, felt free to go to her for sympathy and counsel, sure of an appreciative ear. Her waking hours day and night are spent in speaking of God's goodness." She enjoyed portraiture and worked in the silk industry. She died of malaria at age 55 in September, 1874. The Community's future might have ended differently had Charlotte lived longer; problems with the younger generation seemed to increase after her death.

George Noyes Miller, John and Charlotte Miller's son, went to the Sheffield School and graduated in 1872 from Yale. He had one Community child, artist Kenneth Miller, with Annie Kelly (see above), whom he married after the breakup. Described by an outside journalist, he was a "child of the Community and deeply attached to its principles . . . a young man of thoughtful character and well-educated." He wrote *After the Strike of a Sex*, with large excerpts in chapter 4, and was also a poet. He moved to Niagara Falls to be with J.H. Noyes after the breakup.

John R. Miller was the financier of the Putney Community, having given up business and political aspirations to join the organization in 1841. His financial acumen bridged the gap between the Putney and Oneida Communities and ensured that new industry was established on a sound monetary basis. His chief goal was to support Community publications at whatever cost. He married Charlotte Noyes, John Noyes's sister, and they had three children, Tirzah, George, and Helen, born in the Putney Community and active in the Oneida Community. John died at age forty, some say of overwork.

Tirzah Crawford Miller (Herrick): See Chapter 12.

Daniel Nash was the son of the Reverend Daniel Nash, Charles Grandison Finney's long-time associate in evangelism. He married Sophia Church and they had five children, three born before they joined the Community and twins Ellen and Alice, the first children born in the Community. Daniel was "only a moderate partaker in the social practices of the Community."

Sophia Nash married Daniel, son of the Reverend Daniel Nash. She and Daniel, with the Hatches, the Ackleys, and Hail Waters, were a family association before they joined the Jonathan Burts, who had purchased the land later to be the site of the Oneida Community.

Seymour Nash was the younger son of the Reverend Daniel Nash. He married Sarah Knowles and was converted to Perfectionism by Sarah's sister, Wealthy A. Knowles, and by writings in the New Haven *Perfectionist*. He converted his older brother, Daniel, to Perfectionism in 1839. He was a Community blacksmith.

Sewell Newhouse was born in 1806 and moved to Central New York when he was 14. He made animal traps and sold some to the Oneida Indians, whose language he had learned. He joined the Presbyterian Church and in 1835, received the doctrine of holiness. He married Eveliza Hyde and they joined the Oneida Community on Christmas Day, 1848. Sewell devised improvements on foreign animal traps, with his knack for tempering steel that had eluded other trap makers. By 1864, production grew to 275,000 with the aid of a more mechanical production process introduced by William Inslee. He wrote a trapper's guide. Traps became a major Community industry and the "Oneida Trap" is well-known today.

Some Community members cited in *A Taste of Heaven on Earth*

Corinna Ackley Noyes was born in 1872 in the Oneida Community and married Pierrepont B. Noyes in 1896. She spent time in Washington, D.C. and in Europe with her husband when he went to support a World War I organization and then was appointed to the Rhineland Commission after World War I. She involved herself in many welfare movements, charities, and in the League of Women Voters. Highly intelligent, always gracious, she had a subtle sense of humor.

George Wallingford Noyes was the 52nd Community child of George Washington Noyes and Tirzah Miller, born December 13, 1870, the first of 62 children born in the Stirpiculture period (four died in infancy). George graduated at the top of his class from Cornell University in 1892, a Junior member of Phi Beta Kappa. He worked for Oneida Community, Limited until 1920, when he semi-retired to write Putney and Oneida Community history. He lived as a teenager in Niagara Falls with John Humphrey Noyes, whose son Theodore said, "My father would have swapped all his sons for one-half of George."

Holton V. Noyes, born in March 1871, was the 55th Community child, the son of John Humphrey Noyes and Mary Van Velzer. He was Pierrepont Noyes's partner in New York City at Noyes Brothers, and started two restaurants. He then returned to work for the company's Fruit Department for 28 years, heading it up. His interests and skills were immense: raising prize Holsteins, serving as Agriculture Commissioner for New York State, playing the flute and directing the company band, and writing Oneida Community, Limited's history with Stephen Leonard.

Irene Campbell Noyes, born in June 1873, was the 65th Community child, the daughter of John Humphrey Noyes and Arabelle Woolworth. She graduated Phi Beta Kappa from Cornell University and taught Latin at Mansfield, Pennsylvania, Normal School. She married George Wallingford Noyes in 1899; the couple had three daughters. She taught Sunday School and was a piano teacher.

George Washington Noyes joined the Putney Community at age twenty-two in 1845 and joined the Oneida Community in 1849. He had three Community children and was a strong editorial assistant to his brother, John Humphrey Noyes, writing extensively about spiritual love. He taught Latin, and loved to walk extensively and sketch. He died at age 47 of malaria, four months after his son George Wallingford was conceived. Nearing death, he was not depressed, ". . . cheerful and buoyant through the whole of it," wrote William Woolworth. Community eulogies captured the man: "He has been a promoter of brotherly love in the Community from its commencement . . . more than any other man except John Humphrey Noyes. He realized the blessedness of giving . . . it was a practical feature of his daily life."

Pierrepont B. Noyes was the 49th child born in the Oneida Community in 1870, son of John Humphrey Noyes and Harriet Worden. He wrote about his childhood

APPENDIX

in *My Father's House* and then wrote *A Goodly Heritage* about his adulthood values. He became president of Oneida Community, Limited, in 1910 and instituted profit-sharing and many other generous business and social policies. (See "Spiritual Community to Partnership Corporation," chapter 11). After serving as American High Commissioner of the American Occupation of the Rhineland District in Germany after World War I, he wrote a letter to President Woodrow Wilson warning against harsh treatment of the Germans. He accurately predicted weapons of mass destruction in 1927 in *The Pallid Giant*, meaning "fear." He was appointed by Governor Franklin Roosevelt to the Saratoga Commission, responsible for the construction of its Health Spa. He was a swift sight-reader of music and played the cornet. He died in 1959.

Theodore R. Noyes, the only surviving son of John Humphrey and Harriet Noyes, was born in 1841 in Putney, Vermont. He received a medical degree at Yale in 1867 and later interned at Bellevue in New York City. His wide interests, including surveying and violin making, did not include literal belief in the Bible. For periods he led the Community well in business matters, but it wasn't an ideal match for his objective temperament. With Frank Wayland-Smith, he developed and saw through to success the formation of the joint stock corporation, Oneida Community, Limited.

Victor Noyes grew up in the first Children's House at the Oneida Community and worked as a horticulturalist and salesman, and studied telegraphy in New York City. He was the father of Corinna Noyes, who married Pierrepont B. Noyes.

Emily Otis was born in Welland, Ontario, in 1845, and moved to Bath, New York. She joined the Community with three others attending college there, after being introduced to Perfectionism by Candace Bushnell. She bore a Community child by Edwin Burnham and a second by Charles Cragin. With Lorinda Burt, she cared for the New Haven house for Community men who attended Yale. At the breakup she married "Papa" Kelly, who adopted her children. She had "a magic sense of humor," great honesty, and zest for life.

Theodore Pitt was born in Summit, New Jersey in 1831 and joined the Community in 1853. He worked in the print shop with Noyes's brother, George, and his sister, Harriet Noyes Skinner, and edited the *Circular* for several years. He had one Community child with Mary Van Velzer and married Louisa Tuttle Waters after the breakup, moving first to Niagara Falls and then to a temperance town, Vineland, New Jersey.

Chloe Seymour was born in Westmoreland, New York in 1834 and joined the Community fifteen years after her parents joined in 1849. She was a seamstress, carpet bag maker, and organized the Mansion House linen, as well as tending a garden; she played and sang old Scottish songs and because of her empathy, she became a confidante of the children whom she loved and cared for. "Aunt Chloe" went to Niagara Falls after the breakup.

Henry Seymour received the doctrine of holiness from George Cragin after reading the writings of Noyes, and joined the Community at age 21 on April 9, 1848. Previously a farmer in Westmoreland, he became the Community horticulturist and was said to have uncanny powers of persuasion over all living things, "the magician of orchard and garden." He wrote for the *Circular*, a deep and subtle thinker.

Harriet Noyes Skinner was born in Dummerston, Vermont, in 1817, a younger sister of John Humphrey Noyes. She and her younger sister Charlotte, and younger brother George, were avid converts to John as he visited home in the mid-1830s and discussed his studies and what he learned through meditation on God. They were the first joiners of the Putney Association. She married John Skinner in 1841 and a year later, their son Joseph was born. She was often an editor of the *Circular* and a frequent contributor to Community publications. She taught composition and spelling, among the Community's favorite disciplines.

John Langdon Skinner was born in 1803 in Westmoreland, New Hampshire. He was a Quaker teacher when he heard John Humphrey Noyes preach, and joined the Putney Association in 1839. He married Noyes's sister Harriet in 1841 and they had one son, Joseph. One of the spiritual leaders of the Community and its press, John Skinner was first assistant in writing, editing, and publishing *The Witness* and *The Perfectionist*. His descendants became active in the Community; the road winding in to the back of the Mansion House is Skinner Road.

Joseph Skinner was one of thirteen young men the Oneida Community sent to Yale. He received a Ph.D. from Sheffield Scientific School in 1869 and was on the mathematics and engineering faculty of Yale. He married Community member Ann Hobart, seceding two years before the Community breakup in 1880. Their son Theodore studied architecture at M.I.T., worked at Oneida Community, Limited, and built distinguished houses contiguous to the Mansion House; he designed college buildings in New York and Florida.

Dexter Edson Smith was born in Dorset, Vermont, in 1839, the grandson and son of ministers. He became the first graduate of the University of Iowa and taught Negro freedmen in the South after graduate work at (now) Colgate University. He married Sarah King and they had two children (who died in infancy). They joined the Community in 1867, and had one son, Eugene Deming. He mastered the new art of photography and most of the visual evidence of the middle and later years of the Community is his work. He was especially interested in theories about health. He moved to Santa Ana, California, after marrying Ellen Hutchins at the break-up.

APPENDIX

James Towner was born in Willsboro, New York, in 1823 and married Cinderella Sweet in 1850. He then studied theology, entering the Universalist ministry in Westfield, Ohio. He studied law and was admitted to the Iowa bar in 1859. He joined the Civil War, losing the sight of one eye. After the war he joined the Berlin Heights free love commune. He provided legal advice to Noyes and at the dissolution of the commune, joined the Oneida Community with his wife and three children, six years before its break-up. He opposed the dissolution of the Community, trying to wrest control over Complex Marriage from Noyes. He moved to Santa Ana, California, and became the first judge of newly formed Orange County.

Portia Underhill was born in 1842 and joined the Community in 1865, converted by William Kelly and Candace Bushnell. She was a Community teacher noted for excellent understanding of children. She tended to feelings of special love for George Washington Noyes; then she and Henry Allen became parents of Grosvenor Noyes Allen, but they were separated because of the tendency for exclusive love. They married after the breakup and had a daughter, Hope Allen.

Chester W. Underwood was born in Oneida County in 1825 and joined the Community with his wife, Mary, and their three children in 1859. An influential and popular Community teacher; his was a helpful and cheerful influence in favor of liberal education, which made a deep and immediate impression and left a lasting mark.

Francis (Frank) Wayland-Smith was born Francis Smith in South Hadley, Massachusetts, joining the Community at age ten in 1851 with his widowed mother and brother. He began playing the violin at age 14 and developed into an accomplished musician, playing solo and in Community quartets and quintets, and had a fine singing voice. He wrote and edited for the *Circular*, the *American Socialist*, and the *Quadrangle*. His Community vocations and character development are described in chapter 10, Humanizing Work, first section on "Multitasking." He added "Wayland" to his name after New England divine, Francis Wayland. With Cornelia Worden, Frank had two children, Gerard and Louis Wayland-Smith; he adopted her Community child, Richard Worden Noyes. He was active in Oneida Community, Limited.

Arabelle Woolworth was born in 1850, the 10th child born in the Community, daughter of William Woolworth and Emma Campbell. She had one child with John Humphrey Noyes, Irene. After the community breakup in 1881, "Belle" married Milford Newhouse, the son of Sewell and Eveliza Newhouse. Milford adopted Irene after the breakup.

William Woolworth was born in Long Meadow, Massachusetts, in 1824 and joined the Putney Community in 1846. He married Emma Campbell in 1847 and they

Some Community members cited in *A Taste of Heaven on Earth*

had Helen and Arabelle. He had a son Felix with Carrie Macknet in 1870 whom he married at the breakup, and daughter Agnes (Bliss) with Elizabeth Hutchins in 1871. (Emma seceded in 1854; she died a year later.) William was a farmer, wagon-maker, and member of the Business Board who, in Noyes's absence, was appointed "father of the Community."

Glossary

Antinomianism: The Pauline message of freedom from law, to naïve people or to those with baser motives, meant worldly freedom such as pursuing free love. To attain full growth, one must pass through four stages: infancy and young childhood, primarily concerned with self; the period of friendship or general companionship; and the period of love. It is only when one reaches the fourth stage and becomes a spiritual being that the human being is prepared for absolute freedom (Gal. 5). In the first three stages there is restraint, dependency, and a disagreeable state of things to a certain extent. Human beings are not reborn and free until they come into relationship with God.

Ascending Fellowship: Noyes likened the relationship of children to adults as his was to God: we must be humble and obedient. Those of greater spiritual wisdom were to lead others.

Bible Communism: Based on Acts 2:44–45 and Acts 4:32–34, the Community practiced sharing all things as did those members of the Primitive Church.

Diotrephiasis: A coined word meaning the prideful spirit that rejoices in external prosperity. The more prosperous we are, the more modest we should become.

German Rationalism: A doctrine that denies divine inspiration of the Scriptures. It subjected the Bible to scholarly higher criticism, errors of fact and doctrine, and resolved miracles into legends and myths. This contributed to understanding the meaning of ancient Hebrew words, some of which have been difficult to translate, through context with a word's appearance in several places, and in the culture of the ancient world.

Idolatry: Marriage tends to make partners devote attention to the needs and desires of their spouses, and perhaps become less able to devote sufficient energies to the Lord, as Paul wrote. To love God, and neighbor as oneself, is the object of human life. To achieve love of God, all relationships and activities are to transcend earthly focus; where your treasure is, there your heart will be also. Purity of heart is the foundation for lasting love and peace.

Glossary

Inspiration: Inspiration is infused into the person through his/her spiritual nature by the Holy Spirit as we devote spiritual labor to becoming active listeners to the leading of the divine spirit within. The resulting wisdom is not intellectual exertion, not a human faculty, but a prayerful working of the central life.

Philoprogenetiveness: Parental over-indulgence and excessive attention. The Community emphasized love of all rather than special love for one's own.

Positivism: A system of philosophy originated by Auguste Comte, stating that theology and metaphysics are imperfect modes of knowledge. True knowledge, this view states, is based on natural phenomena and their properties and relations as verified by the empirical sciences.

Providence: Divine guidance or care, especially preserving individuals in danger through intervention."

Special love: Possessiveness and pairing off in the Community was counter to the widening and deepening of love for all. Narrowing of affections blights the individual's potential to love God, the love from which lasting human love springs. The heart should not be contracted with idolatry, exclusive or selfish love in any form. It was considered unhealthy for two people to become exclusively attached—to idolize only each other—however popular infatuation may be. It is a temporary and shaky foundation that often crumbles under the realities and vicissitudes of life.

Stirpiculture: From the Latin *stirps*, a coined word *stirpiculture* means root or stock. Noyes believed that rational, planned propagation would result in a more spiritual race.

Zeitgeist: The dominant perspective, ideology, or climate of a period of time that sets it apart:. The spirit of the times, from the German *Zeit*, meaning "time," and *Geist*, meaning "spirit."

Epilogue Endnotes

1. Great Decisions 2020, Foreign Policy Association, "Modern Slavery and Human Trafficking."
2. Said at Wallingford Community on October 4, 1873.
3. McTaggart, Lynne, Intention Experiment, p. 110.

Bibliography

Barron, Alfred, and George Noyes Miller, eds. *Home-Talks*, Vol. I. Oneida: Published by the Community, 1875.

Brother Lawrence, *Practice of the Presence of God*, translated by Donald Attwater (Springfield, IL, Templegate, 1974), 38.

Cross, Whitney R. *The Burned-Over District: The Social and Intellectual History of Enthusiastic Religion in Western New York,* 1800–1850. Ithaca: Cornell University Press, 1950.

DeMaria, Richard. *Communal Love at Oneida*. New York: Edwin Mellen, 1978.

Edmonds, Walter D. *The First Hundred Years*. Oneida Ltd., 1948.

Fox, Matthew. *Original Blessing*. Inner Traditions Bear & Co., Santa Fe, NM, 1983.

Huxley, Aldous. *Tomorrow and Tomorrow and Tomorrow*. New York: Harper & Brothers, 1952.

James, William. *The Varieties of Religious Experience: a Study in Human Nature*. New York: Random House, Modern Library, 1902.

Miller, George Noyes. *After the Strike of a Sex*. London: William Reeves, 185 Fleet Street, E.C., 1896.

Mutual Criticism. Office of the *American Socialist*: Oneida, New York, 1876.

Noyes, George Wallingford. *John Humphrey Noyes: The Putney Community*. Oneida, New York: 1931.

———. *Religious Experience of John Humphrey Noyes*. New York: Macmillan, 1923.

———. *The Oneida Community: The Oneida Community: Its Relation to Orthodoxy*. Feilding [sic] Star Print. Not dated.

———. Unpublished papers about the Oneida Community.

Noyes, John Humphrey. *The Berean: A Manual for the Help of Those Who Seek the Faith of the Primitive Church*. Putney, VT: Office of the *Spiritual Magazine*, 1847.

———. *Bible Communism: Defining the Relations of the Sexes in the Kingdom of Heaven*, published in 1849 in the *First Annual Report of the Oneida Association*.

———. *Male Continence*, Oneida, New York: Office of the *Oneida Circular*, 1872.

———. *Mutual Criticism*, Oneida, New York: Office of the *American Socialist*, 1876.

Noyes, Pierrepont B. *My Father's House*. New York: Farrar & Rinehart, 1937.

———. *A Goodly Heritage*. New York: Rinehart & Company, 1958.

Noyes, Corinna Ackley. *The Days of My Youth*. Oneida, NY: Mansion House, 1960.

Oneida Circular, Weekly newsletter of the Oneida Community, 13 volumes, 1864–1876.

Origin of the Oneida Community. Corporation of Bible Perfectionists at Putney, VT. Not dated.

Parker, Robert Allerton. *A Yankee Saint: John Humphrey Noyes and the Oneida Community*. New York: G.P. Putnam's Sons, 1935.

BIBLIOGRAPHY

Ratcliff, Nora, ed. *The Journal of John Wesley* 1735–1790. London: Thomas Nelson & Sons, Ltd., 1940.

Robertson, Constance Noyes. *Oneida Community: An Autobiography,* 1851–1876. Syracuse, New York: Syracuse University Press, 1970.

Stace, Walter T. *The Teachings of the* Mystics. New York: Mentor Books, published by The New American Library of World Literature, 1960.

Teeple, John B. *The Oneida Family: Genealogy of a 19th Century Perfectionist Commune.* Oneida Community Historical Committee: Kenwood, Oneida, NY: 1985.

Underhill, Evelyn. *The Essentials of Mysticism.* Oxford, England: Oneworld Publications, 185 Banbury Road, 1995.

Wesley, John. *A Plain Account of Christian Perfection.* Epworth Press: Westminster, London, SW1, 1952.

Worden, Harriet M. *Old Mansion House Memories.* Oneida Ltd., Kenwood, Oneida, NY, 1950.

www.ingramcontent.com/pod-product-compliance
Lightning Source LLC
Chambersburg PA
CBHW080404300426
44113CB00015B/2400